# Key Studies in Sport and Exercise Psychology

# Key Studies in Sport and Exercise Psychology

*David Lavallee, Jean M. Williams and Marc V. Jones*

In collaboration with Mark Allen, Christopher Spray, Heather Peters, Mark Eys, Gareth Morgan, Vikki Krane, Caroline Douglas, Martin I. Jones, Anthony Papathomas, Carrie Scherzer, Kate Goodger

**McGraw-Hill
Higher Education**

Open University Press

Open University Press
McGraw-Hill Education
McGraw-Hill House
Shoppenhangers Road
Maidenhead
Berkshire
England
SL6 2QL

email: enquiries@openup.co.uk
world wide web www.openup.co.uk

and Two Penn Plaza, New York, NY 10121–2289, USA

**British Library Cataloguing in Publication Data**
A catalogue record for this book is available from the British Library

**Library of Congress Cataloging in Publication Data**
The Library of Congress data for this book has been applied for from the Library
of Congress

Commissioning Editor: Ruben Hale
Editorial Assistant: Katy Hamilton
Marketing Manager: Vanessa Boddington
Senior Production Editor: James Bishop

Typeset by RefineCatch Limited, Bungay, Suffolk
Cover design by del norte (Leeds) Ltd
Printed by Bell and Bain Ltd, Glasgow

ISBN-13 978-0-07-711171-7 (pb)   978-0-07-711170-0 (hb)
ISBN-10 0-07-711171-0 (pb)   0-07-711170-2 (hb)

The **McGraw·Hill** Companies

# Contents

# Dedication

I dedicate this book to Ruth, Joseph, Noah and Reuben – David Lavallee

I dedicate this book to all my students who have taught me so much and who have been the primary source of joy and inspiration in my teaching and scholarly pursuits – Jean Williams

I dedicate this book to Helen for all her love and support – Marc Jones

# Preface

*Key Studies in Sport and Exercise Psychology* examines in depth 23 of the most important and influential studies in sport and exercise psychology, what led to the studies, and the impact of the studies on future research and applied work. The studies reflect the breadth of research topics and methodologies used in sport and exercise psychology and thus collectively offer a representation of many of the advances in knowledge and practice within sport and exercise psychology. Unlike other, more traditional readers and anthologies which often only (simply) reproduce writings that are readily available in libraries (and also often accessible via the internet with electronic journal subscriptions), we outline the place of each key study in the field of sport and exercise psychology. A "Background and Context" section is initially provided in order to put the study and its research area into a theoretical, practical, and historical context. This is followed by an abridged version of the "Key Study" itself. Next, a "Subsequent Research and Application" section focuses on research developed since the original study was published, as well as relevant theoretical, methodological, and applied issues. Each chapter concludes with a recommendation of additional readings, along with study questions to stimulate readers to think critically about any theoretical, methodological, application, and ethical implications of the studies. The idea of presenting key studies in this way has been used successfully before in mainstream psychology (e.g., Gross, 2003) and our book is based on this concept.

Each study included in this volume has been summarized in such a way that the substantial character of the original source has been retained while occasionally finer detailed material has been removed. We retained all the section headings as they were employed in the original publication, as well as preserving original language. We felt it was important to retain the original language in order to reflect research writing of that time period (as an example, some older studies used only the male pronoun, even though they included female participants; today, this would be considered sexist language). In some cases, references have been added to the reference list as the original publication did not include them. Occasionally we have also replaced obscure or difficult language with more familiar language for students.

A crucial element in this book was the selection of the key studies. With the breadth and diversity of the field of sport and exercise psychology, we recognize that any attempt to identify important research areas and the "best" study within an area is impossible. That said we selected our studies by initially conducting a thorough review and consultation in order to identify important studies that significantly impacted both thinking at their time of publication and subsequent theories, research initiatives and/or the practice of sport and exercise psychology. Important textbooks and journals in the field were consulted during this process, along with a panel of experts in sport and exercise psychology. These efforts resulted in an initial pool of 92 studies, which did not include key studies from the field of motor behavior as it was felt that an entire, separate volume in this area would be required. Following a further consultation process with experts, 23 studies were selected that reflected the breadth of research topics and methodologies used in sport and exercise psychology. Based on the studies selected the book has been organized into the following five parts: Personality and motivation; Social processes; Psychological characteristics and skills; Personal growth and psychological well-being; and Professional practice and ethics.

Extensive examination of studies has been historically difficult to achieve in general textbooks in the field. Students also often wish to learn more about a particular study or area of research than textbooks can offer or teachers/tutors can provide in a classroom setting. By bringing together a selection of important readings in sport and exercise psychology, we aimed to fill a gap in the literature with a book that is readable and accessible to not only students but also researchers and scholars. As a detailed overview of key studies in the field is not currently available we also try to focus readers' attention on how each area evolved and, by considering the meaning, implication, and impact of the work, how the study contributed to the field of sport and exercise psychology in general. Although it is clearly important to be familiar with current research, we argue that an understanding of current thinking cannot be achieved without understanding past research. It is past research that provided the foundation for, and directed, current thinking. In writing this book we have also kept in mind practitioners, who may find full articles published in journals impractical and time-consuming to read (Speed, Butki, & Andersen, 2001). It is envisioned that this book would be used as a supplementary volume to important undergraduate textbooks in the field, or as a central text for undergraduate or graduate seminars in sport and exercise psychology.

We would like to take this opportunity to thank the following individuals who collaborated with us on chapters within the book: Mark Allen, Caroline Douglas, Mark Eys, Kate Goodger, Vikki Krane, Gareth Morgan, Anthony Papathomas, Heather Peters, Carrie Scherzer, and Christopher Spray. Each of these individuals has been further acknowledged in the table of contents as authors of their respective chapters. We would also like to thank many of the original authors of the key studies for agreeing to have their studies included, and at times, for providing suggestions for edits. Thanks are also extended to all of our colleagues who provided their views on the selection of key studies to be included in this volume, in particular Bob Eklund and Mark Andersen. Finally, we are grateful to all the support we have received from the following people at McGraw-Hill: Ruben Hale, Katy Hamilton, Jon Lee, Shona Mullen, Laura Dent, Jon Reed, and Mark Barratt.

David Lavallee
Jean Williams
Marc Jones

## References

Gross, R. G. (2003). *Key studies in psychology*. London: Hodder Arnold.

Speed, H. D., Butki, H. D., & Andersen, M. B. (2001). The perceived usefulness of sport psychology journal articles for practitioners. In A. Papaioannou, M. Goudas, & Y. Theodorakis (eds), *Proceedings of the 10th World Congress of Sport Psychology* (pp. 82–3). Skiathos, Greece.

# Acknowledgements

The publishers and authors would like to thank the following for permission to reproduce copyright material: American Alliance for Health, Physical Education, Recreation and Dance for "Coping strategies used by more versus less successful U.S. Olympic wrestlers" by D. Gould, R. C. Eklund, and S. A. Jackson (1993), *Research Quarterly for Exercise and Sport*, 64, 83–93, "Self-efficacy and the stages of exercise behavior change" by B. H. Marcus, V. C. Selby, R. S. Niaura, and J. S. Rossi (1992), *Research Quarterly for Exercise and Sport*, 63, 60–6, and "State anxiety among successful and unsuccessful competitors who differ in competitive trait anxiety" by R. Martens and D. L. Gill (1976), *Research Quarterly*, 47, 698–708; the American Psychological Association for "Scrutinizing the skipper: a study of leadership behaviors in the dugout" by J. E. Curtis, R. E. Smith, and F. L. Smoll (Copyright © 1979 by the American Psychological Association), *Journal of Applied Psychology*, 64, 391–400, "The dark side of self and social perception: black uniforms and aggression in professional sports" by M. G. Frank and T. Gilovich (Copyright © 1988 by the American Psychological Association), *Journal of Personality and Social Psychology*, 54, 74–85, and "Conjunctive moderator variables in vulnerability and resiliency research: life stress, social support and coping skills and adolescent sport injuries" by R. E. Smith, F. L. Smoll, and J. T. Ptacek (Copyright © 1990 by the American Psychological Association), *Journal of Personality and Social Psychology*, 58, 360–9; British Psychological Society for "Children's achievement goals and beliefs about success in sport" by J. L. Duda. K. R. Fox, S. J. H. Biddle, and N. J. Armstrong (1992), *British Journal of Educational Psychology*, 62, 313–23; Human Kinetics (Champaign, IL) for "An evaluation of U.S. Olympic sport psychology consultant effectiveness" by D. Gould, S. Murphy, V. Tammen, and J. May (Copyright © 1991 by Human Kinetics Publishers, Inc.), *The Sport Psychologist*, 5, 111–27, "Burnout in competitive junior tennis players: II. Qualitative analysis" by D. Gould, E. Udry, S. Tuffey, and J. Loehr (Copyright © 1996 by Human Kinetics Publishers, Inc.), *The Sport Psychologist*, 10, 341–66, "The effect of cognitive strategies on the free throw shooting performance of young athletes" by C. A. Wrisberg and M. H. Anshel (Copyright © 1989 by Human Kinetics Publishers, Inc.), *The Sport Psychologist*, 3, 95–104, "The influence of the group and its cohesiveness on perception of group-related variables" by L. Brawley, A. Carron, and W. Widmeyer (Copyright © 1993 by Human Kinetics Publishers, Inc.), *Journal of Sport & Exercise Psychology*, 15, 245–66, "The effects of internal and external imagery on muscular and ocular concomitants" by B. D. Hale (Copyright © 1982 by Human Kinetics Publishers, Inc.), *Journal of Sport Psychology*, 4, 379–87,

"Effects of goal specificity, goal difficulty and information feedback on endurance performance" by H. K. Hall, R. S. Weinberg, and A. Jackson (Copyright © 1987 by Human Kinetics Publishers, Inc.), *Journal of Sport Psychology*, 9, 43–54, and "The effects of sport experience in the development of social character: an exploratory investigation" by D. A. Kleiber and G. C. Roberts (Copyright © 1981 by Human Kinetics Publishers, Inc.), *Journal of Sport Psychology*, 3, 114–22; John Wiley & Sons, Inc. for "Attitudes toward eating and body weight in different groups of female adolescent athletes" by J. Brooks-Gunn, C. Burrow, and W. P. Warren (Copyright © 1988 by John Wiley & Sons, Inc.), *International Journal of Eating Disorders*, 7, 749–57; Kluwer Academic Publishers for "Psychology of the elite athlete: an exploratory study" by M. J. Mahoney and M. Avener (1977), *Cognitive Therapy and Research*, 1, 135–41; Lippincott Williams and Wilkins for "Effect of exercise on depression" by T. C. North, P. McCullagh, and Z.V. Tran (1990) in K. B. Pandolf and J.O. Holloszy (eds) *Exercise and Sport Science Reviews*, 18, 379–415; New York Academy of Sciences for "Psychologic characterization of the elite distance runner" by W. P. Morgan and M. Pollock (Copyright © 1977 by New York Academy of Sciences), *Annals of the New York Academy of Science*, 301, 382–403; Pozzi for "The effect of attentional focus on performance of an endurance task" by D. L. Gill and E. H. Strom (1985), *International Journal of Sport Psychology*, 16, 217–23; Taylor & Francis for "Ethical beliefs and behaviors in applied sport psychology: the AAASP ethics survey" by A. Petitpas, B. Brewer, P. Rivera, and J. Van Raalte (Copyright © 1994 by Taylor & Francis, Inc., http://www.taylorandfrancis.com), *Journal of Applied Sport Psychology*, 6, 135–51; University of Illinois Press for "The dynamogenic factors in pacemaking and competition" by N. Triplett (1898), *American Journal of Psychology*, 9, 507–33; V. H. Winston & Son, Inc. for "Self-motivation and adherence to habitual physical activity" by R. K. Dishman, W. Ickes, and W. P. Morgan (1980), *Journal of Applied Social Psychology*, 10, 115–32.

# Author biographies

**David Lavallee** is professor and head of department of sport and exercise science at Aberystwyth University, Wales, UK. His educational qualifications include a master's degree in psychology from Harvard University and a Ph.D. in sport and exercise psychology from the University of Western Australia. He has published seven books, and is editor of *Sport & Exercise Psychology Review*, associate editor of *The Psychologist* and *International Review of Sport and Exercise Psychology*, and editorial board member of the *Journal of Clinical Sport Psychology* and *Psychology of Sport and Exercise*.

**Jean Williams** is a professor in the Department of Psychology at the University of Arizona. She currently teaches courses in stress and coping and psychology of excellence, but has taught sport psychology courses in the areas of social psychology, health and exercise psychology, and performance enhancement psychology. Jean has been an active sport psychology researcher and consultant for over 30 years and has authored over 100 scholarly publications and edited three books. She has served on the editorial boards of four research journals. She is past president of the Association for the Advancement of Applied Sport Psychology.

**Marc Jones** is a reader in sport and exercise psychology at Staffordshire University where he is course tutor for the first online distance learning M.Sc. in sport and exercise psychology. He is an active researcher and has over 25 scholarly publications and has edited two books. In addition Marc also works as a consultant and is accredited by the British Association of Sport and Exercise Sciences and a Chartered Sport and Exercise Psychologist with the British Psychological Society.

# PART 1

## Personality and motivation

# 1

# Personality

Morgan, W. P., & Pollock, M. (1977). Psychologic characterization of the elite distance runner. *Annals of the New York Academy of Science*, 301, 382–403

**Written in collaboration with Mark Allen**

## Background and context

Personality has been one of the foremost subject areas in psychological research since the beginning of the 20th century and many areas of personality research are applicable to sport and exercise settings. For example, the idea that successful sport performance can be predicted by personality traits has intrigued sport psychologists since the early days of Griffith (1928). Other examples of personality research include determining which personality attributes contribute to participation in sport and exercise, how participation in sport and exercise may change personality, or how personality may be associated with maladaptive behaviors in sport (e.g., eating disorders, drug use).

Personality is defined as ". . . those characteristics of the person that account for consistent patterns of feeling, thinking, and behaving" (Pervin & John, 2001: 4), and it is the combination of these characteristics that gives each individual their uniqueness. One of the most important distinctions in personality research was made by Allport and Odbert (1936) who differentiated between underlying personality traits and the more variable personality states. Personality traits (or dispositions) are those aspects of personality that underlie behavior and psychological and emotional responses across situations (states). For example, a basketball player characterized by constant displays of aggression in response to robust opponents may be considered to possess the personality trait of aggressiveness. However, trait theorists recognized that traits alone do not account entirely for individuals' responses as fluctuations do occur across situations. Rather it is the *interaction* of personality traits with the situation that creates a personality state which is the strongest predictor of behavior (Allport, 1937). To illustrate, consider three sprinters, one of whom has a high level of trait anxiety (the tendency to respond with anxiety to threatening situations), the other a moderate level of trait anxiety and one who has a low level of trait anxiety. At a typical race during the season the high trait anxious sprinter feels quite anxious, the moderate trait anxiety sprinter feels a little anxious, whereas the low trait anxious athlete does not feel anxious at all. Later in the season the sprinters reach the Olympic final where all of them feel anxious prior to what is the most important race of their lives. In this scenario it is the environment that is having the strongest impact on the state response. Despite all of the sprinters feeling anxious in this scenario, personality traits will still play a role in predicting the *relative* anxiety levels. That is, it would be expected that the high trait anxious sprinter would still be more anxious than the moderate trait anxious sprinter who would still be expected to be more anxious than the low trait anxious sprinter. The trait-state interactional approach to the study of personality is adopted by most personality researchers (Vealey, 2002). However, Vealey considers the concept of states and traits a rather arbitrary distinction, and suggests that researchers move towards viewing personality characteristics as being on a continuum from "trait-like" to "state-like," rather than two dichotomous categories. That is, some characteristics will manifest themselves across most situations, others occasionally and some rarely.

The key study by Morgan and Pollock used both qualitative and quantitative methods to look at the psychological profiles of elite middle-long distance runners, elite marathon runners, and college middle distance runners. Using a multi-method approach of this nature enabled the researchers to collect complementary data. Interview data typically provides rich, detailed, individual-specific information; while data collected using standardized questionnaires enables comparisons to be made across the different groups of runners and between the runners and participants in other sports. The runners in Morgan and Pollock's key study completed a battery of psychological tests, and it is not possible to provide detailed background information on all of the areas addressed. Accordingly, the focus is on two specific areas that are relevant to subsequent research in sport, and these are Eysenck's (1960, 1970) two-dimensional taxonomy, which provided the theoretical basis for many studies of personality, along with the work on mood states that has been studied extensively in sport and exercise settings in the last 30 years (Terry, 2004). Issues relating to anxiety and attentional processes, which were also addressed in the key study, are covered in detail in Chapters 6 and 13.

Morgan and Pollock's key study adopted Eysenck's (1960, 1970) approach whereby two basic dimensions of personality, labeled *extroversion* and *neuroticism*, formed the basis of human individuality. The extroversion dimension distinguished between those individuals who were unsociable, quiet, and passive (introverts) and those who were sociable, outgoing, and active (extroverts). The neuroticism dimension distinguishes between those who possessed emotional stability (calm, controlled, even-tempered) and those who were emotionally unstable (anxious, full of guilt).

Although it may seem somewhat unusual to include a measure of mood, such as the *Profile of Mood States* (POMS; McNair, Lorr & Droppleman, 1971) in a study on personality, the POMS is proposed to measure typical and persistent mood reactions (McNair *et al.*, 1971). In effect the POMS gives an indication of how an individual is *likely* to feel in a given situation. The POMS is a 65-item self-report questionnaire and measures six distinct mood states of tension, depression, anger, vigor, fatigue, and confusion. Participants typically indicate how they have been feeling during the past week, but the POMS manual also suggests using different time frames (e.g., "right now") depending upon the purpose for assessing mood states. Based on his work exploring the personality characteristics of successful and unsuccessful athletes, Morgan (1968) proposed the "iceberg profile" (also referred to as the mental health model of sport performance), in which athletic success is associated with a higher than normal level of vigor and lower than normal levels of tension, depression, anger, fatigue, and confusion.

The study by Morgan and Pollock was not the first to consider the relationship between personality characteristics and athletic success and even at the time of publication there was a substantial body of research in this area (e.g., Booth, 1958; Flanagan, 1951; La Place, 1954; Lakie, 1962; Merriman, 1960; Ogilvie, 1968). However, a strength of the key study was that it was one of a series of papers published by Morgan and his associates into the personality attributes of athletes from a range of sports (Morgan, 1968; Morgan & Johnson,

1978). This systematic approach to the study of personality attributes greatly facilitated comparisons across sports, levels, and how athletes may differ from non-athletes. The key study not only focused on data comprising state and trait personality profiles but also, interestingly, used qualitative data to explore elite distance runners' cognitive processes *during* competition. While a great deal of information was presented in the original publication, what follows is an abridged version and some of the physiological data and lifestyle data (e.g., amount of coffee drunk) are not presented.

## Key study

The stress imposed during marathon competition is arduous and marathoners have previously been observed to possess unique anatomical and physiological characteristics. However, many athletes appear to meet the anatomical and physiological prerequisites for the marathon, while only a select group of men achieve success in this demanding sport (Costill, 1968). A preliminary study of the personality characteristics of marathoners previously conducted by Morgan and Costill (1972) suggested that athletes from this particular subgroup display unique psychological profiles and were characterized by introversion, stability, and low anxiety levels. However, none of these variables were found to correlate significantly with marathon performance due in part to the homogeneity of the sample (nine males).

The study by Morgan and Costill (1972) should be replicated for several reasons. First of all, while the marathoners reported on were introverted, as measured by the *Eysenck Personality Inventory*, one member of the group who had previously won the Boston Marathon, scored very high on the extroversion measure. His extroversion score, as well as his overall psychological profile, was more like that of the world class wrestlers previously described by Morgan (1968). In other words, it would seem imperative that additional data be generated prior to making an attempt at presenting a psychological stereotype intended to characterize marathoners. It should be noted, however, that an extensive body of literature exists in the field of sport psychology suggesting that individual sport athletes (e.g., runners) are more introverted than team sport athletes, and non-contact athletes (e.g., runners) have typically been observed to be more introverted than contact athletes (Morgan, 1971). Hence, the earlier findings of Morgan and Costill do fit with theoretical expectations to a certain degree. A second reason why their earlier findings should be viewed with caution is that personality structure in sport may well differ as a function of ability level. Therefore, the earlier study of Morgan and Costill may not apply to samples comprised solely of elite marathoners. The present study, unlike the earlier one, is concerned primarily with characterization of elite or world class distance runners.

There are a number of reasons why one might intuitively expect factors of a psychological nature to play an important role in long distance running. First, it appears reasonably clear that endurance performance is governed by both the physical *capacity* and *willingness* of the runner to tolerate the discomfort associated with hard physical work. It appears that substantial differences in both the capacity and willingness to tolerate discomfort exist among marathoners. For example, among finishers of the marathon (26.2 miles or 42.2 km), performance times frequently range from 2 hours 15 minutes to 4 or 5 hours – hence, certainly a considerable difference in capacity, and probably, a fair amount of difference in the willingness to tolerate discomfort. Therefore, the large individual differences widely observed in marathoners have a substantial physiological basis, and the authors in no way intend to suggest otherwise. An attempt will be made in the present paper, however, to examine the extent to which psychological factors can be useful in characterizing the marathoner.

## Procedure

The purposes of this investigation were to (1) compare the psychological characteristics of world class middle-long distance and marathon runners, (2) contrast their psychologic profiles with those of non-world-class runners and athletes from other sports, (3) examine the perceptual processing of "effort sense" information in these runners, and (4) attempt to delineate the factors responsible for *involvement* in competitive running, as well as *adherence* across time.

## Subjects

The runners who served as subjects in this investigation consisted of a group of world class athletes (*n* = 19) and a group of college middle distance runners (*n* = 8). The latter runners, while outstanding by college standards, were not of world class caliber. The world class group was further divided into middle-long distance (*n* = 11) and marathon (*n* = 8) subgroups for comparative purposes.

## Variables

The dependent variables consisted of psychometric test scores obtained from standardized psychological inventories, running histories and race strategies obtained by means of a clinical interview, physiological data obtained during sub-maximal treadmill running, and ratings of perceived exertion obtained during sub-maximal running. The details relating to these dependent variables are outlined below.

*Psychometric Variables.* Each runner completed a battery of psychological inventories. The inventories consisted of the *State-Trait Anxiety Inventory* (STAI; Spielberger, Gorsuch, & Lushene, 1970), *Somatic Perception Questionnaire* (SPQ; Landy & Stern, 1971), *Depression Adjective Checklist* (DACL; Lubin, 1967), *Profile of Mood States* (POMS; McNair, Lorr, & Droppleman, 1971), *Eysenck Personality Inventory* (EPI; Eysenck & Eysenck, 1968), *Physical Estimation and Attraction Scale* (PEAS; Sonstroem, 1974), and the *Hidden Shapes Test* (HST; Watson, 1973). This test battery yielded measures of state and trait anxiety (STAI), perception of somatic activity during "stressful" situations (SPQ), depression (DACL), tension, depression, anger, vigor, fatigue, and confusion (POMS), extraversion, neuroticism, and conformity (EPI), attraction toward physical activity and estimation of physical ability (PEAS), and field dependence (HST).

*Running History and Strategy.* A taped clinical interview lasting approximately 45 minutes to 1 hour was carried out with each runner individually. This interview consisted of questions relating to the runner's current training program, occupation, family structure, diet, use of common drugs (e.g., aspirin, alcohol, coffee, and tea), use of tobacco, sleep patterns, and so on. Also, the runner was asked to respond to each of the following questions in 25 words or less: (1) Explain why you first became involved in competitive running; and (2) Explain why you continue to run competitively. The runners were encouraged to respond spontaneously, describing the first impressions or thoughts that came to mind. The first question was concerned with the general issue of *involvement* (or gravitation), whereas the second was directed toward the matter of *adherence* – two different but interdependent variables. They were also asked to respond to the following question, but unlike the first two questions there was no limit placed on response length – indeed, the runners were encouraged to elaborate on this question as much as possible: (3) Describe what you think about during a long distance run or marathon. What sort of thought processes take place as a run progresses? There is no limit on the length of your response. Please talk in detail about this matter.

Evaluation of data from the psychological inventories was carried out in accordance with specified scoring procedures described in each of the test manuals. Interpretation of the taped interviews was considerably less objective, but it was possible to identify major thematic processes, as well as answer specific questions posed *a priori*. The following hypotheses were tested in this portion of the study:

(H$_1$) The motivational forces responsible for *initial* involvement in running would not be characterized by a single thematic dimension.

(H$_2$) The forces responsible for adherence or continuation in competitive running would be both extrinsic and intrinsic.

(H$_3$) Dissociation of sensory input would represent the principal "cognitive strategy" employed by these world class distance runners during competition.

*Physiological and Perceptual Variables*. Ratings of perceived exertion (RPE) were obtained during submaximal exercise in an attempt to characterize the manner in which these runners processed sensory information relating to physical effort ("effort sense"). The RPE values were obtained using the psycho-physical category scale developed by Borg (1973) and the ratings were made during a submaximal test in which the subjects ran at 10 mph (4.5 m/sec) for seven minutes, and 12 mph (5.5 m/sec) for an additional four minutes on a motor driven treadmill. The grade was maintained at 0% throughout the run.

The RPE scale ranges from 6 to 20, and the odd numbered categories have verbal anchors (7 = very, very light; 9 = very light; 11 = fairly light; 13 = somewhat hard; 15 = hard; 17 = very hard; and 19 = very, very hard). While the perceptual ratings were being obtained, physiological data were simultaneously acquired. This permitted a comparison of factors such as heart rate, oxygen consumption, ventilatory minute volume, and lactate accumulation in the three groups of runners. More importantly, it was thus possible to study the juxtaposition of perceptual ratings and physiologic responsivity.

## Results and Discussion

### Psychometric Data

The means, standard deviations, and standard errors for all of the psychological variables appear in Table 1.1 for the total group ($n = 27$). Also, a one-way ANOVA was performed on these data for the three separate groups, and the means and $F$ ratios resulting from these analyses appear in Table 1.2. Differences between groups are not found to be significant ($p < 0.05$) in Table 1.2.

This analysis revealed that the world class middle-long distance runners and marathon runners did not differ significantly ($p > 0.05$) on any of the 16 variables, nor did these groups differ from the college runners. Indeed, inspection of the mean data reveals a remarkable similarity for the three groups. Therefore, the three groups were combined for purposes of drawing comparisons with other athlete groups, as well as with published norms for college students.

A comparison of the runners in the present study with previously tested high-level U.S. wrestlers (Nagle, Morgan, Hellickson, Serfass, & Alexander, 1975) and rowers (Morgan & Johnson, 1978) appears in Figure 1.1 for data obtained with the POMS. Also, the mean for

**Table 1.1** Raw score means, standard deviations, and standard errors for all runners on each psychological variable

| Variable | Mean (n = 27) | Standard deviation | Standard error |
|---|---|---|---|
| State anxiety | 33.50 | 6.89 | 1.30 |
| Trait anxiety | 31.68 | 9.27 | 1.75 |
| Somatic perception | 20.93 | 5.50 | 1.04 |
| Tension | 10.46 | 5.57 | 1.05 |
| Depression (POMS) | 6.82 | 7.93 | 1.50 |
| Anger | 7.89 | 6.03 | 1.14 |
| Vigor | 21.07 | 5.60 | 1.06 |
| Fatigue | 6.89 | 5.30 | 1.00 |
| Confusion | 7.43 | 4.12 | 0.78 |
| Extraversion | 13.43 | 4.65 | 0.88 |
| Neuroticism | 9.43 | 5.42 | 1.02 |
| Exercise attitude | 42.64 | 4.70 | 0.89 |
| Self-esteem | 26.89 | 5.15 | 0.97 |
| Field dependence | 22.75 | 12.20 | 2.31 |
| Depression (DACL) | 3.96 | 2.70 | 0.51 |
| Conformity | 3.14 | 1.82 | 0.34 |

**Table 1.2** Comparison of raw score means for world class middle-long distance and marathon runners with college middle distance runners on each psychological variable

| Variable | World class runners | | College runners (n = 8) | F |
|---|---|---|---|---|
| | Middle-long distance (n = 11) | Marathon (n = 8) | | |
| State anxiety | 33.82 | 32.75 | 33.75 | 0.06 |
| Trait anxiety | 34.91 | 26.63 | 33.00 | 2.04 |
| Somatic perception | 22.18 | 19.25 | 20.38 | 0.66 |
| Tension | 10.91 | 9.75 | 10.88 | 0.11 |
| Depression (POMS) | 9.18 | 3.88 | 6.88 | 1.01 |
| Anger | 8.73 | 6.75 | 8.13 | 0.23 |
| Vigor | 19.00 | 22.75 | 21.25 | 1.14 |
| Fatigue | 6.81 | 6.38 | 7.88 | 0.16 |
| Confusion | 8.82 | 5.63 | 7.63 | 1.40 |
| Extraversion | 13.27 | 12.75 | 14.88 | 0.44 |
| Neuroticism | 10.27 | 11.00 | 6.50 | 1.66 |
| Exercise attitude | 42.27 | 41.38 | 43.63 | 0.46 |
| Self-esteem | 26.46 | 26.38 | 28.00 | 0.24 |
| Field dependence | 21.27 | 21.75 | 25.63 | 0.30 |
| Depression (DACL) | 4.73 | 4.13 | 3.13 | 0.81 |
| Conformity | 3.73 | 2.25 | 3.38 | 0.46 |

college students (T score = 50) is represented by the solid line, and the broken lines represent a departure of one standard deviation from the mean. It will be noted that the runners possess psychological profiles that are quite similar to high-level athletes in wrestling and crew. How-

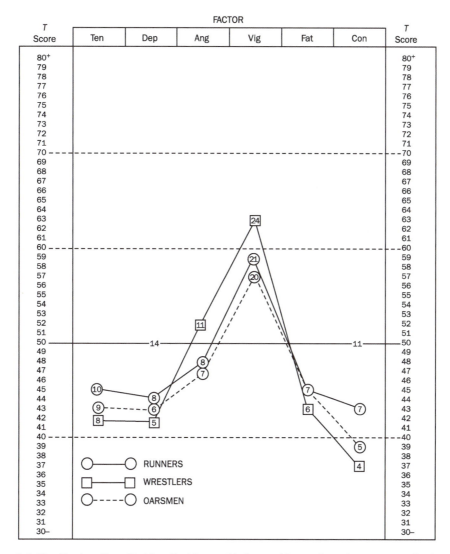

**Figure 1.1** The "iceberg" profile identified for world class athletes. Actual raw score units for tension, depression, anger, vigor, fatigue, and confusion as measured by the *Profile of Mood States* appear in the boxes and circles

ever, all three groups score appreciably *below* the population mean for tension, depression, fatigue, and confusion, and *above* the mean for vigor. These differences favor the athlete samples in every instance, and the observed group profiles for the athletes can be regarded as positive from a mental health standpoint. The observed psychometric configuration can be described as the "iceberg" profile (Morgan, 1968). In other words, high-level athletes score below the mean (surface) on the negative psychological constructs contained in the POMS, but above the mean (surface) for the one positively anchored construct (vigor). The actual raw scores for all of the variables appear in Figure 1.2 for the runners tested in the present study and the previously tested wrestlers and oarsmen, as well as means based on published

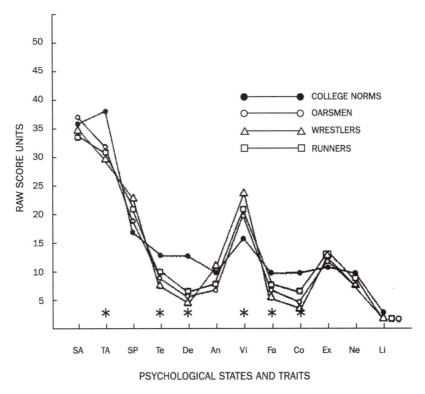

**Figure 1.2** Comparison of selected world class athlete groups with college norms for the complete psychological test battery. The variables in abbreviated form are: state anxiety (SA), trait anxiety (TA), somatic perception (SP), tension (Te), depression (De), anger (An), vigor (Vi), fatigue (Fa), confusion (Co), extroversion (Ex), neuroticism (Ne), and conformity (Li)

norms. Variables *Te* through *Co* in Figure 1.2 constitute data obtained from the POMS, and it will be noted that five of the six significant differences (denoted with asterisks) were accounted for with this scale. Also, the only *trait* variable on which differences existed between the athlete samples and the college norms was that of *trait* anxiety in which the athletes were found to score significantly lower ($p < 0.05$). It should also be noted, and emphasized, that these athlete samples *were not* more extroverted (variable *Ex*) or stable (variable *Ne*) than the college norms, which contradicts a substantial portion of earlier research in the field of sport psychology (Morgan, 1971). Also, the earlier finding that marathoners are more introverted than world class wrestlers was not supported in the present comparison. Further, the marathoners were not more introverted than the general population as reported earlier (Morgan & Costill, 1972). However, the finding that runners are significantly less anxious and depressed than the general population was in agreement with the earlier report of Morgan and Costill. Whether these consistently observed positive differences in *affect* (or mood) represent the result of years of training, or whether long distance runners differ from the outset on these selected behavioral manifestations remains to be demonstrated with longitudinal research. In the meantime, however, since the runners and other athletes possess extroversion and neuroticism scores (*trait* measures) similar to the college norms, it seems quite likely that low anxiety and depression scores (*state* measures) in runners represent a con-sequence of involvement in distance running rather than reflecting an *antecedent* condition.

The observation that these runners, and athletes from other subgroups as well, scored lower than the college norms on tension (POMS) but not on state anxiety (STAI) warrants comment since these variables are presumably tapping the *same* psychological construct. At first glance this appears to be contradictory. However, the "instructional sets" for these two inventories differ in that the respondent is advised to reply in terms of how he or she *feels at this moment* when completing the STAI whereas the "set" used with the POMS requests the subject to reply in terms of "how you have been feeling during the past week including today." Because the tension scale of the POMS and the state anxiety scale of the STAI are highly correlated, it is fair to assume that a lack of complete concordance in the findings was due to elevated state anxiety in these runners at the time of testing, which was due to the test situation *per se*. This view is supported by the finding that these runners scored significantly lower than the college norms on *trait* anxiety as measured by the STAI. Trait anxiety, however, would not be expected to change in a stressful situation since it represents an enduring as opposed to transient (state) variable. Methodological factors such as those cited above are often useful in explaining the many "controversial" or "contradictory" findings that have been found in the field of sport psychology.

## Interview Data

The purpose of the interview data was to (1) test the three hypotheses cited earlier and (2) describe the health behavior of these elite runners. The first hypothesis was *confirmed* in that no single underlying factor or force was responsible for initial involvement in distance running. However, it is noteworthy that none of the runners initially became involved because of the nature of running or its intrinsic appeal. A variety of reasons were given such as peer influence, parental influence, inability to take part in other sports because of body size, a means of getting in shape for another sport such as basketball, and early success in running races held during grade school or junior high school physical education classes.

The second hypothesis was also confirmed in that *adherence* or continuation in competitive running was found to be related to both *extrinsic* and *intrinsic* rewards. The extrinsic rewards related to positive reinforcement resulting from the winning of awards, ability to travel extensively throughout the world, and so on. The intrinsic rewards centered around the sheer joy of running and the sense of well-being resulting from training and competing. Each runner reported that he would continue running for the remainder of his life regardless of whether or not it was possible to continue competing. Hence, the vocational nature of the runner's life style clearly possesses an avocational dimension.

The third hypothesis was rejected, and this represents a major finding in the view of the researchers. *Dissociation* of sensory input did not represent the principal "cognitive strategy," but rather, these elite marathon runners were found to utilize an *associative* strategy. These runners reported that: they paid very close attention to bodily input such as feelings and sensations arising in their feet, calves, and thighs, as well as their respiration; whereas they paid attention to time ("the clock"), pace was largely governed by "reading their bodies"; they identified certain runners they would like to stay with during a given run if possible, but they did not typically employ a "leeching" strategy; during any given marathon they constantly reminded or told themselves to "relax," "stay loose," and so forth; and they typically did not encounter "pain zones" during the marathon, and most of these elite runners dismissed the phenomenon referred to as "the wall" as simply a myth – that is, they did not "come up against the wall" during the marathon run.

Prior work conducted by Morgan (1968) revealed that marathon runners characteristically attempt to "dissociate" sensory input during competition. This research revealed that these athletes are "cognitively active" during competition, but this cognitive activity seldom, if ever, relates to the actual running. The cognitive strategy employed by these athletes can best be regarded as "dissociative cognitive rehearsal." Many runners reconstruct images of past events throughout the marathon. For example, one of the first marathoners interviewed routinely rehearsed or reconstructed his entire educational experience during each marathon. During the run he would age regress himself to first grade and attempt to recall as much as possible about the experience (e.g., the teacher's name and face, the names and faces of other boys and girls in the class, various experiences such as learning to read, print, work with crayons, and paste, playing an instrument in the rhythm band, recess, and so on until his current postdoctoral experiences). Other runners described remarkably similar approaches. For example, another runner always builds a house when he marathons; another writes letters to everyone he owes a letter to; and another listens to a stack of Beethoven records. All rehearsal themes seem to be directed toward the same end – dissociating the painful sensory input.

Unfortunately, the validity of such anthropological reports is always open to question. Therefore, the efficacy of such a procedure has been evaluated under controlled laboratory conditions. Researchers have employed a procedure very similar to that used by Watson (1973) with the exception that the word *down* was used as a "pseudo-matra." Other researchers have documented the effectiveness of a dissociation strategy. For example, using a single-blind, placebo design, Morgan, Horstman, Cymerman, and Stoke (1983) found that a simple dissociation strategy resulted in performance gains that averaged 30% over base-line in contrast with both control and placebo treatments. Their subjects were young adult males, and the endurance task consisted of walking to complete exhaustion at 80% of $\dot{V}_{O_2max}$. The enhanced performance, however, was not associated with cardiovascular, metabolic, or endocrine changes. Hence, the gain in performance took place as a result of the willingness of the subjects to endure or cope with the distress and pain of continued effort.

It has been known for some time that endurance performance can be facilitated by means of hypnosis under a variety of conditions (Morgan, 1972). For example, running performance in the 10,000 meters race, bicycle ergometer sprint speed, shoulder and upper arm endurance, and hand endurance have all been facilitated by means of hypnotic suggestion. It has also been demonstrated more recently that perception of effort during standardized bicycle ergometry can be manipulated hypnotically (Morgan, Hirota, Weitz, & Balke, 1976), and exercise heart rate can be increased, as well as decreased during constant work by means of instrumental conditioning using biofeedback techniques (Arnett, 1974). Therefore, it would seem that either through formal (hypnosis or biofeedback) or informal procedures it would be possible for marathoners to facilitate their performances. Hence, it is not surprising that all of the runners interviewed in our earlier case studies employed various self-taught techniques that can best be viewed as dissociative.

The world class marathoners in the present study, however, did not employ such strategies. Indeed, rather than dissociate, these runners characteristically reported a strategy that we feel can best be viewed as *associative* in nature – not *dissociative*. However, it now becomes clear in retrospect that we were dealing with two rather distinct samples from the marathon community. Our first group consisted of average runners who completed the marathon in times ranging from 3 to 4 hours, whereas the present world class group consisted of several runners who had performed below 2:15 and all of them had performed under 2:20.

## Physiological and Perceptual Data

The selected physiological data presented here are limited to submaximal exercise responsivity in order to better understand the perception of effort. The means and standard deviations for selected physiological variables appear in Table 1.3. Also, a one-way ANOVA was performed on each variable, and the resulting $F$ ratio and associated probability are given for each comparison. The Newman-Keuls procedure described by Winer (1962) was applied when a significant difference for group means occurred.

It will be noted that the three groups did not differ in body weight, percent body fat, or maximal exercise heart rate. A significant difference in groups was observed for maximal aerobic power, and the Newman-Keuls probe revealed that both world class groups scored significantly higher than the college runners. Also, the middle-long distance runners were significantly higher (5 ml/kg min) than the marathon group. A significant difference was also observed for submaximal exercise lactate, with the elite groups scoring significantly lower than the college runners but not differing from each other. This latter finding is understandable since post-hoc analyses revealed the elite groups were running at 84% of maximum while the college group was performing at 95% of maximum during the same submaximal work bout at 12 mph.

The mean perceived exertion ratings for the three groups across the submaximal runs are illustrated in Figure 1.3. The three groups have very similar RPE values during the first two minutes of exercise at 10 mph, and while the elite groups are lower than the college runners at the fourth and sixth minutes, these latter differences are not significant. However, since the elite runners achieved both a perceptual and physiological steady state at 10 mph, and since the college runners had not achieved such states by the sixth minute, it is quite likely that perceptual differences would have emerged with continued running at 10 mph. Once the treadmill speed was increased to 12 mph all groups experienced a significant increase in perception of effort, and at this higher speed the college runners perceived the exercise intensity to be significantly greater than did the elite runners. Also, as noted in Figure 1.3, elite distance runners tend to enter a perceptual steady state at this speed, and, of course, many members of this group compete at a 12-mph pace.

Inspection of Table 1.4 reveals that RPE was significantly correlated with each of the variables, although the magnitude of the correlations differed substantially. Heart rate, for

**Table 1.3** Comparison of selected physiological variables for world class middle-long distance and marathon runners and college middle distance runners

| Variable | World class runners | | College runners (n = 8) | F | p |
| --- | --- | --- | --- | --- | --- |
| | Middle-long distance (n = 11) | Marathon (n = 8) | | | |
| Body weight (kg) | 63.10 | 61.53 | 66.85 | 0.63 | NS |
| Body Fat (%) | 5.79 | 4.63 | 6.81 | 0.85 | NS |
| $\dot{V}_{O_2max}$ (ml/kg·min) | 78.77 | 74.10 | 68.91 | 20.41 | <0.001 |
| Maximum HR (bpm) | 198.73 | 195.75 | 195.12 | 0.63 | NS |
| Submaximal exercise lactate level (mg%) | 30.73 | 31.00 | 69.00 | 18.66 | <0.001 |

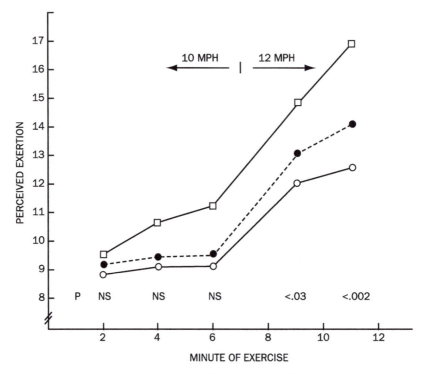

**Figure 1.3** Ratings of perceived exertion in the elite marathon (O–O) and middle-long distance runners (●–●) and the college middle distance runners (□–□)

example, accounted for only 18% of the variance, while lactate accounted for 37% or twice as much of the variance. Ventilatory minute volume was intermediary, accounting for 27% of the variance. Hence, while causality in no way can be argued, it is obvious that lactate accumulation is the single best predictor of the runner's subjective estimate of perceptual cost.

**Table 1.4** Correlation matrix for perceived exertion, heart rate, ventilatory minute volume, and lactate accumulation during submaximal running at 12 mph and 0% Grade (n = 27)

| Variables | Variables | | | |
|---|---|---|---|---|
| | 1 | 2 | 3 | 4 |
| 1. Perceived exertion | – | 0.43* | 0.52† | 0.61† |
| 2. Heart rate (bpm) | | – | 0.14 | 0.44* |
| 3. $\dot{V}_E$ (liter/min) | | | – | 0.65† |
| 4. Lactate (mg%) | | | | – |

* p < 0.05.
† p < 0.01.

## Summary

The findings of this investigation can be interpreted in a straightforward fashion for the most part. First, the psychometric data reveal that elite distance runners resemble outstanding athletes in other sports such as wrestling and rowing, and their *affect* (or mood) seems to be consistently superior to that of the general population. Further, since they do not differ from the general population on personality *traits* such as extroversion-introversion and neuroticism stability (enduring qualities), it is theorized that the positive affective profiles (states) reflect the *consequence* of involvement in distance running, not an *antecedent* or selection factor.

Second, the interview data can be interpreted as suggesting that distance runners belong to a rather unique subculture in various ways besides being affectively one standard deviation from the population mean. Also, their daily investment in running and various forms of training averages 2.5 hours, which clearly has vocational connotations. The interview data also suggests that many motivational forces were operative in terms of initial involvement in running, but the most frequently cited explanations were extrinsic in nature. On the other hand, the reasons for adherence were both extrinsic and intrinsic, and there was not a single runner who did not report that he would continue running once the extrinsic rewards were gone.

The major way in which the elite marathoners studied in this investigation differed from those we have interviewed previously (non-elite), was in their cognitive activity during competition. Whereas the non-elite employ a cognitive strategy designed to *dissociate* painful input, the elite runner *associates* and attempts to process this information, or "read his body" and modulate pace accordingly. The elite runner does not place much emphasis on "the wall" or "pain zones," and there are probably at least two reasons why they differ from the non-elite runner in this respect. First, their physiological superiority permits them to run at a greater percentage of their maximum without encountering discomfort. The elite marathoners, for example, had a mean lactate level of 31 mg% in connection with treadmill running at 12 mph, whereas the less capable runners manifested values twice this level. Also, lactate was found to be the best single predictor of "effort sense" in this study. Second, it is quite likely that elite runners avoid pain zones and fail to come up against the wall simply because they *associate*, i.e., monitor sensory input, and adjust their pace accordingly, with the net result that "pain" is avoided. Of course, and this must be kept in mind, the elite runner can afford the luxury of associating, whereas the non-elite cannot. This overall matter is summarized schematically in Figure 1.4.

On the basis of our interviews it seems reasonable to propose that marathoners might adopt what appear to be two rather divergent "coping strategies." In the one instance it is possible to *dissociate* sensory input because of the discomfort it creates, and in the other case it is possible to cope by means of *associating* or "paying attention to 'bodily' signals." In terms of perception of effort these two cognitive strategies are best viewed as rather diverse approaches with the first basically turning the *perceptostat* on, and the latter turning it off. In work with young adult males the efficacy of dissociation has been demonstrated by Morgan *et al.* (1983) whereby endurance performance has been consistently facilitated. However, their work was carried out under laboratory conditions with continuous monitoring designed to identify biomedical indices that might contraindicate continued exertion.

Since the elite marathon runners consumed significantly less oxygen at the same speed than the middle-long distance runners, and in view of the fact that they did not differ remarkably from a biomechanical standpoint, it would appear that their conscious focus on relaxation, albeit apparently informal, was responsible in part for the lower oxygen consumption. While

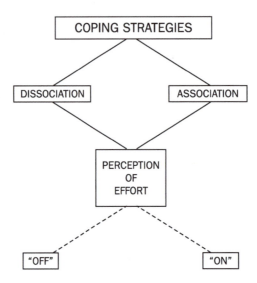

**Figure 1.4** Coping strategies used in the perception of effort

these differences are small when viewed in terms of ml/kg min, extension of such a difference across the distance covered in a marathon takes on a significant meaning. At any rate, whether one's chief concern is with performance or avoidance of trauma, an associative strategy would appear to be more efficacious than a dissociative one. A question that remains unanswered relates to the issue of whether the elite runners learn to employ associative techniques or whether they simply possess this quality. This may be an academic point, however, since individuals can readily be taught to either associate or dissociate (Morgan et al., 1983).

It is concluded that elite marathon runners are very similar from a psychometric stand-point to middle-long distance runners as well as world class athletes in other sports such as wrestling and crew. It is also concluded that elite marathon runners are characterized by positive mental health from an affective standpoint, and this positive affect is regarded as a consequence of training and competition since these world class athletes resemble the general population on most psychological traits. It is further concluded that the major distinguishing psychological dimension of the elite marathoner is in their "effort sense" in that these runners employ an associative cognitive strategy during competition.

## Subsequent research and application

The key study by Morgan and Pollock reported a great deal of qualitative and quantitative data about the psychological make-up of distance runners. Many themes emerged from the key study, and while it is impossible to cover all in detail, the focus is on how subsequent research has developed in three main areas: the validity of predicting athletic success using scores from the POMS; the relationship between personality and performance; and the relationship between personality and participation in sport.

Based on his work exploring the personality characteristics of successful and unsuccessful athletes, Morgan (1968, 1980, 1985) proposed the "iceberg profile," or mental health model of sport performance. However, a number of methodological in-consistencies in Morgan's early studies (e.g., the way in which performance was assessed) led researchers to question the ability of the model to differentiate between successful and less-successful athletes (Prapavessis & Grove, 1991). A meta-analysis by Rowley, Landers, Kyllo, and Etnier (1995) reported that the data from the POMS across 33 studies accounted for less than 1% of the variance in sports performance. While Rowley *et al.* noted that correlating mental health with success is hardly a controversial proposition given that "... psychopathology and success at nearly anything should be inversely correlated" (1995: 186), the data from the POMS did not appear to be able to make the fine distinctions between successful and unsuccessful athletes who may possess similar psychological profiles.

One possibility is that variations in performance requirements across sports may influence the utility of the mental health model in predicting performance (Terry, 1995). For example, in some sports (e.g., boxing, rugby) an angry mood state may facilitate performance. Indeed, winners in Shotokan karate bouts have reported anger scores above the norm (Terry & Slade, 1995). In contrast, in sports where calmness and coordination are valuable assets (e.g., archery) anger may be quite debilitative to performance. Beedie, Terry, and Lane (2000) performed a second meta-analysis of the mood-performance relationship controlling for moderating factors such as type of sport and duration of competition and found that certain sub-scales of the POMS did predict athletic performance in the direction predicted by Morgan. Specifically, a moderate effect size was found for vigor, depression, and confusion, and small effect sizes for anger and tension. Beedie *et al.* also found that the POMS was a better predictor of performance in those sports that are short in duration and those sports involving open skills (e.g., basketball, soccer) rather than closed skills (e.g., rowing, shooting).

One of the criticisms directed at Morgan's (1980, 1985) mental health model is that it emerged from a data-driven approach. Recently, a conceptual model outlining the relationship between the six mood states assessed by the POMS and performance levels was proposed by Lane and Terry (2000). In this model depressed mood serves as a moderator for the effect of other mood constructs on performance. Specifically, the relationship of anger and tension to athletic performance will vary as a function of depressed mood. Anger and tension can be facilitative to performance in the absence of depressed mood but debilitative to performance in the presence of depressed mood, while fatigue and confusion will remain debilitative to performance and vigor facilitative to performance regardless of depressed mood. The model provides an explanation for many of the contradictory findings observed in previous research (Lane, Beedie, & Stevens, 2005), and initial support has been found for many of the hypothesized relationships (Lane, Terry, Beedie, Curry, & Clark, 2001).

Although the POMS has been utilized in a range of sport settings it is not a sport-specific measure. It was initially developed for use with psychiatric patients and as such measures predominantly negative moods (five) compared to positive moods (one). A sport-specific measure of mood derived from the POMS, called the *Brunel Mood Scale* (BRUMS) has been developed (Terry, Lane, Lane, & Keohane, 1999; Terry, Lane, & Fogarty, 2003), and many studies have shown that athletes report a wide range of feeling states beyond those currently classified by POMS sub-scales (Hanin, 2000; Lazarus, 2000). Sport is, at least for most, an enjoyable experience accompanied by many positive feelings, and a more evenly balanced scale would appear more logical. For example, the *Sport Emotion Questionnaire* (SEQ; Jones, Lane, Bray, Uphill, & Catlin, 2005) is proposed to provide a more balanced assessment of emotions in that of the five emotions assessed, two (happiness, excitement) are positive and three are negative (anger, dejection, anxiety).

The relationship between personality characteristics and achievement has been an area of interest for sport psychologists and one that has been hotly debated. Morgan (1980) referred to this as the "credulous-skeptical debate," in which some believe that personality characteristics can be used to predict success in sport (credulous) and others believe that personality characteristics hold no relationship to success (skeptical). While a number of studies have found personality traits to be associated with athletic success (e.g., Evans & Quarterman, 1983; Morgan, O'Connor, Ellickson, & Bradley, 1988), the specific associations have varied considerably, making generalization rather difficult (Vealey, 2002).

Morgan and Pollock adopted Eysenck's (1970) approach to personality and subsequent research using this theoretical framework and reported that athletes exhibit higher extraversion and lower neuroticism when compared to normative data (Kirkcaldy, 1982). In addition to the two dimensions originally proposed by Eysenck (extraversion and neuroticism) a third dimension, psychoticism, was later added to the model (Eysenck & Eysenck, 1976). Individuals high on the psychoticism dimension have a tendency to be egocentric, dominant, antisocial, and have a high level of self-determination. Recent work has reported that individuals attempting to climb Mount Everest have higher scores on extroversion and psychoticism, and lower scores on neuroticism than a normative sample (Egan & Stelmack, 2003). Eysenck's approach was popular, but many psychologists argued that it did not cover the wide variety of factors that contribute to an individual's personality. Developments through the 1980s led to the conceptualization of "the big five" model of personality, in which five basic personality dimensions (neuroticism, extroversion, openness, agreeableness, conscientiousness) each subsume a number of more specific traits (McCrae & Costa, 1987). The extroversion and neuroticism dimensions are as described within Eysenck's theory, while the *openness* dimension distinguishes between those who are open to new experiences (curious, creative, imaginative) and those who like the familiar (conventional, uncreative, unimaginative). The *agreeableness* dimension distinguishes between those who are compassionate (good-natured, trusting, unselfish, forgiving) and those who tend to antagonize (cynical, rude, suspicious, uncooperative), while the *conscientiousness* dimension distinguishes those who are conscientious (organized, reliable, punctual, hardworking) from those who are lackadaisical (unreliable, lazy, easy-going, careless). Although there is still debate regarding how many dimensions should be examined in trait personality research (Barbaranelli & Caprara, 1996; Eysenck, 1991), the five factor model has generally been accepted as the most systematic framework (John, 1990). To date, there has been a limited amount of research using this framework in sport and exercise settings, although one exception is a study by Hughes, Case, Stuempfle, and Evans (2003) which found that participants in a 100-mile race in Alaska reported higher levels of extraversion and openness than normative scores.

Recent research in mainstream psychology has suggested that it may be more beneficial to examine specific aspects of personality (e.g., cautiousness) rather than global personality constructs (e.g., extroversion) in the prediction of performance (Dudley, Orvis, Lebiecki, & Cortina, 2006). This approach has been mirrored by research in sport and exercise settings with researchers focusing on specific aspects of personality considered relevant to sport, such as mental toughness and perfectionism. Mental toughness is proposed by athletes to reflect an ability to cope with the lifestyle demands of the sport and to be more consistent and better than opponents in remaining determined, focused, confident, and in control under pressure (Jones, Hanton, & Connaughton, 2002; Thelwell, Weston, & Greenlees, 2005). In Canadian footballers, adaptive perfectionism, characterized by setting high personal standards and striving hard to achieve them, was positively correlated with task orientation, while maladaptive perfectionism, characterized by a need to avoid failure and a tendency to be over-critical, was positively correlated with ego orientation (Dunn, Dunn, & Syrotuik, 2002). Olympic medal winners have reported high levels of dispositional hope, optimism, and an adaptive approach to perfectionism (Gould, Moffett, & Dieffenbach, 2002). Negative (similar to maladaptive) perfectionism and social physique anxiety are positively associated with disturbed eating attitudes in female athletes (Haase, Prapavessis, & Owens, 2002). Research into the relationship between global psychological traits and performance may have declined, but, in specific fields such as competitive anxiety researchers continue to look at both states and traits as well as how these levels interact to predict theoretical outcomes (e.g., Hanton, Mellalieu, & Hall, 2002).

The development of psychological characteristics has also been an important area of research. Heredity appears to play the largest part in determining personality characteristics (Zuckerman, 1991) and there is evidence that some aspects of personality (e.g., extroversion) may remain relatively stable over a 40-year period spanning childhood and adult life (Hampson & Goldberg, 2006). In sport, researchers have just begun to explore the relationship between genetic make-up and personality. For example, the relationship between the specific genotype of the serotonin transporter 5-hydroxytryptamine (5-HTT) gene, which is proposed to moderate reactions to stress, and positive psychological characteristics in young swimmers has been examined (Golby & Sheard, 2006). While no significant associations were observed, possibly as a result of the small sample size and that the participants had not yet specialized in a single competitive distance, the relationship between genotype and psychological characteristics in athletes remains an area for further research. However, it is also worth noting that heredity is not the sole determinant of personality. The environment also plays a role as does the interaction between heredity and the environment. For example, a child athlete who is extroverted may seek leadership roles and develop leadership skills as a result of being placed in that situation often. Elite athletes themselves have recognized a range of factors as being important in the development of appropriate psychological characteristics with coach and family influence being particularly important (Gould *et al.*, 2002). Participation in sport itself may also impact the development of socially-valued personality traits, such as altruism and cooperation and this is discussed in more detail in Chapter 16.

Many applied implications derive from the research covered in this key study. For example, a number of psychological strategies, such as self-talk, imagery, and relaxation skills have been proposed to enable athletes to develop appropriate psychological states for competition (see Chapter 15). In addition to being used as a tool to predict performance levels, the POMS itself has been used as a tool for diagnosing overtraining syndrome (Morgan, Brown, Raglin, O'Connor, & Ellickson, 1987). Although a natural consequence of developing a body of knowledge outlining the relationship between personality and performance levels is to be able to use personality measures to screen for competition selection, or to encourage participation in sports where the observed attributes may be beneficial, the research is not yet sufficiently advanced for this to be done. Given the many factors that impact sport performance it is arguable whether or not this will ever be achieved.

## Additional readings

Aidman, E., & Schofield, G. (2004). Personality and individual differences in sport. In T. Morris & J. Summers (eds), *Sport psychology: Theory, applications and issues* (2nd ed., pp. 22–47). Milton: Wiley.

Morgan, W. P., Raglin, J. S., & O'Connor, P. J. (2004). Trait anxiety predicts panic behavior in beginning scuba students. *International Journal of Sports Medicine*, 25, 314–22.

Tenenbaum, G., & Bar-Eli, M. (1995). Personality and intellectual capabilities in sport psychology. In D. Saklufske and M. Zeidner (eds), *International handbook on personality and intelligence* (pp. 687–710). New York: Plenum.

Terry, P. C. (2004). Mood and emotions in sport. In T. Morris & J. Summers (eds), *Sport psychology: Theory, applications and issues* (2nd ed., pp. 48–73). Milton: Wiley.

Vealey, R. S. (2002). Personality and sport behavior. In T. Horn (ed.), *Advances in sport psychology* (2nd ed., pp. 43–82). Champaign, IL: Human Kinetics.

## Study questions

1   How useful do you think the iceberg profile is in distinguishing between successful and less successful athletes?

2   What are the strengths and weaknesses of adopting an associative strategy during an endurance event like long-distance running?

3   Can you think of any examples where your personality state in a situation has differed from your personality trait?

4   Do you believe that personality traits contribute to success in sport?

5   Do you think it will ever be possible to use personality measure as a selection tool in sports teams?

## References

Allport, G. W. (1937). *Personality: A psychological interpretation*. New York: Holt.

Allport, G. W., & Odbert, H. S. (1936). Trait-names: A psycholexical study. *Psychological Monographs*, 47 (Whole No. 211).

Arnett, A. J. (1974). The influence of contingent reinforcement on heart rate during exercise. M.S. thesis, University of Wisconsin, Madison.

Barbaranelli, C., & Caprara, G. V. (1996). How many dimensions to describe personality? A comparison of Cattell, Comrey, and the Big Five taxonomies of personality traits. *European Review of Applied Psychology*, 46, 15–24.

Beedie, C. J., Terry, P. C., & Lane, A. M. (2000). The Profile of Mood States and athletic performance: Two meta-analyses. *Journal of Applied Sport Psychology*, 12, 49–68.

Booth, E. G. (1958). Personality traits of athletes as measured by the MMPI. *Research Quarterly*, 29, 127–38.

Borg, G. A. V. (1973). Perceived exertion: A note on "history" and methods. *Medicine and Science in Sports*, 5, 90–3.

Costill, D. L. (1968). *What research tells the coach about distance running*. Washington, DC: AAHPER Publications.

Dudley, N. M., Orvis, K. A., Lebiecki, J. E., & Cortina, J. M. (2006). A meta-analytic investigation of conscientiousness in the prediction of job performance: Examining the intercorrelations and the incremental validity of narrow traits. *Journal of Applied Psychology*, 91, 40–57.

Dunn, J. G. H., Dunn, J. C., & Syrotuik, D. G. (2002). Relationship between multidimensional perfectionism and goal orientations in sport. *Journal of Sport & Exercise Psychology*, 24, 376–95.

Egan, S., & Stelmack, R. M. (2003). A personality profile of Mount Everest climbers. *Personality and Individual Differences*, 34, 1491–4.

Evans, V., & Quarterman, J. (1983). Personality characteristics of successful and unsuccessful black female basketball players. *International Journal of Sport Psychology*, 14, 105–15.

Eysenck, H. J. (1960). *The structure of human personality* (2nd ed.). London: Methuen.

Eysenck, H. J. (1970). *The structure of human personality* (3rd ed.). London: Methuen.

Eysenck, H. J. (1991). Dimensions of personality: 16, 5, or 3? – Criteria for taxonomic paradigm. *Personality and Individual Differences*, 12, 773–90.

Eysenck, H. J., & Eysenck, S. B. G (1968). *Manual for the Eysenck Personality Inventory*. Educational and Industrial Testing Service, San Diego, CA.

Eysenck, H. J., & Eysenck, S. B. G. (1976). *Psychoticism as a dimension of personality*. London: Hodder & Stoughton.

Flanagan, L. A. (1951). A study of some personality traits of different physical activity groups. *Research Quarterly*, 22, 312–23.

Golby, J., & Sheard, M. (2006). The relationship between genotype and positive psychological development in national-level swimmers. *European Psychologist*, 11, 143–8.

Gould, D., Moffett, A., & Dieffenbach, K. (2002). Psychological characteristics and their development in Olympic champions. *Journal of Applied Sport Psychology*, 14, 172–204.

Griffith, C. R. (1928). *Psychology and athletics*. New York: Scribners.

Haase, A. M., Prapvessis, H., & Owens, R. G. (2002). Perfectionism, social physique anxiety and disordered eating: a comparison of male and female athletes. *Psychology of Sport and Exercise*, 3, 209–22.

Hampson, S. E., & Goldberg, L. R. (2006). A first large cohort study of personality trait stability over the 40 years between elementary school and midlife. *Journal of Personality and Social Psychology*, 4, 763–79.

Hanin, Y. L. (2000). Successful and poor performance emotions. In Y. L. Hanin (ed.), *Emotions in sport* (pp. 157–87). Champaign, IL: Human Kinetics.

Hanton, S., Mellalieu, S. D., & Hall, R. (2002). Re-examining the competitive anxiety trait-state relationship. *Personality and Individual Differences*, 33, 1125–36.

Hughes, S. L., Case, S. L., Stuempfle, K. J., & Evans, D. S. (2003). Personality profiles of iditasport ultra-marathon participants. *Journal of Applied Sport Psychology*, 15, 256–61.

John, O. P. (1990). The "Big Five" factor taxonomy: Dimensions of personality in the natural language and in questionnaires. In L. A. Pervin (ed.), *Handbook of personality: Theory and research* (pp. 66–100). New York: Guilford Press.

Jones, G., Hanton, S., & Connaughton, D. (2002). What is this thing called mental toughness? An investigation of elite performers. *Journal of Applied Sport Psychology*, 14, 205–18.

Jones, M. V., Lane, A. M., Bray, S. R., Uphill, M., & Catlin, J. (2005). Development and validation of the Sport Emotion Questionnaire. *Journal of Sport & Exercise Psychology*, 27, 407–31.

Kirkcaldy, B. D. (1982). Personality profiles at various levels of athletic participation. *Personality and Individual Differences*, 3, 321–6.

La Place, J. P. (1954). Personality and its relationship to success in professional baseball. *Research Quarterly*, 25, 313–19.

Lakie, W. L. (1962). Personality characteristics of certain groups of intercollegiate athletes. *Research Quarterly*, 33, 566–73.

Landy, F. J., & Stern, R. M. (1971). Factor analysis of a somatic perception questionnaire. *Journal of Psychosomatic Research*, 15, 179–81.

Lane, A. M., Beedie, C. J., & Stevens, M. J. (2005). Mood matters: A response to Mellalieu. *Journal of Applied Sport Psychology*, 17, 319–25.

Lane, A. M., & Terry, P. C. (2000). The nature of mood: Development of a conceptual model with a focus on depression. *Journal of Applied Sport Psychology*, 12, 16–33.

Lane, A. M., Terry, P. C., Beedie, C. J., Curry, D. A., & Clark, N. (2001). Mood and performance: Test of a conceptual model with a focus on depressed mood. *Psychology of Sport and Exercise*, 2, 157–72.

Lazarus, R. S. (2000). How emotions influence performance in competitive sport. *The Sport Psychologist*, 14, 229–52.

Lubin, B. (1967). *Manual for the Depression Adjective Checklist*. Educational and Industrial Testing Service, San Diego, CA.

McCrae, R. R., & Costa, P. T. (1987). Validation of the five-factor model of personality across instruments and observers. *Journal of Personality and Social Psychology*, 52, 81–90.

McNair, D. M., Lorr, M., & Dropplemam, L. F. (1971). *Manual for the Profile of Mood States*. Educational and Industrial Testing Service, San Diego, CA.

Merriman, J. B. (1960). Relationship of personality traits to motor ability. *Research Quarterly*, 31, 163–73.

Morgan, W. P. (1968). Personality characteristics of wrestlers participating in the world championships. *Journal of Sports Medicine and Physical Fitness*, 8, 212–16.

Morgan, W. P. (1971). Sport psychology. In R. N. Singer (ed.), *Psychomotor domain: Movement behavior* (pp. 193–228). Philadelphia, PA: Lea & Febiger.

Morgan, W. P. (1972). Hypnosis and muscular performance. In W. P. Morgan (ed.), *Ergogenic aids and muscular performance* (pp. 193–233). New York: Academic Press.

Morgan, W. P. (1980). The trait psychology controversy. *Research Quarterly for Exercise and Sport*, 51, 50–76.

Morgan, W. P. (1985). Selected psychological factors limiting performance: A mental health model. In D. H. Clarke & H. M. Eckert (eds), *Limits of human performance* (pp. 70–80). Champaign, IL: Human Kinetics.

Morgan, W. P., Brown, D. R., Raglin, J. S., O'Connor, P. J., & Ellickson, K. A. (1987). Psychological monitoring of overtraining and staleness. *British Journal of Sports Medicine*, 21, 107–14.

Morgan, W. P., & Costill, D. L. (1972). Psychological characteristics of the marathon runner. *Journal of Sports Medicine and Physical Fitness*, 12, 42–6.

Morgan, W. P., Hirota, K., Weitz, G., & Balke, B. (1976). Hypnotic perturbation of perceived exertion: Ventilatory consequences. *American Journal of Clinical Hypnosis*, 18, 182–90.

Morgan, W. P., Horstman, D. H., Cymerman, A., & Stoke, J. (1983). Facilitation of physical performance by means of a cognitive strategy. *Cognitive Therapy and Research*, 7, 251–64.

Morgan, W. P., & Johnson, R. W. (1978). Personality characteristics of successful and unsuccessful oarsmen. *International Journal of Sport Psychology*, 9, 119–33.

Morgan, W. P., O'Connor, P. J., Ellickson, K. A., & Bradley, P. W. (1988). Personality structure, mood states, and performance in elite distance runners. *International Journal of Sport Psychology*, 19, 247–63.

Nagle, F. J., Morgan, W. P., Hellickson, R. O., Serfass, R. C., & Alexander, J. F. (1975). Spotting success traits in Olympic contenders. *The Physician and Sportsmedicine*, 3, 31–4.

Ogilvie, B. C. (1968). Psychological consistencies within the personality of high-level competitors. *Journal of the American Medical Association*, 205, 156–62.

Pervin, L. A., & John, O. P. (2001). *Personality: Theory and research* (8th ed.). New York: Wiley.

Prapavessis, H., & Grove, J. R. (1991). Precompetitive emotions and shooting performance: The mental health and zone of optimal function models. *The Sport Psychologist*, 5, 223–34.

Rowley, A. J., Landers, D. M., Kyllo, L. B., & Etnier, J. L. (1995). Does the iceberg profile discriminate between successful and less successful athletes? A meta-analysis. *Journal of Sport & Exercise Psychology*, 17, 185–99.

Sonstroem, R. J. (1974). Attitude testing examining certain psychological correlates of physical activity. *Research Quarterly*, 45, 93–103.

Spielberger, C. D., Gorsuch, R. L., & Lushene, R. F. (1970). *Manual for the state-trait anxiety inventory*. Palo Alto, CA: Consulting Psychologists Press.

Terry, P. (1995). The efficacy of mood state profiling with elite performers: A review and synthesis. *The Sport Psychologist*, 9, 309–24.

Terry, P. C. (2004). Mood and emotions in sport. In T. Morris & J. Summers (eds), *Sport psychology: Theory, applications and issues* (2nd ed., pp. 48–73). Milton: Wiley.

Terry, P. C., Lane, A. M., & Fogarty, G. J. (2003). Construct validity of the Profile of Mood States – Adolescents for use with adults. *Psychology of Sport and Exercise*, 4, 125–39.

Terry, P. C., Lane, A. M., Lane, H. J., & Keohane, L. (1999). Development and validation of a mood measure for adolescents. *Journal of Sports Sciences*, 17, 861–72.

Terry, P. C., & Slade, A. (1995). Discriminant effectiveness of psychological state measures in predicting performance outcome in karate competition. *Perceptual and Motor Skills*, 81, 275–86.

Thelwell, R., Weston, N., & Greenlees, I. (2005). Defining and understanding mental toughness within soccer. *Journal of Applied Sport Psychology*, 17, 326–32.

Vealey, R. S. (2002). Personality and sport behavior. In T. Horn (ed.), *Advances in sport psychology* (2nd ed., pp. 43–82). Champaign, IL: Human Kinetics.

Watson, L. (1973). *Supernature*. New York: Doubleday.

Winer, B. J. (1962). *Statistical principles in experimental design*. New York: McGraw-Hill.

Zuckerman, M. (1991). *Psychobiology of personality*. Cambridge: Cambridge University Press.

# 2

# Anxiety

Martens, R., & Gill, D. L. (1976). State anxiety among successful and unsuccessful competitors who differ in competitive trait anxiety. *Research Quarterly*, 47, 698–708

## Background and context

Few topics in sport psychology have aroused as much interest as anxiety and this is hardly surprising given the stressful nature of competitive sport settings. Anxiety is characterized by feelings of apprehension and tension along with activation or arousal of the autonomic nervous system (Spielberger, 1966). Thus, anxiety may comprise cognitive (e.g., feelings of apprehension) and physiological (e.g., increased activation of the autonomic nervous system) changes. Competitive anxiety is the anxiety experienced by individuals when placed in a competitive situation, such as a tennis match or athletics meet. The symptoms of competitive anxiety are common to many athletes and examples include increased heart rate, negative thoughts, sweaty palms, images of failure, and butterflies in the stomach.

Most athletes would accept that competitive sport settings can be anxiety inducing. Although athletes desire success they are up against opponents who are equally determined to succeed, are often watched by an audience who are either supportive or hostile (but rarely indifferent), and in many sports the threat of injury, pain, or discomfort is all too real. In short, there is the possibility of public failure, disapproval by significant others, and physical harm. The ability to cope with anxiety is integral to success in competitive sport. Indeed, the term "sport experiment" has been coined, implying that the ability to cope with the pressure of competition, which may lead to increased anxiety levels, is the key factor that will determine success given that athletes, particularly at the elite level, are well matched, technically and physically (Patmore, 1986).

Understanding anxiety and the role it plays in competitive situations is clearly an important endeavor and research at the time of Martens and Gill's paper focused on many aspects. For example, understanding how athletes coped with, or could control, anxiety (e.g., Mahoney & Avener, 1977), how anxiety arising from the presence of others impacted the learning of motor tasks (e.g., Martens, 1969), and how anxiety impacted performance (e.g., Martens, Gill, & Scanlan, 1976).

A primary purpose of Martens and Gill's key study was to continue to investigate the construct validity of a measure of competitive trait anxiety developed by Martens (1977) – the *Sport Competition Anxiety Test* (SCAT). Competitive trait anxiety was defined by Martens and Gill as ". . . a relatively stable personality disposition that describes a person's tendency to perceive competitive situations as threatening or nonthreatening" (Martens &

Gill, 1976: 699). Uncertainty of outcome and importance of outcome are the two constructs that impact a person's perception of threat, which in turn impacts the level of state anxiety (Martens, Vealey, & Burton, 1990). Competitive trait anxiety is thus important as it impacts the level of state anxiety experienced (i.e., actual anxiety at any given moment in time) and therefore possibly performance levels.

The paper by Martens and Gill was published during the early days of research into competitive anxiety. As such, it is not surprising that a primary aim of the study was concerned with determining the validity of available measures. The development of a theoretical base for understanding the influence of emotions, such as anxiety, in sport depends on having valid and reliable measures (Lane, 2004). Early research in any area of psychological inquiry will often be concerned with measurement issues and developing a valid measure ensures that researchers and practitioners are able to have confidence in the values generated. The construct validity of an instrument is demonstrated by evidence that the construct it purports to measure (in this case trait anxiety) is related to other constructs consistent with theoretical predictions (Vealey, 1992). As the SCAT was developed to assess competitive trait anxiety, one way to determine its construct validity was to examine how it predicted actual state anxiety during competition. Martens (1977) considered it important to develop trait anxiety measures for competitive situations, as they would be better able to predict actual state anxiety responses in competitive situations than general measures of trait anxiety.

In order to understand the study, it is important to be familiar with the SCAT. The SCAT is a 15-item inventory in which participants indicate how they typically feel during competitive situations. Two versions of the SCAT were validated, with minor differences in the instructional set and a change to one of the items (Martens, 1977). One version was for use with children between 10 and 14 years of age (SCAT-C; where "C" indicates children) and one for use with participants 15 years and older (SCAT-A; where "A" indicates adults). Martens and Gill used the form SCAT-C in their study. The SCAT-C required participants to indicate how they usually felt when they competed in sports and games. Martens (1977) tried to reduce the response bias by using the title the *Illinois Competition Questionnaire* and not the *Sport Competition Anxiety Test*. To further hide the true aim of the test, five of the items were spurious (e.g., I am a good sport when I compete). The ten items that measure trait anxiety are as follows, and participants respond on a three-item scale where 1 = Hardly Ever; 2 = Sometimes; 3 = Often:

Before I compete I feel uneasy
Before I compete I worry about not performing well
When I compete I worry about making mistakes
Before I compete I am calm (reverse scored)
Before I compete I get a funny (queasy in SCAT-A) feeling in my stomach
Just before competing I notice my heart beats faster than usual
Before I compete I feel relaxed (reverse scored)
Before I compete I am nervous
I get nervous wanting to start the game
Before I compete I usually get uptight

## Key study

The primary purpose of this study was to continue investigating the construct validity of SCAT by testing the hypothesis that persons high in competitive A-trait (trait anxiety) respond in competitive situations with higher levels of A-state (state anxiety) than persons low in competitive A-trait. In recent years several situation-specific trait anxiety scales have been developed because general trait anxiety (A-trait) has been too diverse a construct for predicting accurately how persons behave in all situations. These situation-specific A-trait scales have, in general, shown greater predictive power in the specific situation for which they were developed (Sarason, Davidson, Lighthall, Waite, & Ruebush, 1960).

The theoretical development of competitive A-trait is rooted primarily in the work of Spielberger (1966) and Sarason *et al.* (1960). Competitive A-trait is a relatively stable personality disposition that describes a person's tendency to perceive competitive sport situations as threatening or non-threatening. The SCAT, therefore, was designed to have greater discriminability than general A-trait inventories for identifying persons who tend to perceive competitive situations as threatening or non-threatening. Based on Spielberger's state-trait theory, the basic proposition in this research is that persons high in competitive A-trait respond in competitive situations with higher levels of state anxiety (A-state) than persons low in competitive A-trait.

In addition, this study determined how competition outcome (success-failure) affects A-state levels and how SCAT interacts with competition outcome to predict A-state levels. It was expected that failure would produce higher A-states than success because failure is the more threatening condition, as this has been observed in several previous studies (e.g., Gaudry & Poole, 1972; Millimet & Gardner, 1972). Previous research with general A-trait and success-failure has also shown that success reduced A-state and failure increased A-state more in high A-trait persons than in low A-trait persons. In other words, success reduced the difference between high and low A-trait persons and failure magnified the difference because failure is more threatening. Whether or not SCAT interacts similarly with success-failure is unknown, but the relationship was investigated in this study.

## Method

### Participants and Design

Initially SCAT was administered to 490 fifth- and sixth-grade males and females. Children who scored at the high and low extremes on SCAT were selected to participate in the experimental phase of the study. From the lower quartile (SCAT scores 10–16) 24 males and 24 females were chosen; the same number of males and females were chosen from the upper quartile (SCAT scores 24–30). Participants of each sex and from each level of SCAT were randomly assigned to one of the following success-failure conditions: (a) win 80% of the games ($W_{80}$), (b) win 50% of the games ($W_{50}$), (c) win 20% of the games ($W_{20}$), and (d) a non-competition control condition (NC). Thus, the design of the study was a sex × SCAT × success-failure (2 × 2 × 4) factorial with six participants in each cell.

The dependent variables in the study were periodic measures of A-state as assessed by Spielberger's (1973) *State Anxiety Inventory for Children* (SAIC) and a *Nervous Scale*. The first SAIC (initial) score was obtained when SCAT was administered in the classrooms. Experimental assessments of A-state were then taken immediately prior to the start of the competition (pre-competition), after 10 games (mid-competition) and immediately after the final game (post-competition).

## Apparatus

The motor task consisted of an aluminum maze mounted on a two-dimensional teeter board. By maneuvering two handles located on adjacent sides of the maze the participant controlled the pitch of the board. The task objective was to move a steel ball through the maze as quickly as possible while avoiding numerous cul-de-sacs. A series of 15 microswitches spaced at approximately equal intervals along the maze monitored the progress of the ball through the maze. The microswitches sequentially activated a series of 15 lights on a display panel located above the participant's maze, and simultaneously activated the same light series on the experimenter's master console. The participant's display panel also contained "ready" and "go" lights that provided the starting signal, a digital clock that indicated to the nearest tenth of a second the time taken to complete the maze, and a second row of lights that purportedly monitored the opponent's progress. The master console contained light sequences and digital time clocks for both the participant and opponent, control buttons for the ready-go signal, buttons that manipulated the progress of any opponent, and a button that reset the clocks and lit to the starting position after every game.

The participant's maze and display were located in one room of a mobile van, the master console and a pseudo-computer in an adjacent room. The computer, complete with the several rows of flashing lights and interconnecting wires, purportedly connected the participant with another fifth- or sixth-grader in a similar van at another school for the competition.

## Procedure

Several weeks before the experiment both the SAIC and SCAT, in that order, were administered to the initial 490 participants in their classrooms. Based on their SCAT scores, students were selected as subjects for the experiment.

During the experimental phase of the study the mobile van was driven to each school for the testing. When each participant arrived at the van, the *Nervous Scale* was administered. This scale was a simple linear slide which the participant could position to indicate his/her nervous state. The scale ranged from −50 (calm) to +50 (nervous) with a midpoint of 0 (neutral) and was incremented in units of five.

The participant then entered the experimental room in the van where instructions about the experimental treatment and apparatus were given. The participant was told he/she would be competing with an opponent of the same age and sex who was at another school in a similar van and that the computer would indicate to each of them how both were faring. Instructions for operating the maze were given, one practice trial was allowed, and the participant took his/her place for the competition. The experimenter took her place at the master console and quickly went through the following points, "Ball on start! Grasp the handles! Watch the lights!" After waiting a few seconds, the experimenter announced that the opponent was not yet ready. The SAIC and *Nervous Scale* for the pre-competition score were then obtained. Following that, the participant and experimenter resumed their places and the competition began.

The opponent was generally kept within three lights of the participant's position on the maze during each game, and overall win-loss ratio was manipulated according to a pre-established schedule. The $W_{50}$ group won games 1, 3, 5, 6, 9, 11, 13, 16, 18, and 20; the $W_{20}$ group won games 2, 7, 13, and 16, and the $W_{80}$ group lost those four games. After every game, the participant's time, opponent's time, winner of that game, and cumulative win-loss ratio were announced. The SAIC and *Nervous Scale* mid-competition A-state measures were taken during a break after game 10.

After game 20 the participant was told via the computer how he/she had performed. Performance feedback consisted of the activation of one of three lights (after the computer had gone through a number of gyrations) which labeled the cumulative performance as poor, average, or excellent. The feedback was consistent with the win-loss treatment experienced by the participant. The feedback was not of course, computed by the pseudo-computer but was controlled by the experimenter through the use of hidden switches. The non-competition participants were not ranked and competition was never mentioned during the experiment.

Post-competition A-state measures were taken immediately after participants received their rankings. A special debriefing procedure was used with the $W_{20}$ group to alleviate feelings of failure. In the end, all participants were told they had played well and were asked not to discuss the game or the competition with their classmates until testing at that school was completed.

## Results

This study used a pre-test/post-test design with repeated observations of the treatment effects. The data analysis involved multivariate analysis of covariance (MANCOVA) and multiple regression analysis. A MANCOVA was computed using the pre-, mid-, and post-competition SAIC scores as dependent variables and the initial SAIC score as the covariate. The sex main effect was not significant ($F_{3,77} = 1.50, p < .23$), but the SCAT ($F_{3,77} = 3.04, p < .04$) and success-failure ($F_{9,187.55} = 4.50, p < .0001$) main effects were significant. The multivariate F test treats the three dependent variables as a composite rather than as three separate measures. To assist in the interpretation of the relative contributions of the three dependent variables to the multivariate F, univariate F, and discriminant function coefficients were computed. In addition, the adjusted means, which remove the effects of the covariate, were calculated for each significant effect.

Results of the univariate F tests and discriminant function coefficients for the SCAT main effect are presented in Table 2.1. Although the high SCAT group had higher SAIC scores for all three measures, as indicated by the observed and adjusted means in Table 2.2, the mid-competition measure appeared to be the major contributor to the multivariate F. The mid-competition SAIC had the largest univariate F value, and its standardized discriminant function coefficient was considerably larger than the coefficients for either the pre-competition or the post-competition measures.

As shown in Table 2.2, the differences in the initial A-state levels between high and low SCAT participants were substantial. As a consequence, the covariate altered the pre-competition SAIC scores substantially, as seen by the inspection of the observed and adjusted means. High SCAT participants remained significantly higher in A-state levels than low SCAT participants, but not to the extent shown by the observed means.

**Table 2.1** Additional analysis of covariance results for SCAT main effect

| Dependent variable | df | Univariate F | p | Standardized discriminant function coefficient |
|---|---|---|---|---|
| Pre-competition SAIC | 1, 79 | 4.83 | .03 | −.32 |
| Mid-competition SAIC | 1, 79 | 8.12 | .006 | −1.04 |
| Post-competition SAIC | 1, 79 | 2.07 | .15 | .41 |

High and low SCAT participants differed most in A-state levels at the mid-competition interval, with high SCAT participants experiencing their highest levels of A-state. After completing the competition, the post-competition SAIC adjusted means showed that both high and low SCAT participants decreased their A-state levels substantially.

The univariate $F$ tests and discriminant function coefficients for the success-failure main effect are presented in Table 2.3. Three sets of discriminant function coefficients were obtained because the success-failure factor had three degrees of freedom. Coefficients for the first two discriminant functions are presented; both were statistically significant using Bartlett's chi square test ($p < .05$).

Examining the adjusted mean scores (Table 2.4) among the four success-failure conditions for each dependent variable reveals what occurred. There were few differences among the four treatments at pre-competition. This is entirely understandable because the participants had not yet competed. Overall, the mid- and post-competition SAIC scores were similar. In general, A-state levels increased as the number of games won decreased. A-state levels were low for persons who were winning, particularly at post-competition. While the $W_{50}$ group showed relatively high A-state levels after the first 10 games, they reported quite low A-state levels after completing all 20 games. In comparison, the $W_{20}$ group not only showed high A-state levels at the mid-competition point but also at post-competition. The NC participants remained calm throughout and had a slight tendency to reduce A-state levels as time progressed. These observations are supported by the highly significant univariate $F$ tests (see Table 2.3) for the mid- and post-competition SAIC scores. The evidence shows clearly that

**Table 2.2**  Observed and adjusted SAIC means for the SCAT main effect

| Dependent variable | Low SCAT | High SCAT |
|---|---|---|
| Initial (covariate) SAIC | 27.90 | 33.21 |
| Pre-competition SAIC | | |
|     Observed | 29.00 | 34.00 |
|     Adjusted | 30.17 | 32.83 |
| Mid-competition SAIC | | |
|     Observed | 30.02 | 35.83 |
|     Adjusted | 30.55 | 35.30 |
| Post-competition SAIC | | |
|     Observed | 27.65 | 31.60 |
|     Adjusted | 28.37 | 30.88 |

**Table 2.3**  Additional analysis of covariance results for success-failure main effect

| Dependent variable | df | Univariate F | p | Standardized discriminant function Coefficient 1 | Coefficient 2 |
|---|---|---|---|---|---|
| Pre-competition SAIC | 3,79 | .18 | .91 | .59 | .18 |
| Mid-competition SAIC | 3,79 | 6.66 | .001 | −.61 | −1.39 |
| Post-competition SAIC | 3,79 | 7.72 | .001 | −.70 | −1.23 |
| % of canonical variation | | | | 69.9 | 29.6 |

**Table 2.4** Observed and adjusted SAIC means for the success-failure main effect

| Dependent variable | $W_{80}$ | $W_{50}$ | $W_{20}$ | NC |
|---|---|---|---|---|
| Initial (covariate) SAIC | 29.58 | 31.62 | 29.96 | 31.04 |
| Pre-competition SAIC | | | | |
|     Observed | 31.08 | 31.92 | 31.83 | 31.17 |
|     Adjusted | 31.51 | 31.45 | 32.09 | 30.95 |
| Mid-competition SAIC | | | | |
|     Observed | 30.12 | 35.29 | 37.00 | 29.29 |
|     Adjusted | 30.31 | 35.08 | 37.12 | 29.19 |
| Post-competition SAIC | | | | |
|     Observed | 25.71 | 29.08 | 35.71 | 28.00 |
|     Adjusted | 25.97 | 28.79 | 35.87 | 27.87 |

failure increases A-state levels and, in the case of the $W_{50}$ treatment, when the threat of failure was present (at mid-competition), A-state levels are also elevated. The discriminant function coefficients also corroborated these observations by indicating that the mid- and post-competition variables were the major contributors to the significant multivariate $F$.

The sex × SCAT interaction was not significant ($F_{3,\ 77} = 1.65$, $p < .19$), but the sex × success-failure interaction neared significance at the .05 level ($F_{9,187.58} = 1.83$, $p < .07$). The supplementary analyses indicated that the interaction occurred at the mid-competition point. The univariate $F$ ANOVA ($F_{3,\ 79} = 3.39$, $p < .03$) and the step-down $F$ test ($F_{3,78} = 4.94$, $p < .01$), which used not only the initial SAIC score but also the pre-competition score as covariates, were significant. Additionally, the discriminant function coefficient was substantial ($-1.41$) for the mid-competition score. In Figure 2.1 the sex × success-failure interaction is shown for this mid-competition measure of A-state. Boys are substantially higher than girls in A-state in the $W_{50}$ treatment. Boys remained higher in A-state in the $W_{20}$ treatment than girls, but the girls showed marked increases in their A-state levels when compared to the $W_{50}$, $W_{80}$, and NC treatments.

The SCAT × success-failure interaction was not significant ($F_{9,187.55} = 0.18$, $p < .99$), nor was the sex × SCAT × success-failure interaction ($F_{9,187.55} = 0.48$, $p < .89$) for the SAIC scores. The *Nervous Scale* was not an informative dependent variable. Although the results were similar to those using the SAIC, the scale was generally less sensitive to treatment manipulations and less reliable. Thus, none of the results for the *Nervous Scale* are reported.

A multiple regression analysis was also computed using sex, SCAT, and success-failure as the independent variables, or predictors, and each of the four SAIC scores as dependent variables. The NC condition was not included in the regression analysis; the three success-failure conditions, which represent a linear progression of the number of games won, were coded 1, 2, and 3. Both Sex and SCAT were coded dichotomously (0 or 1). The standardized regression coefficients for three predictors, the multiple correlation coefficients, and the $F$ ratio for each dependent variable are presented in Table 2.5. The standardized regression coefficients were tested using t-tests.

The $F$ test of regression was statistically significant for all four SAIC measures. From Table 2.5 and the previously reported results some very clear trends emerged, SCAT was the major predictor of the initial and pre-competition measures. Once participants began competing, success-failure became a statistically reliable predictor of mid-competition and post-competition A-state levels. Moreover, as participants won and lost more games, success-

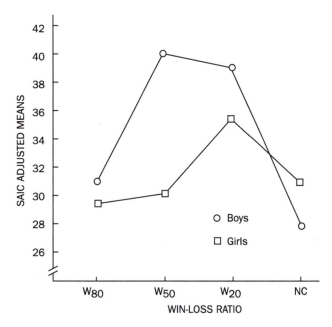

**Figure 2.1** Adjusted means for the sex × success-failure interaction on the mid-competition SAIC scores

**Table 2.5** Summary of the multiple regression results

| | Dependent variables | | | |
|---|---|---|---|---|
| *Standardized regression coefficients* | *Initial SAIC* | *Pre-competition SAIC* | *Mid-competition SAIC* | *Post-competition SAIC* |
| Sex | −.03 | .10 | .27* | .14 |
| SCAT | −.42** | −.45** | −.33** | −.24* |
| Success-failure | .02 | .05 | .31** | .46** |
| Multiple R | .42 | .46 | .53 | .54 |
| R² | .18 | .21 | .28 | .29 |
| F Ratio (df = 3,68) | 4.90** | 6.18** | 8.92** | 9.29** |

*p < .05.
*p < .01.

failure became a more powerful predictor of A-state levels. Although the predictive power of SCAT declined somewhat after the pre-competition measure, the total variance explained by the three predictors increased modestly with each successive measure of A-state. This appears to be largely the consequence of adding the success-failure factor. Sex added significantly to the prediction equation only for the mid-competition SAIC measure. In light of the MANCOVA results, this probably is an indicator that the boys and girls were affected differently by the success-failure manipulation, particularly in the $W_{50}$ condition at the time of the mid-competition measure.

## Discussion

The results in general supported the hypotheses of the study. High SCAT participants manifested higher levels of A-state than low SCAT participants just prior to competition. Somewhat unexpectedly, however, this difference existed to a lesser extent (although significantly) in the initial noncompetitive measure of A-state. This finding renews debate about whether trait anxiety is a chronic or situationally elicited personality variable. Finding that SCAT significantly predicted initial A-state levels suggests that competitive A-trait is a chronic variable. However, because the predictive power of SCAT improved somewhat in the competitive situation, SCAT also was responsive to situational influences. Moreover, when the initial differences in A-state were covaried out, high SCAT participants remained significantly higher in A-state than low SCAT participants at pre-competition. The question as to whether A-trait constructs identify chronic or acute A-state differences has a long history in the anxiety literature (Spence & Spence, 1966) and will require further study as it pertains to competitive A-trait.

While SCAT was a significant predictor of pre-competition A-state levels, this variable in conjunction with the sex and success-failure factor accounted for only 21% of the pre-competitive A-state variance. Is accounting for 21% of the pre-competitive A-state variance noteworthy? For several reasons the answer appears to be yes. The cost of obtaining internal validity in experimental research is often the loss of powerful manipulation of the experimental treatments. The pre-competitive situation fell considerably short of creating the commonly observed anticipatory tension seen prior to actual sport contests. Unlike the usual sport situation, participants came to the experiment with no previous experience with the maze task and little vested interest in the outcome of the competition. Secondly, it is unlikely that any single personality disposition will account for a major part of behavioral variance, particularly when research has shown that situational variables are substantial determinants of behavior.

Evidence to support both these reasons is found in the mid-competition A-state scores. SCAT was a significant predictor of A-state levels at mid-competition. After having played 10 games, participants had some experience with the task but anticipated playing another 10 games. Because they now had also experienced winning and losing, the success-failure factor also became a significant predictor. These two variables, in conjunction with the sex factor, were able to increase the prediction to 28% of the A-state variance at mid-competition.

The success-failure main effect indicated that participants who were highly successful ($W_{80}$ group) maintained low levels of A-state throughout the competition. Their levels of A-state were similar to the NC control group. The $W_{50}$ groups showed high A-state levels after the first 10 games when their destiny was quite uncertain, but reduced their A-state levels to normal after completing the 20 games. The $W_{20}$ groups, however, had high A-state levels not only after the first 10 games, but also after competing in all 20 games. In addition, there was some tendency for boys to be higher in A-state levels than girls in the $W_{50}$ and $W_{20}$ treatments at mid-competition.

Although both SCAT and success-failure significantly predicted mid- and post-competition A-state levels, the two variables did not significantly interact. The failure to observe a SCAT × success-failure interaction appears to be a result of SCAT being insensitive to the outcomes of winning and losing. The highly significant success-failure main effect indicated that A-state levels increased as the number of games won decreased at both mid- and post-competition. Hence, both high and low SCAT persons increased in A-state when they failed and remained relatively calm when they succeeded. These findings are consistent with SCAT's intended purpose – to identify persons who differ in their tendency to become anxious prior to competition, and not how they respond to the consequences of competing.

In conclusion, the results of this study provide clear support for the construct validity of SCAT. The hope of sport psychologists to assist coaches and athletes in understanding individual differences in response to the competitive situation will depend in part on their ability to measure reliably and validly such constructs as competitive A-trait. This study has also shown what most of us have experienced – comfortable levels of A-state when we win and uncomfortably high A-state levels when we lose.

## Subsequent research and application

The study by Martens and Gill was one of 11 cited by Martens (1977) in his original monograph outlining the construct validity of the SCAT. Collectively the findings showed that SCAT scores were better predictors of state anxiety in competitive situations than general measures of trait anxiety and were correlated more strongly with state anxiety in competitive situations than non-competitive situations (Martens *et al.*, 1990). These findings allied to data indicating acceptable internal consistency (Ostrow & Ziegler, 1978) and test-retest reliability (Martens *et al.*, 1990) suggested that the SCAT is an effective predictor of anxiety responses during competitive situations.

The SCAT has since been used in a number of studies. For example, Andersen and Williams (1987) compared the trait anxiety scores of individuals who had also completed the Bem Sex-Role Inventory (Bem, 1974) and were classified as either sex-typed (masculine males, feminine females), cross sex-typed (masculine females, feminine males) or androgynous (males and females who have the characteristics of both genders). The major finding was feminine females reported significantly higher levels of competitive trait anxiety than all other groups. Sonstroem and Bernardo (1982) used the SCAT to explore the relationship between trait anxiety and performance. Trait anxiety had a mediating effect on the relationship between competitive anxiety and basketball performance with high trait anxious individuals demonstrating a more noticeable decrement in performance under conditions of high state anxiety than low, or moderate, trait anxiety individuals.

Interestingly, at the time of Martens and Gill's study, there were no validated measures of competitive state anxiety and they assessed state anxiety using a general measure of anxiety – Spielberger's (1973) *State Anxiety Inventory for Children*. To address this limitation, Martens, Burton, Rivkin, and Simon (1980) developed the *Competitive State Anxiety Inventory* (CSAI). However, soon after the development of the SCAT and the CSAI, sport psychologists rethought the way in which competitive anxiety was conceptualized. In line with test anxiety (e.g., Liebert & Morris, 1967) and clinical psychology (e.g., Davidson & Schwartz, 1976) literature, competitive anxiety was considered to be multidimensional, comprising both cognitive and somatic components (Martens, Burton, Vealey, Bump, & Smith, 1990). Cognitive anxiety refers to ". . . fear of failure and negative expectations about performance" while somatic anxiety refers to ". . . individuals' perceptions of their physiological state" (Hardy, Jones, & Gould 1996: 142). Although it had been recognized that anxiety had both cognitive and somatic aspects (e.g., see the definition by Spielberger at the start of this chapter) anxiety had typically been considered as a unitary construct. That is, an individual was considered to be anxious rather than cognitively anxious, somatically anxious or both cognitively and somatically anxious. Adopting a multidimensional approach to the study of competitive anxiety meant that an individual could be high in cognitive anxiety and low in somatic anxiety, or vice versa, high in both or low in both. Furthermore, cognitive and somatic anxiety would have separate antecedents and relate to performance differently (Parfitt, Jones, & Hardy, 1990), and be affected differently by different anxiety control techniques (Burton, 1990).

The conceptualization of competitive anxiety as a multidimensional construct meant that new measurement tools had to be developed. Smith, Smoll, and Schultz (1990) developed the *Sport Anxiety Scale* (SAS) as a trait measure of multidimensional competitive anxiety. During the development two separate cognitive factors emerged and were labeled "worry" and "concentration disruption", respectively. The SAS therefore provides scores for worry, concentration disruption, and somatic anxiety. Adequate internal consistency of the scales, test-retest reliability and validity data have been reported for the SAS (Smith *et al.*, 1990). The SAS has been used in a number of recent studies. For example, high trait anxious individuals (assessed via the SAS) respond to stress using what would appear to be more maladaptive coping strategies, such as behavioral disengagement, self-blame, humor, denial, and wishful thinking in comparison to low trait anxious individuals (Giacobbi Jr & Weinberg, 2000). However, the factor structure of the SAS has been subject to some criticism (Dunn *et al.*, 2000), and it has also been suggested that Item 1 (I feel nervous) is too ambiguous to capture specific physiological responses, such as increased heart rate, that are typical of somatic anxiety (Prapavessis, Maddison, & Fletcher, 2005). In response Smith, Cumming, and Smoll (2006) have recently proposed a revised version of the SAS addressing these concerns.

Recent work on competitive state anxiety research has largely been driven by the work of Martens and colleagues who developed the *Competitive State Anxiety Inventory – 2* (CSAI–2) and published it alongside a multidimensional theory of competitive state anxiety (MAT; Martens *et al.*, 1990). Similar to the SAS the CSAI–2 was originally developed to assess cognitive and somatic anxiety, but an additional cognitive factor (self-confidence) emerged during the development. The CSAI–2 therefore provides scores for cognitive anxiety, somatic anxiety, and self-confidence. According to MAT each sub-scale relates to performance differently. Specifically, cognitive anxiety has a negative linear relationship, self-confidence a positive linear relationship, and somatic anxiety an inverted-U relationship with performance. However, empirical support for these predictions has been equivocal (Woodman & Hardy, 2001) and competing approaches, such as Hardy and colleagues' catastrophe model of anxiety and performance (Hardy, 1990; Hardy & Fazey, 1987), which requires looking at somatic (physiological arousal) and cognitive anxiety interactions, have also been proposed to describe the relationship between multi-dimensional anxiety and performance.

In addition to *describing* the relationship between competitive anxiety and performance, researchers also strive to *explain* this relationship. Broadly, an individual's emotional state, such as anxiety, could influence motivation along with both physical and cognitive functioning in a competitive sport setting (see Jones & Uphill, 2004a). Examples of potential theories that aim to explain the relationship between competitive anxiety and performance include processing efficiency theory (Eysenck & Calvo, 1992) and the conscious processing hypothesis (Masters, 1992). Interestingly, trait anxiety may also play a greater role in the anxiety performance relationship than initially thought. Trait anxiety is often assumed to impact performance simply through influencing the level of state anxiety. However, Hardy *et al.* (1996) have outlined that a performer's competitive trait anxiety and competitive state anxiety may interact to impact attentional selectivity which in turn may impact performance levels. Specifically, high trait anxious individuals who are also highly state anxious selectively attend towards threatening information (e.g., how well an opponent is performing in a warm-up), while low trait anxious participants who have high levels of state anxiety show an attentional bias away from such information (Eysenck, 1992). Interestingly, this proposition could be used to explain, in part, the findings of Sonstroem and Bernardo (1982) described earlier.

The interaction between trait anxiety, state anxiety, and performance was something explored by Martens and Gill in their study, albeit that they explored the interaction of performance outcome and trait anxiety on state anxiety levels. The impact of performance outcome on emotional states has also been explored by more recent research. Collectively, the findings indicate that competitors respond with positive affect following success and negative affect following a defeat (e.g., Hassmén & Blomstrand, 1995; Wilson & Kerr, 1999). More recent research has demonstrated these affective responses are present in the five days following competition while winning a competition is associated with an increase in well-being, evidenced by a decrease in cold/flu symptom reporting (Jones & Sheffield, in press).

One prominent area of research has focused on understanding how individuals perceive the symptoms they experience during competitive situations. To this end the CSAI–2 has been modified to include a directional sub-scale, the CSAI–2(d), which measures whether the symptoms reported are perceived as being facilitative or debilitative to performance (Jones & Swain, 1992). Athletes with a positive belief in their ability to cope, and in goal attainment, are proposed to interpret their symptoms as facilitative, whereas those with negative expectancies will interpret their symptoms as negative (Jones, 1995). Recent work has extended this line of inquiry to consider a broader range of emotions. Athletes who perceive their anxiety symptoms as facilitative to performance report more positive feelings (e.g., excited, relaxed) and less negative feelings (e.g., tense, angry) than athletes who perceive their anxiety symptoms as debilitative to performance (Jones & Hanton, 2001; Mellalieu, Hanton, & Jones, 2003).

Underpinning much of the research into competitive anxiety has been the development of the CSAI–2 (Martens et al., 1990). However, in recent years the construct validity of the CSAI–2 has been questioned. Broadly, the somatic anxiety sub-scale assesses changes in arousal that may accompany other emotions such as excitement or anger (Kerr, 1997), whereas the cognitive anxiety sub-scale largely assesses if an athlete acknowledges the importance and difficulty of the competition and is mobilizing resources to cope (Lane, Sewell, Terry, Bartram, & Nesti, 1999). In a test of these predictions Jones and Uphill (2004b) asked university athletes to imagine a scenario whereby they were about to compete in the most important competition of the season and to then complete the CSAI–2 as if they were either highly anxious ($n = 83$) or highly excited ($n = 87$). Although it was possible to differentiate participants from the "anxiety" and "excited" groups on the basis of the CSAI–2 mean intensity scores, both the cognitive and somatic anxiety sub-scales from the excited group were substantially higher than the norms reported by Martens et al. (1990). In short, individuals may score highly on the cognitive and somatic anxiety intensity sub-scales of the CSAI–2 if they are experiencing an emotion (e.g., excitement) other than anxiety.

Understanding competitive anxiety has clear applied implications in that it can help in the development of suitable anxiety control techniques for those individuals who experience debilitating levels of anxiety. It is also necessary to evaluate the effectiveness of anxiety control techniques and there are many studies in this area. For example, self-talk, relaxation training, and biofeedback have reduced levels of anxiety and increased performance in a small-bore rifle shooter (Prapavessis, Grove, McNair, & Cable, 1992) and positive self-statements have been used to generate a more positive perception of anxiety symptoms and increase performance in swimmers (Hanton & Jones, 1999).

The study of competitive anxiety is still a vibrant area of research. The work of Martens and colleagues has done much to stimulate interest and provide a theoretical framework for this research. At the present time, there are many competing and complementary theories in addition to those mentioned that aim to explain how anxiety arises (e.g., reversal theory; Apter, 1989) and relates to performance (IZOF; Hanin, 1989). Research has also considered the role of anxiety in physical activity, both in terms of a factor that may impact responses to physical activity, for example the work on social physique anxiety (Focht & Hausenblas, 2003), and in terms of the impact of physical activity on anxiety levels (Taylor, 2000). Finally, the research into anxiety has also acted as a stimulant for research into a broader range of positive (e.g., excitement, happiness) and negative (e.g., anger, dejection) competitive emotions (e.g., Hanin, 2000; Jones, Lane, Bray, Uphill, & Catlin, 2005).

## Additional readings

Gould, D., Greenleaf, C., & Krane, V. (2002). Arousal-anxiety in sport. In T. Horn (ed.), *Advances in sport psychology* (pp. 207–41). Champaign, IL: Human Kinetics.

Lavallee, D., Kremer, J., Moran, A., & Williams, M. (2004). *Sport psychology: Contemporary themes.* London: Palgrave (Chapter 6).

Marchant, D. B. & Morris, T. (2004). Stress and anxiety in sport. In T. Morris and J. Summers (eds), *Sport psychology: Theory, applications and Issues* (pp. 74–100). Milton, Australia: John Wiley & Sons.

Smith, R. E., Smoll, F. L., & Wiechman, S. A. (1998). Measurement of trait anxiety in sport. In J. L. Duda (ed.), *Advances in sport and exercise psychology measurement* (pp. 105–27). Morgantown, WV: Fitness Information Technology, Inc.

Woodman, T., & Hardy, L. (2001). Stress and anxiety. In R. N. Singer, H. A. Hausenblas, & C. M. Janelle (eds), *Handbook of research on sport psychology* (pp. 290–318). New York: John Wiley & Sons.

## Study questions

1   What symptoms of competitive anxiety have you experienced? Are they predominantly cognitive or somatic?

2   Do you believe that competitive anxiety helps you perform better (is facilitative) or has a negative impact on your performance (is debilitative)?

3   What is the potential limitation of assessing state anxiety (as Martens and Gill did) using a measure that is not specific to competitive situations?

4   Which items on the SCAT assess somatic symptoms and which assess cognitive symptoms? Are there some items that are difficult to classify?

5   In the Martens and Gill study performance outcome impacted anxiety levels. What factors contribute to your anxiety levels before and during competition?

## References

Andersen, M. B., & Williams, J. M. (1987). Gender role and sport competition anxiety: A re-examination. *Research Quarterly for Exercise and Sport*, 58, 52–6.

Apter, M. J. (1989). *Reversal theory: Motivation, emotion and personality.* London: Routledge.

Bem, S. L. (1974). The measurement of psychological androgyny. *Journal of Consulting and Clinical Psychology*, 42, 155–62.

Burton, D. (1990). Multimodal stress management in sport: Current status and future directions. In G. Jones & L. Hardy (eds), *Stress and performance in sport* (pp. 171–201). Chichester: Wiley.

Davidson, R. J., & Schwartz, G. E. (1976). The psychobiology of relaxation and related states: A multiprocess theory. In D. I. Mostofsky (ed.), *Behavioral control and modification of physiological activity* (pp. 399–442). Englewood Cliffs, NJ: Prentice Hall.

Dunn, J. G. H., Causgrove Dunn, J., Wilson, P., & Syrotuik, D. G. (2000). Reexamining the factorial composition and factor structure of the sport anxiety scale. *Journal of Sport & Exercise Psychology*, 22, 183–93.

Eysenck, M. W. (1992). *Anxiety: The cognitive perspective*. Hove: Erlbaum.

Eysenck, M. W., & Calvo, M. G. (1992). Anxiety and performance: The Processing Efficiency Theory. *Cognition and Emotion*, 6, 409–34.

Focht, B. C., & Hausenblas, H. A. (2003). State anxiety responses to acute exercise in women with high social physique anxiety. *Journal of Sport & Exercise Psychology*, 25, 123–44.

Gaudry, E., & Poole, C. (1972). The effects of the experience of success or failure on state anxiety level. *Journal of Experimental Education*, 41, 18–21.

Giacobbi Jr, P. R., & Weinberg, R. S. (2000). An examination of coping in sport: Individual trait anxiety differences and situational consistency. *The Sport Psychologist*, 14, 42–62.

Hanin, Y. L. (1989). Interpersonal and intragroup anxiety in sports. In D. Hackfort & C. D. Spielberger (eds), *Anxiety in sports: An international perspective* (pp. 19–28). Washington, DC: Hemisphere.

Hanin, Y. L. (2000). Individual zones of optimal functioning (IZOF) model: Emotions-performance relationships in sport. In Y. L. Hanin (ed.), *Emotions in sport* (pp. 65–89). Champaign, IL: Human Kinetics.

Hanton, S., & Jones, G. (1999). The effects of a multimodal intervention program on performers: II. Training the butterflies to fly in formation. *The Sport Psychologist*, 13, 22–41.

Hardy, L. (1990). A catastrophe model of performance in sport. In G. Jones and L. Hardy (eds), *Stress and performance in sport* (pp. 81–106). Chichester: Wiley.

Hardy, L. & Fazey, J. (1987). *The inverted-U hypothesis: A catastrophe for sport psychology?* Paper presented at the annual conference of the North American Society for the Psychology of Sport and Physical Activity, Vancouver, June.

Hardy, L., Jones, G., & Gould, D. (1996). *Understanding psychological preparation for sport: Theory and practice of elite performers*. Chichester: Wiley.

Hassmén, P., & Blomstrand, E. (1995). Mood state relationships and soccer team performance. *The Sport Psychologist*, 9, 297–308.

Jones, G. (1995). More than just a game: Research developments and issues in competitive anxiety in sport. *British Journal of Psychology*, 86, 449–78.

Jones, G., & Hanton, S. (2001). Pre-competitive feeling states and directional anxiety interpretations. *Journal of Sports Sciences*, 19, 385–95.

Jones, G., & Swain, A. B. J. (1992). Intensity and direction dimensions of competitive state anxiety and relationships with competitiveness. *Perceptual and Motor Skills*, 74, 467–72.

Jones, M. V., Lane, A. M., Bray, S., Uphill, M., & Catlin, J. (2005). Development and validation of the Sport Emotion Questionnaire (SEQ). *Journal of Sport & Exercise Psychology*, 27, 407–31.

Jones, M.V., & Sheffield, D. (in press). The impact of game outcome on the well-being of athletes. *International Journal of Sport and Exercise Psychology*.

Jones, M. V., & Uphill, M. (2004a). Antecedents and consequences of emotion in sport. In D. Lavallee, J. Thatcher, & M. V. Jones (eds), *Coping and emotion in sport* (pp. 9–28). Hauppauge, NY: Nova Science Publishers.

Jones, M. V., & Uphill, M. (2004b). Responses to the competitive state anxiety inventory–2(d) by athletes in anxious and excited scenarios. *Psychology of Sport and Exercise*, 5, 201–12.

Kerr, J. H. (1997). *Motivation and emotion in sport*. Hove: Psychology Press.

Lane, A. M. (2004). Emotion, mood and coping in sport: Measurement issues. In D. Lavallee, J. Thatcher, & M. V. Jones (eds), *Coping and emotion in sport* (pp. 255–71). Hauppauge, NY: Nova Science Publishers.

Lane, A. M., Sewell, D. F., Terry, P. C., Bartram, D., & Nesti, M. S. (1999). Confirmatory factor analysis of the Competitive State Anxiety Inventory–2. *Journal of Sports Sciences*, 17, 505–12.

Liebert, R. M., & Morris, L. W. (1967). Cognitive and emotional components of test anxiety: A distinction and some initial data. *Psychological Reports*, 20, 975–8.

Mahoney, M. J., & Avener, M. (1977). Psychology of the elite athlete: An exploratory study. *Cognitive Therapy and Research*, 1, 135–41.

Martens, R. (1969). Effect of learning a complex motor task in the presence of spectators. *Research Quarterly*, 40, 317–23.

Martens, R. (1977). *Sport Competition Anxiety Test*. Champaign, IL: Human Kinetics.

Martens, R., Burton, D., Rivkin, F., & Simon, J. (1980). Reliability and validity of the Competitive State Anxiety Inventory (CSAI). In C. H. Nadeau, W. C. Halliwell, K. M. Newell, & G. C. Roberts (eds), *Psychology of motor behavior and sport* (pp. 91–9). Champaign, IL: Human Kinetics.

Martens, R., Burton, D., Vealey, R. S., Bump, L. A., & Smith, D. E. (1990). Development and validation of the Competitive State Anxiety Inventory – 2. In R. Martens, R. S. Vealey, & D. Burton (eds), *Competitive anxiety in sport* (pp. 117–90). Champaign, IL: Human Kinetics.

Martens, R., Gill, D. L., & Scanlan, T. K. (1976). Competitive trait anxiety, success-failure and sex as determinants of motor performance. *Perceptual and Motor Skills*, 43, 1199–208.

Martens, R., Vealey, R. S., & Burton, D. (eds) (1990). *Competitive anxiety in sport*. Champaign, IL: Human Kinetics.

Masters, R. S. W. (1992). Knowledge, knerves, and know-how. *British Journal of Psychology*, 83, 343–58.

Mellalieu, S. D., Hanton, S., & Jones, G. (2003). Emotional labeling and competitive anxiety in preparation and competition. *The Sport Psychologist*, 17, 157–74.

Millimet, C. R., & Gardner, D. F. (1972). Trait-state anxiety and psychological stress. *Journal of Clinical Psychology*, 28, 145–8.

Ostrow, A. C., & Ziegler, S. G. (1978). Psychometric properties of the Sport Competition Anxiety Test. In B. Kerr (ed.), *Human performance and behavior* (pp. 139–42). Calgary: University of Calgary.

Parfitt, C. G., Jones, J. G., & Hardy, L. (1990). Multidimensional anxiety and performance. In G. Jones and L. Hardy (eds), *Stress and performance in sport* (pp. 43–80). Chichester: Wiley.

Patmore, A. (1986). *Sportsmen under stress*. London: Stanley Paul.

Prapavessis, H., Grove, J. R., McNair, P. J., & Cable, N. T. (1992). Self-regulation training, state anxiety, and sport performance: A psychophysiological case study. *The Sport Psychologist*, 6, 213–29.

Prapavessis, H., Maddison, R., & Fletcher, R. (2005). Further examination of the factor integrity of the sport anxiety scale. *Journal of Sport & Exercise Psychology*, 27, 253–60.

Sarason, S. B., Davidson, K. S., Lighthall, F. F., Waite, R. R., & Ruebush, B. K. (1960). *Anxiety in elementary school children*. New York: Wiley.

Smith, R. E., Cumming, S. P., & Smoll, F. L. (2006) Factorial integrity of the sport anxiety scale: A methodological note and revised scoring considerations. *Journal of Sport and Exercise Psychology*, 28, 109–12.

Smith, R. E., Smoll, F. L., & Schultz, R. W. (1990). Measurement and correlates of sport-specific cognitive and somatic trait anxiety: The sport anxiety scale. *Anxiety Research*, 2, 263–80.

Sonstroem, R. J., & Bernardo, P. (1982). Intraindividual pregame state anxiety and basketball performance: A re-examination of the inverted-U curve. *Journal of Sport Psychology*, 4, 235–45.

Spence, J. T., & Spence, K. W. (1966). The motivational components of manifest anxiety: Drive and drive stimuli. In C. D. Spielberger (ed.), *Anxiety and behavior* (pp. 291–326). New York: Academic Press.

Spielberger, C. D. (1966). Theory and research on anxiety. In C. D. Spielberger (ed.), *Anxiety and behavior* (pp. 3–22). New York: Academic Press.

Spielberger, C. D. (1973). *Preliminary test manual for the State-Trait Anxiety Inventory for Children.* Palo Alto, CA: Consulting Psychologists Press.

Taylor, A. H. (2000). Physical activity, anxiety, and stress. In S. J. H. Biddle, K. R. Fox, & S. H. Boutcher (eds), *Physical activity and psychological well-being* (pp. 10–45). London: Routledge.

Vealey, R. S. (1992). Personality and sport: A comprehensive view. In T. S. Horn (ed.), *Advances in sport psychology* (pp. 25–59). Champaign, IL: Human Kinetics.

Wilson, G. V., & Kerr, J. H. (1999). Affective responses to success and failure: A study of winning and losing in competitive rugby. *Personality and Individual Differences*, 27, 85–9.

Woodman, T., & Hardy, L. (2001). Stress and anxiety. In R. N. Singer, H. A. Hausenblas, & C. M. Janelle (eds), *Handbook of research on sport psychology* (pp. 290–318.). New York: Wiley.

# 3

# Aggression

Frank, M. G., & Gilovich, T. (1988). The dark side of self- and social perception: Black uniforms and aggression in professional sports. *Journal of Personality and Social Psychology*, 54, 74–85.

## Background and context

Competitive sport is an environment where aggressive acts can often be observed. Examples include the cold, calculating attempt of a soccer player to injure a key member of the opposition, an ice hockey player lashing out angrily at an opponent following a robust challenge, or a tennis player verbally berating an official. The amount and type of aggression does of course differ across sports. Yet, although aggression is more easily associated with sports in which athletes are in physical contact, and achieving physical dominance can contribute substantially to the likelihood of success (e.g., boxing, rugby), even sports that have no physical contact between competitors may contain acts of aggression. For example, a sprinter may verbally abuse his opponent in an attempt to unsettle him. Because aggression occurs in competitive sport (e.g., Kirker, Tenenbaum, & Mattson, 2000), and because it may have consequences for the victim (e.g., injury), the aggressor (e.g., being penalized) and to the sport (e.g., reduced participation rates), understanding why athletes behave aggressively in sport is clearly of interest.

Before discussing the role of aggression in sport it is important to define aggression. In any area of psychology clearly defining the phenomenon, behavior or construct to be studied is crucial to advance knowledge. If researchers use different definitions it becomes impossible to compare findings across different studies and to build a coherent body of knowledge. It is also particularly crucial to define aggression as it is often used in everyday language to describe a wide variety of behaviors. To illustrate, one soccer coach may describe a player as aggressive if she tries to dominate her opponents when physically challenging for the ball. In contrast a different soccer coach may describe a player as aggressive if the player makes deliberate attempts to injure opponents. One definition that includes the commonly accepted components of aggression is provided by Baron and Richardson (1994) who defined aggression as ". . . any form of behavior directed toward the goal of harming or injuring another living being who is motivated to avoid such treatment" (1994: 7). Four aspects of this definition are worth considering in relation to the study of aggression in competitive sport. First, aggression is a behavior, and not a desire to, or fantasy of, harming someone. Second, there must be intent to harm the victim either psychologically or physically. Determining intent can clearly be difficult as identical behaviors may have different intentions (e.g., a baseball pitcher may hit a batter because he intended to, or because he misdirected the pitch). Because aggression can incorporate psychological harm, "trash talking" and "sledging" an opponent can be aggressive behavior. Finally, the intended victim must be living, so, for example, a tennis player cannot behave aggressively towards her racket.

Different types of aggression can be distinguished depending on the goal of the aggressor. Hostile (sometimes called emotional, or reactive) aggression occurs when the primary goal of the aggressor is to harm or make an individual suffer (Baron & Richardson, 1994). Hostile aggression is often accompanied by anger, such as a hockey coach verbally berating a player following a mistake. When the primary goal of an individual is to attain a non-aggressive goal such as helping his basketball team win, and the player deliberately injures the star player on the opposing team in order to enhance his team's chances of success, it is called instrumental aggression (Husman & Silva, 1984). A difficulty with this distinction is that exactly the same behavior (e.g., a clumsy challenge on the basketball court) can be classified as hostile or instrumental aggression depending on the goal of the athlete, which can be difficult to determine.

There are three major explanations of why an individual may behave aggressively. First, aggression can be considered as instinctive and an inherent part of human nature (Freud, 1920; Lorenz, 1981). Thus, aggression is inevitable. However, this approach has been criticized as relying on data from animals that are not subject to the same social controls as humans and ignoring that a human's biological heritage provides the potential for a wide variety of behaviors, such as kindness, which suggest that aggression is not inevitable (Baron & Richardson, 1994).

The remaining two explanations consider in more detail the psychological processes that may lead a person to behave aggressively. The frustration-aggression hypothesis (Dollard, Miller, Doob, Mowrer, & Sears, 1939) proposed that every aggressive action could be traced to a previous frustrating incident and that frustration always led to aggression. However, the link between frustration and aggression is less certain than proposed – for example, frustration may lead to other consequences, such as depression or withdrawal (Seligman, 1975). Accordingly, Berkowitz (1989) revised the frustration-aggression hypothesis and proposed that frustration can produce a readiness to respond aggressively if failing to achieve an anticipated reward (frustration) is accompanied by negative affect (e.g., anger). It is the negative affect that is the fundamental spur to aggressive behavior (Berkowitz, 1993). Berkowitz's revised frustration-aggression hypothesis does provide a mechanism for explaining hostile aggression, but it may not explain instrumental aggression (Widmeyer, Bray, Dorsch, & McGuire, 2002).

The final explanation for aggression is provided by Bandura's (1977) social learning theory. Although Bandura does consider the role of biological (e.g., hormones), emotional (e.g., frustration), and environmental (e.g., being attacked) factors in aggression he also emphasizes the role of learning (Baron & Richardson, 1994). He proposed that many aggressive responses are learned through modeling and whether a person behaves aggressively depends on the pattern of punishments and rewards deemed likely for aggressive behavior. The classic "bobo doll" studies where nursery school children imitated a model's aggressive behavior by behaving aggressively towards a large inflatable doll provided support for these central tenets (Bandura, Ross, & Ross, 1961, 1963a, 1963b). These findings have been criticized, in that aggression towards a doll may be considered something more akin to vigorous play (Apter, 1982). Nevertheless, social learning theory does have important implications as through changing social conditions aggression may be prevented or reduced (Baron & Richardson, 1994).

At the time of Frank and Gilovich's key study there were numerous strands of research covering the broad area of aggression in sport. There was a substantial body of research exploring spectator aggression (e.g., Arms, Russell, & Sandilands, 1979). The research concerning sport participants could broadly be split into that which focused on the consequences of aggression and factors that impacted levels of aggression in sport. Examples of research focusing on the potential consequences of aggression included the work of Widmeyer and Birch (1984) who found a positive relationship between the aggression exhibited by an ice hockey team in the first period and the number of points they scored in a game. Research focusing on factors that impacted levels of aggression found that increased levels of aggression were associated with lower moral reasoning (Bredemeier, Shields, Weiss, & Cooper, 1986), higher physiological arousal (Zillmann, Katcher, & Milavsky, 1972), steroid use (Strauss, Wright, Finerman, & Catlin, 1983), and a higher skill level (Pilz, 1979).

## Key study

This study examined whether wearing black clothing leads both the wearer and others to perceive him or her as more aggressive, and also whether it led the wearer to actually *act* more aggressively. Whereas previous research up until this time had shown that a person's clothing can affect the amount of aggression they express, these studies involved rather contrived situations that raised questions of ecological validity and experimental demand. Frank and Gilovich set out to seek parallel evidence for a link between clothing cues and aggressiveness by specifically examining the effect of the *color* of a person's uniform in an ecologically valid context. In particular, they examined the aggressiveness of teams with black uniforms in two professional "contact" sports. Their specific research question was: do teams with black uniforms appear to play with greater aggressiveness than those with non-black uniforms, and if so, what are the processes that produce this effect?

This key study was, in fact, a series of four separate studies. In the first study, the researchers investigated whether different colored uniforms carry the same connotations as the basic colors themselves (by examining whether the uniforms of the black-uniformed teams in the National Football League (NFL) and the National Hockey League (NHL) look more evil, mean, and aggressive than the uniforms of the non-black-uniformed teams). The penalty records from these two leagues were then analyzed in an archival study (Study 2) to test whether teams with black uniforms are penalized more than their rivals. The researchers then conducted two experiments designed to test whether the results obtained in the archival analysis of penalty records were due to the uniforms' effect on the referees' judgments (Study 3) or on the players' actual behavior (Study 4).

## Study 1

Because a uniform is a complex stimulus, the researchers designed a study to determine whether people's general associations to certain colors also apply to their perceptions of specific colored uniforms. In this study, participants made semantic differential ratings of the uniforms of all teams in the NFL and NHL. The participants were unfamiliar with either football or ice hockey, in that they did not know the rules of either game nor were they able to recognize the uniforms of any of the teams. Such "naive" participants were used in this study to ensure that their ratings were determined solely by the characteristics of the uniforms themselves and not by the reputations of the teams that wear them.

## Participants

The participants (22 females and three males) were run in groups, ten in one group and 15 in another. Participants were shown color slides depicting the uniforms of all NFL and NHL teams. The slides were taken of the official team uniform and color swatches provided by the two leagues. The slides showed the jerseys, pants, socks, and helmets of each team. There were no players modeling the uniforms. Clues to a team's home city were eliminated unless they constituted an integral part of the uniform. The participants rated each uniform on the following five 7-point semantic differential scales: good/bad; timid/aggressive; nice/mean; active/passive; and weak/strong. Each slide was presented for 30 seconds, and the entire experiment lasted 25 minutes.

## Results

Teams in both sports have two uniforms: a "colored" uniform that is dominated by the team's primary color, and a "non-colored" uniform that is almost always predominately white and utilizes the team's primary color only for the trim and the players' numbers. The dark uniforms are worn by the visiting team without exception in the NHL and by the home team on most occasions in the NFL. The researchers considered a team to have a black uniform if at least 50% of its "colored" uniform was black. These criteria resulted in five NFL teams with black uniforms – the Pittsburgh Steelers, the New Orleans Saints, the Los Angeles Raiders, the Cincinnati Bengals, and the Chicago Bears. Likewise, there were five NHL teams with black uniforms – the Vancouver Canucks, the Pittsburgh Penguins, the Philadelphia Flyers, the Chicago Black Hawks, and the Boston Bruins.

The three scales that directly concern badness and aggressiveness – good/bad, nice/mean, and timid/aggressive – were all positively intercorrelated (median $r = .67$). As a result of their statistical and conceptual interconnection, participants' ratings on these three scales were combined to form one overall "malevolence" index. When considering the NFL teams, the black uniforms ($Mdn = 4.97$) had a decidedly more malevolent appearance than the non-black uniforms ($Mdn = 3.85$), Mann-Whitney test, $p < .001$. The results were nearly identical for the NHL teams as well (median malevolence ratings of 5.13 vs. 3.85), $p < .003$.

Less consistent results were obtained on the two other semantic differential ratings. The black uniforms in the NFL were also rated as more "strong" ($Mdn = 5.60$) than the non-black uniforms ($Mdn = 4.65$), Mann-Whitney $Z = 3.03$, $p < .005$, and although there was a similar trend in the ratings of the NHL uniforms (black $Mdn = 5.05$, non-black $Mdn = 4.63$), the difference in these latter ratings was not significant, $p > .20$.

Interestingly, although past research indicates that black is generally seen as a passive color, the black uniforms in both the NFL and the NHL were rated as marginally more active ($Mdns = 4.9$ and 5.15 for football and hockey, respectively) than the non-black uniforms ($Mdns = 4.55$ and 4.65): $Z = 1.89$, $p < .10$, for the NFL; $U = 21$, $p < .10$, for the NHL.

## Discussion

These results suggest that the black uniforms worn by teams in professional football and ice hockey look more malevolent (as well as somewhat more active and strong) than the non-black uniforms worn by other teams. It did not show, however, whether this difference in people's associations to black and non-black uniforms is related to how often these teams are penalized.

## Study 2

The second study examined whether teams with black uniforms were penalized more often than their opponents in non-black uniforms through an archival investigation of official penalty records from 1970 to the most recently completed season (the 1986 season for the NFL and the 1985/6 season for the NHL). Their hypothesis was if the evil connotations of the color black lead those who wear black uniforms to act unusually aggressively, then the teams with black uniforms should be penalized more than other teams.

### The National Football League

Nearly all penalties in professional football involve moving the football a certain distance (usually 5, 10, or 15 yds) away from the goal to which the offending team is heading. The NFL office provided the researchers with complete records of both the number of penalties incurred by each team and the total number of yards penalized. Because penalties for over-aggressiveness are generally more severe (e.g., 15 yards for "spearing," "clipping," or a "headslap") than for infractions having little to do with aggressiveness (e.g., 5 yards for "offsides," "illegal motion," or "delay of game"), the researchers selected the number of yards penalized as the best measure of how aggressively a team plays the game.

All teams were ranked in terms of the number of yards penalized for each of the seasons from 1970 to 1986. The average ranking of the five teams with black uniforms was then calculated and compared to the average to be expected if they were no more likely to be penalized than their opponents (i.e., the average rank of all teams). As predicted, teams with black uniforms in the NFL were uncommonly aggressive: in all but one of the 17 years under investigation these five teams were penalized more yards than one would expect under the appropriate null hypothesis, $p < .02$, using a $z$ score conversion.

### The National Hockey League

Because only three of the five NHL teams – the Boston Bruins, the Chicago Black Hawks, and the Philadelphia Flyers – wore black uniforms during the entire 16-year period under investigation (and the other two switched from non-black to black during this time; the Pittsburgh Penguins during the 1979–80 season and the Vancouver Canucks before the 1978–9 season), the data from the two teams that changed were naturally treated as part of the non-black sample during the earlier years and as part of the black sample after they switched. These teams allowed the researchers to ask an additional question regarding the link between uniform color and aggressiveness: will the *same* team become more aggressive after switching to black uniforms?

In ice hockey, all penalties require the player who committed the infraction to sit out a portion of the game, during which time their team is outnumbered by the opposing team. Players sit out for 2, 5, or 10 minutes depending on the severity of the violation. The NHL office provided the researchers with the total number of minutes each team was penalized per season. The same ranking and comparison procedures were used as those done with the NFL data. As predicted, NHL teams that wear black uniforms were unusually aggressive, in that players on these teams spent more time in the penalty box than expected in each of the last 16 years, $ps < .05$, using $z$ scores.

When the teams from Pittsburgh and Vancouver switched to black uniforms, their penalty minutes increased (Figure 3.1). The difference in penalty minutes (in $z$ scores) before and after

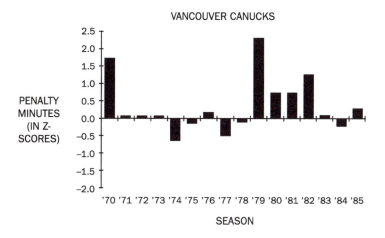

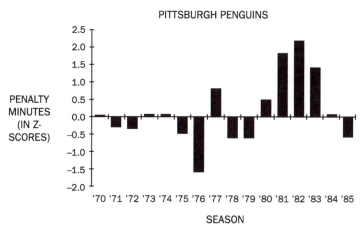

**Figure 3.1** Number of minutes penalized, in *z* scores, for the years 1970–1 (listed as "70") to 1985–6 (listed as "85") for the two National Hockey League teams that switched from non-black to black uniforms

the uniform change was significant for Pittsburgh, $U = 9.5$, $p < .05$, and marginally so for Vancouver, $U = 25$, $p < .15$. To rule out the possibility that these increases in penalty minutes may have stemmed from players playing more energetically and aggressively after *any* kind of change (including a change to a non-black uniform), similar data were examined from another team that switched from blue and gold to red and green uniforms. However, unlike the two teams that switched to black uniforms, this change of colors (and locale) was not accompanied by an increase in penalties.

Even more direct evidence that the color of a team's uniform is connected to how often its players are penalized was obtained by comparing the number of penalty minutes logged by the Pittsburgh Penguins during the first 44 games of the 1979–80 season when they wore blue uniforms, with the corresponding number during the final 35 games when they wore black. During the first 44 games they averaged 8 penalty minutes per game; after switching to black uniforms this average increased to 12 minutes ($Z = 2.16$, $p < .05$).

## Discussion

These data indicate that the uniform color of professional sports teams is related to how aggressively they play the game, as measured by how frequently they are penalized. Teams with black uniforms are overwhelmingly likely to rank near the top of their leagues in penalties. On those rare occasions when a team switched to black uniforms from another color, the switch was accompanied by a dramatic increase in penalties.

This research was initiated with the hypothesis that wearing black uniforms would lead players to play more aggressively than they would with non-black uniforms. However, there are at least two other possible explanations for the finding that teams with black uniforms are penalized more often than their rivals. First, because referees may also associate the color black with evil and aggressiveness, they may view any given action as more malevolent if it is performed by a player in a black uniform. Thus, players in black uniforms may not play the game any more aggressively, but may simply be more likely to be penalized for actions that would be ignored if performed by players wearing non-black uniforms. This explanation is by no means incompatible with the possibility that players in black uniforms actually play more aggressively: these two processes may be jointly responsible for the observed relationship between uniform color and penalties.

A second alternative explanation of these results is less interesting psychologically. According to this interpretation, the observed results are simply due to the fact that the management of certain teams want their players to play aggressively in the belief that doing so will make them more likely to win (during the period under investigation, the black-uniformed teams in the NFL and the NHL did not win a significantly higher percentage of their games than teams with non-black uniforms, Mann-Whitney $Zs < 1$). Operating with this belief, these teams deliberately recruit players who are unusually aggressive. Furthermore, to be consistent with the aggressiveness theme of their organization, they choose black as the color of their team's uniform. According to this interpretation, then, the connection between black uniforms and elevated penalty records is spurious.

Although this latter interpretation has some intuitive appeal, the researchers put forward that it could not serve as an adequate account of the present results. It does not, for example, explain the fact that the two NHL teams that switched to black uniforms experienced an increase in penalties. For one of these teams (the Pittsburgh Penguins) the change took place in the middle of the season and thus was not accompanied by any change in players, coaches, or team philosophy.

At the very least, the researchers felt that such a differential recruitment of aggressive players by black and non-black uniformed teams is neither necessary nor sufficient to explain the main findings reported here, although it may contribute to the results. Moreover, this artifactual interpretation of the results would be rendered even less compelling by any direct experimental evidence in support of the other two, more psychological, interpretations. As a result, the researchers embarked on two experimental studies designed to test whether the results obtained in the archival analysis were due to the uniforms' effect on the referees' judgments or on the players' actual behavior.

## Study 3

To determine whether the archival penalty data reported in Study 2 might stem from the biased judgments of referees, the researchers designed a study in which participants watched video-taped segments of a "staged" football game in which the defensive team was wearing either black or white uniforms. Participants in this study made a series of judgments about the defensive team's actions after each play. Because these actions presented on the videotape were staged by the researchers, they depicted the same events in both the white and black versions. Despite this equivalence, it was hypothesized that the association between black uniforms and aggressiveness would cause participants to question the legality of the defensive team's actions more when they were wearing black uniforms than when they were wearing white.

## Participants

Two groups participated in this experiment. One was a group of 40 knowledgeable football fans who were university students, with 10 of these participants being run in each of the four experimental conditions. The other participants were 20 referees of university and high school football games (with 8–35 years of experience at officiating). These participants were run only in the "color" conditions of this experiment. In essence, this investigation consisted of two separate experiments: a complete $2 \times 2$ factorial experiment with 40 university students as participants, and the other a partial replication (color conditions only) using experienced referees.

## Procedure

All participants were shown a videotape of two football plays involving the same two teams and were asked to make judgments about the actions of the defensive team in each. There were two versions of the videotape: one in which the defensive team wore black uniforms and one in which they wore white (the offensive team wore red in both versions). To ensure that any observed differences in participants' ratings across the black and white versions of these plays could be attributed to the difference in uniform color, it was imperative that the two versions be identical on all other dimensions. With this in mind, the researchers staged the plays with a group of former high school and college football players by taping two versions of the two plays, making every effort to keep them identical. Each play was choreographed such that actions of the defensive team were of borderline compliance with rules of the game. The first play depicted two members of the defensive team grabbing the ball carrier, driving him back several yards, and throwing him to the ground with considerable force; the second play showed a ball carrier trying to leap over a tackler and being violently hit in mid-air by another member of the defensive team.

Because it is impossible to determine whether two versions of such a complex stimulus are in fact identical, the researchers adopted a control procedure to guarantee the validity of their comparison of participants' ratings of the two versions of the same play. In this, they presented the videotapes to different groups of participants in two different ways: in color to one group and with the color removed to the other group. By turning down the color and contrast dials on the videotape monitor, the color of the defensive team's uniforms became a dull gray that varied only slightly in brightness across the two versions. The experiment thus consisted of a $2 \times 2$ between-subjects design with the color of the defensive team's uniforms (black/white) crossed with whether the tape was played with or without color (color/no-color).

Participants were run in one of four groups, with each witnessing two plays, with the defensive team in both plays wearing either black or white uniforms (or the "no-color" presentations of one of these). Before the videotape was shown, participants were read the following instructions: "What we would like you to do is to make referees' judgments of a pair of football plays – plays filmed during a scrimmage between two small-college teams. You will be shown the first play only once, and in slow motion. Then the videotape machine will be stopped, and you will fill out a questionnaire concerning the play you have just witnessed. Once you have completed the questionnaire, the procedure will be repeated for the second play, and then there will be a final questionnaire for you to fill out. Please focus on the defensive team when watching the videotape."

The dependent measures consisted of two sets of questionnaire items. One set was completed after each of the two plays. Participants first indicated on a 9-point Likert-type scale how likely they would be to penalize the defensive team for the play in question, and then they chose one of eight descriptions of the aggressiveness of the defensive team's actions that were ordered in severity (e.g., 8 = "a 'cheap shot' designed to hurt the opposing player," 5 = "legal, but exceedingly aggressive," and 1 = "legal and somewhat non-aggressive"). After watching both plays, participants answered three questions concerning their overall impressions of the defensive team. In particular, participants put an X on a 35-point dotted line to indicate their impression of the defensive team's "aggressiveness," their impression of the team's "dirtiness," and their assessment of the importance of "calling a *tight* game" (i.e., one with a strict interpretation and implementation of the rules) in any game in which the defensive team was a participant to ensure that "aggression does not get out of hand."

## Results

In order to determine whether the referees were more inclined to penalize the defensive team when it was wearing black, their penalty ratings for the two plays were analyzed by a 2 (uniform color) × 2 (play) analysis of variance (ANOVA) with repeated measures on the second factor. This analysis showed the predicted main effect of uniform color to be significant, $F(1, 18) = 6.43$, $p < .05$. As can be seen in the relevant segments of Figure 3.2, the referees were more inclined to penalize the defensive team if they saw the black versions of the two plays ($Ms = 7.2$ and 2.4 for Plays 1 and 2, respectively) than if they saw the white versions ($Ms = 5.3$ and 1.0). There was also a significant, but unimportant, main effect of the play being rated, $F(1, 18) = 38.08$, $p < .0001$, but no significant interaction between uniform color and play, $F < 1$.

Similar results were obtained on the referees' ratings of the aggressiveness of the defensive team's actions in these plays. As with the first measure, the ANOVA revealed a significant main effect of uniform color, $F(1, 18) = 6.52$, $p < .05$; a significant but unimportant main effect of play, $F(1, 18) = 33.05$, $p < .0001$; and no interaction between these two variables, $F < 1$. The defensive team was thought to be more aggressive by the referees who saw the black versions of the two plays ($Ms = 6.1$ and 3.1 for Plays 1 and 2, respectively) than by those who saw the white versions ($Ms = 5.0$ and 2.2).

Because the data provided by the university students included the crucial control conditions of showing the two plays with the color eliminated, their ratings were analyzed by a 2 (uniform color) × 2 ("video condition" – i.e., color/no-color) × 2 (play) ANOVA with repeated measures on the last factor. For participants' penalty ratings, this analysis revealed the hypothesized significant interaction between uniform color and video condition, $F(1, 36) = 16.62$, $p < .001$.

By examining just the data from those participants who saw the two plays *in color*, it was apparent that the results were nearly identical to those provided by the referees (see Figure 3.2). Participants who saw the black versions of the plays were more inclined to penalize the defensive team than were those who saw the white versions. This was true for both Play 1

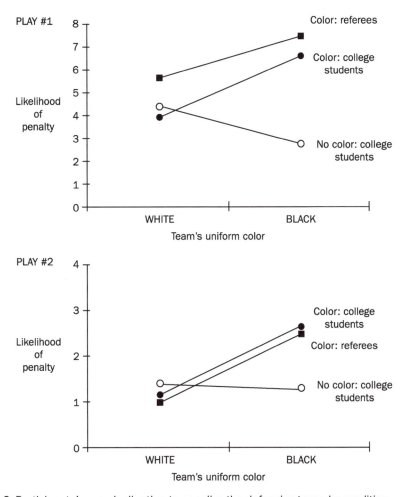

**Figure 3.2** Participants' mean inclination to penalize the defensive team, by condition

(Ms = 6.2 vs. 3.7 for the black and white versions, respectively), F(1, 36) = 7.02, p < .02, and Play 2 (Ms = 2.5 vs. 1.1), F(1, 36) = 7.18, p < .02.

In contrast, an examination of the data from those participants who saw the two plays with the color removed revealed a very different, but equally important, pattern. Among these participants, those who had witnessed the "black" versions of the two plays were not any more inclined to penalize the defensive team than were those who had seen the "white" versions. In fact, for Play 1 the "white" version of the play (M = 4.2) prompted marginally higher penalty ratings than the "black" version (M = 2.6), F(1, 36) = 2.89, p < .10. This produced a significant interaction between uniform color and videotape condition when the data from this play were analyzed separately, F (1, 36) = 9.47, p < .01. Thus, for this play at least, the attempt to make the "black" and "white" versions identical may have been unsuccessful. However, the direction of this asymmetry worked *against* this study's hypothesis: the ratings of the participants in these control conditions of the experiment indicated that the defensive team in the white version of the play may have been "objectively" more aggressive than in the black. For Play 2, the ratings of those who had seen the "black" (M = 1.2) and "white" (M = 1.3) versions were virtually identical, $F < 1$, producing a significant interaction between uniform color and video condition for this play as well, $F(1, 36) = 4.12$, $p < .05$. These control conditions, then, demonstrated that the tendency of both the college students and the referees to be more inclined to penalize the defensive team when it was wearing black cannot be attributed to any inherent difference in the two versions of the two plays.

Similar results were obtained on the university students' ratings of the defensive team's aggressiveness in these two plays. The $2 \times 2 \times 2$ ANOVA revealed the hypothesized significant interaction between uniform color and video condition, $F(1, 36) = 15.34$, $p < .001$. The analysis also produced a significant main effect of play, $F(1, 36) = 19.72$, $p < .0001$, and a marginally significant effect of video condition, $F(1, 36) = 3.24$, $p < .10$. As with the penalty ratings, when the plays were seen in color, those who had seen the black versions of the plays saw marginally more aggressiveness on the part of the defensive team than those who had seen the white versions. This was true of both Play 1 ($Ms = 5.0$ vs. 3.9, for the black and white versions, respectively), $F(1, 36) = 3.46$. $p < .10$, and Play 2 ($Ms = 3.5$ and 2.4), $F(1, 36) = 3.20$, $p < .10$. In contrast, when seen without color, Play 1 yielded higher aggressiveness ratings in the "white" condition ($M = 4.8$) than in the "black" condition ($M = 3.4$), $F(1, 36) = 5.62$, $p < .05$., and Play 2 yielded no difference between conditions ($Ms = 2.4$ and 2.5), $F < 1$. The interaction between uniform color and video condition for each play separately was as follows: For Play 1, $F (1, 36) = 8.93$, $p < .01$; for Play 2, $F (1, 36) = 1.33$. $ns$.

Recall that after watching both plays, participants rated the overall aggressiveness and "dirtiness" of the defensive team and indicated how likely they would be to call a "tight" game in any contest in which the defensive team was one of the participants. For the referees, the results were strong and consistent. Compared to their counterparts who had seen the white versions of the two plays, those who had seen the black versions rated the defensive team as significantly more aggressive ($Ms = 23.3$ vs. 10.0), $F(1, 18) = 8.67$, $p < .01$, and marginally more dirty ($Ms = 16.1$ vs. 9.2), $F(1, 18) = 2.84$, $p < .11$, and, perhaps most important, were significantly more inclined to call a tight game ($Ms = 27.5$ vs. 12.7), $F(1, 36) = 16.47$, $p < .001$.

The analysis of the university students' ratings on these measures revealed consistent, but for the most part less strong, results. After watching the tapes in color, those who had seen the black versions of the plays tended to give higher ratings on all three measures than those who had seen the white versions; in contrast, there were no such differences in participants' ratings when the plays were seen with the color removed. However, the crucial interaction between uniform color and video condition was significant for the dirtiness ratings only, $F(1, 36) = 5.75$, $p < .05$ ($Ms = 17.1$ vs. 9.8 for those who had seen the black and white versions in color, $Ms = 11.4$ vs. 15.6 for those who had seen the same versions, respectively, with the color removed).

## Discussion

These data provide strong support for a "social perception" interpretation of the observed tendency for professional sports teams that wear black uniforms to be penalized more than their rivals. Because people associate the color black with meanness and aggressiveness, they "see" more aggressiveness or more malevolent intent in the actions of players wearing black uniforms. When asked to assume the role of a referee, the participants in this experiment were more likely to penalize the defensive team when its players were wearing black uniforms than when they were wearing white, despite the fact that the actions performed by the players in black uniforms were not in any objective sense more aggressive or illegal. Perhaps the most telling evidence that the inordinate number of penalties amassed by black-uniformed teams is at least partially due to the judgments of referees is that our sample of experienced officials (who actually make the calls in real college and high school football games) indicated that they would call a "tighter" game when the team they had seen was wearing black uniforms.

## Study 4

In order to test whether wearing a black uniform tends to *make* a person more aggressive, the researchers collected data in the form of participants' intended aggressive behavior. Volunteers for an experiment on competition were led to believe that they would be vying against other participants in several competitive events. They were also led to believe that they could exercise some control over which events they were to participate in by selecting their five most preferred events from a list of 12. The 12 events varied in the amount of aggressiveness they called for and were, therefore, assigned point values from the most aggressive (12) to the least aggressive (1), thus allowing the researchers to use participants' choices as a measure of their readiness to engage in aggressive action. Participants' choices were elicited twice: once individually when wearing their usual clothes, and later as a team of three wearing black or white uniforms. The researchers hypothesized that wearing black uniforms would induce participants to view themselves as more mean and aggressive and thus would produce more of a "group shift" (Jaffe, Shapir, & Yinon, 1981) toward aggressive choices.

### Participants and Procedure

In this study, 72 male university students participated in groups of three. To determine their activity preferences, they were asked to individually rank order 5 activities from a group of 12. After making their choices, the participants were outfitted in either white or black uniforms in the guise of facilitating team identity. Then, while the experimenter was supposedly administering instructions to the other team, the three participants in each team were told to discuss their individual choices and to decide as a group on a rank ordering of the five activities they would like to include in the competition. This second ranking allowed the researchers to assess whether participants would choose more aggressive games as a group after donning black uniforms than after putting on white uniforms. To get an overall measure of the aggressiveness of each participant's preferences, the researchers multiplied the point value of his first choice by 5, his second choice by 4, and so forth, and then added these five products. When comparing the choices made by the participants individually (without uniforms) with those made by the same individuals as a group (with uniforms), the researchers compared the average individual choices of the three participants with their group choice.

Finally, as an auxiliary measure of aggression, participants were administered a brief thematic apperception test (TAT; Murray, 1943) to assess their level of aggressive ideation. The TAT, which is one of the most widely used psychological tests in the world, is a projective test of personality. A projective test is one in which a person's patterns of thought, attitudes, observational capacity, and emotional responses are evaluated on the basis of responses to ambiguous test materials. The TAT consists of 31 pictures (Picture 18 was used in this study) that depict a variety of social and interpersonal situations, with participants being asked to tell a story about each picture in order to identify dominant drives, emotions, sentiments, conflicts, and complexes. Participants were given four minutes to write a story based on the following questions: (a) What is happening in the picture?; (b) What is being thought by the characters in the picture?; (c) What has led up to this picture?; and (d) What will happen to the characters in the picture?

After four minutes the experimenter returned, collected the TAT protocols, and thoroughly debriefed the participants. All participants seemed surprised (and many disappointed) to learn that the experiment was over. The debriefing interview also made it clear that none of the participants had entertained the possibility that the color of their uniforms might have been the focus of the experiment.

## Results

The mean levels of aggressiveness in participants' individual and group choices are presented in Table 3.1. As expected, there was no difference in participants' individual choices across the two groups ($Ms = 113.4$ vs. 113.5), because they were not wearing different colored uniforms at the time these choices were made. However, the participants who then put on black uniforms subsequently chose more aggressive games (mean change in aggressiveness = 16.8), whereas those who wore white uniforms showed no such shift (mean change = 2.4). A $2 \times 2$ mixed between/within ANOVA of participants' choices yielded a significant interaction between uniform color and individual/group choice, $F(1, 22) = 6.14, p < .05$, indicating that the pattern of choices made by participants in black uniforms was different from that of those wearing white. Wearing black uniforms induced participants to seek out more aggressive activities, matched-pairs $t(11) = 3.21, p < .01$; wearing white uniforms did not, matched-pairs $t(11) = 1.00$, ns. Participants' TAT stories were scored on a five-point aggressiveness scale (Feshbach, 1955). Stories devoid of aggression received a score of 1, those with a little indirect aggression a score of 2, those with considerable indirect or a little direct aggression a 3, those with direct physical aggression a 4, and those with graphic violence a 5. Two judges who were unaware of the participants' condition made these ratings. The judges' ratings were in perfect agreement on 47% of the stories and were within one point on another 48%. The participants who wore black uniforms also tended to express more aggressive ideation ($M = 3.20$) in their TAT stories than did participants wearing white uniforms ($M = 2.89$), although this difference was not significant, $t < 1$.

**Table 3.1** Mean level of aggressiveness contained in participants' chosen activities, by condition

| | Mean individual choice (without uniforms) | | Group choice (with uniforms) | | Change in aggressiveness | |
|---|---|---|---|---|---|---|
| Uniform color | M | SD | M | SD | M | SD |
| White | 113.4 | 23.9 | 115.8 | 25.4 | +2.4 | 8.5 |
| Black | 113.5 | 18.4 | 130.3 | 22.9 | +16.8 | 18.1 |

## Discussion

The results of this experiment supported the hypothesis that wearing a black uniform can increase a person's inclination to engage in aggressive behavior. Participants who wore black uniforms showed a marked increase in intended aggression relative to those wearing white uniforms. These results, in conjunction with the findings of Study 3, suggested that the excessive penalties amassed by black uniformed teams in professional sports stem from two distinct processes – their own aggressiveness and harsher treatment by the referees.

It should be noted, however, that at this point more confidence can be placed in the role played by the referees than by the players themselves. The effect of referees' judgments was directly assessed by having real referees do what they are paid to do – make judgments about the legality of various actions in the game of football. In contrast, the demonstration that wearing black uniforms increased *participants'* willingness to act aggressively involved only *intended* aggression and did not employ any real football or hockey players as participants. It would have been interesting to have allowed the participants to compete against one another in their chosen activities and see whether those in black uniformed performed more aggressively. The researchers refrained from doing so because of ethical and methodological difficulties. Nevertheless, the results of this experiment make the important point that in a competitive setting at least, merely donning a black uniform *can* increase a person's willingness to seek out opportunities for aggression. If the wearing of a black uniform can have such an effect in the laboratory, there is every reason to believe that it would have even stronger effects in actual sport settings, where many forms of aggression are considered acceptable behavior.

## Subsequent research and application

The findings of Frank and Gilovich's key study indicate that the social cues provided by the color of a uniform impacted on how naive participants, knowledgeable sports fans, and officials perceived athletes. An increasing amount of research has highlighted the important role that social cues, such as clothing and body language, play in sport specific interactions. For example, tennis players reported success to be less likely against potential opponents displaying positive body language, and also rated potential opponents as having a more positive psychological state and more positive psychological characteristics when they displayed positive body language and wore tennis-specific clothing (Greenlees, Buscombe, Thelwell, Holder, & Rimmer, 2005). Not only are social cues important but so are athletes' reputations. Football referees who were asked to make decisions on a series of video clips where two players challenged for the ball awarded significantly more red and yellow cards against a team if they were told that the team had a reputation for aggressive play (Jones, Paull, & Erskine, 2002).

The color black is not the only color proposed to impact how athletes are perceived by others (social perception), and how they perceive themselves (self-perception). In the 2004 Olympics, contestants who were assigned the red uniform or body protectors in boxing, tae kwon do, Greco-Roman wrestling, and freestyle wrestling won more competitions than competitors assigned the blue uniform or body protector (Hill & Barton, 2005). This effect was particularly marked when the competitors were of similar ability. Hill and Barton suggested that this effect may be observed because the color red both impacts the affective state and feelings of dominance of the wearer and is a signal of expressed aggression that may impact the psychological states of opponents.

The validity of the two main explanations for aggression (the revised frustration-aggression hypothesis, social learning theory) for explaining aggressive behavior in sport has also been explored. In a study by Sheldon and Aimar (2001), the aggressive behavior from 11 men's professional ice hockey games was recorded and it was noted whether the aggressive behaviors occurred in a 15-second period before or after a successful or unsuccessful behavior. The results supported social learning theory in that there was a positive relationship between aggression and subsequent successful behavior, but no relationship between unsuccessful performance and subsequent aggression. Thus, performing poorly (and therefore being frustrated) did not appear to be associated with aggression, while aggression appears to be followed, and therefore reinforced, by a successful performance.

A number of other factors have been explored in an attempt to understand why athletes may behave aggressively. An increasing amount of research in sport has sought to explain aggression in terms of a moral-reasoning framework. Lower levels of moral development in an individual athlete are associated with a tendency towards physical and non-physical aggression in sport (Bredemeier, 1994). The moral atmosphere of a team is also important and when an athlete perceives that the team environment sanctions cheating and aggressive behavior they are more likely to view cheating and aggression as appropriate, report a greater intention to engage in cheating and aggression and to have actually done so in the past (Kavassanu, Roberts, & Ntoumanis, 2002; Kavassanu & Spray, 2006). Other factors that contribute to increased or reduced aggression levels include frequency of competition, whereby higher levels of aggression are observed amongst teams that compete more frequently (Widmeyer & McGuire, 1997). Studies have also supported a relationship between steroid use and aggression (e.g., Parrott, Choi, & Davies, 1994) although the inevitability of this link has been disputed (Sharp & Collins, 1998).

Aggression has also been researched as a potential contributory factor to the home advantage phenomenon. The focus on aggression is not surprising as territoriality theories suggest that people identify with places (e.g., home venue) and will protect them against attack (Edwards & Archambault, 1989; McGuire, Courneya, Widmeyer, & Carron, 1992). In addition, Neave and Wolfson (2003) found that soccer players tested for higher levels of testosterone before playing at home compared to away and, in general, research supports a positive (albeit weak) relationship between testosterone levels and aggression (Book, Starzyk, & Quinsey, 2001). In contrast, research by both McGuire et al. (1992) in ice hockey and Jones, Bray, and Olivier (2005) in rugby league found no difference in the levels of aggressive behaviors between home and away teams. There were, however, differences in home and away teams as a function of game outcome. Specifically, McGuire et al. (1992) found that home teams were more aggressive in games they won and away teams were more aggressive in games they lost, while Jones et al. (2005) found that the away teams engaged in more aggressive behaviors in games they lost compared with games they won. There are two potential explanations for these findings. Games with high levels of aggression may favor the home team as they entice the crowd to offer more active involvement in the contest, and in turn energize and motivate the home players (McGuire et al., 1992). Alternatively, games with higher levels of aggression may not favor the home team but be detrimental to the away team as officials are more likely to penalize the away team (Nevill, Balmer, & Williams, 2002).

One of the challenging aspects of researching aggression in sport is determining how aggression can best be measured. Aggression can be assessed using self-report inventories that can determine an intention to aggress in a particular situation, such as the *Judgements About Moral Behavior in Youth Sport Questionnaire* (JAMBYSQ; Stephens, Bredmeier, & Shields, 1997). Trait measures of aggression, such as the *Aggression Questionnaire* (Buss & Perry, 1992) can also be used to give an indication of an individual's likelihood of aggressing. Interestingly, Buss and Perry considered aggression to be a multidimensional construct and the *Aggression Questionnaire* assesses the following four aspects of aggression: physical aggression; verbal aggression; anger and hostility; and individuals may differ in their tendency to respond with different types of aggression. The physical aggression sub-scale has been found to predict the amount of aggressive penalties conceded by high school hockey players during a season (Bushman & Wells, 1998). Because aggression is a behavior, indices of aggressive behavior, such as penalties, have also been used. However, only those penalties that include an attempt to harm should be recorded (Widmeyer & Birch, 1984). A further limitation of using penalties as a measure of aggression is that they will not provide a measure of aggressive acts that occur within the rules of the game, while acts unnoticed by the officials are also not included (Stephens, 1998). In this regard, observational analysis of behavior may be the best opportunity to understand aggression in sport (Kirker et al., 2000).

Aggression is a particularly interesting area to study because it is a moral issue and many psychologists would agree with the sentiments expressed by Tenenbaum, Sacks, Miller, Golden, and Doolin (2000: 318) who suggest that ". . . behaviors intended to harm another are unacceptable in any contact or non-contact sport." It is therefore not surprising that the International Society of Sport Psychology published a position statement outlining several ways in which violence and aggression in sport can be reduced (Tenenbaum, Stewart, Singer, & Duda, 1997). This position statement sparked a debate in the literature about the role of aggression and violence in sport (see Kerr, 1999; 2002; Tenenbaum et al., 2000). It is not possible to consider all the issues raised in the debate here but one crucial issue covered was whether aggression and violence in sport is acceptable.

Leaving aside, for the moment, the issue of violence, let us consider whether aggression has any place in sport. If, as most psychologists agree, aggression is a behavior where there is intent to harm or injure (physically or psychologically) another human being then it would appear that aggression plays a legitimate central role in many competitive sports. Interestingly, merely creating a competitive situation increases aggression (Berkowitz, 1993). The rules of many sports (e.g., boxing, ice hockey, rugby) allow athletes to engage in behaviors that cause physical harm, and behaviors that can cause psychological harm (e.g., trash talking) are rarely legislated against. It could even be suggested that athletes best equipped to harm opponents, physically and psychologically, within the rules of the sport, increase their chances of success.

Many psychologists define the use of behaviors that are legitimate (i.e., within the rules of the game) where the aim is to achieve dominance or assertion (Tenenbaum et al., 1997). As with the earlier classification of hostile and instrumental aggression, a difficulty with this distinction is that exactly the same behavior can be classified as assertive or aggressive depending on the goal of the athlete. This may be difficult as an athlete may not be consciously aware of their goals, or may have multiple goals going into an encounter. For example, a cricket fast bowler may aim to hit a batsman with a short ball because he wishes both to injure him *and* to achieve dominance. However unpalatable, it may be more accurate to accept that competitive sport is aggressive and that aggression may be a necessary requirement for success in many sports. Furthermore much of the pleasure from playing contact sports may be derived from the physical contact and executing physically aggressive plays successfully (Kerr, 2005).

Notwithstanding these issues, there is consensus that aggressive acts outside the rules of the game should be reduced or eliminated. A boxer can hardly complain about being hit on the head during the bout but may legitimately complain about receiving a low blow. In this regard Kerr (2002) cites the argument outlined by Smith (1983: 10) that ". . . volenti non fit injuria – to one who consents no injury is done." A reduction in violence, which is seen as aggression outside the rules of sport (Terry & Jackson, 1985), or what Kerr (2005) terms unsanctioned aggression, is clearly a worthy goal.

An illustration of the types of technique that can be employed to reduce aggression is provided by Brunelle, Janelle, and Tennant (1999) who examined the impact of role playing and self-monitoring strategies in controlling feelings of anger and angry behaviors (which incorporated aggressive behaviors such as arguing and physical retaliation) among competitive soccer players. During the role playing sessions, the players were given the opportunity to practice alternative responses to typical anger inducing situations, such as a poor call by the referee, and this was effective in reducing the angry behaviors exhibited by the players.

## Additional readings

Kerr, J. H. (2005). *Rethinking aggression and violence in sport*. Abingdon: Routledge.

Stephens, D. E. (1998). Aggression. In J. L. Duda (ed.), *Advances in sport and exercise psychology measurement* (pp. 277–92). Morgantown, WV: Fitness Information Technology.

Widmeyer, W. N. (2002). Reducing aggression in sport. In J. M. Silva & D. E. Stevens (eds), *Psychological foundations of sport* (2nd ed., pp. 380–95). Boston, MA: Allyn & Bacon.

Widmeyer, W. N., Bray, S. R., Dorsch, K. D., & McGuire, E. J. (2002). Explanations for the occurrence of aggression: Theories and research. In J. M. Silva & D. E. Stevens (eds), *Psychological foundations of sport* (2nd ed., pp. 352–79). Boston, MA: Allyn & Bacon.

Widmeyer, W. N., Dorsch, K. D., Bray, S. R., & McGuire, E. J. (2002). The nature, prevalence, and consequences of aggression in sport. In J. M. Silva & D. E. Stevens (eds), *Psychological foundations of sport* (2nd ed., pp. 328–51). Boston, MA: Allyn & Bacon.

## Study questions

1   What is the difficulty with using penalties as a proxy measure of aggression as Frank and Golivich did in their second study?

2   Considering the definition of aggression provided by Baron and Richardson are there any sports where aggression is rarely observed? Or is aggression inevitable in all sports?

3   Imagine that you are the commissioner of a contact sport that has declining participation levels because of a series of high profile aggressive incidents (outside the rules of the game) that have led to some serious injuries. How would you apply the principles of social learning theory to reduce aggression in the sport?

4   What are the challenges of measuring aggression in sport?

5   If you were the coach of a team that played in black would you ask the owners if you could change the color of the uniform?

## References

Apter, M. J. (1982). *The experience of motivation. The theory of psychological reversals*. London: Academic Press.

Arms, R. L., Russell, G. W., & Sandilands, M. L. (1979). Effects on the hostility of spectators of viewing aggressive sports. *Social Psychology Quarterly*, 42, 275–9.

Bandura, A. (1977). *Social learning theory*. Englewood Cliffs, NJ: Prentice Hall.

Bandura, A., Ross D., & Ross, S. A. (1961). Imitation of aggression through imitation of aggressive models. *Journal of Abnormal and Social Psychology*, 63, 575–82.

Bandura, A., Ross D., & Ross, S. A. (1963a). Imitation of film-mediated aggressive models. *Journal of Abnormal and Social Psychology*, 66, 3–11.

Bandura, A., Ross D., & Ross, S. A. (1963b). Vicarious reinforcement of imitative learning. *Journal of Abnormal and Social Psychology*, 67, 601–7.

Baron, R. A., & Richardson, D. R. (1994). *Human aggression.* New York: Plenum Press.

Berkowtiz, L. (1989). The frustration-aggression hypothesis: An examination and reformulation. *Psychological Bulletin*, 106, 59–73.

Berkowitz, L. (1993). *Aggression: Its causes, consequences, and control.* London: McGraw-Hill.

Book, A. S., Starzyk, K. B., & Quinsey, V. L. (2001). The relationship between testosterone and aggression: a meta-analysis. *Aggression and Violent Behavior*, 6, 579–99.

Bredemeier, B. (1994). Children's moral reasoning and their assertive, aggressive, and submissive tendencies in sport and daily life. *Journal of Sport & Exercise Psychology*, 16, 1–14.

Bredemeier, B., Shields, D., Weiss, M., & Cooper, B. (1986). The relationship of sport involvement with children's moral reasoning and aggression tendencies. *Journal of Sport Psychology*, 8, 304–18.

Brunelle, J. P., Janelle, C. M., & Tennant, L. K. (1999). Controlling competitive anger among male soccer players. *Journal of Applied Sport Psychology*, 11, 283–97.

Bushman, B. J., & Wells, G. L. (1998). Trait aggressiveness and hockey penalties: Predicting hot tempers on the ice. *Journal of Applied Psychology*, 83, 969–74.

Buss, A. H., & Perry, M. (1992). The Aggression Questionnaire. *Journal of Personality and Social Psychology*, 63, 452–9.

Dollard, J., Miller, N., Doob, I., Mowrer, O. H., & Sears, R. R. (1939). *Frustration and aggression.* New Haven, CT: Yale University Press.

Drabman, R. S., & Thomas, M. H. (1977). Children's imitation of aggressive and prosocial behavior when viewing alone and in pairs. *Journal of Communication*, 27, 199–205.

Edwards, J., & Archambault, D. (1989). The homefield advantage. In J. H. Goldstein (ed.), *Sports, games and play: Social and psychological viewpoints* (2nd ed., pp. 333–70). Hillsdale, NJ: Erlbaum.

Feshbach, S. (1955). The drive-reducing function of fantasy behavior. *Journal of Abnormal and Social Psychology*, 50, 3–11.

Freud, S. (1920). *A general introduction to psycho-analysis.* New York: Boni & Liveright.

Greenlees, I., Buscombe, R., Thelwell, R., Holder, T., & Rimmer, M. (2005). Impact of opponents' clothing and body language on impression formation and outcome expectations. *Journal of Sport & Exercise Psychology*, 27, 39–52.

Hill, R. A., & Barton, R. A. (2005). Red enhances human performance in contests. *Nature*, 435, 293.

Husman, B., & Silva, J. (1984). Aggression in sport: Definitional and theoretical considerations. In J. Silva & R. Weinberg (eds), *Psychological foundations in sport* (pp. 246–60). Champaign, IL: Human Kinetics.

Jaffe, Y., Shapir, N., & Yinon, Y. (1981). Aggression and its escalation. *Journal of Cross-Cultural Psychology*, 12, 21–36.

Jones, M. V., Bray, S. R., & Olivier, S. (2005). Game location and aggression in rugby league. *Journal of Sports Sciences*, 23, 387–93.

Jones, M. V., Paull, G. C., & Erskine, J. (2002). The impact of a team's aggressive reputation on the decisions of association football referees. *Journal of Sports Sciences*, 20, 991–1000.

Kavassanu, M., Roberts, G. C., & Ntoumanis, N. (2002). Contextual influences on moral functioning of college basketball players. *The Sport Psychologist*, 16, 347–67.

Kavassanu, M., & Spray, C. M. (2006). Contextual influences on moral functioning of male youth footballers. *The Sport Psychologist*, 20, 1–23.

Kerr, J. H. (1999). The role of aggression and violence in sport: A rejoinder to the ISSP position stand. *The Sport Psychologist*, 13, 83–8.

Kerr, J. H. (2002). Issues in aggression and violence in sport: The ISSP position stand revisited. *The Sport Psychologist*, 16, 68–78.

Kerr, J. H. (2005). *Rethinking aggression and violence in sport*. Abingdon: Routledge.

Kirker, B., Tenenbaum, G., & Mattson, J. (2000). An investigation of the dynamics of aggression: Direct observations in ice hockey and basketball. *Research Quarterly for Exercise and Sport*, 71, 373–86.

Lorenz, K. (1981). *Foundations of ethology*. New York: Springer-Verlag.

McGuire, E. J., Courneya, K. S., Widmeyer, W. N., & Carron, A. V. (1992). Aggression as a potential mediator of the home advantage in professional ice hockey. *Journal of Sport & Exercise Psychology*, 14, 148–58.

Murray, H. A. (1943). *Thematic Apperception Test manual*. Cambridge, MA: Harvard University Press.

Neave, N., & Wolfson, S. (2003). Testosterone, territoriality, and the "home advantage". *Physiology and Behavior*, 78, 269–75.

Nevill, A. M., Balmer, N. J., & Williams, A. M. (2002). The influence of crowd noise and experience upon refereeing decisions in football. *Psychology of Sport and Exercise*, 3, 261–72.

Parrott, A. C., Choi, P. Y. L., & Davies, M. (1994). Anabolic steroid use by amateur athletes: effects upon psychological mood states. *Journal of Sports Medicine and Physical Fitness*, 34, 292–8.

Pilz, G. A. (1979). Attitudes toward different forms of aggressive and violent behavior in competitive sports: two empirical studies. *Journal of Sport Behavior*, 2, 3–26.

Seligman, M. E. P. (1975). *Helplessness: On depression, development, and death*. San Francisco: W. H. Freeman.

Sharp, M., & Collins, D. (1998). Exploring the "inevitability" of the relationship between anabolic-androgenic steroid use and aggression in human males. *Journal of Sport & Exercise Psychology*, 20, 379–94.

Sheldon, J. P., & Aimar, C. M. (2001). The role aggression plays in successful and unsuccessful ice hockey behaviors. *Research Quarterly for Exercise and Sport*, 72, 304–9.

Smith, M. D. (1983). *Violence and sport*. Toronto: Butterworths.

Stephens, D., Bredmeier, B. J. L., & Shields, D. L. L. (1997). Construction of a measure designed to assess players' descriptions and prescriptions for moral behavior in youth sport soccer. *International Journal of Sport Psychology*, 28, 370–90.

Stephens, D. E. (1998). Aggression. In J. L. Duda (ed.), *Advances in sport and exercise psychology measurement* (pp. 277–92). Morgantown, WV: Fitness Information Technology, Inc.

Strauss, R. H., Wright, J. E., Finerman, G. A. M., & Catlin, D. H. (1983). Side effects of anabolic steroids in weight-trained men. *Physician and Sportsmedicine*, 11, 87–95.

Tenenbaum, G., Stewart, E., Singer, R. N., & Duda, J. (1997). Aggression and violence in sport: An ISSP position stand. *The Sport Psychologist*, 11, 1–7.

Tenenbaum, G., Sacks, D. N., Miller, J. W., Golden, A. S., & Doolin, N. (2000). Aggression and violence in sport: A reply to Kerr's rejoinder. *The Sport Psychologist*, 14, 315–26.

Terry, P. C., & Jackson, J. J. (1985). The determinants and control of violence in sport. *Quest*, 37, 27–37.

Widmeyer, W. N., & Birch, J. S. (1984). Aggression in professional ice hockey: A strategy for success or a reaction to failure? *Journal of Psychology*, 117, 77–84.

Widmeyer, W. N., & McGuire, E. J. (1997). Frequency of competition and aggression in professional ice hockey. *International Journal of Sport Psychology*, 28, 57–66.

Widmeyer, W. N., Bray, S. R., Dorsch, K. D., & McGuire, E. J. (2002). Explanations for the occurrence of aggression: Theories and research. In J. M. Silva and D. E. Stevens (eds), *Psychological Foundations of Sport* (2nd ed., pp. 352–79). Boston, MA: Allyn & Bacon.

Zillmann, D., Katcher, A. H., & Milavsky, B. (1972). Excitation transfer from physical exercise to subsequent aggressive behavior. *Journal of Experimental Social Psychology*, 8, 247–59.

# 4

# Achievement motivation

Duda, J. L., Fox, K. R., Biddle, S. J. H., & Armstrong, N. J. (1992). Children's achievement goals and beliefs about success in sport. *British Journal of Educational Psychology*, 62, 313–23.

**Written in collaboration with Christopher Spray**

## Background and context

Achievement motivation has been a popular area of inquiry in the history of psychology as a scientific discipline. During the last century, various constructs, models, and theoretical frameworks were put forward to explain achievement striving, including need for achievement, attributions, achievement goals, competence perceptions, and implicit theories of ability (Elliot & Dweck, 2005). The focus of the current chapter is on achievement goal theory, which came to the fore in the late 1970s and early 1980s, based initially within educational settings, and led, arguably, by the contributions of John Nicholls (1983, 1984). Published works applying the theory to sport began to emerge in the 1980s (Roberts, 1984). A central figure in the nascent sport-based literature was Joan Duda (Duda, 1980), lead author of this chapter's key study.

A seminal contribution by Maehr and Nicholls (1980) proposed the existence of three achievement goals: ability (ego) goals, task goals, and social-approval goals. Subsequent theoretical and empirical developments in both education and sport led to the "dropping" of social goals as a key area of inquiry. Maehr and Nicholls emphasized that goals determine the meaning of achievement for the individual in that they reflect the purpose of achievement striving and subjective perceptions of success. What is success to one person may not be to another, depending on the goals they pursue. Thus, an individual who is "task-involved" is concerned with self-improvement and task mastery and is likely to feel successful when gains in performance and/or mastery come about, irrespective of the achievements of others. In this state of goal involvement, effort and ability are viewed as positively related – that is, more effort leads to perceptions of higher ability. The individual's purpose (goal) is to develop self-referenced competence. Conversely, an individual who is "ego-involved" is concerned with displaying superior ability to others and is likely to feel successful when performing better than members of a reference group. In this goal involvement state, effort and ability are viewed as inversely related and an individual will feel particularly successful when displaying equal ability but with less effort than others. The individual's purpose is to demonstrate, rather than develop, competence (Nicholls, 1984, 1989).

Nicholls also argued that individuals develop a proneness for task and/or ego involvement. Proneness is deemed to represent a fairly stable tendency (if not a personality *trait*) to define competence in a particular fashion, that is developed via socialization experiences.

Using Nicholls' terminology, people can be *task oriented* (have a tendency toward task involvement states in achievement situations) and/or *ego oriented* (have a tendency toward ego involvement states in achievement situations). The "and/or" in the preceding sentence is a reflection of one of Nicholls' key tenets – that task and ego orientations are orthogonal (independent) constructs and individuals can be characterized by high levels of both, low levels of both or by the dominance of one (i.e., high-ego/high-task, low-ego/low-task, low-ego/high-task, high-ego/low-task).

With the theoretical framework "in place," the next step was to develop an instrument that assessed individuals' ego and task goal orientations in sport. Building on work in the educational sphere, Duda and Nicholls (1992) devised the *Task and Ego Orientation in Sport Questionnaire* (TEOSQ). Once armed with the TEOSQ, researchers were able to reliably assess individuals' goal orientations in sport, and determine the nature of associations between task/ego orientations and a host of motivational and behavioral indices, thereby elucidating the different meanings and experiences attached to sport.

The key study by Duda, Fox, Biddle, and Armstrong was one of the first studies to employ the TEOSQ to assess task and ego goal orientations. It also included the measurement of two additional goals – work avoidance and cooperation – which, at that time, had received attention in education but not in sport. Duda *et al.*'s research focused, firstly, on cognitive correlates of goals, namely beliefs about success. Nicholls had argued that individuals form personal theories of achievement based around their definitions of success (i.e., their goals) and their beliefs about what is necessary in order to be successful in achievement settings. He proposed that conceptually coherent combinations should prevail, whereby a tendency to define success in self- or task-referenced terms (task orientation) is linked with the view that success results from motivation and hard work. On the other hand, a tendency to define success in normative referenced terms (ego orientation) is related with the belief that innate ability (talent) is a necessary determinant of success. Moreover, Nicholls believed that, if winning and showing one's superiority are important to an individual, that person is more likely to do whatever is needed to fulfill that goal. Hence, he hypothesized that the belief that success in sport results from cheating and deceiving others should be related in a positive manner with ego orientation.

Having set out to examine whether goal-belief dimensions would emerge in the sport setting among young people, the second objective of the key study was to establish the relationships between these dimensions and self-reported enjoyment and boredom in sport. Knowledge of the motivation-related correlates of personal theories would be useful, they argued, for researchers and practitioners seeking to optimize children's motivation in sport.

## Key study

The domain of sport has been characterized as a potent and particularly public achievement environment. Similar to the classroom, the relevance of exhibiting ability, performance standards, and competition are hallmarks of the sporting enterprise. For many children, their major exposure to sport occurs within the educational setting. Studies in the United States have indicated that accomplishment in school sport (in contrast to academic classwork) provides an important contribution to students' overall sense of worth and status in the school system. Consequently, recent research has applied and tested the theoretical tenets of contemporary goal perspective theories of achievement in the realm of sport. This literature has indicated that the concepts of task and ego orientation are relevant and meaningful in this context. Studies have shown that the rational interrelationships between goals and beliefs that have emerged in the classroom also exist in sport (e.g., Duda & Nicholls, 1992). Further, there is evidence that the task and ego goal-belief dimensions, or personal theories about achievement, generalize across the academic and sport domains (Duda & Nicholls, 1992). Drawing from this work, it would appear that the determination of children's goal orientations in sport is significant to a greater understanding of this specific achievement context and would carry important implications for how and what is taught in schools. Sports achievement research has, however, largely been conducted with American youth and young adults. Given that achievement goals may be in part culturally determined, it seems important to extend this work to other populations.

## Method

### Sample

A total of 142 children (68 boys and 74 girls) attending middle schools in a small city in south-west England participated in this investigation. Mean age was 10.5 (SD = 0.83) years. Participants were a section of 250 children taking part in a longitudinal project investigating children's physical and psychological development. The main sample had been selected from volunteers after invitations to take part had been offered to the whole cohort of the city's schools.

### Procedures

During an annual testing sessions at a university site, the participants were administered a multi-section inventory (assessing goal orientations, beliefs about success, and satisfaction in sport) by a trained research assistant. The participants were assured that no one but the researchers would see their responses and were encouraged to answer as honestly as possible. The inventory, which can be found in Table 4.1, took approximately 20 minutes to complete.

### Measures

Prior to this data collection, one of the researchers had interviewed six boys and six girls to establish their comprehension of the three-part inventory. As a result, minor wording changes were made to a few items to make them more appropriate for British children. All items were presented in a five-point Likert format ranging from strongly disagree (1) to strongly agree (5). Item means were used to represent subscales in statistical analysis.

*Goal Orientations.* The children's tendency to emphasize task- and ego-involved goals in sport settings was assessed with the 13-item *Task and Ego Orientation in Sport Questionnaire* (TEOSQ; Duda & Nicholls, 1992). Measures of the children's orientation to work avoidance (three items) and focus on cooperation (two items) were also included. These sub-scales had been previously adapted for the sports setting (Duda & Nicholls, 1992) from the *Motivational Orientation Scales*, which have been used extensively in classroom settings (Nicholls, 1989; Nicholls, Cobb, Wood, Yackel, & Patashnick, 1990). The introduction to the goal orientation section of the instrument requested the children to think of when they personally feel most successful in sport and games. The stem for each of the 18 items was "I feel really success-ful in sport and games when . . .". Among the present sample, the task orientation, ego orientation, work avoidance, and cooperation sub-scales demonstrated acceptable internal consistency (alphas were 0.72, 0.78, 0.65, and 0.72, respectively).

*Beliefs About Success.* Drawing from classroom-based and sport research (Duda & Nicholls, 1992; Nicholls, Patashnick, & Nolen, 1985; Nicholls, 1989), the participants were also asked "What do you think is most likely to help kids do well and succeed in sports and games?" Seventeen causes of sport success were presented (see Table 4.1). This measure incorporated three sub-scales assessing children's beliefs that sport achievement stems from (a) motivation/effort, (b) ability, and (c) deception/external factors. To maintain the focus on causes of success (in contrast to the personal criteria underlying subjective success elicited

**Table 4.1**

---

**Goal orientations**

*Task orientation*
   I learn something new that is fun to do
   I learn a new skill and it makes me want to practice more
   I learn a new skill by trying hard
   I work really hard
   Something I learn makes me want to go and practice more
   A new skill I learn really feels right
   I do my very best

*Ego orientation*
   I'm the only one who can do a move or skill
   I can do better than my friends
   The others can't do as well as me
   Others mess up and I don't
   I score the most points or goals
   I'm the best

*Work avoidance*
   I don't have to try hard
   I can skive off
   I don't have anything hard to do

*Cooperation*
   My friends and I help each other improve
   My friends and I help each other do our best

**Beliefs about success**

*Motivation/effort*
   Work really hard
   Always do their best
   Help each other learn
   Like to practice
   Like improving
   Try things that they can't do too well
   Like to learn new skills

*Ability*
   Always try to beat others
   Are better at sport than the others
   Are born naturally good at sport
   Are better than others in tough competition

*Deception*
    Pretend they like their sports/games teacher or coach
    Know how to cheat or bend the rules
    Know how to make themselves look better than they are
    Have the right clothes and equipment
    Are just lucky
    Know how to impress their sports/games teacher or coach

**Satisfaction/interest**

*Enjoyment/interest*
    I usually enjoy playing sport
    I usually find playing sport interesting
    I usually get really involved when I am playing sport
    I usually find that time flies when I am playing sport
    I usually have fun doing sport

*Boredom*
    In sport, I often daydream instead of thinking what I am doing
    When playing sport, I am usually bored
    When playing sport, I usually wish the game would end quickly

by the goal orientation measures), the stem for each item was "Kids succeed if . . .". Among this sample of British children, the motivation/effort, ability, and deception/external factors sub-scales were found to be internally reliable (alphas were 0.83, 0.76, and 0.75, respectively).

*Satisfaction/Interest.* The children responded to eight items, developed by Nicholls and his colleagues (Duda & Nicholls, 1992; Nicholls *et al.*, 1985; Nicholls, 1989), assessing their degree of satisfaction with and interest in sport (see Table 4.1). These items comprise an enjoyment/interest sub-scale (five items) and a boredom sub-scale (three items). Although these sub-scales are related, it has been demonstrated that they are not bipolar opposites of the same construct. On this occasion they were found to be internally consistent (alphas were 0.84 and 0.70 respectively, and moderately correlated, $r = 0.56$).

## Results

### Subscale Means and Standard Deviations

The observed means and standard deviations for each of the measures (by gender and total sample) are presented in Table 4.2. In the sport domain, the children focused primarily on task-oriented and cooperative goals. Both the boys and girls perceived motivation and effort as the major means to sports success. Further, the children generally reported that they found sport enjoyable and interesting and experienced little boredom while engaging in sports/games activities.

### Gender Differences in Goals, Beliefs and Interest

Three separate one-way MANOVAs were conducted, and boys and girls were found to differ significantly in their goal orientations [$F(4,138) = 4.14$, $p < 0.01$], beliefs about success [$F(4,138) = 6.91$, $p < 0.001$], and reported enjoyment of and boredom in sport [$F(4,138) = 7.7$, $p < 0.01$]. Follow-up univariate analyses of variance indicated that the boys were more ego-oriented and reported greater positive affect towards sport than the girls (Table 4.2). Further,

**Table 4.2** Items means and standard deviations

| | Total sample N = 142 | | Males N = 68 | | Females N = 74 | |
|---|---|---|---|---|---|---|
| | *Mean* | *SD* | *Mean* | *SD* | *Mean* | *SD* |
| *Goal orientations* | | | | | | |
| Task orientation | 3.89 | .41 | 3.94 | .39 | 3.89 | .43 |
| Ego orientation | 3.34 | .80 | 3.56 | .80 | 3.14 | .76* |
| Work avoidance | 2.12 | .88 | 2.07 | .93 | 2.17 | .82 |
| Cooperation | 4.40 | .71 | 4.51 | .67 | 4.31 | .74 |
| *Beliefs about success* | | | | | | |
| Motivation/effort | 4.21 | .61 | 4.37 | .58 | 4.07 | .60* |
| Ability | 2.94 | .91 | 3.17 | .90 | 2.72 | .86* |
| Deception/external | 2.35 | .78 | 2.47 | .76 | 2.24 | .78* |
| *Satisfaction/interest* | | | | | | |
| Enjoyment/interest | 4.15 | .79 | 4.35 | .67 | 3.96 | .85* |
| Boredom | 2.03 | .94 | 2.01 | .98 | 2.05 | .90 |

* Indicates gender difference at $p < 0.05$.

boys were more likely to believe that motivation/effort, ability, and deception/external factors result in sport success than girls.

## Inter-relationships Among Goal Orientations and Beliefs

Table 4.3 shows a matrix of correlation coefficients for the goal orientations and beliefs about success in sport. Results confirm that task and ego orientation are separate constructs ($r = 0.11$). Task orientation was strongly and positively correlated with an emphasis on co-operation. Ego orientation was found to be weakly related to work avoidance and cooperation. Work avoidance and cooperation were not related.

**Table 4.3** Intercorrelations among goal orientations and beliefs about success

| | *1* | *2* | *3* | *4* | *5* | *6* |
|---|---|---|---|---|---|---|
| *Goal orientations* | | | | | | |
| 1. Task orientation | – | | | | | |
| 2. Ego orientation | .11 | – | | | | |
| 3. Work avoidance | −.05 | .18* | – | | | |
| 4. Cooperation | .61*** | .20* | −.01 | – | | |
| *Beliefs about success* | | | | | | |
| 5. Motivation/effort | .60*** | .23* | .03 | .61*** | – | |
| 6. Ability | −.04 | .58*** | .28** | −.05 | .27** | – |
| 7. Deception/external | −.15* | .28** | .46*** | −.16* | −.21* | .38*** |

* $p < 0.05$; ** $p < 0.01$; *** $p < 0.001$

Correlation coefficients for beliefs about success in sport showed that a weak relationship ($r = 0.27$) exists between success attributed to effort and that attributed to ability. Beliefs about deception/external factors were negatively related to effort ($r = -0.21$) and showed a stronger positive correlation with success due to ability ($r = 0.38$).

Both task orientation and cooperation corresponded to the view that motivation/effort leads to success ($r = 0.60/-0.61$). A low, negative correlation between these two goal orientations and the belief that success stems from deception/external factors also emerged. Children who scored high on ego orientation and/or work avoidance were more likely to think that deceptive factors or external forces cause success. The perception that the possession of ability results in success was primarily linked to ego orientation ($r = 0.58$) and, to a lesser degree, work avoidance. A weak, positive relationship was revealed between ego orientation and the belief that one becomes successful in sport through hard work and motivation.

To ascertain whether similar goal/belief dimensions to those found in American children would emerge among British children, factor analyses (principal components with both varimax and oblimin rotations) of the four goal orientation and three belief scores were conducted. As shown in Table 4.4, a two-factor solution was revealed (eigenvalues > 1.0). Both rotations produced similar results and the two dimensions which emerged were orthogonal (interfactor correlation = 0.016). Consequently, only the results based on the varimax rotation are reported.

**Table 4.4** Factor analysis of goal orientation and beliefs about success sub-scales

|  | Task dimension | Ego dimension |
| --- | --- | --- |
| Effort belief | .822 |  |
| Cooperation | .822 |  |
| Task orientation | .819 |  |
| Ability belief |  | .828 |
| Deception belief |  | .798 |
| Ego orientation |  | .635 |
| Work avoidance |  | .615 |
| Eigenvalue | 2.23 | 2.11 |
| % of variance | 31.90 | 30.20 |

*Note: Only loadings > 0.40 are printed*

Task orientation, cooperation, and the belief that success stems from motivation/effort loaded on the first factor, labelled Task Dimension. The second factor reflected a very different perspective on sport achievement. Specifically, this Ego Dimension was characterized by an emphasis on ego-oriented and work avoidance goals. Moreover, the beliefs that high ability and deception/external variables lay the basis for sport achievement also loaded on this factor.

## Goal Belief Dimensions and Satisfaction Interest Relationships

Factor scores for each of the two goal/belief dimensions shown in Table 4.4 were calculated and their associations with reported enjoyment/interest and boredom in sport were then determined by correlation coefficients. As can be seen in Table 4.5, a moderately high, positive

**Table 4.5** Intercorrelations between task and ego goal/belief dimensions and indices of interest in the enjoyment of sport

|  | Task dimension | Ego dimension |
|---|---|---|
| Enjoyment/interest | .54*** | .06 |
| Boredom | −.24** | .23** |

** $p < 0.01$; *** $p < 0.001$

association was found between scores on the task dimension and the degree to which the children found sport enjoyable and interesting. The degree of boredom experienced in sport settings was positively correlated with the ego dimension while an inverse relationship between task dimension scores and reported boredom emerged. Both these correlations, however, were quite weak.

## Discussion

The results of this study suggest that this group of 10-year-old boys and girls are primarily task-oriented, value cooperation, and believe that hard work will lead to achievement in sport. Further, when taking the entire sample into consideration, these British youngsters seem to find sport and games enjoyable and not boring. Similar to findings with American youth (Duda & Nicholls, 1992; Nicholls et al., 1985; Nicholls, 1989), a range of individual differences in goal orientations exist among British children. Most importantly, this study has demonstrated that such differences in dispositional goal perspectives provide insight into variations in children's beliefs about success and their affective responses to the sport experience.

When the associations between goals and beliefs about the causes of success were examined, a task dimension or "theory of achievement" was revealed (Nicholls, 1989). This dimension indicated that children who are orientated to personal improvement and skill mastery also believe that success in sport arises through a desire to work hard and do one's best. It seems that to children who primarily operate according to this theory of success, the essence of sport is to work hard and work together. Such children also strongly endorse cooperation. However, this latter finding needs to be tempered as there is a possibility that the items in the cooperation scale may be more heavily weighted towards a task rather than ego orientation.

An orthogonal ego dimension or perspective on achievement also emerged. Although effort and cooperation appeared to play a subordinate role, children who were concerned with demonstrating superior competence were more likely to believe that sport success stems mainly from the possession of high ability. According to Nicholls (1989), believing that talent is the major cause of achievement would most probably result in motivational difficulties among children who have questions concerning their own level of competence. This is also consistent with propositions put forward by Dweck and Leggett (1988).

Interestingly, the ego goal-belief dimension was also linked to an endorsement of work avoidance in the sport setting. Based on the theoretical predictions of Nicholls (1989) and others (Ames, 1984; Ames & Archer, 1988), it would be rational (although not motivationally adaptive) for high ego-oriented children who doubt their competence eventually to define success in terms of not trying or avoiding sport completely. Holding back one's effort and interest is a strategy which may help mask a fragile sense of ability.

The belief that deception/external elements result in success loaded on the ego dimension as well. It is reasonable to expect that, if a child is dependent upon performing better than others, she/he might be more likely to view deceptive tactics and factors outside herself/himself (e.g., luck, equipment) as a viable means to avoid failure (Duda, Olsen, & Templin, 1991). Again, such a belief system would probably not lay the basis for sustained and desirable achievement patterns.

In general, these results indicate that children's goal orientations in sport are logical expressions of their beliefs about the causes of success in sport. Moreover, the goal-belief dimensions which have been identified in studies of American youth are equally manifested in British children. These dimensions represent critical elements on which individual differences in children's personal theories of sport success can be determined. They combine perceptions of what is salient in sport *and* an understanding about how that context operates (Nicholls, 1989).

From the standpoint of trying to optimize motivation in the educational domain, it is important to ascertain the motivation-related correlates of a task versus ego theory of achievement. In this investigation, the authors determined the relationship of children's scores on the task and ego goal/belief dimensions to their reported enjoyment and boredom experienced in sport. Children who held a task-oriented theory of sport achievement found sport activities more fun, interesting, and less boring. In contrast, children who scored high on the ego goal-belief dimension had higher scores on the boredom subscale.

These findings are aligned with previous work examining the interdependencies between dispositional or situationally-induced goal orientations and intrinsic interest (Ames & Archer, 1988; Butler, 1988; Duda & Nicholls, 1992; Nicholls, 1989). The results are also consonant with the predictions stemming from the cognitive evaluation theory of intrinsic motivation (Butler, 1988; Deci & Ryan, 1985).

When an individual holds a task-involved theory of achievement, the assumed antecedents of success are under one's personal control (e.g., trying hard). Moreover, what a person wants to achieve is intrinsic to the task at hand. It is not surprising, therefore, that such a perspective on success would enhance investment in and the joy emanating from achievement experiences.

On the other hand, adhering to an ego-based theory of success entails a focus on the outcome of one's activities. What one is doing is merely a means to an end, namely showing that one is the best (Nicholls, 1989). The subjective evaluation of one's performance, in this case, is dependent on the appraisal of others' performances and not self-referenced. Factors which are less self-determining (e.g., deception, the ability of others, external causes) and not fundamentally under one's internal regulation (e.g., one's athletic ability) are deemed pertinent to future accomplishment. Consequently, it would be expected that children characterized by high scores on the ego goal-belief dimension would be more prone emotionally and attentionally to disengage from sport and games, particularly if they begin to question their own ability.

Children are more likely to be enthusiastic about participating in achievement-related activities when they find these activities enjoyable and absorbing. The present research suggests that fostering a task-oriented interpretation of success would set the stage for more captivating and satisfying experiences and prolonged involvement in sport.

## Subsequent research and application

Duda *et al.*'s study determined the motivation-related correlates of achievement goals in sport. Although a few papers had been published previously employing samples from the United States (e.g., Duda, Olsen, & Templin, 1991), this was one of the first studies to test data from British youth. A plethora of investigations, involving primarily United States- and United Kingdom-based samples, followed suit. Results confirmed the hypothesized links between task orientation and the belief in the utility of effort in bringing about success in sport, and between ego orientation and the belief in the need for ability. These studies encompassed samples involving different sports, ages of participants, and levels of expertise (e.g., Duda & Nicholls, 1992; Duda & White, 1992; Lochbaum & Roberts, 1993; Roberts & Ommundsen, 1996; Roberts, Treasure, & Kavussanu, 1996). Evidence for the association between task orientation and enhanced enjoyment, satisfaction, and intrinsic motivation also emerged in sport and physical activity contexts (e.g., Dorobantu & Biddle, 1997; Duda, Chi, Newton, Walling, & Catley, 1995; Vlachopoulos & Biddle, 1996). Consequently, theorists and researchers have since argued for the promotion of task orientation in sport settings, and proposed that coaches and teachers should try to create a task-involving "climate" that emphasizes self-improvement, effort and cooperation among participants. Promoting competition and intra-group rivalry to identify the best in a class or team, and giving praise only to the most able, are examples of behaviors that should be actively discouraged in order to minimize the perception of an ego-involving climate.

Given the volume of research activity in the achievement goals area throughout the 1990s, Biddle, Wang, Kavussanu, and Spray (2003) conducted a systematic review of research into the correlates of task and ego goal orientations in order to provide summary statements of relationships. These researchers reported a moderate-to-large effect size (ES) of .47 between task orientation and the belief that effort produces success. This ES was derived from 28 studies covering eight different countries. The ES for task orientation and positive affect was .43 (48 studies across 12 countries). A negative ES of −.15 was found for task orientation and negative affect (38 studies across 8 countries). The link between the view that ability produces success and ego orientation was also substantiated (ES = .45). A weak effect emerged regarding the association between ego orientation and negative affect (ES = .07).

Thus, many investigations followed the lead of Duda et al. (1992). Using the same correlational design, researchers broadened the scope of the correlates investigated beyond beliefs about success and affect. A testimony to the sheer volume of achievement goal research in sport throughout the 1990s is the range of correlates of goal orientations identified by Biddle et al., including information processing, moral functioning and sportspersonship, anxiety, use of psychological strategies, beliefs about the purpose of sport, perceived competence, motives for participation, perceptions of significant others' goal orientations, participation, and performance (Biddle et al., 2003; Duda & Whitehead, 1998).

Duda et al.'s key study was characteristic of research in the early 1990s that looked at the individual impact of task and ego goal orientations on athletes' motivation (noting that cooperation and work avoidance goals were encompassed within the task and ego dimensions respectively). However, as reported earlier, Nicholls (1984, 1989) had argued that ego and task orientations are independent constructs and are both present within the individual to different degrees. Two years after the publication of the key study, Fox, Goudas, Biddle, Duda, and Armstrong (1994) produced evidence to support the orthogonality of task and ego orientation among children in sport and they examined the motivational repercussions of the four basic goal combinations. These combinations became known as *goal profiles*. Numerous studies followed looking at the motivational correlates of task and ego profiles. Although researchers have tended to employ a range of data analytic methods to identify the number and nature of profile groups in their samples, the current evidence base suggests that ego orientation may not bring about the same degree of motivational difficulties for an individual who also possesses a high task orientation (a high/high profile), than it may cause in an individual with low task orientation (a high-ego/low-task profile). This finding has been of particular interest to those researchers and practitioners interested in the motivation of elite sport performers because of the highly ego-involving nature of the elite sporting environment that over time is likely to develop/ reinforce in athletes a high ego orientation (Harwood, Cumming, & Fletcher, 2004). Despite these research efforts, however, we currently possess little knowledge regarding how high levels of both goals function effectively together in sport (Harwood, Spray, & Keegan, in press). This has been reflected in a debate which raised the issue of whether an ego orientation is necessary for success in sport and how this should inform the practice of sport psychologists (Duda, 1997; Hardy, 1997, 1998).

In their systematic review of goal orientations research during the 1990s, Biddle *et al.* (2003) were critical of the range of research samples and methods shown in this body of work. Almost all of the studies were cross-sectional in design, precluding inferences of causal relationships. In addition, samples consisted of mostly young people from the United States or United Kingdom. Similarly, in their review of the current state of play in achievement goal research, Harwood *et al.* (in press) caution that achievement goal research may reach a plateau and is in danger of stagnating through repetitive cross-sectional studies that merely identify another correlate of task and ego goal orientations. Harwood *et al.* argue for the need to conceptually (and methodologically) advance our research in order to deepen our understanding of achievement goals in sport.

Arguably the most significant conceptual development since the publication of Duda *et al.*'s key study is the introduction into the literature of the approach/avoidance achievement goal framework (Elliot, 1997, 1999; Elliot & Church, 1997; Elliot & McGregor, 2001). Essentially, Elliot and his colleagues have proposed the existence of four achievement goals, stemming from a two-component analysis of competence: these components are "definition" and "valence." Definition refers to whether competence is self- or other-referenced, in accord with Nicholls' conceptualization of goals. In addition, however, valence refers either to a positive, approach focused event (success, competence), or to a negative, avoidance focused event (failure, incompetence). Combining the definition and valence components results in four goals: mastery approach (Map), mastery avoidance (Mav), performance approach (Pap), and performance avoidance (Pav). Map goals are concerned with self-referenced improvement or task fulfilment, Mav goals are concerned with self-/task-referenced incompetence (i.e., becoming worse at a task), Pap goals entail striving to be better than others, and finally, Pav goals entail not wanting to be worse than others.

Recently, a measure of these four goals has been devised in the sport domain – the *Achievement Goals Questionnaire for Sport* (AGQ-S; Conroy, Elliot & Hofer, 2003). For comparison, the TEOSQ, as used by Duda *et al.* (1992) in the key study, taps only approach forms of goals – task (mastery) and ego (performance). There are other, more subtle, differences between the AGQ-S and the TEOSQ that reflect alternative conceptualizations of goals. For example, the TEOSQ is a measure of a fairly enduring orientation that reflects an individual's personal definition of success. When using the TEOSQ, researchers ask performers to reveal what makes them feel successful in sport. For Elliot and his co-workers, goals are not conceived at the level of a personal disposition. Rather, they are more temporally and situationally-focused to specific contexts, events, or even a moment in time. Moreover, a goal is purely concerned with the aim of behavior; there is no mention in the

AGQ-S of what makes the individual feel successful in sport (Conroy *et al.*, 2003; Elliot & Thrash, 2001).

Consideration of the approach/avoidance achievement goal framework in sport has only just begun (Elliot & Conroy, 2005; Harwood *et al.*, in press; Kingston, Harwood, & Spray, 2006; Spray & Keegan, 2005). Initial investigations support the adaptive nature of Map goals as they have been linked to enjoyment, intrinsic motivation, and a more "positive experience" in sport and physical activity (Cury, Elliot, Sarrazin, Da Fonseca, & Rufo, 2002; Warburton & Spray, 2006). Pap goals are hypothesized to result in some positive consequences such as greater performance but at a cost to the individual in terms of reduced self-determination and heightened anxiety. Pav goals are postulated to bring about overwhelmingly negative consequences. In general terms, the consequences of pursuing Mav goals are expected to be more positive than those associated with the pursuit of Pav goals, but more negative than the repercussions of adopting Map goals (Elliot, 1999). These propositions all await thorough empirical examination in sport, suggesting that there is plenty of ground for achievement goal researchers to cover over the next few years as they unravel the different meanings in sport attached to approach/avoidance goals.

There also remain many intriguing questions to be asked in sport using Nicholls' core concepts (Harwood *et al.*, in press). For example, the key study was one of the first to test Nicholls' theoretical tenets and to utilize the TEOSQ, but it also measured cooperation and work avoidance goals. These latter goals, plus others (e.g., social goals) deserve greater attention in our current research endeavors to find out what makes individuals feel successful in sport.

## Additional readings

Duda, J. L. (2001). Achievement goal research in sport: Pushing the boundaries and clarifying some misunderstandings. In G. C. Roberts (ed.), *Advances in motivation in sport and exercise* (pp. 129–82). Champaign, IL: Human Kinetics.

Duda, J. L. (2005). Motivation in sport: The relevance of competence and achievement goals. In A. J. Elliot & C. S. Dweck (eds), *Handbook of competence and motivation* (pp. 318–35). New York: The Guilford Press.

Elliot, A. J. (2005). A conceptual history of the achievement goal construct. In A. J. Elliot & C. S. Dweck (eds), *Handbook of competence and motivation* (pp. 52–72). New York: The Guilford Press.

Elliot, A. J., & Conroy, D. E. (2005). Beyond the dichotomous model of achievement goals in sport and exercise psychology. *Sport & Exercise Psychology Review*, 1(1), 17–25.

Spray, C. M., & Keegan, R. J. (2005). Beyond the dichotomous model of achievement goals in sport and exercise psychology: Comment on Elliot and Conroy (2005). *Sport & Exercise Psychology Review*, 1(2), 47–9.

## Study questions

1 In what ways did Duda *et al.* argue for the adaptive nature of the task goal-belief dimension and the maladaptive consequences of endorsing an ego goal-belief theory of achievement?

2 What note of caution did Duda *et al.* propose when explaining the relationship between task and cooperation goal orientations?

3 State two differences between Nicholls' and Elliot's conceptualizations of achievement goals.

4   How would you describe your own achievement goals in your sporting endeavors and what are your views concerning what it takes to be successful in sport?

5   Provide two examples, within sport, for each of the four approach/avoidance achievement goals.

## References

Ames, C. (1984). Competitive, cooperative, and individualistic goal structures: A motivational analysis. In R. Ames & C. Ames (eds), *Research on Motivation in Education Student Motivation* (pp. 177–207). New York: Academic Press.

Ames, C., & Archer, J. (1988). Achievement goals in the classroom: students' learning strategies and motivation processes. *Journal of Educational Psychology*, 80, 260–7.

Biddle, S. J. H., Wang, C. K. J., Kavussanu, M., & Spray, C. M. (2003). Correlates of achievement goal orientations in physical activity: A systematic review of research. *European Journal of Sport Science*, 3(5).

Butler, R. (1988). Enhancing and undermining intrinsic motivation: the effects of task-involving and ego-involving evaluation on interest and performance. *British Journal of Educational Psychology*, 58, 1–14.

Conroy, D. E., Elliot, A. J., & Hofer, S. M. (2003). A 2 × 2 achievement goals questionnaire for sport: Evidence for factorial invariance, temporal stability, and external validity. *Journal of Sport & Exercise Psychology*, 25, 456–76.

Cury, F., Elliot, A., Sarrazin, P., Da Fonseca, D., & Rufo, M. (2002). The trichotomous achievement goal model and intrinsic motivation: A sequential mediational analysis. *Journal of Experimental Social Psychology*, 38, 473–81.

Deci, E. L., & Ryan, R. M. (1985). *Intrinsic motivation and self-determination of human behavior*. New York: Plenum.

Dorobantu, M., & Biddle, S. (1997). The influence of situational and individual goals on the intrinsic motivation of Romanian adolescents towards physical education. *European Yearbook of Sport Psychology*, 1, 148–65.

Duda, J. L. (1980). Achievement motivation among Navajo students. *Ethos*, 8, 316–31.

Duda, J. L. (1997). Perpetuating myths: A response to Hardy's 1996 Coleman Griffith Address. *Journal of Applied Sport Psychology*, 9, 307–13.

Duda, J. L., Chi, L., Newton, M. L., Walling, M. D., & Catley, D. (1995). Task and ego orientation and intrinsic motivation in sport. *International Journal of Sport Psychology*, 26, 40–63.

Duda, J. L., & Nicholls, J. G. (1992). Dimensions of achievement motivation in schoolwork and sport. *Journal of Educational Psychology*, 84, 290–9.

Duda, J. L., Olson, L. K., & Templin, T. J. (1991). The relationship of task and ego orientation to sportsmanship attitudes and the perceived legitimacy of injurious acts. *Research Quarterly for Exercise and Sport*, 62, 79–87.

Duda, J. L., & White, S. A. (1992). Goal orientations and beliefs about the causes of sport success among elite skiers. *The Sport Psychologist*, 6, 334–43.

Duda, J. L., & Whitehead, J. (1998). Measurement of goal perspectives in the physical domain. In J. L. Duda (ed.), *Advances in sport and exercise psychology measurement* (pp. 21–48). Morgantown, WV: Fitness Information Technology.

Dweck, C. S., & Leggett, E. L. (1988). A social-cognitive approach to motivation and personality. *Psychological Review*, 95, 256–73.

Elliot, A. J. (1997). Integrating the "classic" and "contemporary" approaches to achievement motivation: A hierarchical model of approach and avoidance achievement motivation. In M. L. Maehr & P. R. Pintrich (eds), *Advances in motivation and achievement* (Vol. 10, pp. 143–79). Greenwich, CT: JAI Press.

Elliot, A. J. (1999). Approach and avoidance motivation and achievement goals. *Educational Psychologist*, 34, 169–89.

Elliot, A. J., & Church, M. A. (1997). A hierarchical model of approach and avoidance achievement motivation. *Journal of Personality and Social Psychology*, 72, 218–32.

Elliot, A. J., & Conroy, D. E. (2005). Beyond the dichotomous model of achievement goals in sport and exercise psychology. *Sport & Exercise Psychology Review*, 1(1), 17–25.

Elliot, A. J., & Dweck, C. S. (2005). Competence and motivation: Competence as the core of achievement motivation. In A. J. Elliot & C. S. Dweck (eds), *Handbook of competence and motivation* (pp. 3–12). New York: The Guilford Press.

Elliot, A. J., & McGregor, H. A. (2001). A 2 × 2 achievement goal framework. *Journal of Personality and Social Psychology*, 80, 501–19.

Elliot, A. J., & Thrash, T. M. (2001). Achievement goals and the hierarchical model of achievement motivation. *Educational Psychology Review*, 13, 139–56.

Fox, K., Goudas, M., Biddle, S., Duda, J., & Armstrong, N. (1994). Children's task and ego goal profiles in sport. *British Journal of Educational Psychology*, 64, 253–61.

Hardy, L. (1997). Three myths about applied consultancy work. *Journal of Applied Sport Psychology*, 9, 277–94.

Hardy, L. (1998). Responses to the reactants on three myths in applied consultancy work. *Journal of Applied Sport Psychology*, 10, 212–19.

Harwood, C., Cumming, J., & Fletcher, D. (2004). Motivational profiles and psychological skills use within elite youth sport. *Journal of Applied Sport Psychology*, 16, 318–32.

Harwood, C., Spray, C. M., & Keegan, R. (in press). Achievement goal theories in sport: Approaching changes and avoiding plateaus. In T. S. Horn (ed.), *Advances in sport psychology* (3rd ed.). Champaign, IL: Human Kinetics.

Kingston, K. M., Harwood, C. G., & Spray, C. M. (2006). Contemporary approaches to motivation in sport. In S. Hanton & S. Mellalieu (eds), *Literature reviews in sport psychology* (pp. 159–97). Hauppauge, NY: Nova Science.

Lochbaum, M. R., & Roberts, G. C. (1993). Goal orientations and perceptions of the sport experience. *Journal of Sport & Exercise Psychology*, 15, 160–71.

Maehr, M. L., & Nicholls, J. G. (1980). Culture and achievement motivation: A second look. In N. Warren (ed.), *Studies in cross-cultural psychology* (Vol. 2, pp. 221–67). London: Academic Press.

Nicholls, J. G. (1983). Conceptions of ability and achievement motivation: A theory and its implications for education. In S. G. Paris, G. M. Olson, & H. W. Stevenson (eds), *Learning and motivation in the classroom* (pp. 211–37). Hillsdale, NJ: Lawrence Erlbaum Associates.

Nicholls, J. G. (1984). Achievement motivation: Conceptions of ability, subjective experience, task choice, and performance. *Psychological Review*, 91, 328–46.

Nicholls, J. G. (1989). *The competitive ethos and democratic education*. Cambridge, MA: Harvard University Press.

Nicholls, J. G., Cobb, P., Wood, T., Yackel, E., & Patashnick, M. (1990). Assessing students' theories of success in mathematics: Individual and classroom differences. *Journal for Research in Mathematics Education*, 21, 109–22.

Nicholls, J. G., Patashnick, M., & Nolen, S. B. (1985). Adolescents' theories of education. *Journal of Educational Psychology*, 77, 683–92.

Roberts, G. C. (1984). Achievement motivation in children's sport. In J. G. Nicholls & M. L. Maehr (eds), *Advances in motivation and achievement: The development of achievement motivation* (Vol. 3, pp. 251–81). Greenwich, CT: JAI Press.

Roberts, G. C., & Ommundsen, Y. (1996). Effect of goal orientation on achievement beliefs, cognition and strategies in team sport. *Scandinavian Journal of Medicine & Science in Sports*, 6, 46–56.

Roberts, G. C., Treasure, D. C., & Kavussanu, M. (1996). Orthogonality of achievement goals and its relationship to beliefs about success and satisfaction in sport. *The Sport Psychologist*, 10, 398–408.

Spray, C. M., & Keegan, R. J. (2005). Beyond the dichotomous model of achievement goals in sport and exercise psychology: Comment on Elliot and Conroy (2005). *Sport & Exercise Psychology Review*, 1(2), 47–9.

Vlachopoulos, S., & Biddle, S. (1996). Achievement goal orientations and intrinsic motivation in a track and field event in school physical education. *European Physical Education Review*, 2, 158–64.

Warburton, V. E., & Spray, C. M. (2006, March). *Examining motivation in physical education across the primary-secondary transition*. Paper presented at the British Psychological Society Annual Conference, Cardiff, Wales.

# 5

# Exercise adherence

Dishman, R. K., Ickes, W., & Morgan, W. P. (1980). Self-motivation and adherence to habitual physical activity. *Journal of Applied Social Psychology*, 10, 115–32.

## Background and context

Exercise psychology is a relatively new field of study which emerged from its sport psychology roots in the 1970s. One primary focus of exercise psychology is to explain the psychological antecedents and consequences of exercise behavior, with exercise behavior referring to structured leisure-time physical activity, such as jogging and swimming, which relate to strength/endurance, cardiopulmonary fitness, flexibility, and/or body composition (Grove & Zillman, 2004). Exercise and physical activity are not one and the same, but there is overlap between the two constructs because physical activity is any movement of the body produced by skeletal muscles (Biddle & Mutrie, 2001).

The field of exercise psychology established itself, in part, alongside the initiation of government programs in the 1960s and 1970s that fostered public involvement in sport in its widest sense. The Council of Europe initiated the "Sport for All" program in 1966, and the United Nations Educational, Scientific, and Cultural Organization (UNESCO) adopted the *International Charter of Physical Education in Sport* in 1978. Both of these initiatives argued that every human being has a fundamental right to access sport- and exercise-related activities and that conditions should be established to enable the widest possible range of the population to regularly participate in these activities. As a result, other countries in the western world (e.g., Australia, Canada) and the developing world began to establish similar, government-funded programs and this, in turn, saw an increase in recognition of the importance of exercise and physical activity for well-being in the 1970s. Although research evidence was still developing at the time, the available studies indicated that more sedentary lifestyles were having harmful effects on general health (e.g., inactivity had been identified as a possible risk factor for coronary heart disease). There were also data to suggest that the adoption of regular exercise can enhance healthy living (e.g., exercise was found to offer psychological benefits to adults, including improvements in anxiety, depression, self-esteem, and mood), and it was recognized that if exercise is no longer a significant part of one's daily routine, then active recreational pursuits (e.g., gardening) might be an appropriate substitute.

The study of motivation has been at the center of developments in research, theory, and applications in exercise psychology since its inception, with motivation to participate in exercise and understanding what sustains such engagement being a central issue (Lavallee, Kremer, Moran, & Williams, 2004). Research prior to the key study had been predominantly atheoretical (Biddle & Mutrie, 2001). Because participation in exercise is a voluntary activity, and consequently subject to human decision-making processes, the factors associated with these processes started to attract research attention in exercise psychology. Furthermore, because most people decide to exercise to enhance their physical and psychological health, and decisions to exercise have much in common with decisions to engage in many other behaviors that influence health (e.g., maintaining a healthy diet, taking medication), exercise was being studied from a psychological perspective as a health behavior.

The key study by Dishman, Ickes, and Morgan was part of a program of research that looked at exercise as a health behavior and sought to determine what factors are most likely to contribute to adherence to exercise and physical activity programs. Adherence is a term used to describe how well a patient or client is complying with a recommendation made to them by a practitioner. Researchers at the time were finding that 40–65% of adults who started fitness programs were not adhering to recommendations, and subsequently dropping-out within several months. Dishman and colleagues were interested in self-motivation with regard to exercise adherence, as they identified this as the variable receiving the most attention in research into adherence to medical treatment programs. They were particularly interested in findings in the medical literature suggesting that those patients most likely to discontinue treatment are those who had previously discontinued treatment of another program. This suggested that stable individual differences in self-motivation may exist at the outset of a program, and thus they wanted to examine self-motivation as a dispositional determinant of adherence to physical activity programs. The term "determinant" is often used to denote a reproducible association (predictive relationship) rather than to imply cause and effect (Dishman & Sallis, 1994: 214). The aim of studying determinants within the context of this chapter is to identify the factors that predict the degree of adherence to exercise-related activity.

The key study involved the construction of a scale to measure self-motivation and subsequent work conducted to validate this construct. Due to the lack of research in the area at the time of the study, the authors initially validated the self-motivation construct in Study 1. Study 2 then used the construct to discriminate between adherers and dropouts of physical activity programs. The authors hypothesized that self-motivation could be measured reliably as a stable disposition, and that it would be positively related to exercise adherence. They also believed that a single unitary trait (i.e., the general disposition to persevere) may operate independently of other psychological variables (e.g., locus of control) that were being studied at the time.

## Key study

The efficacy of vigorous physical activity in the reduction of tension (Byrd, 1963; de Vries, 1968) and anxiety states (Morgan, 1979) is well documented. Not only do subjects consistently report they "feel better" following exercise (Mann, Garrett, Farhi, Murray, & Billings, 1969; Morgan, 1977b; Naughton, Bruhn, & Lategola, 1968), but chronic endurance type activity has also been shown to be effective in reducing or alleviating symptoms of depression (Greist, Klein, Eischens, & Faris, 1978; Morgan, Roberts, Brand, & Feinerman, 1970). In addition, two risk factors in the incidence of cardiovascular disease obesity and hypertension, are known to decrease with chronic exercise (Blackburn, 1976; Boyer & Kasch, 1970), and frequent rhythmic activity involving a large muscle mass is widely employed in cardiac rehabilitation. In summary, there is substantial evidence to support the prevalent belief within the health sciences that habitual physical activity enhances both physiological and psychological well-being.

However, as in many voluntary therapeutic settings, recidivism presents a major impediment to effective treatment. Adult fitness programs typically report adherence rates of only 40–65% (Bruce, Frederick, Bruce, & Fisher, 1976; Massie & Shephard, 1971; Morgan, 1977a; Oja, Teraslinna, Partanen, & Karava, 1975; Oldridge, 1977a, 1977b; Sidney & Shephard, 1976), indicating a substantial dropout percentage among those who volunteer to enter an exercise program. Therefore, from a practical as well as a theoretical standpoint, there exists a need to determine what factors are most likely to contribute to adherence to such programs – a problem that is analogous in many respects to the problem of ensuring patient compliance in many medical treatment programs.

Examination of the medical compliance literature reveals a notable similarity in subject dropout rates for a variety of therapeutic regimens (Baekeland & Lundwall, 1975; Blackwell, 1976; Hunt & Bespalec, 1974; Rosenberg & Raynes, 1973). More specifically, the relapse rates following treatment for the major addictions of smoking, alcoholism, and heroin dependence all follow curves similar to those representing adherence to voluntary exercise programs across 18 months (Morgan, 1977a). These curves are characterized by a rapid and substantial decrease in the percentage of subjects during the initial 3 to 6 months, an asymptote at this point, and a fairly stable plateau across the next 12 to 15 months. This similarity is provocative in suggesting the possible operation of common mechanisms in health care recidivism in general. However, attempts to delineate common predictors of treatment adherence have to date enjoyed qualified, and often minimal, success (Baekeland & Lundwall, 1975).

One of the most frequently examined factors in the medical compliance literature has been motivation (Baekeland & Lundwall, 1975). Furthermore, 34 of 41 studies conducted during the past 20 years which have included motivation as an independent variable have found it to be a significant factor influencing compliance (e.g., Altman, Brown, & Sletten, 1972; Caine, Wijesinghe, & Wood, 1973; Heilbrun, 1973; Wieland & Novack, 1973). However, in the vast majority of the studies, motivation has been a somewhat nebulous construct (Holt, 1967). Almost invariably, its conceptualization has lacked specificity and its involvement has either been inferred subjectively from gross behavioral manifestations or assessed with paper-and-pencil measures considerably lacking in psychometric elegance (Baekeland & Lundwall, 1975: 766–7).

At any rate, the sheer preponderance of the term "motivation" in the medical compliance literature illustrates a general consensus regarding its significance in compliant behavior and suggests the value of assessing this factor in order to predict adherence to habitual physical activity. Somewhat surprisingly, however, this has not yet been done, despite a substantial literature on achievement motivation (Atkinson, 1957; McClelland, Atkinson, Clark, & Lowell, 1953) which has demonstrated that some individuals are much more inclined than others to persist at a task once the task has been initiated. Although causal attributions for success and failure have also been implicated in this general tendency to persist (Weiner, Frieze, Kukla, Reed, Rest, & Rosenbaum, 1972), it is possible that a *general* disposition to persevere may operate somewhat independently of factors that typically have been conceptualized in terms of achievement motive or locus of causality/control. And, even if one were to assume a substantial conceptual overlap between the latter concepts in their relationship to perseverant behavior, the notion of a single, unitary trait reflecting a general disposition to persevere would still be quite appealing. It would not only promise greater conceptual parsimony in accounting for the role of motivation within a treatment or exercise program, but would also greatly simplify the task of operationalizing this variable within such a context.

Beyond these theoretical considerations, there are empirical data which suggest that stable individual differences in self-motivation really do exist. There is, for example, the frequently reported finding in the medical compliance literature that the patients most likely to discontinue treatment are those who previously dropped out of another program (e.g., Zax, 1962). Consistent with this finding is Goldfried's (1969) observation that self-referred patients are less likely to drop out of treatment than are patients referred by others. Results such as these suggest the influence of a general disposition of self-motivation and perseverance; but as we have indicated, earlier attempts to treat motivation within a compliance context have lacked specificity in both conceptualization and assessment.

The purpose of the present research was to examine self-motivation as a dispositional determinant of adherence to programs of strenuous physical activity. The following section describes construction of a scale to measure self-motivation and subsequent work conducted to validate this construct according to the strategy proposed by Cronbach and Meehl (1955). It was hypothesized that self-motivation could be measured reliably as a stable disposition, and that it would be positively related to adherence to programs of habitual physical activity.

## Construction of the Self-Motivation Inventory

An initial pool of 60 test items was written by one of the authors (William Ickes). All of the items in the set concerned an individual's tendency to persevere or to be self-motivated. Items were written in concise, simple sentences and were phrased in the first person with an active voice. Examples of typical items were: "I can persevere at stressful tasks, even when they are physically tiring or painful," and "I have a lot of will power."

The original 60 items were administered, in a 5-point Likert format ranging from 1 ("extremely uncharacteristic of me") to 5 ("extremely characteristic of me"), to 401 undergraduates enrolled in introductory psychology classes at the University of Wisconsin. The sample included both males and females who ranged in age from 17 to 27 years with a mean age of 19.1 and a standard deviation of 1.46. All subjects gave their informed consent prior to participation. In addition to completing the self-motivation items, they also provided self-report information on their age, height, weight, grade point average, and weekly frequency of strenuous physical exercise.

Because two subjects failed to complete the self-motivation questionnaire, subsequent analyses included item response from 399 subjects. The responses to each item were correlated with the summated score for all 60 items and items which correlated less than .30 were deleted. This procedure resulted in the retention of 48 items from the original item pool. Submission of the 48 retained items to alpha factor analysis (Kaiser & Caffrey, 1965) with varimax rotation (Kaiser, 1958) revealed 11 factors with eigenvalues greater than unity which collectively accounted for 40.5% of the total variance. Alpha analysis is so derived as to maximize the internal consistency of each factor and for this reason was the preferred factoring procedure. Inspection of the rotated factor matrix revealed that 40 items loaded at least .30 on a factor and could be considered somewhat univocal in that almost every item loaded on only a single factor (Thurstone, 1947).

Item analysis of these 40 retained items revealed an alpha (Cronbach, 1951) reliability coefficient of .91 and a standard error of measurement modeling 5.84. The alpha coefficient is indicative of exceptionally high internal consistency, and since all 40 items loaded in excess of .30 on the total score, support has been provided for the unitary nature of the underlying construct. A careful reading of the retained items suggested self-motivation to be most illustrative of this construct, and the revised inventory would seem to possess satisfactory validity by appearance.

The resulting Self-Motivation Inventory consists of 19 positively keyed items and 21 items which are keyed negatively. The possible response range is from 40 to 200, with a high score indicative of high self-motivation. Actual responses from the pretest sample of 399 subjects revealed a range of 84 to 184, a mean of 140.5, and a standard deviation of 19.38. Preliminary testing has shown self-motivation to be significantly correlated ($r = .23$, $p < .001$) with self-report of exercise frequency and to be unrelated to age, height, weight, and grade point average. Cross validation of the inventory on a second, independent sample of 48 undergraduates also yielded a high index of internal consistency ($\alpha = .86$) as well as a test-retest reliability of .92 ($df = 46$, $p < .001$, one-month time interval).

Correlations of the Self-Motivation Inventory with other, conceptually-relevant measures suggested the need to obtain behavioral evidence of its discriminant validity. Self-motivation was found to correlate significantly with the Thomas-Zander (1973) Ego-Strength Scale ($r = .63$, $df = 62$, $p < .005$), and the Marlowe-Crowne Social Desirability Scale (Crowne & Marlowe, 1964) ($r = .36$, $df = 62$, $p < .01$). Although the first correlation was expected and tends to reinforce the conceived meaning of the self-motivation construct, the second correlation was a matter of some concern in light of Campbell's (1960) recommendations for establishing the validity of psychological constructs. In order to satisfy these recommendations with respect to discriminant validity, it was necessary to demonstrate that the self-motivation measure predicts its criterion measures better than a measure of a general tendency to respond in a socially desirable way. The following study was conducted as a step toward achieving this goal. It was predicted that, relative to the measures of ego-strength and social desirability, the Self-Motivation Inventory would better predict adherence in a voluntary program of physical activity.

## Validation Study 1

### Method

*Subjects and Adherence Setting.* Subjects in the first validation study were female undergraduates at the University of Wisconsin who had voluntarily elected to participate in the women's crew training program. This program is designed for novice rowers and provides for the development of aspirants for the national-caliber varsity crew. The program is open to any interested women who is eligible under University of Wisconsin and Big Ten Conference rules, and participation is not contingent upon earning a berth in a competitive boat. In fact, there generally are no preliminary "cuts" made prior to the competitive season. The training season begins in early September and continues throughout the harsh Wisconsin winter until initial competition in early spring. Thus, the pre-competitive training season is quite protracted and provides minimal extrinsic behavioral reinforcements.

*Procedure.* Early in the fall semester, as soon as possible after the training program had been organized and workouts begun, subjects were contacted and asked to complete a series of paper-and-pencil measures. These included the Self-Motivation Inventory, the Ego-Strength Scale, and the Marlowe-Crowne Social Desirability Scale. Subjects were informed that the research was designed to determine the intercorrelation of these measures for a sample of students involved in physical education and athletic programs. However, they were not told what specific constructs were being assessed by the measures (the scales were not labeled or referred to by name); nor were they told that any attempt would be made to relate these measures to their performance in the crew training program. Instead, the instructions clearly specified that all data would remain anonymous and be used for statistical purposes only; that the subjects' coaches would never see or have access to their responses; and that the data would have absolutely no bearing on the subjects' eligibility for selection to the crew team the following semester. The instructions further emphasized the importance of giving accurate and honest responses to the items on each of the questionnaires.

Of the 126 females initially participating in the crew training program, 80 (63.5%) agreed to sign a consent form and complete the questionnaires. Due to unusually excessive demands upon practice time and available equipment which resulted from the large subject turnout, a preliminary "cut" became necessary. This cut was made after the first month of training and was based upon coaches' evaluations of early performance and demonstrated potential for competitive rowing. This culling process involved 23 women, 16 of whom had provided questionnaire information. Thus, the data from the remaining volunteer subjects ($N = 64$) provided the basis for the correlations which have been already reported above.

The relatively high response rate helped ensure that the sample was representative of the population from which it was drawn; moreover, any bias due to self-selection was likely to be conservative and work against confirming the research hypothesis, since subjects who lacked the motivation to complete the measures were also more likely to drop out of the training program. In fact, of the 64 subjects for whom questionnaire data were available, 42 (66%) eventually dropped out, while 30 of 35 (86%) women electing not to participate in the study subsequently dropped out ($\chi^2 = 4.60$, $df = 1$, $p < .05$). (Twenty-six of these 30 nonvolunteers discontinued during the first 10 days of training.) The test was likely to be conservative for other reasons as well, since (a) voluntary self-selection for a very rigorous exercise program had probably already reduced the range of self-motivation differences by excluding very low scorers, and (b) the naturalistic, field setting of the research did not permit the degree of control that could be achieved within a laboratory context.

## Results and Discussion

In order to assess adherence to the crew training program over time, an a priori decision was made to compare dropouts with nondropouts at three naturally occurring breakpoints during the year. The test conducted at the first breakpoint compared the scores of nondropouts with those of early dropouts – individuals who withdrew from the program during the first 10 days. It was reasoned that these individuals never really got involved in the program and may have been attracted to it more by curiosity than by any strongly-felt motivation to participate. Accordingly, it was expected that the assessed differences in self-motivation would be greatest when the dropouts and nondropouts were compared at this point.

The test conducted at the second breakpoint was somewhat more stringent, as it included in the dropout group those individuals who had stayed in the program at least 10 days, up to and including the first 8 weeks. During this time, the training took place on the water, the weather was still nice, and the emphasis was merely on developing technique and familiarity with rowing. The more stressful, strenuous conditioning activity took place after this period, when the weather turned cold and the subjects had to leave the frozen lake and work out in the uninviting confines of the boathouse.

The test conducted at the third breakpoint was even more stringent than the second, as it included in the dropout group those individuals who withdrew at least 8 weeks into the program but no later than a time immediately before the formal team "cut" was made prior to the first competition. This competitive cut was made in the 32nd week of training, after the subjects had spent the long, cold winter months training in the boathouse.

The mean self-motivation, social desirability, and ego-strength scores for each of the adherence groups are presented in Table 5.1. Planned comparisons of these data indicated that the mean self-motivation score of the dropouts was significantly ($p < .05$) lower than that of the nondropouts at the first breakpoint and continued to be lower ($ps < .05$) at the second and the third breakpoints (immediately prior to announcement of berths in the competitive boat). In contrast, neither the mean social desirability nor the mean ego-strength scores of the adherence groups differed significantly at any of the breakpoints ($ps > .10$ in all cases). That self-motivation is the specific factor underlying the observed differences is further evidenced by the fact that these differences remained significant ($ps < .07$), even when the data were reanalyzed using the subjects' social desirability and ego-strength scores as covariates. Residuals from the regression of these variables on self-motivation were transformed to standard deviates with a mean of 50 and a standard deviation of 10 to insure positive values. Subsequent results of the previously employed planned comparisons on these residual self-motivation scores are provided in Figure 5.1.

In addition, stepwise multiple regression analysis using the psychometric variables as predictors of adherence revealed that self-motivation entered the regression equation first with a resultant correlation coefficient of .33 ($p < .05$). The subsequent inclusion of social desirability and ego strength did not significantly increase $R^2$. And, in fact, the observed bivariate correlations for these latter two variables were quite small (.05 and .15, respectively).

As an alternative way to view these results, a comparison was made of the percentage of high vs. low self-motivation subjects who remained in the program until the third breakpoint. Based on a median split of the self-motivation scores, the percentage of adherence was only 40.6% (13 out of 32) for subjects with low self-motivation scores, but was 78.1% (25 out of 32) for subjects with high self-motivation scores. This difference was highly significant by a chi-square test ($\chi^2 = 9.32$, $df = 1$, $p < .005$).

Thus, regardless of the perspective from which these data are viewed, they reveal that the disposition of self-motivation is an important factor underlying adherence to a program of

**Table 5.1** Means and standard deviations for the psychometric variables with classification on adherence to the women's crew training program

| Psychometric variables | | Adherence groups | | | |
|---|---|---|---|---|---|
| | | 0–10 days (N = 21) | 10 days to 8 weeks (N = 6) | 8 weeks to 32 weeks (N = 15) | Active at first competition (N = 22) |
| Self-motivation | M | 144.33 | 151.00 | 153.53 | 158.59 |
| | S.D. | 17.98 | 11.35 | 20.07 | 15.37 |
| Social Desirability | M | 17.24 | 15.00 | 16.80 | 17.55 |
| | S.D. | 3.39 | 3.85 | 3.63 | 4.39 |
| Ego strength | M | 12.14 | 12.83 | 12.87 | 13.14 |
| | S.D. | 2.59 | 2.14 | 2.88 | 2.73 |
| Standardized Self-motivation residuals | M | 45.86 | 50.02 | 50.82 | 53.38 |
| | S.D. | 9.46 | 7.37 | 9.21 | 10.75 |

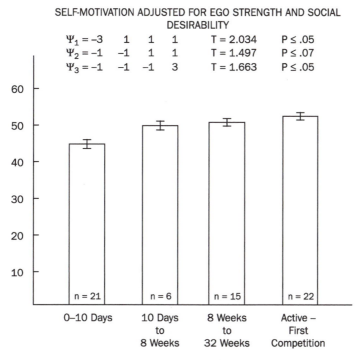

**Figure 5.1** Planned comparison of standardized self-motivation residual scores for dropout groups in women's crew training program

habitual physical activity. It is also clear that related constructs such as social desirability and ego strength do not account for these findings.

Although the previously described results provided considerable evidence for the reliability and behavioral validity of the self-motivation construct, it was desirable to obtain additional information in a context more specifically relating to exercise programs of a therapeutic nature. For this reason, a second validation study was conducted.

## Validation Study 2

Adherence to a program of habitual physical activity has significant implications from the standpoint of preventive medicine (i.e., "wellness") as well as rehabilitation following illness. Rather extensive recidivism rates ranging from 30 to 70% have been reported previously, and the average adherence rate in adult exercise programs has been approximately 50% (Morgan, 1977a). The traditional approach to this particular problem has consisted of attempting to persuade dropouts to become reinvolved. An excellent summary of potential (persuasion strategies has been presented by Wankel and Thompson (1977). Another approach to the problem of adherence would involve the identification and subsequent monitoring of "dropout prone" individuals with an aim toward preventing mortality. Prior to developing such an approach, however, it would first be necessary to characterize individuals in terms of dropout proneness, and this is a problem that is a primary focus of the present work.

Earlier attempts to characterize the type of individual who adheres vs. the type who is likely to drop out of an exercise program have not been successful. Numerous variables which appear to possess predictive ability at an intuitive level have not been found to be useful. It is somewhat surprising, for example, that biologic variables such as age, height, body weight, and initial physical fitness have not been useful in predicting adherence, with the exception of a single study of which the present authors are aware (Dishman, 1981). Moreover, a variety of seemingly relevant psychologic variables such as attitude (affect) toward physical activity, health consciousness, anxiety, or locus of control have also failed to predict adherence (see Morgan, 1977a, for an overview of this research).

In the second validation study, assessment was made of a number of biologic and psychologic variables that seemed intuitively relevant to exercise adherence. Once again, it was hypothesized that among the various psychometric variables employed, self-motivation would best discriminate between adherers and dropouts (i.e., most enhance the prediction of adherence behavior).

## Method

*Subjects and Adherence Setting.* This investigation consisted of a 20-week prospective study involving adult males enrolled in programs of habitual physical activity. This activity consisted of both cardiovascular and muscular endurance training and involved subjects from the following organized exercise programs: Biodynamics Exercise Program, University of Wisconsin-Madison ($N = 16$); LaCrosse Cardiac Rehabilitation and Adult Fitness Programs, University of Wisconsin-LaCrosse ($N = 16$); and The Institute for Aerobics Research, Dallas, Texas ($N = 34$). Subjects included healthy nonrisk individuals as well as those either at risk or symptomatic with regard to coronary heart disease.

Programs administered by the first two cohorts involved medically supervised and prescribed programs by jogging three days per week, while the subjects in the Aerobics Institute program were similarly involved in muscular endurance training of either an isotonic or isokinetic nature. All programs were administered in accordance with guidelines established by the American College of Sports Medicine.

*Procedure.* The nature of all psychological and physiological testing was explained to each volunteer prior to this participation, and any of the subjects' questions except those related to the specific research hypotheses were answered. Subjects were informed of any potential risks or benefits they might incur as a result of participation and told that they were free to withdraw from the study at any time. They were also asked to sign an informed consent document prior to exercise tolerance testing, psychological testing, and involvement in an exercise program. These procedures were standardized for all testing sites.

Assessment was made of various morphologic and physiologic variables; these included body weight, percent body fat, and metabolic capacity. These variables are diagnostic indices that are standardly assessed in conjunction with a medically supervised exercise tolerance test. They were employed in this investigation due to their previously observed relationship to exercise adherence (Dishman, 1981), and in an attempt to characterize the exercise adherer within a psychobiologic framework. Body weight was assessed at each site using calibrated medical scales and was expressed in kilograms (kg), while percent body fat was assessed using a predictive skinfold technique reported by Yuhasz (1965). Metabolic capacity was assessed by means of a predictive measure of oxygen consumption involving graded walking on a motor-driven treadmill. A substandard Balke (Balke & Ware, 1959) protocol was employed at the UW-Madison site while both the UW-LaCrosse and The Institute for Aerobics Research cohorts employed a Bruce, Kusumi, and Hosmer (1973) protocol. A more complete description of these procedures has been published in an article by Dishman and Gettman (1980).

Assessment of the psychological variables required that each volunteer complete a test battery consisting of four standardized questionnaires that were administered in the following sequence: (1) Self-Motivation Inventory (SMO), (2) Physical Estimation and Attraction Scales (PEAS; Sonstroem, 1974), (3) Health Locus of Control Scale (HLC; Wallston, Wallston, Kaplan, & Maides, 1976), and (4) Attitude Toward Physical Activity Scales (ATPA; Kenyon, 1968). A careful review of the exercise science and medical compliance literatures indicated that the constructs underlying these last three measures appeared particularly relevant to the study of exercise adherence; thus, they were employed along with the Self-Motivation Inventory in the present research.

Data regarding adherence to the previously described exercise programs were determined from daily exercise records maintained during the course of the 20-week study period. In the case of the UW-LaCrosse and Aerobics Institute cohorts, attendance records were kept by administrative personnel, while for the UW-Madison cohort this information was provided by subjects in the form of a carefully monitored daily exercise record. Adherence data were quantified in terms of total days of program participation and were also classified discretely according to groups of adherers (i.e., individuals who were involved continuously for the entire 20-week period) or dropouts (i.e., individuals who discontinued participation prior to conclusion of the 20-week period). Due to the relatively short duration of the training program and the subsequently large proportion of adherers (65.2%), a more discrete classification of adherence would have provided too few subjects in each group and violated the homoscedasticity assumption of ANOVA (Box, 1954). Thus, the present dichotomy was preferred.

## Results and Discussion

Results of MANOVA revealed a Wilk's Lambda of .603 and a corresponding $\chi^2$ of 29.06 ($df = 13$; $p < .01$), indicating a significant overall difference between dropouts and adherers on the variables of interest. Application of stepwise multiple discriminant analysis in a post hoc framework revealed that only percent body fat, self-motivation, and body weight contributed significantly ($p < .05$) to this group separation (change in Rao's V was employed as the stepwise criterion). In fact, knowledge of these particular variables permitted accurate classification of subjects into actual adherence or dropout groups for approximately 80% of all cases. Inspection of group means for these variables (Table 5.2) indicated that adherers demonstrated lower values for both percent body fat and body weight but had higher self-motivation scores.

Stepwise multiple regression analysis provided similar results. Percent body fat, self-motivation, and body weight entered the multiple regression consecutively and were the only variables that significantly ($p < .05$) enhanced the prediction of exercise adherence (Table 5.3). Employing these variables in the regression equation yielded a multiple correlation of .67 ($df = 63$; $p < .01$; $R^2 = .45$), accounting for a considerable portion of the variance in adherence behavior.

The influence of percent body fat and body weight on adherence in the present study confirms findings of a previous study by Dishman (1981) regarding biologic factors and adherence behavior. In Dishman's study, which focused on a comparable sample of adult males enrolled in exercise programs, a similar association of percent body fat, total body weight, and adherence was found.

The emergence of self-motivation as the only psychometric variable employed which contributed to the discriminant and regression analyses is notable for several reasons. First of all, these findings support those of Study I in demonstrating that self-motivation discriminated

**Table 5.2** Means and standard deviations of the psychological and biological variables for adherers and dropouts in the adult fitness programs

| Variables | Adherers (N = 43) | | Dropouts (N = 23) | |
|---|---|---|---|---|
| | $\bar{M}$ | S.D. | $\bar{M}$ | S.D. |
| Percent body fat | 19.07 | 5.08 | 24.09 | 7.88 |
| Self-motivation | 158.65 | 16.41 | 143.78 | 26.46 |
| Body weight (kg) | 84.34 | 9.51 | 94.03 | 19.02 |
| Aesthetic experience (ATPA) | 41.47 | 8.40 | 43.22 | 7.54 |
| Health locus of control | 29.81 | 7.20 | 34.04 | 7.38 |
| Ascetic experience (ATPA) | 37.40 | 8.58 | 33.83 | 9.99 |
| Attraction (PEAS) | 37.72 | 8.77 | 33.13 | 11.24 |
| Estimation (PEAS) | 22.65 | 6.80 | 19.13 | 10.35 |
| Catharsis (ATPA) | 39.12 | 6.57 | 37.91 | 8.82 |
| Pursuit of vertigo (ATPA) | 37.51 | 8.85 | 34.17 | 11.01 |
| Social experience (ATPA) | 43.16 | 6.04 | 43.30 | 6.00 |
| Health and fitness (ATPA) | 43.49 | 7.56 | 39.70 | 8.40 |
| Metabolic capacity (METS) | 10.81 | 2.52 | 9.56 | 2.85 |

**Table 5.3** Stepwise multiple regression of psychological and biological variables on total days of exercise program participation

| Number | Variable | Multiple $R^1$ | Multiple $R^2$ | Change in $R^2$ | Bivariate $r$ |
|---|---|---|---|---|---|
| 1 | Percent fat | .49334 | .24339 | .24339 | −.49334 |
| 2 | Self-motivation | .62370 | .38900 | .14561 | .43454 |
| 3 | Body weight | .67349 | .45358 | .06458 | −.27940 |
| 4 | Aesthetic experience | .67714 | .45851 | .00493 | −.11792 |
| 5 | Health locus of control | .68100 | .46376 | .00524 | −.24968 |
| 6 | Ascetic experience | .68793 | .47325 | .00949 | .21593 |
| 7 | Attraction | .68968 | .47566 | .00242 | .19894 |
| 8 | Estimation | .69553 | .48376 | .00810 | .18488 |
| 9 | Catharsis | .69840 | .48777 | .00401 | .07570 |
| 10 | Pursuit of vertigo | .69950 | .48930 | .00153 | .20527 |
| 11 | Social experience | .70008 | .49012 | .00082 | −.14913 |
| 12 | Health and fitness | .70036 | .49050 | .00038 | .22410 |

between exercise subjects on the basis of program adherence whereas other apparently related psychological constructs did not. The failure of psychological constructs such as attitude toward physical activity, locus of control, and health consciousness to predict adherence is consistent with earlier research. It is noteworthy, therefore, that a general or trait-like measure of self-motivation was found to possess greater predictive ability than variables of a more "situation-specific" nature. Secondly, the relationship between exercise adherence and self-motivation was quite substantial in this study ($r = .44$, $p < .05$) and permitted considerably better prediction than did any of the other psychological variables employed. Finally, these findings provide further empirical support for what previously has been primarily only a conceptual relationship between motivation and adherence behavior in therapeutic settings.

Additional discriminant evidence for the validity of self-motivation was obtained in Study II by observing its association with other relevant motivational constructs. Data were available for subsamples on measures of approval motive, i.e., social desirability (Crowne & Marlowe, 1964), and achievement motive (Mehrabian, 1968) as well as health locus of control. Pearson product-moment coefficients indicated that self-motivation was only slightly correlated with an achievement motive ($r = .24$; $df = 28$; $p > .05$), social desirability ($r = .26$; $df = 28$; $p > .05$), and health locus of control ($r = -.23$; $df = 64$; $p > .05$). Although some shared variance between self-motivation and these constructs would be anticipated due to their motivational components, the obtained coefficients suggest that self-motivation does indeed represent a distinct motivational construct. Further evidence for the dispositional nature of self-motivation was provided by a test-retest correlation of .86 ($df = .38$; $p < .01$) over the 20-week test period.

## Conclusions and Implications

In conclusion, this investigation provided evidence for the construct validity of self-motivation through the development of a scale that is logically valid, internally consistent, and reliable. In addition, correlations between self-motivation and social desirability, achievement motive, locus of control, and ego strength provided discriminant and convergent evidence for the validity of this construct. Finally, self-motivation was demonstrated in two field studies to be significantly associated with adherence to programs of physical exercise and to be the best discriminator of adherence behavior when compared to other conceptually relevant psychometric variables. The data from the second field study suggested that prediction of adherence can readily be enhanced by employing two easily measured biologic variables, total body weight and percent body fat, in concert with self-motivation. Both of these biologic variables are ones that are routinely measured in most physical activity programs, and both have been related to adherence in an earlier investigation (Dishman, 1981).

Conceptually, at least, individual differences in self-motivation are considered to be situationally invariant. In the present investigation this point of view was supported for two rather divergent samples – middle-aged adult males involved in health-oriented exercise programs and college-aged females involved in a highly strenuous form of competitive athletics. Therefore, the self-motivation instrument not only possesses demonstrated reliability and internal validity but also appears to be characterized by substantial external validity as well. The instrument has further utility in a pragmatic sense because it is easily administered and objectively scored.

The major findings of this investigation appear to have clear implications for the administration of both preventive medicine and therapeutic exercise programs in that the decision to adhere or to drop out of a prescribed exercise program appears to be largely dependent upon body composition and the behavioral disposition of self-motivation. With respect to self-motivation, it should be emphasized that this particular behavioral disposition exists at the outset of the involvement process. For certain individuals, therefore, aspects of the exercise milieu such as the setting, the exercise leader, or interpersonal relations among subjects may exert only a minor influence upon adherence behavior. The initial diagnosis of subjects who have a high probability of adhering regardless of administrative intervention would permit greater individual attention to the needs of probable dropouts and hopefully enhance program adherence rates. Self-motivation scores, perhaps used in conjunction with percent body fat and body weight values, would appear to have particular utility in this regard.

## Subsequent research and application

Exercise psychology has had a relatively brief history, but has witnessed exponential growth since the publication of the key study. This growth is reflected in a shift in the focus of research within sport and exercise psychology in recent years. In a review of the trends in sport and exercise psychology from 1985–94, exercise-related studies showed an increase of nearly 250% and were the most popular overall when compared to sport (Biddle, 1997). This trend has continued with the fields of sports medicine, public health, and behavioral medicine all showing an increasing interest in exercise psychology (Dishman & Buckworth, 2005), and several journals and professional organizations around the world have added "exercise" to their title. For example, the *Journal of Sport Psychology* became the *Journal of Sport & Exercise Psychology* in 1988 due to the increase in interest in the area. The British Association of Sports Sciences changed its name to the British Association of Sport and Exercise Sciences in 1993. Exercise psychology has also become a popular and important area of study at both the undergraduate and graduate level in universities around the world (Grove, 1995).

The issue of adherence to exercise and physical activity has become a particularly important topic among researchers and practitioners over the last 20 years (Lavallee *et al.*, 2004). Rod Dishman, the first author of the key study, edited a text in 1988 entitled *Exercise adherence: Its impact on public health*. This text, along with a follow-up text published in 1994 entitled *Advances in exercise adherence*, demonstrated that exercise adherence is an established area with clearly defined questions and developing methods. Research on adherence issues in sport and exercise settings beyond the original work of exercise adherence has also increased in recent years. This includes research into sport/exercise adherence behaviors such as injury rehabilitation, primary care exercise referral schemes, psychological skills training, cohesion in sports teams/exercise classes, and fitness training in elite performers. However, the theoretical models arising from the work of Dishman and others have been instrumental in steering these new research initiatives (Bull, 1999).

The key study conducted by Dishman and colleagues was part of a program of research that included a focus on what determinants are most likely to contribute to adherence to exercise and physical activity programs. Research that followed focused on two broad categories of determinants – namely, personal and environmental determinants (Dishman & Buckworth, 2005). The personal factors that influence exercise adherence include individual characteristics (e.g., age, gender) and cognitions and attitudes about behavior (e.g., self-motivation, knowledge, perceived benefits), and of these, self-motivation has been found to be one of the best predictors of exercise adherence. Self-motivation has also been able to distinguish adherents from dropouts across many settings, including cardiac rehabilitation units, preventative medicine clinics, and corporate fitness gyms (Dishman & Sallis, 1994). Evidence suggests that self-motivation may reflect self-regulatory skills, such as effective goal-setting, self-monitoring of progress, and self-reinforcement, which are believed to be important in maintaining physical activity. Combined with other measures, self-motivation has been found to predict adherence even more accurately. For example, when self-motivation scores were combined with percent body fat, about 80% of participants were correctly predicted to be either adherent or dropouts (Dishman, 1981).

Environmental factors can also help or hinder regular participation in physical activity. Research has found that adherence to exercise is influenced by the social environment, and is higher when individuals receive support from their spouse for the activity. Physical environments that promote increased activity, by offering easily accessible facilities and removing real and perceived barriers to an exercise routine, are necessary for the successful maintenance of changes in exercise behavior (Weinberg & Gould, 2007). The characteristics of the physical activity, itself (e.g., intensity and duration of exercise bout), are also important.

Another major development since the study is the increasing use of theoretical models in exercise adherence studies. Research in the area prior to the key study was generally atheoretical and focused predominantly on providing descriptions of non-modifiable factors such as gender, age, and educational level associated with increased attrition from exercise programs (Marcus, Bock, Pinto, Napolitano, & Clark, 2002). Although such epidemiological evidence was useful, few conclusions could be drawn which could help translate research into practice. More recently, however, diversification has occurred with a greater recognition of the importance of systematic testing of theoretical models to explain the reasons for exercise adherence and guide interventions. Broadly, this work has consisted of social cognitive, stage, or ecological approaches to exercise adherence.

Many researchers since the publication of the key study have employed one of a number of social cognitive theories in order to investigate exercise adherence. Social cognitive theories, as discussed further in Chapter 6, seek to understand human cognition, action, motivation, and emotion, and make an assumption that people are active shapers of their environments by being goal-directed, self-regulating, and capable of self-reflection (Maddux, 1993). Bandura (1986) suggests that the personal and environmental factors previously outlined above interact with a person's behavior – and, in fact, are reciprocally interacting determinants. This means that personal and environmental factors affect behaviors (e.g., the access to local parks may affect how often an individual exercises), and also that behaviors affect the personal and environmental factors (e.g., an individual has a degree of control over where they choose to live). For this reason, this model is often referred to as reciprocal determinism.

Researchers have also applied stage models, such as the stages of change model outlined in Chapter 6, in the study of exercise adherence. These models were primarily developed as a framework to describe the different phases involved in the acquisition or cessation of a particular behavior (Marcus, Selby, Niaura, & Rossi, 1992), and have since been applied to the maintenance of a wide range of health-related behaviors – including exercise. In these models, people can be located on a continuum whereby some have not really thought about exercise at all, others are trying to start, whereas others are maintaining the behavior.

The environmental factors discussed above are typically limited to those in the social and cultural environment, and as a result, intervention-based research on exercise adherence often lacks meaningful evaluation of the potential impact of the full range of environmental determinants. The term "ecological" refers to models, frameworks, and/or perspectives rather than a specific set of variables (Dishman & Buckworth, 2005). To address this, some researchers have proposed more comprehensive ecological models and theories that are more inclusive of the many environmental factors that may affect exercise adherence. Ecological theories propose that exercise and behavior are influenced at multiple levels, including intrapersonal (biological), interpersonal (family), institutional (schools), and policy (laws at all levels) factors (Sallis, Cervero, Ascher, Henderson, Kraft,

& Kerr 2006). It has also been proposed that these influences interact with one another. Although all factors are important, researchers are identifying physical environments to be increasingly important in ecological models. In terms of interventions, ecological models may have a direct impact on exercise adherence above that provided by social cognitive and stage-based models, but further research is needed to confirm this proposal.

The challenge to researchers and practitioners interested in exercise adherence is outlined in the development of evolutionary models. These argue that we evolved to be active animals, and are not well equipped to live in a society where food is abundant and in which physical activity has been largely engineered out of daily life (Cordain, Eaton, Sebastian, Mann, Lindberg, Watkins, O'Keefe, & Brand Miller, 2005). Such living conditions have resulted in a large percentage of the population in industrialized societies becoming sedentary and unfit, and often overweight and obese (Biddle & Mutrie, 2001). In short, humans have now adopted lifestyles in industrialized countries that were quite unknown until very recently in terms of human evolution.

Blair (1988, as reported in Biddle & Mutrie, 2001) suggests that four evolutionary periods are important in understanding the relationship between physical activity and health. The pre-agricultural period (up until 10,000 years ago) was characterized by hunting and gathering activities, and exercise levels were high and diet was low in fat. The agricultural period (up until the start of the 19th century) was characterized by reasonably high levels of physical activity and relatively low-fat diets. The industrial period (1800–1945) witnessed the development of the industrialized society with problems associated with overcrowding, poor diets, and inadequate medical care. This trend reversed in the nuclear/technological period (1945–present), which improved public health services and led to less infectious diseases in advanced societies. The health problems did not go away, however, but merely shifted in terms of causes and consequences (Biddle & Murtie, 2001). In essence, the change in lifestyle over time has brought its own health problems. These are sometimes referred to as "hypokinetic diseases," or heart problems caused by a lack of physical activity, and include poor mental health, coronary heart disease, obesity, low back pain, osteoporosis, hypertension, diabetes, and some cancers. The research evidence linking physical activity patterns with such health measures is increasing rapidly (Biddle & Mutrie, 2001), but much more is required before the trend of increasing physical inactivity levels is reversed and exercise adherence rates increase. Indeed, despite our increased knowledge of factors impacting exercise adherence the attrition rate for regular exercise continues to be approximately 50% among individuals who commence exercise programs (Dishman & Buckworth, 2005).

## Additional readings

Biddle, S. J. H., & Mutrie, N. (2001). *Psychology of physical activity: Determinants, well-being and intervention.* London: Routledge.

Bull, S. J. (ed.) (1999). *Adherence issues in sport and exercise.* London: Wiley.

Dishman, R. K. (ed.) (1988). *Exercise adherence: Its impact on public health.* Champaign, IL: Human Kinetics.

Dishman, R. K. (ed.) (1994). *Advances in exercise adherence.* Champaign, IL: Human Kinetics.

Wankel, L. M., & Berger, B. G. (1990). The psychological and social benefits of sport and physical activity. *Journal of Leisure Research, 22,* 167–82.

## Study questions

1  Define adherence, and discuss its importance within the key study.

2  Why were two data collections required to test the hypotheses put forward in the key study?

3  What is a determinant, and what determinants have been found to contribute to exercise adherence since the key study?

4  Discuss some of the theoretical models that have been used in exercise adherence research.

5  Can you think of any other sport and exercise contexts that adherence could be studied in other than those highlighted in this chapter?

## References

Altman, H., Brown, M. L., & Sletten, I. W. (1972). And . . . silently steal away. *Diseases of the Nervous System*, 33, 52–8.

Atkinson, J. W. (1957). Motivational determinants of risk-taking behavior. *Psychological Review*, 64, 359–72.

Baekeland, F., & Lundwall, L. (1975). Dropping out of treatment: A critical review. *Psychological Bulletin*, 82, 738–83.

Balke, B., & Ware, R. (1959). *The status of physical fitness in the air force*. School of Aviation Medicine, United States Air Force.

Bandura A. (1986) *Social foundations of thought and action: A social cognitive theory*. Englewood Cliffs, NJ: Prentice Hall.

Biddle, S. J. H. (1997). Current trends in sport and exercise psychology research. *The Psychologist*, 10(2), 63–9.

Biddle, S. J. H., & Mutrie, N. (2001). *Psychology of physical activity: Determinants, well-being and intervention*. London: Routledge.

Blackburn, H. (1976). Physical activity as primarily preventive in coronary disease. *Proceedings of the International Congress of Physical Activity Sciences*, Quebec City, Canada.

Blackwell, B. (1976). Treatment adherence. *British Journal of Psychiatry*, 129, 513–31.

Blair, S. N. (1988). Exercise within a healthy lifestyle. In R. K. Dishman (ed.), *Exercise adherence: Its impact on public health* (pp. 75–89). Champaign, IL: Human Kinetics.

Box, G. E. P. (1954). Some theorems on quadratic forms applied in the study of analysis of variance problems: I. Effect of inequality of variance in the one-way classification. *Annals of Mathematical Statistics*, 25, 290–302.

Boyer, J. L., & Kasch, F. W. (1970). Exercise therapy in hypertensive men. *Journal of the American Medical Association*, 211, 1668–71.

Bruce, E. H., Frederick, R., Bruce, R. A., & Fisher, L. D. (1976). Comparison of active participants and dropouts in CAPRI cardiopulmonary rehabilitation programs. *American Journal of Cardiology*, 37, 53–60.

Bruce, R. A., Kusumi, F., & Hosmer, I. (1973). Maximal oxygen intake and nomographic assessment of functional aerobic impairment in cardiovascular disease. *American Heart Journal*, 85, 546.

Bull, S. (1999). Preface. In S. Bull (ed.), *Adherence issues in sport and exercise* (pp. xvii–iii). London: Wiley.

Byrd, O. E. (1963). The relief of tension by exercise and a survey of medical viewpoints and practices. *Journal of School Health*, 43, 238–9.

Caine, T. M., Wijesinghe, B., & Wood, R. R. (1973). Personality and psychiatric treatment expectancies. *British Journal of Psychiatry*, 122, 87–8.

Campbell, D. J. (1960). Recommendations for APA test standards regarding construct, trait, and discriminant validity. *American Psychologist*, 15, 546–53.

Cordain, L., Eaton, S. B., Sebastian, A., Mann, N., Lindeberg, S., Watkins, B. A., O'Keefe, J. H., & Brand Miller, J. (2005). Origins and evolution of the western diet: Health implications for the 21st century. *American Journal of Clinical Nutrition*, 81, 341–54.

Cronbach, L. J. (1951). Coefficient alpha and the internal structure of tests. *Psychometrika*, 16, 297–334.

Cronbach, L. J., & Meehl, P. E. (1955). Construct validity in psychological tests. *Psychological Bulletin*, 52, 281–302.

Crowne, D. P., & Marlowe, D. (1964). *The approval motive: Studies in evaluative dependence*. New York: Wiley.

de Vries, H. A. (1968). Immediate and long-term effects of exercise upon resting muscle action potential level. *Journal of Sports Medicine and Physical Fitness*, 8, 1–11.

Dishman, R. K. (1981). Biologic influences on exercise adherence. *Research Quarterly for Exercise and Sport*, 52, 143–59.

Dishman, R. K. (ed.) (1988). *Exercise adherence: Its impact on public health*. Champaign, IL: Human Kinetics.

Dishman, R. K. (ed.) (1994). *Advances in exercise adherence*. Champaign, IL: Human Kinetics.

Dishman, R. K., & Buckworth, J. (2005). Exercise psychology. In J. M. Williams (ed.), *Applied sport psychology: Personal growth to peak performance* (5th ed., pp. 497–518). New York: McGraw-Hill.

Dishman, R. K., & Gettman, L. R. (1980). Psychobiological influences on exercise adherence. *Journal of Sport Psychology*, 2, 295–310.

Dishman, R. K., & Sallis, J. F. (1994). Determinants and interventions for physical activity and exercise. In C. Bouchard, R. J. Shepard, & T. Stephens (eds), *Physical activity, fitness, and health* (pp. 214–38). Champaign, IL: Human Kinetics.

Goldfried, M. R. (1969). Prediction of improvement in an alcoholism outpatient clinic. *Quarterly Journal of Studies on Alcohol*, 30, 129–39.

Greist, J. H., Klein, M. H., Eischens, R. R., & Faris, J. W. (1978). Antidepressant running: Running as a treatment for non-psychotic depression. *Behavioral Medicine*, June, 19–24.

Grove, J. R. (1995) An introduction to exercise psychology. In T. Morris & J. Summers (eds), *Sport psychology: Theory, applications and issues* (pp. 437–55). Brisbane: Wiley.

Grove, J. R., & Zillman, N. (2004). Psychological consequences of exercise: Benefits and potential costs. In T. Morris & J. Summers (eds), *Sport psychology: Theory, applications and issues* (pp. 472–91). Brisbane: Wiley.

Heilbrun, A. B., Jr. (1973). History and self-disclosure in females and early defection from psychotherapy. *Journal of Counseling Psychology*, 20, 250–7.

Holt, W. E. (1967). The concept of motivation for treatment. *American Journal of Psychiatry*, 123, 1388–94.

Hunt, W. A., & Bespalec, D. A. (1974). An evaluation of current methods of modifying smoking behavior. *Journal of Clinical Psychology*, 30, 431–8.

Kaiser, H. F. (1958). The varimax criterion for analytic rotation in factor analysis. *Psychometrika*, 23, 187–200.

Kaiser, H. F., & Caffrey, J. (1965). Alpha factor analysis. *Psychometrika*, 30, 1–14.

Kenyon, G. S. (1968). Six scales for assessing attitude toward physical activity. *Research Quarterly*, 39, 566–74.

Lavallee, D., Kremer, J., Moran, A., & Williams, M. (2004). *Sport psychology: Contemporary themes*. London: Palgrave.

Maddux, J. E. (1993) Social cognitive models of health and exercise behavior: An introduction and review of conceptual issues. *Journal of Applied Sport Psychology*, 5, 116–40.

Mann, G. V., Garrett, H. L., Farhi, A., Murray, H., & Billings, F. T. (1969). Exercise to prevent coronary heart disease. *American Journal of Medicine*, 46, 12–21.

Marcus, B. H., Bock, B. C., Pinto, B. M., Napolitano, M. A., & Clark, M. M. (2002). Exercise initiation, adoption and maintenance in adults: Theoretical models and empirical support. In J. L. Van Raalte & B. W. Brewer (eds), *Exploring sport and exercise psychology* (2nd ed., pp. 185–208). Washington, DC: APA.

Marcus, B. H., Selby, V. C., Niaura, R. S., & Rossi, J. S. (1992). Self-efficacy and the stages of exercise behavior change. *Research Quarterly for Exercise and Sport*, 63, 60–6.

Massie, J. F., & Shephard, R. J. (1971). Physiological and psychological effects of training – a comparison of individual and gymnasium programs, with a characterization of the exercise "drop-out." *Medicine and Science in Sports*, 3, 110–17.

McClelland, D. C., Atkinson, J. W., Clark, R. A., & Lowell, E. L. (1953). *The achievement motive*. New York: Appleton-Century-Crofts.

Mehrabian, A. (1968). Male and female scales of the tendency to achieve. *Educational and Psychological Measurement*, 28, 493–502.

Morgan, W. P. (1977a). Involvement in vigorous physical activity with special reference to adherence. *Proceedings, College Physical Education Conference*, Orlando, Florida.

Morgan, W. P. (1977b). Psychological consequences of vigorous physical activity and sport. In M. Gladys Scott (ed.), *The Academy Papers*. Iowa City: American Academy of Physical Education.

Morgan, W. P. (1979). Anxiety reduction following acute physical activity. *Psychiatric Annals*, 9, 36–45.

Morgan, W. P., Roberts, J. A., Brand, F. R., & Feinerman, A. D. (1970). Psychological effect of chronic physical activity. *Medicine and Science in Sports*, 2, 213–17.

Naughton, J., Bruhn, J. G., & Lategola, M. T. (1968). Effects of physical training on physiologic and behavioral characteristics of cardiac patients. *Archives of Physical Medicine and Rehabilitation*, 49, 131–7.

Oja, P., Teraslinna, P., Partanen, T., & Karava, R. (1975). Feasibility of an 18-months' physical training program for middle-aged men and its effect on physical fitness. *American Journal of Public Health*, 64, 459–65.

Oldridge, N. B. (1977a). Compliance of post M.I. patients to exercise programs. *Proceedings, American College of Sports Medicine Conference on Coronary Artery Disease – Prevention, Clinical Assessment, and Rehabilitation* (pp. 99–107). Oral Roberts University.

Oldridge, N. B. (1977b). What to look for in an exercise class leader. *The Physician and Sports Medicine*, 5, 85–8.

Rosenberg, C. M., & Raynes, A. E. (1973). Dropouts from treatment. *Canadian Psychiatric Association Journal*, 18, 229–33.

Sallis, J. F., Cervero, R., Ascher, W., Henderson, K. A., Kraft, M. K., & Kerr, J. (2006). An ecological approach to creating active living communities. *Annual Review of Public Health*, 27, 297–322.

Sidney, K. H., & Shephard, R. J. (1976). Attitude toward health and physical activity in the elderly: Effects of a physical training program. *Medicine and Science in Sports*, 8, 246–52.

Sonstroem, R. J. (1974). Attitude testing examining certain psychological correlates of physical activity. *Research Quarterly*, 45, 93–103.

Thomas, P., & Zander, A. (1973). Thomas-Zander ego strength scales. In J. P. Robinson & P. R. Shaver (eds), *Measures of social psychological attitudes*. Ann Arbor, MI: Institute for Social Research.

Thurstone, L. (1947). *Multiple factor analysis*. Chicago: University of Chicago Press.

Wallston, B. S., Wallston, K. A., Kaplan, G. D., & Maides, S. A. (1976). Development and validation of the health locus of control (HLC) scale. *Journal of Consulting and Clinical Psychology*, 44, 580–5.

Wankel, L. M., & Berger, B. G. (1990). The psychological and social benefits of sport and physical activity. *Journal of Leisure Research*, 22, 167–82.

Wankel, L. M., & Thompson, C. (1977). Motivating people to be physically active: Self-persuasion vs. balanced decision making. *Journal of Applied Social Psychology*, 7, 332–40.

Weinberg, R. S., & Gould, D. (2007). *Foundations of sport and exercise psychology* (4th ed.). Champaign, IL: Human Kinetics.

Weiner, B., Frieze, I. H., Kukla, A., Reed, L., Rest, S., & Rosenbaum, R. M. (1972). Perceiving the causes of success and failure. In E. E. Jones, D. E. Kanouse, R. H. Kelley, R. E. Nisbett, S. Valins, & B. Weiner (eds), *Attribution: Perceiving the causes of behavior*. Morristown, NJ: General Learning Press.

Wieland, W. F., & Novack, J. L. (1973). A comparison of criminal justice and non-criminal justice related patients in a methadone treatment program. *Proceedings of the Fifth National Conference on Methadone Treatment*, 1, 116–22.

Yuhasz, M. S. (1965). *Physical fitness and sports appraisal laboratory manual*. University of Western Ontario.

Zax, M. (1962). The incidence and fate of the reopened case in an alcoholism treatment center. *Quarterly Journal of Studies on Alcohol*, 23, 634–9.

# 6

# Self-efficacy

Marcus, B. H., Selby, V. C., Niaura, R. S., & Rossi, J. S. (1992). Self-efficacy and the stages of exercise behavior change. *Research Quarterly for Exercise and Sport*, 63, 60–6.

## Background and context

Self-efficacy is an individual's belief in their capabilities to organize and execute the courses of action required to produce given attainments (Bandura, 1997: 3). These beliefs are not judgments about one's skills, but rather are judgments of what an individual can accomplish with these skills (Bandura, 1986). In essence, self-efficacy refers to one's impression of what one is capable of doing. These impressions provide the foundation for human motivation, well-being, and personal accomplishment because unless people believe that their actions can produce the outcomes they desire, they have little incentive to act or persevere when faced with difficulties (Bandura, 1997).

The renowned psychologist, Albert Bandura, developed self-efficacy theory and proposed that "people's level of motivation, affective states, and actions are based more on what they believe than on what is objectively true" (1997: 2). For this reason, a person's behavior can often be better predicted by the beliefs they hold about their capabilities than by what they are actually capable of accomplishing, because self-efficacy beliefs help determine what a person does with the knowledge and skills they have. This explains why an individual's sporting performance sometimes does not match their actual capabilities. For example, many talented people suffer frequent (and sometimes debilitating) bouts of self-doubt about capabilities they clearly possess, just as many individuals are confident about what they can accomplish despite possessing a modest repertoire of skills (Pajares, 1997). However, no amount of confidence or self-appreciation can produce success when requisite skills and knowledge are absent (Pajares & Schunk, 2001).

Bandura (1977), who originally trained as a clinical psychologist, suggested that four sources of information provide the individual with a sense of self-efficacy. These antecedents are performance accomplishments (past experience), vicarious experience (or modeling, which is the observation of others performing successfully), physiological states (e.g., arousal, stamina), and verbal persuasion (e.g., coaching). Maddux (1995) later suggested that two additional sources of self-efficacy may exist, namely emotional states (e.g., anxiety) and imaginal experiences (mental imagery). Of all these sources, performance accomplishments are regarded as the most influential source of efficacy information (Bandura, 1997).

Self-efficacy is an important component of Bandura's (1986) social cognitive theory, which is a more dynamic theory that suggests cognitions (including self-efficacy), behavior, and the environment continually interact in a reciprocal fashion over time. To illustrate, an individual who has a high level of self-efficacy may attend an exercise class, exert a great deal of effort when there and as a result may receive positive reinforcement from the class leader which in turn further raises self-efficacy.

Inspired by Bandura's (1977) theory, and due to the obvious links between beliefs about performance capabilities and actual outcomes, sport and exercise psychology researchers immediately began to examine self-efficacy in numerous settings and contexts. The first studies examined the relationship between self-efficacy and performance in sport and generally found that higher levels of self-efficacy were associated with greater performance (e.g., Feltz, 1988; McAuley, 1985; Weinberg, Gould, & Jackson, 1979). Research was also starting to be conducted on how self-efficacy is related to exercise behavior. For example, self-efficacy predicted the adoption of vigorous physical activity in males and along with exercise knowledge predicted the maintenance of moderate physical activity in females (Sallis, Haskell, Fortmann, Vranizan, Taylor, & Solomon, 1986).

The key study conducted by Marcus, Selby, Niaura, and Rossi looked to extend research on self-efficacy in exercise settings by examining it along with the stages of change model. Prochaska and DiClemente (1983) developed the stages of change model as a framework of stages that individuals progress through in the acquisition and maintenance of a behavior. These stages, at the time of the study, included: precontemplation (i.e., individuals who do not engage in a particular behavior and do not intend to start in the near future); contemplation (i.e., individuals who do not engage in a particular behavior, but have an intention to start in the near future); action (i.e., individuals who are currently engaging in a particular behavior, but have only recently started); and maintenance (i.e., individuals who are currently engaging in a particular behavior, and have been doing so for some time). Another stage, preparation (i.e., individuals who engage in a particular behavior, but not on a regular basis), was one that the authors felt could possibly be distinguished from (and sit between) contemplation and action. At the time of the study, the stages of change model was being validated and applied to a variety of behaviors that included smoking cessation, dietary behavior, and exercise behavior.

## Key study

Research has documented that a large portion of the U.S. population does not participate in regular physical activity (USDHHS, 1991) and approximately 50% of individuals who do join exercise programs drop out during the first three to six months (Carmody, Senner, Manilow, & Matarazzo, 1980; Dishman, 1988). This pattern of attrition is similar to the negatively accelerated relapse curve often seen in tobacco, heroin, and alcohol addiction (Hunt, Barnett, & Branch, 1971). This similarity of patterns is of interest, although research has yet to document common processes involved in starting a positive behavior and stopping negative behaviors (Sonstroem, 1988).

The amount of progress people make as a result of intervention is a function of the stage they are in at the start of treatment programs designed for people who are ready to take action are not successful for people in Precontemplation or Contemplation (Ockene, Ockene, & Kristeller, 1988). Media and other exercise campaigns have had poor results with regard to increasing exercise adoption (Knapp, 1988). This may be due to their educational rather than behavioral and motivational focus or their targeting of the minority of individuals who have already decided to become active.

Two different theoretical models have been useful to researchers interested in understanding and predicting health-related behavior change: (a) the stages-of-change model

(Prochaska & DiClemente, 1983) and (b) self-efficacy theory (Bandura, 1977). A strength of the stages-of-change model is its focus on the dynamic nature of health behavior change. Because this is a dynamic model, the different transitions in adoption and maintenance of exercise behavior described by other researchers (Dishman, 1982; Sallis & Hovell, 1990; Sonstroem, 1988) can be specifically examined. This model suggests that behavior change is not an all-or-nothing phenomenon and that individuals who stop performing a behavior may intend to start again (Sonstroem, 1988). Exercise researchers have recommended that this model be applied to exercise behavior, as the exercise field needs to shift from predictive to process models to better understand behavior change. This model has been successfully applied to a wide range of health behaviors, including smoking, weight control, and mammography (Prochaska & DiClemente, 1983, 1985; Rakowski, Dube, Marcus, Prochaska, Velicer, & Abrams, in press).

Self-efficacy beliefs have, in some instances, been shown to be superior to past performance in predicting future behavior (Bandura, Adams, Hardy, & Howells, 1980; DiClemente, 1981). Self-efficacy beliefs are closely tied to the performance of many behaviors, such as exercise (Sallis et al., 1986; Sallis, Pinski, Patterson, & Nader, 1988), smoking cessation (Condiotte & Lichtenstein, 1981; DiClemente, Prochaska, & Gibertini, 1985), and weight-loss (Bernier & Avard, 1986). Additionally, scores on a smoking-specific self-efficacy measure appear to be related to stage-of-change and success at smoking cessation, with Precontemplators and Contemplators scoring lowest and those in Maintenance scoring highest, although clear differentiation between all stages was not revealed (DiClemente et al., 1985).

The purpose of the present studies was to examine the application of these two models to exercise behavior. The aims of the studies were to (a) develop a scale to measure stages of change for exercise behavior, (b) obtain prevalence information regarding where individuals are distributed along the exercise scale, and (c) test the ability of a self-efficacy measure to differentiate individuals according to stage of readiness to change.

## Study I: Instrument Development

### Method

*Subjects.* Subjects were recruited as part of a statewide worksite health promotion project. Five thousand employees at a Rhode Island division of a government agency were invited to participate, and 1,063 opted to participate in this part of the study. The demographic profile of the sample of 1,063 closely matched that of the entire worksite (see Table 6.1). Seventy-seven percent of the subjects were male, average age was 41.1 (SD = 10.8), and average years of education was 13.6 (SD = 1.9). Most employees were involved in blue-collar occupations.

**Table 6.1** Demographic characteristics

|  | Study I | | Study II | |
|---|---|---|---|---|
|  | Population[a] | Sample | Population | Sample |
| Number of employees | 3,494 | 1,063 | 1,251 | 429 |
| Age (M years) | 41 | 41 | 39 | 41 |
| Sex (% female) | 23 | 23 | 83 | 85 |
| Occupation (% blue collar) | 81 | 77 | 45 | 38 |

[a] Based on data provided by the company.

*Procedure.* Subjects who volunteered for the study completed various questionnaires on exercise and provided basic demographic information and provided informed consent. Subjects also completed questionnaires about their smoking status and about other lifestyle behaviors as part of a large study on health behavior at the worksite. Details concerning the larger study will be reported elsewhere. Subjects were informed their names would be entered in a draw for a $100 prize in return for their participation.

*Instruments.* Two measures were developed. First, a stages-of-change measure, based on a similar measure developed for smoking cessation (Prochaska & DiClemente, 1983) and modified to describe exercise behavior, was constructed (see Figure 6.1). This four-item measure was designed to place subjects into either the Precontemplation, Contemplation, Action, or Maintenance stage. Precontemplation describes an individual who is not engaged in the behavior of interest (i.e., exercise) and has no intention of becoming involved in that behavior in the future. Contemplation describes an individual who is not engaged in the behavior of

|  | Study I |
| --- | --- |
| Stage | Item |
| Precontemplation | I currently do not exercise, and I do not intend to start exercising in the next 6 months. |
| Contemplation | I currently do not exercise, but I am thinking about starting exercising in the next 6 months. |
| Action | I currently exercise some, but not regularly.[a] |
| Maintenance | I currently exercise regularly. |
| Relapse[b] | I have exercised regularly in the past but I am not doing so currently. |

[a] Regular exercise = 3 or more times per week for 20 min or more at each time.
[b] All subjects who endorsed relapse also endorsed another item.

|  | Study II |
| --- | --- |
| Stage | Item |
| Precontemplation | I currently do not exercise, and I do not intend to start exercising in the next 6 months. |
| Contemplation | I currently do not exercise, but I am thinking about starting to exercise in the next 6 months. |
| Preparation | I currently exercise some, but not regularly.[a] |
| Action | I currently exercise regularly, but I have only begun doing so within the last 6 months. |
| Maintenance | I currently exercise regularly, and have done so for longer than 6 months. |
| Relapse[b] | I have exercised regularly in the past but I am not doing so currently. |

[a] Regular exercise = 3 or more times per week for 20 min or more at each time.
[b] All subjects who endorsed relapse also endorsed another item. Relapse is not conceptualized as distinct stage.

**Figure 6.1** Stages of change items

interest but is thinking about becoming involved in the behavior in the near future. Action describes an individual who has initiated some behavior change (i.e., participates in occasional exercise). Maintenance describes an individual who is regularly engaging in the behavior of interest (i.e., participates in activity at least 3 times per week for at least 20 min each time). For example, the Precontemplator would endorse the item, "I currently do not exercise, and I do not intend to start exercising in the next 6 months," whereas the Contemplator would endorse, "I currently do not exercise, but I am thinking about starting to exercise in the next 6 months." A five-point Likert scale was used to rate each item : 1 indicated "strongly disagree" and 5 "strongly agree." Subjects were placed into the stage corresponding to the item they endorsed most strongly (i.e., agree or strongly agree). Any subject not endorsing any item with "strongly agree" or "agree" was not placed into a stage.

Second, a five-item self-efficacy measure (see Figure 6.2) designed to measure confidence in one's ability to persist with exercising in various situations was developed. Items represented the following areas: negative affect, resisting relapse, and making time for exercise. These areas have been shown to be important by other exercise researchers (Sallis *et al.*, 1988) as well as by smoking researchers (Baer & Lichtenstein, 1987). Sallis *et al.* (1988) conducted a principal components factor analysis and found two meaningful exercise self-efficacy factors, resisting relapse and making time for exercise. An 11-point scale was used to rate each item, with 1 indicating "not at all confident" and 11 "very confident." Subjects could also endorse 0, "does not apply to me."

| I am confident I can participate in regular exercise when: | Item-total correlations | |
|---|---|---|
| | Study I | Study II |
| I am tired. | .69 | .65 |
| I am in a bad mood. | .70 | .60 |
| I feel I don't have the time. | .66 | .60 |
| I am on vacation. | .54 | .39 |
| It is raining or snowing. | .63 | .44 |

**Figure 6.2** Self-efficacy items

*Data Analysis*. Frequency counts were used to determine the distribution of individuals on the stages-of-change questionnaire. Stage of change is the independent variable in the analyses. Coefficient alpha (Allen & Yen, 1979) was calculated to determine internal consistency of the self-efficacy measure. Self-efficacy is the dependent variable in the analyses. A one-way ANOVA was performed to assess the relationship between the stages of change for exercise behavior and self-efficacy scores. This was followed up with post hoc comparisons using the Tukey procedure (Keppel, 1982) to determine which stages the self-efficacy measure was able to differentiate. Additionally, chi square analyses and ANOVA were performed to assess the relationship between demographic variables and stage and self-efficacy.

## Results

Results revealed that 8.0% of employees fell in the Precontemplation stage, 21.1% in Contemplation, 36.9% in Action, and 34.0% in Maintenance ($n = 991$; 72 subjects [7%] could not be placed into a stage). For the five-item self-efficacy measure internal consistency was .82 ($n = 917$).

Further results revealed that total scores on the self-efficacy items differentiated employees at different stages, $F(3, 861) = 85.93$, $p < .001$. Proportion of variance accounted for ($\eta^2$) was .23, greatly exceeding Cohen's (1977) definition of a large effect size. Cohen defined small, medium, and large effects as proportions of variance accounted for .01, .06, and .14, respectively. Table 6.2 provides the means and standard deviations for all four groups and Tukey's post hoc comparisons of scores for subjects at the different stages of change are reported in Table 6.3. In all cases Precontemplators were significantly different from subjects in all other stages. A clear pattern emerged, with Precontemplators scoring the lowest and those in Maintenance scoring the highest on the self-efficacy measure. There were no significant relationships between demographic variables and stage of exercise behavior or self-efficacy.

**Table 6.2** Means and standard deviations on the self-efficacy measure in relation to stage in the change process

| Stage | Study I | |
| --- | --- | --- |
| | % of Subjects in stage | Self-efficacy |
| Precontemplation | 8.0 | 16.8 (10.0) |
| Contemplation | 21.1 | 26.5 (11.7) |
| Action | 36.9 | 25.7 (11.3) |
| Maintenance | 34.0 | 36.6 (12.1) |

Note: standard deviations are given in parentheses.

| Stage | Study II | |
| --- | --- | --- |
| | % of Subjects in stage | Self-efficacy |
| Precontemplation | 7.3 | 12.4 (5.1) |
| Contemplation | 23.1 | 17.7 (6.2) |
| Preparation | 30.4 | 18.1 (5.9) |
| Action | 16.6 | 21.6 (6.1) |
| Maintenance | 22.6 | 24.9 (5.7) |

Note: standard deviations are given in parentheses.

## Discussion

Of primary interest in the present study was determining how individuals are distributed along the continuum between the Precontemplation and Maintenance stages of exercise behavior. Results revealed scores on the self-efficacy measure were significantly related to stage in the change process. This measure reliably differentiated most pairings of stages. This finding supports the work of DiClemente et al. (1985) in the area of smoking, who found Precontemplators and Contemplators had the lowest scores and those in Maintenance had the highest scores, although clear differentiation between all stages was not revealed.

**Table 6.3** Tukey post hoc comparison results

|  | Study I | | |
|---|---|---|---|
| *Tukey Test Results* | | | |
| *Significant differences (p < .05) between*: | | | |
| Precontemplation | Contemplation | Action | |
| Contemplation | Maintenance | Maintenance | |
| Action | | | |
| Maintenance | | | |

|  | Study II | | |
|---|---|---|---|
| *Tukey Test Results* | | | |
| *Significant differences (p < .05) between*: | | | |
| Precontemplation | Contemplation | Preparation | Action |
| Contemplation | Action | Action | Maintenance |
| Preparation | Maintenance | Maintenance | |
| Action | | | |
| Maintenance | | | |

Further exploration of the results indicated the present four-stage measure may not adequately describe the sample. Because many subjects clustered in the Action and Maintenance stages, it may be helpful to both better define these stages and possibly add an additional stage, perhaps by adding a time referent to the items and by subdividing the Action stage. DiClemente and Prochaska (1985) and DiClemente *et al.* (1991) have suggested using an intermediary stage, such as Preparation, between the stages of Contemplation and Action. Thus, Action and Maintenance can be divided into Preparation (exercising some, but not regularly), Action (exercising regularly for less than 6 months), and Maintenance (exercising regularly for 6 months or longer).

## Study II: Instrument Refinement

Method

*Subjects.* Four hundred and twenty-nine employees of a Rhode Island medical center, approximately 25% of the employee population, participated in this part of the study. The demographic profile of the sample closely matched that of the entire worksite (see Table 6.1). Eighty-five percent of the subjects were women, average age was 40.5 (SD = 11.0), and average years of education was 13.8 (SD = 2.0). Less than half of the employees were involved in blue-collar occupations.

*Procedure.* The procedure used in Study I was repeated in Study II, including the obtaining of informed consent from participants.

*Instruments.* The two measures used in Study I were modified for use in this study. First, the four-item stages-of-change measure was expanded to a five-item measure to represent

Precontemplation, Contemplation, Preparation, Action, and Maintenance. While the definitions of Precontemplation and Contemplation remained the same, the other definitions were modified. Preparation was defined as the time when one is not only thinking about becoming physically active, but also has started to participate in a limited amount of physical activity. Action was defined as having recently become regularly physically active (at least three times a week for at least 20 min each time), as recommended by the American College of Sports Medicine (ACSM, 1990). Maintenance describes an individual who has been regularly physically active for at least 6 months. As a result of adding time referents to Action and Maintenance and further subdividing the stages, it was hoped the subtleties of the Action and Maintenance stages of change could be more thoroughly explored. A time referent was not used for Preparation, as our interest was in broadly distinguishing it from Contemplation (no exercise) and Action (exercising regularly). Second, the scale ranges on the self-efficacy items were changed from 1–11 to 1–7 as a result of feedback from subjects and a desire to improve response clarity.

*Data Analysis.* The sequence of analyses performed in Study I was repeated in Study II. Additionally, an item reflecting exercise relapse that appeared on the stages-of-change questionnaire in both Study I and Study II was analyzed. Relapsers were those who agreed or strongly agreed with the item "I have exercised regularly in the past, but I am not doing so currently." Although relapse is not conceptualized as a distinct stage in the stages-of-change model (DiClemente *et al.*, 1991), it seemed important to examine which stage relapsers were in at the present time.

## Results

Results revealed that 7.3% of employees fell in the Precontemplation stage, 23.1% in Contemplation, 30.4% in Preparation, 16.6% in Action, and 22.6% in Maintenance ($n = 398$; 31 [7%] subjects could not be placed into a stage). The 138 subjects who endorsed the relapse item fell into the stages as follows: 3.6% in Precontemplation, 35.5% in Contemplation, and 60.9% in Preparation. For the five-item self-efficacy measure internal consistency was .76 ($n = 388$).

Further results revealed that total scores on the self-efficacy items reliably differentiated employees at different stages, $F(4, 369) = 36.57, p < .001$. Proportion of variance accounted for ($\eta^2$) was .28. Post hoc comparisons of scores for subjects in the different stages of change are reported in Table 6.3, which also provides the means and standard deviations for all five groups. Similar to the findings of Study I, Precontemplators were significantly different from subjects in all other stages. Furthermore, all other comparisons were significant except between Contemplation and Preparation. Again, there were no significant relationships between demographic variables and stage or self-efficacy.

## Study III: Instrument Reliability

### Method

*Subjects.* Twenty employees of a Rhode Island Medical Center participated in this part of the study.

*Procedure.* Subjects who volunteered for the study completed the instruments described in Study II on two separate occasions, two weeks apart, after providing informed consent.

## Results

Test-retest (product moment) reliability for the self-efficacy scale over a two-week period was .90 ($n = 20$). The kappa index of reliability for the stages-of-change instrument over a two-week period was .78 ($n = 20$).

## Discussion

The two samples (Study I and Study II) were administered different forms of the stages-of-change measure. However, when the results from the two samples are combined a consistent picture emerges. In the Study I sample, 34.0% of subjects reported exercising at a level that meets the ACSM (1990) criteria for frequency and duration of physical activity (Maintenance). A similar pattern was observed in the Study II sample with 39.2% meeting this criteria (Action and Maintenance). These results are similar to the findings of the Centers for Disease Control 1988 Behavioral Risk Factor Surveillance Survey, which revealed that 35.2% of Rhode Islanders were exercising at the frequency and duration recommended by ACSM (1990).

Although the same pattern prevailed in Study I and Study II, more information about the subjects is available in Study II. Approximately two-thirds of the subjects who are in some phase of Action as identified in Study I are actually in Preparation. Individuals who are in Preparation may only be participating in weekly or monthly physical activity and therefore are distinctly different from those who exercise at least three times per week.

Additionally, many individuals in Preparation also have a history of exercise relapse. Future work utilizing the Preparation stage should attempt to remedy and clarify the limitations present in this investigation, including the lack of a time referent for this stage and the need for more information regarding the exercise history of individuals in this stage (i.e., How many relapses have subjects had? Have they been exercising once or twice a week for a long time?). Further examination of relapsers and the reasons why few give up entirely, some think about starting to exercise again, and many scale back the amount or frequency of exercise they participate in is warranted.

Since 7% of the sample in each study could not be placed into a stage because of their pattern of responding, future work might include development of a yes/no format for items and a scoring algorithm that could place all subjects into a stage. Future work might also include the use of more representative samples and longitudinal designs as the samples of convenience used in these cross-sectional studies may limit the generalizability of these findings. Furthermore, a rigorous test of the stages-of-change model for exercise will require a prospective design and objective information on subjects' exercise behavior.

Further results revealed that, in both Study I and Study II, scores on the self-efficacy measure were significantly related to stage in the change process. Additionally, results of Study III revealed that both the stages of change and the self-efficacy instruments are highly reliable. These results serve to replicate the data on self-efficacy and stages of change in smoking. As is the case with smoking cessation, self-efficacy is closely linked to stage of self-change in physical activity, although clear differentiation between all stages is not present. Further work on developing a self-efficacy measure via a large item pool and the use of principal components factor analysis may help create an instrument where clear differentiation between all stages is possible.

It appears individuals at various stages have different degrees of exercise-specific self-efficacy. This suggests that individuals at the different stages might benefit from interventions that differ in their focus on enhancing efficacy expectations. For instance, those in the early stages of exercise adoption (Precontemplation and Contemplation) might benefit most from informational and motivational experiences designed to increase the appeal of physical activity and to enhance efficacy expectations. Further work in this area will need to be conducted before specific recommendations can be offered.

The primary objective in applying theoretical models such as the stages-of-change model to the study of exercise behavior is to better understand the process of behavior change so that more successful programs can be developed to help people start or continue to be active. Sedentary lifestyle is clearly a behavior that results in increased morbidity and mortality, and numerous physiological and psychological benefits may be accrued from an active lifestyle (Harris, Caspersen, DeFriese, & Estes, 1989). The challenge that remains is to better understand the process of exercise initiation, adoption, and maintenance so that successful programs can be developed.

## Subsequent research and application

Participation in physical activity, whether sport or exercise based, has been found to positively correlate with self-efficacy (Bandura, 1997; Bezjak & Lee, 1990; Biddle & Nigg, 2000; McAuley, Pena, & Jerome, 2001). For example, self-efficacy was positively correlated with intention to be physically active in young people (Hagger, Chatzisarantis, & Biddle, 2001). Adults who are more physically efficacious are likely to attend exercise classes more regularly, expend greater effort, persist longer, have greater success and achieve better health related benefits from a return to exercise than adults with a low sense of physical efficacy (McAuley, 1992; McAuley et al., 2001).

However, the influence of self-efficacy on exercise behavior has been demonstrated to change depending on the stage at which the individual is at with regard to exercise participation. For example, the influence of self-efficacy on exercise participation appears to be stronger in the early stages of exercise adoption (Feltz & Mungo, 1983; Poag & McAuley, 1992). This finding may be explained by the type of efficacy beliefs that are assessed. Crucially, *different* self-efficacy beliefs are thought to be important at different times of exercise participation (Scholz, Sniehotta, & Schwarzer, 2005). To illustrate, a person may have a high degree of task self-efficacy (e.g., I think I can engage in a physically active lifestyle) and this may be important in the initiation of an activity. However, other types of beliefs, such as maintenance self-efficacy (e.g., I will be able to run regularly as I have very flexible working hours) may be more strongly related to continued exercise behavior. This has been empirically demonstrated by Scholz et al. in a study with a large sample of patients undergoing cardiac rehabilitation. They found that task self-efficacy was the strongest predictor of the intention to exercise assessed two weeks into the exercise program. However, it was maintenance self-efficacy that predicted exercise participation both 4 months and 12 months after discharge from the program. Scholz et al. also found that high recovery self-efficacy (belief in the ability to return to exercise after a break) was important for people who had to take a break from the exercise program.

The strong link between self-efficacy and behavior in exercise settings is further supported by research demonstrating that, in line with Bandura's theory, self-efficacy influences behaviors such as activity choice, level of effort, degree of persistence, and achievement (Fontaine & Shaw, 1995; Poag & McAuley, 1992; Propst & Koesler, 1998). Interestingly, the relationship between self-efficacy and exercise behaviors does change across demographic variables. Men, and those with higher socioeconomic status, have been found to be characterized by greater self-efficacy for physical activity compared with women or those with lower socioeconomic status (Allison, Dwyer, & Makin, 1999; Gecas, 1989), although Biddle, Goudas, and Page (1994) found that self-efficacy was a strong predictor of exercise participation for women but not for men, for whom attitude was a better predictor of participation. Furthermore, self-efficacy has been found to increase until middle age where it peaks before decreasing after the age of 60 years (Gecas, 1989).

Self-efficacy is not only an important determinant of exercise behavior but also an important consequence of exercise behavior. That is, successful participation in exercise can increase self-efficacy (e.g., McAuley, Bane, & Mihalko, 1995). This relationship between exercise behaviors and self-efficacy is not surprising given that with repeated success, self-efficacy will increase (performance accomplishments) and a person will be more likely to repeat and sustain their involvement. Alternatively low self-efficacy and unfavorable experiences (low level of performance accomplishments) are more likely to lead to withdrawal. Finally, self-efficacy is also thought to mediate the influence of exercise upon affective responses. For example, participants with a high level of self-efficacy reported exercise to be more enjoyable in comparison to participants with a low level of self-efficacy (McAuley & Courneya, 1992).

Because people operate collectively as well as individually, self-efficacy is both a personal and social construct. Groups and teams can develop a sense of "collective efficacy" in their capacity to achieve desired outcomes and individuals can develop a sense of "proxy efficacy" in significant others (e.g., exercise class leader, coach) to help achieve desired goals (Bandura, 1997). While there is little research in exercise settings into the role of collective efficacy in impacting behavior (possibly because exercise groups are not particularly likely to have a collective goal), research has demonstrated the importance of collective efficacy in sport settings. For example, having completed a strength task, teams whose collective efficacy was then raised (by positive, bogus feedback) performed better on the task the second time, while teams whose collective efficacy was lowered (by negative bogus feedback) performed worse on completing the task a second time even though the teams were comparable in actual strength on the basis of the initial test (Hodges & Carron, 1992). Research has also illustrated that proxy efficacy in the exercise leader is an important contributor to exercise behavior. For example, proxy efficacy in the exercise leader predicted exercise adherence in novice group exercise participants (Bray, Gyurcsik, Culos-Reed, Dawson, & Martin, 2001) and intentions to exercise regularly in participants following completion of a cardiac rehabilitation program (Bray & Cowan, 2004).

The key study, along with other research employing the stages of change model and self-efficacy theory, contributed to the development of an important model of behavior change know as the transtheoretical model (Prochaska, 1994). This model was developed as a framework to describe the different phases involved in the acquisition or cessation of a particular behavior, and has become popular in research related to the maintenance of numerous health-related behaviors, including exercise (e.g., Gorely & Gordon, 1995; Marcus & Simkin, 1993; Nigg & Courneya, 1998). Elements of this model have also been applied within the context of sport psychology practice (e.g., Grove, Norton, Van Raalte, & Brewer, 1999). The model is considered transtheoretical because it encompasses features of the stages of change model and self-efficacy theory (Bandura, 1986), as well as two other theoretical models: processes of change (Prochaska, DiClemente, & Norcross, 1992) and decisional balance (Janis & Mann, 1977). Processes of change are overt or covert activities that individuals use to modify their experiences and/or environment in order to change their behavior(s) (Prochaska *et al.*, 1992), while decisional balance is a process which incorporates self-behavior, self-esteem, and social approval, and consists of the benefits and costs of behavior to both the self and others (Janis & Mann, 1977).

Studies have demonstrated that self-efficacy, the use of the processes of change, and decisional balance are employed uniquely at each stage of change throughout the behavior change process (e.g., Gorley & Gordon, 1995; Marcus & Owen, 1992; Prochaska *et al.*, 1994). However, based on a meta-analysis of the transtheoretical model in relation to exercise and physical activity, Marshall and Biddle (2001) suggested that there is uncertainty as to whether behavior change occurs in a series of stages or along adjacent segments of an underlying continuum. Other criticisms of the model have been put forward in relation to health (e.g., Ashworth, 1997; Bandura, 1997; Bunton, Baldwin, Flynn, & Whitelaw, 2000). As a result, and due to the rise in the popularity and application of the transtheoretical model in sport and exercise psychology, Marshall and Biddle suggest that there is an increasing need to standardize and improve the reliability of measurement in this important area of research.

While there has been a great deal of research into self-efficacy and exercise behaviors, researchers have also considered the link between self-efficacy and sport performance. Research has consistently shown a positive relationship between self-efficacy and sport performance (Moritz, Feltz, Fahrback, & Mack, 2000). In particular self-efficacy has been demonstrated to be strongly related to performance when sport competitors are evenly matched (Kane, Marks, Zaccaro, & Blair, 1996).

Related research in sport has also focused on sport confidence. The term confidence is often used to refer to a belief that a particular outcome can be achieved. This has been reflected in the work of Vealey (1986) who developed a model of sport confidence to consider the role of self-confidence in determining the process of motivation in sporting contexts. Vealey argues that our self-confidence when faced with a particular competition or challenge (otherwise known as "state sport confidence") reflects on both our underlying self-confidence (or "trait sport confidence") and our competitive orientation. Our performance then leads to subjective outcomes (e.g., satisfaction, perceived success) which then influence our competitive orientation and trait self-confidence on future occasions. To support her approach, Vealey developed separate measures of the three core constructs, known as the *Trait Sport-Confidence Inventory*, the *State Sport-Confidence Inventory* and the *Competitive Orientation Inventory*, although primary research based on this model remains scarce (Lavallee, Kremer, Moran, & Williams, 2004).

While recognizing that the term confidence is widely used in sport settings, Bandura (1997) makes it clear that it is distinct from self-efficacy. Specifically, confidence is considered to refer to the strength of a belief but does not specify what that belief is about. More crucially, Bandura goes on to consider that "Confidence is a catchword in sports rather than a construct embedded in a theoretical system. Advances in a field are best achieved by constructs that fully reflect the phenomena of interest and are rooted in theory that specifies their determinants, mediating processes, and multiple effects" (1997: 382). This quote emphasizes the importance of developing and/or applying theory to sport and exercise settings in that it helps to both understand and predict behavior. To explain, using Bandura's theory of self-efficacy it is possible to understand and predict how current experiences impact self-efficacy (because we know the antecedents of self-efficacy, such as performance accomplishments), how self-efficacy impacts behavior (because we know the mediating processes, such as the level of personal goals) and we know the potential outcomes (such as increased level of persistence). Thus, we would know what impact failing to complete an exercise class may have on a first-time exerciser, and whether positive reinforcement should be effective in enhancing self-efficacy.

Understanding the role self-efficacy plays in exercise behavior has obvious applied applications. Because Bandura clearly outlines the determinants of self-efficacy it helps us to understand how self-efficacy can be affected and facilitates the development of interventions designed to enhance it. To illustrate, it can help us to understand the impact that fitness videos may have on exercise behaviors. Many of these videos include attractive-looking women engaging in exercise. While these videos, which are typically aimed at women, have been a popular mechanism for increasing physical activity research has found that if they include "perfect-looking exercisers" they can have a negative impact on self-presentational efficacy (i.e., how confidence that they could present themselves as fit looking and competent exercisers) for both regular and infrequent/non-exercisers (Fleming & Martin Ginis, 2004). This finding was important as self-presentational efficacy was found to predict exercise intention.

While self-efficacy can be affected by a number of factors, a range of potential strategies for enhancing it have been outlined. For example, Dishman and Buckworth (2005) suggest breaking a challenging task into manageable chunks (performance accomplishments), observing someone who is similar successfully performing the exercise behavior (vicarious experiences), the use of encouragement by a significant other (verbal persuasion), and being educated about the normal physiological responses to exercise so these do not cause alarm (physiological states). Building on the work of Maddux (1995), exercise imagery has also been proposed as a potential mechanism for increasing exercise behavior by increasing self-efficacy (Giacobbi, Hausenblas, Fallon, & Hall, 2003). Similar techniques of course can also be applied to enhance self-efficacy in sport (see Zinsser, Bunker, & Williams, 2006). Just like the relationship between self-efficacy and exercise behavior the relationship between self-efficacy level and determinants also changes across demographic variables. For example, Chase (1998) suggests that different age groups rely on different sources of self-efficacy. Encouragement from significant others becomes an increasingly important source of self-efficacy information as we move to adolescence – specifically feedback from coaches and peers. While performance accomplishment has been shown to be important for all age groups, with increasing age the use of effort, comparison, and objective measures of success come to have a more significant bearing on self-efficacy (Chase, 1998).

Central to the continued development of self-efficacy research in sport and exercise settings is that researchers are able to accurately measure efficacy beliefs. Typically, self-efficacy continues to be measured along three dimensions – level (expected level of attainment), strength (certainty that the level will be attained), and generality (the fields across which the person feels capable). While the tendency may have been to regard self-efficacy as a psychological trait, it is more context-specific than a trait. That is, a person who has high self-efficacy toward one activity may not have high efficacy for another although it may generalize across similar activities (Biddle & Nigg, 2000). However, the measurement of self-efficacy can present difficulties. Self-efficacy is an important component of Bandura's (1986) social cognitive theory, which suggests that cognitions (including self-efficacy), behavior, and the environment continually interact in a reciprocal fashion over time. Typically, research in sport and exercise has examined self-efficacy independently – that is, without accompanying analysis of other major aspects of Bandura's social cognitive theory. However, based on social-cognitive theory, self-efficacy is context-dependent and, in turn, any measure must reflect that context (McAuley & Mihalko, 1998). To devise reliable and valid techniques, which are tailored towards particular activities and which reference all three dimensions, presents a real methodological challenge to sport and exercise psychology researchers.

## Additional readings

Bandura, A. (1997). *Self-efficacy: The exercise of control.* New York: W. H. Freeman and Company.

Feltz, D. L., Short, S. E., & Sullivan, P. J. (2007). *Self-efficacy in sport: Research and strategies for working with athletes, teams, and coaches.* Champaign, IL: Human Kinetics.

McAuley, E., & Mihalko, S. L. (1998). Measuring exercise related self efficacy. In J. L. Duda (ed.), *Advances in sport and exercise psychology measurement* (pp. 371–90). Morgantown, WV: Fitness Information Technology.

Moritz, S. E., Feltz, D. L., Fahrbach, K. R., & Mack, D. E. (2000). The relation of self-efficacy measures to sport performance: A meta-analytic review. *Research Quarterly for Exercise and Sport, 71,* 280–94.

Morris, T. (1995). Self-efficacy in sport and exercise. In T. Morris and J. Summers (eds), *Sport psychology: Theory, applications and issues* (pp. 143–72). Brisbane: Wiley.

## Study questions

1  What sources of information can provide individuals with a sense of self-efficacy?

2  What did the authors of the key study find when they included preparation as a stage in Study II (compared to Study I)?

3  What does Bandura outline are the advantages of using self-efficacy, rather than self-confidence, to explain behavior in sport and exercise settings?

4  Along what dimensions is self-efficacy typically measured?

5  What types of behaviors could an exercise leader engage in that may enhance the proxy efficacy of exercisers?

## References

ACSM (American College of Sports Medicine) (1990). Position statement on the recommended quantity and quality of exercise for developing and maintaining cardiorespiratory and muscular fitness in healthy adults. *Medicine and Science in Sports and Exercise, 22,* 265–74.

Allen, M. J., & Yen, W. M. (1979). *Introduction to measurement theory.* Monterey, CA: Brooks/Cole.

Allison, K. R., Dwyer, J. J. M., & Makin, S. (1999). Self efficacy and participation in vigorous physical activity by high school students. *Health Education & Behavior, 26,* 12–24.

Ashworth P. (1997). Breakthrough or bandwagon? Are interventions tailored to stage of change more effective than non-staged interventions? *Health Education Journal, 56,* 166–74.

Baer, J. S., & Lichtenstein, E. (1987). Cognitive assessment. In D. Donovan & G. A. Marlatt (eds), *Assessment of addictive behaviors* (pp. 189–213). New York: Guilford Press.

Bandura, A. (1977). Self-efficacy: Toward a unifying theory of behavioral change. *Psychology Review, 84,* 191–215.

Bandura, A. (1986). *Social foundations of thought and action: A social cognitive theory.* Englewood Cliffs, NJ: Prentice Hall.

Bandura, A. (1997). *Self-efficacy: The exercise of control.* New York: Freeman.

Bandura, A., Adams, N. E., Hardy, A. B., & Howells, G. N. (1980). Tests of the generality of self-efficacy theory. *Cognitive Therapy and Research, 4,* 39–66.

Bezjak, J. E., & Lee, J. W. (1990). Relationship of self-efficacy and locus of control constructs in predicting college students' physical fitness behaviors. *Perceptual and Motor Skills*, 71, 499–508.

Biddle, S., Goudas, M., & Page, A. (1994). Social-psychological predictors of self-reported actual and intended physical activity in a university workforce sample. *British Journal of Sports Medicine*, 28(3), 160–3.

Biddle, S. J. H., & Nigg, C. R. (2000) Theories of exercise behavior. *International Journal of Sport Psychology*, 31, 290–304.

Bray, S. R., & Cowan, H. (2004). Proxy efficacy: Implications for self-efficacy and exercise intentions in cardiac rehabilitation. *Rehabilitation Psychology*, 49, 71–5.

Bray, S. R., Gyurcsik, N. C., Culos-Reed, S. N., Dawson, K. A., & Martin, K. A. (2001). An exploratory investigation of the relationship between proxy efficacy, self-efficacy and exercise attendance. *Journal of Health Psychology*, 6, 425–34.

Bunton, R., Baldwin, S., Flynn, D., & Whitelaw, S. (2000) The "stages of change" model in health promotion: Science and ideology. *Critical Public Health*, 10(1), 55–69.

Carmody, T. P., Senner, J. W., Manilow M. R., & Matarazzo, J. D. (1980). Physical exercise rehabilitation: Long-term dropoutrate in cardiac patients. *Journal of Behavioral Medicine*, 3, 163–8.

Chase, M. A. (1998). Sources of self-efficacy in physical education and sport. *Journal of Teaching in Physical Education*, 18, 76–89.

Cohen, J. (1977). *Statistical power analysis for the behavioral sciences* (rev. ed.). New York: Academic Press.

Condiotte, M. M., & Lichtenstein, E. (1981). Self-efficacy and relapse in smoking cessation programs. *Journal of Consulting and Clinical Psychology*, 49, 648–58.

DiClemente, C. C. (1981). Self-efficacy and smoking cessation maintenance: A preliminary report. *Cognitive Therapy and Research*, 5, 175–87.

DiClemente, C. C., & Prochaska, J. O. (1985). Processes and stages of self-change: Coping and competence in smoking behavior change. In S. Shiffman & T. A. Willis (eds), *Coping and substance abuse* (pp. 319–43). New York: Academic Press.

DiClemente, C. C., Prochaska, J. O., Fairhurst, S., Velicer, W. F., Velasquez, M., & Rossi, J. S. (1991). The process of smoking cessation: An analysis of precontemplation, contemplation and preparation stages of change. *Journal of Consulting and Clinical Psychology*, 59, 295–304.

DiClemente, C. C., Prochaska, J. O., & Gibertini, M. (1985). Self-efficacy and the stages of self-change of smoking. *Cognitive Therapy and Research*, 9(2), 181–200.

Dishman, R. K. (1982). Compliance/adherence in health-related exercise. *Health Psychology*, 1, 237–67.

Dishman, R. K. (1988). Overview. In R. Dishman (ed.), *Exercise adherence* (pp. 1–9). Champaign, IL: Human Kinetics.

Dishman, R. K., & Buckworth, J. (2005). Exercise psychology. In J. M. Williams (ed.), *Applied sport psychology: Personal growth to peak performance* (5th ed., pp. 497–518). New York: McGraw-Hill.

Feltz, D. L. (1988). Self-confidence and sports performance. In K. B. Pandolf (ed.), *Exercise and Sport Science Reviews*, 16, 423–57.

Feltz, D. L., & Mungo, D. A. (1983). A replication of the pathanalysis of the causal elements in Bandura's theory of self-efficacy and the influence of autonomic perception. *Journal of Sport Psychology*, 5, 263–77.

Fleiss, J. L. (1981). *Statistical methods for rates and proportions* (2nd ed.). New York: Wiley.

Fleming, J. C., & Martin Ginis, K. A. (2004). The effects of commercial exercise video models on women's self-presentational efficacy and exercise task self-efficacy. *Journal of Applied Sport Psychology*, 16, 92–102.

Fontaine, K. R., & Shaw, D. F. (1995) Effects of self-efficacy and dispositional optimism on adherence to step aerobic exercise classes. *Perceptual and Motor Skills*, 81, 251–5.

Gecas, V. (1989). The social psychology of self-efficacy. *Annual Review of Sociology*, 15, 291–316.

Giacobbi, P. R., Jr., Hausenblas, H. A., Fallon, E. A., & Hall, C. (2003). Even more about exercise imagery: A grounded theory of exercise imagery. *Journal of Applied Sport Psychology*, 15, 160–75.

Gorely, P. J., & Gordon, S. (1995). An examination of the transtheoretical model on exercise behaviour in older adults. *Journal of Sport & Exercise Psychology*, 17(4), 312–24.

Grove, J. R., Norton, P., Van Raalte, J., & Brewer, B. (1999). Stages of change as an outcome measure in the evaluation of mental skills training programs. *The Sport Psychologist*, 13, 107–16.

Hagger, M., Chatzisarantis, N., & Biddle. S. J. H. (2001). The influence of self-efficacy and past behaviour on physical activity intentions of young people. *Journal of Sports Sciences*, 19, 711–25.

Harris, S. S., Caspersen, C. J., DeFriese, G. N., & Estes, Jr., E. H. (1989). Physical activity counseling for healthy adults as a primary preventive intervention in the clinical setting. Report of the U.S. Preventive Services Task Force. *Journal of the American Medical Association*, 261, 3590–8.

Hodges, L., & Carron, A.V. (1992). Collective efficacy and group performance. *International Journal of Sport Psychology*, 23, 48–59.

Hunt, W. A., Barnett, L. W., & Branch, L. G. (1971). Relapse rates in addictions programs. *Journal of Clinical Psychology*, 27, 455–6.

Janis, I. L., & Mann, L. (1977). *Decision making: A psychological analysis of conflict, choice, and commitments*. London: Methuen.

Kane, T. D., Marks, M. A., Zaccaro, S. J., & Blair, V. (1996). Self-efficacy, personal goals, and wrestlers' self-regulation. *Journal of Sport and Exercise Psychology*, 18, 36–48.

Keppel, G. (1982). *Design and analysis*. Englewood Cliffs, NJ: Prentice-Hall.

Knapp, D. N. (1988). Behavioral management techniques and exercise promotion. In R. Dishman (ed.), *Exercise adherence* (pp. 203–35). Champaign, IL: Human Kinetics.

Lavallee, D., Kremer, J., Moran, A., & Williams, M. (2004). *Sport psychology: Contemporary themes*. London: Palgrave.

Maddux, J. E. (1995). *Self-efficacy, adaptation, and adjustment: Theory, research and application*. New York: Plenum.

Marcus, B. H., & Owen, N. (1992). Motivational readiness, self-efficacy and decision making for exercise. *Journal of Applied Social Psychology*, 22, 3–16.

Marcus, B. H., & Simkin, L. R. (1993). The stages of exercise behavior. *Journal of Sports Medicine and Physical Fitness*, 33, 83–8.

Marshall, S. J., & Biddle, S. J. H. (2001) The transtheoretical model of behavior change: A meta-analysis of application to physical activity and exercise. *Annals of Behavioral Medicine*, 23(4), 229–46.

McAuley, E. (1985). Modeling and self-efficacy: A test of Bandura's model. *Journal of Sport Psychology*, 7, 283–95.

McAuley, E. (1992). The role of exercise cognitions in the prediction of exercise behavior of middle-aged adults. *Journal of Behavioral Medicine*, 15, 65–88.

McAuley, E., Bane, S., & Mihalko, S. L. (1995). Exercise in middle-aged adults: Self-efficacy and self-presentational outcomes. *Preventive Medicine*, 24, 319–28.

McAuley, E., & Courneya, K. S. (1992). Self-efficacy relationships with affective and exertion responses to exercise. *Journal of Applied Social Psychology*, 22, 312–26.

McAuley, E., & Mihalko, S. L. (1998). Measuring exercise related self efficacy. In J. L. Duda (ed.), *Advances in sport and exercise psychology measurement* (pp. 371–90). Morgantown, WV: Fitness Information Technology.

McAuley, E., Pena, M. M., & Jerome, G. J. (2001). Self-efficacy as a determinant and an outcome of exercise. In G. C. Roberts (ed.), *Advances in motivation in sport and exercise* (pp. 235–61). Champaign, IL: Human Kinetics.

Moritz, S. E., Feltz, D. L., Fahrback, K. R., & Mack, D. E. (2000). The relation of self-efficacy measures to sport performance: a meta-analytic review. *Research Quarterly for Exercise and Sport*, 71, 280–94.

Nigg, C. R., & Courneya, K. S. (1998). Transtheoretical model: Examining adolescent exercise behavior. *Journal of Adolescent Health*, 22, 214–24.

Ockene, J., Ockene L, & Kristeller, J. (1988). *Smoking cessation in patients with cardiovascular disease*. Worcester, MA: National Heart, Lung, and Blood Institute Grant.

Pajares, F. (1997). Current directions in self-efficacy research. In M. Maehr & P. R. Pintrich (eds), *Advances in motivation and achievement* (Vol. 10, pp. 1–49). Greenwich, CT: JAI Press.

Pajares, F., & Schunk, D. H. (2001). Self-efficacy, self-concept, and school achievement. In R. Riding and S. Rayner (eds), *Perception* (pp. 239–66). London: Ablex Publishing.

Poag, K., & McAuley, E. (1992). Goal setting, self-efficacy, and exercise behavior. *Journal of Sport & Exercise Psychology*, 14, 352–60.

Prochaska, J. O., & DiClemente, C. C. (1983). Stages and processes of self-change in smoking: Towards an integrative model of change. *Journal of Consulting and Clinical Psychology*, 51, 390–5.

Prochaska, J. O., & DiClemente, C. C. (1985). Common processes of self-change in smoking, weight control, and psychological distress. In S. Shiffman & T. Willis (eds), *Coping and substance use* (pp. 345–63). New York: Academic Press.

Prochaska, J. O., DiClemente, C. C., & Norcross, J. C. (1992). In search of how people change: Applications to addictive behaviors. *American Psychologist*, 47, 1102–14.

Prochaska, J. O., Velicer, W. F., Rossi, J. S., Goldstein, M. G., Marcus, B. H., Rakowski, W., Fiore, C., Harlow, L. L., Redding, C. A., Rosenbloom, D., & Rossi, S. R. (1994). Stages of change and decisional balance for 12 problem behaviors. *Health Psychologist*, 13, 39–46.

Propst, D. B., & Koesler, R. A. (1998). Bandura goes outdoors: Role of self-efficacy in the outdoor leadership development process. *Leisure Sciences*, 20, 319–44.

Rakowski, W., Dube, C., Marcus, B. H., Prochaska, J. O., Velicer, W. F., & Abrams, D. B. (in press). Assessing elements of women's decision-making about mammography. *Health Psychology*.

Sallis, J. F., & Hovell, M. F. (1990). Determinants of exercise behavior. In J. O. Holloszy & K. B. Pandolf (eds), *Exercise and sport sciences review* (Vol. 18, pp. 307–30). Baltimore, MA: Williams & Wilkins.

Sallis, J. F., Haskell, W. L., Fortmann, S. P., Vranizan, K. M., Taylor, C. B., & Solomon, D. S. (1986). Predictors of adoption and maintenance of physical activity in a community sample. *Preventive Medicine*, 15, 331–41.

Sallis, J. F., Pinski, R. B., Patterson, T. L., & Nader, P. R. (1988). The development of self-efficacy scales for health-related diet and exercise behaviors. *Health Education Research*, 3, 283–92.

Scholz, U., Sniehotta, F. F., & Schwarzer, R. (2005). Predicting physical exercise in cardiac rehabilitation: The role of phase-specific self-efficacy beliefs. *Journal of Sport and Exercise Psychology*, 27, 135–51.

Sonstroem, R. J. (1988). Psychological models. In R. Dishman (ed.), *Exercise adherence* (pp. 125–53). Champaign, IL: Human Kinetics.

USDHHS (U.S. Department of Health and Human Services) (1991). *Healthy people 2000: National health promotion and disease prevention objectives* (DHHS Pub No. [PHS] 91–50212). Washington, DC: U.S. Government Printing Office.

Vealey, R. (1986). Conceptualization of sport-confidence and competitive orientation: Preliminary investigation and instrument development. *Journal of Sport Psychology*, 8, 221–46.

Weinberg, R. S., Gould, D., & Jackson, A. (1979). Expectations and performance: An empirical test of Bandura's self-efficacy theory. *Journal of Sport Psychology*, 1, 320–31.

Zinsser, N., Bunker, L., & Williams, J. M. (2006). Cognitive techniques for building confidence and enhancing performance. In J. M. Williams (ed.), *Applied sport psychology: Personal growth to peak performance* (5th ed., pp. 349–81). New York: McGraw-Hill.

# PART 2

## Social processes

# 7

# Social facilitation

Triplett, N. (1898). The dynamogenic factors in pacemaking and competition. *American Journal of Psychology*, 9, 507–33.

**Written in collaboration with Heather J. Peters**

## Background and context

When Norman Triplett, a psychologist from Indiana University, published his research in 1898, psychology was a fledgling field of study in the USA. At that time approximately 32 psychology laboratories existed in the US (Garvey, 1929) and approximately seven psychology research journals were available. The oldest journal had been published for merely 31 years (Green, 2002). Additionally, the American Psychological Association had only been established seven years earlier (Anonymous, 1893). Research methodology and statistics were primitive by today's standards as evidenced by Triplett's study. It was not until the 1900s that theories such as psychoanalysis, behaviorism, and Gestalt psychology came into being (Boeree, 2005).

Triplett's study (1898) regarding the influence of the presence of other individuals on performance (later referred to as social facilitation) is the oldest experimental paradigm in social psychology. His article presents observations and experiments on pacing and competition when cycling and reeling in line on a fishing reel. This study was also the first to look at what we now perceive as a sport psychology phenomenon and some texts (e.g., Weinberg & Gould, 2003) even credit Triplett's research as the beginning of sport psychology in North America. Although motor performance was the arena studied by Triplett, his work did not serve as an impetus for the recognition or development of the field of sport psychology. Even if sport psychology did not begin as early as the late 1800s, Triplett's study is relevant to sport and exercise psychologists considering that both the acquisition and performance of sport skills and physical activity often occur in a social setting.

Triplett's study came from his enthusiasm for bicycle racing and his observation that cyclists often rode faster when they raced in groups or pairs (i.e., were paced) than when they cycled alone. He cites the work of Turner, a fellow cycling enthusiast, who began a three-year study in 1889 that found cyclists with a pacer perform better than those who perform by themselves. Turner believed individuals who set their own pace had more physiological and mental worry that in turn produced higher levels of carbonic, lactic, and uric acid. The increased acid levels diminished the brain's capacity to stimulate muscles, resulting in decreased contractile power and performance.

When Triplett examined official cycling records, he too found that the average times of paced race cyclists (1:55.5 minutes/mile) and competition cyclists (1:50.35 minutes/mile) were faster than those of unpaced race cyclists (2:29 minutes/mile). Triplett did not disagree with Turner's theory (as cited in Triplett, 1898), or other theories of the time (e.g., suction theory, shelter theory, and encouragement theory, which are all outlined in the key study), but he believed additional constructs contributed to the differences. He proposed the dynamogenic factors theory. It states that the presence of another rider serves as a stimulus to arouse the competitive instinct and it, in turn, frees nervous energy that cannot be released when competing alone. Further, the sight of movement in the other cyclist suggests a higher rate of speed and thus inspires greater effort. Triplett reasoned that if his theory of dynamogenesis were true, the effects would occur for other activities requiring muscular effort such as ice skating and foot races.

## Key study

This key study is based on three data collections carried out in the psychological laboratory of Indiana University which attempt to explain the subject of pacemaking and competition. In Part I, Triplett reviewed a copy of the official bicycle records from the *Racing Board of the League of American Wheelmen* at the end of the 1887 season. These records included the times of three types of professional races: (1) unpaced races against time (see Figure 7.1; lower curve); (2) paced races against time, in which a faster bicycle (e.g., a tandem multi-cycle) makes the pace for the rider (middle curve); and (3) actual competition race times against other timed competitors (upper curve). An examination of this archival data led to his follow-up research (Part II) involving an experiment during which participants wound lengths of silk onto a reel, either working alone or alongside a co-actor performing an identical task. In Part III, Triplett briefly discusses another study he conducted in which he found individuals to be able to count numbers faster if they observed a model counting numbers at a fast rate. He also mentions some applications based on this research.

## Part I

Based on the records of the 1887 *Racing Board of the League of American Wheelmen* there are over 2,000 racing wheelmen. Since the records of unpaced efforts against time, shown on the lower curve of the chart (Figure 7.1), are given only to 25 miles, comparisons with the other races are made for the same distance (see also Table 7.1). As is readily seen the time made here is much slower than in the paced race against time. The various factors advanced in explanation are given in detail in the following pages but the fact itself deserves attention at this point. The value of a pace itself is believed by racers to be worth a 20 to 30 second improvement in performance in the mile. The difference between the paced and unpaced race against time is, as seen from Figure 7.1, somewhat greater.

It is well-known that the ability to follow a pace varies with the individual. The paced record from the 3rd to the 10th mile inclusive is held by a racer named Michael. His average gain per mile over another racer (named Senn, the unpaced champion) is 34 seconds. From the 11th mile upward, a different racer (Lesna) holds the paced records. Evidently the pace is not worth so much to him for his average gain per mile is only 29.7 seconds, and a portion of this apparent gain is really due to the increasing exhaustion of the unpaced man, Senn.

As a rule the rider who is fast with a pace is slow without it – and the converse is believed to be true. This is perhaps the reason why the same rider has never held records in both paced and unpaced races. Some of the fastest unpaced riders on the track can ride only a few seconds better with the very best pacemakers, while Michael, whose ability as a "waiter" is

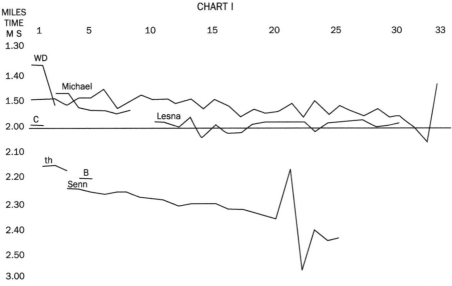

CHART I

Lower curve, unpaced – against time, middle curve, paced – against time, upper curve, paced competition race

**Figure 7.1**

almost marvelous, would fall a comparatively easy victim, his rivals think, in an unpaced race. Success in paced racing presupposes a well trained force of pacers. Michael has confessedly enjoyed greater advantages than their competitors in this respect. The regularity with which he rides is seen in his paced record from 3 to 10 miles. His average rate for these 8 miles was 1 minute and 53 seconds (with a mean variation of less than 0.8 seconds). Other evidences of the constancy of the gain from a pace may be seen through all the records (see Table 7.2).

In these cases a gain in favor of the pace of approximately 25% is shown. However, ratios between records made by different racers, even though they are the product of many riders and entitled to great consideration, have not the absolute certainty that the paced and unpaced time of the same rider would have. While data on this point is difficult to obtain (as riders seldom follow both kinds of racing but specialize in that for which they are best fitted), the best times for one mile of two prominent racers who are good at both types of races are available in

**Table 7.1**

|  | Average time per mile | | Gain over unpaced | Gain percent, over unpaced | Gain percent, competition over paced |
|---|---|---|---|---|---|
|  | Min. | Sec. | Sec. |  |  |
| 25 miles unpaced against time, | 2 | 29.9 |  |  |  |
| "    "    paced    "    " | 1 | 55.5 | 34.4 | 23.9 |  |
| "    "    paced competition | 1 | 50.35 | 39.55 | 26.4 | 3.5 |

**Table 7.2**

| 20 miles | professional, unpaced | is | | 49 min. | 20 | sec. |
|---|---|---|---|---|---|---|
| 25 " | " paced | " | | 49 " | 8.4 | " |
| 20 " | amateur, unpaced | " | | 52 " | 17 | " |
| 25 " | " paced | " | | 51 " | 57.2 | " |
| 80 " | professional, unpaced | " | 3 hr. | 54 " | 53 | " |
| 100 " | " paced | " | 3 " | 52 " | 14 | " |

the records. The gain, in the case of the first, of the paced (1 minute, 39.6 seconds) over the unpaced (2 minutes, 3.8 seconds) is 24.2 seconds – nearly 20%. The second gains 28 seconds (paced = 1 minute, 42 seconds; unpaced = 2 minutes, 10 seconds), nearly 22%.

The upper curve of the chart (Figure 7.1) shows the records made in paced competition races. Here, besides beating the record, the racer is intent on defeating his rivals. This race is started from the tape and in consequence is slightly slower for the first 2 or 3 miles than the time in the paced race against time with flying start. Thereafter the better time made witnesses to the power and lasting effect of the competitive stimulus. For 25 miles the time in this race averages 5.15 seconds per mile, or 3.5%, faster than the paced race against time.

Turner's (1889) research showed that the average gain per mile for the different trials varies from 11.8 seconds to 20 seconds in paced and unpaced races, and from this he asserted that the causes operating to produce the differences noted between paced and unpaced races are directly due to the physiological effects of bodily and mental exercise. Stated briefly: the racer who in a given distance does the greater amount of muscular work burns up the greater amount of tissue and in consequence their blood is more loaded with waste products and they excrete more urea and uric acid than others who do a less amount in the same time. This excretion of nitrogenous products as shown by Turner's experiments is directly proportional to the amount of work done. The blood, surcharged with the poisonous matter, benumbs the brain and diminishes its power to direct and stimulate the muscles, and the muscles themselves, bathed by the impure blood, lose largely their contractile power. Turner asserts further that phosphoric acid is the principal product of brain work, and that carbonic acid, lactic acid and uric acid are excreted in greater quantities during brain work. Therefore, the person racing under conditions to produce brain worry will be most severely distressed.

The production of phosphoric acid by brain work is, however, in dispute. Some observers have found the phosphates diminished, while others have found them present in larger quantities during intellectual labor. As James (1890) suggests, it is a hard problem from the fact that the only gauge of the amount is that obtained in excretions which represent other organs as well as the brain. Turner's (1889) results bear him out, however, in the assertion that a less amount of waste matter was excreted on days when little or no exercise was taken, a greater amount when pacers were used, and the greatest amount when he made his own pace. Basing his position on these physiological facts, Turner states: "Given two riders of equal caliber, properly trained and racing on a fair course, it is impossible (bar falls and similar accidents) for one of them to lead, make fast running and win the race; and the easier the track, the lighter and better the machines ridden, and the faster the time of the race – the longer the distance by which the one following will win." This is known by every rider and accounts for the "loafing" in unpaced competition races, as no rider, unless decidedly superior to their competitors, dares to set the pace.

SOCIAL FACILITATION   117

## Theories Accounting for the Faster Time of Paced and Competition Races

Of the seven or eight theories which have been advanced to date to account for the faster time made in paced as compared with unpaced competitive races and paced races against time as against unpaced races against time, a number need only be stated very briefly. These are grouped according to their nature and first are given two mechanical theories.

*Suction Theory*. Those holding to this as the explanation assert that the vacuum left behind the pacing machine draws the rider following, along with it. Those maintaining this theory believe that the racer paced by a larger machine is at an advantage as the suction exerted is more powerful.

*The Shelter Theory*. This theory posits that the pacemaker or the leading competitor serves as a shelter from the wind, and that "a much greater amount of exertion, purely muscular, is required from a man to drive a machine when he is leading than when he is following, on account of the resistance of the air, and the greater the amount of wind blowing the greater the exertion, and conversely, the greater the shelter obtained the less the exertion." This is the theory held, in general, by racers themselves and also by Turner as a partial explanation of the aid gained from a pace.

*Encouragement Theory*. The presence of a friend on the pacing machine to encourage and keep up the spirits of the rider is claimed to be of great help. The mental disposition has been long known to be of importance in racing as in other cases where energy is expended.

*The Brain Worry Theory*. This theory proposes that "a much greater amount of brain worry is incurred by making the pace than by waiting (following)." The man leading "is in a fidget the whole time whether he is going fast enough to exhaust his adversary; he is full of worry as to when that adversary means to commence his spurt; his nervous system is generally strung up, and at concert pitch, and his muscular and nervous efforts act and react on each other, producing an ever increasing exhaustion, which both dulls the impulse-giving power of the brain and the impulse-receiving or contractile power of the muscles."

*Theory of Hypnotic Suggestions*. A curious theory, lately advanced, suggests the possibility that the strained attention given to the revolving wheel of the pacing machine in front produces a sort of hypnotism and that the accompanying muscular exaltation is the secret of the endurance shown by some long distance riders in paced races.

*The Automatic Theory*. The leader, as has been noted, must use his brain to direct every movement of his muscles. As he becomes more distressed it requires a more intense exertion of will power to force his machine through the resisting air. On the other hand, the "waiter" rides automatically. He has nothing to do but hang on, and his brain having inaugurated the movement leaves it to the spinal cord to continue it and only resumes its functions when a change of direction or speed is necessary. When he comes to the final spurt, his brain, assuming control again, imparts to the muscles a winning stimulus, while the continued brain work of the leader has brought great fatigue.

These facts seem to have a large foundation in general knowledge (e.g., the occurrence in paced trails of a lesser amount of fatigue and the feeling of automatic action that gives the sensation of a strong force pushing from behind). Of course the greater the distance ridden the more apparent becomes the saving in energy from automatic riding, as time is required to establish the movement. It may be remembered, in this connection, that while the average gain of the paced over the unpaced record is 34.4 seconds, the difference between them for the first mile is only 23.8 seconds.

As between the pacer and the paced, every advantage seems to rest with the latter. The two mechanical factors of suction and shelter, so far as they are involved, assist the rider who follows. So the psychological theories, the stimulation from encouragement, the peculiar power induced by hypnotism, and the staying qualities of automatic action, if of help at all, directly benefit the paced rider. The element of disadvantage induced by brain action, on the contrary, belongs more especially to the rider who leads.

*The Dynamogenic Factors.* The remaining factors to be discussed are those which the experiments on competition, detailed in the second part hereof, attempt to explain. No effort is made to weaken the explanative force of the preceding theories, but the facts of this study are given to throw whatever additional light they may.

This theory of competition holds that the bodily presence of another rider is a stimulus to the racer in arousing the competitive instinct; that another can thus be the means of releasing or freeing nervous energy for him that he cannot of himself release; and, further, that the sight of movement in that other by perhaps suggesting a higher rate of speed, is also an inspiration to greater effort. These are the factors that had their counterpart in the experimental study following; and it is along these lines that the facts determined are to find their interpretation.

## Part II

The laboratory competitions below controlled for nearly all the forces outlined in the above mentioned theories. For example, in the 40 seconds the average trial lasted, no shelter from the wind was required, nor was any suction exerted; the only brain worry incident was that of maintaining a sufficiently high rate of speed to defeat the competitors. Furthermore, the shortness of the time and nature of the case, generally, it is doubtful if any automatic movements could be established. On the other hand, the effort was intensely voluntary. It may be likened to the 100 yard dash – a sprint from beginning to end.

## Description of Apparatus

The apparatus for this study consisted of two fishing reels whose cranks turned in circles of one and three-fourths inches diameter. The reels were arranged on a Y-shaped framework clamped to the top of a heavy table with the width of the framework sufficiently far apart to permit two persons to stand side by side while turning the reels. Bands of twisted silk cord ran over the well lacquered axes of the reels and were supported two meters distant by two small pulleys. The records were taken on only one side. The other reel was used merely for pacing or competition purposes. The wheel on the side from which the records were taken communicated the movement made to a recorder, the stylus of which traced a curve on the drum of a kymograph. The direction of this curve corresponded to the rate of turning, as the greater the speed the shorter and straighter the resulting line.

## Method of Conducting the Experiment

Participants practiced turning the reel until they became accustomed to the machine. After a short period of rest the different trials were made with five-minute intervals between to obviate the possible effects of fatigue. A trial consisted in turning the reel at the highest rate of speed until a small flag sewed to the silk band had made four circuits of the four-meter course. A stopwatch recorded the time of the trial. The direction of the curves made on the drum likewise furnished graphic indications of the difference in time made between trials. The actual running time in taking the six trials of a participant was about four minutes, or 40 seconds per trial. The stylus, responding immediately to every change in rate of turning, thus gave clear and accurate indications of the force of competition, of the effects of adverse stimulation, fatigue, and other phenomena.

## Statement of Results

In the course of the work the records of nearly 225 persons of all ages were taken. However, all the tables given below, and all statements made, unless otherwise specified, are based on the records of 40 children taken in the following manner. After the usual preliminaries of practice, 20 participants took six trials in this order: alone, competition, alone, and thus alternating through the six efforts, giving three trials alone and three in competition. The order of trials for the 20 other children was alone, alone, competition, alone, competition, and alone. By this scheme, a trial of either sort, after the first one, by either of the two groups, always corresponds to a different trial by the opposite group. Further, when the participants of the two groups come to their fourth and sixth trials, an equal amount of practice has been gained by an equal number of trials of the same kind. This fact should be remembered in any observation of the time made in trials by any group. During the taking of the records, and afterwards in working them over, it was seen that all cases would fall into two groups: First, those stimulated to either make faster time in competition trials or slower time in competition trials. Second, the small number who seemed little affected by the race.

Tables 7.3, 7.4 and 7.5 are made up from the records of the 40 participants mentioned. The classification was in general determined by the time record as taken by the watch. The first table (Table 7.3) gives the records of 20 participants who were stimulated positively (i.e., presence of another person improved performance). The second table (Table 7.4) contains 10 records of participants who were over-stimulated (i.e., presence of another person decreased performance). The third table (Table 7.5) shows the time of 10 participants who give slight evidence of being stimulated.

The 20 participants given in Group A and Group B, of Table 7.3, in nearly all cases make marked reductions in the competition trials. The averages show large gains in these trials and small gains or even losses for the succeeding trials alone. The second trial for Group A is a competition, for Group B a trial when the participant is alone. The gain between the first and second trials of the first group is 5.6 seconds, between the first and second trials of the second group, 2.52 seconds. The latter represents the practice effect – always greatest in the first trials, the former the element of competition plus the practice. The third trial in Group A – a trial when the participant is alone – is .72 seconds slower than the preceding race trial. The third trial in Group B – a competition – is 4.48 seconds faster than the preceding trial when the participant is alone. By the fourth trial both groups have participated in the same number and type of trials (i.e., two alone and one competition). For Group A the fourth trial is competitive and the gain over the preceding alone trial is 3.32 seconds. For Group B the fourth trial is alone and there is a loss of 1.58 seconds from the time of the preceding competition trial. In like manner prior to the fourth trial there is an equality of conditions for both groups prior to the sixth trial, and again the positive effect of competition plainly appears, the competition trial gaining 2.12 seconds and the alone trial losing .82 seconds with respect to the preceding trials. These are decided differences. The upper curve in Figure 7.2 is a graphical representation of these results.

The 10 participants whose records are given in Table 7.4 are of interest. With them stimulation brought a loss of control. In one or more of the competition trials of each participant in this group the time is very much slower than that made in the preceding trial when

**Table 7.3** Participants stimulated positively
Group A

|  | Age | A | C | A | C | A | C |
|---|---|---|---|---|---|---|---|
| Violet F. | 10 | 54.4 | 42.6 | 45.2 | 41. | 42. | 46. |
| Anna P. | 9 | 67. | 57. | 55.4 | 50.4 | 49. | 44.8 |
| Willie H. | 12 | 37.8 | 38.8 | 43. | 39. | 37.2 | 33.4 |
| Bessie V. | 11 | 46.2 | 41. | 39. | 30.2 | 33.6 | 32.4 |
| Howard C. | 11 | 42. | 36.4 | 39. | 41. | 37.8 | 34. |
| Mary M. | 11 | 48. | 44.8 | 52. | 44.6 | 43.8 | 40. |
| Lois P. | 11 | 53. | 45.6 | 44. | 40. | 40.6 | 35.8 |
| Inez K. | 13 | 37. | 35. | 35.8 | 34. | 34. | 32.6 |
| Harvey L. | 9 | 49 | 42.6 | 39.6 | 37.6 | 36. | 35. |
| Lora F. | 11 | 40.4 | 35. | 33. | 35. | 30.2 | 29. |
| Average | 11 | 47.48 | 41.88 | 42.6 | 39.28 | 38.42 | 36.3 |
| P. E. |  | 6.18 | 4.45 | 4.68 | 3.83 | 3.74 | 3.74 |
| Gains |  |  | 5.6 | .72 | 3.32 | .86 | 2.12 |

Group B

|  | Age | A | A | C | A | C | A |
|---|---|---|---|---|---|---|---|
| Stephen M. | 13 | 51.2 | 50. | 43. | 41.8 | 39.8 | 41.2* |
| Mary W. | 13 | 56. | 53. | 45.8 | 49.4 | 45. | 43.* |
| Bertha A. | 10 | 56.2 | 49. | 48. | 46.8 | 41.4 | 44.4 |
| Clara L. | 8 | 52. | 44. | 46. | 45.6 | 44. | 45.2 |
| Helen M. | 10 | 45. | 45.6 | 35.8 | 46.2 | 40. | 40. |
| Gracie W. | 12 | 6 | 50. | 42. | 39. | 40.2 | 41.4 |
| Dona R. | 15 | 34. | 37.2 | 36. | 41.4 | 37. | 32.8 |
| Pearl C. | 13 | 43. | 43. | 40. | 40.6 | 31. | 35. |
| Clyde G. | 13 | 36. | 35. | 32.4 | 33. | 31. | 35. |
| Lucile W. | 10 | 52. | 50. | 43. | 44. | 38.2 | 40.2 |
| Average | 11.7 | 48.2 | 45.68 | 41.2 | 42.78 | 39. | 39.82 |
| P. E. |  | 5.6 | 4. | 3.42 | 3.17 | 2.89 | 2.84 |
| Gains |  |  | 2.52 | 4.48 | 1.58 | 3.78 | .82 |

* Left-handed
*Note:* A = trial when the participant is alone; C = trial in competition; P. E. = practice effect

the participants are alone. Most frequently this is true of the first trial in competition, but with some was characteristic of every race. In all, 14 of the 25 races run by this group were equal or slower than the preceding when they are alone. This seems to be brought about in large measure by the mental attitude of the participant. An intense desire to win, for instance, often resulted in over-stimulation. Accompanying phenomena were labored breathing, flushed faces and a stiffening or contraction of the muscles of the arm. A number of young children of from 5 to 9 years, not included in our group of 40, exhibited the phenomena most strikingly, the rigidity of the arm preventing free movement and in some cases resulting in an almost total inhibition of movement. The effort to continue turning in these cases was by a swaying of the whole body.

This seems a most interesting fact and confirmatory of the probable order of development of the muscles as given by Stanley Hall (1883) and others. In the case of those sufficiently

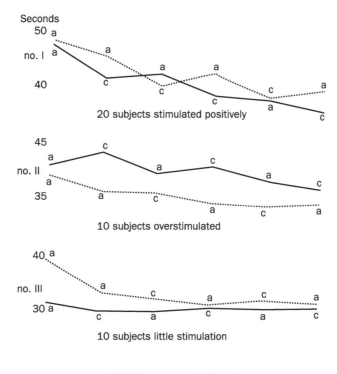

Seconds

50 a

no. I

40

20 subjects stimulated positively

45

no. II

35

10 subjects overstimulated

40.

no. III

30

10 subjects little stimulation

Solid line represents Group A
Dotted line represents Group B

**Figure 7.2**

developed to have the fast forearm movement, fatigue or over-stimulation seemed to bring a recurrence to the whole arm and shoulder movement of early childhood, and if the fatigue or excitement was sufficiently intense, to the whole body movement, while younger children easily fell into the swaying movement when affected by either of the causes named.

It remains one of the ways in which fatigue of a small muscle used in ergographic work will cause the participant to attempt to draw on his larger muscles. This tendency to revert to earlier movements and also old manners of speech is common, when, for any reason, there is interference with the centers of control. It may be said, therefore, that in the work under consideration the chief difference between this group and the large group in Table 7.3, was a difference in control; the stimulation inhibiting the proper function of the motor centers in the one case, and reinforcing it in the other. This, at least, seemed apparent from the characteristics exhibited by the two groups. Observation of the participants of this group show how decided gains were sometimes lost by the participants "going to pieces" at the critical point of the race, not being able to endure the nervous strain. Yet there exists no sharp line of division between participants stimulated to make faster time and those affected in the opposite way. In some instances the nervous excitement acted adversely in every race trial, while in others, a gain in control enabled the participant to make a material reduction in the last competition. These findings suggest that the time record is not always a true index to the amount of stimulation present. Had the trials consisted of but half as many turns the effect of competition as it appears in the tables would have been shown much more constantly. Table 7.4 would have been a smaller group if indeed any necessity existed for retaining it.

**Table 7.4** Participants stimulated adversely

Group A

|  | Age | A | C | A | C | A | C |
|---|---|---|---|---|---|---|---|
| Jack R. | 9 | 44.2 | 44. | 41.8 | 48. | 44.2 | 41. |
| Helen F. | 9 | 44. | 51. | 43.8 | 44. | 43. | 41.2 |
| Emma P. | 11 | 38.4 | 42. | 37. | 39.6 | 36.6 | 32. |
| Warner J. | 11 | 41.6 | 43.6 | 43.4 | 43. | 40. | 38. |
| Genevieve M. | 12 | 36. | 36. | 32.6 | 32.8 | 31.2 | 34.8 |
| Average | 10.4 | 40.84 | 43.32 | 39.72 | 41.48 | 39. | 37.4 |
| P. E. |  | 2.41 | 3.57 | 3.25 | 3.85 | 3.55 | 2.52 |

Group B

|  | Age | A | A | C | A | C | A |
|---|---|---|---|---|---|---|---|
| Hazel M. | 11 | 38. | 35.8 | 38.2 | 37.2 | 35. | 42. |
| George B. | 12 | 39.2 | 36. | 37.6 | 34.2 | 36. | 33.8 |
| Mary B. | 11 | 50 | 46. | 43.4 | 42. | 48. | 36.8 |
| Carlisle B. | 14 | 37. | 35.4 | 35. | 33.4 | 36.4 | 31.4 |
| Eddie H. | 11 | 31.2 | 29.2 | 27.6 | 27. | 26.8 | 28.8 |
| Average | 11.8 | 39.08 | 36.48 | 36.36 | 34.76 | 34.4 | 34.56 |
| P. E. |  | 4.61 | 4.07 | 3.89 | 3.71 | 5.33 | 3.45 |

*Note:* A = trial when the participant is alone; C = trial in competition; P. E. = practice effect

A comparison of the time made by the different groups shows that the participants of Table 7.3 are much slower than those of Table 7.4, and that a still greater difference exists between this group and the participants found in Table 7.5. It may be said that they are slower because of greater sluggishness of disposition, and that the reductions made are largely a result of the subjects warming up. This, indeed, may be a part of the cause for it, but as the larger reductions coincide with the competition trials this cannot be held to completely account for it. A glance over the individual records discovers some facts which furnish a plausible partial explanation, when taken in connection with the following fact. The age at which children acquire control of the wrist movements, a large factor in turning the reel with speed, was found to be about 11 years in general, although a few of the 9 and 10 years had this power. Of the 20 participants composing Table 7.3, seven are 10 years of age or younger, while two others, age 13, are left-handed and being compelled to use the right hand are slow in consequence. So, here are nine participants, a number nearly equal to the group in Table 7.4 or Table 7.5, who had a reason for being slow. Were these omitted from the count, the time of the initial trial would be found not to vary materially from that of Table 7.4.

Besides the lack of muscular development of the younger participants mentioned above, many of the participants of Table 7.3 seemed not to have proper ideals of speed. The desire to beat, if it did nothing else, brought them to a sense of what was possible for them. The arousal of their competitive instincts and the idea of a faster movement, perhaps, in the contestant, induced greater concentration of energy.

The participants in Table 7.5 are a small group who seemed very little affected by competition. They made very fast time, but they are older than the average; their muscular control

**Table 7.5** Participants little affected by competition

Group A

|  | Age | A | C | A | C | A | C |
|---|---|---|---|---|---|---|---|
| Albert P. | 13 | 29. | 28. | 27. | 29. | 27. | 28.6 |
| Milfred V. | 17 | 36.4 | 29. | 29.4 | 30.2 | 30.2 | 32.2 |
| Harry V. | 12 | 32. | 32. | 32.6 | 32.6 | 32.6 | 31.6 |
| Robt. H. | 12 | 31.4 | 31.4 | 32.2 | 35.4 | 35. | 32.4 |
| John T. | 11 | 30.2 | 30.8 | 32.8 | 30.6 | 32.8 | 31.8 |
| Average | 13 | 31.8 | 30.24 | 30.8 | 31.56 | 31.5 | 31.3 |
| P. E. |  | 1.9 | 1.13 | 1.71 | 1.7 | 2.06 | 1.05 |

Group B

|  | Age | A | A | C | A | C | A |
|---|---|---|---|---|---|---|---|
| Lela T. | 10 | 45. | 37.4 | 36.8 | 36. | 37.2 | 38. |
| Lura L. | 11 | 42. | 39. | 38. | 37. | 37. | 38. |
| Mollie A. | 13 | 38. | 30 | 28. | 30. | 30.2 | 29.6 |
| Anna F. | 11 | 35. | 31.8 | 32.4 | 30. | 32. | 30.4 |
| Ora R. | 14 | 37.2 | 30. | 29. | 27.8 | 28.4 | 26.8 |
| Average | 11.8 | 39.44 | 33.64 | 32.84 | 32.16 | 32.96 | 32.16 |
| P. E. |  | 3.11 | 2.88 | 3.03 | 2.75 | 2.69 | 3.71 |

*Note*: A = trial when the participant is alone; C = trial in competition; P. E. = practice effect

was good, and they had the forearm movements. Practice gains while somewhat apparent at first in some cases, are, as shown by the lower curve in Figure 7.2, on the whole, less in amount. Their drum records show fewer fluctuations and irregularities, and less pronounced fatigue curves at the end.

There seems to be a striking analogy between these participants and those racers who are fast without a pace, but can do little or no better in a paced or competition race.

## Observations on the Work

As to the amount of stimulation the odds are apparently with the female sex. The proportion of girls influenced by competition is greater. Of the 40 participants, 14 (or 36.6%) were boys, 26 (63.4%) were girls. In the group of those who were susceptible and influenced positively were 28.6% of the boys and 61.5% of the girls. In the group influenced negatively were 35.7% of the boys and 19.2% of the girls, and in the group not influenced 35.7% of the boys and 19.2% of the girls were found. These figures are deduced from the grouping made on the basis of the time record. An inspection of the graphs indicates that six in Table 7.5 were somewhat stimulated, although it is not made evident from the watch record. Were these participants, consisting of five girls and one boy, to be transferred to their proper table the result would show that 100% of the girls and 71% of the boys showed stimulation.

The gross amount of the effect of competition is also greater in girls. When they were stimulated and had control they made greater gains than the boys and when over-stimulated their losses were greater than those made by the boys. The 16 girls of Table 7.3 gained the average sum of 10 seconds in their competition trials, while the four boys of this group gained an average sum of 8.15 seconds. In Table 7.4 the five girls lost three seconds each, in the course of their competition trials, while the five boys lost less than one second each.

## Influences Affecting the Time of Succeeding Trials When Alone

It is well-known that some racers, who in private practice can go very fast, fail to distinguish themselves when the real race is run in the presence of the public. The weakening effect of nervous agitation has been ascribed as the cause. On the other hand, it has also been suggested that racers increase the energy of their movement when spectators are present. This is a common observation. A boy can turn better handsprings when wishing to impress others with a sense of his accomplishments. A football team plays better ball under the stimulation of the home crowd. Other examples could be instances showing how people respond to various social stimulations. In the records of the 40 participants found in the three groups discussed above, there are 80 cases wherein a competition trial is followed by a trial when the participant is alone. Of these, 45 were made in faster time than the preceding competition trial. Several facts seem to contribute to this result.

First, greater facility in turning naturally follows from the practice gained in former trials. In general, spectators were not permitted during the trials alone, but in a few cases visitors were present. The effect of this would be to stimulate the participant in an alone trial. Then, too, the competition element entered into the trials alone and it was found advisable in some cases to keep from the participant the time made, as there was a constant desire to beat his own or his friend's records, and thus make all the trials competitive. The competition feeling seemed present all the time. It is felt, therefore, that succeeding trials alone are not really non-competitive trials.

In addition, the competition trial was a pattern for after trials, giving a higher ideal of speed and a hint of what was possible for the participant. Féré (1887) remarks that it was his own experience, and that of a majority of experimenters in dynamometrie, "that the second trial was in general stronger than the first, the first trial having the effect of reinforcing the idea of the movement." The same thing seems peculiarly true of the kind of work under discussion. The racer comes to a succeeding alone trial with a reinforced image of the movement. The over-excitement of the former race is gone, but somewhat of its stimulating effect remains and in consequence more than half of the cases equal or exceed the former competitive trial.

## Part III

### The Idea of Movement

We are led to believe from the laboratory competitions detailed in Part II of this article that, besides the bodily presence of a competitor, the idea of his movement, whether gained from sight or sound, had a stimulating effect on the racer. Some participants followed with their eyes the course of the flags during the race and directed their exertions accordingly. Others seemed to be spurred on by the sound of the other machine, gaining some idea of the speed from the noise it made. Either seemed to possess equal power as a stimulus. Thus, supporting this study's assertion that dynamogeny accounts for some of the improvement in performance found when individuals perform with someone versus alone.

A favorite psychological principle of Féré (1887) describes the most important work done in the field of dynamogeny, is that "the energy of a movement is in proportion to the idea of that movement." This study described an experiment by Féré that found that a person began flexing his/her fingers when they observed someone else engaged in the same behaviors, and later research found that individuals who observed someone else counting numbers at a fast rate counted faster than those who did not observe a model. This principle of "ideomotor action" has wide application in human life.

In the cases cited above the observance of motion in another became a stimulus to greater effort. It may, however, have the opposite effect. A correspondence of rhythm of movement seems necessary to make it of aid. Two boys jumping together, or one following immediately at the sight of the other's jump, will not cover the distance possible in jumping alone, because the swaying of the body, and swinging of the arms, not being synchronous or rhythmic become a distraction. So one soon becomes fatigued when walking with a person out of step. Although "ideomotor action" may detrimentally affect performance it is proposed as a mechanism for dynomogeny and thus social facilitation.

## Concluding Statement

From the above facts regarding the laboratory races we infer that the bodily presence of another contestant participating simultaneously in the race serves to liberate latent energy not ordinarily available. This inference is further justified by the difference in time between the paced competition races and the paced races against time. The factors of shelter from the wind, encouragement, brain worry, hypnotic suggestion, and automatic movement, are common to both types of racing, while the competitors participate simultaneously in person only in paced competition races. In the next place the sight of the movements of the pace-makers or leading competitors, and the idea of higher speed, furnished by this or some other means, are probably in themselves dynamogenic factors of some consequence.

## Subsequent research and application

Although Triplett was the first to study social facilitation, Allport coined the term. He defined social facilitation as "an increase in response merely from the sight or sound of others making the same movement" (Allport, 1924: 262). This definition refers to a coaction paradigm in which individuals simultaneously and independently engage in the same activity. By the 1960s the term social facilitation was also used to refer to the effects elicited by the presence of passive spectators. When talking about social facilitation, it is important to note that it does not refer to influences on performance coming from social reinforcement such as harassment or encouragement from fans or teammates nor from competition, thus researchers who studied social facilitation employed passive audiences and coaction designs that discouraged overt rivalry.

Directly following Triplett's study, numerous experiments using different cognitive and motor tasks and both human and animal participants supported the notion of social facilitation, but many studies also contradicted the phenomenon. Use of the term social facilitation persisted despite the fact that the presence of others sometimes impaired and sometimes facilitated performance. By the early 1950s social facilitation research had virtually stopped, largely due to frustration from continued conflicting findings. Interest in social facilitation did not resume until Zajonc, in 1965, made sense of early contradictory findings by noting the pattern that the presence of others tended to improve performance when individuals performed tasks that they knew well or that were simple whereas performance suffered when individuals performed difficult or complex tasks they had yet to learn. Zajonc explained these results based upon drive theory (Spence, 1956), which postulates that increases in drive enhance the probability of emitting the dominant response. Thus, according to Zajonc, the mere physical presence of a spectator or coactor increases drive (i.e., arousal or activation). For example, when an individual first learns a complex task, the incorrect response is dominant and the presence of others will, via increased arousal, produce poorer performance.

Many studies followed in the wake of Zajonc's (1965) theory. Rainer Martens' doctoral dissertation (1968) and subsequent publications (1969a, b, c) provided powerful support for Zajonc's hypothesis and became the prototype for social facilitation research on motor behavior (Landers, Bauer, & Feltz, 1978). Martens' study provided evidence for Zajonc's predictions that the presence of others is a source of arousal and that this presence will inhibit initial stages of motor learning but facilitate later learning. Furthermore, the effects attributed to social facilitation were maintained, that is, they did not decrease over time. These audience effects accounted for 13–15% of the variance in performance, compared to the 2–5% variance typically found in earlier studies.

Martens' support for Zajonc's hypotheses spurred a new wave of research, but the subsequent findings showed small and often inconsistent audience effects [see Landers & McCullagh (1976) for a review]. Rather than questioning Martens' results, the weaker later findings were attributed to methodological shortcomings such as insufficiently eliciting arousal and not specifying a priori the response habit strength of the motor tasks (Landers et al., 1978). Landers et al. decided instead to replicate a portion of Martens' (1969a) study to see if they could duplicate his results. They also found that arousal, via the presence of others, inversely related to performance quality during the initial stage of learning, but could not replicate Martens' constant error and physiological arousal findings during later stages of learning. In addition, they noted that other researchers (e.g., Cohen & Davis, 1973), unlike Martens, clearly demonstrated habituation. Landers et al. (1978) concluded that although some studies have supported Zajonc's (1965) drive theory, the influence of social facilitation on performance is negligible because it typically accounts for only 1–3% of the variance in performance. They proposed that the arousal variability within each person may be too great to detect subtle effects of social facilitation, and that future researchers should examine social situations and individual personality characteristics that are known to be affected by arousal.

Prior to discussing how researchers heeded Landers et al.'s (1978) advice, it is important to discuss another social facilitation development that occurred simultaneously with Martens' findings. In 1968, Cottrell, Wack, Sekerak, and Rittle found that enhanced emission of dominant responses occurred when in the presence of an audience that could evaluate performance, but not when in the presence of blindfolded persons. This finding confirmed their hypothesis that the source of the social facilitation phenomena is the expectation of evaluation from others and its possible consequences, which is a learned source of drive, rather than Zajonc's mere physical presence hypothesis. In terms of the coaction paradigm, Cottrell (1968) argued that it took rivalry (i.e., the ability to see the coactor's performance and outcome relative to your own) to create evaluative potential and thus the social facilitation effect. Some subsequent researchers who manipulated evaluative potential (e.g., expert vs. non-expert, authority figure vs. peer) supported Cottrell et al.'s (1968) proposal, but a meta-analysis review of 241 studies indicated that evaluative pressure does not increase the overall strength of the social facilitation effect (Bond & Titus, 1983). This meta-analysis also found that social facilitation explains only up to 3% of the variance in performance.

Recall that Landers *et al.* (1978) suggested that moderators such as personality characteristics could increase the explanatory value of social facilitation. Allport (1924) may have been the first to discuss such a possibility when he hypothesized that individual differences, in such traits as nervousness and excitability, may influence susceptibility to social facilitation effects. Cox (1966, 1968) found the learning of a complex motor task in the presence of an audience was impaired by high-anxious boys compared to low-anxious boys, but Martens (1969a), with a coincident timing task, and Kozar (1973), with a balancing task, found that level of anxiety did not influence learning. The use of invalid anxiety measures and inconsistent use of any one measure were blamed for the non-significant findings. Eysenck's (1965) distinction between introvert and extrovert personality types may be another possible moderator (Underwood, 1976). Graydon and Murphy (1995) offered support for this proposal when they found that on a table tennis task extroverts performed better than introverts in the presence of an audience whereas the opposite occurred in the alone condition.

In addition to personality characteristics as moderators, the nature of the social situation may moderate social facilitation effects. For example, there is some support for increased social facilitation effects as numbers of audience members and co-actors increase (e.g., Martens & Landers, 1972). Recent research has also demonstrated that type of audience is important. Both Butler and Baumeister (1998), who asked participants to perform a challenging computer game task, and Law, Masters, Bray, Eves, and Bardswell (2003) who asked participants to perform a table tennis task, found that performance declined in front of a supportive audience. One potential explanation for this finding is that participants become more self-focused in front of a supportive audience and consciously focused attention on the task at hand, which for skill-based tasks leads to a detriment in performance (Butler & Baumeister, 1998).

Not only is the nature of the social situation important but so is the nature of the task. Strauss (2002) reviewed social facilitation studies to determine if the type of performance required for the task (i.e., coordination tasks vs. power and stamina tasks) could serve as a moderator. His review supported the claim of Landers and McCullagh (1976) that the classic activation theories of Zajonc (1965) and Cottrell *et al.* (1968) adequately explained social facilitation effects with tasks that require conditioning (i.e., muscle stamina), but that other theories, and particularly attention relevant processes, may provide more explanatory power with tasks that require coordination.

The inability of Zajonc's (1965) drive-theory to explain social facilitation effects more concretely led to alternative theoretical perspectives. Some of these theories include the Yerkes-Dodson (1908) inverted-U hypothesis (Martens, 1974), an attention narrowing/cue utilization perspective (Landers, 1980), alertness hypothesis (Zajonc, 1980), self-attention and control (Carver & Scheier, 1981a, b), attribution theory (Wankel, 1980), distraction-conflict hypothesis (Baron, Sanders, & Baron, 1974; Sanders & Baron, 1975), overload hypothesis (Baron, 1986), capacity model (Manstead & Semin, 1980), and the cognitive-motivational model (Paulus, 1983). Other models have focused on self-presentation (Bond, 1982) or integrated the fields of social facilitation and social loafing (Harkins, 1987). Investigation of these alternative approaches, and future examination of potential moderators, is needed to further clarify our understanding of the effects and potential processes that underlie social facilitation.

Although Triplett's study has been credited with marking the beginning of both social psychology and sport psychology, and for being the catalyst for hundreds of subsequent articles, recently the significance of Triplett's findings have been questioned. Strube (2005) reanalyzed Triplett's data using more advanced statistics and concluded that Triplett found little evidence for social facilitation and that the study probably would not be published today given the current publication standards. However, Strube (2005) concluded that regardless of the results Triplett made a perceptive observation of a real-world phenomenon.

In summary, social facilitation theory predicts that the presence of others, whether as co-actors or observers, facilitates performance on simple tasks and well-learned complex tasks and impairs performance on unlearned complex tasks. These effects occur because the presence of others increases drive and thus the likelihood of emitting the dominant response. It is concluded that if social facilitation effects occur at all, they are usually quite weak. Nevertheless, these effects should be considered when planning the optimal learning and performance environment. For example, current findings indicate, at minimum, that teachers and coaches might motivate better performance on well-learned strength and endurance tasks if they provide for an audience or the presence of other individuals performing the same task.

## Additional readings

Bond, C. F., & Titus, L. J. (1983). Social facilitation: A meta-analysis of 241 studies. *Psychological Bulletin*, 94, 1042–50.

Cottrell, N. B., Wack, D. L., Sekerak, G. J., & Rittle, R. H. (1968). Social facilitation of dominant responses by the presence of an audience and the mere presence of others. *Journal of Personality and Social Psychology*, 35, 245–50.

Landers, D. M., Bauer, R. S., & Feltz, D. L. (1978). Social facilitation during the initial stage of motor learning: A reexamination of Martens' audience study. *Journal of Motor Behavior*, 10, 325–37.

Strauss, B. (2002). Social facilitation in motor tasks: A review of research and theory. *Psychology of Sport and Exercise*, 3, 237–56.

Zajonc, R. B. (1965). Social facilitation. *Science*, 149, 269–74.

## Study questions

1   Social facilitation encompasses what social conditions and what does it not include? For example, would social facilitation researchers study the influence of fans on an athlete's performance?

2   What findings in Part I of Triplett's study motivated Parts II and III?

3   Did Triplett find support for dynamogenic factors as a possible explanation for social facilitation? Explain your answer.

4   How did Cottrell and his colleagues modify Zajonc's theory and is there support for their hypotheses?

5   How may an individual's personality characteristics, the social situation, and the nature of the task (i.e., coordination vs. power and stamina) influence response to social facilitation?

## References

Allport, F. H. (1924). *Social Psychology*. New York: Houghton Mifflon.

Anonymous (1893). The American Psychological Association. *Science*, 21, 34–35.

Baron, R. S. (1986). Distraction-conflict theory. In L. Berkowitz (ed.), *Advances in experimental social psychology* (pp. 1–39). Orlando, FL: Academic Press.

Baron, R. S., Sanders, G. S., & Baron, C. (1974). *Social comparison reconceptualized: Implications for choice shifts, averaging effects, and social facilitation.* Unpublished manuscript, University of Iowa, Iowa City.

Boeree, G. C. (2005). The history of psychology. Retrieved May 30, 2006, from Shippensburg Universities website: http://www.ship.edu/~cgboeree/historyofpsych.html.

Bond, C. F. (1982). Social facilitation: A self-presentational view. *Journal of Personality and Social Psychology*, 42, 1042–50.

Bond, C. F., & Titus, L. J. (1983). Social facilitation: A meta-analysis of 241 studies. *Psychological Bulletin*, 94, 1042–50.

Butler, J. L., & Baumeister, R. F. (1998). The trouble with friendly faces: Skilled performance with a supportive audience. *Journal of Personality and Social Psychology*, 75, 1213–30.

Carver, C. S., & Scheier, M. F. (1981a). *Attention and self-regulation: A control-theory approach to human behavior.* New York: Springer-Verlag.

Carver, C. S., & Scheier, M. F. (1981b). The self-attention-induced feedback loop and social facilitation. *Journal of Experimental Social Psychology*, 17, 545–68.

Cohen, J. L., & Davis, J. H. (1973). Effects of audience status, evaluation, and the time of action on hidden-word problems. *Journal of Personality and Social Psychology*, 8, 101–12.

Cottrell, N. B. (1968). Social facilitation. In C. G. McClintock (ed.), *Experimental social psychology.* New York: Holt, Reinhart, & Winston, 1972.

Cottrell, N. B., Wack, D. L., Sekerak, G. J., & Rittle, R. H. (1968). Social facilitation of dominant responses by the presence of an audience and the mere presence of others. *Journal of Personality and Social Psychology*, 35, 245–50.

Cox, F. N. (1966). Some effects of test anxiety and presence or absence of other persons on boys' performance on a repetitive motor task. *Journal of Experimental Child Psychology*, 3, 100–12.

Cox, F. N. (1968). Some relationships between test anxiety, presence or absence of male persons, and boys' performance on a repetitive motor task. *Journal of Experimental Child Psychology*, 6, 1–12.

Eysenck, H. J. (1965). *Fact and Fiction in Psychology.* London: Penguin.

Féré, C. F. (1887). *Sensation et mouvement.* Paris: Alcan.

Garvey, C. R. (1929). List of American psychology laboratories. *Psychological Bulletin*, 26, 652–60.

Graydon, J., & Murphy, T. (1995). The effect of personality on social facilitation whilst performing a sports related task. *Personality and Individual Differences*, 19, 265–7.

Green, C. D. (2002). Classics in the history of psychology special collections. Retrieved May 30, 2006, from York University, Toronto, Ontario's website: http://psychclassics.yorku.ca/Special/Institutions/#sect2.

Hall, S. G. (1883). The content of children's minds. *Princeton Review*, 11, 249–72.

Harkins, S. G. (1987). Social loafing and social facilitation. *Journal of Experimental Social Psychology*, 23, 1–18.

Kozar, B. (1973). The effects of a supportive and nonsupportive audience upon learning a gross motor skill. *International Journal of Sport Psychology*, 4, 27–38.

Landers, D. M. (1980). The arousal-performance relationship revisited. *Research Quarterly for Exercise and Sport*, 51, 77–90.

Landers, D. M., Bauer, R. S., & Feltz, D. L. (1978). Social facilitation during the initial stage of motor learning: A reexamination of Martens' audience study. *Journal of Motor Behavior*, 10, 325–37.

Landers, D. M., & McCullagh, P. D. (1976). Social facilitation of motor performance. *Exercise and Sport Sciences Reviews*, 4, 125–62.

Law, J., Masters, R. S. W., Bray, S. R., Eves, F., & Bardswell, I. (2003). Motor performance as a function of audience affability and meta knowledge. *Journal of Sport & Exercise Psychology*, 25, 484–500.

Manstead, A. S. R., & Semin, G. R. (1980). Social facilitation effects: Mere enhancement of dominant responses? *British Journal of Social and Clinical Psychology*, 19, 119–36.

Martens, R. (1968). *Effects of an audience on learning and performance of a complex motor skill.* Unpublished doctoral dissertation, University of Illinois at Urbana-Champaign.

Martens, R. (1969a). Effect of an audience on learning and performance of a complex motor skill. *Journal of Personality and Social Psychology*, 12, 252–60.

Martens, R. (1969b). Palmar sweating and the presence of an audience. *Journal of Experimental Social Psychology*, 5, 371–4.

Martens, R. (1969c). Effect on performance of learning a complex motor task in the presence of spectators. *Research Quarterly*, 40, 317–23.

Martens, R. (1974). Arousal and motor performance. *Exercise and Sport Sciences Reviews*, 2, 155–88.

Martens, R., & Landers, D. M. (1972). Evaluation potential as a determinant of coaction effects. *Journal of Experimental Social Psychology*, 8, 347–59.

Paulus, P. B. (1983). Group influence on individual task performance. In P. B. Paulus (ed.), *Basic group processes* (pp. 97–120). New York: Springer.

Sanders, G. S., & Baron, R. S. (1975). The motivating effects of distraction on task performance. *Journal of Personality and Social Psychology*, 32, 291–303.

Spence, K. W. (1956). *Behavior theory and conditioning.* New Haven, CT: Yale University Press.

Strauss, B. (2002). Social facilitation in motor tasks: A review of research and theory. *Psychology of Sport and Exercise*, 3, 237–56.

Strube, M. B. (2005). What did Triplett really find? A contemporary analysis of the first experiment in social psychology. *American Journal of Psychology*, 118, 271–86.

Underwood, G. L. (1976). Social facilitation of individual learning and performance. *International Journal of Sport Psychology*, 7, 143–57.

Wankel, L. M. (1980). Social facilitation of motor performance: Perspective and prospective. In C. H. Nadeau, W. R. Halliwell, K. M. Newell, & G. C. Roberts (eds.), *Psychology of motor behavior and sport – 1979* (pp. 130–48). Champaign, IL: Human Kinetics.

Weinberg, R. S., & Gould, D. (2003). *Foundations of sport & exercise psychology* (3rd ed.). Champaign, IL: Human Kinetics.

Yerkes, R., & Dodson, J. (1908). The relation of strength of stimulus to rapidity of habit formation. *Journal of Comparative Neurology & Psychology*, 18, 459–82.

Zajonc, R. B. (1965). Social facilitation. *Science*, 149, 269–74.

Zajonc, R. B. (1980). Cormpresence. In P. B. Paulus (ed.), *Psychology of group influence* (pp. 35–60). Hillsdale, NJ: Erlbaum.

# 8

# Group dynamics

Brawley, L., Carron, A., & Widmeyer, W. (1993). The influence of the group and its cohesiveness on perception of group-related variables. *Journal of Sport & Exercise Psychology*, 15, 245–66.

Written in collaboration with Mark Eys

## Background and context

Group dynamics represents a field of inquiry dedicated to the examination of group issues. Specifically, Cartwright and Zander (1968) defined the study of group dynamics as the advancement of knowledge regarding the "nature of groups, the laws of their development, and the interrelations with individuals, other groups, and larger institutions" (1968: 7). Under the general umbrella of group dynamics, Carron, Hausenblas, and Eys (2005) highlighted a number of topics involved in this area of study with sport teams. These included member attributes (e.g., athlete to athlete compatibility), group environment (e.g., home field advantage), group structure (e.g., individual roles), group cohesion (e.g., unity of the group), group processes (e.g., group goals), and the outcomes related to both the team and its individuals.

In a review of group dynamics in a sport and physical activity environment, Widmeyer, Brawley, and Carron (2002) highlighted many important issues related to research in this area. Among these was a general suggestion that despite the prevalence of team sports that are present at all levels of competition, "most research conducted within sport has focused on individual participants ... Rarely has the team been studied either unto itself or as a factor that influences individuals, other teams, or larger organizations" (2002: 287).

Contrary to this general statement, the key study conducted by Brawley, Carron, and Widmeyer in this chapter investigated the relationships of a number of group-related variables that fall within the conceptual framework outlined above with volleyball, basketball, ice hockey, and swimming teams. These variables included group cohesion, goal clarity/ influence/participation/certainty, commitment of the team to its goals, and overall team satisfaction with its goals. To put the study into context, it is important to have a general understanding of these variables.

Cohesion, one of the most widely investigated group-related variables in sport, represents "a dynamic process which is reflected in the tendency for a group to stick together and remain united in the pursuit of its instrumental objectives and/or for the satisfaction of member affective needs" (Carron, Brawley, & Widmeyer, 1998: 213). Based on social cognitive and group dynamics theories, a conceptual model of cohesion was developed by Carron, Widmeyer, and Brawley (1985) proposing that distinctions could be made between task and social cohesion from both individual and group orientations. Consequently, their model incorporates four dimensions: (a) individual attractions to the group task (i.e., perceptions of personal involvement in task aspects of the group); (b) individual attractions to the group social (i.e., perceptions of personal involvement in social aspects of the group); (c) group integration task (i.e., perceptions of unity the group possesses regarding task aspects); and (d) group integration social (i.e., perceptions of unity the group possesses regarding social aspects). This conceptualization was utilized in the development of the *Group Environment Questionnaire* (GEQ; Carron *et al.*, 1985), a measure that has been utilized and validated in a number of sport studies (Carron *et al.*, 1998) and has also been modified for use in other settings (e.g., physical activity and exercise groups; Estabrooks & Carron, 2000).

As will be seen, the major component of this study was the examination of group goal-related variables within a team. According to Zander (1971), there are four types of goals that can be set in a group environment: (a) individuals can set goals for themselves (i.e., personal goals); (b) individuals can develop what they believe should be the goals for their team; (c) the team or organization can develop specific goals for each individual; and (d) collective goals can be set whereby the individual team members will (hopefully) come to consensus regarding what constitutes the team's goals. This latter example of setting team or collective goals represents a group process requiring, for their development, the interaction between individual members.

In general, it has been suggested that collective group goals are able to contribute to a group's productivity for five reasons (Weldon & Weingart, 1988). First, as with individual goals, providing objectives that need to be met typically results in an overall increase in effort. Second, when goals are set, groups must develop strategies and plans to meet those goals (i.e., other processes like communication are facilitated). Third, if the goal-setting process is properly conducted, groups will more closely monitor and assess their progress. Fourth, other related communications (e.g., encouragement, shows of affection) could lead to increased morale. Finally, extra-role behaviors (i.e., behaviors outside the expected role) will emerge from individuals that could improve the overall performance of the group.

Despite these suggestions of the potential positive outcomes of group goal-setting, a relatively small amount of research had been conducted prior to the publication of the present key study. As one example, a non-sport examination into the effectiveness of different types of goal-setting (Matsui, Kakuyama, & Onglatco, 1987) revealed that those who set individual goals on their own or in their group did not perform as well on a problem-solving task as those who had developed a collective goal in the group setting.

As another example, and most relevant to the present study, was research conducted by Brawley, Carron, and Widmeyer in 1992. As part of their overall research program, this earlier study sought to determine the *nature* and *prevalence* of team goals in sport. Their findings highlighted that group goals were different for practices and games. Specifically, team practice goals were typically process oriented while, comparatively, team goals for competitive matches were more directed toward the outcome (e.g., winning). One overall finding that was very interesting was that the majority of goals (approximately 70%) set by the groups were extremely vague and general and did not reflect suggested guidelines for setting effective goals (e.g., making them specific, measurable, etc.).

The key study in this chapter extends previous research by taking a comprehensive approach to not necessarily examine the *types* of goals that are set, but rather to progress our knowledge regarding important group processes and the psychological environment surrounding team goals.

## Key study

The general purpose of the study was to examine relationships between two categories of predictor variables (group goal-related variables, and group cohesiveness) and two different criterion variables (group goal satisfaction and amount of participative group goal-setting). The focus was not on the goals actually set but on the form and extent of the proposed relationships as influenced by the group.

Specifically, the first purpose was to determine whether group goal clarity, commitment, behavioral influence, and group cohesion could predict the consequence of team satisfaction with the group goals set for practice and competition. The second purpose was to determine whether there was a relationship between perceptions about participative team goal-setting and perceptions of group goal clarity, commitment, certainty, behavioral influence, and team cohesion. The third and final purpose was to consider the form and extent of the above relationships when examined at midseason and end season so that changes in the relationships over time could be explored relative to the variables assessed.

## Method

### Participants and Design

Athletes ($N = 145$) from 13 adult community and college teams were volunteer participants (mean age = 20.4 years, $SD = 2.32$). The teams were from three different municipalities and competed in the sports of volleyball, basketball, ice hockey, and swimming. Seven of the teams were made up of male athletes and six of female athletes. All teams were from highly competitive, elite leagues. The average number of seasonal competitions was 27 with at least one game per week. Team practices averaged four per week, and athlete attendance was mandatory and regular.

The study design was prospective in nature to allow for the examination of potentially different patterns of the proposed relationships that could emerge at different times in the season. Data were collected at both midseason and end season. The choice of these seasonal time points ensured that (a) group processes had already been in operation for a period of time, and (b) some stability was present in the group (i.e., in contrast to the initial instability characteristic of groups at the beginning of the season). The presence of group stability and regular member interaction provides a context for both the development of group cohesion and the implementation of group goal-setting. The prospective design was chosen to satisfy the cited research need for a more dynamic approach to the study of groups. The comparison of time points represents a step beyond "single snapshot research" characteristic of most sport group investigations.

### Measures

*Group Cohesion.* The GEQ measured cohesion. This instrument is based upon the conceptual model of the cohesion construct by Carron *et al.* (1985) outlined earlier in the Background and context section. The 18-item GEQ assesses four aspects of perceived cohesion in sport groups: individual attractions to the group-task (ATG-T), individual attractions to the group-social (ATG-S), group integration-task (GI-T), and group integration-social (GI-S). The original internal consistency values for the four reported scales are $\alpha = .75, .64, .71$, and $.72$ for ATG-T, ATG-S, GI-T, and GI-S, respectively, and this has been replicated in other studies. These aspects of cohesion are components of two orientations. The first is the orientation from which members view themselves as personally attracted to the group (i.e., individual attractions to the group) and the second is the orientation through which members view their group as a total unit (i.e., group integration). These two orientations are further subdivided into two basic perspectives or concerns: task concerns and social concerns. Thus, two dimensions of members' perceptions of their group's attractiveness for them are examined: ATG-T and ATG-S. Also, two dimensions of members' perceptions of their group's unity are examined: GI-T and GI-S. Each scale has multiple items and is scaled on a 1 to 9 Likert format. The GEQ has been recognized as a valid, reliable instrument in both sport science and in social psychology (e.g., Carron *et al.*, 1998; Dion & Evans, 1992; Widmeyer *et al.*, 1992).

*Goal-related Variables.* A number of goal-related variables were assessed. In all cases, multiple-item scales were developed, and a 1 to 9 Likert-type scale and format was adopted. The psychometric reasons for this are outlined by authors such as Guilford (1954) and Carron *et al.* (1985). All items on these goal scales were drawn from a larger pool of items developed by the investigators. The final selection of items was based upon clarity, readability, face validity, and absence of conceptual confounding as judged by the investigators. The larger sample of items was also piloted with members of two athletic teams for understanding, relevance, and applicability to sport and team. The sum of these criteria reduced the item number to that used for each scale in the questionnaire. All items from each scale were posed twice in any given assessment; once for competition goals and once for practice goals.

1   Goal clarity. This was a 5-item scale with endpoints labeled 1 = *very unclear* to 9 = *very clear*. An example of an item from the scale is "specific steps our team would take to obtain long-term team goals are . . ."
2   Goal influence. This was a 5-item scale that concerned the percentage of the time that goals evoked specific behavioral manifestations that could influence practice and competition behavior/performance. The items were based on the mechanisms that Locke and Latham (1990) suggested as the means by which goals influence behavior and subsequent performance. These mechanisms are directing attention, mobilizing energy expenditure, prolonging effort or persistence, and motivating strategy development. Examples of items and scales are as follows: Team goals "help us be systematic in our play" or "help us persist no matter what." Responses were provided as to the percentage of time that team goals influenced behavior in the manner specified by the item (i.e., 1 = *less than 10% of the time* to 9 = *more than 90% of the time*).
3   Team commitment. Using the previously described item-inclusion criteria, only two items were considered directly relevant. These two items were team commitment in practice and in competition. An example is, "How committed is the team as a whole to the team's goals for practice?" This was scaled 1 = *not at all* to 9 = *very much so*.
4   Team satisfaction. The absolute number of group goals that each athlete identified for practice and competition varied. Consequently, the satisfaction measure was based on the number of team goals stated for each of these situations. For example, if respondents listed one goal for practice, they then rated their perception of the team's satisfaction with that goal. If respondents listed four team goals, they gave four team satisfaction ratings, and a mean was taken as most representative of their responses for practice. Athletes rated how satisfied their team was on a Likert-type scale ranging from 1 = *not at all satisfied* to 9 = *completely satisfied*. This procedure allows for high relevance and salience of group goals for participants while ensuring that the most representative score (i.e., the

mean) was used to reflect their perceptions of their team's satisfaction with group goals for each of practice and competition situations.

5   Participative group goal-setting. Team members were asked to rate the type and extent to which participative group goal-setting occurred on their team. A continuum of participation categories was presented ranging from the coach alone to categories involving an ever-increasing number of team members. In addition, the percentage of time that the teams spent in participative goal-setting as a whole or in part was asked with respect to both practice and competition. Percentage of time was scaled in Likert format, 1 = *10% or less* to 9 = *90% or more*, in response to such questions as, "When team goals are set for practice/competition, what percentage of the time is there participation by the team or part of the team?

6   Goals and goal certainty. Consistent with the conceptual and methodological issues previously described in the introduction, group goals were identified through open-ended questions for both practice and competition. This protocol ensured that naturally occurring, salient group goals were measured. Participants were asked to respond with respect to the team goals they believed their team had. They were only asked to provide goals they believed their team as a whole tried to accomplish. Up to five goals could be listed. Each team member's belief about the certainty his or her team had about reaching the team goals was also assessed. The method of obtaining a most representative value for team certainty of team goals based upon open-ended responses was the same as that described above for team satisfaction with team goals.

## Procedure

This published study by the authors represents part of a larger program of research designed to examine the phenomenology of goals set by groups (Brawley *et al.*, 1992). In this study, two control features were employed. First, to ensure that all athletes were responding with the same type of construct in mind, a definition of goals was provided. The reason for this is that goals can be defined in numerous ways, ranging from performance definitions (Locke & Latham, 1990) to emotional definitions (Hyland, 1988). The definition provided was as follows:

> Goals are usually set out by ourselves or others in order to accomplish certain outcomes. Athletes set out to accomplish personal goals. As well, they often would like their team to accomplish certain goals. Goals help us keep in mind what we want to reach as athletes or as teams. Goals are guides to performance objectives, to practice objectives, to competition objectives. This applies to the individual athlete on a team as well as the whole team.

Second, to ensure the relevance and salience of group goals, the investigators asked participants whether they agreed or disagreed with the definition. If they agreed, they subsequently provided up to *five* goals that their team as a whole had for each practice and competition. The actual content of the team goal was not critical. What was critical was that the goal was not imposed on the team by the investigators and that the team goal had relevance and salience as perceived by that team member. There was no disagreement from any team athletes with the definition provided. Questions concerning clarity, commitment, influence, certainty, and satisfaction with team goals for both practice and competition asked athletes to respond with their salient self-stated goals in mind.

Consistent with the prospective design and the need to provide a more dynamic view of the hypothesized relationships, the questionnaire was administered twice – at midseason (Time 1) and at end season (Time 2). While the length of the season varied depending on the sport, the same relative administration time point was employed. In every instance, the time between assessments was an interval of 6 to 10 weeks. In addition, administration occurred immediately following practice at midweek by trained testers. Testing at competitions was avoided to minimize situational responses.

All participants were assured of the confidentiality of their responses, and all leaders/coaches gave permission for the volunteer testing without requiring that their athletes participate in the study. The mean volunteer compliance for athletes on each team at the initial assessment was 85%. At the second assessment, however, two teams declined participation due to their focus on a key point of competition near the end of their season. This reduced the sample size from $N = 145$ at midseason assessment to $N = 104$ at the end season assessment. For those teams remaining in the study ($N = 11$), the mean compliance of volunteers for the second assessment was 83% of athletes for each team. Therefore, each team complying with both assessments had a majority of their athletes represented.

## Results

One of the purposes of this investigation was to examine whether the form and extent of the relationships between predictor and criterion variables changed or was maintained over time. The form of the relationship refers to whether the same pattern of predictor variables successfully predicts the criterion variable. The extent refers to the magnitude of each variable contributing to the prediction of the criterion. At present, little is known about the form and extent of relationships between group goal satisfaction and its predictors – cohesion and group goal-related variables. The state of our group knowledge in sport is such that we do not want to overlook information that might offer clues about the relationships that exist between these variables for different situational contexts (i.e., practice and competition) at different points in time (i.e., midseason and end season).

Given that more omnibus tests such as canonical correlation would not afford the opportunity for an examination of these form and extent questions, the chosen data analysis procedure was multiple regression. Canonical correlation, while simultaneously correlating the entire set of predictor variables with the entire set of criterion variables, reveals little about the unique pattern of relationships that might exist for each situational context or time. Instead, it provides opportunity to test whether the same pattern of multivariate relationship exists in the variables across situations and time. However, if the changing nature of group development and socialization processes that are ongoing in small groups are considered, it is quite conceivable that those variables that might predict group goal satisfaction at one point in time may not carry the same weight in predicting at a later point in time. It may be more realistic to expect various *dimensions* of multivariable concepts such as cohesion or various moderators of group goals to be related to group goal satisfaction, than it would be to expect the identical pattern of the exact same predictors across both situations and time. Therefore, it was concluded that the separate analyses for each situation (i.e., practice, competition) and each time point (i.e., midseason and end season) was a data analysis strategy that allowed for the examination of proposed relationships without ignoring potentially valuable information.

## Internal Consistency of Measures

Internal consistency analyses were performed on all the goal-related and cohesion variables with the exception of *satisfaction* and *goal certainty*. These variables could not be subjected to these analyses because of the different number and type of goals that had been originally stated by each participant. As a consequence, only mean scores can be reported for each participant. As a result, every athlete had only one score that best represented his or her satisfaction with the self-stated team goals for practice. This also applied for competition.

For similar reasons, internal consistency analyses were also not applicable for goal certainty. The internal consistency values for all other measures are summarized as follows: For the GEQ at both midseason and end season, ATG-S was $r = .63$, ATG-T was $r = .73$, GI-T was $r = .78$, and GI-S was $r = .78$. These values are almost identical to those found in other published studies using the GEQ with teams of this type. The internal consistency values for the remaining scales at practice and competition for both midseason and end season ranged between the two $rs$ reported. For team goal influence ($N$ items $= 5$), the values for $r$ were between .87 and .92; for team goal clarity ($N$ items $= 5$), $r$ was stable at .85; and for team goal commitment ($N$ items $= 2$), r was between .55 and .65. These analyses were performed on the total number of participants available for both midseason and end season ($N = 118$). Recall that members of one individual and one team sport declined to participate at end season. Thus, internal consistency was calculated only on the volunteers compliant with the *entire* study so that instrument reliability could legitimately be considered at each time point as well as across time. All scales were internally consistent (reliable) at two different points in the playing season. Therefore, the instruments in the study were considered to have a degree of face validity reasonable for conducting a preliminary study.

Given that two teams declined to participate in the end season assessment, a reasonable question is whether selective mortality influenced the results for this time point. To check on this, multiple regressions were computed with the midseason data (a) using the total sample and (b) with the two dropout teams removed. The resulting regression results were virtually identical. Also, neither of the dropout teams represented the extremes of performance, arguing against selective attrition for performance-related reasons. Thus selective mortality did not appear to be a problem that would bias multiple regression results and responses from all participants that participated at midseason and end season were used in the analyses that follow.

## Prediction of Team Satisfaction

The prediction of athletes' perceptions of the team's satisfaction with achieving team goals for both practice and competition was accomplished by entering the four cohesion scores (i.e., ATG-T, ATG-S, GI-T, GI-S) plus goal clarity, goal influence, goal commitment, and goal certainty in a backward multiple hierarchical regression equation predicting team satisfaction with team goals. Tables 8.1 and 8.2 illustrate the results. Beta weights for each predictor variable were excluded for brevity as no a priori weighting or order was proposed in this exploratory study. However, it should be noted that all variables reported in models in the tables were significant contributors to the prediction of the criterion variable of team satisfaction ($p < .05$).

*Team Satisfaction with Team Goals for Competition*. Table 8.1 shows the results for competition. Cohesion appears to be the most *common* predictor of the athletes' perceptions of the team's satisfaction with team goals for *competition* at both mid and end season. At end

**Table 8.1** Prediction of team satisfaction with team goals for competition

| Time | Model | DF | R | $R^2adj$ | p |
|------|-------|-----|-----|----------|------|
| Midseason | TS = GI-T + C | 4,141 | .63 | .38 | .0001 |
| End season | TS = I + GI-S + CL | 3,101 | .54 | .27 | .0001 |

Note: TS = team satisfaction; I = team goal influence; GI-T = group integration-task; GI-S = group integration-social; CL = team goal clarity; and C = team goal certainty

**Table 8.2** Prediction of team satisfaction with team goals for practice

| Time | Model | DF | R | $R^2adj$ | P |
|------|-------|-----|-----|----------|------|
| Midseason | TS = I + GI-T | 2, 143 | .47 | .21 | .0001 |
| End season | TS = ATG-T + TCT | 2, 85 | .41 | .15 | .0004 |

Note: TS = team satisfaction; ATG-T = individual attractions to the group-task; TCT = team commitment; I = team goal influence; and GI-T = group integration-task

season, however, goal influence (I), the first entry in the equation, was the strongest predictor of team satisfaction with team goals. This model supports the notion that greater group unity (GI-S) and influence of team goals (e.g., increased effort, focused attention) are related to perceptions of satisfaction with the team's goals for competition.

Table 8.2 provides a summary of the prediction of the athletes' perceptions of their team's satisfaction with their goals for practice. At midseason, goal influence was a strong predictor of perceived team satisfaction. This seems understandable for practice because using drills, practicing strategy, focusing athletes' attention, and expending energy (i.e., mechanisms associated with goal-setting) are often what coaches emphasize as steps to reach team goals for practice. In turn, the practice behaviors directed by mechanisms are related to accomplishable and clear subgoals toward some particular aspect of improvement for competition.

Once again, at end season, an aspect of cohesion (ATG-T) predicted team satisfaction with team goals. Team commitment to team goals explained additional variance beyond that contributed by cohesion. This may be partly a function of the time in the season when athletes were sampled. As the season ends, teams may reaffirm their commitment to some of their team goals.

*Relationships Between Participative Goal Setting, Cohesion, and Goal-Related Variables.* One objective of the study was to determine whether the degree of participation in group goal-setting was in any way related to goal-related variables. The actual degree of participation as measured by a behavioral count of targeted instances of participation in group goal-setting was not possible in this field study. However, like other group measures (e.g., team attributions; Brawley *et al.*, 1992), it is the perception of the amount of team participation by the athlete that is most important. Part of the specific objective stated above was also to determine whether there would be significant differences between group members who perceived a high degree of group participation in group goal-setting and those holding a perception of little group participation in goal-setting.

To examine both aspects of this objective, three steps were involved. First, an extreme-groups analysis was used to obtain groups of athletes who clearly differed in the perceptions of the amount of time their team spent in participative group goal-setting. The idea behind the use of the extreme groups is that these team members are most likely to view the group in a consistent manner and thus would exhibit similarly patterned responses about cohesion and about group goals if these variables are related to perceptions of participative group goal-setting. Should a relationship *not* be evident, no further analysis would be necessary. If athletes who are most extreme in the perceptions do not show the effect, it probably does not occur. Second, the statistical procedure employed was discriminant function analysis because an examination of the relationships described above and a post hoc analysis of the variables discriminating the groups can be conducted with the procedure.

Third, it was assumed that the most common situation in which teams engage in participative group goal-setting is competition. Anecdotal evidence from the coaches in this study partly confirmed this assumption. When questioned, the majority of coaches stated that they engaged in team meetings or discussions with key athletes about setting team goals for various competitions. Coaches stated they rarely did this for practice. Also, 50% of the athletes stated that they perceived that participation in team goal-setting for practice occurred less than half of the time. Seventy percent stated that for practice situations they perceived that the coach sets the team goals, either alone or with just one or two key athletes.

Thus, the discriminant function analysis was performed to analyze the variables discriminating those athletes varying in their perceptions of the amount of participative group goal-setting that occurred on their team for *competition*. This was done for the data collected at both midseason and end season.

Athletes were divided into extreme groups that comprised an approximate upper 30% (i.e., perceived participative group goal-setting occurred more than 90% of the time for competition) and lower 30% (i.e., perceived participative group goal-setting occurred less than 50–60% of the time for competition) of responses to a question about the percentage of time spent participating in team goal-setting. The frequency distribution of responses to the amount of time spent was skewed slightly towards the upper end of the scale. Thus, some teams are perceived as group goal-setting for most competitions, whereas others are perceived as doing this for only one half of the competitions. A $t$ test was conducted to determine whether groups did differ significantly on this perception, and this was confirmed at *both* assessment times ($p < .01$). The groups to be examined were truly different in their perceptions of time spent in team goal-setting for competition (midseason, $M_{high} = 9$ vs. $M_{low} = 3.5$; end season, $M_{high} = 9$ vs. $M_{low} = 2.9$, where $1 = 10\%$ *or less* and $9 = 90\%$ *or more*). Participative goal-setting was operationally defined as occurring if athletes perceived that either part or all of the team worked together to set their goals for competition.

A check on the representation of athletes from each team to extreme groups was made. No single team was over- or underrepresented because two to four athletes from each of the various teams were observed in each extreme group. Tables 8.3 and 8.4 illustrate the means of those variables discriminating high and low extreme groups. As can be seen in Table 8.3, team goal clarity and the group integration-social aspect of cohesion successfully discriminated 68% of the athletes in these extreme groups at midseason, Wilks's lambda = .83, $\chi^2(2, 100) = 18.76, p < .0001$.

Thus, perceived team goal clarity and a social aspect of group cohesion were both characteristic differences between athletes extreme in the amount of team participation they perceived as occurring in the setting of group goals for competition at midseason. As the means in Table 8.3 reflect, for athletes who perceived less team participation in setting team goals for competition, both clarity of those goals and the sense of social cohesion was less, By contrast, when greater participation in setting team goals was perceived, both the clarity of team goals and the perception of cohesion were significantly higher. Independent post hoc analyses (i.e., univariate $F$s) of other goal-related and cohesion variables reflected the same

**Table 8.3** Discriminating athletes' extreme in perceived participative goal-setting at midseason

| Groups | Variables discriminating | | | | |
| | Goal clarity | | GI-S | | |
| | M | SD | M | SD |
| --- | --- | --- | --- | --- |
| Low participation | 33.81 | 6.67 | 27.02 | 5.90 |
| High participation | 37.82 | 4.86 | 30.16 | 4.24 |

*Note:* participation refers to the degree of participation in team goal-setting that is perceived to occur with either part and/or all of the team. Variables discriminating concern team goal clarity and an aspect of team cohesion (i.e., GI-S = group integration-social). A total of 103 participants were in the two extreme groups; 48 in low and 55 in high

**Table 8.4** Discriminating athletes' extreme in perceived participative goal-setting at end season

| Groups | Variables discriminating | | | | |
| | Goal influence | | ATG-T | | |
| | M | SD | M | SD |
| --- | --- | --- | --- | --- |
| Low participation | 37.20 | 5.38 | 26.67 | 5.46 |
| High participation | 41.83 | 3.48 | 30.41 | 5.23 |

*Note:* participation refers to the degree of participation in team goal-setting that is perceived to occur with either part and/or all of the team. Variables discriminating concern the degree team goals influence behavior and an aspect of team cohesion (i.e., ATG-T = individual attractions to the group-task). A total of 59 participants were in the two extreme groups; 30 in low and 29 in high

significant tendency, although they did not add significantly more to the overall discrimination between groups (e.g., team goal influence, $M_{high}$ = 40.1 vs. $M_{low}$ = 37.0; group integration-task, $M_{high}$ = 35.0 vs. $M_{low}$ = 30.2; and team satisfaction with competition goals, $M_{high}$ = 7.9 vs. $M_{low}$ = 7.0, all $p < .01$). All these variables reflected means in the direction predicted.

Table 8.4 reflects the analysis for end season. As can be seen by inspection of the means, a goal-related variable and a cohesion variable again significantly discriminated between the two groups. At end season, the influence of team goals on behaviors such as team persistence or effort (goal influence) and the individual's attractions to the group task (ATG-T) were the primary discriminating variables that successfully classified 75% of the individuals in the two groups who were extreme in their perception of team goal-setting participation, Wilks's lambda = .76, $\chi^2(2, 56) = 15.50$, $p < .004$.

Again there are characteristic goal-related and cohesion differences reflective of individuals who believe that different amounts of participative goal-setting occur on their team. The direction of the means indicates that there is a perception of greater goal influence and group cohesion among team members who perceive their team as actively involved in participative team goal-setting. Independent post hoc analyses of other goal-related and cohesion variables also reflected the same significant tendency, although they did not add significantly to the overall discrimination between groups (e.g., team goal clarity, $M_{high}$ = 36.5

vs. $M_{low} = 33.0$; certainty, $M_{high} = 8.5$ vs. $M_{low} = 7.8$; and group integration-task, $M_{high} = 35.5$ vs. $M_{low} = 31.5$, all $p < .01$).

## Discussion

Both the results of the multiple regression and discriminant function analyses support the general hypothesis that group goal-related variables are indeed related to psychological consequences of perceived team goal-setting. In both analyses results indicated that the group variable of cohesion is (a) related to the psychological consequence of team satisfaction with group goals and (b) greater among those individuals who perceive that their team engages in group goal-setting for competition.

In addition the variables most consistently related (i.e., over time) to group satisfaction with group goals for both practice and competition were (a) the perception that group goals influenced group behavior (i.e., goal task influence by directing attention, motivating energy expenditure or strategy development, and prolonging effort or persistence) and (b) the perception that the team was cohesive in some respect. It is suggested that degree of satisfaction with team goals may be partly associated with the feedback obtained when athletes perceive how much their goals influence the different aspects of team-related behavior. For example, team athletes who perceive that a team goal for practice consistently encourages increased effort and focuses attention on drills designed to achieve the team goal (e.g., in basketball, shifting successfully from a field goal or rebound to a full court press) may perceive team satisfaction with practice goals. This may occur for conditions in which there is feedback that more of the drills have been correctly completed and that the goal itself is being reached, team effort is high and team attention is focused. Thus, it is suggested that the perception of team satisfaction with team goals is, in part, a function of athletes logically drawing on behavioral-influence information which suggests that the team is successfully moving toward its goals.

However, the perception of team goal influence alone may be insufficient to encourage team satisfaction. Another psychological condition that also might need to be present is the extent of perceived team cohesion (i.e., group integration and/or individual attractions to the group). That is, the perceptions that goals influence or fail to influence the group as a whole and the associated degree of team satisfaction with those goals might only be perceived in situations in which team cohesion is concurrently high or low. If the degree of cohesion is perceived as relatively consistent over the season, the degree to which other group goal variables are perceived as affecting one another may be correspondingly related. It seems probable that this would be a tenable hypothesis for future testing based upon the relationships observed in the present study. Whether cohesion is necessary for athletes to perceive both greater team satisfaction with team goals and greater team goal influence, or whether cohesion is a *by-product* of a relationship between group goal influence and group goal satisfaction is also a reasonable question for future investigation.

The results of the present study provide evidence that members of teams view various aspects of group endeavor in consistent, patterned ways. When groups act together, such as in the case of participating as a team in setting team goals, other psychological perceptions that describe "groupness" also occur. In the present study, this included perceptions of group goal influence or clarity and group cohesion. When groups are less involved in participative group actions such as setting team goals, the degree to which group unity and other group goal-related variables are perceived is correspondingly less (as reflected by the univariate post hoc results following the discriminant function analyses). The results suggest that the interactions that occur within a group (e.g., participative goal-setting) may encourage common perceptions about the group (e.g., common beliefs about goals, unity, and satisfaction) among individual members. These results lend some support to the suggestion that cohesion might *relate* to group variables that could affect the achievement of group goals (Austin & Bobko, 1985). Whether this group phenomenon would contribute to the pursuit of group goals and their achievement more effectively on a sport team remains to be investigated in a controlled test. However, having consensus on group goals and acting on them as a team seems more likely to occur when teams are cohesive and have common visions about satisfaction with their efforts towards those objectives.

Thus, results of the present study may have captured a dynamic perspective of group-related and goal-related perceptions suggested by Austin and Bobko (1985). The fact that group cohesion and group goal influence are common predictors at both midseason and end season provides some support for the contention (a) that group goals continue to be perceived as affecting behavior over time (goal influence) and, thus, continue to relate to satisfaction and (b) that group cohesion also continues to relate to goal satisfaction over time. As Moreland and Levine (1988) have suggested, group properties such as cohesion do not exert a static, trait-like influence on the group. Instead, aspects of cohesion change in their influence – a point highlighted by the present results. This finding is consistent with the conceptual model of cohesion that serves as the basis for the GEQ (Carron *et al.*, 1985). Essential to the idea that cohesion is a dynamic process is the notion that multiple dimensions of cohesion bind members to their group but not necessarily the same aspects of cohesion work for every member or for every group (Brawley, 1990). Although the specific aspect of the cohesion construct changed over time, its influence on team satisfaction was maintained for both practice and competition. It is noteworthy that, although group members' perceptions of cohesion change with time, it is still cohesion that is consistently related to team satisfaction, and there is not a change in this general relationship. Finally, it should be noted that the reliable prediction of group satisfaction with goals by various aspects of cohesion confirms and extends results of other studies regarding cohesion and satisfaction.

## Subsequent research and application

The methodology and results of this key study in group dynamics research highlight a number of implications and issues for sport and exercise psychology. First and foremost, it demonstrated the overall importance of group goal-setting and, more specifically, of group variables involved in the success of the group goal-setting process. Some of these variables that were related to team satisfaction with goals for both practice and competition were the group members' perceptions of whether the team's goals were *influencing* its behaviors (i.e., were the goals helping them be successful) as well as the amount of group cohesion present. In the case of the former, as the authors noted in the discussion, providing feedback regarding the achievement of team goals (an often cited recommendation for goal-setting programs) could be seen to facilitate the members' beliefs that they are making progress and consequently would be related to greater satisfaction.

With regard to cohesion, the results of this study have provided a possible future research direction that may be able to respond to Brawley's (1990) call for a greater under-standing as to *why* there is a positive cohesion-performance relationship (Carron, Colman, Wheeler, & Stevens, 2002). While only one potential piece of the puzzle, this study indicated that a higher level of cohesion may be related to better perceptions of goal influence and goal satisfaction. The authors noted that future research should determine whether (a) cohesion is *necessary* to allow for greater perceptions of goal related variables or (b) "cohesion is a by-product" (Brawley *et al.*, 1992: 258) of the goal-setting environment. It could logically be hypothesized that one potential reason cohesion is related to performance is that a more united team may be more likely to participate in group goal-setting, view their goals as being influential, and be more satisfied with the group's goals, consequently leading to increased performance.

As the importance of group goal-setting was demonstrated in this key study, a second implication has been that it has prompted subsequent research to continue to examine its use and effectiveness in sport and exercise domains. In 2002, for example, Dawson, Bray, and Widmeyer re-examined the use of the four types of goals outlined by Zander (1971) by intercollegiate athletes. Their results supported and extended previous research in that the athletes reported utilizing all four of these types of goals and that they were strongly committed to and aware of the team's collective goals. Their discussion also highlighted issues for future research and practice. One of these issues was that it will be important to keep in mind that with the vast array of goals existing in a team environment, athletes may have difficulty prioritizing or reconciling different or conflicting objectives. This could occur, for example, if an individual's goal does not fit within the team's framework or collective goal. Their suggestion was to have the coach establish clearly what the priorities are for the team.

Obviously, a delicate balance exists as there is natural interplay between individual and team goals. Burton, Naylor, and Holliday (2001) noted that both team and individual goals are important for performance enhancement and cited previous research (e.g., Jackson & Williams, 1985) predicting that the presence of team goals *without* specific goals for its individual members could lead to social loafing (i.e., "the reduction of individual effort that occurs when people are involved with group activities"; Carron *et al.*, 2005: 7).

One question that has been investigated related to the above is whether setting individual or collective goals is better for individual performance. Johnson, Ostrow, Perna, and Etzel (1997) conducted a study to examine this issue with novice bowlers. Their study initially established baseline bowling performance scores during the first two weeks of the protocol. This was followed by randomly separating participants into either an individual goal-setting group or a collective goal-setting group. Their results demonstrated that the individuals who set group goals significantly improved their performance whereas the other participants did not.

A third issue that should be raised is concerned with methodology in group dynamics research. In their summary of research in this area, Widmeyer *et al.* (2002) noted a number of pitfalls that should be avoided when examining social scientific topics in sport and exercise. The study summarized in this section provides a very good example for researchers of how to effectively proceed (i.e., avoid the pitfalls) in studying group dynamics. For example, one pitfall they noted was the failure to develop and utilize theoretical frameworks. In the current key study, its purpose and hypotheses were strongly founded in theory (e.g., Austin & Bobko, 1985; Locke & Latham, 1985) and its results and discussion provided additional information on the psychological processes related to group goal-setting and cohesion; further developing our knowledge in this area.

A second pitfall noted by Widmeyer *et al.* (2002) was the tendency for researchers to examine groups at only one point in time. Given that the development and processes of any group are constantly changing (i.e., dynamic), their suggestion was that we should be utilizing longitudinal designs. As is obvious in the case of this key study, Brawley *et al.* have adhered to this recommendation by examining their groups at both midseason and end season points of time.

A final relevant pitfall avoided by the current study was that the investigators examined the group environment from a multivariate standpoint. Widmeyer *et al.* (2002) noted that a limitation of many group dynamics studies is that they approach this area from a univariate standpoint (i.e., examining one variable in relation to another). This study recognized and predicted the complex psychological environment surrounding group goals and examined many facets including goal influence, satisfaction, clarity, etc. in addition to perceptions of cohesion. In the end, our knowledge regarding the interplay of these variables (as opposed to just the relationship between participation in a goal-setting program and satisfaction for example) is greatly enhanced and will serve to inform the practical application of this type of intervention.

Finally, another issue arising from this key study is the applied importance of individual participation when setting collective goals. In their discussion, the authors suggested that when individuals are less involved in the goal-setting process it is less likely that other group-related variables (i.e., cohesion) will be perceived as being strong. As they noted, "interactions that occur within a group (e.g., participative goal-setting) may encourage common perceptions about the group (e.g., common beliefs about goals, unity, and satisfaction) among individual members" (2002: 258). This strategy has been subsequently employed in a comprehensive team goal-setting program outlined by Widmeyer and colleagues (Widmeyer & Ducharme, 1997; Widmeyer & McGuire, 1996). Their program is based heavily on the participation of individual members culminating in the development of collective goals. This program utilizes four phases in which many of the principles of goal-setting are employed. First, athletes are educated with regard to the benefits of goal-setting and proper techniques of setting those goals.

The second phase is the time when participation from the athletes is crucial. In this phase, each athlete is initially asked to develop what he or she believes to be approximately five critical goals for the team to achieve in a set period of time (e.g., the next two weeks or next five games) based on information/statistics presented to them. The next step in this phase is to group four or five team members in a sub-group to discuss the goals they developed individually and come to consensus regarding what they believe should be the team's goals. The final step in this phase is to then have the sub-groups join together (i.e., the team as a whole), present each of their goals, and come to consensus as a team on the four or five goals they wish to pursue. The benefits of this approach is that every member of the team will have had a chance to voice their thoughts in a more comfortable environment (i.e., the sub-group) and hopefully will feel ownership over the goals that the team eventually agrees upon. The final two phases monitor and chart the progress of the team and revisits the goals that were set after the predetermined period of time (e.g., two weeks or five games) so that they can be adjusted or changed if necessary.

While there have been subsequent studies in group goal-setting conducted since the publication of this key study, a number of questions remain regarding the process and effectiveness of group goal-setting in different domains, sports, group sizes, and competitive levels, to name just a few variables. This study has provided our field of group dynamics and sport and exercise psychology as a whole with evidence of the importance of group processes surrounding goal-setting and is a solid template from which to develop research protocols in the future.

## Additional readings

Burton, D., Naylor, S., & Holliday, B. (2001). Goal setting in sport: Investigating the goal effectiveness paradox. In R. N. Singer, H. A. Hausenblas, & C. M. Janelle (eds), *Handbook of sport psychology* (2nd ed., pp. 497–528). New York: Wiley.

Carron, A. V., Colman, M. M., Wheeler, J., & Stevens, D. (2002). Cohesion and performance in sport: A meta-analysis. *Journal of Sport & Exercise Psychology*, 24, 168–88.

Dawson, K. A., Bray, S. R., & Widmeyer, W. N. (2002). Goal setting by intercollegiate sport teams and athletes. *Avante*, 8, 14–23.

Widmeyer, W. N., Brawley, L. R., & Carron, A. V. (2002). Group dynamics in sport. In T. Horn (ed.), *Advances in sport psychology* (pp. 285–308). Champaign, IL: Human Kinetics.

Widmeyer, W. N., & Ducharme, K. (1997). Team building through team goal-setting. *Journal of Applied Sport Psychology*, 9, 97–113.

## Study questions

1   List the four dimensions of cohesion proposed by Carron *et al.* (1985) and provide a brief explanation for each.

2   According to Weldon and Weingart (1988), why might collective goals contribute to the effectiveness of the group?

3   Describe four types of goals that could be present on interactive sport teams as outlined by Zander (1971).

4   What are the six goal-related variables examined in this key study? Briefly describe each of them.

5   Outline the pitfalls that Widmeyer *et al.* (2002) urge researchers in the social sciences to avoid.

## References

Austin, J. T., & Bobko, P. (1985). Goal-setting theory: Unexplored areas and future research needs. *Journal of Occupational Psychology*, 58, 289–308.

Brawley, L. R. (1990). Group cohesion: Status, problems, and future directions. *International Journal of Sport Psychology*, 21, 355–79.

Brawley, L. R., Carron, A. V., & Widmeyer, W. N. (1992). The nature of group goals in sport teams: A phenomenological analysis. *The Sport Psychologist*, 6, 323–33.

Burton, D., Naylor, S., & Holliday, B. (2001). Goal setting in sport: Investigating the goal effectiveness paradox. In R. N. Singer, H. A. Hausenblas, & C. M. Janelle (eds), *Handbook of sport psychology* (2nd ed., pp. 497–528). New York: Wiley.

Carron, A. V., Brawley, L. R., & Widmeyer, W. N. (1998). The measurement of cohesiveness in sport groups. In J. L. Duda (ed.), *Advances in sport and exercise psychology measurement* (pp. 213–26). Morgantown, WV: Fitness Information Technology.

Carron, A. V., Colman, M. M., Wheeler, J., & Stevens, D. (2002). Cohesion and performance in sport: A meta-analysis. *Journal of Sport & Exercise Psychology*, 24, 168–88.

Carron, A. V., Hausenblas, H. A., & Eys, M. A. (2005). *Group dynamics in sport* (3rd ed.). Morgantown, WV: Fitness Information Technology.

Carron, A. V., Widmeyer, W. N., & Brawley, L. R. (1985). The development of an instrument to assess cohesion in sport teams: *The Group Environment Questionnaire. Journal of Sport Psychology*, 7, 244–66.

Cartwright, D., & Zander, A. (1968). *Group dynamics: Research and theory.* New York: Harper & Row.

Dawson, K. A., Bray, S. R., & Widmeyer, W. N. (2002). Goal setting by intercollegiate sport teams and athletes. *Avante*, 8, 14–23.

Dion, K. L., & Evans, C. R. (1992). On cohesiveness: Reply to Keyton and other critics of the construct. *Small Group Research*, 23, 242–50.

Estabrooks, P. A., & Carron, A. V. (2000). The *Physical Activity Group Environment Questionnaire*: An instrument for the assessment of cohesion in exercise classes. *Group Dynamics: Theory, Research, and Practice*, 4, 230–43.

Guilford, J. P. (1954). *Psychometric methods* (2nd ed.). New York: McGraw-Hill.

Hyland, M. E. (1988). Motivational control theory: An integrative framework. *Journal of Personality and Social Psychology*, 55, 642–51.

Jackson, J. M., & Williams, K. D. (1985). Social loafing on difficult tasks: Working collectively can improve performance. *Journal of Personality and Social Psychology*, 49, 937–42.

Johnson, S. R., Ostrow, A. C., Perna, F. M., & Etzel, E. F. (1997). The effects of group versus individual goal-setting on bowling performance. *The Sport Psychologist*, 11, 190–200.

Locke, E. A., & Latham, G. P. (1985). The application of goal-setting to sports. *Journal of Sport Psychology*, 7, 205–22.

Locke, E. A., & Latham, G. P. (1990). *A theory of goal-setting and task performance*. Englewood Cliffs, NJ: Prentice Hall.

Matsui, T., Kakuyama, T., & Onglatco, M. L. (1987). Effects of goals and feedback on performance in groups. *Journal of Applied Psychology*, 72, 407–15.

Moreland, R. L., & Levine, J. M. (1988). Group dynamics over time: Development and socialization in small groups. In J. E. McGrath (ed.), *The social psychology of time: New perspectives* (pp. 151–81). Newbury Park, CA: Sage.

Weldon, E., & Weingart, L. R. (1988, August). *A theory of group goals and group performance*. Paper presented at the Annual Meeting of the Academy of Management, Anaheim, CA.

Widmeyer, W. N., Brawley, L. R., & Carron, A. V. (2002). Group dynamics in sport. In T. Horn (ed.), *Advances in sport psychology* (pp. 285–308). Champaign, IL: Human Kinetics.

Widmeyer, W. N., Carron, A. V., & Brawley, L. R. (1992). Group cohesion in sport and exercise. In R. Singer, M. Murphy, & L. K. Tennant (eds), *Handbook of research on sport psychology* (pp. 672–92). New York: Macmillan.

Widmeyer, W. N., & Ducharme, K. (1997). Team building through team goal-setting. *Journal of Applied Sport Psychology*, 9, 97–113.

Widmeyer, W. N., & McGuire, E. J. (1996, May). *Sport psychology for ice hockey*. Presentation to Ontario Intermediate Coaching Clinic, Waterloo, ON.

Zander, A. (1971). *Motives and goals in groups*. New York: Academic Press.

# 9

# Leadership

Curtis, J. E., Smith, R. E., & Smoll, F. L. (1979). Scrutinizing the skipper: A study of leadership behaviors in the dugout. *Journal of Applied Psychology*, 64, 391–400.

**Written in collaboration with Gareth Morgan**

## Background and context

Much of the research interest surrounding youth sports concerns the role that adults play in the process. For instance, it is apparent that coaches can have a significant influence on children through the environment they create, the attitudes and values they emphasize, the targets they establish with their athletes, as well as the behaviors they demonstrate. Thus, an appreciation of the coach's role, and its subsequent implications, has given rise to a popular area of research within sport psychology.

Most athletes gain their first sport experiences under the guidance of volunteer coaches. Although many of these coaches are knowledgeable in the technical aspects of their chosen sport, they rarely have any formal training in the processes required to create a positive psychological environment. Thus, it was during the mid-1970s to early 1980s, following a rapid growth in organized youth sports participation, that the study of coaching behaviors emerged. Essentially, acknowledging the development of this complex social system, the area of youth sport interactions attracted the interests of researchers keen to understand the impact of sport participation on athletes' psychosocial development.

Specifically, researchers became interested in what coaches do, such as the frequency with which they delivered instruction, praise, and punishment. In essence, researchers studied coaching *behaviors* and not "traits" or characteristics. Additionally, they wanted to know the psychological dimensions that underpin such behaviors, and how such observable behaviors impacted on children's perceptions of the whole sport experience. Researchers from this initial period developed hypotheses based on psychological theories developed outside of sport, such as social learning theory and psychoanalytic theory. While this integration of related theories was deemed applicable, Smith, Smoll, and other leading researchers at this time indicated that the most pertinent inquiries were likely to grow from theories and research formulated in reference to the actual phenomenon of interest, youth sport.

As a result, Smith, Smoll, and their colleagues embarked on a program of research that was guided by a mediational model of coach-athlete interactions. The basic elements of this model (Smoll, Smith, Curtis, & Hunt, 1978) are:

Coach behaviors ⟶ Athlete perception
and recall ⟶ Athletes' evaluative reactions

The model specifies that the impact of coaches' behaviors on athletes is essentially determined by the significance athletes assign to them. Thus, the way that athletes interpret the various aspects of their coaches' behaviors that they remember affects the way that they evaluate their experiences in sport. With this grounding, Smith and Smoll then sought to establish a method of gathering information on these aspects of their model.

To measure leadership behaviors, the Coach Behavior Assessment System (CBAS) was created, enabling the direct observation and coding of coaches' actions during practices and games (Smith, Smoll, & Hunt, 1977). Behavioral observation systems had been devised for use within educational settings in the 1960s. As academic interest in youth sport developed in the 1970s, so too did the emergence of several other systematic observation instruments. Ultimately, researchers developed behavioral assessment tools to accommodate the specific line of inquiry with which they were most concerned. Hence, Smith and Smoll acquired the support of Earl Hunt, a renowned cognitive psychologist, to assist in the formation of their instrument.

The 12 behavioral categories contained within the CBAS are split into two major classes of behaviors: reactive and spontaneous. *Reactive* behaviors are responses to immediately preceding athlete or team behaviors – either desirable performance, or moments of observed effort, mistakes, or misbehaviors by the athletes. *Spontaneous* behaviors are initiated by the coach and are not a response to a distinct preceding event. The spontaneous class is subdivided into game-related and game-irrelevant behaviors. Thus, application of the CBAS involves recording basic interactions between the situation and the coach's behavior.

Whereas the coaches' behaviors were relatively simple to observe and record, collecting data on players' perceptions would prove more complex. Smith, Smoll, and Curtis (1978) elected to interview children to establish their perceptions and recall of how their coach behaved, and their attitudes towards him or her and other aspects of their sport experience. Analysis of such data enabled the researchers to generate conclusions based on their mediational model.

## Key study

A controversial issue surrounding organized sports programs for children concerns how a coach's behavior affects the experience of players. For example, coaches are often accused of overemphasizing the importance of winning to the detriment of their players' enjoyment of sports. Although the public media focuses attention on this topic, little scientific evidence is available concerning the impact of coaching behaviors on children.

Studying interactions between coaches and players holds implications not only for the psychology of sport, but also for the field of leader-group relations. In fact, sports offer an excellent setting for studying the behaviors of leaders. Ilgen and Fujii (1976) stressed the importance of field studies relating group performance and morale to behavioral data on leaders. They suggested that both the greater importance of a leader's behavior to subordinates and the increased time for interactions that occur in a field setting may produce stronger relationships than what had been obtained in the laboratory.

In this study, behavioral data on Little League Baseball coaches were obtained from trained observers, players, and the coaches themselves. In addition, data were collected on won-lost records and players' attitudes toward their experience. Data were collected over two seasons, allowing a replication of the first year's results. These data also allowed a field replication of the results obtained by Ilgen and Fujii (1976) in a laboratory simulation concerning different sources of information on leader behavior.

## Method

### Participants

Coaches of youth baseball teams (i.e., Little League) in the United States were studied during the 1976 and 1977 seasons. The 1976 sample consisted of 51 male coaches who had given their permission to be observed during league games, and 542 of their players (83% of total, all male, 8–15 years of age) who were available for interviews at the close of the season. The coaches studied had from 0 to 17 years of coaching experience ($M = 6.8$, $SD = 4.3$). The 51 teams were drawn from three levels of competition separated by age: minors (8–9 years), majors (10–12 years), and seniors (13–15 years). The 1977 sample was limited to teams in the majors and seniors divisions. All 31 coaches from the leagues selected were observed, 19 of whom had been included in the 1976 sample. These coaches had from 0 to 22 years of coaching experience ($M = 8.3$, $SD = 6.4$). From these 31 teams, 325 players were interviewed at the close of the season (82% of all players).

### Procedures

The *Coaching Behavior Assessment System* (CBAS) is a data collection technique that permits the classification of coaching behaviors into 12 categories. These categories are divided between reactive behaviors (responses to good performance, mistakes, or misbehaviors) and spontaneous behaviors (self-initiated responses that may be relevant or irrelevant to the game). The organization of the 12 CBAS behaviors is presented in Table 9.1.

Research assistants (31 in 1976 and 18 in 1977) initially completed an audiovisual training sequence that taught them how to collect CBAS data as observers. In using the CBAS, observers positioned themselves behind the team bench, where the coach could be heard and seen clearly. For the entire game, the observer recorded every behavior the coach directed toward players into one of the 12 CBAS categories.

Each coach was observed for three to six games, with approximately 280 behaviors being coded during each game. A behavioral profile was formulated for each coach as follows: for each game, the frequency of each behavioral category was divided by the total number of behaviors coded for that game, yielding a proportion for each category; and the proportions for each category were then averaged across games to create the average proportion of behaviors belonging to each category. These proportions are reported as percentages.

### Player Perceptions and Attitudes

At the conclusion of each season, trained research assistants who had not participated as observers went to the home of each player and conducted a structured interview. The interview began by giving the player a description and examples of each of the 12 CBAS behavioral categories. The player was then asked to indicate how often his coach engaged in each of the 12 behaviors on a scale from 1 (*never*) to 7 (*almost always*). Later in the interview, the player answered 10 questions measured on a 7-point scale (*least favorable* to *most favorable*) about his attitudes toward his coach, team, and baseball.

Scores from the 10 attitudinal items measured during 1976 were entered into a factor analysis (Smith, Small, & Curtis, 1978), and two factors emerged reflecting players' feelings

**Table 9.1** The coaching behavior assessment system

| Behavior | Definition |
|---|---|
| | **Reactive behaviors** |
| Responses to desirable performance | |
| Reinforcement | A positive, rewarding reaction (verbal or nonverbal) to a good play or good effort |
| Nonreinforcement | Failure to respond to a good performance |
| Responses to mistakes | |
| Encouragement after a mistake | A positive, consoling reaction to a player following a mistake |
| Technical instruction after a mistake | Instructing a player how to correct a mistake he has just made |
| Punishment | A negative reaction, verbal or nonverbal, following a mistake |
| Punitive technical instruction | Technical instruction, following a mistake, that is given in a harsh or sarcastic manner |
| Ignoring a mistake | Failure to respond to a player mistake |
| Response to misbehavior | |
| Keeping control | Reactions intended to restore or maintain order among team members |
| | **Spontaneous behaviors** |
| Game related | |
| General technical instruction | Spontaneous instruction in the techniques and strategies of the sport (not following a mistake) |
| General encouragement | Spontaneous encouragement that does not follow a mistake |
| Organization | Administrative behavior that sets the stage for play by assigning duties, responsibilities, positions, etc. |
| Game irrelevant | |
| General communication | Interactions with players unrelated to the game |

toward the coach and toward the team. Based on this analysis, attitudinal criteria were developed by summing intercorrelated items into two composites: (a) attitude toward the coach – How much did you like playing for your coach? How much would you like having the same coach again next year? How much do you like your coach? How much do your parents like your coach? How much does your coach like you? How much does your coach know about baseball?; and (b) attitude toward the team – How well did the players on your team get along? How well did you like the other players on your team?

Lower bound estimates of internal consistency (Cronbach's alpha) for these two composites were .94 and .86, respectively. Based on the 1976 results, a revised set of items was chosen for use in 1977 (with attitudes toward the coach and the team measured by reduced sets of items, and a new item being added concerning how good the coach was at teaching baseball).

Team perceptions of the 12 CBAS behaviors and team attraction toward each coach and team were computed as average scores on the appropriate measures across members of each team. In aggregating data to the team level, the researchers were not trying to minimize the importance of studying the effect of coaching behavior on individual players. However, limitations inherent in this field study restricted their ability to collect data at the individual player level. That is, the speed with which coaching behaviors had to be recorded limited the observer's ability to identify and record the player toward which the behavior was directed, and many behaviors were directed toward groups of players.

## Coach Self-Perceptions

Coaches were asked to indicate how frequently they engaged in each of the 12 CBAS behaviors. These responses were made on the same 7-point scale used by the players (*never* to *almost always*).

## Data Analysis

The initial analyses investigated the extent to which coaching behaviors were stable over time, and whether observers, players, and coaches agreed on their perceptions of these behaviors. The next phase involved correlating observed behaviors and ratings of the 12 CBAS categories by players and coaches with team attitudes toward the coach and team and the won-lost record. In addition, multiple regressions were performed to determine the extent to which these criteria were related to behavioral data provided by observers, players, and coaches. The multiple correlations reported represent step-wise results in which only variables contributing significantly to the overall prediction (significant *b* weights) were entered into the analysis. Squared multiple correlations, adjusted to account for the number of cases and predictors (Theil, 1971), are also reported.

## **Results**

### Behavioral Data

*Means*. Data presented in Table 9.2 indicate that the behaviors most frequently observed across all coaches during both years were general technical instruction, general encouragement, and reinforcement. The least frequently observed behaviors were keeping control, punishment, and punitive technical instruction, each accounting for no more than 2% of total game behaviors. The mean profiles of coaching behaviors provided by players and coaches were similar to each other across both years. Both coaches and players perceived coaches as engaging in punishment, punitive technical instruction, nonreinforcement, and ignoring mistakes less often than other behavior. Means for these four behaviors typically fell below 3.6 on a 7-point scale compared to means above 4.1 for other behaviors.

*Consistency*. Table 9.2 also presents correlations between 1976 and 1977 observed player-perceived, and self-rated behavioral data for the 19 coaches who were studied during both years. Significant correlations were obtained on seven of the 12 observed categories and were largest for punitive behaviors and general encouragement. Fewer significant correlations occurred between 1976 and 1977 scores on player-perceived and self-rated coaching behaviors, and these correlations occurred primarily for punitive behaviors. Thus, although there was some consistency in the frequency of observed behaviors across years, players and coaches were most aware of this consistency in punitive behaviors.

*Intersource Agreement*. Correlations representing intersource agreement on each of the 12 behaviors among observers, players, and coaches are presented in Table 9.3. During 1976 there was agreement on six of the 12 behavioral categories in the data provided by observers and players. These categories involved primarily reinforcement and reactions to mistakes.

**Table 9.2** Means for observed, player-perceived, and self-rated behaviors and correlations between 1976 and 1977: results for coaches appearing in both samples

| Behavior | Observed | | | Player perceived | | | Self-rated | | |
|---|---|---|---|---|---|---|---|---|---|
| | M | | | M | | | M | | |
| | 1976 (51) | 1977 (31) | r (19) | 1976 (51) | 1977 (31) | r (19) | 1976 (50) | 1977 (30) | r (19) |
| Reinforcement | 17.1 | 23.7 | .36 | 5.31 | 5.53 | .26 | 6.56 | 6.07 | .14 |
| Nonreinforcement | 4.2 | 3.1 | .50* | 2.71 | 2.65 | −.19 | 1.96 | 1.93 | .52* |
| Encouragement after mistakes | 3.1 | 3.9 | .40* | 5.24 | 5.56 | .44* | 5.82 | 5.10 | .32 |
| Technical instruction after mistakes | 4.2 | 3.3 | .50* | 5.32 | 4.91 | .35 | 5.90 | 6.23 | .42* |
| Punishment | 1.8 | 1.6 | .64** | 2.51 | 2.29 | .76** | 3.00 | 3.53 | .46* |
| Punitive technical instruction | 1.0 | .8 | .68** | 2.71 | 2.41 | .65** | 4.09 | 3.60 | .58** |
| Ignoring mistakes | 3.7 | 1.7 | .09 | 2.89 | 2.80 | .23 | 3.28 | 2.77 | −.16 |
| Keeping control | 1.7 | 1.3 | .37 | 5.37 | 5.11 | −.02 | 5.78 | 5.50 | .27 |
| General technical instruction | 27.4 | 22.7 | .44* | 5.33 | 4.84 | .11 | 6.02 | 5.50 | −.14 |
| General encouragement | 21.3 | 30.8 | .73** | 5.67 | 6.04 | .38 | 6.46 | 4.93 | .37 |
| Organization | 8.4 | 4.8 | .32 | 5.63 | 5.71 | .14 | 5.90 | 5.70 | .33 |
| General communication | 6.1 | 2.8 | .11 | 4.68 | 4.32 | .35 | 4.74 | 4.17 | .09 |

*Note*: means for observed behaviors represent percentages, whereas means for player-perceived and self-rated behaviors represent responses on a 7-point scale. Numbers in parentheses are *ns*
* p′.05
** p′.01

During 1977, however, this agreement was limited primarily to punitive behaviors. With the exception of punishment, there was little agreement between perceptions of their own behavior by coaches and the data provided by observers and players.

## Relationships With Criteria

*Attitude Toward the Coach*. Correlations of the team's attitude toward the coach with observed behaviors, team perceptions, and self-ratings by the coach on the 12 CBAS categories are presented for both samples in Table 9.4. Adjusted $R^2$ values indicated that the largest percentage of variance in team attitude toward the coach was related to team perceptions of behavior, especially during 1977 (76%). During 1977, correlations for team perceptions of all but two CBAS categories achieved significance. Among observer data, keeping control correlated negatively with attitudes toward the coach during both years. Although significant relationships were also obtained for observed general communication during both years, the direction of the relationship differed from one year to the next. Inspection of scatterplots indicated that the 1976 result was accounted for entirely by two coaches in the youngest league with extreme scores on general communication. Little relationship was obtained for coach self-ratings during either year.

*Attitude Toward the Team*. Table 9.5 presents correlations of intra-team attraction with the

**Table 9.3** Correlations among observers', coaches', and players' behavioral data

| Behavior | Observers and players | | Observers and coaches | | Players and coaches | |
|---|---|---|---|---|---|---|
| | 1976 (51) | 1977 (31) | 1976 (50) | 1977 (30) | 1976 (50) | 1977 (30) |
| Reinforcement | .38** | .29 | .19 | .13 | −.04 | .00 |
| Nonreinforcement | .14 | .12 | .21 | .02 | .20 | .13 |
| Encouragement after mistakes | .37** | −.07 | .01 | .35* | .23 | .13 |
| Technical instruction after mistakes | .31* | .03 | .19 | .01 | .06 | .18 |
| Punishment | .54** | .59** | .45** | .17 | .26* | .53** |
| Punitive technical instruction | .45** | .46** | .13 | .27 | .06 | .25 |
| Ignoring mistakes | .06 | .28 | −.02 | −.08 | .23 | .23 |
| Keeping control | −.08 | −.06 | −.02 | .05 | .20 | .28 |
| General technical instruction | −.03 | −.30* | .05 | .21 | .01 | −.05 |
| General encouragement | .05 | .21 | .03 | .12 | .09 | .09 |
| Organization | −.11 | −.06 | −.07 | −.07 | .22 | .13 |
| General communication | .26* | .26 | .10 | −.03 | .14 | .31* |

Note: numbers in parentheses are ns
* $p' .05$
** $p' .01$

**Table 9.4** Correlations of behavioral categories with attitude toward the coach

| Behavior | Observed behavior | | Team perceptions | | Coach self-rating | |
|---|---|---|---|---|---|---|
| | 1976 (51) | 1977 (31) | 1976 (51) | 1977 (31) | 1976 (50) | 1977 (30) |
| Reinforcement | .20 | .05 | .17 | .43** | .00 | .13 |
| Nonreinforcement | .09 | .05 | −.07 | −.48** | .01 | .19 |
| Encouragement after mistakes | .08 | −.13 | .33* | .68** | .13 | .20 |
| Technical instruction after mistakes | .08 | .10 | .31* | .41** | −.06 | .03 |
| Punishment | −.02 | −.26 | −.27 | −.64[a]** | −.02 | −.14 |
| Punitive technical instruction | −.10 | −.21 | −.40[a]** | −.61** | −.20 | .05 |
| Ignoring mistakes | .01 | .18 | .16 | −.25 | −.19 | .05 |
| Keeping control | −.31* | −.33[a]* | .21 | .16 | −.02 | −.07 |
| General technical instruction | .16 | −.27 | .42[a]** | .52** | −.02 | .30 |
| General encouragement | −.11 | .22 | .39** | .64[a]** | −.14 | .02 |
| Organization | .12 | −.08 | .28* | .70[a]** | .05 | .02 |
| General communication | −.47[a]** | .32[a]* | −.03 | .47** | .29[a]* | .19 |
| R | .47** | .46* | .54** | .89** | .29* | |
| Adjusted $R^2$ | .22 | .16 | .30 | .76 | .08 | |

Note: numbers in parentheses are ns
[a] This category was entered into the multiple regression analysis
* $p' .05$
** $p' .01$

**Table 9.5** Correlations of behavioral categories with attitudes toward the team

| Behavior | Observed behavior | | Team perceptions | | Coach self-rating | |
|---|---|---|---|---|---|---|
| | 1976 (51) | 1977 (31) | 1976 (51) | 1977 (31) | 1976 (50) | 1977 (30) |
| Reinforcement | .30* | .08 | .17 | .44** | −.02 | .14 |
| Nonreinforcement | .07 | −.05 | −.10 | −.47** | −.02 | −.08 |
| Encouragement after mistakes | .07 | −.29 | .04 | .69ª** | .01 | .15 |
| Technical instruction after mistakes | .07 | −.27 | .12 | .21 | .07 | −.07 |
| Punishment | .04 | −.34* | −.23 | −.54** | −.08 | −.12 |
| Punitive technical instruction | −.14 | −.44ª** | −.33* | −.45** | −.26 | −.10 |
| Ignoring mistakes | .03 | .07 | −.08 | .01ª | −.02 | .00 |
| Keeping control | −.23* | −.59ª** | .15 | .12* | −.04 | −.29 |
| General technical instruction | .01 | −.09 | .15 | .37* | −.02 | .37ª* |
| General encouragement | −.09 | .26ª | .43ª** | .55ª** | −.11 | −.06 |
| Organization | .15 | −.31* | .07 | .46** | .08 | −.02 |
| General communication | −.43ª** | .44ª** | −.12 | .58ª** | .05 | .15 |
| R | | .43** | .85** | .43** | .90** | | .37* |
| Adjusted $R^2$ | | .18 | .68 | .18 | .77 | | .14 |

Note: numbers in parentheses are *ns*
ª This category was entered into the multiple regression analysis
* p′ .05
** p′ .01

behavioral data on coaches for both samples. These results were similar to those presented for team attitude toward the coach. That is, significant correlations were obtained for player ratings of most CBAS categories during 1977. The 1976 results, however, were not as strong. Among observed behaviors, the correlations for keeping control and general communication with intrateam attraction were almost identical to those obtained with team attitude toward the coach. During 1977, however, additional negative relationships were obtained for punitive behaviors and organization. Adjusted $R^2$ values indicated that during 1977, substantial variance in intra-team attraction was related to both observed behaviors and team perceptions (68% and 77%, respectively). Results for coach self-ratings were generally weak.

*Team Performance.* Correlations of the team's won-lost record with behavioral data for both samples are presented in Table 9.6. Coaches of losing teams in the 1977 sample were observed engaging in proportionately more reactions to player mistakes and misbehaviors than were winning coaches. As seen by their players, coaches of losing teams were more punitive toward mistakes, whereas coaches of winning teams were more reinforcing and engaged in more spontaneous behaviors. Adjusted $R^2$ values indicated that slightly more variance in won-lost records was related to team perceptions than to observed behavior. Again, correlations for coach self-ratings were weak.

Moderate similarities in the correlations of behavioral data both with won-lost records and team attitudes suggested a possible relationship among these criteria. As is apparent in Table 9.7, there was a modest relationship between the won-lost record and team attitudes toward the coach in the 1976 sample, but stronger relationships were evident in the 1977 results. When the 1976 sample was separated into divisions, the won-lost record was correlated with team attitude toward the coach in the older major and senior divisions, but not in the

**Table 9.6** Correlations of behavioral categories with the won-lost record

| Behavior | Observed behavior | | Team perceptions | | Coach self-rating | |
|---|---|---|---|---|---|---|
| | 1976 (51) | 1977 (31) | 1976 (51) | 1977 (31) | 1976 (50) | 1977 (30) |
| Reinforcement | .08 | −.01 | .44[a]** | .18 | .15 | .11 |
| Nonreinforcement | .27[a]* | .07 | −.34** | −.17 | −.02 | .11 |
| Encouragement after mistakes | −.09 | −.15 | .40** | .34** | .33[a]** | .20 |
| Technical instruction after mistakes | −.14 | −.31[a]* | .29* | .14 | .17 | .02 |
| Punishment | −.35[a]** | −.37* | −.42[a]** | −.53[a]** | −.32* | −.30 |
| Punitive technical instruction | −.20 | −.32* | −.31* | −.45** | .19 | −.30 |
| Ignoring mistakes | −.08[a] | −.32* | −.08 | −.12 | −.04 | .04 |
| Keeping control | −.01 | −.42[a]** | .08 | .09 | .07 | −.04 |
| General technical instruction | .06 | −.19 | .18 | .20 | .11 | .16 |
| General encouragement | −.11 | .38* | .36** | .35* | .02 | −.11 |
| Organization | .02 | −.24 | .20 | .37* | .02 | −.01 |
| General communication | .06 | .16 | .09 | .51[a]** | .07 | .14 |
| R | .51** | .52* | .52** | .63** | .33** | |
| Adjusted $R^2$ | .26 | .22 | .27 | .35 | .11 | |

*Note:* numbers in parentheses are *n*s
[a] This category was entered into the multiple regression analysis
* p´.05
** p´.01

**Table 9.7** Correlations of the won-lost record with attitudes toward the coach and team

| Group | Coach | Team |
|---|---|---|
| 1976 sample[a] | .26* | .15 |
| Minors[b] | .15 | .07 |
| Majors and seniors[c] | .40* | .28 |
| 1977 sample[d] | .50** | .59** |

[a] n = 51; [b] n = 23; [c] n = 28; [d] n = 31
* p´.05; **p´.01

minors. Although relationships among criteria differed across divisions in the 1976 sample, few differences occurred across divisions in relationships between behavioral data and the criteria.

## Discussion

The data reported in this study demonstrated relationships between data on coaching behaviors and team performance and morale, and also identified which aspects of a coach's behavior were most salient to the criteria studied. The findings revealed that the strongest agreement on assessments of coaching behavior among observers, players, and coaches concerned punitive behaviors. Although punishment and punitive technical instruction accounted for only 3% of the coaching behavior observed, players seemed especially sensitive to punitiveness in their perceptions of a coach. Agreement on other behaviors among the three sources of behavioral data was weak and inconsistent. These relationships between coaching behaviors and team perceptions represent the first link in determining how a coach affects team morale.

The second link in the mediational model predicted that team attitudes toward the coach would be more highly related to perceptions of his behavior than to his actual behavior. Assuming that the data provided by observers is the best approximation of actual coaching behavior, this prediction was supported and replicated. In both samples, team perceptions of most behavioral categories were related to attitudes toward the coach, while observed behavior in only two CBAS categories exhibited such relationships.

On the other hand, the prediction of the mediational model in accounting for players' attitudes toward their team was not strongly supported. The direct relationships of attitudes toward the team with observed behaviors were about as strong as those with team perceptions of behavior. It was curious that observed coaching behaviors were more strongly related to attitudes toward the team than to those toward the coach during 1977, However, the observed behavior that related most strongly to intra-team attraction was keeping control, and its relative frequency may provide one index of team harmony.

Data on coaching behaviors from observers and players were also related to team performance. Although observers may have been aware of the score during a game, there was little evidence to suggest that this knowledge affected their observations. When compared to winning coaches, proportionately more of the observed behaviors of coaches on losing teams were reactions to player mistakes and misbehaviors. This result is not surprising, since players on losing teams usually make more mistakes. Furthermore, players perceived coaches of losing teams as more punitive and less supportive than winning coaches. Team performance was related to team attitudes primarily in the older age groups.

The findings reported in this study are valuable in applying the principles and techniques of behavioral science to improving organized athletic programs, especially those for children. These data suggest that some improvement in team performance or morale might result from training coaches how to interact more effectively with players, in addition to instruction on conditioning and athletic techniques. Focusing on the training of coaches, however, implies that their behavior is a causal factor in team performance and morale. Unfortunately, causality could not be tested directly in this study. An attempt to establish causal relationships between actual coaching behaviors and team performance or morale might best proceed by analyzing the reciprocal relationships among selected variables.

## Subsequent research and application

The data generated by the key study provided some initial scientific information on coach-player interactions and also a solid foundation from which Smith and Smoll developed "a set of coaching do's and don'ts" including a three-hour educational program, called Coach Effectiveness Training (CET; Smith, Smoll, & Curtis, 1979), to teach them. The CET program involves providing participants with both verbal and written behavioral guidelines that are intended to assist coaches in their attempts to communicate effectively with young athletes, to gain their respect, and to relate effectively to their parents. Emphasis is also placed on the need for sensitivity and responsiveness to individual differences among athletes. More specifically, the behavioral guidelines emphasize the desirability of increasing four specific behaviors: reinforcement (for effort as well as good performance), mistake-contingent encouragement, corrective instruction (given in an encouraging and supportive fashion), and technical instruction (spontaneous instruction in the techniques and strategies of the sport). Coaches were also urged to decrease non-reinforcement, punishment, and punitive instruction and to avoid having to use regimenting behaviors (keeping control).

Smith and Smoll's next phase of research focused on determining the effectiveness of modifying coaching behaviors through the application of CET. These studies compared trained and untrained coaches and their respective athletes on five areas of outcome variables. The researchers hypothesized the following outcomes for the CET participants: observed and perceived (by their players) behavioral differences for the coaches relative to their training; an increase in children's positive reactions to their coach, teammates, and sport experience; an increase in general self-esteem levels of the children, especially those particularly low in self-esteem; a reduction in the children's sport performance anxiety; and, seen as a combination of the preceding factors, a reduction in the likelihood that children drop out of their sport programs.

The identified variables were initially tested in two focused studies of CET (Smith *et al.*, 1979; Smoll, Smith, Barnett, & Everett, 1993), while subsequent studies replicated the original findings (e.g., Smith & Smoll, 1990; Smith, Zane, Smoll, & Coppel, 1983; Smith, Smoll, & Barnett, 1995). Essentially, Smith and Smoll's subsequent investigations have generated results that support the hypotheses made in the previous paragraph. The trained coaches in their research were better liked and were rated as better teachers by their players, their players reported that they had more fun playing sport, and a higher level of attraction among teammates was found despite the fact that their teams did not differ from controls in win-loss records. Consistent with a self-esteem enhancement model, children with low self-esteem who played for the trained coaches displayed a significant increase in general self-esteem over the course of the season; their low self-esteem counterparts in the control group did not change. Additionally, the children who played for the CET coaches revealed lower levels of performance anxiety than did the control children.

The subsequent research conducted by Smith, Smoll and colleagues has culminated in a much greater understanding of this area of study. This enhanced knowledge has led to further refinements to the original mediational model put forward by Smith, Smoll, and colleagues; suggesting that various cognitive and affective processes are involved at the mediational level (Smoll & Smith, 1989). The athletes' perceptions and reactions are likely to be affected not only by the coach's behaviors, but also by other factors, such as the athlete's age, what he or she expects of coaches (normative beliefs and expectations), and certain personality variables such as self-esteem and anxiety. In recognition of this, the basic three-element model has been expanded to reflect these factors (Smoll & Smith, 1989). The expanded model specifies a number of situational factors as well as coach and athlete characteristics that could influence coach behaviors and the perceptions and reactions of athletes to them.

The development of Smoll and Smith's (1989) mediational model, along with progress made by other researchers in the area, has only enhanced the great levels of interest in sports coaching research. A specific area of interest for sport psychology researchers has centred on the feedback provided by coaches towards high and low expectancy athletes. Using Smith *et al.*'s (1977) CBAS to code coaches' behaviors, Horn (1984) found no differences in feedback patterns to high and low expectancy junior high softball players during practice sessions. Rejeski, Darracott, and Hutslar (1979), however, identified that high expectancy children in youth basketball received more positive reinforcement whereas low expectancy children received more general instruction.

Further research has followed up on this initial work with high and low expectancy athletes participating at a more elite level. Sinclair and Vealey (1989), in their study of elite field hockey teams, established that high expectancy athletes received more overall, specific, and evaluative feedback in contrast to low expectancy athletes receiving more prescriptive feedback. In the most recent research in this area, Solomon, Striegel, Eliot, Heon, Maas, and Wayda (1996) found that coaches supplied significantly greater rates of feedback to high expectancy players within two college basketball squads.

Several more recent studies (Allen & Howe, 1998; Amorose & Horn, 2000; Amorose & Weiss, 1998; Black & Weiss, 1992) have researched coaching behaviors without the use of systematic observation. Whilst still using the categories from the CBAS, these investigations have been explicitly concerned with athletes' perceptions of their coaches' behaviors and also sought to evaluate the impact of these perceived behaviors on particular psychological outcomes related to the athletes. Summarized conclusions from these studies reveal that coaches' use of encouragement and informative feedback following athletes' performance attempts increased the athletes' perceptions of competence, success, and intrinsic motivation. In related research that examined athletes' perceptions of coaching behaviors, but that did not use the CBAS categories, Kenow and Williams (1992, 1999) found that athletes with higher anxiety and lower self-confidence and compatibility with their coach were more likely to negatively evaluate coaching behaviors.

Other researchers have opted to investigate the behaviors of coaches in studies that were less focused on psychological outcomes, but which have still generated findings that are of interest to the field of sport psychology. For instance, behavioral investigations have been conducted into coaches' in-game versus in-practice behaviors (e.g., Chaumeton & Duda, 1988; Wandzilak, Ansorge, & Potter, 1988), male versus female coaches' behaviors (e.g., Lacy & Goldston, 1990; Millard, 1996), successful versus unsuccessful coaches' behaviors (e.g., Bloom, Crompton, & Anderson, 1999; Seagrave & Ciancio, 1990), experienced versus inexperienced coaches' behaviors (e.g., Jones, Housner, & Kornspan, 1997; van der Mars, Darst, & Sariscsany, 1991), and the stability of coaches' behaviors over time (Miller, 1992; Seagrave & Ciancio, 1990).

The numerous investigations conducted into coaches' behaviors have created a vast amount of descriptive information on coaches' behaviors as well as their impact on athletes. However, while research on coaching behaviors has provided insight into the coaching process, our understanding of the thought processes underlying the behaviors is limited (Abraham & Collins, 1998). To extend this line of research, it has been suggested that direct observation techniques be supplemented with methods for exploring the thought processes of coaches (Jones et al., 1997). Therefore, recent investigations (e.g., Potrac, Jones, & Armour, 2002) have sought to gain further insights into the rationale underpinning the behaviors demonstrated by coaches.

## Additional readings

Bloom, G. A., Crompton, R., & Anderson, J. E. (1999). A systematic observation study of the teaching behaviors of an expert basketball coach. *The Sport Psychologist*, 13, 157–70.

Smith, R. E., & Smoll, F. L. (2005). Assessing psychosocial outcomes in coach training programs. In D. Hackfort, J. L. Duda, & R. Lidor (eds), *Handbook of research in applied sport psychology: International perspective* (pp. 293–316). Morgantown, WV: Fitness Information Technology.

Smith, R. E., & Smoll, F. L. (2007). The antecedents and consequences of coaching behaviors: A social-cognitive approach. In S. Jowett & D. Lavallee (eds), *Social psychology in sport*. Champaign, IL: Human Kinetics.

Smoll, F. L., & Smith, R. E. (2006). Development and implementation of coach training programs: Cognitive-behavioral principles and techniques. In J. M. Williams (ed.), *Applied sport psychology: Personal growth to peak performance* (5th ed., pp. 458–80). Boston, MA: McGraw-Hill.

Vealey, R. S. (2005). *Coaching for the inner edge*. Morgantown, WV: Fitness Information Technology.

## Study questions

1 Describe the mediational model of coach-athlete interactions as proposed by Smith, Smoll and colleagues.

2 Outline the behavioral categories of the CBAS.

3 Describe the procedures employed in the key study, including the strengths and weaknesses of the observation method.

4 How have Smith and Smoll conducted research in which the focus was to modify coaching behaviors through the application of CET and to evaluate the success of the intervention program?

5 Are the qualities of the best coaches you know similar or different to the qualities outlined in the key study?

## References

Abraham, A., & Collins, D. (1998). Examining and extending research in coach development. *Quest*, 50, 59–79.

Allen, J. B., & Howe, B. (1998). Player ability, coach feedback, and female adolescent athletes' perceived competence and satisfaction. *Journal of Sport & Exercise Psychology*, 20, 280–99.

Amorose, A. J., & Horn, T. S. (2000). Intrinsic motivation: Relationships with collegiate athletes' gender, scholarship status, and perceptions of their coaches' behavior. *Journal of Sport & Exercise Psychology*, 22, 63–84.

Amorose, A. J., & Weiss, M. R. (1998). Coaching feedback as a source of information about perceptions of ability: A developmental examination. *Journal of Sport & Exercise Psychology*, 20, 395–420.

Black, S. J., & Weiss, M. R. (1992). The relationship among perceived coaching behaviors, perceptions of ability, and motivation in competitive age-group swimmers. *Journal of Sport & Exercise Psychology*, 14, 309–25.

Bloom, G. A., Crompton, R. & Anderson, J. E. (1999). A systematic observation study of the teaching behaviors of an expert basketball coach. *The Sport Psychologist*, 13, 157–70.

Chaumeton, N. R., & Duda, J. L. (1988). Is it how you play the game or whether you win or lose? The effect of competitive level and situation on coaching behaviors. *Journal of Sport Behavior*, 11, 157–74.

Horn, T. S. (1984). Expectancy effects in the interscholastic setting: Methodological considerations. *Journal of Sport Psychology*, 6, 60–76.

Ilgen, D. R., & Fujii, D. S. (1976). An investigation of the validity of leader behavior descriptions obtained from subordinates. *Journal of Applied Psychology*, 61, 642–51.

Jones, D. F., Housner, L. D., & Kornspan, A. S. (1997). Interactive decision making and behavior of experienced and inexperienced basketball coaches during practices. *Journal of Teaching in Physical Education*, 16, 454–68.

Kenow, L. J., & Williams, J. M. (1992). Relationship between anxiety, self-confidence, and the evaluation of coaching behaviors. *The Sport Psychologist*, 6, 344–57.

Kenow, L. J., & Williams, J. M. (1999). Coach-athlete compatibility and athlete's perception and evaluative reactions to coaching behaviors. *Journal of Sport Behavior*, 22, 251–9.

Lacy, A. C., & Goldston, P. D. (1990). Behavior analysis of male and female coaches in high school girls' basketball. *Journal of Sport Behavior*, 13, 29–39.

Millard, L. (1996). Differences in coaching behaviors of male and female high school soccer coaches. *Journal of Sport Behavior*, 19, 19–31.

Miller, A. W. (1992). Systematic observation behavior similarities of various youth sport soccer coaches. *The Physical Educator*, 49, 136–43.

Potrac, P., Jones, R., & Armour, K. (2002). "It's all about getting respect": The coaching behaviors of an expert English soccer coach. *Sport, Education and Society*, 7, 183–202.

Rejeski, W., Darracott, C., & Hutslar, S. (1979). Pygmalion in youth sport: A field study. *Journal of Sport Psychology*, 1, 311–19.

Seagrave, J. O., & Ciancio, C. A. (1990). An observational study of a successful Pop Warner football coach, *Journal of Teaching in Physical Education*, 9, 294–306.

Sinclair, D. A., & Vealey, R. S. (1989). Effects of coaches' expectations and feedback on the self-perceptions of athletes. *Journal of Sport Behavior*, 12, 77–91.

Smith, R. E., & Smoll, F. L. (1990). Self-esteem and children's reactions to youth sport coaching behaviors: A field study of self-enhancement processes. *Developmental Psychology*, 26, 987–93.

Smith, R. E., Smoll, F. L., & Barnett, N. P. (1995). Reduction of children's sport performance anxiety through social support and stress-reduction training for coaches. *Journal of Applied Developmental Psychology*, 16, 125–42.

Smith, R. E., Smoll, F. L., & Curtis, B. (1978). Coaching behaviors in little league baseball. In F. L. Smoll & R. E. Smith (eds), *Psychological perspectives in youth sports* (pp. 173–201). New York: Hemisphere.

Smith, R. E., Smoll, F. L., & Curtis, B. (1979). Coaching effectiveness training: A cognitive-behavioral approach to enhancing relationship skills in youth sport coaches. *Journal of Sport Psychology*, 1, 59–75.

Smith, R. E., Smoll, F. L., & Hunt, E. B. (1977). A system for the behavioral assessment of athletic coaches. *Research Quarterly*, 48, 401–7.

Smith, R. E., Zane, N. W., Smoll, F. L, & Coppel, D. B. (1983). Behavioral assessment in youth sports: Coaching behaviors and children's attitudes. *Medicine and Science in Sport and Exercise*, 15, 208–14.

Smoll, F. L., & Smith, R. E. (1989). Leadership behaviors in sport: A theoretical model and research paradigm. *Journal of Applied Social Psychology*, 19, 1522–51.

Smoll, F. L., Smith, R. E., Curtis, B., & Hunt, E. (1978). Toward a mediational model of coach-player relationships. *Research Quarterly*, 49, 528–41.

Smoll, F. L., Smith, R. E., Barnett, N. P., & Everett, J. J. (1993). Enhancement of children's self-esteem through social support training for youth sport coaches. *Journal of Applied Psychology*, 78, 602–10.

Solomon, G. B., Striegel, D. A., Eliot, J. F., Heon, S. T., Maas, J. L., & Wayda, V.K. (1996). The self-fulfilling prophecy in college basketball: Implications for effective coaching. *Journal of Applied Sport Psychology*, 8, 44–59.

Theil, H. (1971). *Principles of econometrics*. New York: Wiley.

van der Mars, H., Darst, P., & Sariscsany, M. J. (1991). Practice behaviors of elite archers and their coaches. *Journal of Sport Behavior*, 14, 103–12.

Wandzilak, T., Ansorge, C. J., & Potter, G. (1988). Comparison between selected practice and game behaviors of youth sport soccer coaches. *Journal of Sport Behavior*, 11, 78–88.

# PART 3

## Psychological characteristics and skills

# 10

# Characteristics and skills of elite athletes

Mahoney, M.J., & Avener, M. (1977). Psychology of the elite athlete: An exploratory study. *Cognitive Therapy and Research*, 1, 135–41.

**Written in collaboration with Vikki Krane**

## Background and context

Prior to Mahoney and Avener's key study, little research existed in North America regarding whether there was an optimal psychological state for peak performance or if psychological factors and use of psychological skills might distinguish successful from less successful athletes. Although books had been written that addressed the psychological aspects of performance, such as Griffith's (1928) *Psychology of athletics*, Lawther's (1951) *Psychology of coaching*, Gallwey's (1974) *The inner game of tennis*, and Vanek and Cratty's (1970) *Psychology and the superior athlete*, they did not present a database to address these critical concerns. Without a sufficient understanding of the mental side of performance, there is no foundation for improving performance through psychological skills training. Thus, the prevalence of mental skills training with athletes did not occur until well after the key study by Mahoney and Avener.

Eastern Europe was an exception to the preceding. The iron curtain countries had a long history of enhancing elite athletes' performance through applied research and direct interventions (Salmela, 1984). Garfield and Bennet (1984) reported that the extensive investment in athletic research began early in the 1950s as part of the Soviet space program's efforts to teach cosmonauts how to control psychophysiological processes (e.g., heart rate, muscle tension) while in space. They also cited the Director of the Leipzig Institute of Sports in East Germany, Kurt Tittel, as saying that the impressive victories by East German and Soviet athletes during the 1976 Olympics were partly due to new training methods similar to psychic self-regulation.

Within North America, Williams and Straub (2006) noted that "Coaches showed interest in the psychological aspects of athletic competition even before there was a science called sport psychology" (2006: 1). They gave the example of Knute Rockne, the 1920s coach of the fighting Irish of Notre Dame who popularized the pep talk as an important part of his coaching repertoire. Athletes have also recognized the importance of the mental side of performance. In 1974, Jack Nicklaus wrote that golf is 90% mental and mental preparation is the single most critical element in peak performance. Roger Bannister, the Englishman who first broke the four-minute mile barrier, credits mental preparation for part of his success (Bannister, 1955). After winning seven gold medals in swimming at the 1976 Olympic Games, Mark Spitz was quoted as saying "At this level of physical skill, the difference between winning and losing is 99 percent psychological."

Considering the criticalness of psychological skills and factors to sport performance, it is surprising that so few North American and European researchers had globally addressed these concerns prior to this chapter's key study in which Mahoney and Avener designed a questionnaire to compare the psychological differences between two elite groups of male gymnasts. The members of one group made the 1976 Olympic team and the other qualified for the final Olympic trials but failed to make the team. In addition to the questionnaire, Mahoney and Avener interviewed the gymnasts at various stages of the competition. Their research also exemplifies the shift in the late 1970s to sport psychology reflecting a more cognitive focus, that is, a growing interest in studying athletes' thoughts and images (Williams, 1986).

We should also note that the same year as this key study, Ravizza (1977) published the research from his doctoral dissertation in which he interviewed 20 male and female athletes from 12 sports and a variety of competitive levels regarding their "greatest moment" in sport. Over 80% of the athletes reported having perceptions such as no fear of failure, no thinking of performance, total immersion in the activity, effortless performance, feeling in complete control, a time-space disorientation (usually slowed down), and a narrow focus of attention. Another exception to the limited prior research was Suinn's (1972) study in which he reported that relaxation training and visualization improved the performance of ski racers. Both Ravizza's and Mahoney and Avener's design and findings provided the prototype for future studies and laid the initial foundation for understanding the role psychological factors and skills play in sport performance.

## Key study

Although coaches and physical educators have long been interested in the relevance of psychology for their professional tasks, psychologists have been somewhat slower in their recognition of sport as a legitimate area of research focus. This discrepancy seems to be rapidly diminishing, however, and the interface between psychology and athletic competition could hardly seem more promising. Not only is sport a major aspect of contemporary society, but the athletes themselves have been repeatedly emphasizing the significance of psychology to their endeavors. To these must be added the incomparable research opportunities afforded by competitive athletics. In a discipline which spends considerable time laboring over the selection and reliability of dependent variables, the allure of straightforward physical measures is noteworthy. Speed, distance, and height constitute the primary assessment criteria in sport and offer substantial improvements over the precision of popular psychometric indices. One wonders why these two disciplines have not interacted more extensively in the last few decades.

The present study was an exploratory attempt to examine some of the psychological aspects of athletic competitors. Specifically, elite male American gymnasts were interviewed and administered a questionnaire in an effort to determine psychological factors that might be related to their athletic competence.

## Method

In accordance with the United States Olympic Committee's guidelines, selection of the U.S. men's gymnastics team required a series of qualifying meets. At the semifinals in May, 1976, the top 24 U.S. gymnasts vied for advancement to the Olympic trials. Because of a tie for 12th place, 13 gymnasts advanced to the final Olympic trials held in June, 1976. That competition was designed to select the Olympic team – consisting of six individuals and one alternate. Forty-eight hours prior to this final qualifying meet, the 13 gymnasts were given a standardized questionnaire which inquired about various aspects of their personality, self-concept, and the strategies they employed in training and competition. Representative items on the questionnaire asked participants in the study to rate their frequency of gymnastics dreams, to estimate the extent to which they used mental imagery, and to categorize the kinds of private monologues they experienced during competition. Questionnaire items employed an 11-point Likert-type scale, and participants were interviewed at various stages of the competition.

## Results

One of the 13 gymnasts submitted an un-scorable questionnaire and was, therefore, eliminated from the study. Responses of the other 12 were submitted to point bi-serial correlational analyses, using final competitive grouping as the dichotomous variable (i.e., Olympic team versus non-qualifiers). It was hypothesized that psychological differences between these two elite groups would probably be less pronounced than differences between elite and less exceptional gymnasts. Because of this consideration and the small subject sample, an arbitrary critical significance level was not employed in this study. The final competitive grouping – and therefore the selection of the Olympic team – was accomplished by summing each individual's score across 24 separate performances (six compulsory and six optional routines in both the semifinal and final meets). Scoring on each event was done by four independent judges sanctioned by the United States Gymnastics Federation (USGF). In accordance with USGF rules, an athlete's score for any given performance was determined by discarding the highest and lowest mark awarded them and then averaging the remainder. This system yielded an assessment method which sampled broadly across the six gymnastics events and the two separate competitive meets.

Correlations between specific questionnaire responses and final competitive grouping are summarized in Table 10.1. Given the relatively small sample size, the magnitude of some of the correlations is striking. The better gymnasts tended to be more self-confident ($r = .57$) and reported a higher frequency of gymnastics dreams ($r = .45$). Within those dreams, the better athletes tended to see themselves performing with a moderate degree of success ($r = .55$).

Another interesting trend was for the better gymnasts to think more about gymnastics in everyday situations ($r = .78$). They reported "talking to themselves" extensively during training and competition ($r = .62$). The Olympic team qualifiers also reported varying reliance on types of mental imagery. All the finalists said that they used imagery extensively, but the better athletes reported a higher frequency of "internal" rather than "external" images ($r = -.51$). This distinction refers to the perspective of the imagery. In external imagery, a person views himself from the perspective of an external observer (much like on a videotape) and with internal imagery the orientation is the same perspective as one has when actually performing. It is interesting to note that in prior studies of mental practice with athletes researchers have reported that the benefits of this cognitive rehearsal strategy may be moderated by the controllability of the image (Corbin, 1972). Some basketball players, for example, have reported that the ball refuses to bounce when they try to practice free throws in imagery. In the present study there did not appear to be any clear relationship between imagery control and final competitive grouping ($r = -.34$).

Attributionally, the better athletes tended to underemphasize the role of poor judging in

**Table 10.1** Correlations between grouping (Olympic team vs. nonqualifiers) and specific responses

| Item | Correlation |
| --- | --- |
| 1. Self-confidence | .57 |
| 2. Hours of training per week | .27 |
| 3. Structuredness of life-style | −.15 |
| 4. Frequency of gymnastics dreams | .45 |
| 5. Identity of dream character | −.40 |
| 6. Dream focus (practice vs. competition) | .25 |
| 7. Degree of success in dream | .55 |
| 8. Temporal character of dream (past/future) | −.29 |
| 9. Change in dream frequency prior to a meet | −.58 |
| 10. Dream realism (tragic/perfect) | −.16 |
| 11. Anxiety 1 week prior to meet | −.35 |
| 12. Anxiety 1 day prior to meet | .00 |
| 13. Anxiety 1 hour prior to meet | .49 |
| 14. Anxiety in dressing room | .54 |
| 15. Anxiety while warming up | .19 |
| 16. Anxiety while chalking up prior to worst event | .08 |
| 17. Anxiety while chalking up prior to best event | −.06 |
| 18. Anxiety while performing worst event | −.16 |
| 19. Anxiety while performing best event | −.42 |
| 20. Keeping track of personal standing during meet | −.24 |
| 21. Feeling "behind" just prior to last event | −.45 |
| 22. Feeling "ahead" just prior to last event | −.42 |
| 23. Perceived nearness to own potential | .15 |
| 24. Frequency of gymnastics thoughts | .78 |
| 25. Attention given to audience | .48 |
| 26. Attention given to current move | −.52 |
| 27. Attention given to past move | .44 |
| 28. Attention given to next move | .42 |
| 29. Frequency of thinking about mistakes during performance | .12 |
| 30. Frequency of imagery use in training and competition | .03 |
| 31. Difficulty in controlling imagery | −.34 |
| 32. Imagery perspective (internal/external) | −.51 |
| 33. Imagery clarity | .17 |
| 34. Frequency of self-talk in training and competition | .62 |
| 35. Frequency of instructional self-task | .29 |
| 36. Frequency of critical self-talk | .12 |
| 37. Frequency of complimentary self-talk | −.04 |
| 38. Combined reliance on imagery and self-talk | .00 |
| 39. Ability to concentrate | .00 |
| 40. Difficulty in recovering from a break | −.36 |
| 41. Attribution of failures to injuries | −.22 |
| 42. Attribution of failures to poor judging | .59 |
| 43. Attribution of failures to nervous tension | .17 |
| 44. Attribution of failures to poor preparation | −.31 |
| 45. Setting standards relative to personal past performance | −.30 |
| 46. Setting standards relative to peers' performance in meet | .26 |
| 47. Setting standards relative to perfection | .06 |
| 48. Frequency of self-doubts about gymnastic ability | −.08 |

| Item | Correlation |
|------|------------|
| 49. Preperformance psyching strategy (reassurance/challenge) | .11 |
| 50. Attribution of success to innate ability | .16 |
| 51. Attribution of success to training | .40 |
| 52. Attribution of success to mental attitude | −.59 |
| 53. Attribution of success to coaching | −.26 |

their past performance failures ($r = .59$). Interestingly, they did not rate mental attitude as a significantly influential factor in their success ($r = −.59$). Within an actual performance, it is noteworthy that the less successful gymnasts tended to focus more of their attention on the move they were currently executing ($r = −.52$).

One other factor which seemed to differentiate these highly competent athletes was their anxiety patterns prior to and during athletic competition. The present investigation found apparent differences in the reported anxiety patterns of the successful (those who went on to the Montreal Olympics) and unsuccessful (those who failed to make the team) gymnasts. Information on these patterns was obtained via the aforementioned questionnaire, which asked participants to rate their typical degree of anxiety at various stages of athletic competition. As shown in Figure 10.1, the relatively small differences between the two groups prior to competition were in the direction of the better athletes being more anxious. During the crucial moments of actual performance, however, this pattern reversed. It is important to note that neither group was non-anxious during the competition. Supplementing their subjective reports of anxiety level, interviews suggested that the more successful athletes tended to "use" their anxiety as a stimulant to better performance. The less successful gymnasts seemed to arouse themselves into near-panic states by self-verbalizations and images which belied self-doubts and impending tragedies.

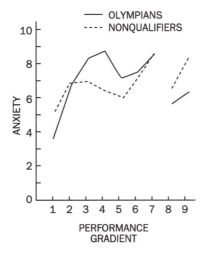

**Figure 10.1** Anxiety ratings during competitive preparation and performance. Performance gradient key: (1) 1 week prior to meet; (2) 1 day prior to meet; (3) 1 hour prior to meet; (4) dressing at meet; (5) warming up; (6) chalking up before best event; (7) chalking up before worst event; (8) performing best event; (9) performing worst event

In addition to the correlations between questionnaire items and final gymnastics performance, intercorrelations among response items were examined. These finding revealed that the more a gymnast attributed his success to training, the more hours he spent in the gym ($r = .86$). More interestingly, perhaps, was the finding that amount of training correlated with frequency of gymnastics dreams ($r = .65$). Gymnasts who tended to talk to themselves in a coaching, self-instructional format also tended to be more self-confident ($r = .93$). Doubts about one's gymnastic abilities correlated with having more tragic dreams ($r = .91$), and those individuals whose dreams were unrealistically perfect reported greater difficulty in controlling their imagery ($r = .81$). A relatively relaxed and unstructured life-style (as opposed to a regimented one) was associated with greater performance anxiety ($r = .82$).

## Discussion

This study was an exploratory attempt to delineate psychological factors which might be important to athletic performance. Due to its correlational design and restricted sample, no causal or general conclusions can be made. The main purpose of the study, however, was to identify candidates for further scrutiny and controlled experimental manipulation. This function was served and a variety of research-worthy paths were suggested. First, it would appear that sport-related dreams could offer additional information on the psychological functioning of the competitive athlete. The content and frequency of those dreams might provide supplementary information and suggestive guidelines for helping the athlete to focus on specific problem areas (e.g., self-doubts, tragic imagery, etc.). In addition, the fantasies of the athlete – both verbal and visual – may serve a dual-purpose role in athletic counseling and coaching. On the one hand, they may reflect the athlete's current attitudes and perceptions about himself and/or a given performance task. As such, they may serve important assessment functions. When systematically addressed via structured meditation exercises (Mahoney, 1974), these cognitive phenomena may also become a means to therapeutic improvement. The athlete can learn, for example, to monitor and modify specific performance-related images. Would training and practice in internal imagery improve athletic performance? This is but one of the questions suggested by the present data. Finally, the different styles of coping with anxiety prior to and during competition suggest the possibility that athletes could be trained not to "fight" anxiety but to capitalize on its energizing correlates in a manner which is conducive to improved performance. The procedures developed by "cognitive behavior therapists" may prove particularly helpful in this regard (Mahoney, 1974).

It is worth emphasizing that the present study dealt with a very small and select sample of athletes in one very restricted sphere of competition. Whether similar results will be obtained with other samples, more refined instruments, or different athletic specialties remains to be examined. However, we now seem to be entering an era which will witness greater intimacy between the disciplines of sport and psychology. Exploratory efforts such as the present one will, it is hoped, provide directions and means for furthering such interchange.

## Subsequent research and application

Mahoney and Avener's study quickly piqued the interest of many sport psychologists. It became an impetus for a long line of replication and follow-up studies examining athletes' use of psychological skills. Soon after the study, several researchers modified Mahoney and Avener's questionnaire to use it with other samples. Meyers, Cooke, Cullen, and Liles (1979) compared more and less skilled athletes on a university racquetball team. Highlen and Bennett (1979) compared the psychological characteristics of qualifiers and non-qualifiers for Canadian national wrestling teams and, in a follow-up study (1983), examined elite Canadian divers and wrestlers attempting to qualify for the Pan American Games. Across these samples, compared to the non-qualifiers, the qualifiers reported fewer self-doubts, higher confidence, better concentration, less anxiety, and more imagery use. Using an adaptation of Highlen and Bennett's inventory, Gould, Weiss, and Weinberg (1981) assessed the cognitive and behavioral strategies used by university wrestlers competing in the Big Ten Conference championship. Consistent with previous research, the placers had higher self-confidence, perceived themselves closer to their maximum potential, were better able to recover from mistakes, and mentally prepared for competition by focusing their attention.

Recognizing the need for a psychometrically stronger questionnaire, Mahoney, Gabriel, and Perkins (1987) revised the original and called the new one the *Psychological Skills Inventory for Sport* (PSIS). The PSIS, which is scored with 5-point Likert scales, contains 45-items that fall into six constructs: anxiety management, concentration, self-confidence, motivation, mental preparation, and team orientation. Its stronger psychometric properties led to greater use by future researchers. For example, in a series of studies that assessed the mental skills of university rodeo athletes (Meyers, LeUnes, & Bourgeois, 1996), equestrian athletes (Meyers, Bourgeois, LeUnes, & Murray, 1999), and telmark skiers (Trafton, Meyers, & Skelly, 1997), higher skilled athletes reported better anxiety management and concentration and higher confidence and motivation than less skilled athletes, thus corroborating Mahoney and Avener's findings.

Thomas, Murphy, and Hardy (1999) described the PSIS as what has "probably been the most popular and useful instrument for the assessment of psychological skills" (1992: 697). For example, when surveyed, US Olympic sport psychology consultants rated the PSIS as the most useful test of psychological skills available at that time (Gould, Tammen, Murphy, & May, 1989). Nevertheless, Mahoney and Avener's original questionnaire (and its PSIS revision) would not hold up to today's more stringent psychometric expectations (Murphy & Tammen, 1998).

Subsequent researchers developed other scales to assess psychological characteristics and skills. For example, Smith, Schutz, Smoll, and Ptacek's (1995) *Athletic Coping Skills Inventory* (ACSI) measures how athletes cope with competitive stress. The revised, and currently used, version has seven sub-scales: coping with adversity, peaking under pressure, goal setting/mental preparation, concentration, freedom from worry, confidence and achievement motivation, and coachability (ACSI-28; Smith *et al.* 1995). Research with the ACSI-28 showed that scores were predictive of US minor league baseball players' continued involvement in the league three years later (Smith & Christensen, 1995) and scores from a Greek translation distinguished between competitive levels of basketball players (Goudas, Theodorakis, & Karamousalidis, 1998).

Thomas *et al.* (1999) developed the *Test of Performance Strategies* (TOPS), which measured psychological strategies used in competition and in practice: relaxation, activation, goal setting, imagery, self-talk, emotional control, automaticity, attentional control (practice only), and negative thinking (competition only). Using the TOPS, they found that international athletes, compared to less elite athletes, reported using more relaxation, activation, self-talk, emotional control, goal setting, imagery, and negative thinking (Thomas *et al.*, 1999); and Jackson, Thomas, Marsh, and Smethurst (2001) found that psychological skill use, particularly controlling activation/anxiety, thoughts, and emotions, positively related to flow experiences. Lane, Harwood, Terry, and Kareageorghis (2004) tested the factorial structure of the TOPS with adolescent athletes and concluded that further scale development is necessary because the factor structure is questionable.

Thomas and colleagues (Thomas & Over, 1994; Thomas, Schlinker, & Over, 1996) emphasized the need for sport-specific assessment of mental skills, and developed and used several (e.g., the *Golf Performance Survey*, the *Ten-Pin Bowling Performance Survey*). Golfers with lower handicaps (less than 11) had better concentration, mental preparation, automaticity, and more commitment compared to high handicap golfers (greater than 20) (Thomas & Over, 1994). More skilled bowlers did more planning and evaluation and reported superior confidence in their equipment and technique, interest in improving, mental toughness, competitiveness, and consistency than the less skilled bowlers (Thomas *et al.*, 1996).

Durand-Bush, Salmela, and Green-Demers (2001) developed the *Ottawa Mental Skill Assessment Tool* (OMSAT). It tests athletes' use of relaxation, activation, stress reactions, fear control, focusing, refocusing, imagery, goal setting, mental practice, mental planning, confidence, and commitment. They compared the OMSAT responses of Canadian elite (national or international competitors) and competitive (university or provincial sport club) athletes and found that elite athletes had higher scores on focusing, refocusing, stress reactions, confidence, and commitment.

Other scales have entered the arena of psychological skills assessment, yet little research has been done with them. These include the *Psychological Performance Inventory* (Loehr, 1984) and the *Sport-Related Psychological Skills Questionnaire* (Nelson & Hardy, 1990). The findings across all the studies in this area, regardless of the instrumentation used, were very similar in that more successful athletes have better psychological skills and use them more often and more effectively than less successful athletes. Continuation of this essential area of research, first initiated by Mahoney and Avener, requires valid and reliable instrumentation. Although many advances have occurred, in 1998 Murphy and Tammen concluded their review of psychological skill measurement by noting that further psychometric development is still needed. Almost ten years later, this conclusion still is fitting.

Another way to investigate athletes' use of mental skills, quite simply, is to talk with them about it. As qualitative research has gained acceptance in sport psychology, more researchers are using this methodology to study the development and use of psychological skills in athletes. In particular, studies have focused on elite (primarily Olympic) athletes. In one of the earliest and largest studies in this genre, Orlick and Partington (1988) interviewed 75 Canadian Olympic athletes about their mental readiness and mental control during the 1984 Olympics. Athletes identified as "the best" (i.e., Olympic or world medalists) reported being highly committed, having clear goals, mentally preparing for training, setting daily goals, having well developed imagery skills, extensively using simulation training, having systematic precompetition and competition plans, systematically evaluating performances post-competition, and having strong refocusing skills. Perhaps obvious today, they concluded that "mental readiness is an extremely important factor influencing an athlete's performance" (1988: 129) and that mental readying is a learned skill.

Following up on Orlick and Partington's work, Gould and his colleagues conducted a series of qualitative investigations with members of the US Olympic wrestling team and found that good performances were associated with compliance with mental preparation plans and pre-competition routines, and being confident, focused, and optimally aroused (Gould, Eklund, & Jackson, 1992). Specifically, as outlined in the key study in Chapter 11, these athletes controlled their thoughts by blocking distractions, positive thinking, and prayer; used a narrow, immediate focus of attention; followed set competition routines; controlled arousal; and used imagery (Gould, Eklund, & Jackson, 1993). Skills that were well learned, or automatic, were most effective. Similar findings occurred in subsequent studies assessing 1990 Olympians' and national champion figure skaters' use of mental skills and coping strategies (Gould, Finch, & Jackson, 1993; Gould, Guinan, Greenleaf, Medbery, & Peterson, 1999; Greenleaf, Gould, & Dieffenbach, 2001).

Clearly, a continuing need for subsequent research is the development of theoretically grounded and psychometrically sound assessment instruments. This likely would entail revision and additional testing of currently available scales. As we become more confident with assessment instruments, we can consider new avenues of research. For example, an area where additional research is needed is in the assessment of psychological skills training programs. Intervention studies often examine changes in performance as an indication of success. It would be extremely valuable to have pre- and post-intervention assessments of psychological skill proficiency and use in addition to performance outcome measures. Fournier, Calmels, Durand-Bush, and Salmela's (2005) research provides a prototype for such research. They tested the effects of a ten-month psychological skills training program with adolescent nationally-ranked gymnasts. The athletes completed the OMSAT on multiple occasions throughout the study, providing support for the effectiveness of their intervention.

Mahoney and Avener initiated an essential area of research within applied sport psychology. Understanding psychological skill use is useful for both researchers and consultants. Following from the initial study by Mahoney and Avener, we seem to have fairly consistent findings supporting that successful and elite athletes use psychological skills. Further, these athletes are adept at controlling their anxiety, thoughts, and attention; systematically use imagery and goal setting; and develop specific routines for precompetition, competition, and refocusing. These skills, when learned and practiced, are perceived as beneficial. Future researchers and practitioners need to build upon and apply this knowledge base.


## Additional readings

Krane, V., & Williams, J. M. (2006). Psychological characteristics of peak performance. In J. M. Williams (ed.), *Applied sport psychology: Personal growth for peak performance* (5th ed.) (pp. 207–27). Palo Alto, CA: Mayfield.

Mahoney, M. J., Gabriel, T. J., & Perkins, T. S. (1987). Psychological skills and exceptional athletic performance. *The Sport Psychologist*, 1, 181–99.

Murphy, S., & Tammen, V. (1998). In search of psychological skills. In J. L. Duda (ed.), *Advances in sport and exercise psychology measurement* (pp. 195–209). Morgantown, WV: Fitness Information Technology.

Orlick, T., & Partington, J. (1988). Mental links to excellence. *The Sport Psychologist*, 2, 105–30.

Ravizza, K. (1977). Peak experiences in sport. *Journal of Humanistic Psychology*, 17, 34–40.


## Study questions

1   What psychological characteristics distinguished the Olympic qualifiers from the non-qualifiers in Mahoney and Avener's study?

2   Compare and contrast the research design and results obtained by the 1977 studies of Mahoney and Avener and Ravizza.

3   What differences existed in research and practice in North America and Eastern Europe prior to the key study?

4   Name and describe some of the scales developed to assess psychological skills.

5   What quantitative and qualitative approaches have been used to assess psychological skills?

## References

Bannister, R. (1955). *The four-minute mile*. New York: Dodd, Mead.

Corbin, C. B. (1972). Mental practice. In W. P. Morgan (ed.), *Ergogenic aids and muscular performance* (pp. 93–118). New York: Academic Press.

Durand-Bush, N., Salmela, J. H., & Green-Demers, I. (2001). *The Ottawa Mental Skills Assessment Tool* (OMSAT-3). *The Sport Psychologist*, 15, 1–19.

Fournier, J. F., Calmels, C., Durand-Bush, N., & Salmela, J. H. (2005). Effects of a season-long PST program on gymnastic performance and on psychological skill development. *International Journal of Sport and Exercise Psychology*, 3, 59–78.

Gallwey, W. T. (1974). *The inner game of tennis*. New York: Random House.

Garfield, C. A., & Bennett, H. Z. (1984). *Peak performance: Mental training techniques of the world's greatest athletes*. Los Angeles: Tarcher.

Goudas, M., Theodorakis, Y., & Karamousalidis, G. (1998). Psychological skills in basketball: Preliminary study for development of a Greek form of the *Athletic Coping Skills Inventory*-28. *Perceptual and Motor Skills*, 86, 59–65.

Gould, D., Eklund, R. C., & Jackson, S. A. (1992). 1988 U.S. Olympic wrestling excellence: I. mental preparation, precompetitive cognition, and affect. *The Sport Psychologist*, 6, 358–82.

Gould, D., Eklund, R. C., & Jackson, S. A. (1993). Coping strategies used by U.S. Olympic wrestlers. *Research Quarterly for Exercise and Sport*, 64, 83–93.

Gould, D., Finch, L. M., & Jackson, S. A. (1993). Coping strategies used by national champion figure skaters. *Research Quarterly for Exercise and Sport*, 64, 453–68.

Gould, D., Guinan, D., Greenleaf, C., Medbery, R., & Peterson, K. (1999). Factors affecting Olympic performance: perceptions of athletes and coaches from more and less successful teams. *The Sport Psychologist*, 13, 371–94.

Gould, D., Tammen, V., Murphy, S., & May, J. (1989). An examination of U.S. Olympic sport psychology consultants and the services they provide. *The Sport Psychologist*, 3, 300–12.

Gould, D., Weiss, M., & Weinberg, R. (1981). Psychological characteristics of successful and non-successful Big Ten wrestlers. *Journal of Sport Psychology*, 3, 69–81.

Greenleaf, C., Gould, D., & Dieffenbach, K. (2001). Factors influencing Olympic performance: Interviews with Atlanta and Nagano U.S. Olympians. *Journal of Applied Sport Psychology*, 13, 154–84.

Griffith, C. R. (1928) *Psychology of athletics*. New York: Scribner's.

Highlen, P. S., & Bennett, B. B. (1979). Psychological characteristics of successful and nonsuccessful elite wrestlers: An exploratory study. *Journal of Sport Psychology*, 1, 123–37.

Highlen, P. S., & Bennett, B. B. (1983). Elite divers and wrestlers: A comparison between open- and closed-skill athletes. *Journal of Sport Psychology*, 5, 390–409.

Jackson, S. A., Thomas, P. R., Marsh, H. W., & Smethurst, C. J. (2001). Relationships between flow, self-concept, psychological skills, and performance. *Journal of Applied Sport Psychology*, 13, 129–53.

Lane, A. M., Harwood, C., Terry, P. C., & Kareageorghis, C. I. (2004). Confirmatory factor analysis of the *Test of Performance Strategies* (TOPS) among adolescent athletes. *Journal of Sports Sciences*, 22, 803–12.

Lawther, J. D. (1951). *Psychology of coaching*. Englewood Cliffs, NJ: Prentice-Hall.

Loehr, J. E. (1984, March). How to overcome stress and lay at your peak all the time. *Tennis*, 66–76.

Mahoney, M. J. (1974). *Cognition and behavior modification*. Cambridge, MA: Ballinger.

Mahoney, M. J., Gabriel, T. J., & Perkins, T. S. (1987). Psychological skills and exceptional athletic performance. *The Sport Psychologist*, 1, 181–99.

Meyers, A. W., Cooke, C. J., Cullen, J., & Liles, L. (1979). Psychological aspects of athletic competitors: A replication across sports. *Cognitive Therapy and Research*, 3, 361–6.

Meyers, M. C., Bourgeois, A. E., LeUnes, A., & Murray, N. G. (1999). Mood and psychological skills of elite and sub-elite equestrian athletes. *Journal of Sport Behavior*, 22, 399–409.

Meyers, M. C., LeUnes, A., & Bourgeois, A. E. (1996). Psychological skills assessment and athletic performance in collegiate rodeo athletes. *Journal of Sport Behavior*, 19, 132–46.

Murphy, S., & Tammen, V. (1998). In search of psychological skills. In J. L. Duda (ed.), *Advances in sport and exercise psychology measurement* (pp. 195–209). Morgantown, WV: Fitness Information Technology.

Nelson, D., & Hardy, L. (1990). The development of an empirically validated tool for measuring psychological skill in sport (abstract). *Journal of Sports Sciences*, 8, 71.

Nicklaus, J. (1974). *Golf my way*. New York: Simon & Schuster.

Orlick, T., & Partington, J. (1988). Mental links to excellence. *The Sport Psychologist*, 2, 105–30.

Ravizza, K. (1977). Peak experiences in sport. *Journal of Humanistic Psychology*, 17, 34–40.

Salmela, J. H. (1984). Comparative sport psychology. In J. M. Silva, III & R. A. Weinberg (eds). *Psychological foundations of sport* (pp. 23–4). Champaign, IL: Human Kinetics.

Smith, R. E., & Christensen, D. S. (1995). Psychological skills as predictors of performance and survival in professional baseball. *Journal of Sport & Exercise Psychology*, 17, 399–415.

Smith, R. E., Schutz, R. W, Smoll, F. L., & Ptacek, J. T. (1995). Development and validation of a multidimensional measure of sport-specific psychological skills: the *Athletic Coping Skills Inventory*-28. *Journal of Sport & Exercise Psychology*, 17, 379–98.

Suinn, R. M. (1972). Behavioral rehearsal training for ski racers. *Behavior Therapy*, 3, 519.

Thomas, P. R., Murphy, S. M., & Hardy, L. (1999). *Test of Performance Strategies*: development and preliminary validation of a comprehensive measure of athletes' psychological skills. *Journal of Sports Sciences*, 17, 697–711.

Thomas, P. R., & Over, R. (1994). Psychological and psychomotor skills associated with performance in golf. *The Sport Psychologist*, 8, 73–86.

Thomas, P. R., Schlinker, P. J., & Over, R. (1996). Psychological and psychomotor skills associated with prowess at ten-pin bowling. *Journal of Sports Sciences*, 14, 255–68.

Trafton, T. A., Meyers, M. C., & Skelly, W. A. (1997). Psychological characteristics of the telemark skier. *Journal of Sport Behavior*, 20, 465–76.

Vanek, M., & Cratty, B. J. (1970). *Psychology and the superior athlete*. New York: Macmillan.

Williams, J. M. (1986). Psychological characteristics of peak performance. In J. M. Williams (ed.), *Applied sport psychology: Personal growth to peak performance* (pp. 123–32). Mountain View, CA: Mayfield Publishing Co.

Williams, J. M., & Straub, W. (2006). Sport psychology: Past, present, future. In J. M. Williams (ed.), *Applied sport psychology: Personal growth to peak performance* (pp. 1–14). Mountain View, CA: Mayfield Publishing.

# 11

# Coping with stress

Gould, D., Eklund, R. C., & Jackson, S. A. (1993). Coping strategies used by more versus less successful U.S. Olympic wrestlers. *Research Quarterly for Exercise and Sport*, 64, 83–93.

## Background and context

One of the most interesting features of competitive sport is that athletes often have to perform in stressful situations. Stress can be considered as ". . . a relationship between the person and the environment that is appraised by the person as relevant to his or her well-being and in which the person's resources are taxed or exceeded" (Folkman & Lazarus, 1985: 152). An illustration from sport would be an athlete appraising whether they are able to perform to the best of their ability in an important competition, against a talented opponent, in front of a hostile crowd. Examples of stressors (sources of stress) identified by athletes include negative significant-other relationships, expectations and pressures to perform, and negative aspects of organizational systems and culture (Gould, Jackson, & Finch, 1993; Scanlan, Stein, & Ravizza, 1991).

Coping is considered integral to the stress process and has been conceptualized from both a trait and process perspective. If coping is viewed from a trait perspective then athletes are considered to apply a relatively fixed set of coping strategies across different time points and situations. However, in the extant literature coping in sport is typically viewed as a dynamic process. In this regard coping can be defined as ". . . constantly changing cognitive and behavioral efforts to manage specific external and/or internal demands that are appraised as taxing or exceeding the resources of the person" (Lazarus & Folkman, 1984: 141). Because coping is central to the stress process athletes do not necessarily experience a negative psychological or emotional state in response to stressors. Athletes with a positive belief in their ability to cope, and in goal attainment, are proposed to interpret their competitive anxiety symptoms as facilitative to sport performance, whereas those with negative expectancies are proposed to interpret their competitive anxiety symptoms as debilitative to sport performance (Jones & Swain, 1992). Perceptions of the ability to cope with a situation may also impact physiological responses. Individuals who performed a task in front of an audience (stressor) are found to record different physiological responses depending on whether they perceive the task as a challenge or a threat (Blascovich, 1992).

Coping behaviors are typically classified into one of two categories (Lazarus & Folkman, 1984). Problem-focused coping involves taking action to change the person-stressor relationship. For example, listening to music over a pair of headphones may block out the noise of a hostile crowd that may have been a stressor for the athlete. Emotion-focused coping, on the other hand, attempts to regulate the emotional states associated with, or resulting from, the stressor. For example, an athlete who is feeling particularly anxious may engage in a breathing technique in an attempt to reduce the intensity of the anxiety. Individuals do not typically rely on one strategy but rather combine problem-focused and emotion-focused coping when dealing with a stressor (Folkman & Lazarus, 1985). Because coping is central to the stress process and it can determine athletes' psychological and emotional responses to stressors, an important task for sport psychologists is to determine what types of strategies athletes use to cope with stressors associated with competition. At the time the key study was published few studies had considered this. Exceptions were two papers by Madden and colleagues. The first collected data from 21 middle distance runners who were asked to indicate how they would cope during a slump in form. The most consistently reported strategies were seeking social support, increased effort and resolve, and problem-focused coping (Madden, Kirkby, & McDonald, 1989). In the second study 133 basketball players were asked to indicate how they would cope with 20 stressful situations that can arise during a basketball game (e.g., poor refereeing decisions, missing free throws). Participants who felt the situations were most stressful sought more social support, increased effort and resolve, and engaged in more problem-focused coping and wishful thinking compared with athletes who felt the situations were less stressful (Madden, Summers, & Brown, 1990). Although valuable, both of these studies had the limitation of only considering how athletes responded to hypothetical scenarios rather than actual sport settings.

One way in which it is possible to understand how athletes cope with the stressors associated with competition is to ask highly successful athletes what type of strategies they use. It was this approach that Gould, Eklund, and Jackson utilized in this study. Although some studies had used a qualitative approach in sport psychology (e.g., Cohn, 1990, 1991; McCaffrey & Orlick, 1989; Orlick & Partington, 1988; Scanlan, Stein, & Ravizza, 1989) this approach was not widely used in the field at the time the study was conducted.

## Key study

The study by Gould et al. comprised a series of interviews with US wrestlers who competed in the 1988 Seoul Olympics. This study was one of three papers that resulted from the interviews with the wrestlers – the other two reported the wrestlers' mental preparation and pre-competitive psychological state (Gould, Eklund, & Jackson, 1992a) and psychological state during competition (Gould, Eklund, & Jackson, 1992b). Although Gould et al. in the key study anticipated that the coping strategies outlined by athletes could be categorized as either problem-focused or emotion-focused they decided to categorize the coping strategies inductively. That is, they adopted no predetermined way in which to categorize coping strategies. This approach allowed themes and categories to emerge from the quotes that may not have been observed if the researchers had been "forced" to categorize coping strategies as either emotion or problem-focused. The researchers felt that this approach was appropriate given the paucity of previous research on the coping strategies among elite athletes which meant that they could not be sure that these two categories would adequately capture the range of coping strategies used by athletes.

## Method

### Participants

All 20 of the 1988 US Olympic wrestlers, ten freestyle and ten Greco Roman, voluntarily served as participants for this investigation. The participants ranged in age from 21 to 31 years, with a mean age of 26 ($M = 26.6$; $SD = 2.4$). On average these Olympians had six years of senior international wrestling experience ($M = 5.7$; $SD = 3.1$), although some wrestlers were participating in their first year of senior international wrestling whereas others had as many as 11 years of experience. Finally, six of the 20 Olympians (30%) won medals in the 1988 Olympic Games, including two gold, one silver, and three bronze medals.

### Instrument

An interview guide was developed for the study to facilitate and standardize the acquisition of the qualitative data. The guide was based on previous interview research with Olympic athletes by Orlick and Partington (1988), and also on issues and concerns identified by US wrestling in commissioning this investigation. Using a guide helps minimize interviewer effects by asking subjects the same questions in the same words and in the same order of presentation (Patton, 1987). The interview guide sections included the following: (1) background and readiness information; (2) Olympic goals and expectations; (3) unforeseen positive and negative events; (4) mental skills used/means of developing mental skills; (5) coping strategies employed; (6) mental preparation strategies; (7) coaching recommendations; and (8) recommendations for improving wrestler preparation.

Several pilot interviews were conducted prior to the initiation of the investigation with individuals with relevant experience (e.g., collegiate wrestlers and an elite marathon athlete knowledgeable in sport psychology). Evaluative information from the pilot interviews was used to refine the interviewer's skills. In particular, to avoid biasing participant responses, efforts were made to ensure that the interviewer adopted a neutral, impartial stance in efforts to probe answers (Backstrom & Hursch-Ceasar, 1981).

Following an extensive discussion of awareness of expectations of others and unforeseen experiences, the wrestlers were asked the question: "How did you try to cope with adversity from the negative effects of expectations and unforeseen experiences? Tell us about the coping strategies." The results presented in the key study focused on the responses to this question and subsequent probes.

### Procedures

Within six months after the 1988 Olympic Games all of the wrestlers were contacted by telephone, explained the nature of the investigation, and asked to participate. It was emphasized that all data would be kept strictly confidential and that only group or sub-group (e.g., medal vs. non-medal winning wrestlers) data would be reported. All 20 of the Olympic wrestlers agreed to participate and were sent a copy of the interview guide containing all of the interview questions. The interviews were completed within 6 to 12 months after the Olympics.

Although it would have been most desirable to have the interviews conducted closer to the time of the Olympic Games or during the competition itself, because of the salience of the Olympic Games in the lives of these athletes the authors believed that there was little decay in the athletes' recollections of the Olympic experience. Other qualitative researchers investigating the experiences of Olympians have conveyed similar beliefs (Orlick & Partington, 1988) and have noted that simple recall of this salient event stimulated physical responses such as sweating, muscular tension, increased heart rate, etc. among study participants. In addition, whereas trivial information in laboratory investigations has been found to be retained only for a short period of time, autobiographical memory, particularly of memorable events, has been found to be much more resilient (Ashcraft, 1989; Wagenaar, 1986).

All interviews were conducted by phone due to geographical limitations, were tape-recorded in their entirety, and lasted between 90 and 120 minutes. The authors noted that the interviewer is at a disadvantage in phone interviews because he or she cannot react to the nonverbal behaviors of the participant, but that this is offset by the fact that the participants cannot react to nonverbal behaviors of the interviewer. Lastly, the authors noted that the anonymity of the phone may have had the advantage of allowing the participants to freely disclose their feelings. The second author of the key study conducted all the interviews, thus providing a constant across the interviews. He was a former international wrestler and hence familiar with sport terminology and circumstances. In addition, this researcher was trained and had previous experience in qualitative research methodology.

## Data Analysis

An eight-step procedure was used to prepare and analyze the qualitative data generated in this investigation. Each of these steps is outlined and described below.

1   All 20 tape-recorded interviews were transcribed verbatim, resulting in 750 single-spaced pages of interview data.
2   Two investigators (the first and third authors of the key study) read and reread all 20 transcripts until they became completely familiar with them. Both investigators had a background in qualitative research methodology and had previously conducted qualitative research.
3   Independently, the first and third authors identified raw data themes (quotes or paraphrased quotes that captured major ideas conveyed) characterizing each wrestler's responses within the coping subsection of the interview and developed ideographic profiles or summary abstracts of each wrestler. Subsequently, through extensive discussion, consensus was obtained on a joint profile for each wrestler as well as on a list of subsection raw data themes characterizing each subject.
4   The interviewer and the two other investigators extensively discussed the ideographic profiles of each wrestler and all raw data themes until consensus was reached. Hence, agreement among all three investigators or triangular consensus (Lincoln & Guba, 1985) had to be reached on all 20 ideographic profiles and all raw data themes. When disagreements between investigators emerged, the investigators would restudy the transcripts and re-discuss points of contention. The viewpoint of the interviewer was considered especially salient in settling interpretative disputes because he conducted the interviews and had the advantage of talking directly to the study participants.
5   Sectional raw data themes characterizing each wrestler in Step 4 were compiled across wrestlers. This resulted in a listing of raw data themes within each subsection encompassing the sum total of responses by all 20 wrestlers.
6   An inductive analysis was conducted to identify common themes of greater generality from the lists of subsection raw data themes generated in Step 5 (Scanlan, Ravizza, & Stein, 1989). Second-level themes were labeled "higher order themes," while the highest level

themes (those of greatest abstraction) were labeled "general dimensions." Triangular consensus was reached at each level of analysis.

7    As an additional verification of the inductive analysis, the raw data themes, higher order themes, and general dimensions were tested by conducting a deductive analysis whereby the investigators went back to the original transcripts and verified that all themes and dimensions were represented. This process also allowed the investigators to record the number of wrestlers who cited each theme, higher order theme, and/or general dimension and to record the total number of citations.

8    Extensive scrutiny of interview transcripts was conducted to compare sub-group coping efforts. In particular, medal versus non-medal winning and Greco Roman and freestyle wrestlers were compared.

## Results

### Inductive Analysis of Coping Strategies

Figure 11.1 shows the 39 raw data themes extracted from the transcripts regarding coping strategies. Subsequently these raw data themes were organized into 11 higher order theme. Finally, these 11 higher order themes were further abstracted into four general dimensions, which were considered an accurate synopsis of coping strategies used by the US wrestlers in Seoul. The four dimensions arrived at were (a) thought control strategies, (b) task focus strategies, (c) emotional control strategies, and (d) behavioral based strategies. These dimensions are not considered mutually exclusive. Rather they were distinct, albeit inter-twined, threads of the larger fabric of coping with the circumstances associated with the Olympic Games.

Table 11.1 reports the percentage of individuals who identified each of the dimensions and higher order themes. Although some higher order themes are representative of the comments of a relatively small percentage of the total group, it was considered important to characterize all of the responses to the coping queries. Additionally, wrestlers usually identified more than one coping strategy, and as a consequence the total of numbers appearing for higher order themes within a dimension can exceed the number of wrestlers who represented that dimension. For example, in the dimension of emotional control strategies the number of wrestlers mentioning the two higher order themes (9) exceeds the number representing the overall dimension (8). The observation that wrestlers identify more than one coping strategy is consistent with the notion that coping is a dynamic, complex process.

*Thought Control Strategies.* Thought control strategies were found to be the most often reported coping strategies used. Nineteen raw data themes cited by 16 (80%) wrestlers were organized into five higher order themes, which were subsequently conceptualized into the dimension of thought control strategies through an inductive process. The dimension of thought control was considered to collectively reflect efforts by the athletes to impose order or constraint on their thought content in some general sense. Coping strategies conceptualized under this dimension were reflected in 80% of the interview transcripts. The higher order themes from which the coping dimension of thought control strategies was abstracted were labeled "blocking distractions," "perspective taking," "positive thinking," "coping thoughts," and "prayer."

The most frequently referred to higher order theme within the dimension of thought control strategies was "blocking distractions" and simply referred to efforts by the wrestlers to deny

| Raw data themes | Higher order themes | Dimension |
|---|---|---|
| Block things out – let nothing interfere<br>Put previous match out of mind<br>Focus out that have to wrestle Korean<br>Focus out referee<br>Not focusing on opponent<br>Thought stopping<br>Put mistakes out of mind<br>Not let injuries bother me | Blocking distractions | Thought control strategies |
| Rational self-talk<br>Focus on what you can control<br>Not get caught up in Olympics; treat as any other tournament<br>Put things in perspective<br>Try not to put too much pressure on self | Perspective taking | |
| Positive thinking<br>Write positive affirmations<br>Remember previous victories<br>Focus on strengths | Positive thinking | |
| Learn to cope through experience<br>Use adversity as a stimulus | Coping thoughts | |
| Prayer | Prayer | |
| Tunnel vision<br>Take it one match at a time<br>Focus on match at hand<br>Analyze mistakes then focus on next match<br>Task-focused self-talk<br>Focus on what you want to do<br>Just keep fighting | Narrow, more immediate focus | Task focus strategies |
| Concentrate on goals | Concentrate on goals | |
| Stay relaxed and control breathing<br>Try to get to the same emotional/mental state before each match<br>Walkman with music or relaxation tape | Arousal control | Emotional control strategies |
| Visualization | Visualization | |
| Surround self with "at ease" people<br>Separate self from others<br>Make alternate plans, plan ahead, budget time<br>Rest<br>Distract self with other activities | Change/control the environment | Behavioral strategies |
| Follow same routine<br>No emotional reaction – don't look upset | Follow set routine | |

**Figure 11.1**   Hierarchical development of coping strategy dimensions

**Table 11.1** Number and percentage of wrestlers ($N = 20$) providing raw data themes falling into major categories

| Coping strategy dimension/Higher order theme | Number | Percentage |
| --- | --- | --- |
| **Thought control strategies** | 16 | 80 |
| Perspective taking | 7 | 35 |
| Positive thinking | 5 | 25 |
| Coping thoughts | 2 | 10 |
| Prayer | 2 | 10 |
| **Task focus strategies** | 8 | 40 |
| Narrow, more immediate focus | 7 | 35 |
| Concentrate on goals | 1 | 5 |
| **Emotional control strategies** | 8 | 40 |
| Arousal control | 7 | 35 |
| Visualization | 2 | 10 |
| **Behavioral strategies** | 8 | 40 |
| Change/control the environment | 6 | 30 |
| Follow a set routine | 3 | 15 |

access to their consciousness of distracting, irrelevant, or irritating thoughts. This was abstracted from comments such as the following:

> I focus on having tunnel vision . . . I eliminate anything that's going to interfere with me. I don't have any side doors, I guess, for anyone to come into. I make sure that nothing interferes with me.

Similarly, this higher order theme can be evidenced in the following quotation regarding coping with injury:

> It seems that you just put it behind you. It's just like this is a three-day tournament, if you can't suck it up for three days, you shouldn't be in the sport. It's an injury sport . . . You really just don't let it bother you. You just don't let it distract you.

The second most frequently referred to higher order theme within the dimension of thought control strategies was "perspective taking." Thirty-five percent of the wrestlers made comments abstracted into this higher order theme. Perspective taking involved attempts at rational thinking to place the event within a subjectively reasonable mental framework in which the wrestler felt comfortable or in control. This higher order theme can be evidenced in the following wrestler quotation:

> A lot of times I just think about what other people have to deal with. You know, handicapped men or starving men or something like that and just kind of put it into the total perspective. Knowing that, hey, I am doing pretty good over here.

The third most frequently referred to higher order theme within the dimension of thought control strategies, mentioned by 25% of the wrestlers, was "positive thinking." Positive thinking involved the mental activity of actively attempting to view unforeseen events, distracting or negative circumstances in a positive light, or, alternatively, replacing negative thoughts with corresponding positive images. This higher order theme was reflected in comments such as the following:

> I just tried to look at most everything that happens in a positive manner. Try not to doubt yourself. Once you start doubting yourself like maybe I should have run that extra mile, or maybe I should have done this, they can take over pretty easy in a tense situation. You have to try to stay positive . . . I would say you can't overdo it positively, but you have got to stay on a pretty even keel;

and

> If you get knocked down to one knee or something, there are two ways you can interpret it. You can say "he's destroying me, making me look bad" or you can say "well he only knocked me down on my knee, he didn't score, I feel good, I feel strong, he's getting tired." I think it's always been important to really respect my opponent and be positive in my own response to myself because if you are negative, you will just talk yourself down into being nothing.

The higher order theme of "coping thoughts" within the dimension of thought control strategies was mentioned by 10% of the athletes and involved efforts to use adversity as a stimulus or placing the situation in the context of past experiences. The final higher order theme of "prayer" in this dimension was also mentioned by 10% of the wrestlers and involved the diversion of thoughts to an appeal for divine intervention, inspiration, or support.

*Task Focus Strategies*. Task focus strategies for coping as a dimension was interpreted from a total of eight raw data themes present in 40% of the interview transcripts. These eight raw data themes were then organized into two higher order themes. The higher order themes from which the coping dimension of task focus strategies was abstracted were "narrow, more immediate focus" and "concentrating on goals."

The dimension of task focus strategies was considered to reflect efforts to control thought content by the wrestlers on a very specific, limited spectrum. The most frequently referred to higher order theme (by 35% of the wrestlers) within this dimension was that of a "narrow, more immediate focus." This characterization refers to efforts to concentrate on the match at hand and very immediate process demands while ignoring the implications of past and present performance outcomes. Descriptions of coping strategies through task focus can be found in the following quotations:

> I just stayed positive and focused on putting it behind me and not thinking about it any-more . . . and then just started thinking about the next match;

and

> I just tried to focus on my individual, I do best when I prepare myself and know what I need to do individually . . . You just try to focus on your matches.

The other related higher order coping theme identified by a single wrestler related to attempts to concentrate on goals and objectives the wrestler had set for himself for the tournament and is consistent with conceptualization of this dimension with the exception that the time frame is less immediate.

*Emotional Control Strategies*. The dimension of emotional control strategies was considered to reflect wrestlers' efforts to control their feeling state or activation level. This dimension was interpreted from themes present in 40% of the interviews represented in four raw data themes. These four raw data themes were then organized into two higher order themes. The higher order themes from which the coping dimension of emotional control strategies was abstracted were "arousal control" and "visualization."

The most frequently referred to higher order theme within this dimension was that of "arousal control" through the use of relaxation, breathing control, music or relaxation tapes, and other attempts to arrive at a more optimal emotional-mental state. Thirty-five percent of the wrestlers made comments conceptualized within this higher order theme. Breathing control was the most often reported single technique used within this dimension of coping strategies (20% of the wrestlers). Visualization was also used by 10% of the wrestlers in this regard.

*Behavioral Based Strategies*. The dimension of behavioral based strategies was considered to reflect coping efforts characterized by the enactment of overt behavioral responses. The dimension of behavioral based strategies for coping was interpreted from seven raw data themes present in 40% of the interview transcripts. These seven raw data themes were then organized into two higher order themes. The higher order themes from which the coping dimension of behavioral based strategies was abstracted were "changing or controlling the environment" and "following a set routine."

The most frequently referred to higher order theme within this dimension (cited by 30% of the wrestlers) was that of "changing or controlling the environment." Behavioral strategies that the wrestlers used to change or control their environment included such strategies as surrounding self with "at ease people," separating self from others, making alternate plans to avoid dealing with irritants, and distracting self with other activities. For example, one wrestler demonstrated the use of this general strategy in the following quotation:

> A lot of times I would walk away from it. Say it was lunch time, 11:45, and I didn't feel like dealing with the crowd. I would have just gone downstairs and got a couple of cookies and a soda and then ate lunch later on when the crowd wasn't there instead of going over there. Kind of an avoidance. And then there was like just going and grabbing a buddy. "Hey [buddy], what are you doing, you know, let's listen to music, let's play cards, let's play checkers" – you know, take an outlet with something familiar to me.

Similarly, the strategy of adhering to a predetermined, familiar, ingrained behavioral routine to minimize uncertainty and focus attention was identified as useful in this regard. This coping strategy was evidenced in the specific warm-up routines that wrestlers used to prepare for matches and also in preplanned behaviors for dealing with adverse incidences such as bad calls by the referee. One wrestler described his routine for dealing with bad calls in the following way:

> I tried not to get very emotional. I didn't say anything to the referee . . . I didn't look at the coaches, I didn't make any body gestures or anything. The things I did was to breathe as deep as I could, took like three deep breaths and just looked at my opponent and just walked back to the middle. Didn't even listen to the refs. Just tried to focus them out and keep concentrating on the match.

In addition to the evidence of a particular behavioral routine, this quotation also contains elements relevant to "emotional control" and "task focus" themes. Hence, this quotation also illustrates that the coping efforts of the Olympic wrestlers were not limited to particular strategies or single approaches to dealing with a particular stressor. Rather, it can be seen that coping is a dynamic, complex process involving any number of strategies in combination.

## Coping Sub-group Comparisons

In examining interview transcripts for differences between medalists and non-medalists, it was found that the salient differences in ability to cope with adversity appeared to lay in the extent to which the individual's strategies were well practiced and internalized. The medalists seemed to have their strategies internalized to such an extent that these strategies acted as automatized buffers to adversity, that is, the medalist strategies appeared to be so well learned that the wrestler did not have to consciously engage them when faced with a potentially threatening circumstance. Rather, like a well-learned athletic skill, the coping strategy was quickly initiated without a great deal of thought. This type of automated coping response also had the advantage of buffering or minimizing the effect of aversive events because either the stress caused by the aversive event or the aversive event itself was dealt with immediately, before its negative ramifications could gain momentum. As one wrestler described this:

> Something I've always practiced is to never let anything interfere with what I'm trying to accomplish at a particular tournament. So what I try to do is if something is trying to bother me, it's an automatic effect for me to completely empty my mind and concentrate on the event coming up . . . My coping strategy is just to completely eliminate it from my mind, and I guess I'm blessed to be able to do that.

Because of the automatized buffering nature of the coping strategies of the medalists, these wrestlers seemed to perceive adversity as less threatening or even in a positive light. This was inferred not only through descriptions of coping efforts (as above) and the less frequent reference to adverse conditions but also through the lesser intensity of the references to adversity.

In contrast, the nonmedalists did not seern to have their coping strategies as well developed, practiced, or internalized and hence tended to have to consciously engage coping strategies in response to perceptions of stress or adversity. Whereas the medalists seemed to be able to maintain a relatively stable and positive emotional level because of their automatized coping strategies, nonmedalists experienced more of an emotional roller-coaster effect as a consequence of cycles of experiencing perceptions of threat followed by implementation of coping strategies. The following quotation of a nonmedalist regarding the stress of his Olympic experience illustrates this roller-coaster effect:

> I had a tape, a relaxation tape, that I would listen to, and it seemed to give me moments of relief I guess because I was able to listen to the tape . . . It got to the point where what you would try to do was not think about wrestling and get your mind on other things. But inevitably . . . you would bind up and get tight, pulse would pick-up and your palms and legs and hands or feet are sweating and you go through that thing trying to relax or trying to sleep and I would resort to my relaxation tape. I don't think I coped very well with it really.

## Problem-focused vs. Emotion-focused Coping

Because of the lack of previous research on sport coping strategy, it was deemed most appropriate to use qualitative methodology and inductive data analysis in this investigation. As an additional tool of analysis the investigative team attempted to deductively categorize the 39 coping strategy raw data themes contained in Figure 11.1 into Folkman and Lazarus's (1985) problem- or emotion-focused coping categories to investigate the hypothesis that coping strategies could be characterized as such. It was found that the qualitative data were not amenable to simple interpretation within this framework. Coping is a dynamic, complex process in which the athlete can simultaneously be striving to both manage the person/stressor environment and regulate distressing emotions. The same strategy may also be used in one instance to regulate emotions and in another to manage the environment. Hence, it is perhaps not surprising that this analysis was unsuccessful. The unsuccessful attempt to use Folkman and Lazarus's coping strategy dichotomy to interpret these data reinforces the complex nature of coping efforts.

## Discussion

The wrestlers reported that they faced a great deal of adversity throughout the Olympic Games and employed a variety of coping strategies to deal with this adversity. These included the use of (a) thought control strategies (blocking distractions, perspective taking, positive thinking, coping thoughts, and prayer), (b) task focus strategies (narrow, more immediate focus, concentrating on goals), (c) behavioral-based strategies (changing or controlling the environment, following a set routine), and (d) emotional control strategies (arousal control, visualization).

Of the coping strategies used, thought control strategies were employed by the highest percentage of wrestlers (80%), whereas task focus, emotional control, and behavioral strategies were reflected in a much smaller number of transcripts (40%). Unfortunately, reasons for this discrepancy are not readily apparent; however, it is possible that the majority of wrestlers more often experienced cognitive (as opposed to somatic) stress and more often employed cognitively-based coping strategies. This would be consistent with Burton's (1990) "match hypothesis" that coping strategies are most effective if linked to the domain in which stress is being experienced. The wrestlers may have also found cognitive strategies more effective and for that reason more wrestlers may employ them. It would be fruitful to examine these issues in future investigations.

In accordance with the observations of Compas (1987) and Folkman and Lazarus (1985), it was apparent that the coping efforts of the Olympic wrestlers were not limited to particular strategies nor single approaches to dealing with a particular stressor. Rather, the process of coping is a dynamic complex one involving any number of strategies, often in combination. These observations are also consistent with the conceptual underpinning of multimodal approaches to stress management such as the SMT (Smith, 1980; Smith & Ascough, 1985), SIT (Meichenbaum, 1977, 1985), and COPE (Anshel, 1990). Hence these stress management programs should be further examined and refined within the sporting context. For example, studies need to be conducted to determine which aspects of these multidimensional programs (e.g., physical relaxation, imagery, cognitive restructuring) are related to coping effectiveness and how these specific strategies interact with one another. Moreover, it would be useful to determine when specific components of these stress management programs are used and for what purposes.

In comparing the medalists and nonmedalists, the most important finding derived from the wrestlers' comments was in the degree of automaticity in coping strategies found in medal-winning wrestlers. Non-medal-winning wrestlers did not have their coping strategies as well learned or internalized and had to consciously engage them when faced with adversity. Lazarus and Folkman's (1984) contentions regarding stress as a transactional process between the person factors and objective environment are salient. This finding reflects the need to automatize coping strategies through long-term development and implementation, thus influencing the relationship between person factors and stress stimuli.

However, Lazarus and Folkman (1984) have argued that it is important to limit the conceptualization of coping behaviors to effortful or purposeful reactions to stress while excluding reflexive, instinctive, or automatic reactions to the environment. In the absence of such delimitation virtually all responses to the environment could qualify as coping behaviors. Compas (1987), while acknowledging that a broader conceptualization is problematic, points out that purposeful responses may become automatic with sufficient repetition. Such automatized mastery responses, while not requiring conscious control, in some degree still represent planned adaptive or coping behavior. Such well-learned, purposefully acquired skills seem relevant, even necessary, in the context of intensely competitive events such as the Olympic Games.

Although our in-depth examination of the interview transcripts suggested that coping strategy automaticity was strongly related to coping effectiveness and superior performance, other factors could account for this relationship. For example, nonmedalists might have made external attributions regarding coping whereas medalists may have retrospectively minimized adversity or difficulty in coping. Hence, although the investigative team did not believe that this was the case, the possibility of such an attributional bias cannot be ruled out. Some caution must therefore be used in interpreting the automaticity findings.

## Subsequent research and application

In response to stressors associated with sport competition athletes do use a range of coping strategies. For example, active coping/planning, increased effort and positive reappraisal were used more frequently by young golfers than other coping strategies (Gaudreau, Blondin, & Lapierre, 2002). The most frequently used coping strategies identified by 110 Norwegian and Danish Olympic athletes were acceptance, positive redefinition, and growth and active coping (Pensgaard & Duda, 2003). Members of a female soccer team participating at the World Cup reported using ten separate coping strategies (e.g., positive self-talk, family support, on-field task communication) to cope with the stressors associated with a major tournament (Holt & Hogg, 2002).

Athletes not only use coping strategies in order to deal with competition related stressors, but also to deal with injury and retirement from competition. Members of the Canadian Alpine ski team reported that they used both cognitive (e.g., keep a positive perspective) and behavioral (e.g., try alternative treatments) strategies in coping with injury and illness (Bianco, Malo, & Orlick, 1999). Data from 48 former elite-level athletes indicated that when retiring from sport a range of coping strategies were used, most frequently, acceptance, positive reinterpretation and growth, planning, active coping mental disengagement, and the seeking of social support for emotional reasons (Grove, Lavallee, & Gordon, 1997).

In support of the notion that coping is a dynamic process research has demonstrated that the type of coping strategies employed may change across the competition period

(Gaudreau *et al.*, 2002), differ according to the stressor, and whether the stressor is appraised as harmful, threatening or challenging (Anshel, Jamieson, & Raviv, 2001). Furthermore, situational factors, rather than personal disposition, best predicted the coping response in basketball players (Anshel & Kaissidis, 1997). Individual differences may however have some influence on the type of coping strategy employed. Females used higher levels of social support to cope with competition (Crocker & Graham, 1995) and more emotion-focused coping strategies to cope with injury (Johnson, 1997). Gender and goal orientations were found to be important factors in determining the coping strategies employed in a study with 69 Norwegian Olympic athletes (Pensgaard & Roberts, 2003). A task orientation was associated with more adaptive coping strategies (e.g., active coping and positive redefinition and growth). For females a high score on the ego dimension was associated with less use of active coping, planning and more use of denial. Winter Olympic athletes employed more redefinition and growth strategies than Winter Paralympic athletes (Pensgaard, Roberts & Ursin, 1999). High trait anxious individuals respond to stress using more behavioral disengagement, self-blame, humor, denial, and wishful thinking in comparison to low trait anxious individuals (Giacobbi Jr & Weinberg, 2000). Finally, in the case of athletes who had retired a strong athletic identity was positively related to the venting of emotions, mental disengagement, behavioral disengagement and reliance on denial, social support, suppression of competing activities and seeking of emotional support (Grove *et al.*, 1997).

There are a number of interesting issues that arise from the key study and the subsequent research into coping in sport. First, of particular interest was that Gould, Eklund, and Jackson chose to analyze the data using an inductive approach. There is some debate about whether or not data can ever be analyzed solely inductively in that researchers are likely to begin any study with at least some understanding of what might be found (Biddle, Markland, Gilbourne, Chatzisarantis, & Sparkes, 2001). Furthermore, if the categories are not predetermined this can lead to different categories emerging in each study making synthesis of findings from a number of studies difficult. As an illustration Gould and colleagues explored the coping strategies used by 17 senior US national champion figure skaters using an inductive approach (Gould, Finch, & Jackson, 1993). This time 13 general dimensions were identified (e.g., rational thinking and self-talk, pre-competitive mental preparation, and anxiety management) in contrast to the 4 identified by Gould, Eklund, and Jackson in the key study. Although Gould *et al.* (1993) did note there was an overlap between the majority of themes found in both studies, applying a common theoretical framework to categorize the findings makes the synthesis of findings across different studies easier.

It is also difficult to synthesize the data on coping in sport because of the range of quantitative measures used and theoretical frameworks employed. For example, coping has been assessed using a range of inventories. They include the *COPE* (e.g., Pensgaard & Roberts, 2003), *Modified-COPE* (e.g., Gaudreau *et al.*, 2002), the *Coping Strategies Inventory* (e.g., Anshel *et al.*, 2001), and the *General Coping Questionnaire* (e.g., Johnson, 1997). Examples of differing theoretical frameworks include classifying coping strategies as approach or avoidance (e.g., Anshel *et al.*, 2001), active/problem-focused or avoidance/withdrawal (Kim & Duda, 2003) or emotion- or problem-focused (e.g., Pensgaard & Duda, 2003). Of course there is no requirement that all studies should use the same theoretical framework or the same measure and indeed there are similarities between the theoretical frameworks employed and the measures used. Yet it does illustrate that building a "body of knowledge" and synthesizing the findings is challenging when different approaches are used.

Research has not only considered how athletes cope with stressors but also with the emotions that arise from those stressors. In a study with 62 golfers, Gaudreau *et al.* (2002) assessed the coping strategies employed and affect experienced before, during, and after a golf competition. They found that positive reappraisal was an effective coping strategy in enabling golfers who had not performed up to expectations to reduce the negative affect experienced. In addition they suggested that to facilitate goal attainment and a positive emotional state, athletes should engage in active coping, planning and positive reappraisal during competition but refrain from engaging in behavioral disengagement. Qualitative research with 12 elite athletes from a range of sports (e.g., golf, athletics, rugby) found that problem-focused coping (e.g., increased task related effort) accounted for 24% and emotion-focused coping (e.g., imagery) accounted for 76% of the reported strategies used to cope with the emotions experienced during competition (Uphill & Jones, 2004).

While research has typically focused on athletes' abilities to cope with negative events, understanding how athletes cope with positive events and positive emotions is also worthy of investigation. While positive events and positive emotions are common in sport, athletes report that positive emotions are associated with performance decrements (Hanin, 2000) and that sources of stress may result from positive events (Gould *et al.*, 1993). Jackson, Mayocchi, and Dover (1998) have explored this important area and reported that after winning an Olympic gold medal athletes used a range of coping strategies (e.g., cognitive restructuring, social support) to cope with the changes they experienced (e.g., loss of single-minded motivation and intensity, loss of focus, being overly focused on outcomes).

The notion that coping with positive events and positive emotions is a challenge for athletes relates to an emerging field from the stress and coping literature; that of emotion regulation. Emotion regulation refers to ". . . the processes by which individuals influence which emotions they have, when they have them, and how they experience and express these emotions" (Gross, 1998: 275). Emotion regulation is considered distinct from coping in a number of ways, in that the primary focus of coping is on decreasing negative emotional experience, and emotion regulation may include processes not traditionally considered in the coping literature such as maintaining or augmenting positive emotions (Gross, 1998). The notion of emotional regulation rather than coping with emotion may be particularly relevant to sport given that not only do athletes have to reduce or eliminate emotions that may be harmful to performance but they also want to generate emotions that may have a positive impact on performance. Even within one contest an athlete may be continuously regulating their emotions in order to maintain performance levels. For example, a rugby union hooker may want to experience some levels of anxiety and excitement to benefit from the increases in anaerobic power associated with these high-arousal emotions (Perkins, Wilson, & Kerr, 2001) but be in a calm focused state when having to throw the ball into the lineout. According to Lazarus (1999) only appraisals of harm, threat, or challenge (which leads to negative emotions) warrant the use of coping resources. Yet athletes may also want to be able to "cope" with positive emotions, such as intense excitement or happiness that may have a negative impact on sport performance (Uphill & Jones, 2004). For example, a tennis player close to his first tournament win may wish to control his feelings of excitement and happiness in case the emotion has a negative impact on attention.

## Additional readings

Biddle, S. J. H., Markland, D., Gilbourne, D., Chatzisarantis, N. L. D., & Sparkes, A. C. (2001). Research methods in sport and exercise psychology: Quantitative and qualitative issues. *Journal of Sport Sciences*, 19, 777–809.

Lane, A. M. (2004). Emotion, mood and coping in sport: Measurement issues. In D. Lavallee, J. Thatcher, & M. V. Jones (eds), *Coping and emotion in sport* (pp. 255–71). Hauppauge, NY: Nova Science Publishers.

Richards, H. (2004). Coping in sport. In D. Lavallee, J. Thatcher, & M. V. Jones (eds), *Coping and emotion in sport* (pp. 29–51). Hauppauge, NY: Nova Science Publishers.

Smith, R. E., & Smoll, F. L. (2004). Anxiety and coping in sport: Theoretical models and approaches to anxiety reduction. In T. Morris & J. Summers (eds), *Sport psychology: Theory, applications and issues* (pp. 294–321). Brisbane: Wiley.

## Study questions

1   What are the potential limitations of gathering data from interviews conducted over the phone?

2   What is the point of comparing medal-winning wrestlers with non-medal-winning wrestlers and are there any dangers in using objective outcome criteria to classify success?

3   How did Gould *et al.* explain the difference observed in the coping strategies employed by the medallists and nonmedallists?

4   What type of coping strategies do you employ and are they similar to those mentioned by the wrestlers?

5   Why might males and females differ in the coping strategies they employ?

## References

Anshel, M. H. (1990). Toward validation of a model for coping with acute stress in sport. *International Journal of Sport Psychology*, 21, 58–83.

Anshel, M. H., Jamieson, J., & Raviv, S. (2001). Cognitive appraisals and coping strategies following acute stress among skilled competitive male and female athletes. *Journal of Sport Behavior*, 24, 128–43.

Anshel, M. H., & Kaissidis, A. N. (1997). Coping style and situational appraisals as predictors of coping strategies following stressful events in sport as a function of gender and skill level. *British Journal of Psychology*, 88, 263–76.

Ashcraft, M. H. (1989). *Human memory and cognition*. Glenview, IL: Scott, Foresman.

Backstrom, C. H., & Hursch-Ceasar, G. (1981). *Conducting interviews: Survey research* (2nd ed., pp. 237–308). New York: John Wiley & Sons.

Bianco, T., Malo, S., & Orlick, T. (1999). Sport injury and illness: Elite skiers describe their experiences. *Research Quarterly for Exercise & Sport*, 70, 157–69.

Biddle, S. J. H., Markland, D., Gilbourne, D., Chatzisarantis, N. L. D., & Sparkes, A. C. (2001). Research methods in sport and exercise psychology: Quantitative and qualitative issues. *Journal of Sport Sciences*, 19, 777–809.

Blascovich, J. (1992). A biopsychosocial approach to arousal regulation. *Journal of Social and Clinical Psychology*, 11, 213–37.

Burton, D. (1990). Multimodal stress management in sport: Current status and future directions. In J. G. Jones & L. Hardy (eds), *Stress and performance in sport* (pp. 171–201). New York: John Wiley & Sons.

Cohn, P. J. (1990). An exploratory study on sources of stress and athlete burnout in youth golf. *The Sport Psychologist*, 4, 95–106.

Cohn, P. J. (1991). An exploratory study on peak performance in golf. *The Sport Psychologist*, 5, 1–14.

Compas, B. E. (1987). Coping with stress during childhood and adolescence. *Psychological Bulletin*, 101, 393–403.

Crocker, P. R. E., & Graham, T. R. (1995). Coping by competitive athletes with performance stress: Gender differences and relationships with affect. *The Sport Psychologist*, 9, 325–38.

Folkman, S., & Lazarus, R. S. (1985). If it changes it must be a process: Study of emotion and coping during three stages of a college examination. *Journal of Personality & Social Psycholog*, 48, 150–70.

Gaudreau, P., Blondin, J.-P., & Lapierre, A.-M. (2002). Athletes' coping during a competition: relationship of coping strategies with positive affect, negative affect, and performance-goal discrepancy. *Psychology of Sport & Exercise*, 3, 125–50.

Giacobbi Jr, P. R., & Weinberg, R. S. (2000). An examination of coping in sport: Individual trait anxiety differences and situational consistency. *The Sport Psychologist*, 14, 42–62.

Gould, D., Eklund, R. C., & Jackson, S. A. (1992a). 1988 U.S. Olympic wrestling excellence: I. Mental preparation, precompetitive cognition, and affect. *The Sport Psychologist*, 6, 358–82.

Gould, D., Eklund, R. C., & Jackson, S. A. (1992b). 1988 U.S. Olympic wrestling excellence II: Thoughts and affect occurring during competition. *The Sport Psychologist*, 6, 383–402.

Gould, D., Finch, L. M., & Jackson, S. A. (1993). Coping strategies used by national champion figure skaters. *Research Quarterly for Exercise & Sport*, 64, 453–68.

Gould, D., Jackson, S., & Finch, L. (1993). Sources of stress in national champion figure skaters. *Journal of Sport & Exercise Psychology*, 15, 134–59.

Gross, J. J. (1998). The emerging field of emotion regulation: An integrative review. *Review of General Psychology*, 2, 271–99.

Grove, J. R., Lavallee, D., & Gordon, S. (1997). Coping with retirement from sport: The influence of athletic identity. *Journal of Applied Sport Psychology*, 9, 191–203.

Hanin, Y. L. (2000). Successful and poor performance and emotions. In Y. L. Hanin (ed.), *Emotions in sport* (pp. 157–87). Champaign, IL: Human Kinetics.

Holt, N. L., & Hogg, J. M. (2002). Perceptions of stress and coping during preparations for the 1999 women's soccer world cup finals. *The Sport Psychologist*, 16, 251–71.

Jackson, S. A., Mayocchi, L., & Dover, J. (1998). Life after winning gold: II. Coping with the change as an Olympic gold medallist. *The Sport Psychologist*, 12, 137–55.

Johnson, U. (1997). Coping strategies among long-term injured competitive athletes. A study of 81 men and women in team and individual sports. *Scandinavian Journal of Medicine and Science in Sports*, 7, 367–72.

Jones, G., & Swain, A. (1992). Relationships between sport achievement orientation and competitive state anxiety. *The Sport Psychologist*, 6, 42–54.

Kim, M., & Duda, J. L. (2003). The coping process: Cognitive appraisals of stress, coping strategies, and coping effectiveness. *The Sport Psychologist*, 17, 406–25.

Lazarus, R.S. (1999). *Stress and emotion: A new synthesis*. London: Free Association Books.

Lazarus, R. S., & Folkman, S. (1984). *Stress, appraisal, and coping*. New York: Springer Publishing Company.

Lincoln, Y. S., & Guba, E. G. (1985). *Naturalistic inquiry*. Newbury Park, CA: Sage.

Madden, C. C., Kirkby, R. J., & McDonald, D. (1989). Coping styles of competitive middle distance runners. *International Journal of Sport Psychology*, 20, 287–96.

Madden, C. C., Summers, J. J., & Brown, D. F. (1990). The influence of perceived stress on coping with competitive basketball. *International Journal of Sport Psychology*, 21, 21–35.

McCaffrey, N., & Orlick, T. (1989). Mental factors related to excellence among top professional golfers. *International Journal of Sport Psychology*, 20, 256–78.

Meichenbaum, D. (1977). *Cognitive behavior modification: An integrative approach*. New York: Plenum.

Meichenbaum, D. (1985). *Stress inoculation training*. New York: Pergamon.

Orlick, T., & Partington, J. (1988). Mental links to excellence. *Sport Psychologist*, 2, 105–30.

Patton, M. Q. (1987). *How to use qualitative methods in evaluation*. Newbury Park, CA: Sage.

Pensgaard, A. M., & Duda, J. L. (2003). Sydney 2000: The interplay between emotions, coping, and the performance of Olympic-level athletes. *The Sport Psychologist*, 17, 253–67.

Pensgaard, A. M., & Roberts, G. C. (2003). Achievement goal orientations and the use of coping strategies among Winter Olympians. *Psychology of Sport & Exercise*, 4, 101–16.

Pensgaars, A. M., Roberts, G. C., & Ursin, H. (1999). Motivational factors and coping strategies of Norwegian paralympic and Olympic winter sport athletes. *Adapted Physical Activity Quarterly*, 16, 238–50.

Perkins, D., Wilson, G. V., & Kerr, J. H. (2001). The effects of elevated arousal and mood on maximal strength performance in athletes. *Journal of Applied Sport Psychology*, 13, 239–59.

Scanlan, T. K., Stein, G. L., & Ravizza, K. (1989). An in-depth study of former elite figure skaters: II. Sources of enjoyment. *Journal of Sport & Exercise Psychology*, 11, 65–82.

Scanlan, T. K., Stein, G. L., & Ravizza, K. (1991). An in-depth study of former elite figure skaters: III. Sources of stress. *Journal of Sport & Exercise Psychology*, 13, 103–20.

Scanlan, T. K., Ravizza, K., & Stein, G. L. (1989). An in-depth study of former elite figure skaters: I. Introduction to the project. *Journal of Sport & Exercise Psychology*, 11, 54–64.

Smith, R. E. (1980). Development of an integrated coping response through cognitive-affective stress management training. In I. G. Sarason & C. D. Spielberger (eds), *Stress and anxiety* (Vol. 7, pp. 265–80). Washington, DC: Hemisphere.

Smith, R. E., & Ascough, J. C. (1985). Induced affect in stress management training. In S. Burchfield (ed.), *Stress: Psychological and physiological interactions* (pp. 359–78). New York: Hemisphere.

Uphill, M., & Jones, M. V. (2004). Cognitive-motivational-relational-theory as a framework for coping with emotions in sport. In D. Lavallee, J. Thatcher & M. V. Jones (eds), *Coping and Emotion in Sport* (pp. 75–89). Hauppauge, NY: Nova Science Publishers.

Wagenaar, W. A. (1986). My memory: A study of autobiographical memory over six years. *Cognitive Psychology*, 18, 225–52.

# 12

## Cognitive strategies

Wrisberg, C. A., & Anshel, M. H. (1989). The effect of cognitive strategies on the free throw shooting performance of young athletes. *The Sport Psychologist*, 3, 95–104.

### Background and context

The performances of athletes are often being evaluated, whether it is in relation to others (e.g., opponents, teammates), personal standards (e.g., previous time) or a particular outcome (e.g., "I must finish the marathon"). Achieving success in sport, however it is defined, is difficult given that athletes are often competing against others, sport can by very physically demanding, and there are many psychological challenges (e.g., expectations) to be overcome. Little wonder then that sport psychologists are interested in understanding how psychological techniques can be employed to help athletes perform to the best of their ability. The four basic psychological skills are imagery, relaxation, goal-setting, and self-talk – the "workhorses in the applied sport psychology canon" (Andersen, 2000: ix). Simply, we can control what we aim for and how we judge success (goal-setting), what is going on in our mind (imagery and self-talk), and how "pumped-up" or calm we are (relaxation). Before discussing the usefulness of interventions utilizing these skills, we will first explore, briefly, each of the skills in turn.

A goal is ". . . what an individual is trying to accomplish; it is the object or aim of an action" (Locke, Shaw, Saari, & Latham, 1981: 126). Goal-setting has been demonstrated to be an effective technique for enhancing performance in sport and exercise settings. Goals can improve performance by directing attention and action, regulating the amount of effort exerted, and in particular maintaining this effort until the goal is reached (persistence), and motivating people to develop alternative strategies in their attempts to reach their goal (Locke *et al.*, 1981). While goal-setting is often used in a systematic and considered manner prior to entering practice or competition, the focus on appropriate goals is also important during performance itself and an athlete may use self-talk, or cue cards, to remain focused on the goals during competition. Further information on goal-setting is contained in Chapter 15.

Self-talk can be conceptualized as cognition (thinking) in its broadest sense, but more typically it is conceptualized more narrowly as athletes' overt (said out loud) and covert self-verbalizations. From an applied perspective, self-talk is a versatile strategy and athletes have reported using it to enhance the learning and execution of the correct skills, devise suitable strategies, control arousal levels, maintain and enhance motivation, focus attention, increase self-confidence, be mentally prepared, and cope with difficult circumstances.

Imagery involves the recreation of an event in our mind and can involve some or all of the senses related to the event. For example, a 100-meter sprinter imaging the start of the race may feel her fingers resting on the track, hear the starter's orders and feel herself push powerfully off the blocks as she hears the starter's gun. In relation to sport performance, imagery can help enhance skilled performers change cognitions and regulate arousal levels. Further information on imagery is contained in Chapter 14.

A number of strategies have been proposed to help athletes relax, probably because the ability to cope with the pressure of competition, particularly at the highest levels, is seen as central to success (Patmore, 1986). Harris (1986) classified relaxation techniques as muscle-to-mind, which are more physical in nature (e.g., deep breathing, progressive muscular relaxation) or mind-to-muscle, which are more cognitive in nature (e.g., imagery of a quiet place, meditation). Although muscle-to-mind techniques focus predominantly on relaxing the participant physically, they also help psychological relaxation. Similarly, mind-to-muscle techniques predominantly relax the person psychologically but also help with physical relaxation. Being able to relax is an important skill that enables athletes to develop greater sensitivity to their bodily feelings and responses, and to regulate arousal depending on the needs of the situation (Harris, 1986). Relaxation techniques have been applied effectively, often as part of a package of techniques, to help athletes cope with the pressure of competition (Mace, Eastman, & Carroll, 1987).

The use of psychological skills came to the fore with the cognitive-behavioral approach to behavior modification in the 1970s (e.g., Mahoney, 1974). This approach emphasizes that cognitions play a vital role in emotional and behavioral responses. At the time, this line of thinking represented a shift from the behaviorist approach, which had dominated until this point. Cognition is central in determining an individual's response to situations because an individual does not respond to a real environment, but rather to a perceived one (Mahoney, 1974). It therefore follows that a potential way of changing how an individual reacts or behaves in a certain situation is to alter these cognitive processes. Furthermore, an individual's cognitive processes are subject to the same laws of learning as overt behaviors (Kendall & Hollon, 1979). So, for example, by reinforcing the correct cognitions, by imagining performing well and by effectively coping in a difficult situation, an athlete may feel more confident of success and less anxious when they actually come to perform in that situation.

The key study by Wrisberg and Anshel focused on two psychological skills: imagery and a relaxation response. At the time there was a healthy body of research exploring the applicability of cognitive strategies to athletes. For example, psychological skills were applied to improve performance in darts, over and above that of a control group (Straub, 1989). Psychological skills had also been combined in packages. Examples include cognitive-affective stress management training (Smith, 1980) where the skills are practiced and rehearsed in conditions which approximate the actual situations in which they will eventually be employed under conditions of high emotional arousal; and stress inoculation training (Meichenbaum, 1977) which involves the participants using the skills as they are exposed to small, manageable units of stress which are gradually increased. These training programs have been applied to sport settings to help athletes control anxiety levels and prevent performance decrement. For example, novice abseilers reported lower levels of distress following stress inoculation training than a control group (Mace & Carroll, 1985), while youth volleyballers reported a better service reception (but not different anxiety levels) following cognitive-affective stress management training (Crocker, Alderman, & Smith, 1988).

There was comparatively less research interest into the application of psychological skills with young athletes, although Wrisberg and Anshel outlined that some research had at the time shown that young male athletes were able to develop relaxation skills (Blais & Vallerand, 1986; Kulakova, Bassiyuni, & Chernikova, 1980). Understanding how young athletes respond to psychological skills training is an important endeavor. If young athletes are able to utilize these psychological skills effectively, then there are potential benefits in terms of speed of development and performance levels, with the athlete laying a solid psychological foundation for their future career.

## Key study

The purpose of the present study was to explore the potential benefit of various types of mental training on the free throw shooting performance of young basketball players who were participants at a summer sports camp. The cognitive strategies selected for instruction were relaxation and imagery.

## Method

### Participants

Forty boys ranging in age from 10.2 to 12.4 years ($M = 11.6$ years) participated in the study. They were registered in a 6-week coed sports camp, the purpose of which was to teach a variety of sports skills in a competitive environment. Each participant was skilled in basketball free throw shooting prior to the study, as determined by an assessment by his group counselor and his own evaluation of basketball shooting skill.

### Equipment

All equipment and dimensions of the task were within the YMCA guidelines for boys' competitive junior basketball. A basketball was tossed from a distance of 12 feet (3.35 m) to a basketball hoop 8-foot (2.44 m) high. A stopwatch was used to regulate the length of between-trial intervals, during which time a cognitive task was practiced.

### Procedure

Prior to the first trial participants were randomly assigned to one of four groups: (a) a group that learned and practiced mental imagery during the treatment phase of the study, (b) a group that learned and attempted an arousal adjustment strategy, (c) a group that combined imagery with arousal adjustment techniques, and (d) a no-strategy (control) group.

Each participant watched a model demonstrate the correct technique for basketball free throw shooting accompanied by verbal reminders about important features of the skill to enhance performance. The boys then attempted 20 free throws with an inter-trial interval of 45 seconds. Between tosses they read selected portions of a book entitled *Basketball for young champions* (Antonacci & Barr, 1960) that was commensurate with fourth-grade reading ability. They were told that questions would be asked from the material at the end of the 20 trials. Ostensibly, this prevented mental rehearsal of the task. After completion of baseline trials each participant was asked a question from a list of possible questions about the game of basketball (e.g., "Describe the correct technique for the bounce pass"). Boys in the three treatment groups were then taught a cognitive strategy by an instructor for a period of 15 minutes while those in the control group reviewed additional written information. The experimental treatments included mental imagery (I), arousal adjustment (A), and the combined use of imagery and arousal adjustment (A+I). The latter group was first introduced to the relaxation response followed by the imagery technique.

Imagery training followed the guidelines proposed by Orlick (1986). While standing at the free throw line the performer was asked to (a) observe the basket for a few seconds, (b) close his eyes, (c) feel confident in making the shot, (d) mentally picture "through the mind's eye" standing at the free throw line (i.e., mentally reproduce what he saw at the free throw line – the basket – rather than what he would see if watching another person shoot), (e) concentrate on taking the shot while blocking out other sights and sounds, (f) mentally rehearse making several perfect shots while using the proper form, and (g) feel very confident and happy after each successful shot.

Arousal adjustment training involved the learning of a relaxation response technique (Benson, 1985) that consisted of practice in reducing arousal levels. Emphasis on arousal reduction was given in light of the fact that free throw shooting is typically accompanied by higher arousal associated with nervousness and/or the vigorous physical activity required by the game of basketball. Moreover, participants in this study appeared to be relatively nervous about succeeding in the task. Therefore it was reasoned that reducing arousal, not elevating it, would be a more practical cognitive technique to perform prior to basketball free throw shooting.

The participants learned the four steps of the relaxation response: (a) keep the mind free of visual and auditory distractions (Benson, 1985, actually suggests a quiet environment, which of course is not practical in competitive basketball); (b) use a mental device such as a sound, word, or phrase (e.g., "soft hands," "no tension") repeated silently to prevent "mind wandering" and stop distracting thoughts; (c) maintain a passive "let it happen" attitude (Benson suggests that participants not worry about how well they are performing the technique); and (d) assume a comfortable position to eliminate muscular tension – in this case by holding the ball in front of the body with arms fully extended and head tilted forward to relax neck, shoulders, and upper limbs.

A second 15-minute instructional period was held the following day to allow additional rehearsal of the techniques learned on Day 1. To examine the effect of selected cognitive strategies on free throw shooting performance, the respective groups practiced the cognitive techniques they had learned and then attempted 10 free throw shots separated by a period of 45 seconds.

Between trials all participants read from the same basketball book described earlier. Participants in the three experimental groups read for 30 seconds and then practiced their assigned cognitive strategy for 15 seconds before attempting the shot. Control participants read for the entire 45 seconds. To assure that they paid attention to the reading material, all participants were told they would be asked a question on the history of basketball at the end of the session. To enhance external validity and simulate actual basketball free throw shooting conditions, all participants were allowed to engage in what was for them normal preshot preparation habits such as bouncing or aiming the basketball.

Immediately after the last trial on Day 2, participants were asked one question about the history of basketball. Experimental participants were then asked to respond to two questions: "To what extent did you actually use the strategy you learned – always, often but not always, occasionally, rarely, or never?" "If you did not use the technique you were taught, what *did* you think about?" Control participants were asked what they thought about while attempting their shots. All participants in the cognitive strategy groups indicated that they "always" used the treatment they were taught. Thus it appeared that the novelty and uniqueness of the learned mental approach facilitated its adherence during the experiment. Three control participants also admitted that they "occasionally" took a deep breath before the shot in order to relax.

## Results

In spite of the fact that the boys were randomly assigned to groups and that the basketball ability of all was judged by trained counselors to be between good and excellent, a significant group difference in free throw percentage was obtained on pretraining trials (Table 12.1). Therefore, in order to assess the effects of the various cognitive strategies implemented by participants prior to each shot, an analysis of covariance (ANCOVA) was performed on the post-training free throw percentage scores using pretraining free throw percentage as the covariate. The adjusted mean free throw percentages for each group on the post-test are shown in Figure 12.1. The best performance was evidenced by the imagery-plus-arousal-adjustment (A+I) group. Results of the ANCOVA revealed a significant groups effect, $F(3,35) = 3.79, p < .01$, and subsequent significant, $p < .05$, pairwise contrasts were found between the scores of the combined group (A+I) and those of both the arousal adjustment and the control groups.

**Table 12.1** Free throw percentages for each group on the pretest and post-test

| Group | Pretest | | Post-test | |
|---|---|---|---|---|
| | M | SD | M | SD |
| Control | 38 | 16 | 39 | 25 |
| Arousal | 68 | 11 | 57 | 19 |
| Imagery | 36 | 19 | 49 | 29 |
| Combined | 63 | 14 | 79 | 10 |

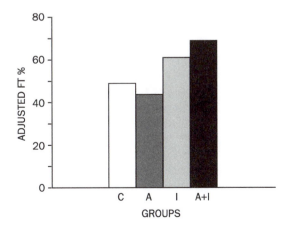

**Figure 12.1** Adjusted mean free throw percentages for each group on the post-test

## Discussion

The purpose of this study was to determine the extent to which various cognitive strategies currently being practiced by many adult athletes could be learned and effectively used by younger athletes. The results offer empirical support for the efficacy of a preshot strategy involving a combination of relaxation and imagery on the free throw shooting performance of young basketball players. It should also be noted that the design employed in the present study involved a long wait between shots, reducing the possibility that a shooting rhythm could be sustained. Thus it is likely that the test situation represented a challenge to the performers' ability to mobilize concentration for each shot. That the boys were able to acquire and effectively use the combined strategy is particularly impressive in light of the fact that time constraints imposed by the summer camp situation prevented the type of extended practice of cognitive techniques advocated by proponents of mental training (Smith, 1987; Suinn, 1983; Vealey, 1986). However, further research is needed to determine the optimal conditions (e.g., length of practice time, spacing of sessions) under which younger performers may learn and effectively use cognitive strategies to enhance sport performance and whether positive effects can be produced on repeated occasions.

The present results are consistent with those of Kolonay (1977), who found that a combination of relaxation and imagery resulted in better free throw performance for male college basketball players than did either preshot technique by itself. Although the visuomotor behavior rehearsal method (Suinn, 1972a, 1972b) was not strictly taught to participants in the combined group, the results are consistent with those of a number of experiments demonstrating the potential of VMBR in enhancing the closed skill performance of older athletes (Hall & Erffmeyer, 1983; Noel, 1980; Weinberg *et al.*, 1981).

Why the arousal adjustment group performed the poorest during test trials is somewhat difficult to explain. Perhaps arousal was reduced to lower than optimal (i.e., underaroused) levels. If so, additional practice in arousal adjustment techniques may be required for younger participants. It is also possible that too much attention to the act of releasing muscle tension may have diverted these boys' attention from the cues necessary for optimal performance. As Nideffer (1985) has suggested, it is important for the athlete to redirect attention to a task-relevant cue following tension reduction in order to maximize response productivity. Such a process may have occurred in the preshot preparation of the combined group which included arousal adjustment followed by a focus on performance-relevant cues (e.g., the rim and "seeing" the ball going through the basket).

Of particular interest was the anecdotal observation that boys in the cognitive strategy groups appeared extremely receptive and enthusiastic about gaining a mental edge that they felt might enhance their skill performance. Such a response is consistent with the results of studies indicating that young athletes are particularly motivated by opportunities/techniques that promote skill development (Gill *et al.*, 1983; Klint & Weiss, 1987).

In summary, the present study appears to offer support for the notion that young athletes are able to learn and use cognitive techniques to enhance their performance. It remains to be determined whether there is a minimum age at which mental strategies may be effectively learned and utilized. Cross-sectional studies employing a variety of age groups should help resolve this issue. Further investigation is also needed to determine whether learned cognitive strategies are generalizable by young athletes to actual game/competition settings.

## Subsequent research and application

There is compelling evidence that interventions, comprising psychological skills training, can be applied effectively to sport settings. Often interventions are applied to help athletes control competitive anxiety, and cognitive-behavioral programs have been successfully applied to help control anxiety and prevent performance decrement as a result of increased levels of anxiety in sport (Mace, 1990). More generally, psychological skills have been found to improve performance in 85% of published studies across a wide variety of sports (Weinberg & Williams, 2006).

While there is evidence supporting the efficacy of psychological skills there are many challenges for those wishing to conduct research in this area. The key study by Wrisberg and Anshel is an important example of a control group design and this is typical of much of the research into psychological skills. In these studies a group which receives an intervention is typically compared on performance and psychological variables with a control group. However, acquiring a control group for a study can sometimes be difficult if the coach wants all the athletes to receive the intervention in the belief that it will enhance performance. A further difficulty comes in interpreting the results. Non-significant data from groups may mask any small but consistent improvements in performance that have practical significance for the athlete (Bryan, 1987) or that the treatment worked for some individuals (Mace, 1990). As controlled studies should consist of homogeneous groups it can be argued that this problem should not apply. However, it is often difficult to obtain large numbers of participants who are homogeneous on all relevant characteristics, particularly skill level. This was evidenced in Wrisberg and Anshel's key study, where a substantial variation across groups in performance levels was reported during the pretest phase. The need for suitable sample sizes comprising homogenous participants has resulted in many controlled studies consisting of novice participants (e.g., Mace & Carroll, 1985) and there is an obvious limitation in generalizing results gained from novice participants to more experienced, skillful performers.

The relatively small sample size in the key study (with only ten participants in each group) also highlights an important issue in psychological research: that of power. In conducting an experimental study researchers are trying to see if the independent variable (in the key study this was the cognitive strategies) impacts the dependent variable (in the key study this was performance). The power of the study refers to the ability to detect a difference (in the key study this was the change in performance following the intervention) and is dependent on the number of participants, the alpha level set, and the effect size. Simply, if the number of participants in the groups is too small then the test will not have sufficient power to detect differences that may in fact be quite meaningful. Of course the opposite can also occur and studies with very large numbers of participants can report statistically significant results that are not especially meaningful. The meaningfulness of a difference is termed the effect size. The effect size refers to the size of the treatment effect and can be calculated by finding the difference between the two means (e.g., pre- and post-intervention) and dividing by the standard deviation of either group (Cohen, 1988). An effect size of 0.2 was tentatively labeled small, 0.5 medium, and 0.8 labeled large by Cohen. A glance at Figure 12.1 indicates that the imagery group did perform substantially better than the control group and arousal-only group. With greater participant numbers the differences between the imagery group and these two groups may have been significant. To illustrate, if we take Cohen's (1988) suggestion that for behavioral research a power of 0.8 is required then at a 0.05 level of probability a follow up t-test comparing the difference in performance between the imagery group and control group would have required 26 participants in each group to detect a large effect size. Thus, with more participants, Wrisberg and Anshel may have concluded that imagery on its own was an effective intervention. Indeed by looking at Table 12.1 it can be seen that the imagery group improved by 36% from pretest to post-test while the combined skill group (which was significant) improved by 25%.

The small sample size may also help to explain why the group that used the relaxation technique alone performed poorest during the post-test trials in relation to their pretest scores, because relatively few participants performing poorly could affect the mean score of the entire group. It may also reflect a further challenge with group-based intervention studies, which is ensuring that all the participants are sufficiently trained in the psychological skill in question. The ability to relax can take a number of sessions and insufficient practice may be a cause for relaxation training failing (Williams & Harris, 2006), however, in Wrisberg and Anshel's key study the participants only had two sessions (held over two days) to practice the technique. Notwithstanding the challenges of group-based intervention studies in general, and of teaching relaxation skills specifically, there is a substantial body of evidence that has supported the efficacy of relaxation skills as a technique to both cope with stress (e.g., Mace, 1990) and enhance performance (Greenspan & Feltz, 1989; Myers, Whelan, & Murphy, 1996). However, it is important that sport psychology consultants are aware of how relaxation skills may be perceived by athletes. For example, when reflecting on his consultancy with the England Women's Cricket team, Bull (1995) felt that relaxation training was not well-received by the players and a strategy too far-removed from competition.

There are clearly a number of challenges that researchers must address when conducting experimental research with large groups to determine the efficacy of psychological skill techniques. Accordingly, there has been a call for researchers to also use a single case approach where appropriate (Hrycaiko & Martin, 1996; Mace, 1990). A single-case approach negates the need for large numbers of participants and enables the practitioner to provide more individualized, as opposed to standardized, training. There are many different types of single case approach. For example, a case study will typically be descriptive and lack sufficient experimental control to rule out the threats to validity that more rigorous single case designs may include (Kratochwill, Mott, & Dodson, 1984). An example may be the description of an intervention to help an athlete control stress, which is lacking in objective pre- and post-intervention data. An example of a case study in sport is the work of Mace et al. (1987) with an elite gymnast.

It is, however, possible to bring a similar level of rigor to that utilized in typical experimental designs in which a control group is compared on performance to experimental group(s) and these more rigorous studies employ a single-case research design. For example, the athlete's behavior (or psychological response) is repeatedly measured, and a baseline established, so that various trends in the data can be examined as the treatment is introduced, and even possibly withdrawn (Kratochwill et al., 1984). In effect the participant acts as their own control by comparing changes following the intervention to the baseline (control) phase. One common design is an AB design where the variable of interest (e.g., performance, or a psychological construct such as anxiety) is recorded during a baseline phase (A) and compared to that recorded after the intervention (B). For example, a psychologist interested in applying a relaxation technique to help a young athlete cope with the pressure of competition may record her anxiety levels over a series of eight competitions before administering the intervention and monitoring anxiety levels in a subsequent eight competitions. Examples of AB designs in sport include work with a county golfer (Uphill & Jones, 2005) and a cricket bowler (Barker & Jones, 2005).

Of course, with an AB design it is possible that any observed differences may be a consequence of normal development and not due to the intervention. More robust designs whereby the intervention is withdrawn (ABA) or withdrawn and then reintroduced (ABAB) can also be used. If the variable of interest changes in line with the introduction or withdrawal of the intervention then it is possible to have confidence that the changes occurred as a result of the intervention. Although with psychological interventions this may not always be possible as, for example, an athlete may not want to stop using a relaxation strategy that they perceive is useful, although there are examples of this being achieved (e.g., Heyman, 1987).

A characteristic of single case-research designs is demonstrating the replicability of effects (Kratochwill *et al.*, 1984). While this can be done by observing changes in the dependent variables following the introduction, removal, and reintroduction of the intervention as in ABAB designs it is also possible to achieve this with multiple baseline across participants designs. In sport the typical multiple baseline design involved the collection of baseline and post-intervention data across several individuals. The validity of the intervention is determined by observing changes in the dependent variable(s) following the introduction of the intervention. If similar changes are observed across participants this provides support for the efficacy of the technique employed. There are many examples of multiple baseline studies in sport demonstrating the effectiveness of psychological skills interventions. These include studies with tennis players (Mamassis & Doganis, 2004), basketball players (Swain & Jones, 1995), tri-athletes (Thelwell & Greenlees, 2001), soccer players (Johnson, Hrycaiko, Johnson, & Halas, 2004) and swimmers (Hanton & Jones, 1999).

The key study by Wrisberg and Anshel was important in that it empirically tested how cognitive strategies could be effectively applied to enhance sport performance. Furthermore, one of the main aims of the key study was to explore the effectiveness of cognitive strategies with young performers. Children and adolescents are typically under-represented as a research group in the sport psychology literature (Vealey, 1988, 1994), yet psychological skills training programs have been applied to young athletes (e.g., Gould, 2002; Orlick & McCaffrey, 1991). Encouragingly, preliminary results suggest that psychological skills are of value to young athletes and can be taught in a school or sport setting (Smith & Smoll, 2002). However, in working with young children it is crucial that consultants are aware of developmental aspects. That is, our behavior and psychological processes may change over time and moderate the impact of a psychological skills intervention (Petlichkoff, 2004). As cognitive and social developmental changes occur so might the type and nature of required psychological skills change. For example, children up to 12 years of age will have quite a poor understanding of time (Piaget, 1969), and as such having a "long-term goal" will have little meaning for the child. Thus, an adult may be able to understand that to achieve a long-term goal a series of smaller goals will be useful, but research suggests that younger children will find this problematic (Bandura & Schunk, 1981).

The increasing empirical basis for the effectiveness of psychological techniques (Weinberg & Williams, 2006) and a desire on the behalf of athletes and coaches to perform to the best of their ability means that sport psychologists are often called upon to work with performers across all ages, sports, and levels of ability. The experiences of psychologists working with athletes are increasingly well documented and provide a valuable resource for students, recently qualified psychologists and experienced professionals alike (e.g.,

Andersen, 2000, 2006; Bull, 1995; May & Brown, 1989). When delivering psychological skills to athletes a number of guidelines have been outlined by Weinberg and Williams (2006). The guidelines consider the way a psychologist interacts with clients (e.g., emphasizing the importance of psychological skills training), when psychological skills training should occur (e.g., as much as possible psychological skills should be integrated with physical skills in practice), the importance of detailed assessment, choosing the right skills, and evaluating the program effectiveness.

Clearly, psychological skills are not only applied to competitive sport settings. Sport psychologists are also beginning to recognize that they have skills that can be applied to a range of achievement settings such as business professionals and military personnel (Lavallee, Kremer, Moran & Williams, 2004). Furthermore, the psychological skills learnt in a sport setting can also be applied to other life pursuits, such as academics and a job interview (Weinberg & Williams, 2006). Athletes can also use psychological skills when injured, such as an athlete using positive self-talk to maintain motivation during rehabilitation exercises or using a relaxation intervention or imagery to enhance healing (Williams & Scherzer, 2006). Finally, psychological skills can also be effectively used in exercise settings, for example goal-setting may be an effective strategy to help motivate an individual who has just begun an exercise program (Dishman & Buckworth, 2006).

## Additional readings

Andersen, M. B. (ed.) (2000). *Doing sport psychology*. Champaign, IL: Human Kinetics.
Andersen, M. B. (ed.) (2006). *Sport psychology in practice*. Champaign, IL: Human Kinetics.
Mace, R. D. (1990). Cognitive behavioural interventions in sport. In G. Jones and L. Hardy (eds), *Stress and performance in sport* (pp. 203–30). Chichester: Wiley.
Morris, T., & Thomas, P. (2004). Applied sport psychology. In T. Morris & J. Summers (eds), *Sport psychology: Theory, applications and issues* (2nd ed., pp. 236–77). Chichester: Wiley.
Weinberg, R. S., & Williams, J. M. (2006). Integrating and implementing a psychological skills training program. In J. M. Williams (ed.), *Applied sport psychology: Personal growth to peak performance* (5th ed., pp. 425–57). New York: McGraw-Hill.

## Study questions

1 Why might the use of relaxation techniques lead to a reduction in performance on some sports tasks?

2 What types of psychological skills (if any) do you use to ensure that you perform to the best of your ability in a sport setting?

3 Outline the strengths of using a single-case design to explore the effectiveness of psychological skills. Can you also think of any weaknesses?

4 If you are planning to conduct a group study to determine the effectiveness of a psychological intervention why is it important to consider the amount of participants you should recruit?

5 Why is it important to include a detailed pre- and post-intervention assessment when engaging in a psychological intervention with an athlete?

## References

Andersen, M. B. (ed.) (2000). *Doing sport psychology*. Champaign, IL: Human Kinetics.
Andersen, M. B. (ed.) (2006). *Sport psychology in practice*. Champaign, IL: Human Kinetics.

Antonacci, R.J., & Barr, J. (1960). *Basketball for young champions*. New York: McGraw-Hill.

Bandura, A. & Schunk, D. H. (1981). Cultivating competence, self-efficacy and intrinsic interest. *Journal of Personality and Social Psychology*, 41, 586–98.

Barker, J. B., & Jones, M. V. (2005). Using hypnosis to increase self-efficacy: A case study in elite judo. *Sport and Exercise Psychology Review*, 1, 36–42.

Benson, H. (1985). The relaxation response. In A. Monat & R. S. Lazarus (eds), *Stress and coping: An anthology* (2nd ed., pp. 315–21). New York: Columbia University Press.

Blais, M.R., & Vallerand, R.J. (1986). Multimodal effects of electromyographic biofeedback: Looking at children's ability to control precompetitive anxiety. *Journal of Sport Psychology*, 8, 283–303.

Bryan, A. J. (1987). Single-subject designs for evaluation of sport psychology interventions. *The Sport Psychologist*, 1, 283–92.

Bull, S. J. (1995). Reflections on a 5-year consultancy program with the England women's cricket team. *The Sport Psychologist*, 9, 148–63.

Cohen, J. (1988). *Statistical power analysis for the behavioral sciences* (2nd ed.). Hillsdale, NJ: Erlbaum.

Crocker, P. R. E., Alderman, R. B., & Smith, F. M. R. (1988). Cognitive-affective stress management training with high performance youth volleyball players: Effects on affect, cognition, and performance. *Journal of Sport & Exercise Psychology*, 10, 448–60.

Dishman, R. K., & Buckworth, J. (2006). Exercise psychology. In J. M. Williams (ed.), *Applied sport psychology: Personal growth to peak performance* (5th ed., pp. 616–37). New York: McGraw-Hill.

Gill, D.L., Gross, J.B., & Huddleston, S. (1983). Participation motivation in youth sport. *International Journal of Sport Psychology*, 14, 1–14.

Gould, D. (2002). Sport psychology: Future directions in youth sport research. In F. L. Smoll & R. E. Smith (eds), *Children and youth in sport: A biopsychosocial perspective* (2nd ed., pp. 565–89). Dubuque, IA: Kendall/Hunt.

Greenspan, M. J., & Feltz, D. L. (1989). Psychological interventions with athletes in competitive situations: A review. *The Sport Psychologist*, 3, 219–36.

Hall, E.G., & Erffmeyer, E.S. (1983). The effect of visuo-motor behavioral rehearsal with videotaped modeling on free throw accuracy of intercollegiate female basketball players. *Journal of Sport Psychology*, 5, 343–6.

Hanton, S., & Jones, G. (1999). The effects of a multimodal intervention program on performers: II. Training the butterflies to fly in formation. *The Sport Psychologist*, 13, 22–41.

Harris, D.V. (1986). Relaxation and energizing techniques for regulation of arousal. In J. M. Williams (ed.), *Applied sport psychology: Personal growth to peak performance* (pp. 185–208). Mountain View, CA: Mayfield Publishing Company.

Heyman, S. R. (1987). Research interventions in sport psychology: Issues encountered in working with an amateur boxer. *The Sport Psychologist*, 1, 208–23.

Hrycaiko, D. W., & Martin, G. L. (1996) Applied research studies with single subject designs: Why so few? *Journal of Applied Sport Psychology*, 8, 183–99.

Johnson, J. J. M., Hrycaiko, D. W., Johnson, G. V., & Halas, J. M. (2004). Self-talk and female youth soccer performance. *The Sport Psychologist*, 18, 44–59.

Kendall, P. C., & Hollon, S. D. (1979). Cognitive-behavioral interventions: Overview and current status. In P. C. Kendall & S. D. Hollon (eds), *Cognitive-behavioural interventions: Theory, research and procedures*. New York: Academic Press.

Klint, K. A., & Weiss, M. R. (1987). Perceived competence and motives for participating in youth sports: A test of Harter's Competence Motivation Theory. *Journal of Sport Psychology*, 9, 55–65.

Kolonay, B. J. (1977). *The effects of visuo-motor behavior rehearsal on athletic performance*. Unpublished master's thesis. Hunter College, The City University of New York.

Kratochwill, T. R., Mott, S. E., & Dodson, C. L. (1984). Case study and single-case research in clinical and applied psychology. In A. S. Bellack (ed.) *Research methods in clinical psychology* (pp. 55–99). Oxford, UK: Pergamon Press.

Kulakova, E. A., Bassiyuni, M., & Chernikova, O. A. (1980). Psychological self-regulation as a means of improvement of sports mastership of young gymnasts. *Theory and Practice of Physical Culture*, 2, 31–4.

Lavallee, D., Kremer, J., Moran, A., & Williams, M. (2004). *Sport psychology: Contemporary themes*. London: Palgrave.

Locke, E. A., Shaw, K. N., Saari, L. M., and Latham, G. P. (1981). Goal setting and task performance: 1969–1980. *Psychological Bulletin*, 90, 125–52.

Mace, R. D. (1990). Cognitive behavioral interventions in sport. In G. Jones and L. Hardy (eds), *Stress and performance in sport*. (pp. 203–30). Chichester: Wiley.

Mace, R. D., & Carroll, D. (1985). The control of anxiety in sport: Stress inoculation training prior to abseiling. *International Journal of Sport Psychology*, 16, 165–75.

Mace, R., Eastman, C., & Carroll, D. (1987). The effects of stress inoculation training on gymnastics performance on the pommelled horse: A case study. *Behavioral Psychotherapy*, 15, 272–9.

Mahoney, M. J. (1974). *Cognition and behavior modification*. Cambridge, MA: Ballinger.

Mamassis, G., & Doganis, G. (2004). The effects of a mental training program on juniors pre-competitive anxiety, self-confidence, and tennis performance. *Journal of Applied Sport Psychology*, 16, 118–37.

May, J. R., & Brown, L. (1989). Delivery of psychological services to the U.S. alpine ski team prior to and during the Olympics in Calgary. *The Sport Psychologist*, 3, 320–9.

Meichenbaum, D. (1977). *Cognitive behavior modification: An integrative approach*. New York: Plenum.

Meyers, A. W., Whelan, J. P., & Murphy, S. M. (1996). Cognitive behavioral strategies in athletic performance enhancement. In M. Hersen, R. M. Eisler, & P. M. Miller (eds), *Progress in behavioral modification* (Vol. 30, pp. 137–164). Pacific Grove, CA: Brooks/Cole.

Nideffer, R.M. (1985). *Athletes' guide to mental training*. Champaign, IL: Human Kinetics.

Noel, R.C. (1980). The effect of visuo-motor behavior rehearsal on tennis performance. *Journal of Sport Psychology*, 2, 221–6.

Orlick, T. (1986). *Psyching for sport: Mental training for athletes*. Champaign, IL: Leisure Press.

Orlick, T., & McCaffrey, N. (1991). Mental training with children for sport and life. *The Sport Psychologist*, 5, 322–34.

Patmore, A. (1986). *Sportsmen under stress*. London: Stanley Paul.

Petlichkoff, L. M. (2004). Self-regulation skills for children and adolescents. In M. R. Weiss (ed.), *Developmental sport and exercise psychology* (pp. 269–88). Morgantown, WV: Fitness Information Technology.

Piaget, J. (1969). *The child's conception of time*. London: Routledge & Keegan Paul.

Smith, D. (1987). Conditions that facilitate the development of sport imagery training. *The Sport Psychologist*, 1, 237–47.

Smith, R. E. (1980). A cognitive affective approach to stress management for athletes. In C. A. Nadeau, W. R. Halliwell, K. M. Newell, and G. C. Roberts (eds), *Psychology of motor behavior and sport* (pp. 54–72). Champaign, IL: Human Kinetics.

Smith, R. E. & Smoll, F. L. (2002). Youth sports as a behavior setting for psychosocial inter-ventions. In J. L. Van Raalte & B. W. Brewer (eds), *Exploring sport and exercise psychology* (2nd ed., pp. 341–71). Washington, DC: American Psychological Association.

Straub, W. F. (1989). The effect of three different methods of mental training on dart throwing performance. *The Sport Psychologist*, 3, 133–41.

Suinn, R. (1972a). Behavior rehearsal training for ski racers: Brief report. *Behavior Therapy*, 3, 210–12.

Suinn, R. (1972b). Removing emotional obstacles to learning and performance by visuo-motor behavior rehearsal. *Behavior Therapy*, 3, 308–10.

Suinn, R. (1983). Imagery and sports. In A. Sheikh (ed.), *Imagery: Current theory, research, and application* (pp. 507–34). New York: Wiley.

Swain, A., & Jones, G. (1995). Effects of goal-setting interventions on selected basketball skills: A single-subject design. *Research Quarterly for Exercise and Sport*, 66, 51–63.

Thelwell, R. C., & Greenlees, I. A. (2001). The effects of a mental skills training package on gymnasium triathlon performance. *The Sport Psychologist*, 15, 127–41.

Uphill, M. A., & Jones, M. V. (2005). Coping with and reducing the number of careless shots: A case study with a county golfer. *Sport and Exercise Psychology Review*, 2, 14–22.

Vealey, R. (1986). Imagery training for performance enhancement. In J. Williams (ed.), *Applied sport psychology: Personal growth to peak performance* (pp. 209–34). Palo Alto, CA: Mayfield.

Vealey, R. S. (1988). Future directions in psychological skills training. *The Sport Psychologist*, 2, 318–36.

Vealey, R. S. (1994). Current status and prominent issues in sport psychology interventions. *Medicine and Science in Sport and Exercise*, 26, 495–502.

Weinberg, R.S., Seabourne, T. G., & Jackson, A. (1981). Effects of visuo-motor behavior rehearsal, relaxation, and imagery on karate performance. *Journal of Sport Psychology*, 3, 228–38.

Weinberg, R. S., & Williams, J. M. (2006). Integrating and implementing a psychological skills training program. In J. M. Williams (ed.), *Applied sport psychology: Personal growth to peak performance* (5th ed., pp. 425–57). New York: McGraw-Hill.

Williams, J. M., & Harris, D. V. (2006). Relaxation and energizing techniques for regulation of arousal. In J. M. Williams (ed.), *Applied sport psychology: Personal growth to peak performance* (5th ed., pp. 285–305). New York: McGraw-Hill.

Williams, J. M., & Scherzer, C. B. (2006). Injury risk and rehabilitation: Psychological considerations. In J. M. Williams (ed.), *Applied sport psychology: Personal growth to peak performance* (5th ed., pp. 565–94). New York: McGraw-Hill.

# 13

# Attention and concentration

Gill, D. L., & Strom, E. H. (1985). The effect of attentional focus on performance of an endurance task. *International Journal of Sport Psychology*, 16, 217–23.

## Background and context

The construct of attention has attracted considerable research interest since the start of experimental psychology. Abernethy, Summers, and Ford (1998) claimed that "understanding attention . . . has been one of, if not the, central research issue" (1998: 175) within cognitive psychology. Among its many definitions, attention denotes a concentration of mental activity (Matlin, 2002), where concentration is the ability to focus mental effort on the task at hand while ignoring distractions. When athletes and coaches talk about concentration they are typically referring to the focus of attention on task *relevant* cues and thus an athlete is "not concentrating" when their focus of attention is on task *irrelevant* cues. Athletes are required to display different types of attention when performing. They are required to selectively attend to some stimuli in preference to others (e.g., a tennis player is better off focusing on an opponent's body position before they serve rather than a heckler in the crowd). Athletes also have to engage in divided attention when they perform two or more tasks concurrently, such as, dribbling a soccer ball and scanning the pitch for a suitable pass. Given the range of stimuli that an athlete could attend to during performance (e.g., crowd, coach, opponents, own thoughts, physical state) and the importance of attention for successful performance (Moran, 1996), the study of attention in sport is clearly essential.

Over the years, mainstream psychology theorists have conceptualized the construct of attention by employing an array of metaphors. For example, attention has been compared to a physical device (i.e., a filter) that screens information as it flows into the mind. Attention has also been likened to a spotlight that can illuminate or enlarge what we focus on in the world, as well as a zoom lens that can broaden or narrow our attentional focus in the same way that one can adjust the focus of a camera. The ability of people to do two or more tasks concurrently, through divided attention, has been described as being possible because of a pool of mental energy that can be divided up between tasks (Kahneman, 1973) or a series of separate pools that can be allocated to different tasks (Wickens, 1984).

At the time of Gill and Strom's study, attentional processes were predominantly measured from a psychometric (or "individual differences") paradigm in sport psychology, although the mainstream was also beginning to examine attention with neuroscientific and dual-task approaches. The psychometric approach to the measurement of attention is based on the assumption that people can provide valuable self-report evidence on their own focusing habits, skills, and preferences. Based on this assumption, sport psychologists have attempted to measure individual differences in attentional processes in athletes using specially designed questionnaires. Nideffer's (1976) *Test of Attentional and Interpersonal Style* (TAIS) is one of the most popular inventories in this subject area, and is used as a screening device in many field settings to measure people's attentional processes.

The TAIS, which contains 144 items and is organized into 17 different sub-scales, proposes that people's attentional focus varies simultaneously along two independent dimensions – direction and width. Within this model, direction refers to the target of one's focus (i.e., either external or internal), while attentional width ranges along a continuum from a broad focus (where one is aware of many stimulus features at the same time) to a narrow one (where irrelevant information is excluded effectively). The dimensions of width and direction may also be combined factorially to yield four hypothetical attentional styles (e.g., a narrow-external attentional focus in sport is used when a darts player looks at the board before throwing, while a narrow-internal focus is required when a tennis player mentally rehearses a serve). The study by Gill and Strom is based on this framework of attentional styles by Nideffer, and specifically tested whether participants would perform more repetitions of an endurance task when using a narrow-external focus than when using a narrow-internal focus.

## Key study

The application of psychological principles to sport has increased dramatically in recent years. Most applied sport psychology programs involve cognitive-behavioral techniques, and typically, attentional control strategies are important components of such programs. However, little empirical evidence exists to support the use of such techniques, and few studies have examined the appropriateness and effectiveness of varying attentional styles for varying sport tasks.

Nideffer (1976) is one of the few researchers to examine attentional constructs in relation to sport, and proposes that the appropriate width and direction combination can enhance performance. He also specifically advocates a narrow-internal focus for increasing pain tolerance and performance on endurance tasks. Further support for the use of a narrow-internal focus with endurance tasks comes from Morgan and Pollock's (1977) study, which – as outlined in Chapter 1 – showed that world-class distance runners used an associative strategy, or a narrow-internal focus on body sensations, whereas non-elite runners used a dissociative or distraction strategy.

Although the work of Nideffer and Morgan and Pollock is widely cited to support the contention that an internal focus on body sensations enhances endurance performance, considerable empirical work indicates that distraction, or an external focus, improves endurance performance. As early as 1898 Welch found that feelings of muscular fatigue on a strength task set in later when the task was accompanied by a visual distraction. Other studies demonstrate that distraction strategies increase pain tolerance in nonsport settings (e.g., Spanos, Horton, & Chaves, 1975), and research on endurance performance provides some evidence of the benefits of dissociation (e.g., Pennebaker & Lightner, 1980). In fact, Morgan and Pollock did not claim that an associative strategy was advantageous for all endurance tasks and specifically noted that distraction may enhance endurance performance. In subsequent experiments, Morgan and his colleagues (e.g., Morgan, Horstman, Cymerman, & Stokes, 1983) demonstrated that a dissociative cognitive strategy resulted in superior endurance performance on a treadmill task when compared to control and placebo conditions.

The aim of this study was to test the influence of attentional focus, as defined within Nideffer's model, on the performance of an endurance task through a controlled laboratory experiment that involved a within-subjects design. Despite the previous findings by Nideffer and Morgan and Pollock, it was felt that stronger experimental evidence existed to suggest that an external focus would enhance endurance performance. The hypothesis, therefore, was that individuals would perform more repetitions of a leg lift task when using a narrow-external focus than when using a narrow-internal focus.

## Method

### Participants and Design

All 34 female volunteers, age 18 to 22, were members of intercollegiate teams. All participants performed on the quadriceps machine in two separate sessions, using an internal focus in one session and an external focus in the other. Individuals were randomly assigned to two groups with Group 1 using the internal focus in the first session and the external focus in the second, and Group 2 using the external focus in the first and the internal focus in the second. The design, then, was a Group X Internal/External focus (2 × 2) design with Internal/External focus as a within-subjects factor.

### Procedure

Each participant was scheduled for two 15-minute sessions with the second session scheduled two days after the first. At the beginning of each session the experimenter read the procedures and set the weight that the participant normally used [weights ranged from 13.6 kg (30 lb) to 40.8 kg (90 lb) and the two groups did not differ in the weights used].

When doing the task the participant sat upright with their knees bent over the end of the bench and their hand holding the sides of the bench. For one repetition the legs were lifted to full extension of the knee and then returned to the starting position without stopping. A metronome was used to illustrate the pace and two practice trials were performed with the metronome. The study participant was then asked to perform as many repetitions as possible and to stop when they could not do a full repetition. For the internal focus the participants was instructed to focus all of their attention on the feelings in their legs while performing the exercise, and for the external focus they were asked to focus on a collage fixed .91 m (3 ft) in front of their eye.

Participants also completed a questionnaire at the end of the session about their thoughts and feelings during performance. This questionnaire was used to help insure that individuals focused as instructed, as well as to assess subjective reactions to the attentional manipulation. For the second session, participants used the attentional focus that they had not used during the previous session and all other procedures remained the same.

## Results

### Manipulation Check

At the end of each session participants were asked to describe their thoughts and feelings during performance. Open-ended responses indicated that individuals did, indeed, focus as instructed. Nearly all (94%) internal responses specifically referred to feelings of pain, strain or tension in the legs, and similarly, 94% of external responses referred to specific things on the collage.

## Performance Results

A Group by Internal/External focus repeated measures analysis of variance ($2 \times 2$ ANOVA) on the performance data yielded a significant Internal/External main effect [$F(1,32) = 6.18$, $p <$ .05], and a Group by Internal/External interaction [$F(1,32) = 4.26$, $p < .05$]. As hypothesized, more repetitions were performed when the external focus (Mean = 20.2) than the internal focus (Mean = 17.5). The interaction represents a day effects with a tendency to perform more repetitions on the second day (Mean = 20.0) than the first day (Mean = 17.7), but that effect is weaker than the Internal/External main effect. Group 1, who used the internal focus first and the external focus second, showed greater improvements from the internal focus (Mean = 17.1) to the external focus (Mean = 22.2) than Group 2. However, it is notable that Group 2, who used the external focus on the first day, still performed more repetitions with the external focus (Mean = 18.2) and dropped slightly when using the internal focus on Day 2 (Mean = 17.8).

## Questionnaire Responses

Questionnaire responses were consistent with performance results. At the end of each session, participants were asked if the attentional focus that had used that day helped, hindered, or had no effect. Following the internal focus session, 15 respondents indicated that the internal focus helped, 16 indicated that it hindered and three reported no effect. Chi-square analyses indicated that the three choices were not used equally [chi-square (2) = 9.24, $p <$ .01], but the number of help and hinder responses did not differ significantly. Following the external focus session, 28 respondents indicated that the external focus helped, four that it hindered and two reported no effect. Again, the three choices were not used equally [chi-square (2) = 36.95, $p < .01$]. Unlike the responses to the internal focus, though, significantly more respondents (28) indicated that the external focus helped than hindered (4) [chi-square (1) = 18, $p < .01$].

Additional two-way chi-square analyses using the Group classification indicated that the group did not affect the choices in either the internal or external session. Thus, reactions to the internal focus were mixed, but the external focus was seen as helping nearly all participants.

At the end of the session, after participants had used both the internal and external focus, they were asked to indicate which attentional strategy they found easier to use. Significantly [chi-square (1) = 14.24, $p < .01$] more individuals chose the external focus (28) than the internal focus (6). A second question asked respondents which strategy they would use in the future. Again, significantly [chi-square (1) = 11.77, $p < .01$], more individuals chose the external focus (27) than the internal focus (7). Additional two-way chi-square analyses indicated that the group classification did not affect performance. Thus, individuals performed more repetitions with an external focus than an internal focus, as hypothesized, and questionnaire responses indicated a clear preference for the external focus.

## Discussion

The findings that individuals preferred the external focus and performed more repetitions when using the external focus than the internal focus confirm the hypothesis, but they are somewhat inconsistent with Morgan and Pollock's (1977) widely cited work with marathon runners. Several differences between the two studies may account for the discrepancy. First, Morgan and Pollock's study was not a controlled experiment designed to compare the efficacy of two attentional strategies, but a report of cognitive styles used by a selected sample of runners. As well as that difference in purpose and design, the two studies used quite different samples and tasks. Apparently Morgan and Pollock's elite runners could deal with pain and actually used it to enhance performance. Non-elite runners in Morgan and Pollock's study, however, used a dissociation or distraction strategy. Perhaps the leg left task of the current study is more like the task for the non-elite runners. In both cases the primary goal seems to be to keep going or maintain performance in the face of pain and fatigue. It appears that elite runners monitor body sensations to pace themselves, and they need to note pain that could indicate malfunction or injury. In the leg extension task, though, monitoring body sensations has no obvious benefit. As noted in the introduction, Morgan and Pollock stated that distraction often increases pain tolerance and performance on endurance tasks, and cited the specificity of their sample and activity when discussing their findings.

It should be noted that a few participants in this study specifically stated that they needed to associate with body feelings and the pain in their legs to concentrate and push themselves further. Even though the findings indicate that the external focus yielded superior performance and was preferred by most, it was not universally preferred by all. Perhaps this is a key to the applications of many cognitive techniques in sport. Certain techniques may prove effective for particular tasks or in particular situations, but even then, some preferences and idio-syncrasies of athletes need not be eliminated.

## Subsequent research and application

Recent research has considered the impact of attentional focus on performance, this time on a task requiring fine motor control. Perkins-Ceccato, Passmore, and Lee (2003) found that the direction of attention affected performance on a golf task differently depending on skill level. Specifically, on a golf pitching task high-skilled golfers were more consistent when they had an external focus of attention (concentrating on hitting the ball as close to the target as possible) while the low-skilled performers were more consistent when they had an internal focus of attention (concentrating on the form of the golf swing). These findings are interesting as they highlight how a focus of attention inwards may lead to a reduction in performance for skilled athletes when required to perform a fine motor control task. This concurs with one potential explanation for the negative impact of anxiety on performance levels, which is that athletes, when anxious, will have a tendency to focus attention inwards and on the mechanics of the movement (Masters, 1992). This "paralysis by analysis" leads to a worse performance level than if the athlete did not attempt to consciously control the mechanics of the movement.

Anxiety may not only impact the direction of attention it may also impact other aspects of attentional focus. For example, under conditions of high arousal (that often accompanies anxiety, as well as other emotions such as anger) an individual's focus of attention is proposed to be narrower than under conditions of low arousal (Easterbrook, 1959). This narrowing in attentional width may have a positive effect on performance if it blocks out unimportant distractions, but a negative effect if task relevant cues are missed. Anxious individuals may also display an increased tendency to be distracted by peripheral cues (Janelle, 2002). Moran, Byrne, and McGlade (2002) demonstrated this in a study with gymnasts and proposed two potential explanations for this effect. It may have occurred because individuals attempted to compensate for the attentional narrowing associated with anxiety with more fixations in peripheral areas. Alternatively, attentional focus may have been governed by the subjective importance of cues rather than their location in the visual field and if there are potentially threatening cues in the periphery of the visual field then an athlete may find themselves drawn to those cues (e.g., a climber switching attention from the rock face to the steep drop). Indeed, previous research has demonstrated that individuals high in anxiety selectively attend to threatening stimuli (Mathews & Macleod, 1994).

While it is possible to classify attention in terms of whether it is directed towards internal or external factors it is probably more important to consider *what* an athlete is attending to. This is particularly relevant when considering that the thoughts an athlete is attending to can have very different effects on performance depending on whether the thoughts relate to positive or negative outcomes. To explain, while an athlete may have thoughts about what she should do, and should not do, in a particular situation she may very well do the one thing she was trying really hard to avoid (as in a golfer who tells herself the one thing she must not do is "hit her drive right and into the water" and then proceeds to do exactly that!). This phenomenon is explained by Wenger's (1994) theory of ironic processes of mental control where an ironic process refers to the ". . . tendency to feel, act, and think in ways that are opposite to the intended direction of emotion, behavior, and cognition" (Janelle, 1999: 2002). Ironic processes occur when an athlete suppresses thoughts about what they should not do. According to Wenger (1994), when this occurs the athlete will engage in a conscious search for thoughts that are different from the suppressed thought, which would be consistent with the desired (and more pleasant) state. At the same time the athlete will engage in an unconscious process whereby they monitor for signs that are incompatible with what they want to achieve (so that these can be dealt with and performance remain unaffected). In normal circumstances this works well and the conscious operating system focused on a positive goal state dominates. However, when an athlete is then placed under a high mental load (e.g., anxiety, time pressure) the unconscious (and ironic) system prevails because the conscious operating system is disrupted while the unconscious monitoring system remains unaffected. This results in the athlete doing, under pressure, the very things she was trying to avoid.

While researchers have been particularly interested in the construct of attention, assessing it, like many other psychological constructs, is a difficult process. Nideffer's (1976) TAIS is one of the most popular psychometric tests of attention in sport psychology, and among its advantages are the fact that it seems to make intuitive sense to coaches and athletes (Bond & Sargent, 1995) and that some athletes who had been rated by their coaches as "good concentrators" in competition have scored significantly lower on the broad external focus and broad internal focus sub-scales than did "poor concentrators" (Wilson, Ainsworth, & Bird, 1985). Unfortunately, these advantages must be weighed against the issue of whether athletes are capable of evaluating their own attentional processes using self-report instruments (Boutcher, 2002). The TAIS also assesses perceived, rather than actual, attentional skills. Therefore, it is not always possible to be sure that athletes who complete it are distinguishing accurately between what they actually do and what they would like us to believe that they do in everyday situations requiring attentional processes. Furthermore, scores on the TAIS did not predict how visual information was processed on a computer-based task (Dewey, Brawley, & Allard, 1989), or the performance of basketballers in a task requiring attention and decision-making skills (Vallerand, 1983). Lastly, scores on the TAIS failed to differentiate between athletes of different skill levels in sports in which selective attention is known to be important (Summers & Ford, 1990).

Although the psychometric paradigm is a popular but limited approach to the measurement of attentional processes in athletes, it has yielded a promising new instrument that measures concentration skills. In 2000, Hatzigeorgiadis and Biddle developed the *Thought Occurrence Questionnaire for Sport* (TOQS) that assesses the degree to which athletes experience cognitive interference from distracting thoughts (e.g., about previous mistakes that they have made) during competition. This test contains three sub-scales which use a standard stem item ("During the competition, I had thoughts . . .") that measures "task-related worries" (e.g., ". . . that other competitors are better than me"), "task-irrelevant thoughts" (e.g., ". . . about what I'm going to do when I'll go home") and "thoughts of escape" (". . . that I cannot stand it any more"). The reliability of each of these sub-scales appears to be impressive but the construct validity of the TOQS has not been established fully to date.

Researchers have also begun recently to search for reliable psychophysiological and/or neural substrates of attentional processes in athletes. Among the most popular indices of attention that have been studied in this regard is heart rate, and there is now evidence of cardiac deceleration among elite rifle-shooters just before they pull the trigger (Boutcher, 2002). This finding is interesting because it suggests that expert target shooters appear to be able to switch on their attention at will. Other techniques that are being employed include electroencephalographic (EEG) measures and event-related potential (Hatfield & Hillman, 2001), but unfortunately these have some conceptual and methodological limitations that curtail their usage in sport psychology including them being costly and time-consuming to administer and interpret. Moreover, although functional imaging techniques are very useful in helping to identify brain regions associated with certain tasks, they do not illuminate the psychological mechanisms which underlie cognitive activities (Cowey, 2001).

Attentional processes in athletes have also been measured recently by using the dual-task paradigm, which comes from experimental psychology (Abernethy, 2001). This theory proposed that attention may be defined operationally in terms of the interference between two tasks (a primary task and a secondary task) that are performed simultaneously. If these two tasks can be performed as well simultaneously as individually, then it suggests that at least one of them was automatic (i.e., demanding minimal attentional resources). However, if the primary task is performed less well when it is combined with the secondary task, then both tasks are believed to require some attentional resources. In the dual-task paradigm, two tasks are typically performed over three conditions. In condition one, the person has to perform the primary task on its own. In condition two, she or he must perform the secondary task on its own. In condition three, the tasks are performed concurrently.

When this method has been applied to sport psychology, the primary task usually consists of a self-paced or closed skill (i.e., one that can be performed without interference from others – e.g., target-shooting in archery) whereas the secondary task typically requires the subject to respond to a predetermined "probe" signal (e.g., an auditory tone). Following comparison of performance between these three conditions, conclusions may be drawn about the attentional demands of the primary and secondary tasks. Using this method, sport psychologists are usually interested in people's performance in condition three – the concurrent task situation. In this condition, participants are required to perform a primary task that is interrupted periodically by the presentation of the stimulus. When this probe signal occurs, the person has to respond to it as rapidly as possible. It is assumed that the speed of responding to the probe is related inversely to the momentary attention devoted to the primary task. Therefore, if a primary task is cognitively demanding, then a decrement should be evident in secondary task performance. But if the performance of the secondary task in the dual-task condition does not differ significantly from that evident in the relevant control condition, then it may be assumed that the primary task is relatively effortless (or automatic).

To date, unfortunately no consensus has emerged about the best combination of methods to use when assessing athletes' attentional processes. Despite its ingenuity, the dual-task paradigm from experimental psychology is rarely used to measure attentional processes in athletes for a number of reasons (Abernethy et al., 1998). For example, few criteria are available to guide researchers on the selection of appropriate secondary tasks in this method. Also, it is difficult to generate baseline measures for the performance of primary and secondary tasks. The self-report paradigm is, therefore, still perhaps the most popular of those available on account of its brevity, convenience and simplicity. Of course, a major problem with this approach is that few self-report measures of attention deal explicitly with concentration skills.

In terms of applications, concentration and attention have been found to be vital for success in sport, and studies of "peak performance" experiences (descriptive evidence) and research on the efficacy of concentration strategies on athletic performance (experimental evidence) supports this claim. Studies of peak performance experiences highlight the importance of absorption or concentration in the task at hand (e.g., Jackson, 1996; Kimiecik & Jackson, 2002). To explain, in these coveted but elusive states of mind, there appears to be no difference between what athletes are thinking about and what they are doing. This fusion of thought and action lies at the heart of what has been termed the "flow" experience. Thus, Jackson, Thomas, Marsh, and Smethurst (2001) defined flow as a "state of concentration so focused that it amounts to absolute absorption in an activity" (2001: 130). Similarly, Kimiecik and Jackson (2002) concluded that a "complete focus on the task at hand stands out as the clearest indication of flow" (2002: 506). Paradoxically, athletes often report feeling that their minds were empty during peak performances.

Given an appropriate focus of attention for performance is important it is no surprise that a number of strategies to enhance concentration have been proposed. Two categories of strategies have been outlined (Moran, 1996) and include training exercises (e.g., simulation training) or techniques that can be used during competition (e.g., performance routines). Regardless of the specific strategy employed the aim is to ensure that athletes focus attention on actions that they can control and are relevant to successful performance. There is evidence that strategies proposed to enhance concentration are associated with improvements in performance. For example, Mallett and Hanrahan (1997) found that sprinters who had been trained to use race plans that involved deliberately focusing on task-relevant information cues ran faster than those in baseline (control) conditions. Similarly, research suggests that the use of "associative" concentration techniques (in which athletes are trained to concentrate on bodily signals such as heart beat, respiratory signals, and kinaesthetic sensations) is associated with faster performance in running (Masters & Ogles, 1998; Morgan, 2000) and swimming (Couture, Jerome, & Tihanyi, 1999). However, there is very limited evidence that concentration enhancing strategies actually lead to an increase in concentration. For example, weekly completion of a concentration grid exercise did not enhance concentration in collegiate soccer players (Greenlees, Thelwell, & Holder, 2006) and there is little empirical evidence for the effectiveness of simulation training (Moran, 2004), or the use of key words (Lavallee, Kremer, Moran, &

Williams, 2004) in enhancing concentration. One recent exception is a study by Calmels, Berthoumieux and d'Arripe-Longueville (2004) who reported that an imagery program was effective in enhancing the selective attention ability of three softball players. Given the importance of an appropriate focus of attention there is clearly a need for research into the efficacy of concentration enhancement techniques.

## Additional readings

Abernethy, B. (2001). Attention. In R. N. Singer, H. A. Hausenblas, & C. M. Janelle (eds), *Handbook of research in sport psychology* (2nd ed., pp. 53–85). New York: Macmillan.

Abernethy, B., Summers, J. J., & Ford, S. (1998). Issues in the measurement of attention. In J. L. Duda (ed.), *Advances in sport and exercise psychology measurement* (pp. 173–93). Morgantown, WV: Fitness Information Technology.

Greenlees, I., & Moran, A. P. (eds) (2003). *Concentration skills training in sport.* Leicester: The British Psychological Society.

Moran, A. P. (1996). *The psychology of concentration in sport performers: A cognitive analysis.* Hove: Psychology Press.

Wegner, D. M. (1994). Ironic processes of mental control. *Psychological Review*, 101, 34–52.

## Study questions

1   Why did Gill and Strom ask the participants in this study to complete a questionnaire at the end of the experiment about their thoughts and feeling during performance?

2   How did the researchers explain that their findings were inconsistent with Morgan and Pollock's?

3   Outline the limitations of employing the TAIS in research with athletes.

4   Explain how sport psychology research can measure attention by using the dual-task paradigm.

5   What are the potential threats to your focus of attention (distractions) when competing?

## References

Abernethy, B. (2001). Attention. In R. N. Singer, H. A. Hausenblas, & C. M. Janelle (eds), *Handbook of research in sport psychology* (2nd ed., pp. 53–85). New York: Macmillan.

Abernethy, B., Summers, J. J., & Ford, S. (1998). Issues in the measurement of attention. In J. L. Duda (ed.), *Advances in sport and exercise psychology measurement* (pp. 173–93). Morgantown, WV: Fitness Information Technology.

Bond, J., & Sargent, G. (1995). Concentration skills in sport: An applied perspective. In T. Morris and J. Summers (eds), *Sport psychology: Theory, applications and issues* (pp. 386–419). Brisbane: Wiley.

Boutcher, S. H. (2002). Attentional processes and sport performance. In T. S. Horn (ed.), *Advances in sport psychology* (2nd ed., pp. 441–57). Champaign, IL: Human Kinetics.

Calmels, C., Berthoumieux, C., & d'Arripe-Longueville, F. (2004). Effects of an imagery training program on selective attention of national softball players. *The Sport Psychologist*, 18, 272–96.

Couture, R. T., Jerome, W., & Tihanyi, J. (1999). Can associative and dissociative strategies affect the swimming performance of recreational swimmers? *The Sport Psychologist*, 13, 334–43.

Cowey, A. (2001). Functional localisation in the brain: From ancient to modern. *The Psychologist*, 14, 250–4.

Dewey, D., Brawley, L. R., & Allard, F. (1989). Do the TAIS attentional-style scales predict how visual information is processed? *Journal of Sport and Exercise Psychology*, 11, 171–86.

Easterbrook, J. A. (1959). The effect of emotion on cue utilization and the organization of behavior. *Psychological Review*, 66, 183–201.

Greenlees, I., Thelwell, R., & Holder, T. (2006). Examining the efficacy of the concentration grid exercise as a concentration enhancement exercise. *Psychology of Sport and Exercise*, 7, 29–39.

Hatfield, B. D., & Hillman, C. H. (2001). The psychophysiology of sport: A mechanistic understanding of the psychology of superior performance. In R. N. Singer, H. A. Hausenblas, & C. M. Janelle (eds), *Handbook of research in sport psychology* (2nd ed., pp. 362–86). New York: Macmillan.

Hatzigeorgiadis, A., & Biddle, S. J. H. (2000). Assessing cognitive interference in sport: Development of the *Thought Occurrence Questionnaire for Sport*. Anxiety, Stress and Coping, 13, 65–86.

Jackson, S. A. (1996). Toward a conceptual understanding of the flow experience in elite athletes. *Research Quarterly for Exercise and Sport*, 67, 76–90.

Jackson, S. A., Thomas, P. R., Marsh, H. W., & Smethurst, C. J. (2001). Relationships between flow, self-concept, psychological skills, and performance. *Journal of Applied Sport Psychology*, 13, 129–53.

Janelle, C. M. (1999). Ironic mental processes in sport: Implications for sport psychologists. *The Sport Psychologist*, 13, 201–20.

Janelle, C. M. (2002). Anxiety, arousal and visual attention: A mechanistic account of performance variability. *Journal of Sports Sciences*, 20, 237–51.

Kahneman, D. (1973). *Attention and effort*. Englewood Cliffs, NJ: Prentice Hall.

Kimiecik, J. C., & Jackson, S. A. (2002). Optimal experience in sport: A flow perspective. In T. S. Horn (ed.), *Advances in sport psychology* (2nd ed., pp. 501–27). Champaign, IL: Human Kinetics.

Lavallee, D., Kremer, J., Moran, A., & Williams, M. (2004). *Sport psychology: Contemporary themes*. London: Palgrave.

Mallett, C. J., & Hanrahan, S. J. (1997). Race modelling: An effective cognitive strategy for the 100m sprinter? *The Sport Psychologist*, 11, 72–85.

Masters, K. S., & Ogles, B. M. (1998). Associative and dissociative cognitive strategies in exercise and running: 20 years later, what do we know? *The Sport Psychologist*, 12, 253–70.

Masters, R. S. W. (1992). Knowledge, knerves, and know-how. *British Journal of Psychology*, 83, 343–58.

Mathews, A., & Macleod, C. (1994). Cognitive approaches to emotion and emotional disorders. *Annual Review of Psychology*, 45, 25–50.

Matlin, M. W. (2002). *Cognition* (5th ed.). Fort Worth, TX: Harcourt Brace.

Moran, A. P. (1996). *The psychology of concentration in sport performers: A cognitive analysis*. Hove: Psychology Press.

Moran, A., Byrne, A., & McGlade, N. (2002). The effects of anxiety and strategic planning on visual search behavior. *Journal of Sports Sciences*, 20, 225–36.

Moran, A. P. (2004). *Sport and exercise psychology: A critical introduction*. Hove: Routledge.

Morgan, W. P. (2000). Psychological factors associated with distance running and the marathon. In D. T. Pedloe (ed.), *Marathon medicine* (pp. 293–310). London: The Royal Society of Medicine Press.

Morgan, W. P., Horstman, D. H., Cymerman, A., & Stokes, J. (1983). Facilitation of physical performance by means of a cognitive strategy. *Cognitive Therapy and Research*, 7, 251–64.

Morgan, W. P., & Pollock, M. L. (1977). Psychological characterization of the elite distance runner. *Annals of the New York Academy of Science*, 301, 382–403.

Nideffer, R. M. (1976). *The inner athlete*. New York: Thomas Crowell.

Pennebaker, J. W., & Lightner, J. M. (1980). Competition of internal and external information in an exercise setting. *Journal of Personality and Social Psychology*, 39, 165–74.

Perkins-Ceccato, N., Passmore, S. R., & Lee, T. D. (2003). Effects of focus of attention depend on golfers' skill. *Journal of Sports Sciences*, 21, 593–600.

Spanos, N., Horton, C., & Chaves, J. (1975). The effects of two cognitive strategies on pain threshold. *Journal of Abnormal Psychology*, 84, 677–81.

Summers, J. J., & Ford, S. K. (1990). *The Test of Attentional and Interpersonal Style:* An evaluation. *International Journal of Sport Psychology*, 21, 102–11.

Vallerand, R. J. (1983). Attention and decision making: A test of the predictive validity of the *Test of Attention and Interpersonal Style* (TAIS) in a sport setting. *Journal of Sport Psychology*, 5, 449–59.

Welch, J. C. (1898). On the measurement of mental activity through muscular activity. *American Journal of Physiology*, 1, 283–306.

Wenger, D. M. (1994). Ironic processes of mental control. *Psychological Review*, 101, 34–52.

Wickens, C. D. (1984). Processing resources in attention. In R. Parasuraman & D. R. Davies (eds), *Varieties of attention* (pp. 63–102). New York: Academic Press.

Wilson, V., Ainsworth, M., & Bird, E. (1985). Assessment of attentional abilities in male volleyball players. *International Journal of Sport Psychology*, 16, 296–306.

# 14

# Imagery

Hale, B. D. (1982). The effects of internal and external imagery on muscular and ocular concomitants. *Journal of Sport Psychology*, 4, 379–87.

## Background and context

Athletes often report that imagery is an essential part of their training and performance routines. For example, in a sample of 160 Canadian athletes from the 1984 Olympic team, 99% reported using imagery as a mental preparation strategy (Orlick & Partington, 1988). Imagery can be conceptualized as ". . . quasi-sensory and quasi-perceptual experiences of which we are self-consciously aware and which exists for us in the absence of those stimulus conditions that are known to produce their genuine sensory or perceptual counterparts" (Richardson, 1969: 2–3). Simply, imagery means the creation or re-creation of an event in our mind.

Imagery involves not only "seeing" things, but as Richardson points out it may involve any of the senses related to an event. For example, a tennis player imagining a serve might notice the touch and weight of the ball in one hand and the tennis racquet in the other, feel the arm and body movement associated with tossing the ball in the air and hitting the perfect slice serve, hear the ball come off the racquet and whizzing through the air, see the ball land and bounce past his opponent. If he is imagining serving on a hot day he may even smell his sweat and taste the salt on his lip. In addition to activating relevant senses, it is important that the imagery also creates the emotions associated with the sport experience (Martens, 1982). For example, in the tennis example, the player might create a calm feeling before serving and feelings of satisfaction and joy after hitting a great serve.

Imagery is a frequently used psychological technique and around the time of Hale's key study research had considered the effectiveness of imagery used in combination with relaxation techniques to enhance performance (e.g., Noel, 1980; Weinberg, Seabourne, & Jackson, 1981) and control stress (e.g., Suinn, 1972). Most of the research was however focused on the use of imagery as a technique to improve learning and performance (e.g., Clark, 1960) and there existed extensive reviews supporting the effectiveness of imagery in this regard (Corbin, 1972; Richardson, 1967a, b), including a review limited to just sport and motor behavior research from 1970 to 1982 (Martens, 1982).

The key study by Hale added to the literature by exploring the physiological changes that occurred as a result of imagery. This is an important area of research as an understanding of what changes occur at a physiological level may help explain how imagery can be used to aid learning and performance of a skilled movement. Much of the research investigating the physiological changes associated with imagery focused on muscular activity. This is assessed using a technique called electromyography (EMG) which measures the electrical activity of a muscle. Early research had already reported that imagery was accompanied by low-level muscular activity (e.g., Carpenter, 1894; Jacobson, 1931). If low-level muscular activity had the same pattern as that which occurred during the actual movement then it would strengthen the same neural pathways and could provide feedback to the imager enabling them to make adjustments to the motor skill for future performances (Corbin, 1972). Thus, by imagining a motor skill the athlete is getting a similar benefit to physically practicing the task in that they are able to "hone" the correct movement pattern from the peripheral feedback associated with the neuromuscular activity. This proposal for why imagery works has been referred to a *psychoneuromuscular* explanation (e.g., Richardson, 1967b).

The key study by Hale sought to build on the literature in a number of ways. First, Jacobson's study (1931) had demonstrated that low-level muscular activity did not always occur in response to imagery but that it depended on the nature of the imagery used. Specifically, low-level muscular activity was reported in the biceps when participants were asked to "imagine bending the right arm" or "imagine lifting a 10-pound weight." However, when participants were asked to "visualize bending their right arm" Jacobson observed no activity in the biceps but did observe some in the ocular muscles. Hale made a link between Jacobson's findings and research from Mahoney and Avener (1977) which reported that gymnasts who qualified for the US Olympic team reported greater use of internal, rather than external, imagery. That is, the successful gymnasts tended to imagine from "within their own body" – as a person would normally see the world (internal perspective). In contrast imaging from an external perspective means that the person sees themselves from outside their body, as if they were watching themselves on TV. In the key study Hale tested whether the type of perspective adopted would impact the physiological responses, in the same way that the different instructional set provided by Jacobson (1931) did.

In order to explain why a different imagery perspective (internal versus external) might lead to different responses Hale drew on Lang's (1979) bio-informational theory. According to Lang images are comprised of a series of logical relationships between concepts, termed propositions. During imagery a stimulus proposition is activated which describes the content of the image. For example, if an individual were to imagine taking a penalty flick in a field hockey match she may see the goal and hear her team-mates. Accompanying stimulus propositions are response propositions, which describe the emotional, physiological, and behavioral responses. For example, the hockey player may experience some anxiety but feel the correct movement patterns associated with a successful penalty flick. From Lang's description of stimulus and response propositions Hale inferred that external images would be primarily composed of ocular activity response propositions, while internal imagery would contain greater muscular activity response propositions.

## Key study

The purpose of this study was to investigate a primary assumption inherent to the ideo-motor (psychoneuromuscular) principle. Based on predictions drawn from Lang's (1979) bio-informational theory, this research sought to replicate in a controlled laboratory setting Jacobson's (1931) site-specific findings. Participants were hypothesized to produce more biceps electromyography (EMG) activity during internal compared to external images of a dumbbell curl. Because concomitant ocular activity is not crucial to a neuromuscular explanation of mental practice effects and Jacobson's ocular findings involved a medically unfeasible technique, with only a small subject population ($N = 3$), the hypothesis replicating his ocular results was considered secondary in importance. Previous researchers (Corbin, 1972; Richardson, 1967a) had also suggested that prior physical experience and recency of overt practice were influential factors on mental practice. Therefore, experienced weightlifters with recent prior practice were hypothesized to generate greater biceps EMG concomitance. In addition, several analyses tested possible relationships between vividness and concomitant amplitude (Shaw, 1940) and individual differences in imagery ability and style (Epstein, 1980).

## Method

### Participants

Male university students and faculty ($N = 48$) were recruited based on prior experience as "experienced" ($N = 24$) weightlifters (regularly lifted at least twice a week for 3 months prior to the investigation) or "inexperienced" ($N = 24$) lifters (did not regularly lift twice a week for 3 months preceding).

### Procedure

Participants first completed a 7-point *Imagery Exercise Questionnaire* (adapted from Epstein, 1980) of an imagined dumbbell curl in order to obtain information on possible individual differences in imagery perspective style, control, and vividness which might influence subsequent localized concomitance. The kinesthetic and visual sub-scales of the Bett's QMI *Vividness of Imagery Scale* (Sheehan, 1967) were also completed. Each subject rated the vividness of 10 test images on a 7-point scale.

Two Beckman standard silver-silver chloride electrodes were longitudinally attached over the motor endpoint of the dominant biceps brachii muscle, and a reference electrode was placed on the ventral wrist area. EMG activity was amplified, integrated, and printed by a Coulbourn (Model S10–21) portable modular biofeedback system at 6-sec intervals. Amplifier gain was set at 20,000 for baseline and covert activity and reduced to 5,000 for overt lifting. High and low pass filters narrowed measurement to 8–250 Hz. Another connection transferred the amplified data directly to one channel of a dual-channel Sencore (Model PI63) oscilloscope to allow continuous signal monitoring.

Two Beckman miniature silver-silver chloride electrodes were also attached vertically above the eyebrow and below the dominant eye in a straight line configuration. EOG data were amplified, integrated, and printed by a second channel component of the Coulbourn system. The gain was fixed at 20,000 for all overt and covert recordings, and high and low pass filters restricted the measurement range. Amplified EOG data were also transmitted to the second channel of the oscilloscope to permit visual monitoring.

Based on prior classification by weight lifting experience, subjects were randomly assigned to either a delayed imaginary lifting condition (25–30 min after overt lifting; $N = 24$) or an immediate imaginary lifting condition (5–10 min after overt biceps curls; $N = 24$). Possible order effects for imagery perspective were negated by first presenting the internal perspective to half of each group and the external perspective first to the other half (subsequent non-significant *t*-tests supported this assumption).

After EMG and EOG signal checks of printed output and oscilloscope activity, subjects underwent either the delayed or immediate group protocol while reclining on a cot. For the immediate imagery group, a 1-min pre-relaxation baseline (10 6-sec periods) was recorded to assess tonic activity level at muscular and ocular sites. Then a 20-min abbreviated progressive relaxation tape (adapted from Bernstein & Borkovec, 1973) was played in order to reduce residual muscle tension. Next, subjects sat and performed 10 biceps curls (6-sec EMG and EOG samples were recorded) with a 25 lb (11.34 kg) dumbbell while their attention was focused on the kinesthetic sensations in their biceps. Another 1-min post-lifting baseline was recorded almost immediately after they returned to a reclining position. In the delayed imagery group, all baseline and overt recordings duplicated the length and number of the immediate group's protocol, but the overt lifting occurred 25–30 min before the imagery conditions (prior to the relaxation procedure).

While reclining supinely on the cot, half of the participants in each group underwent the internal imagery protocol first and the other half received the external imagery instructions first. To begin a protocol, each person viewed five filmed trials of an 8mm film loop depicting the dumbbell curl from either a first-person or third-person visual perspective to further equate the exactness of the imagery manipulations. Each participant performed a practice imagery trial and 10 6-sec trials of each imagery perspective. In the internal imagery condition, participants were urged to "imagine what it feels like in your biceps to lift the 25 lb dumbbell" (muscular response propositions; Lang, 1979), and before the external imagery condition the emphasis was to "visualize what it looks like to lift the 25 lb dumbbell" (ocular response propositions; Lang, 1979). After each internal and external trial, subjects rated the vividness of the kinesthetic and visual sensations, respectively, on the same 7-point scale as the *Imagery Exercise Questionnaire*. Tonic activity at both sites was carefully monitored between trials via the oscilloscope to ensure that concomitant activity was not due to extraneous activation of a baseline shift. Participants were continually encouraged to remain relaxed between trials and not to isometrically contract the biceps or flex the elbow during imagination. During debriefing, all participants stated that they had successfully imaged from both perspectives.

## Results

### EMG Biceps Responses

The 10 trials of each imagery perspective condition were first averaged into one cumulative score. The post-relaxation baseline average score (10 trials) was then subtracted from the imagery average to yield a difference score for each subject in each perspective.

A $2 \times 2 \times 2$ (lifting experience × recency of lift × imagery perspective) analysis of variance with a repeated measure on the last factor revealed a significant within-subjects main effect for imagery perspective, $F(1,44) = 15.46$, $p < .001$. This finding suggested that the internal imagery perspective (mean difference score of .64 uV) produced greater biceps activity than the external imagery perspective (mean difference score of .08 uV) as predicted (see Table 14.1). No other significant main effects or interactions appeared.

### EOG Ocular Responses

EOG difference data were formulated in an identical manner as EMG data. Another $2 \times 2 \times 2$ (lifting experience × recency of lift × imagery perspective) repeated measures ANOVA resulted in nonsignificant values for all between- and within-subjects main effects and interactions.

**Table 14.1** Mean difference scores and standard deviations of biceps EMG and ocular EOG for imagery conditions (in uV)

|  | Internal imagery | | External imagery | |
|  | M | SD | M | SD |
| --- | --- | --- | --- | --- |
| Biceps EMG | .64[a] | 1.04 | .08[a] | .39 |
| Ocular EOG | .54 | 19.23 | −1.74 | 17.94 |

[a] The within-subjects main effect for biceps EMG difference scores during imagery conditions was significant, $p < .001$

## Relaxation Effects

The relaxation procedure (Bernstein & Borkovec, 1973) provided a means of physiologically monitoring tonic baseline activation and more closely replicated Jacobson's protocol (1931). Two dependent $t$-tests (paired scores method) were calculated on average pre-relaxation and post-relaxation baseline scores (10 consecutive 6-sec trials) for EMG and EOG data. Post-relaxation EMG scores were lower than pre-relaxation scores $t(48) = 1.97$, $p = .055$, and post-relaxation EOG scores were significantly lower than pre-relaxation records, $t(48) = 3.53$, $p < .001$. The relaxation procedure helped ensure a stable baseline during the imagery manipulations by reductions in muscular (mean difference of .18 uV) and ocular (mean difference of 8.41 uV) activity.

## Vividness Ratings and Concomitant Responses

Subjective vividness ratings of kinesthetic sensations (scale of 1–7) after each internal imagery trial were correlated with EMG biceps difference scores for each trial. Only on trials 7 and 10, small negative associations ($r = -.40$ and $-.33$, $p < .05$, respectively) appeared, implying that on most trials kinesthetic sensation awareness was not significantly related to biceps activity. For EOG data, subjective visual vividness ratings (scale of 1–7) were correlated with each EOG trial difference score. No significant correlations occurred, which indicated that visual vividness was not significantly related to concomitant ocular amplitude.

## Betts Subscale Ratings and Concomitant Responses

Subjects were classified post hoc as high (10 or less points; $n = 13$) or low (16 or more points; $n = 15$) scorers in kinesthetic imagery ability on the Betts sub-scale. A conservative Behrens-Fisher statistic computed on the two samples of internal EMG difference scores was nonsignificant, $t'(26) = -1.13$, $p > .05$, which indicated that kinesthetic imagery clarity was not a good predictor of biceps response amplitude during internal imagery. Statistical power was .82 at the .025 level for a one-tailed test.

Participants were also classified as high (10 or less points; $n = 11$) or low (17 or more points; $n = 11$) in visual vividness ability on the basis of the Betts visual sub-scale. Another Behrens-Fisher statistic on external EOG difference scores was again nonsignificant, $t'(20) = 1.07$, $p > .05$. Statistic power was .67 at the .025 level for this one-tailed test. Visual imagery ability was not associated with degree of ocular amplitude during external imagery.

### Natural Imagery Style and Concomitant Physiological Responses

Thirty-eight men were classified post hoc as "internals" ($N = 25$) or "externals" ($N = 13$) on the basis of the *Imagery Exercise Questionnaire*. A Behrens-Fisher statistic computed on internal EMG difference scores was nonsignificant, $t'(36) = .25$, $p > .05$. Statistical power was only .12 at the .025 level.

Another Behrens-Fisher statistic with external EOG difference scores produced non-significant results, $t'(36) = 1.35$, $p > .05$. Statistical power was .97 at the .025 level. In both cases, imagery style was not a viable classification of amount of concomitant muscular or ocular efference.

## Discussion

Jacobson's (1931) site-specific muscular activation finding was partially replicated by the EMG data. The internal imagery perspective did indeed produce substantial localized concomitance while the external imagery did not. This result further implies that imagery which more totally involves the individual in visual and kinesthetic experiences (muscular response propositions; Lang, 1979) is more likely to produce localized neuromuscular outflow than merely visualizing an action.

Other independent variables (prior lifting experience and recency of lift) failed to differentiate between subjects in concomitant physiological responses. Although previous literature reviews (Corbin, 1972; Richardson, 1967b) suggested that prior physical experience and recency of overt practice were critical prerequisites for maximal mental practice gains, apparently the 10 overt trials may have been sufficient prior experience to equate subjects with visual and kinesthetic task feedback. Schramm's (1967) data indicate that immediate, prior task experience can significantly enhance localized muscle responses during imagery. Furthermore, the time difference between lifting and imagery was only a matter of minutes between the two groups, which may not have been sufficiently distinct to clearly manipulate the recency independent variable.

Based on Jacobson's (1931) finding of isolated ocular activity occurring during "visualization," the secondary hypothesis predicted that external, not internal, imagery would generate EOG increments. Although this failure to replicate is not critical to motor behavior research, some examination of possible explanations is warranted. As stated previously, any direct comparison to Jacobson's findings was methodologically impossible since Jacobson's use of needle electrodes (EMG) inserted into the recti muscles was medically unfeasible.

Furthermore, it is possible that internal imagery instructions contained more powerful response propositions (Lang, 1979) for ocular movements than external instructions, thereby resulting in enhanced ocular concomitants during the former condition. Future investigations must carefully control the quantity and quality of response propositions in the image script.

Because the eye exhibits continuous movement, Oster and Stern (1978) have advised that the stereotypical eye shift movements be recorded prior to treatment manipulation so they may serve as a more valid baseline comparison of imagery outflow. Programmed computer identification of desired movements would greatly ensure the selection of particular ocular components; an average amplitude reading at rest is an unsatisfactory baseline because of inclusion of extraneous movements. A more accurate quantification of each eye movement is required if Jacobson's prediction is to be more reliably tested.

The individual differences in imagery ability and natural imagery style that previous reviewers (Corbin, 1972; Richardson, 1967a) had identified as mediating factors also did not differentiate between subjects by physiological concomitants. The findings involving imagery ability failed to replicate Shaw's (1940) observation with only three participants that greater arm muscle response during imagined lifting seemed to be linked to imagery vividness. Perhaps, as Lang's (1979) theory states, subject interpretive bias occurs in content-based ratings, and this does not accurately reflect the presence or absence of stimulus or response propositions in the image structure. According to Lang, participants must be first behaviorally trained to produce crucial response propositions in their images before predictions of correlations between vividness reports and physiological responses can be validly tested.

In accordance with Epstein's (1980) findings concerning imagery style, the data supported the notion that it may not be possible "to characterize subjects as strictly internal or external imagers because an individual's images varied considerably both within and between images" (1980: 218); style seems to be more a function of the scene imagined (Epstein, 1980), or more precisely, a function of the presence or absence of particular response propositions (Lang, 1979). According to Bauer and Craighead (1979), the crucial determinant of efference pattern is not imagery perspective per se, but attentional focus (on bodily reactions). Translated into motor behavior mechanisms, this prediction suggests that *kinesthetic* imagery should control localized neuromuscular effector patterns during mental practice.

The original ideomotor principle (Carpenter, 1894) asserted that mental practice is an effective learning aid because it produces neuromuscular activation patterns identical to those occurring during the same overt movement execution. The theorized neuromuscular feedback from this innervation continually "perfects" the controlling motor execution plan in the brain. Before any final judgment is rendered on this theory, more sophisticated EMG research, where amplitude, frequency, and duration patterns of a large number of contributing muscles would be simultaneously analyzed by an on-line computer, is necessary in order to reveal the complete picture of neuromuscular activation during covert movements.

Further examination of Lang's (1979) theory reveals many testable hypotheses applicable to motor behavior research. First, his prediction that response propositions determine effector outflow pattern deserves thorough investigation with sport tasks. In addition, the nature of response propositions in motor skill imagery and adequate means of evoking them must be determined. Lang's recent research (Lang, Kozak, Miller, Levin, & McLean, 1980) on a behavioral training program for increasing elicitation of specified response propositions and localized efference has direct application to sport psychology. If his theory is supported, then athletes could be trained to enhance vividness and efference generation (through reinforcement or biofeedback), and individual differences in imagery ability might be reduced. Then all sport participants might be able to receive maximal benefits from mental practice training.

## Subsequent research and application

The finding of Hale's key study that muscular activity was greatest with internal imagery contributed to a belief among sport psychologists that internal imagery was preferable to external imagery (Callow & Hardy, 2004). Specifically, it supported the assertion that kinesthetic aspects of a movement were harder to recreate with external imagery. More recent evidence suggests that imaging from an external perspective does not necessarily mean that kinesthetic aspects of the image cannot be achieved. For example, participants using external or internal imagery to rehearse a wheelchair slalom task and a gymnastic task reported experiencing kinesthetic imagery with the same frequency (White & Hardy, 1995). Weightlifters who regularly used imagery with either an internal or external perspective were equally effective in creating appropriate muscle firing in the biceps and triceps when imaging a bicep curl with their preferred imagery perspective (Vigus & Williams, 1987). Also, in a sample of sport science students kinesthetic imagery correlated positively with external visual imagery (Callow & Hardy, 2004). In short, internal and kinesthetic are not synonymous but refer to different aspects of imagery – the perspective and the modality, respectively (MacIntyre & Moran, 2003; Morris, Spittle, & Watt, 2005).

A central tenet of Hale's key study was that low-level muscular activity could occur as a result of some types of imagery. The suggestion that this activity has the same pattern as that which occurs during the actual movement, has been a popular concept in sport psychology and underpins *psychoneuromuscular* explanations for imagery's effectiveness in improving learning and performance. Indeed research has demonstrated, in line with the findings of Hale's key study, that low-level muscular activity can occur as a result of imagery. For example Bakker, Boschker, and Chung (1996) found EMG activity in the biceps to be higher when participants imagined doing a dumbbell curl. These findings were replicated by Slade, Landers, and Martin (2002) who also found elevated activity in the biceps and triceps of individuals who imagined dumbbell and manipulandum curls. However, the research has not yet supported the proposition that the low-level muscular activity has the same pattern as that which occurs during the actual movement. For example, when Slade *et al.* examined the pattern of biceps/triceps EMG activity it did not mirror the muscular activity observed during an actual curl. Also, in a footnote in the key study (but not reprinted in this abridged version) Hale also reported that during an exploratory investigation the percentage of biceps and triceps activity that occurred during overt and imagined lifting was different.

Indeed Hale and colleagues (Hale, Holmes, Smith, Fowler, & Collins, 2003) feel that research supports a functional equivalence model to explain imagery's effectiveness in learning and refining a motor skill (e.g., Jeannerod, 1994; Kosslyn, Ganis, & Thompson, 2001) and not a psychoneuromuscular explanation. That is, imagery can be an effective way of improving performance on a motor skill because the pattern of activity in the brain (and not the muscles as proposed by psychoneuromuscular explanations) is similar to that during the actual performance of a motor skill (Holmes & Collins, 2001). What differs between imagery of a motor skill and actual motor performance is that during imagery the movement is consciously blocked, or largely suppressed at some level of the cortico-spinal flow (Holmes & Collins, 2001). The muscular activity observed during Hale's key study (and the Bakker *et al.*, 1996 and Slade *et al.*, 2002 studies) could therefore be considered as a "leakage" that has occurred because the movement has not been completely inhibited (Jeannerod, 1997). In support of the functional equivalence approach imagery interventions that include greater perceptual information (which may be expected to stimulate more neural pathways in the brain) produced greater improvements in golf putting performance (Smith & Holmes, 2004). However, while the functional equivalence approach shows promise, Callow and Hardy (2005) note that based on the research evidence the degree of coincidence between the neural activity observed in motor imagery and that observed in motor activity is debatable.

Lang's bioinformational theory has been used as a theoretical basis to guide imagery research in sport settings. It has also been expanded since Hale conducted his key study to include meaning propositions which define the significance of the image, the likelihood of events and the potential consequences of an action (Lang, 1984). Imagery involving stimulus and response propositions improved performance on a field hockey penalty flick greater than imagery that involved only stimulus propositions (Holmes, Smith, Whitemore, Collins, & Devonport, 2001). Interestingly, Smith and Collins (2004) reported that the brain activity and performance did not differ between imagery focused on stimulus propositions and imagery focused more on response propositions on a strength task (increasing finger strength) but did differ on a cognitive task (computer game). They suggest that in order to improve performance on a cognitively oriented motor task a deeper level of processing is needed as these tasks are more complex and this occurs when the imagery is focused on response propositions.

In the years since Hale's key study there has been empirical support for many potential uses for imagery. Imagery has been used as a strategy to enhance self-efficacy and self-confidence (Callow, Hardy & Hall, 2001; Feltz & Reissinger, 1990), regulate emotions (Jones, Mace, Bray, MacRae, & Stockbridge, 2002), and as a technique to develop selected attention in softballers (Calmels, Berthoumieux & d'Arripe-Longueville, 2004). Athletes have also reported using imagery to help in the recovery from injury (e.g., Ievleva & Orlick, 1991). While research explicitly testing the effectiveness of imagery as a technique to facilitate injury rehabilitation is limited, there is reason to believe it may be effective in this regard. For example, imagery was an effective adjunctive technique to physical practice in improving the range of movement at the hip joint (Williams, Odley, & Callaghan, 2004).

Not surprisingly given the range of potential outcomes, there are different types of imagery. The type of imagery employed by the athlete will depend on what he or she wishes to achieve. Drawing on earlier research (Hall, Mack, Paivio, & Hausenblas, 1998; Paivio, 1985) a conceptual model of imagery use in sport settings has been proposed by Martin, Mortiz, and Hall (1999). In this model, five types of imagery are outlined. "Motivational-specific" imagery represents specific goals and goal-oriented behaviors such as imagining winning a race and receiving the congratulations of friends and family. "Motivational general-mastery" imagery refers to effective coping and mastery of challenging situations. For example, imagining feeling confident while standing on the first tee of a crucial golf tournament. "Motivational general arousal" imagery focuses on emotions and physio-logical changes in conjunction with sport competition. For example, recalling the feeling of anxiety associated with a crucial free throw in basketball or happiness associated with winning a crucial competition. "Cognitive-specific" imagery refers to specific sport skills, such as, executing a perfect soccer penalty kick. Finally, "cognitive general" imagery refers to competitive strategies. For example, a rugby player imaging particular attacking or defensive plays. These five types of imagery are functionally orthogonal which means that it is possible for an athlete to experience two or more types simultaneously (Martin *et al.*, 1999). It is crucial that the type(s) of imagery used should be consistent with, and appropriate for, the desired outcome(s). For example, motivational-specific imagery might be an effective strategy for increasing motivation on a cold, wet, windy training night but is unlikely to improve skill acquisition in a specific sport task – a function better served by cognitive-specific imagery.

Imagery is most often used as a strategy for the acquisition and practice of motor skills, and this use of imagery has the most robust empirical support. Since Hale's key study two meta-analyses have attested to imagery's effectiveness in this regard (Driskell, Cooper, & Moran, 1994; Feltz & Landers, 1983). Both reported similar findings in that imagery can benefit performers across all levels of experience and ability. However, imagery was found to be more effective for tasks with a cognitive component which provides some support for the notion that imagery is primarily a cognitive activity that mimics perceptual, motor, and emotional experiences in the brain (Lavallee, Kremer, Moran, & Williams, 2004) and not by stimulating peripheral muscular activity (which would support a psychoneuromuscular explanation).

Imagery is very much a technique used by athletes in the "real world" and research has investigated the nature and extent of what athletes *actually use* imagery for. Not surprisingly athletes tend to use imagery most during the competition period compared to practice (Munroe, Giacobbi Jr, Hall, & Weinberg, 2000; Weinberg, Butt, Knight, Burke, & Jackson, 2003) and in tough/difficult situations when the pressure is high (Weinberg *et al.*, 2003). Athletes reported using imagery for learning skills, rehearsing game plans and strategies, setting goals, controlling arousal and stress and to maintain and enhance self-confidence (Munroe *et al.*, 2000). Athletes also use imagery during the off-season and particularly athletes of a provincial and national skill compared to regional athletes (Cummings & Hall, 2002a). These provincial and national level athletes also engaged in more imagery during a typical week than did recreational athletes (Cummings & Hall, 2002b). Typically the imagery used by athletes is positive (Hall, Rodgers, & Barr, 1990; Munroe *et al.*, 2000), and this is important as imaging failure has a negative effect on performance (e.g., Nordin & Cummings, 2005; Taylor & Shaw, 2002).

Although less common, a growing body of research is documenting the application of imagery to exercise settings. Exercise participants reported using imagery for similar cognitive and motivational reasons to sports participants (Hausenblas, Hall, Rodgers, & Munroe, 1999). Specifically, Hausenblas *et al.* reported that exercisers used appearance imagery (e.g., imagine getting healthier and improving their physical appearance), technique imagery (e.g., imagining the steps to a particular exercise), and energy imagery (e.g., imagery to get "psyched up"). Exercisers use appearance imagery the most (Gammage, Hall, & Rodgers, 2000), and more frequent exercisers use imagery more often than less frequent exercises (Gammage *et al.*, 2000; Hausenblas *et al.*, 1999). Further, women use appearance imagery more so than men, but men use more technique imagery (Gammage *et al.*, 2000). Given the increasingly sedentary nature of western populations, continued research into exercise imagery is a worthwhile endeavor given that it may be a useful intervention to enhance exercise behavior by increasing motivation and self-efficacy to engage in exercise and physical activity (Giacobbi Jr, Hausenblas, Fallon, & Hall, 2003).

One of the major difficulties faced by psychologists is determining whether a participant in an experiment or an athlete with whom they are consulting is actually using imagery, and if yes, to determine the nature of that imagery experience. For example, is there any way of knowing whether their image of a dumbbell curl is similar to what the psychologist expects? In his key study Hale used a self-report questionnaire to collect data on vividness and kinesthetic sensations and whether participants could successfully image the task from the perspective required. This method of collecting data is common, and since Hale's key study a number of self-report measures have been developed to assess participants' imagery ability as well as when, and how, imagery is used.

Notwithstanding the debate about the psychometric qualities of these tests (Morris *et al.*, 2005) the measures are limited in that they are subject to contamination from a response set such as social desirability (Moran, 2004). Participants are likely to portray themselves as having a good or vivid imagination, regardless of their skills in this area (Moran, 2004). Recently, however, advances in brain imaging techniques make it possible to measure the areas of the brain which are activated during imagery (Jeannerod, 1994; Kosslyn *et al.*, 2001). This provides an experimentally sound way of assessing participants' imagery experiences and validating self-report measures of imagery ability and type. For example, currently it is possible to assess the validity of current self-report measures of imagery ability, and develop new measures, by assessing their relationship with spatial tasks requiring the use of imagery (Dean & Morris, 2003). The same could be done by assessing the relationship between self-report measures of imagery ability and actual brain activity.

Imagery is a technique that has clear applied implications for athletes in practice and competition, athletes in rehabilitation, and exercise participants. One of the challenges, therefore, facing psychologists is how best to deliver imagery interventions. A number of guidelines for practitioners in setting up an imagery program have been outlined by Vealey and Greenleaf (2006). These include guidelines on introducing imagery to athletes, helping athletes evaluate their imagery ability, and basic training for developing the core aspects of vividness, controllability, and using imagery to increase self-awareness of relevant thoughts and feelings. Imagery that is vivid (incorporates as many of the senses as possible to make it realistic) and includes both stimulus and response propositions should be more effective (Smith & Holmes, 2004). Interestingly, in addition to the "regular" five senses (sight, hearing, taste, smell, and touch) humans possess other senses such as proprioception (body awareness) or nociception (the perception of pain) and exploring how these senses are incorporated into imagery is an area for further research. Controllability is also critical so that the imagery can be manipulated for the intended purpose and so that the imagery is kept positive and not negative. Further, imagery should be integrated into practice sessions so that it becomes a consistent part of training, while integrating imagery into a pre-performance routine ensures it becomes a consistent part of competition. Finally, it is particularly important that athletes practice imagery, as just like any other skill, practice strengthens the ability to use imagery.

## Additional readings

Hall, C. R. (2001). Imagery in sport and behavior. In R. Singer, H. A. Hausenblas, & C. M. Janelle (eds.), *Handbook of sport psychology* (pp. 529–49). New York: John Wiley.

Hale, B. D., Seiser, L., McGuire, E. J., & Weinrich, E. (2005). Mental imagery. In J. Taylor & G. S. Wilson (eds), *Applying sport psychology: Four perspectives* (pp. 117–35). Champaign, IL: Human Kinetics.

Morris, T., Spittle, M., & Watt, A. P. (2005). *Imagery in sport*. Champaign, IL: Human Kinetics.

Murphy, S. M., & Martin, K. A. (2002). The use of imagery in sport. In T. Horn (ed.), *Advances in sport psychology* (pp. 405–39). Champaign, IL: Human Kinetics.

Vealey, R. S., & Greenleaf, C. A. (2006). Seeing is believing: Understanding and using imagery in sport. In J. M. Williams (ed.), *Applied sport psychology: Personal growth to peak performance* (5th ed., pp. 306–48). New York: McGraw-Hill.

## Study questions

1 Why did Hale control for weightlifting experience in the study?

2 Do you use imagery for any sport and exercise related aspects? Using Martin *et al.*'s (1999) model, outline what type(s) of imagery you use and for what outcomes?

3 What are some of the challenges faced by researchers interested in exploring how imagery works?

4 Why is it important to incorporate a range of senses when devising an imagery script?

5 Outline one major research question that imagery researchers should address in the future?

## References

Bakker, F. C., Boschker, M. S. J., & Chung, T. (1996). Changes in muscular activity while imagining weight lifting using stimulus or response propositions. *Journal of Sport & Exercise Psychology*, 18, 313–24.

Bauer, R. M., & Craighead, W. E. (1979). Psychophysiological responses to the imagination of fearful and neutral situations: The effects of imagery instructions. *Behavior Therapy*, 10, 389–403.

Bernstein, D. A., & Borkovec, T. D. (1973). *Progressive relaxation training: A manual for the helping professions.* Champaign, IL: Research Press.

Callow, N., & Hardy, L. (2004). The relationship between kinaesthetic imagery and different visual imagery perspectives. *Journal of Sports Sciences*, 22, 167–177.

Callow, N., & Hardy, L. (2005). A critical analysis of applied imagery research. In D. Hackfort, J. L. Duda, & R. Lidor (eds), *Handbook of research in applied sport and exercise psychology: International perspectives* (pp. 37–58). Morgantown, WV: Fitness Information Technology.

Callow, N., Hardy, L., & Hall, C. (2001). The effects of a motivational general-mastery imagery intervention on the sport confidence of high-level badminton players. *Research Quarterly for Exercise & Sport*, 72, 389–400.

Calmels, C., Berthoumieux, C., & d'Arripe-Longueville, F. (2004). Effects of an imagery training program on selective attention of national softball players. *The Sport Psychologist*, 18, 272–96.

Carpenter, W. B. (1894). *Principles of mental physiology* (4th ed.). New York: Appleton.

Clark, L. V. (1960). Effect of mental practice on the development of a certain motor skill. *Mental Practice and Motor Skill*, 31, 560–9.

Corbin, C. B. (1972). Mental practice. In W. P. Morgan (ed.), *Ergogenic aids and muscular performance.* New York: Academic Press.

Cummings, J., & Hall, C. (2002a). Athletes' use of imagery in the off-season. *The Sport Psychologist*, 16, 160–72.

Cummings, J., & Hall, C. (2002b). Deliberate imagery practice: the development of imagery skills in competitive athletes. *Journal of Sports Sciences*, 20, 137–45.

Dean, G. M., & Morris, P. E. (2003). The relationship between self-reports of imagery and spatial ability. *British Journal of Psychology*, 94, 245–73.

Driskell, J. E., Cooper, C., & Moran, A. (1994). Does mental practice enhance performance? *Journal of Applied Psychology*, 79, 481–92.

Epstein, M. L. (1980). The relationship of mental imagery and mental rehearsal to performance on a motor task. *Journal of Sport Psychology*, 2, 211–20.

Feltz, D. L., & Landers, D. M. (1983). The effects of mental practice on motor skill learning and performance: A meta-analysis. *Journal of Sport Psychology*, 5, 25–57.

Feltz, D. L., & Reissinger, C. A. (1990). Effects of in-vivo emotive imagery and performance feedback on self-efficacy and muscular endurance. *Journal of Sport and Exercise Psychology*, 12, 132–43.

Gammage, K. L., Hall, C. R., & Rodgers, W. M. (2000). More about exercise imagery. *The Sport Psychologist*, 14, 348–59.

Giacobbi Jr., P. R., Hausenblas, H. A., Fallon, E. A., & Hall, C. A. (2003). Even more about exercise imagery: A grounded theory of exercise imagery. *Journal of Applied Sport Psychology*, 15, 160–75.

Hale, B., Holmes, P., Smith, D., Fowler, N., & Collins, D. (2003). Give those men a cigar (but no light): A reply to Slade, Landers, and Martin. *Journal of Sport & Exercise Psychology*, 25, 402–9.

Hall, C., Mack, D. E., Paivio, A., & Hausenblas, H. (1998). Imagery use by athletes: development of the *Sport Imagery Questionnaire. International Journal of Sport Psychology*, 23, 1–17.

Hall, C., Rodgers, W. M., & Barr, K. A. (1990). The use of imagery by athletes in selected sports. *The Sport Psychologist*, 4, 1–10.

Hausenblas, H. A., Hall, C. R., Rodgers, W. M., & Munroe, K. J. (1999). Exercise imagery: Its nature and measurement. *Journal of Applied Sport Psychology*, 11, 171–80.

Holmes, P. S., & Collins, D. J. (2001). The PETTLEP approach to motor imagery: A functional equivalence model for sport psychologists. *Journal of Applied Sport Psychology*, 13, 60–83.

Holmes, P. S., Smith, D., Whitemore, L., Collins, D., & Devonport, T. (2001). The effect of theoretically-based imagery scripts on hockey penalty flick performance. *Journal of Sport Behavior*, 24, 408–19.

Ievleva, L., & Orlick, T. (1991). Mental links to enhanced healing: An exploratory study. *The Sport Psychologist*, 5, 25–40.

Jacobson, E. (1931). Electrical measurements of neuromuscular states during mental activities. *American Journal of Physiology*, 96, 115–21.

Jeannerod, M. (1994). The representing brain: Neural correlates of motor intention and imagery. *Behavioral and Brain Sciences*, 17, 187–245.

Jeannerod, M. (1997). *The cognitive neuroscience of action*. Oxford: Blackwell Publishers.

Jones, M. V., Mace, R. D., Bray, S. R., MacRae, A., & Stockbridge, C. (2002). The impact of motivational imagery on the emotional state and self-efficacy levels of novice climbers. *Journal of Sport Behavior*, 25, 57–73.

Kosslyn, S. M., Ganis, G., & Thompson, W. L. (2001). Neural foundations of imagery. *Nature Reviews: Neuroscience*, 2, 635–42.

Lang, P. J. (1979). A bio-informational theory of emotional imagery. *Psychophysiology*, 16, 495–512.

Lang, P. J. (1984). Cognition in emotion: concept and action. In C. E. Izard, J. Kagan, & R. B. Zajonc (eds), *Emotions, cognition and behavior* (pp. 192–226). New York: Cambridge University Press.

Lang, P. J., Kozak, M. J., Miller, G. A., Levin, D. N., & McLean Jr., A. (1980). Emotional imagery: Conceptual structure and pattern of somato-visceral response. *Psychophysiology*, 17, 179–92.

Lavallee, D., Kremer, J., Moran, A., & Williams, M. (2004). *Sport psychology: Contemporary themes*. London: Palgrave.

MacIntyre, T., & Moran, A. (2003). Learning through imagery functions from a sport psychology perspective. *Journal of Mental Imagery*, 27, 121–5.

Mahoney, M. J., & Avener, M. (1977). Psychology of the elite athlete: An exploratory study. *Cognitive Therapy and Research*, 1, 135–41.

Martens, R. (1982). Imagery in sport. In M. L. Howell & A. W. Parker (eds), Proceedings of the Australian Sports Medicine Federation International Conference. Vol. 8, *Sports medicine: Medical and scientific aspects of elitism in sport*, pp. 213–30.

Martin, K. A., Moritz, S. E., & Hall, C. R. (1999). Imagery use in sport: A literature review and applied model. *The Sport Psychologist*, 13, 245–68.

Moran, A. P. (2004). *Sport and exercise psychology: A critical introduction*. London: Routledge.

Morris, T., Spittle, M., & Watt, A. P. (2005). *Imagery in sport*. Champaign, IL: Human Kinetics.

Munroe, K. J., Giacobbi Jr., P. R., Hall, C., & Weinberg, R. (2000). The four Ws of imagery use: Where, when, why, and what. *The Sport Psychologist*, 14, 119–37.

Noel, R. C. (1980). The effect of visuo-motor behavior rehearsal on tennis performance. *Journal of Sport Psychology*, 2, 221–6.

Nordin, S. M., & Cummings, J. (2005). More than meets the eye: Investigating imagery type, direction, and outcome. *The Sport Psychologist*, 19, 1–17.

Orlick, T., & Partington, J. (1988). Mental links to excellence. *The Sport Psychologist*, 2, 105–30.

Oster, P. J., & Stern, J. A. (1978). Electrooculography. In I. Martin & P. H. Venables (eds), *Techniques in psychophysiology*. London: Wiley.

Paivio, A. (1985). Cognitive and motivational functions of imagery in human performance. *Canadian Journal of Applied Sport Sciences*, 10, 22s–28s.

Richardson, A. (1967a). Mental practice: A review and discussion: Part I. *Research Quarterly*, 38, 95–107.

Richardson, A. (1967b). Mental practice: A review and discussion: Part II. *Research Quarterly*, 38, 263–73.

Richardson, A. (1969). *Mental imagery*. New York: Springer.

Schramm, V. (1967). *An investigation of EMC responses obtained during mental practice*. Unpublished masters thesis, University of Wisconsin.

Shaw, W. A. (1940). The distribution of muscular action potentials to imaginal weight lifting. *Archives of Psychology*, 35(247), 5–50.

Sheehan, P. W. (1967). A shortened form of Betts questionnaire upon mental imagery. *Journal of Clinical Psychology*, 23, 386–9.

Slade, J. M., Landers, D. M., & Martin, P. E. (2002). Muscular activity during real an imagined movements: A test of inflow explanations. *Journal of Sport & Exercise Psychology*, 24, 151–67.

Smith, D., & Collins, D. (2004). Mental practice, motor performance, and the late CNV. *Journal of Sport & Exercise Psychology*, 26, 412–26.

Smith, D., & Holmes, P. (2004). The effect of imagery modality on golf putting performance. *Journal of Sport & Exercise Psychology*, 26, 385–95.

Suinn, R. (1972). Behavior rehearsal training for ski racers. *Behavior Therapy*, 3, 519–20.

Taylor, J. A., & Shaw, D. F. (2002). The effects of outcome imagery on golf-putting performance. *Journal of Sports Sciences*, 20, 607–13.

Vealey, R. S., & Greenleaf, C. A. (2006). Seeing is believing: Understanding and using imagery in sport. In J. M. Williams (ed.), *Applied sport psychology: Personal growth to peak performance* (5th ed., pp. 306–48). New York: McGraw-Hill.

Vigus, T. L., & Williams, J. M. (1987). *The effect of skill level and imagery experience on EMG activity and patterning during internal and external imagery*. North American Society for Psychology of Sport and Physical Activity, Vancouver, BC, June.

Weinberg, R., Butt, J., Knight, B., Burke, K. L., & Jackson, A. (2003). The relationship between the use and effectiveness of imagery: An exploratory investigation. *Journal of Applied Sport Psychology*, 15, 26–40.

Weinberg, R. S., Seabourne, T. G., & Jackson, A. (1981). Effects of visuo-motor behavior rehearsal, relaxation, and imagery on karate performance. *Journal of Sport Psychology*, 3, 228–38.

White, A., & Hardy, L. (1995). Use of different imagery perspectives on the learning and performance of different motor skills. *British Journal of Psychology*, 86, 169–80.

Williams, J. G., Odley, J. L., & Callaghan, M. (2004). Motor imagery boosts proprioceptive neuromuscular facilitation in the attainment and retention of range-of-motion at the hip joint. *Journal of Sports Science and Medicine*, 3, 160–6.

# 15

# Goal-setting

Hall, H. K., Weinberg, R. S., & Jackson, A. (1987). Effects of goal specificity, goal difficulty, and information feedback on endurance performance. *Journal of Sport Psychology*, 9, 43–54.

**Written in collaboration with Caroline Douglas**

## Background and context

The importance placed on having a goal can be viewed through a variety of anecdotal accounts in the autobiographies of many athletes and coaches. Given this importance of goal-setting and the abundance of research on goal-setting in general psychology, surprisingly little research had occurred within the realm of sport psychology prior to the key study. Nevertheless, based on the research that existed at that time and reports from sport psychologists who used goal-setting interventions with athletes, Gould (1986) concluded that goal-setting had been shown not only to enhance the performance of athletes, but had been linked to positive changes in psychological states such as anxiety, confidence, and motivation. Little was known, however, regarding the most effective way to employ goal-setting.

One way in which it is possible to understand how goals are believed to enhance performance is to examine the purpose of goal-setting. The practice of assigning specific goals to individuals emerged out of efforts in management and industrial/organizational (I/O) psychology to increase the productivity of manufacturing workers. Goal-setting was considered to be a technique of scientific management (Taylor, 1911) that involved motivational leadership. This approach would later evolve into the contemporary business leadership strategy of management by objectives (MBO). Central to the MBO style is the practice of identifying specific performance objectives and potential constraints in order to develop a method of goal attainment (Ordiorne, 1978).

Using these hypotheses of scientific management, Locke (1968) suggested a goal-directed theory of motivation based on a more direct relationship between goals and individual performance – a link previously overlooked in leadership motivation models that focused on the development of efficiency. Locke's premise was based on the intention of the individual and the impact of different goals. His key assertions were that difficult goals are more effective than easy goals and specific goals produce a higher level of performance than "do your best" goals or no goals. A goal is defined as ". . . what an individual is trying to accomplish; it is the object or aim of an action" (Locke, Shaw, Saari, & Latham, 1981: 126). Locke *et al.* further define it as "attaining a specific standard of proficiency on a task, usually within a specified time limit" (1981: 145).

In a comprehensive review of I/O goal-setting studies undertaken between 1969 and 1980, Locke *et al.* (1981) established empirical support in both field and laboratory settings for the premise that goals positively influence task performance. In 99 out of 110 examined studies, results showed positive effects, leading the researchers to conclude that ". . . the beneficial effect of goal setting on task performance is one of the most robust and replicable findings in the psychological literature" (1981: 145). Locke *et al.* proposed the following four underlying mechanisms to explain exactly how goals influenced performance: goals direct action by focusing attention; goals mobilize and regulate effort on a task; goals enhance persistence; and goals motivate development of problem-solving strategies in attempts to reach a goal. These explanations were subsequently challenged by assertions that they were merely tautological statements. Moreover, the mechanisms fail to elaborate on the matter of why an athlete can have goals in place but still fail to attain those goals, even if the individual has both motivation and the necessary physical ability (Kuhl, 1984).

The gap between I/O psychology research and sport was effectively bridged by Locke and Latham's (1985) contention that goal-setting should work more effectively in sport than in business because performance measurements, such as points scored or shots attempted, are entirely objective. Locke and Latham, therefore, called for sport- and exercise-based studies by suggesting specific hypotheses each with practical examples of where and how goals should be relevant (e.g., in competition, training, for developing self-confidence, and in the development of long-term strategies).

There were very few sport-based investigations at the time of Hall, Weinberg, and Jackson's key study that had examined Locke and Latham's (1985) goal-performance relationship. A notable exception is a study by Weinberg, Bruya, and Jackson (1985) which tested the effects of randomly assigned goal conditions on the performance of a sit-up task on university students enrolled in fitness courses. Results showed no significant performance differences between "do your best" goals and "specific difficult" goals, a finding that was in complete contrast with the majority of I/O research, which had shown overwhelming support for the superiority of specific goals (Locke *et al.*, 1981).

In light of this result, as well as other unpublished sport studies also conducted in field settings, the key study sought to understand how goal-setting manifests in sport by firstly undertaking a laboratory-based test in which grip strength endurance was measured by a hand dynamometer. The purpose of the research was both to test goal specificity, as previously examined by Weinberg *et al.* (1985), and also to study goal-setting strategies by examining the contention that goals combined with feedback enhance performance more effectively than using just goals *or* feedback alone (Locke *et al.*, 1981). Although Hall *et al.* acknowledged the possible effects of participants competing against each other, and that setting covert goals may have impacted findings in previous sport and exercise studies (i.e., 83% of control participants in the Weinberg *et al.* study in 1985 admitted setting personal targets), they sought to initially explore more general effects.

## Key study

One purpose of this study was to test Locke's (1968) basic assumption that participants assigned specific difficult goals will perform better than those assigned generalized "do your best" goals. This assumption was tested in a motor skill situation utilizing an endurance task requiring considerable effort and persistence. Specifically, it was hypothesized that the more difficult improvement goal would lead to better performances than the less difficult improvement goal and also that participants in both specific goal groups would be superior to those participants with "do best" goals.

A further basic assumption outlined by Locke *et al.* (1981) is that for goal-setting to be effective, the goals must be accompanied by performance feedback. Attempts to separate the effects of feedback from the effects of goal-setting were made in many early studies (e.g., Locke, 1968; Locke & Bryan, 1968, 1969; Locke, Cartledge, & Koeppel, 1968). Results from these studies indicated that knowledge of results (KR) independently was not enough to improve performance, but could be a necessary condition for goals to improve performance. Locke *et al.* (1981) concluded that neither goals alone nor KR alone is sufficient to improve performance, but rather both are necessary to facilitate improvement.

Bandura and Simon (1977) emphasized how goals and feedback are reciprocally dependent, with feedback being most effective as an adjunct to goals when the task is divided into trials and feedback is provided following each one. They found that overweight clients in a weight clinic who kept daily records of their food consumption but did not set goals to reduce consumption did not alter their eating habits and performed similarly to a control group who neither kept records nor set specific goals. Clients who did set specific goals and also kept daily records of food intake consumed significantly less than the control group.

In the sport and motor performance literature, there is little doubt that feedback plays a critical role in both learning and performance (Newell, 1974; Schmidt, 1982), although it can be presented in various forms and at different times. Due to the requirements of a particular motor skill, the form or timing of feedback may have differing effects on task performance. Concurrent feedback occurring during the performance may regulate the moment-to-moment performance of particular tracking skills such as catching, throwing to a moving target, or steering a car (Stallings, 1982). Terminal feedback occurs following a performance and is much more widely used in aiding motor performance than is concurrent feedback because administering feedback during performance is often difficult. Stallings (1982) suggests that physical educators tend to rely on terminal feedback as their only alternative. However, skills involving performing against a clock are likely to improve if feedback is administered during the event. Thus, another purpose of this study was to test the notion that concurrent feedback provided as an adjunct to goals would lead to greater performance enhancement than terminal feedback.

## Method

### Preliminary Procedures

A pilot study was conducted with 20 male college students to determine at what level to set specific hard goals. Participants were tested in a do best condition to ascertain if performance would improve significantly in the absence of goal-setting instructions.

Using a hand dynamometer, participants were tested for maximum grip strength. Once this was established, participants had three minutes to recover from the effects of fatigue. The participants were then placed in either a terminal or concurrent feedback condition and were asked to hold a contraction of one-third maximum tension for as long as possible. Simonson (1971) found that a contraction of one-third maximum tension would result in performances of approximately three minutes, allowing the effects of other variables to be measured. Once participants could no longer hold this contraction at one-third maximum tension, they were given a 20-min rest period. Following this, they were asked to hold a second contraction at one-third maximum tension. This enabled the determination of mean performance improvements for subjects in a do best condition, which for the pilot study group was 2.9%.

Questionnaire results indicated that if given the option to set their own goals, participants would set them at 35% above the baseline endurance performance, and would not accept goals of 47% above the baseline level. However, they were obviously overestimating their abilities in setting these extremely high goals considering that the mean improvement from Trial 1 to Trial 2 was just 2.9%. Dossett, Latham, and Mitchell (1979) found that when subjects participated in the goal-setting process, high goals were established. However, no performance differences occurred between participants assigned hard goals by an experimenter and those who participated in the process and set higher goals. Therefore, based upon both the performance improvements of 2.9% from the first to second trial and evidence suggesting that subjects participating in the goal-setting process would set extremely high goals, it was decided that goals of 15 and 25% above the baseline level would be assigned. These were deemed to be difficult and very difficult, respectively, when compared to the pilot group's performance.

Expressed in absolute terms, specific hard goals were either 40 seconds (s) (15% above the group mean score on the pilot study) or 70 s (25% above the group mean score on the pilot study) over the score attained on the first endurance trial. It was decided that the goals should be assigned by the experimenter rather than allowing participants to set their own goals. This decision was based on the conclusions of Locke *et al.* (1981) that no consistent evidence suggests that participation in setting goals leads to either greater commitment or better task performance than having assigned goals when goal level is controlled.

## Participants and Design

The participants for the study were 94 male students enrolled at a university in the Southwest. All the participants were assigned randomly to a 40-s or 70-s improvement goal or a do best goal and received either concurrent or terminal feedback on their performance.

## Task

A Lafayette 4205 hand dynamometer was used to secure an index of general bodily strength and also to obtain an index of endurance or fatigue. While performing the three trials, participants were seated at a table and placed their dominant arm (determined by asking the study participant) along a line drawn at a 30° angle on the table placed in front of them, so as to standardize the testing procedure.

## Procedures

A total of three trials were given to all participants. The first trial was a pretest used to obtain a basal (maximum) strength measurement and to determine initial strength differences between the groups. Following this pretest trial, a three minute rest period was given to enable the participants to recover from the effects of fatigue. Participants then performed the first experimental trial in which they were asked to perform the task at one-third maximum tension for as long as possible.

*Feedback Manipulation.* Participants were given feedback regarding their performance on both the first and second experimental trials in one of two forms. Those given concurrent feedback had a digital timer placed directly in front of them during their performance, whereas participants given terminal feedback were simply told how long they had held the contraction following their performance. Once participants could no longer hold the isometric contraction at one-third maximum tension, they were given a 20 minute rest period before undertaking the second experimental trial. The length of the rest period was based on Lind's (1983) findings that the recovery of the ability to exert maximum tension after fatigue in isometric contractions of one-third maximum tension was 90% complete after seven minutes and 100% complete after 20 minutes.

*Goal Specificity and Difficulty Manipulation.* Following the 20 minute rest period, each participant was randomly assigned to a goal difficulty condition and given a set goal, based upon initial performance on the first experimental trial. In many previous studies, specific hard goals were arbitrarily assigned; in the present study, however, the goal difficulty was determined from the results of a pilot study. The two levels of specific goal difficulty were set by asking subjects to perform at least 40 s or at least 70 s above their initial performance levels. These goals represented a 15 and 25% improvement (in absolute terms) above the group mean score for a do best condition on the pilot test. Finally, a control condition was included whereby participants were simply told to do their best.

The specific goals were reflected in absolute terms rather than as percentages of individual performances because performance ceilings are more likely to influence those who scored high on experimental Trial 1 than those who scored low. Specifically, a 25% goal for a subject with a high score is far greater in absolute terms than the same 25% goal for an individual with a low score. Schmidt (1982) alludes to this by stating that as performance improvements occur, psychological or physiological ceilings present a barrier. As these ceilings are approached, smaller performance improvements are possible than when performances are at an intermediate or low level.

Once participants had been assigned their goals, they were then asked to complete a pre-experimental questionnaire to determine whether or not they accepted the specific set goals, because when specific hard goals are assigned they must be accepted by the subject in order to have any positive effects upon performance (Locke *et al.*, 1981), To increase the likelihood of goal acceptance, subjects were informed that if they reached the set goal, they would receive $1. Locke *et al.* (1981) stressed that incentives affect the individual's degree of goal commitment. In essence, the offer of monetary rewards leads to participants expending more effort to attain the goal than not offering money.

In terms of expectancy theory, monetary rewards endow goal success with a higher valance than no money. Further, Deci and Porac (1978), investigating intrinsic and extrinsic motivation, suggested that monetary rewards that encourage the attainment of competence on a task (reaching a challenging goal) may enhance rather than decrease interest in the task. The do best group was given the same monetary incentive as the other two goal-difficulty groups; however, participants were told they must achieve an undisclosed standard (20% above their first endurance performance) known only to the experimenter. In addition to goal acceptance, participants in the 40- and 70-s goal conditions were asked to rate how difficult and realistic their goal was along with their commitment to achieving this goal on a 0-to-100 scale.

After participants had been assigned their goals and goal acceptance had been assessed, they performed the second experimental trial holding the contraction at one-third maximum tension. Once again participants received either concurrent or terminal feedback in the same manner as in the first experimental trial. Following this trial, participants were asked to complete a post-experimental questionnaire in order to assess various feelings and cognitions related to their performance on a 0-to-100 scale.

## Results

### Performance

A 2 × 3 × 2 (feedback × goal specificity × trials) analysis of variance (ANOVA) with repeated measures on the last factor was employed to analyze the performance data. A significant trials effect, $F(1, 88) = 54.95$, $p < .001$, was found with participants performing significantly better on the second trial ($M = 262.37$) than on the first trial ($M = 224.54$). Results also indicated a significant goals-by-trials interaction, $F(2, 88) = 13.1$, $p < .001$, and simple main effects analysis for each goal condition across trials showed that the 40- and 70-s goal groups improved significantly ($p < .05$) from Trial 1 to Trial 2. No significant improvement was found for the "do your best" condition. In addition, concerning differences among goal-setting conditions at each trial, results revealed there were no significant differences on Trial 1. However, on Trial 2 the 40-s goal group was significantly better ($M = 285.65$) than the do best group ($M = 233.22$). No significant differences were found between the concurrent and terminal feedback conditions. The goal-by-trials interaction is depicted in Figure 15.1. Performance means are presented in Table 15.1.

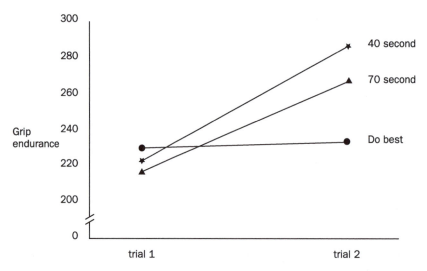

**Figure 15.1** Goal-by-trials interaction

**Table 15.1** Performance means for grip endurance

| Feedback | Do best | SD | 40 | SD | 70 | SD |
|---|---|---|---|---|---|---|
| Trial 1 | | | | | | |
| Terminal | 225.31 | (84.22) | 223.68 | (85.49) | 209.73 | (93.34) |
| Concurrent | 238.66 | (95.48) | 223.81 | (60.65) | 226.00 | (63.82) |
| Trial 2 | | | | | | |
| Terminal | 227.31 | (63.85) | 284.87 | (82.51) | 243.13 | (98.98) |
| Concurrent | 239.43 | (72.88) | 286.43 | (81.64) | 290.31 | (79.33) |

## Questionnaire

Results from the pre-experimental questionnaire were analyzed by a 2 × 3 (feedback × goal specificity) ANOVA and indicated no significant between-group differences on any of the questions. The means clearly reveal that both goal groups felt the goal was realistic ($M = 73$) and difficult ($M = 74$), as well as indicating a very high degree of commitment ($M = 89$) and confidence in attaining the goal ($M = 73$). Finally, all the subjects indicated that they accepted the goal.

Results from the post-experimental questionnaire revealed a significant goal main effect, $F(2, 93) = 3.94$, $p < .03$, for the question, "How well did you perform on the task?" Newman Keuls post hoc analysis revealed the 40-s goal group ($M = 82.50$) indicated they performed significantly better than the do best group ($M = 72.58$). A significant goal main effect was also found for the question, "Were you successful on the task?", $F(2, 93) = 5.80$, $p < .01$. Newman Keuls post-hoc analysis revealed that the 40-s goal difficulty group ($M = 79.37$) and the do best goal group ($M = 74.19$) felt they were more successful than the 70-s goal group ($M = 57.41$). These results reflect the fact that fewer participants in the 70-s goal condition reached their goal (46%) than in the 40-s condition (68%).

A significant feedback main effect was found on the question, "How important was the feedback to the way you performed?", $F(1, 93) = 12.55$, $p < .001$. The concurrent feedback group ($M = 80.85$) indicated that feedback was much more important to the way they performed than did the terminal feedback group ($M = 59$). A significant feedback main effect was also found on the question, "Was the feedback helpful to your performance?", $F(1, 93) = 12.31$, $p < .001$. Participants in the concurrent feedback group ($M = 79$) indicated that feedback was more helpful than did subjects in the terminal feedback group ($M = 58$).

A further significant feedback main effect was found on the question, "How often did you use the feedback?", $F(1, 93) = 11.16$, $p < .001$. Participants in the concurrent feedback group ($M = 67$) indicated that they used the feedback more often than did subjects in the terminal feedback group ($M = 46$). Although significant feedback main effects were found for a number of questions on the post-experimental questionnaire, these differences were not reflective of the performances on the task of the two feedback groups in that no significant differences occurred between the two groups. No other questions reached significance.

## Discussion

The goal-by-trials interaction supports the findings from the industrial psychology literature that participants with specific hard or challenging goals outperform individuals with do best goals (Locke et al., 1981). However, this interaction is not wholly consistent with the prediction of Locke (1968), who suggested a positive linear relationship between goal difficulty and task performance given goal acceptance by the subjects. Results from the pre-experimental questionnaire revealed that all participants in the two specific difficult goal conditions accepted the goals prior to the task, stating high levels of commitment to their goals. Post-experimental questionnaire information revealed that participants continued to accept their goals throughout the task. Locke would suggest, therefore, that a positive linear relationship would occur with the 70-s group performing best and the do best group showing no significant improvement. The 40-s group would perform at a level between the 70-s group and the do best group. However, no significant differences occurred between the two difficult goal groups; both performed similarly, that is, significantly better on the second trial than on the first. The performance of the do best group, as hypothesized, showed no significant improvement from Trial 1 to Trial 2, and only the 40-s group performed significantly better than the do best group.

A number of explanations can be put forward to account for these findings. First, the 40-s goal group's performance, being unexpectedly similar to that of the 70-s group, could possibly be explained by the findings of Locke (1966) and Garland (1982), who found that when subjects are assigned low performance standards, they invariably overshoot them and perform above the level of the assigned goal. Although pre-experimental questionnaire findings indicated that both the 40- and 70-s goal groups believed the goal to be difficult based upon their first trial performance, this was not verified by the performance results. That is, 68% of the 40-s goal group overshot the goal (41% by over 30 s) compared with 46% of the 70-s goal group (only 9% by over 30 s). Therefore, if the 40-s goal was in fact perceived as a low performance standard, this could explain the similar performance of both specific goal groups.

Another explanation of both specific goal groups' similar performance could be that once participants in the 40-s goal group achieved their assigned goals, they set new goals and were motivated to work toward achieving them. Participants in the 70-s goal group achieved their goals less often (46% compared to 68% of the 40-s group), perhaps believing that their physical capacities were close to being reached once they achieved the goal. Consequently, they did not set new goals or perhaps set smaller goals than the 40-s group. Along these lines, the findings revealed that of the participants who reached their goal of 40 s, 97% continued to hold the contraction compared to only 50% of the participants who reached their goal in the 70-s group. Although there are no specific data as to whether the 40-s group did set further goals, it nevertheless could explain the similar performance results of the two goal-setting groups.

A further explanation of why no significant differences were found between the 40- and 70-s goal groups may lie in the fact that 54% of participants in the 70-s goal group did not reach their goal. This would indicate that at some stage prior to releasing the contraction on the second experimental trial, those subjects ceased to accept the goal. They may have considered a 70-s improvement goal to be too difficult, and although performance improvements occurred, achieving significantly greater performance improvements than the 40-s goal group may require performing multiple trials on the task. This would expand the time frame during which participants could strive to reach their goal. Locke et al. (1981) support this contention, suggesting that longer time spans probably will progressively increase the differences between subjects with hard goals and those without hard goals.

Performance results in this study did show some consistency with previous literature governing goal-setting and sport. The superior performance of the specific goal-setting groups on the second trial supports the findings of both Botterill (1977) and Barnett and Stanicek (1979), who found that participants who set specific hard goals performed better than those who were instructed to do their best. However, these findings are inconsistent with a number of field experiments investigating the effect of goal-setting in sport by Hall, Weinberg, and Jackson (1983) using a circuit training task, by Weinberg et al. (1985), and by Hall and Byrne (1986) using a sit-up task. These studies found no significant differences between participants given specific difficult goals and do best goals.

This study, utilizing a laboratory setting, differed sharply from the aforementioned field experiments, which may account for the conflicting findings. First, the task employed in the present study was a novel task and as such held little meaning to the participants. A task such as this might therefore be highly suited to a motivational technique such as goal-setting in order to encourage optimal performance. Alternatively, most sporting activities or tasks are often highly motivating to the participant and are often directed consistently toward meeting a standard or achieving a goal. Thus, the activity itself may be a more salient motivational factor than the technique of goal-setting in such situations.

Second, this study was able to control for the effects of extraneous variables that in field settings may be highly influential on the goal-setting manipulation. For example, the three field experiments mentioned all used students from physical education classes as their experimental populations. Although no specific competition instructions were given, it is possible that due to lack of control the participants in the do best groups were in fact setting goals due to competition with other members of the class. Latham and Baldes (1975) and Komaki, Barwick, and Scott (1978) found evidence of this, concluding that goal-setting plus feedback led to competition among the subjects. Locke (1968) also suggested that competition could lead people to set higher goals than they otherwise would. Likewise, White, Mitchell, and Bell (1977) found that telling participants their performance would be compared to that of others had a powerful effect on task performance independent of a separate goal manipulation. Therefore, if competition becomes the most salient motivational factor influencing performance, then the effects of goal-setting are likely to be overridden. Those with do best goals will then adopt other people's performance standards as their own, resulting in no significant performance differences between those with specific difficult goals and those with do best goals. Further research is needed, however, regarding the effects of competition on goal-setting in sport.

Close scrutiny of the performance data would seem to suggest that participants favored concurrent feedback somewhat more than terminal feedback, particularly in the 70-s goal condition. However, no significant performance differences were found between the feedback groups, a finding that was not hypothesized. However, it is possible that regardless of the form it takes, feedback may be a necessary requirement if goals are to improve performance (Locke *et al.*, 1981). Although both forms of feedback are considered to be informational, they may lead to different strategies regarding how the information is used. This may explain why, regardless of the similar performances of the two feedback groups, there were significant differences in their associated cognitions. Specifically, participants in the concurrent condition, compared to those in the terminal feedback condition, indicated that the feedback was more important, more helpful to performance, and used more often. Participants in the concurrent feedback condition had the clock in front of them so they could pace their performance.

An interesting observation regarding strategic use of the feedback and verified by post-experimental questionnaire findings revealed that feedback was not used continuously throughout the performance. Even in the concurrent feedback condition where the timer was located directly in front of the participants, many indicated that looking at the time early in the second trial had a demoralizing effect because they were so far away from the goal. Feedback became more salient toward the latter part of the trial as the goal was approached.

## Subsequent research and application

Despite being one of the first studies to provide support for the superiority of specific goals over do-best conditions, results of the key study also showed similar performance levels between the respective difficult and very difficult goal conditions, even with goal difficulties being personalized for each participant. Subsequent studies, therefore, attempted to address the social comparison factor that Hall *et al.* had negated in order to determine whether competition between subjects – a factor that would be near unavoidable in a sport-based setting – was preventing results as robust as in I/O research.

To limit the competition effects that hindered prior studies because participants could view each other, Hall and Byrne (1988) attempted to control for spontaneous goal-setting across different conditions by assigning one of four conditions (long-term goals, long-term goals plus experimenter-set goal, long-term goals plus subject-set goal, and do-best goals) for a sit-up task in separate classes of college students enrolled in weight training classes. Results demonstrated that while all four classes significantly improved performance, the classes with long-term goals plus experimenter-set and subject-set goals performed significantly better than the do-best (control) classes. However, questionnaire results indicated over 55% of the do-best group had spontaneously set their own goals and 56% of all subjects admitted to having been competitive during the tasks. Weinberg, Jackson, and Bruya (1990) attempted to replicate Hall and Byrne's control of competition effects in university fitness classes, but this time maintained the same teacher across their three conditions (do-best goals, moderately hard goals, very hard goals). With standardized teacher motivation, no significant differences were shown between the conditions but 32% of the control participants and 27% in the specific groups (38% overall) were revealed to have spontaneously set goals. Similar results were provided in two studies comprising a field based sit-up task with students in fitness classes and a laboratory-based study on grip strength endurance (Weinberg, Bruya, Garland, & Jackson, 1990). Participants were assigned to realistic or unrealistic goal conditions, and in both studies no significant effects were shown in any condition. Results also showed that of the do-best group 41% of participants in the sit-up task and 24% in the grip endurance had set personal short-term goals.

Locke's (1991) response to this series of unequivocal findings was to attribute the results to the existence of major methodological flaws in sport and exercise research, including the focus on "do your best" goals, inappropriate measurement of personal goals (e.g., not knowing what personal goals participants have set in response to the goal being assigned), and the assumption that specific goals in their own right lead to better performances. In an extended debate, Weinberg and Weigand (1993) suggested that individuals who were already involved in sports would have a higher level of motivation for performing physical tasks than those of participants performing work-related tasks in industry. In turn, Locke (1994) dismissed any claims as to the uniqueness of sport settings, believing subjects in I/O studies to be just as motivated because they were similarly made up of student volunteers seeking course credits for participation. Locke's (1991, 1994) indicated that the reason for a lesser number of significant differences between do-best and specific goal conditions was a lack of experimental precautions to prevent participants setting their own spontaneous covert goals, which renders both conditions identical. In retort Weinberg and Weigand (1996) commented that while competition can be controlled in a laboratory setting this did not reflect the real world of sport, and therefore offered limited ecological validity. Locke's (1994) recommendation that goals should be specific and difficult to yield better performance is countered by a confusion caused by the definition of a "difficult" goal. As Weinberg (1994) observed, while a goal must be challenging, the sport psychology literature very clearly favors the use of realistic goals with athletes.

Burton (1993) proposed the following four key issues that might explain null findings in sport settings: small sample size; athletes operating close to their performance potential; task complexity; and individual differences. To specifically address these issues and methodological concerns, Kyllo and Landers (1995) conducted a meta-analysis of sport and exercise studies in this area. Results indicated that goal-setting caused performance improvement above baseline levels by an effect size (ES) of 0.34. Trends indicated that goal-setting could be potentially enhanced if short-term and long-term goals were combined (ES = 0.48), if the individual set their own goals (0.62), if the goal was made public (0.79), or by setting outcome (end result relative to others) goals (0.93). Furthermore, an effect size of 0.53 was found for the use of moderate goals, which offered support for the suggested use of realistic goals over difficult, specific goals (Weinberg, 1994).

A prominent deviation from the research published in the immediate period following the key study by Hall *et al.* is a longitudinal intervention study by Burton (1989) that examined goal-setting as a trainable psychological skill. Burton trained collegiate swimmers in the use of performance goals, which are improvement goals based on the individual's previous performance. Performance goals are more flexible and controllable than outcome goals, as they allow athletes to constantly adjust goal difficulty levels so that they are challenged. Burton reported the first instance of more flexible (performance) goals having superiority over outcome goals. However, Burton did not specifically test performance goals against outcome goals, but rather made an assumption by comparing the race times of goal-setting trained athletes against non-trained athletes.

A new direction was based on the work of Hardy and Jones (1994), who observed in the literature the use of a goal type that directs focus onto a specific procedural element of technique, called a "process" goal. Process goals focus on task-relevant strategies and procedures that the person needs to do in order to have a good performance. They are used in immediate situations to enable individuals to focus on specific task demands. Through a goal-setting skills training program for golfers, Kingston and Hardy (1997) provided support for the positive impact of both process and performance goals. This highlighted how different goal types can help athletes who, on the one hand want to win, but on the other want to improve their technique and motivation.

With a plethora of research having explored whether or not goals work, the literature began to emphasize that future research should be directed toward the consideration of potential underlying mechanisms such as individual behaviors regarding goal acceptance and goal commitment (Hardy & Jones, 1994; Kyllo & Landers, 1995; Weinberg, 1994, 1998). In two major studies conducted in collegiate (Burton, Weinberg, Yukelson, & Weigand, 1998) and Olympic (Weinberg, Burton, Yukelson, & Weigand, 2000) settings, results demonstrated both athletes and coaches used goal-setting extensively, yet, paradoxically, they rated goals as only moderately effective in enhancing performance. Athletes who experienced the most success with goal-setting were shown to plan and use goal implementation strategies.

Based on the paucity of research in this area, Burton, Naylor, and Holliday (2001) suggested this lack of action planning to be the most feasible factor in accounting for why goal-setting was less effective in sport. The four issues previously highlighted by Burton (1993) were subsequently explored with larger sample sizes that were comparable with I/O research, and action planning became part of a revised goal implementation process that involved the following: setting goals; evaluating barriers to goal attainment; developing goal commitment; constructing an action plan; obtaining feedback; evaluating goal attainment; and reinforcing goal achievement (Burton *et al.*, 2001). This seven-phase goal setting model for developing and implementing procedures for goal attainment highlighted that goals themselves do not determine whether intentions are accomplished (Elbe, Szymanski, & Beckmann, 2005) and that any flaws in action planning may greatly limit goal attainment. Goal-directed action may, in fact, be disabled by a lack of planning, initiation, and commitment to completion, none of which are necessarily issues of motivation, but rather facets of volition (Latham, 2000).

Goal-setting continues to be one of the most important areas of research within sport and exercise psychology, with studies extending beyond enhancing individual sport performance in recent years. For example, research in sport and exercise has found goal-setting to be effective in enhancing personal growth, life skills, and health-enhancing behavior (e.g., Danish, 1997; Harmon *et al.* 2005). With research expanding into such areas, it is important that future studies focus on how to make goals more effective because the effectiveness of a goal-setting program relies on the interaction of the coach, exercise leader, or sport psychologists with the motivation of the specific participants and the specific environmental constraints (Weinberg & Butt, 2005).

## Additional readings

Beckmann, J. (2002). Interaction of volition and recovery. In M. Kellmann (ed.), *Enhancing recovery: Preventing underperformance in athletes* (pp. 269–82). Champaign, IL: Human Kinetics.

Burton, D., Naylor, S., & Holliday, B. (2000). Goal setting in sport. In R. N. Singer, M. Murphy, & L. K. Tennant (eds), *Handbook of research on sport psychology* (pp. 497–528). New York: Macmillan.

Gould, D. (2005). Goal setting for peak performance. In J. M. Williams (ed.) *Applied sport psychology: Personal growth to peak performance* (5th ed., pp. 240–59). Madison, WI: McGraw-Hill.

Hardy, L., & Jones, G. (1994). Current issues and future directions: Performance related research in sport psychology. *Journal of Sports Sciences*, 12, 61–92.

Weinberg, R. (2002). Goal setting in sport and exercise: Research to practice. In J. L. Van Raalte & B. W. Brewer (eds) *Exploring sport and exercise psychology* (2nd ed., pp. 25–48). Washington, DC: American Psychological Association.

## Study questions

1   What are the stages of the goal-setting process that an athlete needs to consider when attempting to achieve their goals?

2   Which assumptions of Locke *et al.*'s (1981) goal-setting theory did Hall, Weinberg, and Jackson seek to examine?

3   What performance influencing factors might be relevant when undertaking goals in real world sport settings? How did Hall, Weinberg, and Jackson attempt to control for these factors?

4   Why are the findings of Hall, Weinberg, and Jackson unique in the goal-setting literature?

5   Why might an athlete require a variety of goal types to help achieve success?

## References

Bandura, A., & Simon, K. M. (1977). The role of proximal intentions in self-regulation of refractory behavior. *Cognitive Therapy and Research*, 1, 177–93.

Barnett, M., & Stanicek, J. A. (1979). Effect of goal setting on achievement in archery. *Research Quarterly*, SO, 328–32.

Botterill, C. (1977). *Goal setting and performance on an endurance task*. Paper presented at the Canadian Psycho Motor Learning and Sport Psychology Conference, Banff, Alberta.

Burton, D. (1983). *Evaluation of goal setting training on selected cognitions and performance of collegiate swimmers*. Unpublished doctoral dissertation, University of Illinois.

Burton, D. (1989). Winning isn't everything: Examining the impact of performance goals on collegiate swimmers' cognitions and performance. *The Sport Psychologist*, 3, 105–32.

Burton, D. (1993). Goal setting in sport. In R. N. Singer, M. Murphy, & L. K. Tennant (eds), *Handbook of research on sport psychology* (pp. 467–91). New York: Macmillan.

Burton, D., Naylor, S., & Holliday, B. (2001). Goal setting in sport. In R. N. Singer, M. Murphy, & L. K. Tennant (eds), *Handbook of research on sport psychology* (pp. 497–528). New York: Macmillan.

Burton, D., Weinberg, R. S., Yukelson, D., & Weigand, D. A. (1998). The goal effectiveness paradox in sport: Examining the goal practices of collegiate athletes. *The Sport Psychologist*, 12, 404–18.

Danish, S. J. (1997). Going for the goal: A life skills program for adolescents. In G. Albee & T. Gullota (eds), *Primary prevention works* (pp. 291–312). Thousand Oaks, CA: Sage.

Deci, E. L., & Porac, J. (1978). Cognitive evaluation theory and the study of human motivation. In M. R. Lepper & D. Greene (eds), *The hidden costs of reward* (pp. 149–76). Hillsdale, NJ: Erlbaum.

Dossett, D. L., Latham, G. P., & Mitchell, T. R. (1979). The effects of assigned versus participatively set goals, knowledge of results, and individual differences when goal difficulty is held constant. *Journal of Applied Psychology*, 64, 291–8.

Elbe, A., Szymanski, B., & Beckmann, J. (2005). The development of volition in young elite athletes. *Psychology of Sport and Exercise*, 6, 559–69.

Garland, H. (1982). Goal levels and task performance: A compelling replication of some compelling results. *Journal of Applied Psychology*, 67, 245–8.

Gould, D. (1986). Goal setting for peak performance. In J. Williams (ed.), *Applied sport psychology: Personal growth to peak performance* (pp. 133–48). Palo Alto, CA: Mayfield.

Hall, H. K., & Byrne, A. T. J. (1986, June). *Goals, subgoals: Their effects on the performance on an endurance task.* Paper presented at NASPSPA Conference, Scottsdale, AZ.

Hall, H., & Byrne, T. (1988). Goal setting: Clarifying anomalies. *Journal of Sport & Exercise Psychology*, 10, 189–92.

Hall, H. K., Weinberg, R. S., & Jackson, A. (1983). *The effects of goal setting upon the performance of a circuit training task.* Paper presented at the Texas Association for Health, Physical Education, Recreation and Dance Conference, Corpus Christi, TX.

Hardy, L., & Jones, G. (1994). Current issues and future directions: Performance related research in sport psychology. *Journal of Sports Sciences*, 12, 61–92.

Harmon, A. L., Westerberg, A. L., Bond, D. S., Hoy, K. N., Fries, E. A., & Danish, S. J. (2005). Cancer prevention among rural youth: Building a "Bridge" to better health with genealogy. *Journal of Cancer Education*, 20, 103–7.

Kingston, K. M., & Hardy, L. (1997). Effects of different types of goals on processes that support performance. *The Sport Psychologist*, 11, 277–93.

Komaki, J., Barwick, K. D., & Scott, L. R. (1978). A behavioral approach to occupational safety: Pinpointing and reinforcing safe performance in a food manufacturing plant. *Journal of Applied Psychology*, 64, 434–45.

Kuhl, J. (1984). Volitional aspects of achievement motivation and learned helplessness: Toward a comprehensive theory of action control. In B. A. Maher (ed.), *Progress in experimental personality research* (Vol. 13, pp. 99–171). New York: Academic Press.

Kyllo, L. B., & Landers, D. M. (1995). Goal-setting in sport and exercise: A research synthesis to resolve the controversy. *Journal of Sport & Exercise Psychology*, 17, 117–37.

Latham, G. P. (2000). Motivate employee performance through goal setting. In E. A. Locke (ed.), *Handbook of principles of organization behavior* (pp. 107–17). Malden, MA: Blackwell.

Latham, G. P., & Baldes, J. J. (1975). The practical significance of Locke's theory of goal setting. *Journal of Applied Psychology*, 64, 434–45.

Lind, A. R. (1983). *Physiology of exercise.* New York: Macmillan.

Locke, E. A. (1966). The relationship of intentions to level of performance. *Journal of Applied Psychology*, 51, 324–9.

Locke, E. A. (1968). Toward a theory of task motivation and incentives. *Organizational Behavior and Human Performance*, 3, 157–89.

Locke, E. A. (1991). Problems with goal-setting research in sports – and their solution. *Journal of Sport & Exercise Psychology*, 13, 311–16.

Locke, E. A. (1994). Comments on Weinberg and Weigand. *Journal of Sport & Exercise Psychology*, 8, 212–15.

Locke, E. A., & Bryan, J. F. (1968). Goal setting as a determinant of the effect of knowledge of score and performance. *American Journal of Psychology*, 81, 398–406.

Locke, E. A., & Bryan, J. F. (1969). Knowledge of score and goal level as determinants of work rate. *Journal of Applied Psychology*, 53, 59–65.

Locke, E. A., Cartledge, N., & Koeppel, J. (1968). Motivational effects of knowledge of results: A goal setting phenomenon? *Psychological Bulletin*, 70, 474–85.

Locke, E. A., & Latham, G. P. (1985). The application of goal setting to sports. *Journal of Sport Psychology*, 7, 205–22.

Locke, E. A., & Latham, G. P. (1990). *A theory of goal setting and task performance*. Englewood Cliffs, NJ: Prentice-Hall.

Locke, E. A., Shaw, L., Saari, M., & Latham, G. P. (1981). Goal setting and task performance: 1969–1980. *Psychological Bulletin*, 90, 125–52.

Newell, K. M. (1974). Knowledge of results and motor learning. *Journal of Motor Behavior*, 6, 235–44.

Ordiorne, G. S. (1978). MBO: A backward glance. *Business Horizons*, 21(5), 14–24.

Schmidt, R. (1982). *Motor control and learning: A behavioral emphasis*. Champaign, IL: Human Kinetics.

Simonson, E. (1971). *Physiology of work capacity and fatigue*. Springfield, IL: C.C. Thomas.

Stallings, L. M. (1982). *Motor learning: From theory to practice*. St Louis: C.V. Mosby.

Taylor, F. W. (1911). *Principles of scientific management*. New York: Harper & Brothers.

Weinberg, R. (1994). Goal setting and performance in sport and exercise settings: A synthesis and critique. *Medicine and Science in Sports and Exercise*, 26, 469–77.

Weinberg, R. (1998). Goal setting in sport and exercise: Research to practice. In J. L. Van Raalte & B. W. Brewer (eds), *Exploring sport and exercise psychology* (pp. 3–24). Washington, DC: American Psychological Association.

Weinberg, R. S. & Butt, J. (2005). Goal setting in sport and exercise domains: The theory and practice of effective goal setting. In D. Hackfort, J. L. Duda, & R. Lidor (eds), *Handbook of research in applied sport and exercise psychology: International perspectives* (pp. 129–46). Morgantown, WV: Fitness Information Technology.

Weinberg, R. S., Bruya, C., Garland, H., & Jackson, A. (1990) Effect of goal difficulty and positive reinforcement on endurance performance. *Journal of Sport & Exercise Psychology*, 12, 144–56.

Weinberg, R. S., Bruya, L.D., & Jackson, A. (1985). The effects of goal proximity and goal specificity on endurance performance. *Journal of Sport Psychology*, 7, 296–305.

Weinberg, R. S., Burton, D., Yukelson, D., & Weigand, D. (2000). Perceived goal practices of Olympic athletes: An exploratory investigation. *The Sport Psychologist*, 14, 279–95.

Weinberg, R. S., Jackson, A., & Bruya, L. D. (1990). Goal setting and competition: A reaction to Hall and Byrne. *Journal of Sport & Exercise Psychology*, 12, 92–7.

Weinberg, R. S., & Weigand, D. A. (1993). Goal setting in sport and exercise: A reaction to Locke. *Journal of Sport & Exercise Psychology*, 15, 88–96.

Weinberg, R. S., & Weigand, D. A. (1996). Let the discussions continue: A reaction to Locke's comments on Weinberg and Weigand. *Journal of Sport & Exercise Psychology*, 18, 89–93.

White, S. E., Mitchell, T. R., & Bell, C. H., Jr. (1977). Goal setting evaluation apprehension and social cues as determinants of job performance and job satisfaction in a simulated organization. *Journal of Applied Psychology*, 62, 665–73.

# PART 4

Personal growth and psychological well-being

# 16

# Character development and sportsmanship

Kleiber, D. A., & Roberts, G. C. (1981). The effects of sport experience in the development of social character: An exploratory study. *Journal of Sport Psychology*, 3, 114–22.

**Written in collaboration with Martin I. Jones**

## Background and context

Sport participation for young people is a social phenomenon. It is widely accepted that sport participation has a substantial and growing presence in many countries across the world with tens of millions of children and adolescents participating in organized sport. In the USA alone Ewing, Seefeldt, and Brown (1996) estimated that 48 million children and adolescents, between the ages of 5 and 17, participate in sport. As such, organized sport represents a major source of activity and entertainment for children and adolescents across the world.

In addition to sport being a social phenomenon of "where the kids are" the writings and declarations of philosophers, theologians, politicians, and educators have led to the portrayal of sport as a forum for teaching values, skills, and character virtues that transfer into other life domains. For example, Pope John Paul II called sport "a total valorization of the body, a healthy spirit of competition, an education in the values of life, the joy of living". However, whether participating in sport can really promote the development of character is a debate in sport psychology that has re-emerged on a regular basis since the 1930s (Weiss & Gill, 2005).

Character has received a great deal of attention across the fields of philosophy, psychology, sociology, sport science, and physical education over the past century. However, a clear definition of character has proved elusive. From a psychological perspective, character connotes enduring qualities that make up a person's personality in addition to moral and ethical attributes (Power & Khemlkov, 1998). From this perspective, character has typically been studied in terms of morality and socially valued qualities. Moral character is traditionally conceptualized as the ability to deduce the right course of action in any particular situation (Kohlberg, 1981) and the ability to construct moral balances (agreements between people of what is right) in interactive moral dialogues (e.g., open verbal negotiation; Haan, 1983). Social character is usually conceptualized as the skills, traits, and virtues valued by society, for example, prosocial behaviors such as leadership, self-control, social cooperation, honesty, altruism, empathy, optimism, commitment, dedication, and so forth (McCloy, 1930).

At the time of the Kleiber and Roberts study, the majority of research in character development through sport reflected similar research trends as those found in mainstream psychology. Specifically, there had been a gradual shift away from the study of individual personality traits as a indicator of character (e.g., Messick, 1939) to the moral, ethical behaviors associated with having character. Prior to the key study, one of the only other papers that espoused the value of sport as a forum for social (rather than moral) character development was a paper by McCloy (1930) published in the first volume of the journal *Research Quarterly*. McCloys' seminal paper demonstrated one of the first attempts to outline a process of seeking specific character developments through well-planned physical activities (i.e., through physical education). McCloy provided the foundations of learning by which physical educators may teach character, more specifically, a list of character objectives that could be learned through physical education (e.g., leadership, social cooperation, etc.) and types of activities conducive to character building. In addition to forwarding the argument of character development through physical education, McCloy also proposed criteria to facilitate the transfer of character to other life domains, methods of character measurement, and potential research directions for character education. The current chapter focuses specifically on social character development. For a review of moral character and the influence of sport participation on moral character development see Shields and Bredemeier (1995).

The antithesis of McCloys' (1930) arguments was presented by Ogilvie and Tutko (1971). They stated, "We found no empirical support for the tradition that sport builds character. Indeed there is evidence that athletic competition limits growth in some areas" (1971: 61). Both the McCloy and Ogilvie and Tutko papers were largely based on the authors' personal experiences, assumptions, and anecdotal evidence. At the time of the Kleiber and Roberts (1981) study, a paucity of research examined whether the development of character was (or was not) susceptible to participation and/or competition in sport. As a result, a reasonable degree of ambiguity existed regarding whether sport did build character.

Consequently, Kleiber and Roberts designed the key study of this chapter as a field-based experiment to assess the susceptibility of social character (specifically prosocial behaviors of cooperation and altruism) in childhood to the influence of organized sport. Kleiber and Roberts stated that findings from previous comparison studies between athletes and non-athletes were suspect because when differences were found it was impossible to determine if the differences were there to begin with or if they were attributable to sport participation (Stevenson, 1975). Additionally, well controlled experimental and longitudinal studies were lacking. Moreover, sport is not a laboratory-based activity. Therefore, Kleiber and Roberts (1981) felt a field experiment of actual sport participation over a two-week period, lending a degree of ecological validity to the investigation, was best suited to the study of character development.

## Key study

The impact of sport on social development has been largely ignored. There is certainly logic, if not a great deal of evidence, for the position that organized sport provides a forum for teaching responsibility, conformity, and subordination for the greater good, and for shaping achievement behavior by encouraging persistence, delay of gratification, and even a degree of risk taking. But even to the extent that such behaviors are the consequences of sport, the generalization that "sport builds character" does not sit well with those who see athletes as less-than-model citizens.

The most well-known attack on this position was in a report by Ogilvie and Tutko (1971). They argued (from a database that was not presented) that, if anything, the qualities of character and personality associated with athletes are likely to have been established before they engaged in sport. They pointed out that such things as achievement orientation, respect for authority, endurance, and self-control are selected for rather than nurtured by sports, and that the competitive nature of sport forces those with lesser amounts of these qualities out of sport. Goffman (1967) has suggested that sport is the ideal setting for the display of such qualities of character as courage, gallantry, integrity, and composure (Loy, McPherson, & Kenyon, 1978); but whether or not the display seems to reinforce such qualities is a question for additional research.

Such possibilities argue strongly for more careful consideration of the role of sport in character development. This study is thus an attempt to move in that direction while reflecting three specific concerns: (a) that the construct of "character" be adequately defined and delimited, (b) that the scope of the study be limited to a more manageable subset of behaviors within the broad domain of "character development," and (c) that movement be made beyond a "correlates of sport participation" model to one that seeks to establish actual effects.

The term "character" is rarely used any more in studies of personality and social behavior. The use of the term among psychologists may be traced back to Freud (1901/1960) and other psychoanalysts (Fenichel, 1945; Fromm, 1947). Originally, it was used almost synonymously with "personality," referring somewhat more generally to personality structure; use of the term was modified, however, by Fromm (1947) and later by Allport (1961) to reflect those traits or qualities that are culturally valued and, more specifically, that reflect ethical or morally appropriate orientations and behavior. This perspective was reflected also in one of the more extensive studies of character development (Peck & Havighurst, 1960).

Culturally valued traits include those that are primarily individualistic, such as courage, achievement motivation, independence, and perseverence, and those that reflect positive interpersonal behavior, such as generosity, fairness, and cooperativeness. Although allowing for the need to assess the impact of sport on the individual dimensions of character, it was to the more social aspects of character – as valued by American culture – that this investigation was directed. Nevertheless, it is important to note that the research was prompted by a question about the basic compatibility of certain individual and social values in the sport context. Specifically, it was speculated that to the extent that achievement behavior is fostered through an emphasis on competitiveness, prosocial behavior, such as giving and cooperating, may be undermined. Indeed, a substantial body of evidence from laboratory settings leads to this conclusion (e.g., Bryan, 1977).

Although studies of personality change and antisocial behavior (e.g., aggression) are common in research on sport, attention to prosocial behavior and moral development has been scant. On the other hand, sport is essentially competitive and the effects of competition on prosocial behavior has been the subject of a substantial body of research on child development (Bryan, 1977). On that subject, the studies of Madsen and Kagan and their students are noteworthy, suggesting a tendency for American children especially to become more irrationally rivalrous and competitive with age (e.g., Kagen & Madsen, 1972). Their explanation is that winning is so culturally emphasized that to act differently in an ambiguous situation is at most times inconceivable. It follows that organized sport may be one of those contexts that forms and reinforces such tendencies (Sadler, 1973).

Studies of the effects of competition have revealed that it reduces prosocial tendencies, such as helping and sharing (e.g., Barnett & Bryan, 1974; McGuire & Thomas, 1975), and increases antisocial tendencies (e.g., Berkowitz, 1972; Gelfand & Hartman, 1978; Rausch, 1965), and all these effects are exacerbated by losing. But much of this research has been done in the laboratory, with the "game" usually defined by artificial conditions. It may be that in the context of organized sports, with ties to coaches, teams, and the community at large, any negative effects of competition are mitigated. Indeed, the argument is often advanced that cooperation is not antithetical to competition in sport, but rather that association and co-operation are necessary to promote, establish, and enact a sporting event (e.g., Lüeschen, 1970). And this would be especially true in team play where one has to play a role in an organized unit.

Thus, one might expect that the value of "sportsmanship," which is based on a commitment to the primacy of justice and cooperation, would flourish in the sport context. But existing evidence indicates that such principles are less, rather than more, commonly endorsed by regular sport participants (e.g., Kroll & Peterson, 1965). Furthermore, the research by Webb (1969) and others (e.g., Loy, Birrell, & Rose, 1976) has shown that with age and sport experience, the value of fairness becomes increasingly subordinated to the values of competence and comparative success (i.e., winning).

An important related question is whether or not sport competition generates or undermines empathic responses. Empathy is the basis of such prosocial responses as sharing, giving, and helping (see Bryan, 1977); concern for and understanding of others are necessary predispositions. There is some evidence that competition inhibits empathic responses, and indeed, elite athletes, the ones who have weathered years of simulated conflict, have been described as aloof and insensitive (Ogilvie & Tutko, 1971). The suggestion is that a certain distancing is necessary for competitive success. On the other hand, most sports participants commonly experience failure, and if empathy for opponents' failures and losses is not particularly adaptive in this context, empathy for one's teammates who fail to perform effectively is probably quite common and socially adaptive.

The period of eight to 12 years is thought to be especially critical in the process of prosocial development. It is a time when children move out of an egocentric view of the world into one in which the perspectives of others pervade their consciousness. In that manner social experience leads potentially to the emergence of an understanding of the values of equality and reciprocity and to a growing regard for mutual agreement and positive justice (Damon, 1977; Piaget, 1932; Turiel, 1980).

## Method

### Participants

Participants ($N = 54$) were fourth and fifth grade children (mean age 10.9 years) from two public elementary schools in Illinois in the United States. Parental permission was obtained. Although there was some variation in race, ethnic background, and socioeconomic status, the sample was predominantly white and middle class. Of the total group, 28 were boys and 26 were girls.

### Testing

The participants were given the *Social Behavior Scale* (Knight & Kagen, 1977) before and after the experimental manipulation. This instrument assesses altruistic vs. rivalrous behavioral tendencies. The scale provides for a continuum of responses between those extremes as illustrated in Figure 16.1. The four alternatives differ in the outcomes they provide and the social motives they probably satisfy. As shown in Figure 16.1, the alternative on the far right satisfies motives for altruism and group enhancement. The next alternative, also prosocial,

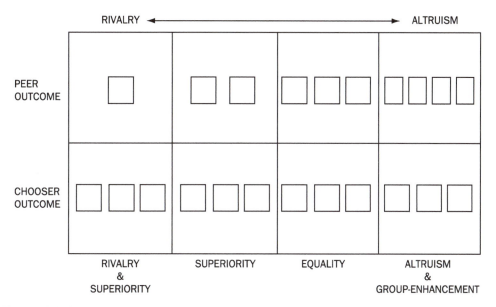

**Figure 16.1** The *Social Behavior Scale*

offers equality. The third alternative offers superiority, and the alternative on the far left satisfies motives of rivalry and superiority.

## Procedure

Prior to the experimental manipulation, each participant was given the *Social Behavior Scale*. Participants were taken from the classroom to a room where the testing was explained and conducted, and were told that this was an opportunity to do a little exercise (but *not* "to play a game") for which a prize could be earned. They were told that they would choose 10 times among the four alternatives on the scale shown in Figure 16.1 (actually a 30 cm × 120 cm cardboard), that each choice would provide poker chips for themselves and for another child in another school, and that those chips would be exchanged for a prize. The prizes were four different quality pens, graded for the participant according to the number of chips each was worth. Because the participant could only get 30 chips, the second best pen was the best that was available to him/her, but by choosing the most altruistic alternatives (alternatives three or four), on most trials, the "other child" would receive the best.

Two experiments were conducted and children were assigned randomly to each experiment. On the pre-test, neither of the experimenters knew which child was an experimental or control group participant. Further, the choice board was reversed for each successive participant to control for position effects. The same procedures were followed for the post-test, but at this point, the experimenter knew which condition each child was in.

*Experimental Manipulation.* In each of the two schools, a two-week "Kick-Soccer World-Series" was organized for participants assigned to the experimental condition. A game was played during the 20-minute free recess period for eight days. With the exception of the first day, which was used for organization, practice, and the dividing of teams, a game was played each day and the final score established a winning and losing team. Two male graduate research assistants served as coaches and "drafted" the players after seeing them play kickball in their normal fashion on the first day. All the children were volunteers and were told by the experimenter of the plan to have a Kick-Soccer World-Series over the next two weeks and that they would be assigned to one of the two teams for that period. They were also told that scores were to be kept each day and that at the end of the two-week period, the team that had won the most games would be declared champions and each player on the winning team would receive a trophy. All participants were told that they would receive a participation certificate.

Following the experimental manipulation, the winners were declared and given their trophies, the losers were given participation certificates, and all were thanked for their participation. Anecdotally, the children wanted to repeat the series, and other children who were not included wanted to become involved. Indeed, it was difficult to restrict the games only to those children for whom parental permission had been secured.

*Assessment of Previous Participation.* The participants, all of whom participated in a second interview study conducted by the experimenters, were also asked about previous sport experience. A determination was made of the number of years of active participation in each sport played on an organized team, that is with a coach, regular teammates, and a formal schedule.

## Results

On a subjective, qualitative level, the manipulation was apparently effective in creating a realistic sport competition experience. Although the investigators did not intend to create an excessive amount of tension, crying occurred on three occasions largely as a result of perceived failure or injustice, and quarreling took place at regular intervals with a fist fight even following one game. The experimenters had a good deal of ambivalence about the value and worth of the experiment at this point, but there was enough apparent positive affect from the children to justify continuing. In any case, these effects provided evidence that a sufficient level of psychological investment in the activity had at least been created. The fact that the two "series" were both relatively close in outcome may also have contributed.

On the pre-test with the *Social Behavior Scale*, it was discovered that those boys and girls with the most sport experience were significantly more likely to deny gift-redeemable chips to other children ($r = -.33$ for boys and $-.39$ for girls). Both of these correlations were significant at the .05 level.

The mean number of tokens given in total and on the last trial, Trial 10, is presented in Table 16.1. To control for initial differences, pre-test scores were subtracted from post-test scores and the changes were subjected to a two-way, sex by treatment ANOVA. Although the male participants in the experimental groups showed the greatest change in the total number of chips given to the other child, the mean change was not significantly different from the other three groups. Subsequent analyses, grouping on win-loss, and controlling the effects of previous sport experience through covariance also failed to reveal any differences. Prior to the experimental manipulation, however, it was argued that Trial 10 would be the last chance for children to effectively increase or decrease the sum of the other child's accumulation and might, therefore, be important in its own right. When mean change scores were analyzed, a significant treatment by sex interaction materialized, $F(1,54) = 4.75$, $p < .05$. Newman-Keul post-hoc tests revealed that experimental male participants gave reliably fewer chips on Trial 10 after the sport experience (see also Figure 16.2). No differences between either of the control groups and the female experimental group were evident. Boys who were in the experimental sport group showed a mean response between rivalry and superiority on Trial 10.

**Table 16.1** Tokens given before and after sport experience

| Total Other | Means | | | | Change |
|---|---|---|---|---|---|
| | Pre | | Post | | |
| | M | SD | M | SD | |
| Experimental Group | | | | | |
| Males (n = 16) | 25.47 | 4.32 | 23.53 | 5.85 | −1.94 |
| Females (n = 13) | 24.23 | 5.30 | 24.40 | 7.04 | .17 |
| Control Group | | | | | |
| Males (n = 12) | 21.38 | 5.44 | 20.46 | 6.55 | −.92 |
| Females (n = 13) | 26.08 | 6.27 | 24.62 | 5.58 | −1.46 |
| Trial 10 | | | | | |
| Experimental Group | | | | | |
| Males | 2.65 | .86 | 1.71 | .85 | −.94 |
| Females | 2.23 | 1.09 | 2.48 | 1.39 | .25 |
| Control Group | | | | | |
| Males | 1.77 | .72 | 1.77 | 1.01 | .00 |
| Females | 2.33 | 1.23 | 2.25 | 1.14 | −.08 |

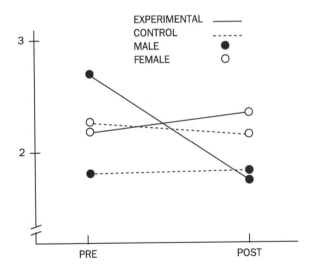

**Figure 16.2** Tokens given on Trial 10 before and after sport experience

## Discussion

This attempt to determine the effects of sport experience on social character and social behavior must be regarded as exploratory. The question of generality remains largely unanswered. Although there were some indications that the sport experience created had an effect on the altruistic tendencies of male participants, the impact occurred only on the last trial, and the researchers were left with the question of whether a more effective manipulation of the conditions (e.g., a longer period of time) would have affected altruistic tendencies more effectively. Of course, one could argue as easily that more extensive involvement would have generated more intra-team responsiveness rather than more rivalrous behavior.

The fact that an experimental effect was only found for male participants bears some consideration. It may be dismissed as an artifact in that the pre-test scores were somewhat higher for that group, and changes may have merely reflected a regression to the mean. The researchers observed, however, that male participants were generally more "caught up" in the activity and took more responsibility in directing and controlling the action. Of course, the researchers may also entertain the contention that boys and girls do indeed respond differently to competitive situations in our culture. It may be that girls' rivalrous responses are so strongly inhibited in general, or cooperative responses so strongly reinforced, or both, that short-term manipulations are less likely to have an influence. Whatever the explanation, future research on the effects of sport on social behavior should examine sex differences.

The interesting correlational evidence that sport participants were more likely to deny gift-redeemable chips to peers is also worth considering further. Apparently, those children who were more experienced in competitive sports were more rivalrous than those with less sport experience. It still cannot be stated that organized sport necessarily forms and reinforces such tendencies – it may be that the more competitive children are merely the survivors in sport – but it does lead one to speculate that the emphasis upon winning in organized sport may lead the children to become more rivalrous in social interactions with other children. Certainly, the evidence of Kagen and Madsen (1972) supports this speculation, and it may be argued that the results of this study are consistent with such an interpretation.

Based upon these findings, it may be argued that to the extent that competition is allowed to dominate the interpersonal relationships in children's sports, their potential for actually facilitating the development of prosocial behavior is entirely lost. This need not be the case, however. In the future, investigators might well examine practices that are likely to mitigate the negative effects of competition: First, coaches can emphasize a "team concept" and utilize team-building experiences to promote interdependence; second, coaches and league officials can influence players to regard opponents as "associates" who make the game possible (see Lüeschen, 1970); and, finally, players may be given more responsibility in the process of playing so that natural expressions of generosity and goodwill, or "gallantry" in Goffman's (1967) words, are allowed to emerge.

Although this investigation has provided some evidence that sport competition in childhood may have the effect of reducing some prosocial tendencies, it cannot be asserted that it undermines the development of character in general. Furthermore, the evidence presented here suggests that sport may influence boys and girls differently in this regard. Generally, however, this investigation must be regarded as preliminary. Consideration of other qualities of character, attempts to examine various sports and various age groups, assessment of the influence of coaches and other significant observers, and more sophisticated longitudinal or quasi-experimental field research designs will all be needed to adequately determine the role of sport in character development.

## Subsequent research and application

Weiss and Gill (2005) recently investigated the trends in sport and exercise psychology over the past 75 years. One hot topic was that of sportsmanship/moral development, on which many articles related to character development were housed (e.g., McCloy 1930). Weiss and Gill suggested that even though research paradigms and methodologies had changed the dominant themes tended to re-emerge. This is certainly true in the case of character development. Although Kleiber and Roberts were unable to support the assumption that sport builds character, the belief that sport participation can have a beneficial effect on the development of social character has remained popular among coaches, athletes, sport administrators, physical educators, and sport philosophers (Danish, Petitpas, & Hale, 1995; Docheff, 1998; Fisher, 1998; Gough, 1998; Jones & McNamee, 2000; Sage, 1998). The number of published articles in sport psychology journals diminished during the 1980s, however, and it wasn't until the early 1990s that this area of research re-emerged under the new heading of life skills. One potential explanation of the re-emergence of this topic was given by Miller and Kerr (2002). During the 1990s there was a growing awareness of the costs of an exclusive pursuit of performance excellence, for example, the high profile case of steroid use in Canadian sprinter Ben Johnson at the 1988 Seoul Olympics and the death of US gymnast Christie Heinrich from an eating disorder (Miller & Kerr, 2002). In essence, it appeared that sport *produced characters* rather than *building character* (Ogilvie & Tutko, 1971). As such researchers began to focus on the positive aspects of sport participation and how they could be fostered to ensure performance and personal excellence (Miller & Kerr, 2002).

In addition to the swing in the media, the recent shift toward positive psychology (Gould, 2002; Seligman & Csikszentmihalyi, 2000), positive youth development in developmental psychology (Larson, 2000), and the role leaders play in team climate (e.g., Kavussanu & Spray, 2006) has led to increased interest in sport as a context for developing life skills.

In sport psychology literature the term "life skills" has largely replaced character, but there is substantial crossover between the two areas of research; for example, life skills encompass many of the aspects of social character (e.g., leadership, teamwork, communication, organization, etc.). The main difference is that life skills are clearly defined and are objective skills as opposed to the socially constructed, conceptually problematic, values of character (Chung, 2003). The World Health Organization (1999) defines life skills as the ability for adaptive and positive behavior that enables individuals to deal effectively with the demands and challenges of everyday life; similarly, life skills training has been defined as the formalized teaching of requisite skills for surviving, living with others, and succeeding in a complex society (Hamburg, 1990). Furthermore, Danish, Petitpas, and Hale (1995) provided the following life skills that potentially could be learned through sport: to perform under pressure; to make good decisions; to set and attain goals; to have self-control; to evaluate yourself; to be organized; to handle both success and failure; to recognize your limitations; to be flexible to succeed; to communicate with others; to work with people you don't necessarily like; to respect others; to accept others' values and beliefs; to work within a system; to compete without hatred; to push yourself to the limit; to take risks, to make a commitment and stick to it; to be dedicated; to accept responsibility for your behavior; and to be self-motivated.

To date, life skills have primarily been taught to sports participants via two methods. The first method is through coaching, but this method has proven problematic. In a study by Gilbert and Trudel (2001) of an ice hockey coach, one of the coach's goals was to promote personal development, however the only strategy reported to accomplish this was to emphasize academics by not allowing the team captain to travel to several games so that he could spend the time studying. McCallister, Blinde, and Weiss (2000) uncovered similar results when studying 22 volunteer softball and baseball coaches. Although the coaches talked about teaching life skills they found it difficult to indicate how life skills were taught; rather it was assumed that athletes learned life skills as a byproduct of participating in sport.

As a result of the lack of evidence to support the view of coaches developing life skills, an alternative approach has been sought.

This alternative method is through applied life skills programs that link sport skills with life skills. Examples of life skills programs include *Going for the Goal* (GOAL; Danish & Nellen, 1997), *Sports United to Promote Enjoyment and Recreation* (SUPER; Danish, Fazio, Nellen, & Owens, 2002), *The First Tee* (Petlichkoff, 2004), and *Play It Smart* (Petitpas, Van Raalte, Cornelius, & Presbrey, 2004). Although rigorous published evaluations of these programs are few in number, those that exist generally find positive outcomes, suggesting life skills are developed through the implementation of life skills programs. For example, Papacharisis, Goudas, Danish, and Theodorakis (2005) conducted two studies using an eight session version of SUPER with Greek schoolchildren, aged between 10 and 12. The first study involved 40 female volleyball players on two teams; the second study involved 32 male soccer players from two teams. In each study, one team served as the experimental group who were taught the abbreviated version SUPER, and the other as the control group who received no instruction. In both studies measurements were taken of physical skills; knowledge of the SUPER program; and self-beliefs about one's ability to set goals, to problem solve, and to think positively. Results revealed no difference between the groups before the intervention, however, following the SUPER program the experimental group had higher scores in their self-beliefs to use goal-setting, think positively, and problem solve compared to the control group. Furthermore, participants taught the abbreviated SUPER program demonstrated an increase in program knowledge and improvement in physical skills between pre- and post-tests compared to participants in the control group.

Although such examples are promising caution should be taken. Specifically, many of the aforementioned life skill programs only target one life skill. For example, both the SUPER and GOAL programs focus on goal-setting, while omitting many others. Therefore, can these programs be regarded as life skills programs or just goal-setting programs? Furthermore, the belief that life skills are transferred from sport to other life domains is based on assumption. The lack of current research evidence to support these claims limits the legitimacy of the extant life skills research; however, it opens many new doors for future research and development in this area.

In summary, the area of social character development and more specifically life skills development has become an increasingly popular area of academic research within sport psychology. With the development of new life skills programs, sport psychologists, coaches, athletes, and sport administrators have the resources to facilitate the learning of a broad range of life skills. To ensure optimal future developments, however, researchers and practitioners must also implement a comprehensive system of evaluation and research (Petitpas, Cornelius, Van Raalte, & Jones, 2005) that determines if it is the sport experience or other extraneous variables that build character.

## Additional readings

Danish, S. J., Fazio, R. J., Nellen, V. C., & Owens, S. S. (2002). Teaching life skills through sport: Community-based programs to enhance adolescent development. In J. L. Van Raalte & B. W. Brewer (eds), *Exploring sport and exercise psychology* (2nd ed., pp. 269–88). Washington, DC: American Psychological Association.

Gould, D., Collins, K., Lauer, L., & Yongchul Chung, Y. (2006). Coaching life skills: A working model. *Sport & Exercise Psychology Review*, 2, 4–12.

Miller, S. C., Bredemeier, B. J. L., & Shields, D. L. L. (1997). Sociomoral education through physical education with at risk children. *Quest*, 49, 114–29.

Papacharisis, V., Goudas, M., Danish, S., & Theodorakis, Y. (2005). The effectiveness of teaching a life skills program in a sport context. *Journal of Applied Sport Psychology*, 17, 247–54.

Shields, D. L. L., & Bredemeier, B. J. L. (1995). *Character development in physical activity*. Champaign, IL: Human Kinetics.

## Study questions

1   Outline how character has been conceptualized within psychology and other disciplines.

2   Compare the arguments put forward by McCloy (1930) and Ogilvie and Tutko (1971).

3   How do the authors of the key study explain the experimental effect found only for male participants?

4   How does the World Health Organization define life skills, and what are some of the life skills that sport psychologists have suggested could be learned through sport?

5   Describe the two methods through which life skills have primarily been taught to sports participants.

## References

Allport, G. W. (1961). *Pattern and growth in personality*. New York: Holt, Rinehart & Winston.

Barnett, M. A., & Bryan, J. H. (1974). Effects of competition with outcome feedback on children's helping behavior. *Developmental Psychology*, 10, 838–42.

Berkowitz, L. (1972). Sports competition and aggression. In I. Williams & L. Wankel (eds), *Fourth Canadian symposium on psychology of motor learning and sport*. Ottawa: University of Ottawa.

Bryan, J. H. (1977). Prosocial behavior. In H. L. Ham (ed.), *Psychological processes in early education*. New York: Academic Press.

Chung, Y. (2003). *Teaching life skills to high school football players: Strategies identified by Play It Smart academic coaches*. Ph.D. thesis. University of North Carolina at Greensboro.

Damon, W. (1977). *The social world of the child*. San Francisco: Jossey-Bass.

Danish, S. J., Fazio, R. J., Nellen, V. C., & Owens, S. S. (2002). Teaching life skills through sport: Community-based programs to enhance adolescent development. In J. L. Van Raalte & B. W. Brewer (eds), *Exploring sport and exercise psychology* (2nd ed.) (pp. 269–88). Washington, DC: American Psychological Association.

Danish, S., & Nellen, J. (1997). New roles for sport psychologists: teaching life skills through sport to at-risk youth. *Quest*, 49, 100–13.

Danish, S., Petitpas, A., & Hale, B. (1995). Psychological interventions: A life development model. In S. M. Murphy (ed.), *Sport psychology interventions* (pp. 19–38). Champaign, IL: Human Kinetics.

Docheff, D. (1998). Character development and physical education – summation. *The Journal of Physical Education, Recreation & Dance*, 69, 24–5.

Ewing, M. E., Seefeldt, V. D., and Brown, T. P. (1996). *Role of organized sport in the education and health of American children and youth*. New York: Carnegie Corporation of New York.

Fenichel, O. (1945). *The psychoanalytic theory of neurosis*. New York: W. W. Norton.

Fisher. S. (1998). Developing and implementing a K-12 character education program. *The Journal of Physical Education, Recreation & Dance*, 69, 21–3.

Freud, S. (1960). *The psychopathology of everyday life*. In *Standard edition* (Vol. 6). London: Hogarth Press (originally published 1901).

Fromm, E. (1947). *Man for himself*. New York: Rinehart.

Gelfand, D. M., & Hartman, D. P. (1978). Some detrimental effects of competitive sports on children's behavior. In R. A. Magill, M. J. Ash, & F. L. Smoll (eds), *Children in sport: A contemporary anthology*. Champaign, IL: Human Kinetics.

Gilbert, W. D., & Trudel, P. (2001). Learning to coach through experience: Reflection in model youth sport coaches. *Journal of Teaching Physical Education*, 21, 16–34.

Goffman, E. (1967). *Interaction ritual*. Chicago: Aldine.

Gough, R. W. (1998). A practical strategy for emphasizing character development in sport and physical education. *The Journal of Physical Education, Recreation & Dance*, 69, 18–20.

Gould, D. (2002). Sport psychology in the new millennium: The psychology of athletic excellence and beyond. *Journal of Applied Sport Psychology*, 14, 137–8.

Haan, N. (1983) An interactional morality of everyday life. In N. Haan *et al.* (eds) *Social science as moral inquiry*. New York: Columbia University Press.

Hamburg, B. A. (1990). *Life skills training: Preventative interventions for young adolescents*. Washington, DC: Carnegie Council on Adolescent Development.

Jones. C., & McNamee, M. (2000). Moral reasoning, moral action and the moral atmosphere of sport. *Sport Education and Society*, 5, 131–46.

Kagen, S., & Madsen, M. C. (1972). Experimental analyses of cooperation and competition of Anglo-American and Mexican children. *Developmental Psychology*, 6, 49–59.

Kavussanu, M., & Spray, C. M. (2006). Contextual influences on moral functioning of male youth footballers. *The Sport Psychologist*, 20, 1–23.

Kleiber, D. A. and Roberts, G. C. (1981). The effects of sport experience in the development of social character: An exploratory investigation. *Journal of Sport Psychology*, 3, 114–22.

Knight, G. P., & Kagen, S. (1977). Development of prosocial and competitive behaviors in Anglo-American and Mexican-American children. *Child Development*, 48, 1385–94.

Kohlberg, L. (1981). *Essays on moral development: Vol. 1. The philosophy of moral development*. San Francisco, CA: Harper & Row.

Kroll, W., & Peterson, K. H. (1965). Study of values test and collegiate football teams. *Research Quarterly*, 36, 441–7.

Larson, R. (2000). Toward a psychology of positive youth development. *American Psychologist*, 55, 170–83.

Loy, J., Birrell, S., & Rose, P. (1976). Attitudes held toward agonistic activities as a function of selected social identifies. *Quest*, 26, 81–95.

Loy, J., McPherson, B., & Kenyon, G. (1978). *Sport and social systems*. Reading, MA: Addison-Wesley.

Lüeschen, G. (1970). Cooperation, association and contest. *Journal of Conflict Resolution*, 4, 21–34.

McCallister, S. G., Blinde, E. M., & Weiss, W. M. (2000). Teaching values and implementing philosophies: Dilemmas of the youth coach. *Physical Educator*, 57, 35–46.

McCloy, C. H. (1930). Character building through psychical education. *Research Quarterly*, 1, 41–61.

McGuire, J., & Thomas, M. H. (1975). Effects of sex, competence and competition on sharing behavior in children. *Journal of Personality and Social Psychology*, 32, 490–4.

Messick, J. D. (1939). *Personality and character development*. New York: Fleming H. Revell Company.

Miller, P. S., & Kerr, G. A. (2002). Conceptualizing excellence: Past, present, and future. *Journal of Applied Sport Psychology*, 14, 140–53.

Ogilvie, B. C., & Tutko, T. A. (1971). Sport: If you want to build character, try something else. *Psychology Today*, 5, 60–3.

Papacharisis, V., Goudas, M., Danish, S., & Theodorakis, Y. (2005). The effectiveness of teaching a life skills program in a school-based sport context. *Journal of Applied Sport Psychology*, 3, 247–54.

Peck, R. F., & Havighurst, R. J. (1960). *The psychology of character development*. New York: Wiley.

Petitpas, A., Van Raalte, J. L., Cornelius, A., & Presbrey, J. (2004). A life skills development program for high school student-athletes. *The Journal of Primary Prevention*, 24, 325–34.

Petitpas, A., Cornelius, A., Van Raalte, J., & Jones, T. (2005). A framework for planning youth sport programs that foster psychosocial development. *The Sport Psychologist*, 19, 63–80.

Petlichkoff, L. M. (2004). Self-regulation skills for children and adolescents. In M. R. Weiss (ed.), *Developmental sport and exercise psychology* (pp. 273–92). Morgantown, WV: Fitness Information Technology.

Piaget, J. (1932). *The moral judgement of the child*. New York: Harcourt & Brace.

Power, F. C., & Khemlkov, V. T. (1998). Character development and self esteem: Psychological foundations and educational implications. *International Journal of Educational Research*, 27, 539–51.

Rausch, H. L. (1965). Interaction sequences. *Journal of Personality and Social Psychology*, 22, 487–99.

Sadler, W. A. (1973). Competition out of bounds: Sport in American life. *Quest*, 19, 124–32.

Sage, G. (1998). Does sport affect character development in athletes? *The Journal of Physical Education, Recreation & Dance*, 69 (1), 15–18.

Seligman, M., & Csikszentmihalyi, M. (2000). Positive psychology: An introduction. *American Psychologist*, 55, 5–14.

Shields, D., & Bredemeier, B. (1995). *Character development and physical activity*. Champaign, IL: Human Kinetics.

Stevenson, C. L. (1975). Socialization effects of participation in sport: A critical review of the research. *Research Quarterly*, 46, 287–301.

Turiel, E. (1980). Domains and categories in social cognitive development. In W. Overton (ed.), *The relationship between social and cognitive development*. Hillsdale, NJ: Erlbaum.

Webb, H. (1969). Professionalization of attitudes toward play among adolescents. In G. S. Kenyon (ed.), *Aspects of contemporary sport sociology*. Chicago: The Athletic Institute.

Weiss, M. R., & Gill, D. L. (2005). What goes around comes around: Re-emerging themes in sport and exercise psychology. *Research Quarterly for Exercise and Sport*, 76 (supplement), S71–87.

World Health Organization (1999). *Partners in life skills education*. Geneva: World Health Organization, Department of Mental Health.

# 17

# Exercise and psychological well-being

North, T. C., McCullagh, P., & Tran, Z. V. (1990). Effect of exercise on depression. In K. B. Pandolf & J. O. Holloszy (eds), *Exercise and Sport Science Reviews*, 18, 379–415. Baltimore: William & Wilkins.

**Written in collaboration with Anthony Papathomas**

## Background and context

The benefits of exercise to physical health are becoming widely accepted. Robust evidence exists suggesting that people who are physically active are less prone to illnesses such as coronary heart disease (CHD), hypertension, and osteoporosis amongst others. In the case of CHD, exercise is considered a key factor in its prevention. The benefits of exercise on *mental health* are struggling to achieve similar acceptance levels among medical authorities, despite a wealth of anecdotal evidence and a growing empirical research base. The key study by North, McCullagh, and Tran is important as it made a first attempt to scientifically unify the research findings of the time, taking an initial step towards acquiring a consensus as to the effects of exercise on mental health.

The World Health Organization (2001) acknowledge the great difficulty in comprehensively defining mental health. Although a variety of definitions exist, it is agreed that mental health is not merely the absence of a given mental disorder but the presence of emotional and psychological well-being. A multitude of mental disorders exist and these place a massive burden on the individual, their loved ones, and society. A more recent report by the World Health Organization (2005) estimates one in four of us will experience a mental health problem at some point in our lives. The report goes on to state that the cost to national economies is billions yet still the demand for treatment far outweighs the care provided. If exercise, with its positive physical side-effects and relatively inexpensive nature, is shown to be an effective treatment and preventative of certain mental disorders, then some of the huge financial strain and, crucially, individual suffering may be substantially alleviated. This is an important goal and the motivation for both the key study and this line of research in general.

Prior to the North *et al.* study, findings were both encouraging and diverse. Exercise was related to better cognitive functioning (Mutrie & Knill-Jones, 1986) and improved self-esteem (Sonstroem, 1984). From a clinical perspective Chamove (1986) reported transient improvements in the symptoms of schizophrenic patients after exercise. In reference to clinical anxiety, Martinsen, Hoffart, and Solberg (1989) engaged patients in an eight-week exercise program and found anxiety levels significantly reduced. These exploratory investigations, and similar ones, show promise but are not addressed as extensively in the literature because most exercise researchers have opted instead to study mood states disorders.

Anecdotally many of us appreciate the lift in mood we experience after a bout of exercise, be it a "good run" or a "refreshing swim." Biddle and Mutrie (2001) view mood as a global set of affective states experienced on a day-to-day basis, and studies have shown that moderate intensity exercise can lead to transient and longer-term enhancement in mood and affect in mentally healthy populations (Moses, Steptoe, Matthews, & Edwards, 1989; Steptoe & Bolton, 1988). If enhanced psychological well-being can occur in normal populations then can exercise raise "clinically low" mood levels in depressed individuals?

Much of exercise and mental health research has addressed depression, and it is the specific focus of the key study in question. According to the DSM-IV-TR, a manual providing clinical definitions of mental disorders and used in practice by psychologists and psychiatrists for purposes of diagnosis, clinical depression is a debilitative mental illness characterized primarily by at least two weeks of depressed mood or loss of interest (American Psychiatric Association, 2000: 349). It further stipulates that this must also be accompanied by at least four other depressive symptoms such as loss of appetite, decreased energy, feelings of guilt, and difficulty concentrating. A recent study showed European prevalence of clinically severe depression to be at least 5% (Paykel, Brugha, & Fryers, 2005). Similar values have previously been found in Australia and the USA (Lehtinen & Joukamaa, 1994). Clearly, depression represents one of the more widespread mental disorders and is worthy of the research attention it has received.

So can exercise reduce symptoms of depression? Tentative questions of this nature were prompted by epidemiological studies that showed higher levels of physical activity are associated with lower levels of depression (Farmer, Locke, Moscicki, Dannenberg, Larson, & Radloff, 1988; Stephens, 1988). Though such cross-sectional data is intriguing it cannot tell us the direction of this relationship – does physical activity lead to less depression or does depression lead to less physical activity? Experimental studies are necessary to identify a possible causal relationship, and these have produced similarly intriguing results. Prior to the key study, exercise groups were found to show lower depression levels when compared to no treatment controls (Doyne, Ossip-Klein, Bowman, & Osborn, 1987). Similarly, exercise groups experienced equivalent reductions in depression when compared to groups receiving therapy (Fremont & Craighead, 1987). There was also a finding that exercise and psychotherapy combined reduced depression significantly more than either treatment alone (Simons, McGowan, Epstein, Kupfer, & Robertson, 1985). The authors of the key study sought to integrate the findings of these experimental studies and thus reveal the general extent to which exercise decreases depression and how best it to do it, as well as other relevant questions. This goal was achieved through a meta-analysis which is a statistical technique that combines the results of all the studies on a given issue to produce an overall value known as an effect size. The derived effect size illustrates whether one variable (e.g., exercise) causes a change in a dependent variable (e.g., depression). Specifically, a high effect size corresponds to a strong causal relationship and a low effect size corresponds to a weak causal relationship. Meta-analyses are often used in the medical profession to assess whether a treatment is effective for a given condition.

## Key study

Depression is one of the most common complaints of adults who seek psychotherapy, and mood disorders are the most prevalent disorder in western society (Taylor & Abrams, 1981). In fact, the American Psychiatric Association reports that 4.5–9.3% of females and 2.3–3.2% of males in the USA currently have a major depressive disorder. One potential psychosomatic treatment for reducing depression is exercise. Some recent studies indicate that exercise may be an antidepressant (Brown, Ramirez, & Taub, 1978; Doyne, Chambless, & Beutler, 1983; Greist, 1977; Greist, Klein, Eischens, & Faris, 1978, Greist, Eischens, Klein, & Faris, 1979) and others have shown no significant effect of exercise on depression (Morgan, Roberts, Brand, & Feinerman, 1970; Morgan, Roberts, & Feinerman, 1971; Perri & Templer, 1985). From a clinical perspective, Greist (1977), a psychiatrist, suggests that many patients would do better if they used running rather than psychoanalysis to decrease their depression. Greist qualifies this statement by suggesting that running does not resolve an individual's existential problems, but may offer temporary relief (similar to aspirin for a headache).

Previous reviews of the effect of exercise on depression have used the traditional approach, from which only subjective conclusions could be drawn. Therefore, relationships between such variables as exercise mode, length of exercise program, initial depression level, and the effect of exercise on depression are not yet clear. Thus, an objective statistical integration of studies investigating the effects of exercise on depression would help clarify this area of research. The purpose of this study was to provide a comprehensive review of the literature on the effect of exercise on depression. Both meta-analysis and traditional review methodologies (a review of proposed mechanisms for the antidepressant effect of exercise) were employed by the researchers, but the meta-analysis is the primary focus of this chapter.

## Meta-Analysis of the Effect of Exercise on Depression

Understanding the current scientific data on a topic is a requisite for investigators to proceed with future research. Reviews of literature serve to differentiate which hypotheses the literature supports and which remain in question for future research. Given the discrepant findings in this area of research, it is likely that a narrative review of literature would conclude that there were no consistent findings in this body of literature. It would also be difficult for a narrative review to address the effect of independent variables like mode of exercise, subject populations, etc. on depression in these studies. Due to the proliferation of research reports on the effect of exercise on depression in recent years, a method of reviewing that is systematic, quantitative, and replicable would contribute to a more objective view of the effect of exercise on depression research.

### Introduction to Meta-Analysis

To overcome some of the limitations of a traditional review, Glass (1976) developed a methodology for the statistical review of literature. According to Glass, McGraw, and Smith (1981), the essential characteristic of meta-analysis ". . . is the statistical analysis of the summary findings of many empirical studies" (1981: 21). Meta-analysis is a quantitative approach to reviewing research that uses a variety of statistical techniques for sorting, classifying, and summarizing information from the findings of many experimental studies. It is a systematic and replicable procedure that overcomes many of the problems associated with the traditional narrative review.

The purpose of the meta-analysis methodology includes: (a) to increase statistical power for primary endpoints and subgroup analysis, (b) to resolve conflicts when studies disagree, (c) to improve estimates of effect size, and (d) to answer questions not posed by authors of individual studies (Sacks, Berrier, Reitman, Ancona-Bark, & Chalmer, 1987).

## Meta-Analysis Procedures

*Problem Formulation.* As a preface to this present meta-analysis, a pilot meta-analysis was completed, using studies evaluating the effect of exercise on depression. This pilot meta-analysis, based on a random sample of the studies that had been located for potential inclusion, helped refine the research questions and coding sheet used in the present meta-analysis. There were only two criteria for studies to be included in this meta-analysis. First, each study must have had at least one outcome measure of depression related to exercise or fitness; and second, data (published in English) must have been available prior to June 1, 1989. Cross-sectional, longitudinal, published, and unpublished studies were included.

*Literature Search.* In a meta-analysis, the literature search is analogous to the collection of data in an experimental study. Thus, the search procedures must be explicated to the extent that it could be replicated by other researchers. The literature search is the point in a meta-analysis where the greatest bias may occur. Thus, a thorough description of the search procedures used to locate studies is provided so the reader can determine the representativeness and completeness of the database.

Initially, approximately 20 current, relevant studies, and one review of literature were read to select key words and determine important characteristics of these studies. Using these key words, an initial search was done on ERIC (Educational Resource Information Center). This search served to identify other key words and additional studies for possible inclusion. The final list of key words was then used to search title, descriptor words, and the abstract (where possible). Computer searches were conducted at the University of Colorado. Tran and Weltman (1985) indicated that only 35% of the studies included in their meta-analysis were identified through computer searches, so the present search for studies also included the following strategies: books searched through a university computerized card catalog, cross-referencing of studies in the reference lists from all previously located studies, abstracts from annual professional meetings, a bibliography of over 1400 psychology of exercise articles from Dr Michael Sachs (personal communication) and a citation search of seven frequently used studies were used to locate updated articles in the Social Science Citations and Science Citations Indexes.

*Coding Sheet.* The coding sheet included the following types of variables: publication (author, publication date, etc.), subject characteristics (age, gender, health status, etc.), design (level of internal validity, depression scale used, etc.), and exercise treatment (length of program, intensity, and duration of session, etc.).

*Definition of Effect Size.* Every outcome measure found in the studies that was included in this meta-analysis was transformed into an effect size (ES). See the original publication for a description of how the authors computed ES.

*Definition of Depression.* Classifying depression can be difficult. The American Psychiatric Association (APA, 1987) developed the most universally accepted classification system of mental disorders. Major forms of depression as the primary illness are classified as mood disorders, or organic mood syndromes. Mood disorders are divided into two major sub-classifications, bipolar disorders and depressive disorders, both of which have additional subcategories. The American Psychiatric Association (1987) also lists depression as an associated feature (symptomatic of a primary disorder, or a secondary disorder) of a large variety of other psychiatric disorders including: psychosis, schizophrenia, dementia, some adjustment and anxiety disorders, and bereavement. Depression is ubiquitous as an illness, or a symptom of an illness, in both the psychological and medical literature. The aforementioned differences in definition suggest a lack of universal agreement on how to diagnose, classify, and measure depression. This meta-analysis included all reported forms of depression.

*Definition of Exercise.* The American College of Sports Medicine (1986) defines three types of exercise: (a) cardiorespiratory or aerobic endurance, (b) muscular strength and endurance, and (c) flexibility. In this meta-analysis, the first two categories were considered exercise, because they both require an elevated metabolic rate.

## Data Analysis Procedures

*Problems of Inferential Testing.* F tests with unequal Ns per cell and multiple comparison techniques are not robust with respect to violations of homogeneity of variance and normality assumptions. Therefore, tests of homogeneity of variance and normality were made. In all cases these assumptions were violated to some degree. Thus, reported $p$ values are on the liberal side. In addition, most inferential tests assume independence of observations. In this meta-analysis, several ESs may have been calculated from a single study, each computed from the same group of subjects. Because the ES was the dependent measure in this meta-analysis, some of the ESs are correlated and therefore not independent. Because of this correlation, reported $p$ values may be liberal, and reported standard deviations too small.

*Weighting of ES.* Because large samples more frequently produce statistically significant findings and more precise estimates than do small samples, some measure of weighting should be incorporated. Precisely what weight to assign to each ES in an aggregation of data is an extremely complex question that cannot be answered adequately by giving each ES equal weight regardless of sample size. Because the sampling variance of ES is approximately proportional to the inverse of sample size, the use of sample size to weigh each ES is reasonably close to optimal so this is the procedure chosen for this meta-analysis.

*Overall Results.* A $z$ test was used to determine if the overall mean ES ($\overline{ES}$) was significantly different from zero. A $\overline{ES}$ that was significantly different from zero is comparable to rejecting the null hypothesis in an experimental study. A probability level of 0.05 was used to determine statistical significance for all results.

*Analysis of Variables.* Each variable is presented individually in a section corresponding to the research question it addresses. Descriptive, inferential, and correlational analyses are presented as appropriate. Descriptive statistics are reported for categories of the variables analyzed and include: the $\overline{ES}$, standard deviation, number of ESs (N of ESs), and number of studies those ESs came from (N of studies). Pearson correlation coefficients and point-biserial correlation coefficients are reported, where appropriate, to quantify the magnitude and direction of the relationships between independent variables and ES. Where significant correlational relationships were found, $r^2$ is also reported.

*Inferential Analysis of Categorical Variables.* One-way or two-way analysis of variance (ANOVA) for categorical variables, with ES as the dependent measure, was used to determine if significant differences existed among categories in variables with two or more levels. To increase statistical power, only categories with seven or more ESs were included in the ANOVAs. The $\Omega^2$ (omega squared) statistic was reported for each significant one-way ANOVA to provide an indication of the magnitude of the relationship between ES and the variable analyzed (Hays, 1973). Categorical variables have significance of z scores reported for each variable category where appropriate. The z scores indicate whether an $\overline{ES}$ was significantly different from zero and is comparable to rejecting the null hypothesis in an experimental study. When a one-way ANOVA was significant, post hoc, pairwise multiple comparisons were computed using the Newman-Keuls multiple comparison test.

*Reliability of Coding Procedures.* Coding of studies was done by one investigator. The reliability of this coding was checked by an independent investigator who calculated eight ESs from six randomly selected studies. The ES for the author's and independent investigator's eight ES calculations were –0.64 and –0.65, respectively. The correlation between the two sets of ESs was high ($r = 0.99$).

## Research Questions

To assess both the overall effect of exercise on depression and the influence of independent variables, six research questions were proposed. (*a*) Does exercise affect depression level? (*b*) Does the source of subjects influence the outcome of the effect of exercise on depression? (*c*) Do study design, methods employed, or publication variables affect the outcome of exercise on depression studies? (*d*) What subject populations (age, gender, initial level of depression, health status, etc.) decrease depression with exercise? (*e*) What mode and duration of exercise affect depression? (*f*) What is the magnitude of the antidepressant effect of exercise compared with other treatments?

## **Overall Results and Discussion**

Each section of the results addresses one of the research questions investigated in this meta-analysis. Data for 19 variables are reported according to the research question that each variable addresses. Most variables have missing cases due to missing or unclear information from the studies coded or too small a number of ESs in a variable category to be included in the analysis. Each variable is discussed in terms of the data presented and compared to other authors' findings where applicable. Meta-analysis methodology is still a relatively new statistical procedure, so for clarification, the following descriptions of important components of the results are provided. (*a*) A negative mean effect size (ES) in this meta-analysis indicates that exercise groups decreased depression scores more than comparison groups. For example, a ES of –0.50 indicates that subjects in exercise groups decreased their depression scores an average of one-half of a standard deviation unit more than subjects in comparison groups. (*b*) The term "comparison group" is used in this meta-analysis, because all studies of the effect of exercise on depression have been included in this synthesis of studies, regardless of the type of group to which the exercise group was compared. Comparison groups included, control, leisure activity, and psychotherapy groups, among others. The influence of different comparison groups was evaluated and results presented within the variable comparison groups. (*c*) The *z* scores presented throughout this chapter are measures of how different an ES is from zero. An ES of zero indicates that the change in depression scores for exercise groups and comparison groups was the same. (*d*) The $\Omega^2$ values reported with all significant one-way ANOVAs were a measure of how much variance was accounted for by the variable being analyzed (analogous to $r^2$ for correlations). (*e*) To increase the power of the analysis of categorical variables, only categories with seven or more ESs were analyzed. These categorical variables are presented in tables. Categories are listed in order, starting with the largest negative ES to the least negative ES except with ordinal categorical variables, and these are tabled in the order of the variable categories. (*f*) Only the overall results section includes all ESs in the analysis. In subsequent reporting of variables, all acute exercise ESs were dropped from the analysis, because they were found to be significantly different than ESs from chronic exercise and could confound the results (see overall results). Thus, all analysis presented after the overall results section includes only ESs calculated from exercise programs and follow-up measurements of exercise programs (chronic exercise).

## Results and Discussion of: Does Exercise Affect Depression Level?

*Overall Results.* A total of 80 studies met the criteria for inclusion in this meta-analysis and yielded 290 ESs (Table 17.1). Each study provided an average of 3.8 ESs, with a range from 1 to 36 ESs. The overall $\overline{ES}$ was −0.53, which was significantly different from zero. The range of ESs was −3.88 to +2.05. The $\overline{ES}$ indicated that in the studies coded, depression scores decreased approximately one-half of a standard deviation more in exercise groups than in comparison groups. Thus, overall, exercise groups received antidepressant benefits from exercise because they decreased depression scores more than comparison groups.

The overall results were categorized to determine if there was a difference between a single exercise session, exercise programs, and follow-up measurements, since these could be quite different. Single exercise session included all measurements of the effect of acute exercise, exercise programs measured the effect of multisession exercise programs, and follow-up measurements were measurements taken after an exercise program had been previously terminated. All three categories were significantly different from zero (Table 17.1) indicating that exercise was a beneficial antidepressant in all three situations. The one-way ANOVA type of measurement was significant ($F_{2,290} = 4.32$, $p < 0.02$, $\Omega^2 = 0.02$). Post hoc pairwise comparisons indicated that single exercise session was significantly different from exercise programs, but not different from follow-up.

In this meta-analysis, the effect of exercise on depression was different for acute exercise (single exercise session) and for exercise programs, but both were effective antidepressants. This suggests that the antidepressant effect of exercise may begin in the first session of exercise, contradicting the findings of several studies (Browman & Tepas, 1976; Morgan *et al.*, 1971; Walker, Floyd, Fein, Cavness, Lualhati, & Feinberg 1978). The group of 38 ESs in the follow-up category indicate that the effect of exercise may persist beyond the end of exercise programs. The degree that subjects continued to exercise during the follow-up periods was not reported in most of the studies coded, so it is not clear whether continued exercise is necessary for a continued antidepressant effect. However, it is encouraging to identify a method (exercise) of treating depression that apparently has both an immediate and long-term effect.

The overall results indicated that exercise was an effective antidepressant and are consistent with the findings in several previous reviews (Folkins & Sime, 1981; Martinsen, 1987; Morgan, 1969; Ransford, 1982; Sachs, 1982; Taylor, Sallis, & Needle, 1985) and contradicted other reviews (Hughes, 1984; Weinstein & Meyers, 1983). However, the overall results included all subject populations, modes of exercise, length of exercise programs, etc . . . and

**Table 17.1** Overall effects of exercise on depression

|  | N of ESs | N of studies | $\overline{ES} \pm SD$ |
|---|---|---|---|
| Total data | 290 | 80 | −0.53 ± 0.85*** |
| Type of measurement |  |  |  |
|    Exercise programs | 226 | 76 | −0.59 ± 0.89*** |
|    Follow-up | 38 | 7 | −0.50 ± 0.80*** |
|    Single exercise session | 26 | 10 | −0.31 ± 0.44*** |

Mean effect size is significantly different from zero at: *** $p < 0.001$

close inspection of the data presented in this chapter offers some contradictions to several widely accepted beliefs regarding the effects of exercise on depression. Although the overall results indicated that exercise was, in general, an effective antidepressant, it is important to determine how other factors may moderate this overall effect. To accomplish this, the previously stated research questions were examined. Subsequent data reported in this chapter were determined using only ESs calculated from programs and follow-up measurements and do not include single exercise session ESs. This was done to evaluate the effect of chronic exercise on depression.

## Results and Discussion of: Does the Source of Subjects Influence the Outcome of the Effect of Exercise on Depression?

*Source of Subjects.* There were five sources of subjects analyzed for the studies coded (Table 17.2). A one-way ANOVA of source of subjects with ES indicated that the groups were heterogeneous ($F_{4,238} = 9.66$, $p < 0.001$, $\Omega^2 = 0.13$). The variance accounted for by the source of subjects was not high, but considerably greater than most other single variables analyzed in this meta-analysis.

**Table 17.2** Effect sizes for source of subjects

| Source of subjects | N of ESs | N of studies | ES ± SD |
|---|---|---|---|
| Medical/psychological patients | 46 | 21 | −0.94 ± 1.16*** |
| High school students | 12 | 3 | −0.60 ± 0.93* |
| Health club members | 27 | 2 | −0.49 ± 1.31* |
| Community citizens | 100 | 20 | −0.49 ± 0.60*** |
| College students/faculty | 58 | 20 | −0.16 ± 0.60* |

Mean effect size is significantly different from zero at: * $p < 0.05$ and *** $p < 0.001$

The medical/psychological patients category included ESs from studies using subjects receiving medical and/or psychological treatment and had the largest negative ES. The post hoc analysis found significant differences between the medical/psychological patient category and all other four categories, indicating that exercise decreased depression more in individuals recruited from medical or psychological facilities than individuals recruited from other locations. These findings support Folkins and Sime (1981) who suggested that exercise is most effective as an antidepressant for subjects who are the most physically and psychologically unhealthy at the outset of an exercise program. In summary, the source of subjects influenced the outcome of the studies coded, and subjects receiving medical and/or psychological care demonstrated the greatest decrease in depression with exercise.

## Results and Discussion of: Do Study Design, Methods Employed, or Publication Variables Affect the Outcome of Exercise on Depression Studies?

Methodological variables can influence the outcome of a meta-analysis and all meta-analyses should code for methodological weaknesses and make a posteriori rather than a priori decisions about how methodology affects study outcomes (Glass *et al.*, 1981). Six variables have been included in this section to address the effects of study design, methods employed, and publication information on the outcome of exercise studies on depression.

*Form of Publication.* The form of publication was important to analyze, because a previous meta-analysis by Smith (1980) found that ESs from theses and journals were not only significantly different, but also in opposite directions. There were two categories analyzed (Table 17.3). The published category included ESs from published articles and books, and the unpublished category included all unpublished doctoral dissertations and master's theses. A one-way ANOVA of form of publication was significant ($F_{1,265} = 7.30$, $p < 0.01$, $\Omega^2 = 0.02$). The published studies had a significantly larger negative ES than the unpublished studies. In other words, results of published studies showed greater decreases in depression for exercise groups than unpublished studies. These results, like Smith's (1980) indicate the importance for reviewers to include unpublished studies to avoid biasing their reviews.

*Purpose of Exercise.* Purpose of exercise had four categories (Table 17.3). The medical rehabilitation category included ESs from studies that used subjects receiving medical care and exercise as part of their treatment (coronary disease, pulmonary disease, kidney failure, and alcohol and drug addiction patients). The psychological rehabilitation category included ESs using exercise as a treatment for psychological problems. The general health category contained all ESs from studies that used subjects that exercised to promote and/or maintain well-being. The academic experiment category included ESs from studies where the only purpose of exercise was to participate in an academic experiment.

All groups significantly decreased depression scores (Table 17.3). A one-way ANOVA was significant ($F_{3,247} = 11.16$, $p < 0.001$, $\Omega^2 = 0.11$). Post hoc pairwise comparisons indicated that the medical rehabilitation category was significantly different from the other three categories, and no other differences were found. The decreased depression of the psychological rehabilitation group supports several previous reviews that have indicated that exercise is an antidepressant for subjects in need of psychotherapy to treat depression (Browman, 1981; Folkins & Sime, 1981; Ledwidge, 1980; Mellion, 1985; Simons, Epstein, McGowan, Kupfer, & Robertson, 1985; Taylor *et al.*, 1985). Subjects in medical rehabilitation have received very little attention in most reviews and individual studies. Only one previous review has addressed the medical rehabilitation population (Taylor *et al.*, 1985) and indicated that the effect of exercise on depression in postmyocardial infarction patients was not clear. However, in this

**Table 17.3** Effect sizes for form of publication, purpose of exercise, and exercise location

| Variable | N of ESs | N of studies | $\overline{ES} \pm SD$ |
|---|---|---|---|
| Form of publication | | | |
| Published | 131 | 42 | $-0.69 \pm 0.99$*** |
| Unpublished | 136 | 31 | $-0.37 \pm 0.72$*** |
| Purpose of exercise | | | |
| Medical rehabilitation | 44 | 13 | $-0.97 \pm 1.24$*** |
| Academic experiment | 9 | 5 | $-0.67 \pm 0.44$*** |
| Psychological rehabilitation | 65 | 15 | $-0.55 \pm 0.76$*** |
| General health | 133 | 31 | $-0.29 \pm 0.56$*** |
| Exercise location | | | |
| Home | 9 | 3 | $-1.34 \pm 1.63$** |
| Medical facility | 26 | 15 | $-0.68 \pm 0.80$*** |
| Community center | 60 | 8 | $-0.68 \pm 0.68$*** |
| University/college | 115 | 29 | $-0.24 \pm 0.88$** |

Mean effect size is significantly different from zero at: ** $p < 0.01$ and *** $p < 0.001$

meta-analysis, the medical rehabilitation group decreased depression with exercise more than any other group. Medications were not addressed in most of the studies coded and are not accounted for in this meta-analysis, which may confound the medical rehabilitation and psychological rehabilitation results. Because depression is a common secondary symptom of individuals with physical disease, exercise may prove to be a cost-effective means to provide both physical and psychological rehabilitation for individuals with physical illness.

*Exercise Location.* Exercise location was analyzed to determine if exercising in different environments influenced the outcome of the effect of exercise on depression. Exercise took place in four types of locations (Table 17.3). The one-way ANOVA with ES was significant ($F_{3,206}$ = 4.14, $p < 0.01$, $\Omega^2 = 0.04$). Post hoc pairwise comparisons indicated that the home category was significantly different from the community center and university/college categories. Thus, exercising at home led to a greater decrease in depression than exercising in a university/college or community center setting. No other significant pairwise differences were found.

In this meta-analysis, exercise significantly decreased depression regardless of exercise location. The reason for the significant difference between the home and both the community center and university/college categories was not clear. The nine ESs in the home category were from only three studies, so the results need to be interpreted cautiously. Seven of the nine ESs in this category used subjects with a purpose of exercise being medical rehabilitation. The medical rehabilitation group had the largest negative $\overline{ES}$ in the variable purpose of exercise. A two-way ANOVA of exercise location and purpose of exercise with ES as the dependent measure found a significant main effect for exercise location ($F_{3,199} = 4.13$, $p < 0.001$), a significant main effect for purpose of exercise ($F_{3,199} = 7.19$, $p < 0.001$), but no significant interaction ($F_{4,199} = 0.80$, $p > 0.05$).

*Group Assignment.* One of the criticisms of meta-analysis has been the combining of studies that have good internal validity with studies that do not (Eysenck, 1978). Two variables (group assignment and degree of internal validity) were coded to evaluate the effect of the quality of experimental design on the outcome of the effect of exercise on depression studies. Six categories of group assignment were analyzed (Table 17.4).

All $z$ scores were significantly different from zero, indicating that exercise groups lowered depression scores significantly more than comparison groups across all categories of group assignment. The one-way ANOVA was significant ($F_{5,252} = 2.63$, $p < 0.05$, $\Omega^2 = 0.03$) but no significant post hoc pairwise differences were found. Previous reviewers have been critical of

**Table 17.4** Effect sizes for group assignment and degree of internal validity

| Variable | N of ESs | N of studies | $\overline{ES} \pm SD$ |
|---|---|---|---|
| Group assignment | | | |
| Random assignment | 110 | 27 | −1.30 ± 1.11*** |
| Cross-sectional study | 11 | 6 | −0.71 ± 0.45*** |
| Convenient groups | 11 | 6 | −0.43 ± 0.64* |
| Matching groups | 42 | 5 | −0.41 ± 0.51*** |
| One group pre-post | 9 | 4 | −0.30 ± 0.34** |
| Self-selected groups | 75 | 20 | −0.27 ± 0.74*** |
| Degree of internal validity | | | |
| High | 60 | 11 | −0.47 ± 1.14*** |
| Medium | 62 | 20 | −0.94 ± 1.02*** |
| Low | 139 | 41 | −0.34 ± 0.63*** |

the methods used for studies investigating the effect of exercise on depression (Folkins & Sime, 1981; Hughes, 1984; Ledwidge, 1980; Morgan, 1969; Simons et al., 1985; Weinstein & Meyers, 1983). However, in this meta-analysis, group assignment had no differential effect on the outcome of exercise on depression level.

*Degree of Internal Validity.* The variable degree of internal validity also addressed the quality of experimental design. Internal validity scores were determined according to the methods suggested by Glass et al. (see Glass et al., 1981: 83) with high, medium, and low categories. All ESs were significantly different from zero (Table 17.4). A one-way ANOVA of internal validity was significant ($F_{2,258} = 4.97$, $p < 0.01$, $\Omega^2 = 0.03$). Post hoc comparisons indicated that the medium category had a significantly larger negative ES than both the high and low categories. The Pearson correlation coefficient for internal validity with ES was not significant ($N = 261$, $r = -0.08$, $p > 0.05$). To determine if degree of internal validity was affected by whether a study was published or unpublished, a two-way ANOVA of the degree of internal validity with published versus unpublished, with ES as the dependent measure, was computed. There was a significant main effect for degree of internal validity ($F_{2,255} = 4.10$, $p < 0.05$), a significant main effect of published versus unpublished ($F_{1,255} = 5.11$, $p < 0.05$) but no significant interaction ($F_{2,255} = 2.13$, $p > 0.05$). The two-way ANOVA was used to determine if there was any relationship between the quality of design of studies and whether the study had been published. Because all of the unpublished studies in this meta-analysis were from dissertations or theses, it justifies the importance of including them. In this meta-analysis, exercise decreased depression regardless of the degree of internal validity of the study design. This finding may help allay the concerns pointed out by authors who have suggested that readers interpret the studies on exercise and depression cautiously because of poor study design (Browman, 1981; Folkins & Sime, 1981; Hughes, 1984; Simons et al., 1985).

*State Versus Trait Measurements.* Evaluating the effect of state and trait measurement scales on the outcome of exercise on depression studies is important. State scales reflect subjects' affect at that point in time, and trait scales reflect subjects' more enduring personality traits. Folkins and Sime (1981) have suggested that exercise studies do not demonstrate global personality trait changes. A one-way ANOVA was not significant ($F_{1,251} = 2.13$, $p > 0.05$). Because trait scores are likely to change more slowly than state scores, a two-way ANOVA of state versus trait measurements and length of exercise program, with ES as the dependent measure, was computed. There was a nonsignificant main effect for state versus trait ($F_{1,216} = 0.32$, $p > 0.05$), the main effect for length of exercise program was significant ($F_{6,216} = 12.65$, $p < 0.001$), and no two-way interaction was found ($F_{3,216} = 0.11$, $p > 0.05$). The lack of interaction needs cautious interpretation because of the low number of ESs in some of the cells for analysis (Table 17.5).

Only 11% of the total number of ESs used a trait scale. Trait measurements were used primarily on middle-aged subjects (who had the largest negative ES in the variable age

**Table 17.5** Effect sizes for state versus trait measurements

| State vs. trait | N of ESs | N of studies | $\overline{ES} \pm SD$ |
|---|---|---|---|
| Trait | 27 | 16 | $-0.91 \pm 0.83$*** |
| State | 226 | 59 | $-0.45 \pm 0.90$*** |

Mean effect size is significantly different from zero at: *** $p < 0.001$

category) so a two-way ANOVA was performed to determine if there was an interaction between state versus trait measurements and age category, using ES as the dependent measure. The main effect for state versus trait measurements was not significant ($F_{1,214} = 1.37, p > 0.05$), the main effect of age category was significant ($F_{2,214} = 4.00, p < 0.05$), and there was no significant interaction ($F_{1,214} = 0.16, p > 0.05$). In this meta-analysis, ESs using trait scales had as large a negative mean value as ESs using state scales. The two-way ANOVAs performed were not able to explain this finding. The data suggest that in the studies coded, exercise changed depression as a personality trait, as well as a temporary mood state, contradicting two previous reviews (Browman, 1981; Folkins & Sime, 1981). No interactions were found between state and trait measures and length of exercise program, or age category. Future studies with serial comparisons using both state and trait depression scales simultaneously may be able to provide insight into any interaction that may exist between state and trait depression changes and length of exercise programs.

## Results and Discussion of: What Subject Populations Decrease Depression with Exercise?

Determining who (what subject populations) can decrease depression with exercise was addressed by analyzing the seven variables discussed in this section.

*Mean Age and Age Category.* The age of subjects from the ESs analyzed ranged from 11 to 55 years. The mean age for all ESs was $31.8 \pm 12.4$ years. A significant, negative correlational relationship was found between mean age and ES ($N = 170, r = -0.16, p < 0.05$). A negative relationship suggests that the older the subjects, the greater the decrease in depression with exercise. Age category was coded, because many studies did not provide a mean age, but did provide enough information to determine the age category of study subjects (Table 17.6). The z scores indicate that exercise significantly decreased depression across all age categories. The one-way ANOVA was significant ($F_{2,230} = 3.83, p < 0.003, \Omega^2 = 0.02$); however, no significant post hoc differences were found. In this meta-analysis, exercise significantly decreased depression in all age groups analyzed; unfortunately, there were not enough data on the elderly population to include in the analysis.

*Gender.* Gender included the ESs from studies that used either 100% male, or 100% female subjects (Table 17.6). The ESs for males and females were not significantly different ($F_{1,133} = 0.20, p > 0.05$). These data suggest that exercise was an equally effective antidepressant for both genders.

**Table 17.6** Effect sizes for age category and gender

| Variable | N of ESs | N of studies | $\overline{ES} \pm SD$ |
|---|---|---|---|
| Age category | | | |
| Middle aged (25–64 years) | 161 | 41 | −0.74 ± 0.95*** |
| College (18–24 years) | 55 | 17 | −0.23 ± 0.62** |
| Young (<18 years) | 17 | 5 | −0.49 ± 0.78* |
| Gender | | | |
| Males | 53 | 20 | −0.82 ± 1.09*** |
| Females | 82 | 16 | −0.45 ± 0.86*** |

Mean effect size is significantly different from zero at: * $p < 0.05$, ** $p < 0.01$, and *** $p < 0.001$

*Health Status.* Health status was analyzed to help determine which subject populations benefit from exercise as an antidepressant (Table 17.7).

Mean ESs ranged from −2.31 for the hemodialysis category, to −0.29 for the apparently healthy category (Table 17.7). Mean ESs of all categories of health status were significantly different from zero, indicating that exercise was an effective antidepressant for all groups analyzed. A one-way ANOVA was significant ($F_{6,245} = 9.75$, $p < 0.001$, $\Omega^2 = 0.17$). Post hoc pairwise comparisons of means indicated that the hemodialysis category was significantly different from all other groups; schizophrenic was significantly different from depressed, athlete, feeling down, and apparently healthy groups; and the postmyocardial infarction group was significantly different from the feeling down and the apparently healthy groups.

The subjects in the postmyocardial infarction category showed a large decrease in depression with exercise, contradicting several individual studies (Mayou, 1983; Naughton, Bruhn, & Lategola, 1968; Stern & Cleary, 1982; Stern, Gorman, & Kaslow, 1983) and a review (Taylor *et al.*, 1985) that suggested that the antidepressant effect of exercise is not clearly documented in postmyocardial infarction patients. However, these data are in agreement with Kavanaugh, Shephard, Tuck, and Qureshi (1977) who found a significant reduction in depression in postmyocardial infarction patients who participated in a 4-year running program.

The data in this meta-analysis suggest that exercise substantially reduced depression in all the health status categories analyzed. Health status had one of the largest $\Omega^2$ values in this meta-analysis, indicating that the health of the population being studied accounted for more of the variance than most of the other variables coded. This meta-analysis of studies suggests that apparently healthy subjects significantly decreased depression scores with exercise, contrary to some previous research (Folkins & Sime, 1981; Morgan *et al.*, 1970; Simons *et al.*, 1985), but in agreement with the findings of Folkins, Lynch, and Gardner (1972). The effect of the initial level of subjects' health is analyzed further in the next two variables.

*Healthy and Unhealthy Subjects.* The variable healthy and unhealthy subjects had three categories, apparently healthy subjects, subjects under medical treatment, and subjects requiring psychological treatment (Table 17.7). This variable was analyzed to determine if there

**Table 17.7** Effect sizes for health status and healthy and unhealthy subjects

| Variable | N of ESs | N of studies | $\overline{ES} \pm SD$ |
|---|---|---|---|
| Health status | | | |
| Hemodialysis patient | 7 | 3 | −2.31 ± 1.02*** |
| Schizophrenic | 7 | 1 | −1.43 ± 1.07***[a] |
| Postmyocardial infarction | 19 | 7 | −0.95 ± 1.28***[a] |
| Depressed | 100 | 21 | −0.55 ± 0.90***[a,b] |
| Athlete | 7 | 6 | −0.42 ± 0.33***[a,b] |
| Feeling down | 18 | 1 | −0.36 ± 0.43***[a,b] |
| Apparently healthy | 94 | 33 | −0.29 ± 0.62***[a,b] |
| Healthy and unhealthy subjects | | | |
| Under medical treatment | 26 | 9 | −0.97 ± 1.32*** |
| Requiring psychological treatment | 132 | 97 | −0.60 ± 0.87*** |
| Apparently healthy | 105 | 40 | −0.31 ± 0.60*** |

Mean effect size is significantly different from zero at: *** $p < 0.001$
[a]Significantly different from hemodialysis patient ($p < 0.05$)
[b]Significantly different from postmyocardial infarction ($p < 0.05$)

was a difference in the response to exercise in these three subject populations. The subjects under medical treatment group consisted of ESs from studies that used medical rehabilitation patients as subjects (post-myocardial infarction, high cardiovascular risk, pulmonary, and hemodialysis patients). The category of subjects requiring psychological treatment was ES from studies using subjects who had been identified in need of psychotherapy or were requesting help for mood problems. The apparently healthy group included all ESs from studies that used subjects who were generally healthy and not in need of either medical rehabilitation or psychotherapy (like subjects exercising for general health, athletes, etc.).

All three ESs were significantly different from zero. The one-way ANOVA was significant ($F_{2,260} = 17.15$, $p < 0.001$, $\Omega^2 = 0.11$). Post hoc pairwise comparisons indicated that the medical group was significantly different from both the healthy and psychological groups, but there was no significant difference between the psychological and healthy groups. Some studies and reviews have stated that exercise may only help decrease depression in subjects that are already depressed (Folkins & Sime, 1981; Morgan et al., 1970; Simons et al., 1985). These results indicate that all three groups decreased depression with exercise and the apparently healthy population decreased depression with exercise to a similar extent as subjects seeking psychotherapy, but less than subjects receiving medical treatment.

*Initial Depression Level.* Initial depression level is a dichotomous variable that was analyzed to evaluate the antidepressant effect of exercise on subjects who were initially depressed and nondepressed (Table 17.8). Browman (1981) has stated that there is a relationship between the initial level of anxiety or depression, and the amount of change in depression with exercise. In a similar vein, Simons et al. (1985) have suggested that clinically depressed populations can decrease depression with exercise, but evidence in nonclinical populations needs clarification.

Both the depressed and nondepressed categories were significantly different from zero and no significant difference was found between these categories ($F_{1,261} = 1.22$, $p > 0.05$). In this meta-analysis, ES was not related to the initial depression level, and both subjects who were initially depressed and nondepressed decreased depression with exercise, contradicting statements of several authors who have indicated that exercise may be useful only in decreasing depression in subjects who are initially depressed (Folkins & Sime, 1981, Morgan et al., 1970; Simons et al., 1985).

*Depression Category.* Depression category was included on the coding sheet in an attempt to determine how subjects with different depression diagnoses were affected by exercise.

**Table 17.8** Effect sizes for initial depression level and depression category

| Variable | N of ESs | N of studies | $\overline{ES} \pm SD$ |
|---|---|---|---|
| Initial depression level | | | |
|   Nondepressed | 143 | 53 | −0.59 ± 0.91*** |
|   Depressed | 120 | 22 | −0.53 ± 0.84*** |
| Depression category | | | |
|   Reactive | 3 | 2 | −0.67 ± 0.65* |
|   Situational | 2 | 2 | −0.75 ± 0.03*** |
|   Major | 1 | 1 | −0.61 |
|   Unipolar | 14 | 2 | −0.60 ± 0.83** |
|   Dysphoric | 1 | 1 | −0.10 |

Mean effect size is significantly different from zero at: * $p < 0.05$, ** $p < 0.01$, and *** $p < 0.001$

Exercise has been stated to be beneficial to individuals who are mildly or moderately depressed (Browman, 1981; Ledwidge, 1980; Mellion, 1985). Depression categories were determined by the classification provided by the author(s) of each coded study. A total of 21 ESs from eight studies had depression category coded (Table 17.8). The three categories that had more than one ES were significantly different from zero. Thus, in the studies coded, exercise was an effective antidepressant for subjects diagnosed with unipolar, reactive, and situational depression. Because there are so few studies using subjects with diagnosed depression, additional studies are needed to clarify how exercise effects depression in each diagnostic group.

## Results and Discussion of: What Mode and Duration of Exercise Affect Depression?

To evaluate the effect of mode and duration of exercise programs on depression, three variables were analyzed and their results are presented.

*Primary Mode of Exercise.* Five categories of primary mode of exercise were coded (Table 17.9). The various aerobic categories included ESs from studies where subjects used a variety of forms of aerobic activity like jogging and swimming rather than just one aerobic activity.

Walk and/or jog and jogging were the most frequent forms of exercise treatments in the studies coded. The z scores indicate that all modes of exercise analyzed were effective antidepressants. The one-way ANOVA of primary mode of exercise was significant ($F_{4,224} = 3.59$, $p < 0.01$, $\Omega^2 = 0.04$). Multiple comparisons found weight training significantly different from all the other groups. Most authors have suggested that aerobic, and not necessarily anaerobic, exercise decreases depression (Antonelli, 1982; Folkins & Sime, 1981; Sachs, 1982). There was a sufficient number of ESs from studies using aerobic forms of exercise to suggest that aerobic exercise in general was an effective antidepressant. This finding is consistent with Sachs (1982) who suggested that all exercises that are vigorous, uninterrupted for a period of time, and require less cognitive focus and decision making than daily life may be useful psychotherapeutic forms of exercise. However, the data in this meta-analysis suggest that anaerobic exercise was also an effective antidepressant. Thus, anaerobic exercise may also be psychotherapeutic. Additional research is needed before strong generalizations can be made regarding the effect of anaerobic exercise on depression.

*Length of Exercise Program.* The variable length of exercise program was divided into 4-week categories (Table 17.10). The z scores indicated that exercise was an effective antidepressant across all categories. The one-way ANOVA of length of exercise program with ES was significant ($F_{6,230} = 13.41$, $p < 0.001$, $\Omega^2 = 0.24$) and accounted for 24% of the total variance. There was a wide range of ESs. The largest negative ES was at 21–24 weeks (−2.93)

**Table 17.9** Effect sizes for primary mode of exercise

| Primary exercise | N of ESs | N of studies | $\overline{ES} \pm SD$ |
|---|---|---|---|
| Weight training | 7 | 2 | −1.78 ± 0.82*** |
| Various aerobic | 54 | 18 | −0.67 ± 1.22*** |
| Walk and/or jog | 89 | 24 | −0.55 ± 0.92*** |
| Aerobic class | 13 | 7 | −0.56 ± 0.74** |
| Jogging | 66 | 15 | −0.48 ± 0.38*** |

Mean effect size is significantly different from zero at: ** $p < 0.01$ and *** $p < 0.001$

**Table 17.10** Effect sizes for length of exercise program

| Length in weeks | N of ESs | N of studies | ES ± SD |
|---|---|---|---|
| >24 | 11 | 6 | −2.00 ± 1.11***[b] |
| 21–24 | 4 | 1 | −2.93 ± 0.91*** |
| 17–20 | 6 | 1 | −0.97 ± 0.44****[a,b] |
| 13–16 | 7 | 6 | −0.41 ± 0.39**[a,b] |
| 9–12 | 94 | 22 | −0.31 ± 0.84****[a,b] |
| 5–8 | 104 | 22 | −0.30 ± 0.71****[a,b] |
| ′4 | 11 | 4 | −0.11 ± 1.17****[a,b] |

Mean effect size is significantly different from zero at: ** $p < 0.01$ and *** $p < 0.001$
[a]Significantly different from >24 weeks ($p < 0.05$)
[b]Significantly different from 21–24 weeks ($p < 0.05$)

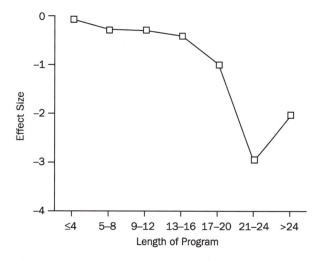

**Figure 17.1** The relationship between length of exercise program and effect size

and the least negative ES value was at less than or equal to 4-weeks of exercise (−0.11). A post hoc pairwise comparison found 11 significant pairwise differences between means. The relationship between length of exercise program and ES is depicted in Figure 17.1.

In this integration of studies, the variable length of exercise program accounted for more of the total variance according to the $\Omega^2$ value than any other variable analyzed. The relationship between the length of exercise program and the effect of exercise on depression level has rarely been discussed in previous reviews. Simons et al. (1985) discussed the length of exercise programs in regard to the time it takes to demonstrate a change in cardiovascular conditioning, but not in terms of the optimal length to decrease depression. In this meta-analysis of studies, all lengths of programs significantly decreased depression, the total length of exercise programs influenced the amount of depression change, and the greatest decreases in depression were seen in programs of 17 weeks or longer.

*Total Number of Exercise Sessions.* The variable total number of exercise sessions quantifies the total number of exercise sessions that was recommended by the research investigators that their subjects participate in during the exercise program. The mean total number of exercise sessions was 30.0 ± 34.6 with a range of 3 to 468 sessions. A significant correlational relationship was found ($N = 204$, $r = -0.27$, $p < 0.001$, $r^2 = 0.07$) between total number of exercise sessions and ES. There was one data outlier (greater than 3 standard deviations above the mean). When this outlier was dropped from the analysis, the correlation improved ($N = 203$, $r = -0.33$, $p < 0.001$, $r^2 = 0.11$). These data, like the variable length of exercise program, suggest that the longer the exercise program and greater the total number of exercise sessions, the greater the decrease in depression with exercise.

*Intensity, Frequency, and Time per Session.* Intensity of exercise was coded; however, insufficient data were found to include in the analysis. The number of times exercise was performed per week, and the length of exercise session were both found to have no influence on ES.

## Results and Discussion of: What Is the Magnitude of the Antidepressant Effect of Exercise Compared with Other Treatments?

*Comparison Group.* The variable comparison group was analyzed to evaluate the magnitude of the antidepressant effect of exercise compared with other treatments as well as nontreatments. Eight categories were analyzed (Table 17.11) and the following is a description of these groups. The no treatment group received no treatment (the traditional control group in an experimental study); waiting list subjects were waiting to receive an antidepressant treatment; the less run/exercise comparison group participated in less exercise or running than the exercise treatment group; the relaxation group participated in relaxation therapy; the enjoyable activity ESs were from studies where subjects participated in a nonexercise activity of their choice; the psychotherapy group received psychological counseling; the anaerobic comparison group was a special situation where the two treatment groups both exercised, one aerobically and the other anaerobically (the aerobic group was coded as the exercise group and the anaerobic group was coded as the comparison group); the exercise plus psychotherapy group received both exercise and psychotherapy treatments. The z scores indicate that all comparison group categories were significantly different from zero except psychotherapy and anaerobic exercise. This suggests that exercise was as effective an antidepressant as psychotherapy and that anaerobic exercise was as effective in reducing depression as aerobic exercise. The exercise plus psychotherapy category had a significantly positive ES indicating

**Table 17.11** Effect sizes for comparison group

| Comparison group | N of ESs | N of studies | $\overline{ES} \pm SD$ |
|---|---|---|---|
| No treatment | 43 | 24 | −0.71 ± 1.03***[a,b] |
| Waiting list | 32 | 6 | −0.54 ± 0.91***[a,b] |
| Less run/exercise | 9 | 7 | −0.29 ± 0.46***[a,b] |
| Relaxation | 9 | 4 | −0.50 ± 1.15[a,b] |
| Enjoyable activity | 27 | 9 | −0.39 ± 0.55***[a,b] |
| Psychotherapy | 35 | 11 | −0.19 ± 0.71[a,b] |
| Anaerobic exercise | 14 | 2 | +0.20 ± 0.67 |
| Exercise + psychotherapy | 7 | 3 | +0.81 ± 0.57*** |

Mean effect size is significantly different from zero at: *** $p < 0.001$
[a]Significantly different from anaerobic exercise
[b]Significantly different from exercise + psychotherapy

that exercise was not as effective an antidepressant as exercise plus psychotherapy. In other words, exercise plus psychotherapy was a better antidepressant than exercise alone. The one-way ANOVA of comparison group was significant ($F_{7,168} = 8.44$, $p < 0.001$, $\Omega^2 = 0.23$). Post hoc pairwise comparisons revealed 12 pairs of significantly different ESs.

The first two categories, no treatment and waiting list, are control group categories. The z scores indicate that, when an exercise treatment was compared with a control group that was not receiving any treatment, exercise was an effective antidepressant. This finding is in agreement with most previous reviews (Folkins & Sime, 1981; Martinsen, 1987; Morgan, 1969; Ransford, 1982; Sachs, 1982, Taylor *et al.*, 1985) but contradicts others (Hughes, 1984; Weinstein & Meyers, 1983). The less run/exercise category suggests that in the seven studies coded comparing an exercise group to an easier exercise group, the easier exercise was not as effective an antidepressant. This finding suggests that there may be an optimal level of physical activity to reduce depression. In this meta-analysis, exercise and relaxation were equally effective antidepressants. However, this finding must be viewed with caution due to the small number of ESs and studies in the relaxation category. One of the proposed mechanisms of the antidepressant effect of exercise is the time out/distraction hypothesis that states that distraction from daily worries may be the antidepressant agent, not exercise itself. The data in the enjoyable activity category indicate that exercise was a significantly better antidepressant than enjoyable activities and do not support this hypothesis.

Most studies that have evaluated the effect of exercise on depression have used aerobic activity for the exercise treatment. The 14 ESs from the two studies that used anaerobic exercise as the comparison group indicate that anaerobic exercise was at least as good of an antidepressant as aerobic exercise. Additional studies using anaerobic exercise are needed to determine the reliability of these findings.

The results comparing exercise with psychotherapy indicate that, in the studies coded, exercise was as good an antidepressant treatment as psychotherapy and is in agreement with the study by Greist *et al.* (1978) and the review by Simons *et al.* (1985). However, additional data are needed to clarify this comparison.

When exercise and psychotherapy were combined as co-treatments these co-treatments decreased depression significantly more than exercise alone. These results are consistent with Simons *et al.* (1985), who proposed that exercise may potentiate the outcome of psychotherapy in reducing depression, and Ledwidge (1980), who suggested that exercise has an antidepressant effect, and would be well utilized as an adjunct to psychotherapy. The results of exercise plus psychotherapy suggest that an additive effect of treatments may exist. Due to the small number of studies available, additional data are needed to clarify how exercise and exercise plus psychotherapy, compare with psychotherapy as antidepressant treatments.

## Meta-Analysis Conclusions

*Does Exercise Affect Depression Level?* The overall results of this meta-analysis indicate that, in the studies coded, both acute and chronic exercise significantly decreased depression, and the antidepressant effect continued through follow-up measures.

*Does the Source of Subjects Influence the Outcome of Exercise on Depression?* All source of subject groups decreased depression with exercise, and subjects, requiring medical or psychological care demonstrated the largest decreases. This variable accounted for a relatively substantial amount of the variance in this meta-analysis.

*Do Study Design, Methods Employed, or Publication Variables Affect the Outcome of Exercise on Depression Studies?* Six variables were analyzed to address the above question:

form of publication, purpose of exercise, exercise location, group assignment, degree of internal validity, and state versus trait measurements. Published studies reported a significantly larger decrease in depression than unpublished studies. Medical rehabilitation subjects demonstrated a greater decrease in depression than did other groups in the purpose of exercise category. The degree of internal validity affected the outcome of the studies included. Both state and trait depression scores decreased with exercise.

*What Subject Populations Decrease Depression with Exercise?* Subjects from most of the populations coded demonstrated decreased depression with exercise including: all age groups, both males and females, subjects in all categories of health status, apparently healthy subjects, subjects involved in medical or psychological rehabilitation, subjects who were initially depressed, and those who were not depressed.

*What Mode and Duration of Exercise Affect Depression?* In this meta-analysis, all modes of exercise were effective antidepressants including anaerobic exercise. The longer the exercise program and the greater the total number of exercise sessions, the larger the decrease in depression.

*What Is The Magnitude of the Antidepressant Effect of Exercise Compared with Other Treatments?* Exercise was a better antidepressant than relaxation and enjoyable activities. Exercise was as effective in decreasing depression as was psychotherapy. Anaerobic exercise was as potent an antidepressant as aerobic exercise. Exercise plus psychotherapy was better than exercise alone in reducing depression.

## Recommendations

The following recommendations are offered for future research and to future reviewers: Additional studies are needed using the following subject populations: subjects exercising in their home, young, elderly, patients with diagnosed mood disorders, and patients with diagnosed medical illnesses (drugs need to be controlled in these studies). Studies using serial measurements of both state and trait depression scales are needed to help clarify the onset and magnitude of the antidepressant effect of exercise. Cardiovascular, and muscular strength measurements need to be evaluated in regard to changes in depression level with exercise. Different forms of exercise, particularly strength training and other anaerobic exercises, need additional evaluation for their potential antidepressant effects. Intensity of exercise needs to be quantified to determine if there is a differential effect. Follow-up studies are needed to determine if the antidepressant effect is maintained as exercise is continued or discontinued. Methodology needs to be addressed to continue to improve the validity of the studies in this area. Additional studies are needed to determine the effectiveness of exercise as a cotreatment with psychotherapy in treating depression. A theoretical model of the antidepressant effect of exercise that includes the effects of acute, short-term, and habitual exercise needs to be developed.

## Subsequent research and application

Since the publication of the key study by North *et al.* research within the field has grown considerably both in terms of quantity and profile. Indeed, within three years of its publication the *International Journal of Sport Psychology* dedicated an entire issue to the topic of "Exercise and Psychological Well-Being," with two articles focusing on depression (Bosscher, 1993; Martinsen, 1993). A contemporary exercise and mental health text (Faulkner & Taylor, 2005) has addressed the role of exercise on such diverse environments as drug and alcohol rehabilitation, smoking cessation and crime reduction. There can be few clearer indications as to the establishment of exercise and mental health as a prominent line of inquiry.

As would be expected from such a comprehensive review, North *et al.* provided detailed recommendations for future study. Perhaps one of the more telling suggestions was that "methodology needs to be addressed to continue to improve the validity of the studies in this area" (1990: 408). This is an important and accurate criticism that also highlights the key weakness of the North *et al.* study itself. If a meta-analytic review seeks to combine the results of individual studies and produce an "overall value," then the significance of that value is dependant on the quality of studies from which it was derived. The studies included in the key study had three fundamental flaws. First, many participants were not diagnosed as clinically depressed. How can the effects of exercise on depression be tested if study participants are not actually depressed? Second, many samples were not randomly assigned to treatment and control groups. Randomizing samples ensures groups did not differ prior to the administration of exercise and hence observed effects can be more readily attributed to the effect of the treatment as opposed to an existing group characteristic. Third, several studies failed to adopt a no treatment (i.e., no exercise) control group. Comparison of the treatment to a control group helps assess whether lowering of depression may have occurred regardless (e.g., tendency for high scorers to simply "regress to the mean").

Subsequent meta-analyses have sought to update and improve on North *et al.* by only including studies with certain important design features. For example, a meta-analysis by Craft and Landers (1998) incorporated 30 studies, all of which involved clinically depressed participants. A considerable overall effect size (ES) of −.72 was identified. Interestingly, when isolating the analysis to studies using participants with moderate to severe depression the ES rises to −.88 which is significantly higher than the −.34 revealed when only including studies involving mild to moderate depression scores. This suggests exercise may be most beneficial when treating more severe forms of depression, an important consideration for health professionals. Also of practical importance is the finding that exercise is as effective as other treatments (e.g., group/individual therapy and behavioral interventions) in reducing depression. The meta-analysis provided little insight into the relationship between depression and specific exercise characteristics (e.g., How much? How often? How hard?) or "moderating variables" as they are also known. Knowledge is generally lacking in this area, which is problematic in terms of effective exercise prescription. Craft and Landers (1998) did identify that exercise programs lasting nine to twelve weeks (ES = −1.18) showed significantly greater reductions in depression than those of eight weeks or less (ES = −.54). Differences within other related moderating variables however, such as exercise type, duration, intensity, and days per week, could not be ascertained. One interpretation of this is that these factors have no bearing on the exercise-depression relationship though it is more likely that research simply hasn't afforded them the necessary attention. Critically, it should be acknowledged that some of the studies included by Craft and Landers did not involve randomized controlled trials (RCTs). RCTs are experiments that include random assignment and an appropriate control group. Given this methodological weakness few concrete conclusions can be made from the findings.

Lawlor and Hopker (2001) did specify RCTs as a requirement for inclusion in their meta-analysis, and as a consequence only managed to accumulate 14 studies. Again, results were encouraging with exercise significantly reducing depression compared with no treatment controls (ES = −1.1). Also as with Craft and Landers (1998) exercise was as effective as other treatment methods (e.g., cognitive therapy and antidepressant use). A less positive similarity to its meta-analysis predecessors is the lack of discussion regarding moderating variables. Only *type* of exercise was addressed and no differences were found between anaerobic and aerobic activity. In general, the authors interpreted their findings with great caution suggesting that though RCTs were evident they were "concealed adequately in only three studies" (1998: 736).

A recent meta-analysis by Stathopoulou, Powers, Berry, Smits, and Otto (2006) stipulated both clinical samples and RCTs for inclusion with a mere 11 studies meeting this criteria. Crucially, the established trend was maintained with an ES of 1.42 in favor of exercise over control conditions. Closer scrutiny of the studies analyzed reveals that some of the control and treatment groups were subject to confounding variables. For example the Armstrong and Edwards (2003) study employed a *multi-intervention* as a treatment condition that incorporated exercise and social support. While depression levels did decrease, causation cannot be totally attributed to exercise. Similarly, 6 of the 11 studies used did not adopt a *pure control* (i.e., no form of treatment provided) with low level exercise, health education, meditation, and "treatment as usual" all serving as conditions for comparison. Again, deciphering the full effect of exercise is therefore difficult. Additionally, a much larger number of studies is necessary if the results of a meta-analysis are to have a significant impact in this field (Dishman, 1995).

It is important to acknowledge the role of the key study, as well as the other discussed meta-analyses, in emphasizing experimental weaknesses and hence promoting more meticulous methodologies. It has been shown that even when experimental rigor is ensured exercise continues to be an effective treatment for depression. For example, just a year after the key study, McNeil, LeBlanc, and Joyner (1991) conducted an RCT on an elderly depressed sample. Participants were randomly assigned to either experimenter accompanied walking, a social contact control and a waiting-list control. Both exercise and social contact significantly reduced depression though only exercise reduced somatic symptoms of depression.

While continuing to encourage more rigorous scientific evidence such as that provided by McNeil *et al.* (1991) many experts believe certain conclusions can now be drawn as to the effects of exercise on depression. For example, Mutrie (2000) produced the following five consensus statements based on the extant literature base:

1   Physical activity is associated with decreased risk of developing clinically defined depression.

2   Aerobic exercise and resistance training may be used to treat depression, usually as an adjunct to standard treatment.

3   The anti-depressant effect of exercise is of the same magnitude as that found from other psychotherapeutic techniques.

4   There is support for a causal link between exercise and decreased depression.

5   No negative effects of exercise have been noted in depressed populations.

Interestingly, these statements are not dissimilar to many of the concluding comments stated in the key study. Evidently, although recent times have witnessed research that encompasses more rigorous and appropriate experimental procedures, the positive findings of past research have still occurred. Regardless, to date, exercise is rarely considered a viable treatment option by mental health service providers (Callaghan, 2004). It may be that in the first instance exercise is prescribed as an adjunctive treatment (i.e., a treatment used together with the primary treatment, such as exercise with prescribed medication). This adjunctive function has received inconsistent results thus far with some studies suggesting increased benefits (Mather, Rodriguez, Guthrie, McHarg, Reid, & McMurdo, 2002; Veale, Le Fevre, Pantelis, De Souza, Mann, & Sargeant, 1992) and others implying no additive effect (Fremont & Craighead, 1987). In a recent review, Landers and Arent (2007) comment that exercise combined with psychotherapy is more effective than either method alone, but that a similar relationship has not yet been established with regards to exercise combined with drugs. Nevertheless, an adjunctive approach could make exercise prescription more common, as therapists can still retain the security of more familiar, traditional treatment options.

While the relatively small number of quality RCTs is central to exercise's struggle for acceptance as a valid treatment tool, there also exists a range of deeper rooted obstacles concerning both professional practice issues and "real world" applicability. From a practical standpoint there is some contention as to whether or not depressed populations can adhere to exercise long enough for long term benefits. Those with a negative view may consider that in normal populations exercise participation rarely reaches above the 50% mark (King, 1994) and in clinical populations (i.e., CHD patients) compliance can be as low as 20% (Biddle, Fox, & Edmund, 1994). It can therefore be argued that the difficulty of adherence may be accentuated in the clinically depressed who regularly experience symptoms of fatigue and reduced energy (Lawlor & Hopker, 2001). Contrary to this, Babyak et al. (2000) found that at six-month follow-up, exercise adherence in a depressed sample was as high as 66%. Pertinently, this was higher than adherence to medication, which was as low as 26%. The suggestion here therefore is that patients may be just as prone to cease medication use as they are exercise, if not more so. It is worth noting however that research studies always risk an element of "selection bias" (i.e., depressed participants volunteering for an exercise study are potentially more likely to be receptive to it).

Of great relevance to adherence levels is the exact nature of the exercise required to gain a reduction in depression. Should benefits only accrue with frequent high intensity exercise then adherence is likely to be challenging. As previously discussed, a number of meta-analyses in the area have failed to shed light as to the most beneficial mode, frequency, intensity, and duration. There is a definite need to establish some form of "dose-response" relationship particularly if exercise is to be prescribed. Dunn, Trivedi, Kambert, Clark, and Chambliss (2005) addressed this issue in a sample of clinically depressed individuals. Participants were randomly assigned to one of four aerobic exercise conditions that reflected differing levels of energy expenditure. Flexibility training was deployed as an exercise placebo control. It was found that the higher dose of exercise of 17.5 kcal/kg/week (e.g., 30 min moderate intensity exercise most days of the week), which was consistent with public health guidelines (Taylor, Coffee, Berra, Iaffaldano, Casey, & Haskell, 1984), was most effective in reducing symptoms of depression. Future research must look to build on these findings and add to the knowledge of the exercise-depression dose-response relationship.

There appears to be an element of resistance within the professional practice of clinical psychology. In a sample of 250 psychotherapists McEntree and Halgin (1996) found that the most common reason provided for not discussing exercise as therapy with clients was that it was perceived as inappropriate. Specifically, it was considered too prescriptive (i.e., authoritarian and insensitive to individual needs). Further, many therapists believed their work pertained to the mind and not the body. Similarly, Faulkner and Biddle (2001) conducted semi-structured interviews with course directors of clinical psychology doctoral programs. Although half of those interviewed were positive about the role of exercise in mental health, other findings were less encouraging. For example, some perceived exercise lacked the sophistication necessary to tackle depression and very few actually recommended it. Interestingly, there was also a limited knowledge of the exercise and mental health research base and exercise interventions did not form a significant part of course content. Researchers should look to assess how such negative perceptions can be changed at both individual and institutional levels.

In conclusion, exercise and mental health, and in particular the effect of exercise on depression, has become a prominent line of research within sport and exercise psychology. While a number of methodological issues remain, current consensus statements stipulate that exercise is effective in reducing symptoms of clinical depression (Mutrie, 2000). Add to this the negligible side-effects of exercise (e.g., sore muscles, fatigue, minor injury) and the well documented physical benefits (reduced risk of CHD, hypertension, arthritis) and there appears no valid reason why it should not be considered as a valuable treatment option. Subsequent studies must further investigate the dose-response relationship between exercise and depression as well as continue to explore the practical, real-world barriers documented by Faulkner and Biddle (2001).

## Additional readings

Dunn, A. L., Trivedi, M. H., Kambert, J. B., Clark, C. G., & Chambliss, H. O. (2005). Exercise treatment for depression: Efficacy and dose response. *American Journal of Preventive Medicine*, 28, 1–8.

Faulkner, G., & Biddle, S. (2001). Exercise and mental health: It's just not psychology! *Journal of Sports Sciences*, 19, 433–44.

Mutrie, N. (2000). The relationship between physical activity and clinically defined depression. In S. J. H. Biddle, K. R. Fox, & S. H. Boutcher (eds) *Physical activity and psychological well being* (pp. 46–62). London: Routledge.

O'Neal, H. A., Dunn, A. J., & Martinsen, E. W. (2000). Depression and exercise. *International Journal of Sport Psychology*, 31, 110–35.

Stathopoulou, G., Powers, M. B., Berry, A. C., & Smits, J. A. J. (2006). Exercise interventions for mental health: A quantitative and qualitative review. *Clinical Psychology: Science and Practice*, 13, 179–93.

## Study questions

1 In exploring the relationship between exercise and depression, what is the advantage of experimental studies over epidemiological research?

2 Explain the technique of meta-analysis and outline in what ways it is useful.

3 Discuss three methodological criticisms of the exercise and depression experimental research base.

4 According to the results of the key study, how does exercise fair as a treatment for depression in relation to each of the documented comparison treatments?

5 Identify findings from the key study that provide support for consensus statements 1 and 2 (Mutrie, 2000).

## References

American College of Sports Medicine (1986). *Guidelines for exercise testing and prescription*. Philadelphia, PA: Lea & Febiger.

American Psychiatric Association (1987). *Diagnostic and statistical manual of mental disorders, third edition*. Washington, DC: American Psychiatric Association.

American Psychiatric Association (2000). *Diagnostic and statistical manual of mental health disorders, fourth edition, text revision*. Washington, DC: American Psychiatric Association.

Antonelli, F. (1982). Sport and depression therapy. *International Journal of Sport Psychology*, 13, 187–93.

Armstrong, M. E., & Edwards, H. (2003). The effects of exercise and social support on mothers reporting depressive symptoms: A pilot randomized controlled trial. *International Journal of Mental Health Nursing*, 12, 130–8.

Babyak, M. A., Blumenthal, J. A., Herman, S., Khatri, P., Doraiswamy, M., Moore, K., Craighead, W. E., Baldewicz, T. T., & Krishnan, K. R. (2000). Exercise treatment for major depression: Maintenance of therapeutic benefit at 10 months. *Psychosomatic Medicine*, 62, 633–8.

Biddle, S. J. H., Fox, K., & Edmund, L. (1994). *Physical activity in primary care in England*. London: Health Education Authority.

Biddle, S. J. H., & Mutrie, N. (2001). *Psychology of physical activity: Determinants, well-being and interventions*. London: Routledge.

Bosscher, R. J. (1993). Running and mixed physical exercises with depressed psychiatric patients. *International Journal of Sport Psychology*, 24, 170–84.

Browman, C. P. (1981). Physical activity as a therapy for psychopathology: A reappraisal. *Journal of Sports Medicine and Physical Fitness*, 21, 192–7.

Browman, C. P., & Tepas, D. I. (1976). The effects of presleep activity on all-night sleep. *Psychophysiology*, 13, 536–40.

Brown, R. S., Ramirez, D. E., & Taub, J. M. (1978). The prescription of exercise for depression. *The Physician and Sportsmedicine*, 6, 34–7, 40–1, 44–5.

Callaghan, P. (2004). Exercise: A neglected intervention in mental health care? *Journal of Psychiatric and Mental Health Nursing*, 11(4), 476–783.

Chamove, A. S. (1986). Positive short-term effects of activity on behaviour in chronic schizophrenic patients. *British Journal of Clinical Psychology*, 25, 125–33.

Craft, L. L., & Landers, D. M. (1998). The effect of exercise on clinical depression and depression resulting from mental illness: A meta-analysis. *Journal of Sport & Exercise Psychology*, 20, 339–57.

Dishman, R. K. (1995). Physical activity and public health: Mental health. *Quest*, 47, 362–85.

Doyne, E. J., Chambless, D. L., & Beutler, L. E. (1983). Aerobic exercise as a treatment for depression in women. *Behavioural Therapy*, 14, 434–40.

Doyne, E. J., Ossip-Klein, D. J., Bowman, E. D., & Osborn, K. M. (1987). Running versus weight lifting in the treatment of depression. *Journal of Consulting and Clinical Psychology. Special Issue: Eating Disorders*, 55(5), 748–54.

Dunn, A. L., Trivedi, M. H., Kambert, J. B., Clark, C. G., & Chambliss, H. O. (2005). Exercise treatment for depression: Efficacy and dose response. *American Journal of Preventive Medicine*, 28(1), 1–8.

Eysenck, J. H. (1978). An exercise in mega-illness. *American Psychologist*, 33, 517b.

Farmer, M., Locke, B., Moscicki, E., Dannenberg, A., Larson, D., & Radloff, L. (1988). Physical activity and depressive symptoms: The NHANES I epidemiologic follow-up study. *American Journal of Epidemiology*, 128, 1340–51.

Faulkner, G., & Biddle, S. (2001). Exercise and mental health: It's just not psychology! *Journal of Sports Sciences*, 19, 433–44.

Faulkner, G. E. J. & Taylor, A. H. (2005). *Exercise, health and mental health: Emerging relationships*. London: Routledge.

Folkins, C. H., Lynch, S., & Gardner, M. M. (1972). Psychological fitness as a function of physical fitness. *Archives of Physical Medicine and Rehabilitation*, 53, 503–8.

Folkins, C. H., & Sime, W. E. (1981). Physical fitness training and mental health. *American Psychologist*, 36, 373–89.

Fremont, J., & Craighead, L. W. (1987). Aerobic exercise and cognitive therapy in the treatment of dysphoric moods. *Cognitive Therapy and Research*, 11(2), 241–51.

Glass, G. V. (1976). Primary, secondary and meta-analysis of research. *Educational Research*, 5, 3–8.

Glass, G. V., McGraw, B., & Smith, M. L. (1981). *Meta-analysis in social research*. Beverly Hills, CA: Sage Publications.

Greist, J. H. (1977). *Run to reality*. Milwaukee: Bulfin.

Greist, J. H., Eischens, R. R., Klein, M. H., & Faris, J. W. (1979). Antidepressant running. *Psychiatric Annals*, 9, 23–33.

Greist, J. H., Klein, M. H., Eischens, R. R., & Faris, J. (1978). Running as a treatment for non-psychotic depression. *Behavioral Medicine*, 5, 19–24.

Hays, W. L. (1973). *Statistics for the social sciences*. New York: Holt, Rinehart & Winston.

Hughes, J. R. (1984). Psychological effects of habitual aerobic exercise: A critical review. *Preventive Medicine*, 13, 66–84.

Kavanaugh, T., Shephard, R. J., Tuck, J. A., & Qureshi, S. (1977). Depression following myocardial infarction: The effects of distance running. *Annals of the New York Academy of Sciences*, 301, 1029–38.

King, A. C. (1994). Clinical and community interventions to promote and support physical activity participation. In R. K. Dishman (ed.), *Advances in exercise adherence* (pp. 183–212). Champaign, IL: Human Kinetics.

Landers, D. M., & Arent, S. M. (2007). Physical activity and mental health. In G. Tenenbaum and R. C. Eklund (eds), *Handbook of sport psychology* (3rd ed.). London: Wiley.

Lawlor, D. A., & Hopker, S. W. (2001). The effectiveness of exercise as an intervention in the management of depression: Systematic review and metaregression analysis of randomised controlled trials. *British Medical Journal*, 322(7289), 763–6.

Ledwidge, B. (1980). Run for your mind: aerobic exercise as a means of alleviating anxiety and depression. *Canadian Journal of Behavioural Science*, 12, 127–40.

Lehtinen, V., & Joukamaa, M. (1994). Epidemiology of depression: Prevalence, risk factors and treatment situation. *Acta Psychiatrica Scandinavia*, 377, 7–10.

Martinsen, E. W. (1987). The role of aerobic exercise in the treatment of depression. *Stress Medicine*, 3, 93–100.

Martinsen, E. W. (1993). Therapeutic implications of exercise for clinically anxious and depressed patients. *International Journal of Sport Psychology*, 24, 185–99.

Martinsen, E. W., Hoffart, A., & Solberg, O. (1989). Comparing aerobic with nonaerobic forms of exercise in the treatment of clinical depression: A randomized trial. *Comprehensive Psychiatry*, 30(4), 324–31.

Mather, A. S., Rodriguez, C., Guthrie, M. F., McHarg, A. M., Reid, I. C., & McMurdo, M. E. (2002). Effects of exercise on depressive symptoms in older adults with poorly responsive depressive disorder: Randomised controlled trial. *British Journal of Psychiatry*, 180, 411–15.

Mayou, A. (1983). A controlled trial of early rehabilitation after myocardial infarction. *Journal of Cardiac Rehabilitation*, 6, 387–402.

McEntree, D. J., & Halgin, R. P. (1996). Therapists attitudes about addressing the role of exercise in psychotherapy. *Journal of Clinical Psychology*, 52, 48–60.

McNeil, J. K., LeBlanc, E. M., & Joyner, M. (1991). The effect of exercise on depressive symptoms in the moderately depressed elderly. *Psychology and Ageing*, 6, 487–8.

Mellion, M. B. (1985). Exercise therapy for anxiety and depression. *Postgraduate Medicine*, 77, 59–66.

Morgan, W. P. (1969). Physical fitness and emotional health: A review. *American Corrective Therapy Journal*, 23, 124–7.

Morgan, W. P., Roberts, J. A., Brand, F. R., & Feinerman, A. D. (1970). Psychological effect of chronic physical activity. *Medicine and Science Sports and Exercise*, 2, 213–17.

Morgan, W. P., Roberts, J. A., & Feinerman, A. D. (1971). Psychological effect of physical activity. *Archives of Physical Medicine and Rehabilitation*, 52, 422–5.

Moses, J., Steptoe, A., Matthews, A., & Edwards, S. (1989). The effects of exercise training on mental well-being in the normal population: A controlled trial. *Journal of Psychosomatic Research*, 33, 47–61.

Mutrie, N. (2000). The relationship between physical activity and clinically defined depression. In S. J. H. Biddle, K. R. Fox, & S. H. Boutcher (eds), *Physical activity and psychological well being* (pp. 46–62). London: Routledge.

Mutrie, N., & Knill-Jones, R. (1986). Psychological effects of running: 1985 survey of Glasgow People's Marathon. In J. H. McGregor & J. A. Moncur (eds), *Sport and Medicine: Proceedings of VIII Commonwealth and International Conference on Sport, Physical Education, Dance, Recreation and Health* (pp. 186–90). London: E & F. N. Spon.

Naughton, J., Bruhn, J. G., & Lategola, M. T. (1968). Effects of physical training on physiological and behavioral characteristics of cardiac patients. *Archives of Physical Medicine and Rehabilitation*, 49, 131–7.

Paykel, E. S., Brugha, T., & Fryers, T. (2005). Size and burden of depressive disorders in Europe. *European Neuropsychopharmacology*, 15, 411–23.

Perri, S., & Templer, D. I. (1985). The effects of an aerobic exercise program on psychological variables in older adults. *International Journal of Aging and Human Development*, 20, 167–72.

Ransford, C. P. (1982). A role for amines in the antidepressant effect of exercise: A review. *Medicine and Science in Sports and Exercise*, 14, 1–10.

Sachs, M. L. (1982). Exercise and running: effects on anxiety, depression, and psychology. *Humanistic Education and Development*, 21, 51–7.

Sacks, H. S., Berrier, K., Reitman, D., Ancona-Bark, V. A., & Chalmer, T. C. (1987) Meta-analysis of randomized controlled trials. *New England Journal of Medicine*, 316, 450–5.

Simons, A. D., Epstein, L. H., McGowan, C. R., Kupfer, D. J., & Robertson, R. J. (1985). Exercise as a treatment for depression: an update. *Clinical Psychology Review*, 5, 553–68.

Simons, A. D., McGowan, C. R., Epstein, L. H., Kupfer, D. J., & Robertson, R. J. (1985). Exercise as a treatment for depression: An update. *Clinical Psychology Review*, 5, 553–68.

Smith, M. L. (1980). Sex bias in counseling and psychotherapy. *Psychological Bulletin*, 87, 392–407.

Sonstroem, R. J. (1984). Exercise & self-esteem. *Exercise and Sport Sciences Reviews*, 12, 123–55.

Stathopoulou, G., Powers, M. B., Berry, A. C., Smits, J. A. J., & Otto, M. W. (2006). Exercise interventions for mental health: A quantitative and qualitative review. *Clinical Psychology: Science and Practice*, 13(2), 179–93.

Stephens, T. (1988). Physical activity and mental health in the United States and Canada: Evidence from our population surveys. *Preventive Medicine*, 17, 35–47.

Steptoe, A., & Bolton, J. (1988). The short-term influences of high and low intensity physical exercise on mood. *Psychology and Health*, 2, 91–106.

Stern, M. J., & Cleary, P. C. (1982). The national exercise and heart disease project long-term psychosocial outcome. *Archives of Internal Medicine*, 142, 1093–8.

Stern, M. J., Gorman, P. A., & Kaslow, K. L. (1983). The group counseling versus exercise therapy study. A controlled intervention with subjects following myocardial infarction. *Archives of Internal Medicine*, 143, 719–25.

Taylor, C. B., Coffee, T., Berra, K., Iaffaldano, R., Casey, K., & Haskell, W. L. (1984). Seven-day activity and self-report compared to a direct measure of physical activity. *American Journal of Epidemiology*, 120, 818–24.

Taylor, C. B., Sallis, J. F., & Needle, R. (1985). The relation of physical activity and exercise to mental health. *Public Health Reports*, 100, 195–202.

Taylor, M. A., & Abrams, R. (1981). Prediction of treatment response in mania. *Archives of General Psychiatry*, 38, 800–2.

Tran, Z. V., & Weltman, A. (1985). Differential effects of exercise on serum lipid and lipoprotein levels seen with changes in body weight: A meta-analysis. *Journal of the American Medical Association*, 254, 919–23.

Veale, D., Le Fevre, K., Pantelis, C., De Souza, V., Mann, A., & Sargeant, A. (1992). Aerobic exercise in the adjunctive treatment of depression: A randomised controlled trial. *Journal of the Royal Society of Medicine*, 85, 541–4.

Walker, J. M., Floyd, T. C., Fein, G., Cavness, C., Lualhati, R., & Feinberg, I. (1978). Effects of exercise on sleep. *Journal of Applied Physiology*, 44, 945–51.

Weinstein, W. S., & Meyers, A. W. (1983). Running as a treatment for depression: Is it worth it? *Journal of Sports Psychology*, 5, 288–301.

World Health Organization (2001). *Mental health: New understanding, new hope. The World Health Report 2001*. Geneva: World Health Organization.

World Health Organization (2005). *The world health report 2005*. Geneva: World Health Organization.

# 18

# Eating disorders

Brooks-Gunn, J., Burrow, C., & Warren, W. P. (1988). Attitudes toward eating and body weight in different groups of female adolescent athletes: *International Journal of Eating Disorders*, 7, 749–57

**Written in collaboration with Carrie Scherzer**

## Background and context

Historically, society has pressured girls and women to maintain a low weight through modalities such as the media's portrayal of the ideal body shape as one of thinness (Striegel-Moore, Silberstein, & Rodin, 1986). The pressures to be thin may lead to body dissatisfaction and eating disorders, some of which may result in such disturbed eating behaviors and perceptual/attitudinal distortions that they are potentially life threatening and require clinical treatment. Although 90% of disordered eating occurs with females (American Psychiatric Association, 1994), boys and men are not immune to the problem. They can also have the additional pressure to maintain a muscular physique. The *Diagnostic and Statistical Manual of Mental Disorders* (DSM-IV) lists criteria for three categories of clinical eating disorders: anorexia nervosa (AN), bulimia nervosa (BN), and eating disorder not otherwise specified (EDNOS) (American Psychiatric Association, 2000). Individuals with AN refuse to maintain normal body weight for their height and weight and have an intense fear of weight gain despite being underweight. Their distorted perception of body shape and weight and fear of weight gain lead to highly restrictive and ritualized eating behaviors, irrational food beliefs, and amenorrhea (the absence of a menstrual period in a woman of reproductive age). In contrast, BN is characterized by episodes of binge eating (i.e., eat large amounts in a short time and/or feel out of control during the eating episode) followed by compensatory behaviors such as self-induced vomiting, diuretic or laxative use, fasting/dieting, or excessive exercising. Like the anorexic, the bulimic's self-evaluation is also highly influenced by body shape and weight. Individuals diagnosed with EDNOS have some, but not all, of the criteria for either AN or BN. AN affects approximately 0.5–1% of females in late adolescence and early adulthood and BN affects about 1–3% of adolescent and young adult females and approximately 0.1–0.3% of males (American Psychiatric Association, 2000).

It may seem like many athletes are afflicted with these disorders, but that is largely due to media portrayals. One tragic example is Christy Henrich, a gymnast who at 4′11″ went from weighing 95 pounds at the apex of her career in 1988 to just 52 pounds some six years later when she died. A judge told Christy she needed to lose weight to make the Olympic team. She never realized her dream of making it to the Olympic Games, and her body finally shut down just four years after she retired from her sport ("Illness attacks mind and body," 1994). Despite the fact that other examples of athletes with eating disorders may come to mind, the reality is that few athletes meet the criteria for a clinical diagnosis. Nevertheless, many athletes have eating disorders that fall short of the diagnostic criteria, and their problems are severe enough to lead to disturbed body images and other serious psychological, physical, and behavioral disturbances. For example, the same year as the key study, a survey of close to 700 college student-athletes by Burckes-Miller and Black (1988) classified many college athletes as having disordered eating because they fell somewhere on the continuum between having an eating disorder to normal eating behaviors. A later study (Wichmann & Martin, 1993) reported as many as 62% of college athletes engaging in some form of disordered eating. Such eating disorders are often referred to as "sub-clinical" or, in the case of AN, as anorexic athletica, a term coined by Pugliese, Lifshitz, Grad, Fort, and Marks-Katz (1983).

Determining disordered eating behaviors and attitudes is often done using questionnaires (e.g., Sundgot-Borgen & Corbin's 1987 study with athletes) as they are practical, but it is best to have medical practitioners and psychologists conduct diagnostic interviews when determining clinical eating disorders. Prior to the key study, two questionnaires had been devised by Garner and colleagues that were valid and reliable in differentiating between people with and without tendencies towards eating disorders. One is the 64-item *Eating Disorders Inventory* (EDI; Garner, Olmstead, & Polivy, 1983), which assesses attitudes and behaviors related to eating and body shape (i.e., sub-scales drive for thinness, bulimia, body dissatisfaction) as well as traits (i.e., sub-scales ineffectiveness, perfectionism, interpersonal distrust, interoceptive awareness, maturity fears) identified by clinical theorists as fundamental to the psychopathology of anorexia nervosa. The other is the 40-item *Eating Attitudes Test* (EAT; Garner & Garfinkel, 1979), which is a self-report measure, designed to indicate disordered eating patterns among sub-clinical populations. The EAT contains three sub-scales: dieting; bulimia; and oral control. It also has a 26-item, abbreviated version, which is highly correlated with the original measure ($r = .98$; Garner *et al.*, 1983). The EAT has been widely used as a screening measure for eating disorders, and a cut-off total score of 20 has been recommended as indicative of disordered eating patterns (Garner & Garfinkel, 1979). The EAT exhibits high internal reliability in both clinical ($\alpha = .90$) and sub-clinical ($\alpha = .83$) populations (Garner *et al.*, 1983).

Even before the key study in this chapter, researchers had theorized that there was a connection between athletic participation and disordered eating. For example, Leon (1984) discussed the differences between primary and secondary anorexia in athletes, suggesting that both may be present in athletes and athletes with primary anorexia may use athletic participation as an expression of the disorder. After interviewing 60 male runners, Yates, Leehey, and Shisslak (1983) proposed that obligatory male runners were similar to individuals with anorexia nervosa, however, when Weight and Noakes (1987) attempted to replicate and extend their findings by examining the incidence of anorexia in female distance runners, they found that abnormal eating attitudes and behaviors, including anorexia, were no more common in competitive female runners than the general population.

In 1986, Richert and Hummers tested the hypothesis that physical activity, more specifically hyperactivity or excessive physical activity, is one of the earliest signs of AN. When studying college students, they found that a group determined to be at risk of developing an eating disorder spent more hours per week jogging than a group of peers. These findings led them to propose that jogging might be the exercise of choice for college students at risk of developing an eating disorder because it is a culturally acceptable activity and might satisfy the need of an anorexic to constantly seek others' approval.

Although the previous studies began to put athletic involvement and disordered eating together, it was the key study by Brooks-Gunn, Burrow, and Warren that first examined whether differences in sport type might differentially influence pressure to stay thin and attitudes toward eating. They empirically examined body weight and attitudes toward eating in adolescent girls who either did not participate in sport or who participated in aesthetic (i.e., ballet, figure skating) or non-aesthetic sports (i.e., swimming).

## Key study

Low weight and delayed menarche (i.e., the time in a girl's life that menstruation first begins) are common characteristics of female athletes, especially those who compete in competitive sports (e.g., Frisch, Wyshak, & Vincent, 1980; Warren, 1980). Variations have been found to occur across studies, however, and these differences have been attributed, in part, to the type of sport, the competitiveness of the individual athlete, and the process of selection for particular sports. Comparing the characteristics of adolescents in different athletic groups may help explain variations in physical characteristics across different sports, and at least two dimensions of sports endeavor may be identified that are likely to be associated with weight and menarcheal age: the body size and shape preferred by a particular athletic endeavor and the energy expended in training for a sport. In the present study, adolescents were compared who engaged in three sports that varied on these two dimensions.

Although sports are similar in that high standards of technical proficiency are demanded of nearly all elite athletes, some may differ in terms of requirements for body shape and size. For example, low weight is required of gymnasts, figure skaters, and dancers, all of whom are likely to be delayed maturers. In contrast, low weight is not demanded of swimmers, volleyball players, and other athletes. Requirements for thinness may sometimes go beyond what is necessary for the performance of a certain athletic endeavor, thus becoming an esthetic preference. The most obvious example is the ballet dancer who, unless they are very thin, may not be accepted into a national company regardless of talent. The demand for dancers to have very low weights is a fairly recent phenomenon often attributed to Balanchine's esthetic preferences (Vincent, 1981). Although body size is to a large part genetically determined, it is influenced by environmental factors (Garn & Clark, 1976). Diet, exercise, or a combination of the two may affect body size.

Although most elite athletes train for numerous hours a day, sports differ on caloric expenditure. On the average, for example, recreational tennis and cycling are classified as moderate activity and cross-country skiing, running (7 mph), and swimming (crawl stroke) as hard activity; the approximate energy expenditure per hour is estimated to be 25–75% higher for activities in the latter than the former category. Estimates of specific athletic endeavors have been calculated, based on $VO_2$ maximum estimates. About 200 kcal are expended in a typical ballet class, as compared to about 500 kcal in swimming and skating (based on a weight of 50–53 kg).

The present study compared dancers, swimmers, figure skaters, and non-athletes with regard to weight, attitudes about eating, and menarcheal age. Dancers and figure skaters, who are required to maintain low weights, were expected to have lower weight for height, more negative attitudes about eating, and later menarche than swimmers, who are not required to maintain low weights. In addition, the dancers were expected to engage in more dieting behavior in order to maintain their low weight than the figure skaters, given that in general the dancers expend less energy in training than the skaters. The swimmers, by contrast, were expected to exhibit little if any dieting behavior because low weight is not required and because caloric expenditure is relatively high.

## Method

### Participants

Female adolescent non-athletes ($n = 424$) and athletes ($n = 161$) aged 14–18 were surveyed. The athlete participants included 25 figure skaters who were competing in the sectionals (regionals) or nationals, 64 ballet dancers who attended one of three national ballet company schools where initial and yearly auditions are required, and 72 swimmers who competed regionally or nationally. Participants in all three sports practiced at least four days a week and were training for regional or national competition (or, in the case of the dancers, for entrance into a national company). The mean number of hours of practice a week was 15.72 (SD = 6.58) for dancers, 14.89 (SD = 9.82) for swimmers, and 21.09 (SD = 9.36) for figure skaters; the difference between the skaters and the other two groups was significant ($p < .01$).

All the athlete participants were White except for three Black and three Asian skaters. (Findings with and without the Black and Asian skaters were similar.) Families were middle to upper-middle class (based on Hollingshead & Redlich's *Social Class Scale*; Hollingshead & Redlich, 1958). Age, familial background, and sibship size were comparable for the three groups. A group of 424 females (age range = 14–18) not involved in competitive athletics was surveyed for comparison purposes. The family demographics of this group were similar to the athletes; no differences in age, family, social class, or sibship size were seen.

### Procedure

After obtaining parental permission (written informed consent), participants filled out a survey at their school or at the end of practice in groups of 5–10 with a research assistant present to answer questions. They were weighed and measured in private. Participants were paid for their participation. Over 70% participated, an acceptable rate for previous studies of adolescents (e.g., Brooks-Gunn, Petersen, & Eichorn, 1985).

### Measures

All participants reported their current weight and height, and the dancers, non-athletes, and swimmers had height and weight measured two times (with averages of the two taken). The self-report data are used for group comparison purposes, as all participants had these measures. Self-reports of height-weight are quite accurate in cohorts of adults, and have been used in many studies (e.g., Palta, Prineas, Berman, & Hannan, 1982; Stunkard & Albaum, 1981). In adolescent girls, correlations between self-reported and measured weight are .97 or better; for height, the correlations are .80 or better (Brooks-Gunn, Warren, Rosso, & Gargiulo, 1987). In this study, the correlations between self-reported and measured weight were .95 and .97 for the dancers and non-athletes and .85 and .90 for height. Self-reported weights were on the average 1 kg less than actual weights for the two groups.

Body mass was estimated using the formula weight/height$^2$ (kg/m$^2$); body mass or ponderal indices are highly related to one another and provide approximations of leanness (Keys, Fidanza, Karvonen, Kimura, & Taylor, 1972). Direct measures of body fat were not able to be obtained because many of the schools/teams did not approve the measurement of skinfold thickness (a common problem at the time of the study in American school-based studies of adolescents; Brooks-Gunn et al., 1987). Body fat formulas were not used because of statistical problems, lack of adequate normative samples, and possible overestimates of fat in athletes (Loucks, Horvath, & Freedson, 1984). However, the ponderal index is highly correlated with total body fat as measured by hydrostatic weighing in adolescent girls ($r = .89$; Roche, Siervogel, Chumlea, & Webb, 1981).

Participants were asked to report the age (in years) and date (year and month) of menarche. Adolescent reports of menarcheal status are accurate (Brooks-Gunn et al., 1987). Athlete participants also indicated their number of hours in practice per week, their number of practices/dance classes a week, and the age at which they began training.

Participants completed the abbreviated (26-item) version of the EAT with items reworded for use with adolescents. All items are rated on a 6-point Likert-type scale (from *Always* to *Never*), with the item average taken (range = 1–6). A score of 4.10 is similar to Garner and Garfinkel's original cut-off score of 20 for the EAT. The scale exhibits high stability over a 2-year period ($r = .65$, $p < .001$), and scores are related to weight, maturational timing, context, and nutritional intake in adolescent dancers and non-dancers (Brooks-Gunn & Warren, 1985). The sub-scales are Dieting ("I am on a diet much of the time"), Bulimia ("I have the impulse to throw up after meals"), and Oral Control ("I feel that others pressure me to eat").

Participants were also asked how much they would like to weigh at their present height. One scale from the EDI was included; this scale, Perfectionism, has been linked to eating problems (Garner et al., 1983).

## Results

Comparisons were made between the four groups in terms of physical characteristics, menarcheal age, attitudes toward eating, weight concerns, and self-image. One-way ANOVAs were performed (using the Bonferroni method). If a significant difference was found, comparisons between the groups were done using Student's *t*-test. Chi-square statistics were used to compare the number of premenarcheal and postmenarcheal girls in each group.

### Height and Weight

The dancers and skaters weighed 6–7 kg less than the swimmers and non-athletes (Table 18.1). In contrast, swimmers and non-athletes were taller than the dancers and skaters, who were similar to one another. The dancers and skaters were comparatively leaner than the swimmers and non-athletes. All girls wished to weigh about 2–3 kg less than their reported weight. The dancers and skaters wished to weigh less than the swimmers and non-athletes, and the dancers less than the skaters.

### Eating Behavior

Dancers and skaters had higher dieting, bulimia, and oral control scores than the swimmers and non-athletes. The dancers had higher dieting and lower oral control scores than the skaters. Dancers and skaters had higher perfectionism scores than the other two groups.

**Table 18.1** Mean scores for physical characteristics, eating behavior, and self-image for dancers, skaters, swimmers, and nonathletic adolescent girls [means and (standard deviations)]

|  | Dancers[a-c] | Skaters[d,e] | Swimmers[f] | Non-athletes |
|---|---|---|---|---|
| Chronological age | 15.63(1.25) | 15.73(1.18) | 15.63(1.24) | 15.66(1.36) |
| Physical characteristics |  |  |  |  |
| Weight (kg) | 46.84(6.33) | 48.23(5.56) | 54.91(6.16) | 54.27(6.92) |
| Height (cm) | 163.04(5.31) | 160.73(5.97) | 165.84(5.97) | 165.51(6.93) |
| Ponderal index | 17.45(1.90) | 18.62(1.28) | 20.02(2.04) | 19.93(2.43) |
| Menarcheal age | 13.29(1.25) | 13.61(1.50) | 12.93(1.34) | 12.72(1.08) |
| Percent premenarcheal | 25%(16) | 24%(6) | 4%(3) | 6%(23) |
| Eating behavior |  |  |  |  |
| Diet | 3.63(1.41) | 3.34(1.44) | 2.94(1.23) | 3.16(1.40) |
| Bulimia | 3.26(1.25) | 3.37(0.52) | 2.49(1.04) | 2.43(1.18) |
| Oral control | 2.97(1.15) | 3.32(0.48) | 2.41(0.76) | 2.18(0.95) |
| EAT total | 3.19(1.00) | 3.34(0.34) | 2.62(0.67) | 2.59(0.87) |
| Self-image |  |  |  |  |
| Perfectionism | 3.70(1.18) | 3.41(0.53) | 3.06(1.29) | 3.03(1.14) |
| Weight want | 43.98(4.96) | 46.24(4.61) | 52.08(4.70) | 50.67(5.28) |

[a] All differences between dancers and non-athletes significant
[b] All differences between dancers and swimmers significant
[c] Differences between dancers and skaters were only significant for diet, oral control, and weight want
[d] All differences between skaters and non-athletes significant except dieting
[e] All differences between skaters and swimmers significant
[f] No differences between swimmers and non-athletes significant

## Menarcheal Age

The dancers and skaters had a later menarcheal age than did the swimmers (Table 18.1). In addition, 4–5 times as many skaters and dancers than swimmers and non-athletes were premenarcheal (25% versus 5%). Given the relatively large number of postmenarcheal dancers and skaters, the menarcheal ages reported here are underestimates. Girls were classified as late maturers based on menarcheal age. Girls who were ±1.2 years from the population mean were classified as early or late (menarcheal age for white American adolescents is 12.7–12.8; Zacharias, Rand, & Wurtman, 1976). Girls who reached menarche at or after 14 years of age or who were still premenarcheal were classified as late maturers. Two-thirds of the skaters, 56% of the dancers, 31% of the swimmers, and 25% of the nonathletes were late maturers ($\chi^2$, $p < .01$). The comparison group's menarcheal age was similar to population norms (Zacharias et al., 1976), was not different from the swimmers' menarcheal age, but was earlier than that of the dancers and skaters (Table 18.1).

## Discussion

As expected, skaters and dancers were lighter and leaner than swimmers, possibly reflecting the demands for low weight seen in these two groups. Indeed, when asked what they would like to weigh, skaters and dancers would like to weigh about 6–7 kg less than swimmers, suggesting that the differential sport demands are well recognized by the adolescents themselves.

Additionally, skaters and dancers were shorter than swimmers, which may be indicative of the physical requirements of their sports (spins, leaps) and/or alterations in the timing of skeletal growth. For example, adolescent swimmers may have advanced skeletal age and dancers may have delayed skeletal growth. Variations in delayed menarche also were found for the skaters and dancers. The menarcheal age of the swimmers in this study was similar to non-athletes and was not particularly delayed, as other studies have reported (i.e., means tend to be 13.1; Meleski, Shoup, & Malina, 1982).

Clearly, these physical differences among athletic groups (menarcheal age, height, weight, and body mass) in part are associated with genetic factors. In addition, to become a highly competitive athlete, a stringent process of selection occurs, which leads to very few reaching an elite standard. Unfortunately, prospective studies of adolescent athletes that have examined those who leave the sport, or do not become elite athletes, and how they differ on physical characteristics pre-pubertally than those who stay in the sport, are rare.

At the same time, environmental factors influence weight and menarcheal age, including intensity and duration of exercise and restricted food intake. The three groups did not differ on onset of training. Duration of current training did differentiate groups; however, since the skaters reported practicing more hours, on average, than did the other two groups. And the energy expenditure probably differs for these three athletic groups; based on estimated caloric expenditure per hour for the three groups (keeping in mind that in this study no data were collected on caloric expenditure, or $VO_2$ max, which will differ for individuals within any sport or competitive level), the swimmers and skaters were probably expending more energy than the dancers.

Finally, and most importantly, the dancers and skaters were exhibiting more restraint eating and binge/purge eating than were the swimmers. The negative eating attitudes of the skaters and dancers were comparable to those reported for adult dancers (Garner & Garfinkel, 1980). However, they were not indicative of a high incidence of self-reported eating disorders (based on cut-off scores using Garner and Garfinkel's criteria, only 5% of the dancers and none of the other athletes had very high EAT scores). The key study authors postulated that their eating attitudes were in response to the low weights required by their professions. These findings are similar to those reported for male college wrestlers, nordic skiers, and swimmers, with the wrestlers having higher negative eating attitude scores than the other two groups, presumably because of weight requirements (Enns, Drewnowski, & Grinker, 1987). At the same time, skaters had lower dieting and higher oral control scores than dancers. Oral control is negatively associated with weight while dieting is positively associated with weight in other adolescent samples (Brooks-Gunn & Warren, 1985), suggesting that high dieting scores may reflect concerns with weight and counterregulatory behavior (cycles of dieting followed by cycles of bingeing). Although speculative, the researchers hypothesized that the higher dieting scores of the dancers compared with the skaters, in the face of the two groups' similar weight, is a response to the fact that the dancers are expending less energy than the skaters.

Whether actual nutritional intake differed for the three groups of athletes is not known; however, in a study of adult dancers, negative eating attitude scores (indicative of dieting and bulimia) were related to lower levels of protein and fat intake (Hamilton, Brooks-Gunn, & Warren, 1986), and overall caloric intake and nutrients may be below the minimal daily requirement even before controlling for energy drain in adult dancers and gymnasts. Premenarcheally trained college athletes may consume fewer calories than postmenarcheally trained athletes (Frisch et al., 1981). Nutrition intake may affect girls differently as a function of body size; if lighter girls are affected more than heavier girls, the effects of dieting may be more pronounced in some sports than in others, particularly in those with stringent weight requirements.

In brief, in a comparison of three groups of competitive adolescent athletes, dancers, and skaters were lighter and leaner than swimmers, in accordance with the weight requirements of the former two groups. Additionally, the dancers and skaters had higher eating problem scores than swimmers, again probably indicative of professional demands. Dancers exhibited more restraint and less oral control than skaters, perhaps because low weights are difficult to maintain given the fairly low energy demands required for dance. High dieting generally may be more common in adolescents and young women who must maintain low weight for professional reasons and even for those who wish to be thin (Striegel-Moore *et al.*, 1986) who are not expending much energy (and calories) in the form of work or exercise.

## Subsequent research and application

There has been a surge of research in the area of eating disorders and athletes since the Brooks-Gunn *et al.* key study. Some studies have found that athletes and dancers have higher rates of disordered eating compared to their respective counterparts (e.g., Anshel, 2004; DiBartolo & Shaffer, 2002; Sundgot-Borgen, 1993; Sundgot-Borgen & Torstveit, 2004) and others find no difference between athletes and non-athletes (e.g., Ashley, Smith, Robinson, & Richardson, 1996; Fulkerson, Keel, Leon, & Door, 1999). Although the question remains as to whether people who are worried about their weight and body shape are attracted to physical activities of high demand or whether dedication to regular exercise may heighten concern about weight, body shape, and dieting, there is some evidence that exercise level (defined as weekly mileage) and muscle dysmorphia (i.e., men who perceive themselves as less muscular than they actually are) correlate with eating disorder problems (e.g., Kiernan, Rodin, Brownell, Wilmore, & Crandall, 1992; Olivardia, Pope, Borowiecki, & Cohane, 2004).

Evidence also exists for the possibility that physical activity may contribute to the development of an eating disorder. In a study of hospitalized eating disordered patients, Davis, Kennedy, Ravelski, and Dionne (1994) found that more than 75% of the patients had engaged in excessive exercise and 60% had been competitive athletes prior to the onset of their disorder. At the other end of the spectrum, Petrie (1996) suggests that participation in sport may serve as a protective function. He found that both male and female collegiate athletes tended to be more satisfied with their bodies and to feel more effective than their non-athlete peers. Other researchers also provide support for the protective role of athletics in that they demonstrated a lower risk for eating disorders among athletes compared to non-athletes (e.g., DiBartolo & Shaffer, 2002; Hausenblas & McNally, 2004; Reinking & Alexander, 2005; Wilkins, Boland, & Albinson, 1991).

The equivocal findings in eating disorder studies have been influenced by methodological problems such as the use of different measurement instruments (some with questionable psychometric properties), inconsistent definitions/classifications for the disordered eating construct, small or non-representative samples, non-matched control groups of non-athletes, failure to consider contextual problems within the sport environment, rarity of structured diagnostic interviews, and sole use of cross-sectional as opposed to longitudinal methodologies (see Petrie and Greenleaf (2007) for a more thorough discussion of these issues and how to correct them).

In addition to the preceding methodological concerns, eating disorders is one area within sport and exercise psychology that could be sensitive to social desirability bias. Social desirability is the inclination to present oneself in a manner that will be viewed as socially acceptable by others. Having this predisposition can cause difficulties in psychological research in that it can confound results. When social desirability cannot be controlled directly within a study, researchers will often ask participants to complete a questionnaire that measures this type of responding (e.g., the *Marlowe-Crown Scale*, Crowne & Marlowe, 1960). If participants answer in a socially desirable manner on such a questionnaire, it can be assumed that they are responding similarly throughout the study. Depending upon the aims of the research, respondents that answer predominantly in a socially desirable way are often eliminated from the data analysis. Fortunately, Tilgner, Wertheim, and Paxton (2004) found that the EAT-26 was free from social desirability bias, which suggests that this bias did not confound the results of the key study.

Even with these methodological problems and the numerous equivocal findings, the writers of review articles (Garner & Rosen, 1991; Garner, Rosen, & Barry, 1998; Petrie & Greenleaf, 2007) and meta-analyses (Hausenblas & Carron, 1999; Smolak, Muren, & Ruble, 2000) have concluded that the overall findings suggest that athletes are slightly more likely than non-athletes to have eating disorders, sub-clinical eating disorders are more prevalent than clinical eating disorders in athletes, and female athletes are more likely than male athletes to meet the criteria of clinical and sub-clinical eating disorders. Other conclusions, such as Petrie and Greenleaf's (2007) report that competitive level and sport type influence eating disorders, have also been noted. The most likely occurrence, and highest prevalence, exists in sports and physical activities that emphasize esthetics, leanness, or that have weight requirements (e.g., gymnastics, figure skating, diving, ballet, cheerleading, distance runners, wrestlers, bodybuilders). For example, female gymnasts reported sub-clinical prevalence rates (engaged in some type of disordered eating) as high as 60% (Petrie, 1993), 38% to 54% of figure skaters reported elevated EDI and EAT scores (Monsma & Malina, 2004; Rucinski, 1989), and 43% of male wrestlers engaged in some type of pathogenic weight control behavior (e.g., fasting, self-induced vomiting) with 1.7% of them meeting the DSM-III criteria for BN (Oppliger, Landry, Foster, & Lambrecht, 1993). In contrast, the few studies that compared non-elite high school athletes and non-athletes found no differences in disordered eating attitudes and behavior (Fulkerson *et al.*, 1999; Smolak *et al.*, 2000; Taub & Blinde, 1992).

To better understand eating disorders in athletes, and to stimulate a more sophisticated and effective approach for future study, Petrie and Greenleaf (2007) proposed an etiological model that identifies risk factors, moderator variables that might influence the direction and intensity between the risk factor and eating disorders, and mediational pathways that explain why the relationship occurs. According to the model, it is the individual's internalization of the thin-ideal (the mediator) that explains how general societal and sport-specific pressures (the predictors) lead to the development of body dissatisfaction and eating disorders (the outcome). The model theorizes that consistent exposure to general (e.g., media images, wishes of family and friends) and sport-specific pressures (e.g., esthetic or weight demands of sport, team weigh-ins, emphasis on appearance rather than skill, coach and teammates feedback) increases the likelihood of internalizing society's body-ideal and overemphasizing physical shape/size and attractiveness. The end result is increased risk of dissatisfaction with one's own looks/body and engaging in some type of disordered eating behavior or behavior such as excessive exercise. Examples of moderator variables hypothesized to increase the vulnerability of certain athletes to these effects are perfectionism, low self-esteem, and a poor self-concept.

Petrie and Greenleaf's (2007) etiological model (i.e., its risk factors, moderators, and mediational pathways) also provides a theoretical basis for designing eating disorders prevention and treatment programs. Most of what is presently known about such programs comes from intervention studies with non-athletes. For example, a meta-analysis by Stice and Shaw (2004) determined that the most successful programs target at-risk populations of participants age 15 and over, entail interactions amongst the participants, have more than one session, are presented as "body acceptance" or "healthy body" programs rather than one for eating disturbances, and typically include both a cognitive component to alter negative self-attitudes (e.g., body dissatisfaction) and a behavioral component designed to encourage nutritious eating, regular exercise, and other healthy behaviors. In addition to doing the preceding, Petrie and Greenleaf (2007) recommend including wait-list and placebo control groups and obtaining follow-up measures for six months to a year post-intervention when conducting intervention research. Although knowledgeable sport psychology consultants can conduct prevention programs, treatment for actual eating disorders is best left to qualified, licensed mental health providers.

In summary, despite the tremendous growth in what is known about athletes and eating disorders since the publication of the key study, many questions still remain. We do know, however, that far too many athletes are still at risk of or engaging in some form of disordered eating. Petrie and Greenleaf's (2007) etiological model provides a good foundation for designing theoretically based research to advance understanding regarding which athletes are most at risk of eating disorders, why they are at risk, and how best to design intervention programs to prevent and treat eating disorders.

## Additional readings

Petrie, T. A. (1996). Differences between male and female college lean sport athletes, nonlean sport athletes, and nonathletes on behavioral and psychological indices of eating disorders. *Journal of Applied Sport Psychology*, 8, 218–30.

Petrie, T. A., & Greenleaf, C. A. (2007). Eating disorders in sport: From theory to research to intervention. In G. Tenenbaum & R. Eklund (eds), *Handbook of sport psychology* (3rd ed., pp. 352–78). Hoboken, NJ: John Wiley & Sons.

Smolak, L., Murnen, S. K., & Ruble, A. E. (2000). Female athletes and eating problems: A meta analysis. *International Journal of Eating Disorders*, 27, 371–80.

Stice, E., & Shaw, H. (2004). Eating disorder prevention programs: A meta-analytic review. *Psychological Bulletin*, 130, 206–27.

Sundgot-Borgen, J. (1994). Risk and trigger factors for the development of eating disorders in female elite athletes. *Medicine and Science in Sports and Exercise*, 26, 414–19.

## Study questions

1   How could athletic participation serve as a buffer against developing an eating disorder?

2   According to reviews and meta-analyses, what conclusions have been reached regarding research into eating disorders and athletic participation?

3   How did the methodology of the Brooks-Gunn *et al.* study differ from previous research on eating disorders and athletes? How has it influenced later research?

4   Explain social desirability and list some areas within sport and exercise contexts that might be sensitive to participants' interpretations of social desirability.

5   One of the goals of eating disorders research is to improve prevention and treatment programs. What do we know about how to design and assess intervention programs?

# References

American Psychiatric Association (1994). *Diagnostic and statistical manual of mental disorders* (4th ed.). Washington, DC: APA.

American Psychiatric Association (2000). *Diagnostic and statistical manual of mental disorders* (text revision). Washington, DC: APA.

Anshel, M. H. (2004). Sources of disordered eating patterns between ballet dancers and non-dancers. *Journal of Sport Behavior*, 27, 115–33.

Ashley, C. D., Smith, J. F., Robinson, J. B., & Richardson, M. T. (1996). Disordered eating in female collegiate athletes and collegiate females in an advanced program of study: A preliminary investigation. *International Journal of Sport Nutrition*, 6, 391–401.

Brooks-Gunn, J., Petersen, A. C, & Eichorn, D. (eds) (1985). Time of maturation and psychosocial functioning in adolescence. Special issue. *Journal of Youth and Adolescence*, 14 (3/4).

Brooks-Gunn, J., & Warren, M. P. (1985). Effects of delayed menarche in different contexts: Dance and nondance students. *Journal of Youth and Adolescence*, 14, 285–300.

Brooks-Gunn, J., Warren, M. P., Rosso, J., & Gargiulo, J. (1987). Validity of self-report measures of girls' pubertal status. *Child Development*, 58, 829–41.

Burckes-Miller, M. E., & Black, D. R. (1988). Behaviors and attitudes associated with eating disorders: Perceptions of college athletes about food and weight. *Health Education Research*, 3, 203–8.

Crowne, D. P., & Marlowe, D. (1960). A new scale for social desirability independent of psychotherapy. *Journal of Consulting Psychology*, 24, 349–54.

Davis, C., Kennedy, S. H., Ravelski, E., & Dionne, M. (1994). The role of physical activity in the development and maintenance of eating disorders. *Psychological Medicine*, 24, 957–67.

DiBartolo, P. M., & Shaffer, C. (2002). A comparison of female college athletes and nonathletes: Eating disorder symptomatology and psychological well-being. *Journal of Sport and Exercise Psychology*, 24, 33–41.

Enns, M. P., Drewnowski, A., & Grinker, J. A. (1987). Body composition, body size estimation, and attitudes towards eating in male college athletes. *Psychosomatic Medicine*, 49, 56–64.

Frisch, R. E., Gotz-Welbergen, A. V., McArthur, J. W., Albright, T., Witschi, J., Bullen, B., Birnholz, J., Reed, R. B., & Hermann, H. (1981). Delayed menarche and amenorrhea of college athletes in relation to age of onset of training. *Journal of the American Medical Association*, 246, 1559–63.

Frisch, R. E., Wyshak, G., & Vincent, L. (1980). Delayed menarche and amenorrhea in ballet dancers. *New England Journal of Medicine*, 303, 17–19.

Fulkerson, J. A., Keel, P. K., Leon, G. R., & Door, T. (1999). Eating-disordered behaviors and personality characteristics of high school athletes and nonathletes. *International Journal of Eating Disorders*, 26, 73–9.

Garn, S. M., & Clark, D. C. (1976). Trends in fatness and the origins of obesity. *Pediatrics*, 57(4), 443–56.

Garner, D. M., & Garfinkel, P. E. (1979). The eating attitudes test: An index of the symptoms of anorexia nervosa. *Psychological Medicine*, 9, 273–9.

Garner, D. M., & Garfinkel, P. E. (1980). Sociocultural factors in the development of anorexia nervosa. *Psychological Medicine*, 10, 647–56.

Garner, D. M., Olmstead, M. P., & Polivy, J. (1983). Development and validation of a multidimensional eating disorder inventory for anorexia nervosa and bulimia. *International Journal of Eating Disorders*, 2, 15–34.

Garner, D. M., & Rosen, L. W. (1991). Eating disorders among athletes: Research and recommendations. *Journal of Applied Sport Science Research*, 5, 100–7.

Garner, D. M., Rosen, L. W., & Barry, D. (1998). Eating disorders among athletes. *Child and Adolescent Psychiatric Clinics of North America*, 7, 839–57.

Hamilton, L. H., Brooks-Gunn, J., & Warren, M. P. (1986). Nutritional intake of female dancers: A reflection of eating disorders. *International Journal of Eating Disorders*, 5, 925–34.

Hausenblas, H. A., & Carron, A. V. (1999). Eating disorder indices and athletes: An integration. *Journal of Sport & Exercise Psychology*, 21, 230–58.

Hausenblas, H. A., & McNally, K. D. (2004). Eating disorder prevalence and symptoms for track and field athletes and nonathletes. *Journal of Applied Sport Psychology*, 16, 274–86.

Hollingshead, A. B., & Redlich, F. C. (1958). *Social class and mental illness: A community study*. New York: John Wiley & Sons.

Illness attacks mind and body: Eating disorder killed world-class gymnast (July 29, 1994). *St. Louis Post-Dispatch*, p. B5.

Keys, A., Fidanza, F., Karvonen, M. J., Kimura, N., & Taylor, H. L. (1972). Indices of relative weight and obesity. *Journal of Chronic Diseases*, 25, 329–43.

Kiernan, M., Rodin, J., Brownell, K., Wilmore, J., & Crandall, C. (1992). Relation of level of exercise, age, and weight-cycling history to weight and eating concerns in male and female runners. *Health Psychology*, 11, 418–21.

Leon, G. R. (1984). Anorexia nervosa and sports activities. *The Behavior Therapist*, 7, 9–10.

Loucks, A. B., Horvath, S. M., & Freedson, P. S. (1984). Menstrual status and validation of body fat prediction in athletes. *Human Biology*, 56, 383–92.

Meleski, B. W., Shoup, R. F., & Malina, R. M. (1982). Size, physique, and body composition of competitive female swimmers 11 through 20 years of age. *Human Biology*, 54, 609–25.

Monsma, E. V., & Malina, R. M. (2004). Correlates of eating disorders risk among female figure skaters: A profile of adolescent competitors. *Psychology of Sport and Exercise*, 5, 447–60.

Olivardia, R., Pope, H. G., Borowiecki, J. J., & Cohane, G. H. (2004). Biceps and body image: The relationship between muscularity and self-esteem, depression, and eating disorder symptoms. *Psychology of Men and Masculinity*, 5, 112–20.

Oppliger, R. A., Landry, G. L., Foster, S. W., & Lambrecht, A. C. (1993). Bulimic behaviors among interscholastic wrestlers: A statewide survey. *Pediatrics*, 91, 826–31.

Palta, M., Prineas, R. J., Berman, R., & Hannan, P. (1982). Comparison of self-reported and measured height and weight. *American Journal of Epidemiology*, 115, 223–30.

Petrie, T. A. (1996). Differences between male and female college lean sport athletes, nonlean sport athletes, and nonathletes on behavioral and psychological indices of eating disorders. *Journal of Applied Sport Psychology*, 8, 218–30.

Petrie, T. A., & Greenleaf, C. A. (2007). Eating disorders in sport: From theory to research to intervention. In G. Tenenbaum & R. C. Eklund (eds), *Handbook of Sport Psychology* (3rd ed., pp. 352–78). Hoboken, NJ: John Wiley & Sons.

Pugliese, M. T., Lifshitz, F., Grad, G., Fort, P., & Marks-Katz, M. (1983). Fear of obesity: A cause for short stature and delayed puberty. *New England Journal of Medicine*, 30(9), 513–18.

Reinking, M. F., & Alexander, L. E. (2005). Prevalence of disordered-eating behaviors in undergraduate female collegiate athletes and nonathletes. *Journal of Athletic Training*, 40, 47–51.

Richert, A. J., & Hummers, J. A. (1986). Patterns of physical activity in college students at possible risk for eating disorder. *International Journal of Eating Disorders*, 5, 757–63.

Roche, A. F., Siervogel, R. M., Chumela, W. C., & Webb, P. (1981). Grading body fatness from limited anthropometric data. *American Journal of Clinical Nutrition*, 34, 2831–8.

Rucinski, A. (1989). Relationship of body image and dietary intake of competitive ice skaters. *Journal of American Dietetic Association*, 89, 98–9.

Smolak, L., Muren, S. K., & Ruble, A. E. (2000). Female athletes and eating problems: A meta-analysis. *International Journal of Eating Disorders*, 27, 371–80.

Stice, E., & Shaw, H. (2004). Eating disorder prevention programs: A meta-analytic review. *Psychological Bulletin*, 130, 206–27.

Striegel-Moore, R., Silberstein, L., & Rodin, J. (1986). Toward an understanding of risk factors for bulimia. *American Psychologist*, 41, 246–63.

Stunkard, A. J., & Albaum, J. M. (1981). The accuracy of self-reported weights. *American Journal of Clinical Nutrition*, 34, 1593–9.

Sundgot-Borgen, J. (1993). Prevalence of eating disorders in elite female athletes. *International Journal of Sport Nutrition*, 3, 29–40.

Sundgot-Borgen, J., & Corbin, C. B. (1987). Eating disorders among female athletes. *Physician and Sportsmedicine*, 15, 89–96.

Sundgot-Borgen, J., & Torstveit, M. K. (2004). Prevalence of eating disorders in elite athletes is higher than in the general population. *Clinical Journal of Sports Medicine*, 14, 25–32.

Taub, D., & Blinde, E. (1992). Eating disorders among adolescent female athletes: Influence of athletic participation and sport team membership. *Adolescence*, 27, 833–48.

Tilgner, L., Wertheim, E. H., & Paxton, S. J. (2004). The effect of social desirability on adolescent girls' responses to an eating disorders prevention program. *International Journal of Eating Disorders*, 35, 211–16.

Vincent, L. M. (1981). *Competing with the sylph: Dancers and the pursuit of the ideal body.* Kansas City, KS: Andrews & McMeel.

Warren, M. P. (1980). The effects of exercise on pubertal progression and reproductive function in girls. *Journal of Clinical Endocrinology Metabolism*, 51, 1150–7.

Weight, L. M., & Noakes, T. D. (1987). Is running an analog of anorexia? A survey of the incidence of eating disorders in female distance runners. *Medicine and Science in Sports and Exercise*, 19, 213–17.

Wichmann, S., & Martin, D. R. (1993). Eating disorders in athletes. *Physician and Sportsmedicine*, 21, 126–35.

Wilkins, J. A., Boland, F. J., & Albinson, J. (1991). A comparison of male and female university athletes and nonathletes on eating disorder indices: Are athletes protected? *Journal of Sport Behavior*, 14, 129–43.

Yates, A., Leehey, K., & Shisslak, C. M. (1983). Running – An analogue of anorexia? *New England Journal of Medicine*, 308, 251–5.

Zacharias, L., Rand, W. M., & Wurtman, R. J. (1976). A prospective study of sexual development and growth in American girls: The statistics of menarche. *Obstetrical and Gynecological Survey* 31, 325–37.

# 19

## Substance abuse

Yesalis, C. E., Herrick, R. T., Buckley, W. E., Friedl, K. E., Brannon, D., & Wright, J. E. (1988). Self-reported use of anabolic-androgenic steroids by elite power-lifters. *The Physician and Sports Medicine*, 16, 91–4, 96–8.

### Background and context

People participate in sport and exercise while using drugs for several reasons. Some require medication for legitimate medical reasons, including chronic conditions such as hypertension or acute conditions such as injuries. Others, however, take drugs illegally in order to enhance sporting performance and their physical appearance. While all drugs have the common characteristic of altering a physiological process within the body (usually to treat, prevent, or diagnose disease), performance-enhancing drugs are intended to affect the quality of physical movement (Anshel, 2005).

The use of performance-enhancing substances in sports dates back to ancient times, when Olympians in Greece were reported to have "eaten special foods and taken special medicines to increase their ability to perform" and the gladiators of ancient Rome used stimulants to "combat fatigue and pain while fighting" (Wadler & Hainline, 1989). As early as the 19th century, professional cyclists were using substances such as caffeine and cocaine in order to enhance their performance (Yesalis & Bahrke, 2005), and, according to Anshel (2005), the first recorded drug-related fatality occurred in 1886 when a cyclist died as a result of the stimulants he was taking during a race. In modern times, drug use and abuse has spread to Olympic and professional sports, as well as non-competitive sport and exercise settings.

Drug use is a behavior that can be characterized in different ways. For example, occasional drug use that is motivated by peer pressure can be classified as experimental, while recreational drug users are those who sometimes take them and experience no adverse effect. Drug abuse, on the other hand, consists of the regular use of drugs for at least one month, and involves continued use despite knowledge of having a persistent social, occupational, psychological, or physical problem that is exacerbated by the use of the substance and/or recurrent use in situations that physically hazardous (e.g., driving a car while on drugs) (American Psychiatric Association, 1994).

Drug use in sports has become the subject of considerable research in recent years. This research has revealed that some sport and exercise participants have been using an alarming number of illegal substances in order to enhance their performance and/or physical appearance. This is surprising given the accumulating evidence revealing the negative psychological and physiological risks associated with some performance-enhancing drugs, including increased blood pressure, mood swings, and heightened levels of aggression. Long-term use has also been found to be a contributor to seizures, strokes, and heart attacks, and the development of liver and kidney disease. However, these negative side-effects can be overshadowed by the "win-at-all-costs" attitude of some individuals who view the rewards of success as so great that they outweigh the risks. Two research surveys conducted in the 1980s illustrate this.

Dr Gabe Mirkin, a sports physician, initially asked more than 100 elite runners at the start of a marathon the following question: "If I could give you a pill that would make you an Olympic champion but kill you in five years, would you take it?" The results revealed that more than 50% of the athletes said they would take the pill. Dr Bob Goldman (1984) tried to replicate the study with 198 other elite-level athletes from a variety of sports (including weightlifters, discus throwers, shot-putters, sprinters, swimmers, and other athletes) because he wondered whether this willingness to die was idiosyncratic to runners. Goldman's question was: "If I had a magic drug that was so fantastic that if you took it once you would win every competition you would enter for the next five years, but it had one minor drawback – it would kill you in five years after you took it – would you still take the drug?" A total of 103 (52%) athletes answered yes, thus expanding the findings beyond marathon runners.

Performance-enhancing substances are often referred to as ergogenic drugs, where sports ergogenics refers to any technique that improves performance beyond what would be possible through natural ability (i.e., genetics) and training alone (Williams, 1998). The International Olympic Committee (IOC) uses the term *doping* to refer to the use of substances in any form alien to the body or of physiological substances in abnormal amounts and with abnormal methods by healthy persons with the exclusive aim of attaining an artificial and unfair increase of performance in competition (Prokop, 1970). The World Anti-Doping Agency, which was established in 1999, has a list of hundreds of banned substances that it regularly updates. The IOC has classified five doping categories that are banned from international competition, including stimulants, beta-blockers, diuretics, narcotic analgesics, and steroids. The technique of blood doping is also banned (Anshel, 2005).

Stimulant drugs such as cocaine and most diet suppressants can improve performance by increasing alertness through the inhibition of mental and physical fatigue. Stimulants increase the rate, and hence the work capacity, of the heart, central nervous system, and respiratory system. Beta-blockers, on the other hand, aid performance by slowing down the heart rate, decreasing anxiety, steadying natural body tremors, and reducing signs of nervousness. These have been used in sports in which steady hands are required, such as rifle shooting, archery, bowling, and golf. Diuretics, which are sometimes used by jockeys, wrestlers, and boxers in order to make weight in competitions, increase the rate at which water and salts leave the body as urine. Narcotic analgesics are anti-inflammatory drugs that are used by athletes for their pain-killing properties. They can produce feelings of well-being and invincibility, and allow injured competitors to continue playing through considerable pain. They can also, however, reduce performance in some sports due to their sedative effect. Finally, blood doping typically involves removing units of blood from an athlete months before a competition, freezing and storing the blood, and then infusing the red blood cells back into the athlete immediately before competition. All of these drugs and techniques have serious side-effects (Bell & Doege, 1987).

Of all the known ergogenic drugs used and abused by athletes, steroids are probably the most widely publicized. Steroids are used by individuals to increase muscle size, strength, and power (Bahrke, Yesalis, & Brower, 1998). The proper term for steroids is anabolic-androgenic steroids, where anabolic refers to growing or building and androgenic refers to generating male sexual characteristics. There are more than 100 different types of steroid, with various combinations of anabolic and androgenic properties. The key study by Yesalis, Herrick, Buckley, Friedl, Brannon, and Wright focused specifically on steroids.

At the time of the key study there was considerable debate about the level of use of steroids among sports participants. Two studies published in the same year as the key study provided some evidence about prevalence. The first study, conducted by Buckley *et al.* (1988) found that nearly 7% of over 3,000 male high school students in the USA had used steroids and that over two-thirds of those that had used steroids started using them when they were 16 years old or younger. In a study with nearly 500 head football coaches in American high schools, Duda (1988) found that 12% admitted to suspecting or knowing one or more athletes who had used steroids. With little known about the psychology of drug use in sport, and the focus at the time on prevalence of steroid use, Yesalis and colleagues designed a study to measure the self-reported rate of previous steroid use where steroids were obtained, and attitudes regarding steroid use, testing, why chose to use/not use, and any health and performance effects from using.

## Key study

Anabolic-androgenic steroids are a group of synthetic compounds that are structurally related to the natural male sex hormones. In the 1930s male sex steroids were isolated and chemically characterized, and their anabolic effects were elucidated. It was at this time that it was suggested by Boje (1939) that their use might enhance athletic performance.

Steroid use is perceived by the media, sports medicine and athletic communities, and the public, to have grown to epidemic proportions (Strauss, 1987). There is some disagreement, however, as to whether the current level of use is increasing or decreasing (Cowart, 1987). Given the degree of concern about the potential health effects of these drugs (American College of Sports Medicine, 1987) reasonable estimates of the size and characteristics of the population at risk should be established. Catlin (1987) suggests estimates of the incidence of steroid use based on the results of drug testing at major sports events (e.g., the Olympic Games, Pan American Games, and college football bowl games) should be interpreted cautiously for two reasons: (1) athletes know about drug tests prior to competition, and (2) the detection time for some steroids – especially oral steroids – is short (i.e., a few days to several weeks).

Thus, it seems that to escape detection athletes have avoided certain long-lasting injectable steroids that may have a detection time of up to six months or longer, in favor of oral steroids and injectable testosterone. Based on recent United States Olympic Committee pronouncements, it seems that some athletes have had themselves tested by laboratories in order to determine the doses of particular steroids to their own biochemistry; thus they know when to stop use prior to official testing during competition. Research suggests that athletes usually discontinue oral steroids two to four weeks and testosterone esters (which are injectable) three to six weeks before testing (Di Pasquale, 1987).

Athletes view steroids primarily as training drugs. Because the effects of steroids on physiologic capacities and performance linger for a significant time after steroids are discontinued, athletes can use them during training and stop before being tested at the time of competition. Thus it appears likely, based on anecdotal information, that steroid users who abstain for a time continue to have enhanced capacities relative to non-users. Not considered here is the impact of purported masking drugs such as robnecid or the use of "designer" steroids. The efficacy of either strategy in subverting the testing process has not been scientifically documented (Di Pasquale, 1987).

Surprisingly, there have been few attempts to measure the incidence or prevalence of steroid use among a designated population of athletes in which use is expected to be high. Other studies of steroid use typically have not identified the population at risk and have relied on a self-selected sample. The opportunity arose to survey competitors at the 1987 National Championship of the United States Powerlifting Federation (USPF).

## Methods

Sixty-one athletes competed in the USPF national championship; all were asked to complete a questionnaire that included items about steroids (including previous use, attitudes, and health effects). Participation was voluntary, and no identifiers (such as name or weight class) were included. Although the competitors were tested for steroid use, we did not ask questions that would have allowed us to identify recent users. The athletes were given the questionnaires during weigh-in. They placed the completed form in a sealed ballot box, which was not opened until after the competition. Forty-five (74%) of the 61 participants completed the questionnaire.

Because analysis of the data revealed rates of steroid use that were far lower than expected, we selected a random sub-sample of 50 competitors for a follow-up telephone survey. One of the authors, who was known to most of the competitors, interviewed 20 of these athletes within seven months after the competition. The other 30 could not be located. The interview consisted of only one question: "Have you ever used anabolic steroids?" It was not possible to link the results of the questionnaire with those of the telephone interview. Thus there were two samples from the same population of competitors with an unknown amount of overlap.

## Results

Fifteen (33%) of the 45 competitors who completed a questionnaire acknowledged having used steroids; their mean age was 27 years (range = 20–39). However, 11 (55%) of the 20 competitors interviewed by phone reported previous steroid use. Some of the users reported also having taken diuretics, amphetamines, and human growth hormone.

Of the 15 users, 11 (73%) thought drug testing was beneficial; nine (60%) favored stopping steroid use in sports. However, they seemed somewhat skeptical about the efficacy of drug testing in stopping steroid use (Table 19.1). Their uncertainty is consistent with the fact that nine (75%) indicated that for testing to be effective, it must take place several times throughout the year and must be conducted on a random, unannounced basis. This is in contrast to current practice, in which athletes are tested only at championship events. Also, most of the users denied that drug testing had motivated them to use oral rather than injectable steroids prior to competition.

Those participants who did not acknowledge steroid use were asked to indicate as many as four reasons to explain why they did not use the drugs (Table 19.2). The reason noted most frequently was that they saw no need to use them; next were reasons related to health effects.

The mean age of the users when they started using the drugs was 21.5 years (range = 17–27) (Table 19.3). They had used steroids for about eight cycles; the median length of each cycle was six to nine weeks. The longest continuous period of steroid use was almost three

**Table 19.1** Attitudes about steroids and reported use of other drugs among 15 power lifters who used steroids

| Survey item | No. | % |
| --- | --- | --- |
| Drug testing has helped stop steroid use (agree) | 5 | 33 |
| How many times per year should athletes be tested for steroid use? | | |
| 1 | 0 | 0 |
| 2 | 3* | 25 |
| 4 | 3* | 25 |
| > 4 | 0 | 0 |
| Unannounced random tests throughout the year | 6* | 50 |
| What other drugs have you used? | | |
| Diuretics | 7 | 47 |
| Amphetamines | 5 | 30 |
| Human growth hormone | 3 | 20 |

*Note:* * 12 respondents

**Table 19.2** Reasons given by 30 power lifters for not using steroids

| | No. | % |
| --- | --- | --- |
| No need to use them | 25 | 83 |
| Concerned about health effects | 24 | 80 |
| Did not want the side-effects | 16 | 53 |
| Illegal | 13 | 43 |
| Against my beliefs | 12 | 40 |
| Recovered from injury/illness without them | 4 | 13 |
| Others would disapprove | 3 | 10 |
| Other | 3 | 10 |
| Fear of being caught | 2 | 7 |
| Too expensive | 2 | 7 |
| Hard to get | 0 | 0 |

months. Eleven (73%) of the users identified the "black market" (defined in this survey as other athletes and gym owners/managers) as their primary source. Ten (67%) indicated improved athletic performance and seven (47%) stated prevention of injury as the main reason for using the drugs. In addition, about half the users indicated that they had decreased their dosages and that steroids were harder to obtain; only one third agreed that drug testing influenced their level of use of steroids.

Nine of 13 users (69%) said they were more concerned than they had been five years ago about the safety of steroid use (Table 19.4). Two (15%) said they were not concerned; none said they were less concerned. Most said they would discontinue use if it were proved beyond doubt that these drugs would shorten their life expectancy or significantly increase the probability of getting liver cancer or having a heart attack. Eleven of 13 users (85%) indicated that they would quit using steroids if they were "absolutely assured" that their fellow competitors no longer used them. Approximately half listed physician, pharmacist, or medical literature as their principal source of information on steroids; the other half indicated fellow athletes or

**Table 19.3** Some survey results of 15 steroid users

|  | No. | % |
|---|---|---|
| **Median length of cycle (wk)** |  |  |
| < 6 | 4 | 27 |
| 6–9 | 5 | 33 |
| 10–12 | 6 | 40 |
| > 12 | 0 | 0 |
| **Primary source of steroids** |  |  |
| Black market* | 11 | 73 |
| Physician or pharmacist | 3 | 20 |
| Mail order | 1 | 7 |
| **Main reason for use†** |  |  |
| Improved athletic performance | 10 | 67 |
| Treatment of injury | 4 | 27 |
| Prevention of illness/injury | 3 | 20 |
| Appearance or other personal reasons | 2 | 13 |
| Mean longest cycle of use | 12 wk |  |
| Mean age at first use of steroids | 21.5 yr |  |
| Mean number of cycle of use | 7.9 |  |

Note: * other athletes, gym owners/managers, † respondents could select up to two reasons

coaches. Signs and symptoms most frequently experienced while taking steroids included heightened sex drive, acne, increased body hair, and fluid retention.

## Discussion

To our knowledge this is the first systematic survey of steroid use among elite power lifters. Previous information came from the results of drug tests at competitive events and from other sources such as personal communications. It is disconcerting that the level of steroid use reported here is at great odds with our anecdotal information. One of the authors discussed our findings with two former elite power lifters, who said that there was significant underreporting of steroid use and that at the national level of competition, virtually every power lifter they knew had used steroids at least once. The contention that there was some deception on the part of the respondents is seemingly supported by the increased percentage of competitors who admitted to steroid use when they were questioned on the telephone by someone they knew (55% by telephone interview vs. 33% by questionnaire). Thus, it is possible that the level of trust they felt with the interviewer was a greater factor to them than anonymity.

Furthermore, the fact that "no need to use them" (probably interpreted as "they won't improve my performance") was the most common reason given by self-identified nonusers is consistent with a hypothesis of underreporting. Reasons relating to health concerns are believable, but the notion that elite power lifters do not think that steroids enhance strength and muscle mass is contrary not only to current scientific thought (Haupt & Rovere, 1984; Wright & Stone, 1985) but also to numerous comments made by athletes to the press.

One reason for the underreporting in our survey might be that even though the respondents were assured of personal anonymity, they wanted to protect the reputation of their sport. The difficulty of convincing athletes to be open about steroid use has been described as viewing

**Table 19.4** Survey responses of 15 power lifters regarding health-related aspects of steroid use

| Survey item | No. | % |
|---|---|---|
| **Concern about safety of steroid use compared with five years ago** | | |
| More concerned | 9* | 69 |
| Less concerned | 0 | 0 |
| About the same | 2* | 15 |
| Not concerned | 2* | 15 |
| **Would discontinue use if it were proved beyond doubt that they would** | | |
| Shorten my life expectancy by 2–5 years | 8* | 62 |
| Triple my risk of liver cancer | 11† | 79 |
| Triple my risk of heart attack before age 40 | 11* | 85 |
| **Primary source of information on health effects** | | |
| Other athletes or coach | 7 | 47 |
| Physician/pharmacist/medical literature | 8 | 53 |
| **Signs and symptoms experienced while taking steroids** | | |
| Increased sex drive | 9 | 60 |
| Acne | 8 | 53 |
| Increased body hair | 7 | 47 |
| Fluid retention | 6 | 40 |
| Elevated blood pressure | 5 | 33 |
| Sleeplessness | 5 | 33 |
| Increased irritability | 5 | 33 |
| Greasy skin/hair | 4 | 27 |
| Euphoria (feeling of well-being) | 4 | 27 |
| Increased appetite | 4 | 27 |
| Loss of scalp hair | 3 | 20 |
| Elevated level of liver enzymes | 3 | 20 |
| Altered cholesterol levels | 3 | 20 |
| Muscle spasms | 2 | 13 |
| Decreased appetite | 2 | 13 |
| Decreased sex drive | 2 | 13 |
| Depression | 2 | 13 |
| Increased number of headaches | 1 | 7 |
| Gynecomastia | 1 | 7 |
| Enlarged prostate | 1 | 7 |
| Increased urine output | 0 | 0 |

*Note*: * 13 respondents, † 14 respondents

the "tip of a large, well-developed, but very covert and private subculture" (Pope & Katz, 1988). The underreporting of drug use may be the outcome of a possible lack of trust and communication between members of the athletic and scientific/medical communities. This could be a function of poor understanding on the part of researchers and physicians of the motivation of athletes. In addition, it could be that the medical community lost credibility when it denied that steroids enhance performance. Athletes were told at that time that any weight gained while taking steroids was merely the result of fluid retention and that any strength gain was probably psychological (a placebo effect).

On the other hand, the self-reporting of other types of illicit drug use has been found to yield reasonably valid, reliable results (e.g., Petzel, Johnson, & McKillip, 1973). Therefore this method (i.e., a survey of self-reported use) is worthy of consideration when investigating steroid use.

After careful consideration, we concluded that there was a significant but unknown amount of underreporting in our survey; thus our results probably represent the lower boundary of steroid use among this group of athletes. However, to dismiss our findings based solely on hearsay evidence and conventional wisdom is premature and is at odds with accepted standards of scientific inquiry. It must be realized that this area of research is complex and fraught with difficulty. Future studies should take into account the potential problem of under-reporting by considering alternative strategies to enhance reporting and accuracy; for example, they might use questions that are less direct (i.e., projective techniques), interviewers who are athletes (i.e., insiders), a questionnaire that is mailed to the respondent's home, or the randomized response method.

Among the acknowledged steroid users (as well as nonusers), there was significant pessimism regarding the efficacy of drug testing as it is currently practiced. Coupled with the fact that most of these athletes realize that drug testing for steroids needs to be random, unannounced, and conducted throughout the year, this pessimism suggests that elite athletes are reasonably well-informed regarding detection of steroids. However, three power lifters tested positive for steroids at the national competition, but we have no way of knowing if these athletes identified themselves in our survey as users or nonusers, or if they even participated.

Another noteworthy finding is that five of the 15 self-reported steroid users stated that one of their main reasons for use was "prevention or treatment of injuries." Although not considered appropriate in most countries, the use of steroids to assist in recovery from surgery or musculoskeletal injury is common in the Soviet Union.

The side-effects most often reported by the steroid users (e.g., heightened libido, acne, and increased body hair) are similar to those reported elsewhere (e.g., Pope & Katz, 1988). On the surface they probably would not seem serious – let alone deleterious – to the user, nor would they likely cause the athlete to discontinue use. However, nine of the 15 users indicated that they were more concerned about the safety of steroids than they were five years ago. Most of them stated that they would stop using steroids if research "proved beyond a doubt" that steroids affect longevity or the risk of major illness. One might infer from these responses that power lifters are unsure of the long-term effects of these drugs. This is probably the case, because research on deleterious but transient, generally symptom-less changes has been inconclusive regarding the long-term outlook (e.g., Wright & Stone, 1985). The demonstrated interest in the health effects of steroids and the hypothetical willingness of the respondents to stop using them might temper the suggestion that athletes would risk serious harm or death in order to win.

## Subsequent research and application

Following the publication of the key study, research on drug use in sport continued to focus primarily on performance-enhancing drugs, and in particular, anabolic steroids and the prevalence rates of drug use and abuse across the world. Several large-scale studies among adolescents and young adults revealed some interesting trends, from which the sport psychology community started to extract important information. For example, Canadian researchers found that nearly 3% of 16,000 high school students had used banned substances in order to attempt to enhance sport performance and/or improve their body image

(Melia, Pipe, & Greenberg, 1996). Similar studies conducted in Australia (Australian Sports Medicine Federation, 1989), South Africa (Schwellnus, Lambert, Todd, & Juritz, 1992), Sweden (Nilsson, 1995), and the United Kingdom (Williamson, 1993) also reported overall prevalence rates between 1% and 3%. However, in a review of studies conducted in the USA from 1988 to 1996, Yesalis, Barsukiewicz, Kopstein, and Bahrke (1997) found mixed trends in steroid use (i.e., decreased, stable, increased) among both female and male high school-age students. Such inconsistent results led researchers to consider, as Yesalis and colleagues did in their study, the extent to which underreporting of genuine drug use was occurring.

In one study by Mark Anshel, who is perhaps the most prolific writer on the psychology of drug use in sports, interviews were conducted with 126 university athletes (32 female, 94 male) in the USA competing in nine sports (Anshel, 1991). To overcome the issue of underreporting, information about the participants' personal use was not included in the interviews. Overall, 64% revealed that they were aware of drug use on their team, 72% of males and 40% of females indicated that a team-mate took a drug that a user knew was illegal or banned from their sport, and 43% acknowledged that athletes use drugs for the purpose of enhancing performance as opposed to recreational use.

Despite the problems associated with underreporting, specific trends started to emerge with regard to who is more likely to use drugs in sport. Studies have suggested that higher usage is more likely in males compared to females, student-athletes compared to non-athletes, and participants in specific sports that require assets such as muscular power, strength, and speed compared to sports lacking such requirements. Steroid users are also more likely to use other drugs, alcohol, and tobacco. This finding is somewhat surprising given that steroid users are attempting to improve their strength and/or appearance, yet they would jeopardize their health or sport performance by using other drugs (Yesalis, Kennedy, Kopstein, & Bahrke, 1993).

As research progressed in this area, researchers started to focus in more depth on the psychological reasons (motivation) to take drugs beyond the already known physical (including enhancing sport performance, and controlling weight) and social (including peer pressure) reasons. In a study conducted by Tricker and Connolly (1997) among college athletes (which reported an 8% rate of anabolic steroid use over a lifetime and a 1% use within the past six months), nearly 12% of the athletes studied indicated that they would use steroids "under the right circumstances," which was defined as the ability to achieve their athletic potential without testing positive for use. Other researchers have found competitiveness and the desire to win, perfectionism (i.e., a set of self-defeating thoughts and behaviors aimed at reaching excessively high unrealistic goals), fear of failing, and the "Superman complex" (i.e., a tendency to not only want to overachieve but to feel that you are expected to achieve) to be motives for steroid use by athletes (Anshel, 2005; ISSP, 1993).

Some athletes believe that the use of performance-enhancing drugs is so widespread in their sport that they, too, need to take drugs to be competitive. When this belief is present, these individuals may also have the view that the use of performance-enhancing drugs does not skew competition or discount the magnitude of their own accomplishments, it merely increases the absolute level of performance equally across all elite competitors (Wadler & Hainline, 1989).

Research into the identification of the effects associated with steroid use also continued as a focus after the key study, with primary emphasis on determining adverse health effects. Researchers have confirmed that steroid use can have negative effects on the liver, on reproductive and cardiovascular systems, and can even result in death, but the incidence of such adverse effects is reported to be low (Berning, Adams, & Stamford, 2004). A number of psychological and behavioral effects as a result of steroid use have also been reported in the literature, including reduced self-esteem and increased stress and anxiety (Evans, Weinberg, & Jackson, 1992).

Also, as noted in Chapter 6, research has suggested that steroid use can lead to increased levels of aggression (Parrott, Choi, & Davies, 1994). Although studies with animals have found clear evidence to make this link, research with humans is yet to be confirmed. One possibility is that people who are potentially aggressive are more likely to use steroids (Williams, 1998). Alternatively, some steroid users may take drugs with an expectation that they will cause aggression, seeing this as desirable for competition and/or training. A study conducted by Su *et al.* (1993) outside of sport found significant increases among a male population in violent feelings, anger, hostility, and irritability as a result of anabolic steroid use. In this study, a small dose of the steroid and a placebo were administered to two matched groups of research participants with no predisposing pathology, with neither the researchers nor the participants knowing who received the drug and who received the placebo until the end of the study. Such studies, which are referred to as "double-blind" experiments due to both the researchers and participants being unaware of who was administered the drug, are difficult to conduct as it is dangerous to use steroids in studies with large dosages taken by participants. Moreover, trials with smaller doses may not provide valid comparisons with how steroids are actually used by athletes in real life.

Maganaris, Collins, and Sharp (2000) have also tested the hypothesis that athletes may improve their performance in sport based purely on the expected benefits of steroid use. In this study the researchers administered a placebo (saccharin) to a sample of competitive power lifters who had never used, and were relatively naïve about, the impact of steroids in order to delineate expectancy effects. Although each participant was not told about the true nature of the study at this time, they all gave informed consent to taking part in the trial of a "new steroid." Halfway through the study, the participants were disclosed the true nature of the study. All participants showed significant improvements in performance following the first trial, and these results largely dissipated when they were informed as to the true nature of the drug.

Some studies have examined both positive and negative effects of drug use. Olrich (1999), for example, investigated the psychological perceptions of use and discontinuance of steroids among male body builders. His qualitative investigation involved interviews with ten male body builders (age range 18–57 years), five of whom had taken and discontinued usage of steroids, and five who were still taking steroids. The perceptions of usage were found to be overwhelmingly positive, as they felt more alert and "tuned-in" to their bodies, had increased self-confidence, had heightened aggressiveness – which they viewed generally in a positive way – and perceived an increase in peer recognition. They also stated that they were dependent on the mental edge provided by steroids. With such a multiplicity of positives being derived from steroid use, it was found that psychological dependency occurred, suggesting that this represents a form of addiction. Further, they had a desire to maintain the benefits accrued by the use of steroids and an urge to avoid the negative ramifications associated with a loss of muscle mass. Since this study, there is other evidence to support the theory that steroid use can be motivated more by avoidance of unpleasant withdrawal effects on stopping the drug than the positive effects on exercise and physique (Berning *et al.*, 2004).

In order to protect the health and safety of athletes and promote fair play in competition, virtually all organizations overseeing sporting competitions oppose the use of performance-enhancing drugs such as steroids. This has led to more and more athletes being tested, and subsequently, more being caught. Disciplinary actions towards coaches, trainers, and medical practitioners are being taken if they are found to encourage and support drug use among their athletes. Although the quality of drug testing has improved, problems still exist in terms of potential false positives, athletes learning how to beat the latest testing protocol, as well as athletes not always knowing what is on the banned list (Yesalis, 2000). Nevertheless, the fear of testing positive and risking disqualification or sanction clearly deters a certain percentage of athletes considered at risk for drug use, but others continue to use drugs and either hope to, or try to, beat the system.

Several education programs have been developed to prevent the use of steroids, including the ATLAS (Adolescents Training and Learning to Avoid Steroids) programs in the USA. Numerous psychological strategies have also been proposed as ways to control drug abuse, including the development of resources to cope with the demands of competitive sport, monitoring of athletes' attitudes and behaviors, and professional counseling (Anshel, 2005). It should be noted, however, that it is unlikely that a sport psychologist should continue to work with an athlete who they discover is using banned drugs, not only because it may implicate the practitioner in something that it is illegal but also because such actions contradict what the sport psychologist is trying to achieve – the fostering of self-control and self-determination, and an attempt to maximize the athlete's true potential (Lavallee, Kremer, Moran, & Williams, 2004).

Research on the psychology of drug use continues to expand, and the work of Yesalis *et al.* has significantly influenced empirical investigations. The extant research has identified an alarming number of performance-enhancing drugs used by individuals to improve sports performance and enhance physical appearance, along with the health risks associated with these drugs. It is, therefore, surprising that the incidence of drug use in sport and exercise settings has not decreased, and, in some instances, has increased.

## Additional readings

Anshel, M. H. (2005). Drug abuse in sport: Causes and cures. In J. M. Williams (ed.), *Applied sport psychology: Personal growth to peak performance* (5th ed., pp. 505–40).

Anshel, M. H. (2005). Substance use and abuse: Chemical roulette in sports. In S. Murphy (ed.), *The sport psych handbook* (pp. 255–78). Champaign, IL: Human Kinetics.

Evans, M., Weinberg, R., & Jackson, A. (1992). Psychological factors related to drug use in college athletes. *The Sport Psychologist*, 6, 24–41.

ISSP (International Society of Sport Psychology) (1993). The Use of anabolic-androgenic steroids (AAS) in sport and physical activity. *The Sport Psychologist*, 7, 4–7.

Sharp, M., & Collins, D. (1998). Exploring the "inevitability" of the relationship between anabolic-androgenic steroid use and aggression in human males. *Journal of Sport & Exercise Psychology*, 20, 379–94.

## Study questions

1   What did Mirkin and Goldman find in their surveys with athletes?

2   What are the five doping categories that have been banned from international competition by International Olympic Committee?

3  What reasons are given for the underreporting in the key study?

4  What are some of the challenges of trying to conduct research in this area?

5  What is a double-blind experiment, and why it is difficult to conduct this type of experiment when researching drug use in sport?

## References

American College of Sports Medicine (1987). Position stand on the use of anabolic-androgenic steroids in sports. *Medicine and Science in Sports and Exercise*, 19, 534–9.

American Psychiatric Association (1994). *Diagnostic and statistical manual on mental disorders, fourth edition* (DSM-IV). Washington, DC: American Psychiatric Press.

Anshel, M. H. (1991). Causes for drug abuse in sport: A survey of intercollegiate athletes. *Journal of Sport Behavior*, 14, 283–307.

Anshel, M. H. (2005). Drug abuse in sport: Causes and cures. In J. M. Williams (ed.), *Applied sport psychology: Personal growth to peak performance* (5th ed., pp. 505–40). Madison, WI: McGraw Hill.

Australian Sports Medicine Federation (1989, October). *Survey of drug use in Australian sport* (2nd ed.). Canberra, ACT: Australian Sports Drug Agency.

Bahrke, M. S., Yesalis, C. E., & Brower, K. J. (1998). Anabolic-androgenic steroid abuse and performance-enhancing drug among adolescents. *Child and Adolescent Psychiatric Clinics of North America*, 7, 821–38.

Bell, J. A., & Doege, T. C. (1987). Athletes' use and abuse of drugs. *The Physician and Sportsmedicine*, 15(3), 99–108.

Berning, J. M., Adams, K. J., & Stamford, B. A. (2004). Anabolic steroid usage in athletics: Facts, fiction, and public relations. *Journal of Strength and Conditioning Research*, 18, 908–17.

Boje, O. (1939). Doping. *Bulletin of the Health Organization of the League of Nations*, 8, 439–469.

Buckley, W. E., Yesalis, C. E., Friedl, K. E., Anderson, A., Streit, A. L., & Wright, J. E. (1988). Estimated prevalence of anabolic steroid use among male high school seniors. *Journal of the American Medical Association*, 260(23), 3441–5.

Catlin, D. (1987). Detection of drug use by athletes. In R. H. Strauss (ed.), *Drugs and performance in sports* (pp. 103–20). Philadelphia, PA: WB Saunders Co.

Cowart. V. (1987). Some predict increased steroid use in sports despite drug testing, crackdown on suppliers. *Journal of the American Medical Association*, 257(22), 3025, 3029.

Di Pasquale, M. (1987). *Drug use and detection in amateur sports* (Update 4). Warkworth, Ontario: MGD Press.

Duda, M. (1988). Gauging steroid use in high school kids. *The Physician and Sportsmedicine*, 16(8), 16–17.

Evans, M., Weinberg, R., & Jackson, A. (1992). Psychological factors related to drug use in college athletes. *The Sport Psychologist*, 6, 24–41.

Goldman, B. (1984). *Death in the locker room: Steroids and sports*. South Bend, IN: Icarus Press.

Haupt, H. A., & Rovere, G. D. (1984) Anabolic steroids: A review of the literature. *American Journal of Sports Medicine*, 12, 469–84.

ISSP (International Society of Sport Psychology) (1993). The use of anabolic-androgenic steroids (AAS) in sport and physical activity. *The Sport Psychologist*, 7, 4–7.

Lavallee, D., Kremer, J., Moran, A., & Williams, M. (2004). *Sport psychology: Contemporary themes*. London: Palgrave.

Maganaris, C., Collins, D., & Sharp, M. (2000) Expectancy effects and strength training: Do steroids make a difference? *The Sport Psychologist*, 14, 272–8.

Melia, P., Pipe, A., & Greenberg, L. (1996). The use of anabolic-androgenic steroids by Canadian students. *Clinical Journal of Sport Medicine*, 6, 9–14.

Nilsson, S. (1995). Androgenic anabolic steroid use among male adolescents in Falkenburg. *European Journal of Clinical Pharmacology*, 48, 9–11.

Olrich, T. W. (1999). Perceptions of benefits and losses associated with the use and discontinuance of anabolic-androgenic steroids among male bodybuilders. *Journal of Personal and Interpersonal Loss*, 4, 231–42.

Parrott, A. C., Choi, P. Y. L., & Davies, M. (1994). Anabolic steroid use by amateur athletes: Effects upon psychological mood states. *Journal of Sports Medicine and Physical Fitness*, 34, 292–8.

Petzel, T. P., Johnson, J. E., & McKillip, J. (1973). Response bias in drug surveys. *Journal of Consulting and Clinical Psychology*, 40, 437–9.

Pope, H., & Katz, D. (1988). Affective and psychotic symptoms associated with anabolic steroid use: Case reports and survey findings. *American Journal of Psychiatry*, 145, 487–90.

Prokop, L. (1970). The struggle against doping and its history. *Journal of Sports Medicine and Physical Fitness*, 10, 45–8.

Schwellnus, M. P., Lambert, M. I., Todd, M. P., & Juritz, J. M. (1992). Androgenic anabolic steroid use in matric pupils. A survey of prevalence of use in the western Cape. *South African Medical Journal*, 82(3), 154–8.

Strauss, R. H. (1987). Anabolic steroids. In R. H. Strauss (ed.), *Drugs and performance in sports* (pp. 59–67). Philadelphia, PA: WB Saunders Co.

Su, T. P., Pagliaro, M., Schmidt, P. J, Pickar, D., Wolkowitz, O., & Rubinow, D. R. (1993) Neuro-psychiatric effects of anabolic steroids in male normal volunteers. *Journal of the American Medical Association*, 269, 2760–4.

Tricker, R., & Connolly, D. (1997). Drugs and the college athlete: An analysis of the attitudes of student athletes at risk. *Journal of Drug Education*, 27, 105–19.

Wadler, G. I., & Hainline, B. (1989). *Drugs and the athlete*. Philadelphia: F. A. Davis Company.

Williams, M. H. (1998). *The ergogenics edge: Pushing the limits of sports performance*. Champaign, IL: Human Kinetics.

Williamson, D. (1993). Anabolic steroid use among students at a British college of technology. *British Journal of Sports Medicine*, 27, 200–1.

Wright, J., & Stone, M. (1985). NCSA statement on anabolic drug use. *National Strength and Conditioning Association Journal*, 7(5), 45–59.

Yesalis, C. E. (2000). *Anabolic steroids in sports and exercise* (2nd ed.). Champaign, IL: Human Kinetics.

Yesalis, C., & Bahrke, M. S. (2005). Anabolic steroid and stimulant use in North American sport between 1850 and 1980. *Sport in History*, 25, 434–51.

Yesalis, C., Barsukiewicz, C., Kopstein, A., & Bahrke, M. (1997). Trends in anabolic-androgenic steroid use among adolescents. *Archives of Pediatric and Adolescent Medicine*, 151, 1197–206.

Yesalis, C., Kennedy, N., Kopstein, A. & Bahrke, M. (1993). Anabolic-androgenic steroid use in the United States. *Journal of the American Medical Association*, 270(10), 1217–21.

# 20

# Injury

Smith, R. E., Smoll, F. L., & Ptacek, J. T. (1990). Conjunctive moderator variables in vulnerability and resiliency research: Life stress, social support and coping skills and adolescent sport injuries. *Journal of Personality and Social Psychology*, 58, 360–9.

## Background and context

Booth (1987) reported that over 17 million sport injuries occur per year and other data suggests that each year nearly half of all amateur athletes suffer an injury that precludes participation (Garrick & Requa, 1978; Hardy & Crace, 1990). For sanctioned sport activities with high school and college athletes, estimates are that each year over 30% will be injured and hundreds of millions of dollars spent on treatment of those injuries (Meeuwisse & Fowler, 1988; National Collegiate Athletic Association, 1992; Requa, 1991). The personal devastation and economic costs of sport injuries are so serious that they merit a better understanding of what contributes to them, with the ultimate goal that such knowledge might lead to prevention interventions. Although many of the causes of sport injuries are physical in nature (e.g., nature of the sport, poor physical conditioning or biomechanics, bad weather or playing surface conditions) or simply bad luck, psychological and social factors have also been found to influence vulnerability and resiliency to injury.

Two decades prior to Smith, Smoll, and Ptacek's key study, Holmes (1970) found that 50% of University of Washington football players who experienced high levels of major stressful life events during the 12 months prior to the football season experienced an injury requiring either missing at least three days of practice or one game in contrast to only 25% and 9%, respectively, for players with moderate and low levels of life stress. This research stemmed from Holmes and Rahe's (1967) development of the *Social Readjustment Rating Scale* (SRRS), a questionnaire that ranks the magnitude of 40 life change events (e.g., breakup of a relationship, death/significant illness of a loved one, taking a vacation) often experienced in the general adult population. The premise behind the scale is that experiencing major life events places demands on the organism to adapt and, therefore, stress on the body and thus an increased risk for negative outcomes such as illness and accidents.

The next life event and sport injury study (Bramwell, Masuda, Wagner, & Holmes, 1975) found an even stronger relationship between life stress and football injuries when they modified the SRRS to better fit athletes by deleting less relevant events and adding 20 events such as troubles with head coach, being dropped from the team, and difficulties with eligibility. All subsequent research with football players (Coddington & Troxell, 1980; Cryan & Alles, 1983; Passer & Seese, 1983) supported the initial findings, but equivocal results occurred with attempts to generalize the findings to sport participants outside of football (Lysens, van den Auweele, & Ostyn, 1986; Williams, Haggert, Tonymon, & Wadsworth, 1986; Williams, Tonymon, & Wadsworth, 1986).

The 1970s and 1980s also saw many researchers try to identify personality factors (e.g., tough-minded vs. tender-minded, outgoing vs. shy) that might put athletes at risk of injury (e.g., Irvin, 1975; Jackson *et al.* (1978); Valiant, 1981). One study (Passer & Seese, 1983) even examined whether personality variables (i.e., trait anxiety, competitive trait anxiety, locus of control) might moderate the influence of life events on injury occurrence. In addition to this design advancement, Passer and Seese also improved upon prior measurement of life event stress by using a questionnaire that allowed respondents to give their own rating of the impact of the life event and whether they perceived the event to be positive or negative. Research within the life stress and illness area tended to find that only negative life events correlated with negative outcome (e.g., Thoits, 1983; Vinokur & Selzer, 1975). As hypothesized, Passer and Seese found only negative events influenced injury occurrence, but their moderator variables did not affect the relationship. As outlined in the key study section, moderator variables specify the conditions under which an independent (or predictor) variable exerts its effects on a dependent (or criterion) variable. This is different to a mediator variable, which describes how and why certain psychological effects occur by accounting for the relationship between the independent and dependent variables.

Although less common, a few early sport injury researchers examined life event stress and levels of coping resources such as stress management, other psychological coping skills, good nutritional and sleeping habits, and social support (e.g., the presence of others whom we know value and care for us and on whom we can rely, Sarason, Levine, Basham, & Sarason, 1983). Coping resources did not moderate the life stress-injury relationship, but they contributed directly to the likelihood of injury (Hardy, Prentice, Kirsanoff, Richman, & Rosenfeld, 1987; Williams *et al.*, 1986). See Bergandi (1985) and Crossman (1985) for reviews of personality and other psychological factors related to sport injury.

The narrow scope (i.e., failure to adequately consider the interaction of personal and situational variables that can influence stress reactions) and atheoretical nature of early attempts to identify psychosocial injury risk factors led Andersen and Williams (1988) to propose a multi-component theoretical model of stress and injury. They proposed that most psychological variables, if they influence injury at all, probably do so through a linkage with stress and the resulting stress response. More specifically, they hypothesized that athletes with a lot of stress in their lives and who have poor coping resources (e.g., psychological coping skills, social support) and personality characteristics that exacerbate stress are more likely to become injured compared to athletes who do not have this high-risk profile. Increased injury risk occurs because these athletes perceive a wider variety of performance situations as stressful and therefore have an elevated stress response. Particularly disastrous is the resulting increase in muscle tension and attention disruptions such as failure to detect relevant cues in the periphery and delayed responses to cues in the central field of vision.

According to the model, coping resources and personality can directly influence the stress response and resulting injury risk, or they can do so by moderating the effects of major life events and minor events such as daily irritants or hassles. In other words, having coping resources and desirable personality characteristics may serve a protective or buffering function from the injury effects of high life events/hassles and the failure to have them may exacerbate the injury effects of high life events/hassles. Further, the presence of a single desirable variable would probably not be as effective a moderator as multiple variables. The model also proposes that reducing the risk factors and stress response through interventions such as relaxation and concentration training and building social support can lower injury rates.

## Key study

As a result of inconsistent patterns of data obtained in studies of stressful life events and outcome measures, and the typically minor portion of illness outcome variance accounted for (Schroeder & Costa, 1984), this study set out to test the possibility that certain moderator variables may influence the relation between life events and sport injury vulnerability (or, conversely, the resiliency). A moderator variable is a qualitative or quantitative variable that affects the nature, direction, or strength of a relation between an independent or predictor variable and a dependent or criterion variable (Arnold, 1982; Baron & Kenny, 1986). Identification of moderator variables that influence the stress-injury relationship can help find subgroups of athletes who may be at particular risk of injury and toward whom intervention programs might be targeted.

The researchers focused their analytic strategy on determining the extent to which individual differences in athletes' social support and psychological coping skills scores, both singly and in combination, affected the magnitude of the correlations between major and minor life events and injury measures. The selection of social support and coping skills as potential moderators was based not only on the central role these constructs occupy within contemporary theories of stress and coping, but also on the fact that personal and environmental resources may be relatively independent of one another (Lazarus & Folkman, 1984). Statistical independence is an important factor in the ability to determine whether these psychosocial resources operate in a conjunctive or a disjunctive fashion. Evidence that social support and coping skills operate in a conjunctive manner requires that the combination of these variables in a set pattern (e.g., low-low, high-low) results in a notable increment in the amount of injury variance accounted for by life event scores over that accounted for when either moderator is considered alone (a disjunctive relationship).

On the basis of previous findings that negatively appraised events are more consistently related to negative outcomes than are positively appraised events, it was hypothesized that negative events would be the strongest predictors of subsequent injury. The researchers also hypothesized that subjects' appraisals of their social support and the adequacy of their psychological coping skills would moderate the life event-injury relation in a disjunctive manner, that is, the strongest stress-injury association would occur among subjects who were low in both social support and coping skills. In a more exploratory vein, the researchers also assessed relations between minor events and injuries, as well as the possible contribution of events appraised as positive. They did not have an empirical or theoretical basis for making differential predictions for minor and major negative events, because both major events and daily hassles have been shown to be potential risk factors in various studies (e.g., Cohen, 1988; Lazarus & Folkman, 1984; Sarason, Sarason, & Johnson, 1985). Positive events, on the other hand, have not been significantly related to injuries in previous studies (e.g., Passer & Seese, 1983; Williams, Tonymon, & Wadsworth, 1986), but this investigation allowed the researchers to assess their possible role with a more extensive measure that provided separate scores for major and minor positive events.

## Methods

### Subjects

The subjects were 250 male and 201 female high school varsity athletes ranging in age from 14–19 years ($M = 16.23$, $SD = 1.11$). The athletes participated in boys' and girls' basketball, boys' wrestling, or girls' gymnastics at 13 high schools in the United States. These sports were selected in order to provide a range of individual, team, contact, and non-contact sports. Data were obtained from a total of 41 teams in the three sports.

### Measures and Procedure

A prospective research design was implemented. At each of the schools, the athletes completed a series of questionnaires in a group setting in the week prior to the beginning of the sport season. The inventories included measures of recent life events, levels of social support experienced by the athlete, and self-perceived adequacy of psychological coping skills. Injury data were then collected over the course of the season.

*Life Experiences.* Life events were measured using a modified version of the *Adolescent Perceived Events Scale* (Compas, Davis, Forsythe, & Wagner, 1987). This questionnaire contains 197 specific life changes generated by a large sample of high school students (e.g., "getting good grades or progress reports," "pressures or expectations by parents," "getting a driver's license or learner's permit," and "parents getting divorced"). None of the items involved previous injuries. The response format was modified by the researchers for this study so that for each item, the subjects indicated whether or not the event had been experienced in the past six months. If an event had been experienced, the subjects indicated whether they perceived it as positive or negative at the time it occurred. They also classified the event as either a major event that had long-term consequences for them or as a "day-to-day" event that did not. Scores were calculated for the total numbers of major and minor life events of a positive and negative nature reported by the subjects. The researchers also calculated total positive and negative event scores and a total events score.

*Social Support.* The subjects also completed measures of the amount and quality of social support available to them from 20 different individuals (e.g., mother, father, coach, and best friend) and groups (e.g., their teammates and clubs or religious groups to which they belonged). The social support measure was derived from one used previously by Cauce, Felner, and Primavera (1982) to assess adolescents' subjective appraisals of the individual and group components of their social support network. Because athletes were being studied, the researchers added items for assistant coach, trainer, team physician, and athletic religious organizations to assess the athletic environment in greater detail. On separate scales, the athletes indicated the extent to which each individual and group could be counted on to provide them with (a) emotional support and caring, and (b) help and guidance on a scale ranging from *not at all helpful* (1) to *very helpful* (5). Scores were summed to provide overall measures of the two varieties of social support. The range of possible scores on each of the scales was 20–100. On a separate sample of 94 athletes not included in this study, the social support scale had one-week test-retest reliability of .87 for emotional support and .88 for help and guidance. The two social support components correlated .88 with one another.

*Psychological Coping Skills.* To assess self-perceived adequacy of coping skills, the subjects completed the *Athletic Coping Skills Inventory* (Smith, Smoll, & Schutz, 1988). This scale consists of 42 behavioral self-report items designed to measure a range of general coping skills within a sport context. These include the ability to control arousal and to concentrate and think clearly under stress, the tendency to set specific goals and to engage in problem-solving strategies, and the ability to relate effectively to authority figures and to profit from corrective feedback. The following are sample items: "I play relaxed under intense pressure"; "I set my own performance goals for each practice"; and "If a coach criticizes or yells at me, I correct the mistake without getting upset about it." Each item was rated on a 4-point Likert-type scale ranging from *not at all* (0) to *very much so* (3). Total scores on the scale can range from zero to 126. One-week test-retest reliability was .88 in an independent sample of 94 athletes (Smith *et al.*, 1988). Although the *Athletic Coping Skills Inventory* measures a variety of specific skills, it has substantial inter-item correlations and high internal consistency (Cronbach's alpha = .90). The total score used in this study is assumed to reflect the self-perceived adequacy of an individual's range of cognitive, emotional control, and behavioral coping skills within the sport setting.

*Injury Assessment.* A sport injury was defined in this study as a medical problem resulting from athletic participation that restricted subsequent participation for at least one day beyond the day of its occurrence. To provide a more objective measure of injury than that derived from the retrospective self-reports of the athletes, the researchers hired the coaches of the 41 teams as project research assistants and trained them in the injury recording system. Each day during the sport season, the coaches indicated on a special team roster any athlete who was unable to participate fully in practices or contests. The coaches also recorded the reason for non-participation (injury, illness, or absence for some other reason). Several times each week, the researchers contacted the coaches by telephone and their data was collected for later analysis. To reduce possible underreporting of injuries by coaches because of concerns that injuries might reflect unfavorably on their coaching competence, the researchers emphasized to them that the goal of the study was to identify athlete characteristics that might be related to injury, and not to assess differences between teams or coaches. The coaches were assured that data from all the teams would be combined for the data analysis.

The total number of days of non-participation because of injury over the course of the season (i.e., time loss) served as the injury measure. To ensure the comparability of this measure across teams and sports, the data were corrected for differential exposure to possible injury by dividing the number of days lost because of injury by the total number of days the team practiced or competed minus the number of days lost because of injury, illness, or absence (i.e., the number of days on which there was no opportunity to incur injury).

## Results

Complete data were obtained on all the variables of interest from 424 of the 451 subjects. Descriptive statistics for this data are presented in Table 20.1. The social support variable is the perceived availability of help and guidance. As noted earlier, the two social support scales correlated so highly that they can be considered to be tapping the same construct. Help and guidance was chosen for moderator analyses because it yielded greater homogeneity of variance for negative life events within the various subgroups chosen to test for moderator effects (even though the overall pattern of results was identical for the emotional support variable). The data of Table 20.1 indicate that the athletes reported more positive than negative life events, and minor events were reported more frequently than major events within both the positive and negative classes.

Overall, 31% of the sample sustained at least one injury during the course of the season. Injury rates ranged from 25% in boys' basketball to 41% in wrestling. The mean number of days

**Table 20.1** Means and standard deviations of predictor, moderator, and outcome variables

| Variable | M | SD |
| --- | --- | --- |
| Minor positive events | 36.01 | 11.81 |
| Major positive events | 13.70 | 8.32 |
| Minor negative events | 18.58 | 10.08 |
| Major negative events | 12.91 | 9.40 |
| Social support | 51.90 | 12.01 |
| Coping skills | 72.41 | 16.17 |
| Exposure-corrected time loss (days) | .03 | .09 |

Note: $N = 424$

lost per injury was 5.46 ($SD = 7.17$), and the median time loss per injury was three days. The figure shown in Table 20.1 is the exposure-corrected injury time loss measure. Because the injury time loss distribution was positively skewed, the researchers subjected the scores to the logarithmic transformation recommended by Cohen and Cohen (1983: 261) for treatment of time data in order to reduce a potential spurious influence of extreme scores.

## Correlational Analyses

Product-moment correlations of the life event, social support, and coping skills measures with the outcome measure of exposure-corrected injury time loss are presented in Table 20.2. None of the life event variables were significantly related to subsequent injuries. The social support and coping skills measures were also uncorrelated with injuries.

To assess potential moderator effects involving the social support and coping skills variables, correlations were computed between the life event measures and injuries for groups of subjects who fell within the upper and lower thirds of the social support or coping skills distributions. Event-injury correlations involving minor positive, major positive, and minor negative events were unaffected by differences in social support, coping skills, or by any combination of social support and coping skills. However, as shown in Table 20.3, these variables did affect the relation between major negative events and subsequent injuries.

Because the social support and coping skills measures shared little common variance ($r = .17$), they were treated as separate and independent psychosocial resources. To assess possible disjunctive moderator influences, correlations between major negative life events and subsequent injury time loss were computed separately for subjects falling in the upper and lower thirds of the two distributions. The correlation between the life event and injury measures was somewhat higher for subjects low in social support than for those who reported high levels of support, but neither coefficient was significant.

The influence of differences in coping skills on the stress-injury relation was stronger than was the case for social support. As shown in Table 20.3, the correlation between negative life events and subsequent injury was significant for athletes who reported low levels of coping skills, and nearly 6% of the injury time loss variance was accounted for in terms of negative life events within this group of athletes. No relation existed for subjects who fell within the upper third of the coping skills distribution.

Next, possible conjunctive moderator effects of social support and coping skills were assessed by selecting subgroups of athletes who fell within the upper or lower thirds of the

**Table 20.2** Correlation of life event, social support, and coping skills measures with exposure-corrected injury time loss

| Variable | r |
|---|---|
| Minor positive events | −.02 |
| Major positive events | .07 |
| Minor negative events | .04 |
| Major negative events | .09 |
| Social support | −.07 |
| Coping skills | −.03 |

Note: N = 424

**Table 20.3** Means, standard deviations, and correlations between major negative life events and log injury time loss as a function of high and low social support and high and low coping skills

| Moderator variables | n | Life events | | Time loss[a] | | |
| | | M | SD | M | SD | r |
|---|---|---|---|---|---|---|
| Social support | | | | | | |
| Low | 124 | 12.38 | 8.96 | −3.79 | 1.28 | .15 |
| High | 137 | 12.43 | 9.50 | −3.98 | 1.15 | .03 |
| Coping skills | | | | | | |
| Low | 123 | 14.22 | 8.97 | −3.95 | 1.15 | .24* |
| High | 126 | 12.25 | 9.83 | −3.90 | 1.24 | .07 |

Note: high and low = upper and lower thirds of the distributions
[a] Logarithmic transformation of exposure-corrected time loss; greater time loss is reflected in a lower negative score
* $p < .05$

distributions on both measures. Because the measures of social support and coping skills are nearly orthogonal, it was possible to select groups of athletes who were high on both psychosocial asset measures, low on both, or high on one and low on the other. Conjunctive moderation requires that the correlation between negative events and subsequent injuries be maximized by some combination of social support and coping skills. As noted earlier, one hypothesis for the study was that vulnerability to the impact of life stress would be greatest for subjects who were deficient in both environmental (social support) and personal (coping skills) assets.

Descriptive statistics for the four groups of athletes on the life change measure and on the transformed injury variable are presented in Table 20.4. Analyses of variance revealed that the four groups did not differ significantly in the number of major negative life events they reported, nor did they differ in injury time loss, $Fs(3, 168) = 1.45$ and $1.52$, respectively, $p > .10$. The researchers also regressed the injury measure on negative life change separately for each group to ensure that the Y (injury) intercepts were similar for the four groups, because radical differences in intercepts might pose difficulties in positing vulnerability or resiliency effects even if the correlation coefficients differ (Cohen & Edwards, 1989). The intercepts were

**Table 20.4** Means, standard deviations, and correlations between major negative life events and log injury time loss as a function of combined social support and coping skills

| Social support/ coping skills | n | Life events | | Time loss[a] | | |
|---|---|---|---|---|---|---|
| | | M | SD | M | SD | r |
| Low–low | 47 | 12.88 | 9.72 | −3.75 | 1.27 | .47* |
| Low–high | 33 | 14.55 | 8.34 | −4.23 | 0.78 | .22 |
| High–low | 40 | 12.95 | 9.60 | −3.83 | 1.28 | .13 |
| High–high | 53 | 10.95 | 9.11 | −3.79 | 1.32 | .13 |

Note: high and low = upper and lower thirds of the distributions
[a] Natural logarithmic transformations of exposure-corrected time loss; greater time loss is reflected in a lower negative score
* $p < .01$

very similar for the four groups, with the widest difference being less than .5 SE of the constant (intercept).

The correlations between life change and subsequent injury time loss for the four social support-coping skills groups are also presented in Table 20.4. These results provide strong evidence for a conjunctive moderator influence. Consistent with the proposed hypothesis for this study, subjects low in both of the psychosocial assets exhibited the strongest correlation between major negative life events and subsequent injuries. A notable increment in systematic variance occurred, with 22% of the injury variance being accounted for by the life event variable within this group. This is more than triple the amount of variance accounted for by the sum of the two moderator variables considered separately. No other combination of social support and coping skills yielded a statistically significant stress-injury correlation. The statistical test for differences among three or more correlation coefficients (Edwards, 1984: 74) revealed that the coefficients differed significantly, $\chi^2(3, N = 173) = 12.59, p < .01$.

A follow-up test of conjunctive moderator effects considered groups that were even more extreme in psychosocial assets, falling in the upper and lower quartiles of the social support and coping skills distributions. Again, the groups did not differ in negative life events or in injury time loss, and the regression intercepts were very similar. In the low-low group, the correlation increased to $r(29) = .55, p < .01$, accounting for more than 30% of the injury variance. For the other three groups, none of the correlations were significant; all were low and negative in direction. Even with the reduction in number of subjects in these more extreme groups, the difference among the correlation coefficients remained significant, $\chi^2(3, N = 98) = 8.71$, $p < .05$.

## Moderated Regression Analysis

Correlational analyses are the most direct approach for assessing the amount of variance in an outcome variable accounted for by a predictor within specific subgroups defined by moderator variables. The correlational approach is appropriate on statistical grounds, provided that restriction in range in the predictor variable and differential measurement error in the dependent variable are not present in the subgroups defined by the moderator variable(s) (Arnold, 1982; Cohen & Cohen, 1983). Restriction in range does not appear to be a problem in our data, and there is no apparent basis for attributing differential measurement error to the injury time loss data (which were recorded by the coaches).

Despite the appropriateness of the correlational approach to the data in this study, the most frequently recommended approach to assessing moderator influences is moderated regression analysis involving a predictor variable, a moderator variable, and a product term (Baron & Kenny, 1986). A hierarchical regression analysis is carried out so that the unique increment in variance accounted for by the product term (the "interaction" between the predictor and the moderator) can be assessed (Cohen & Cohen, 1983). Moderated regression analysis was applied to assess the extent to which this approach would be sensitive to moderator effects that resulted in a predictor-criterion relation within only a small portion of the total data set (in this case, approximately 10% of the sample defined by scores in the lower thirds of the social support and coping skills distributions). A hierarchical regression analysis was carried out, with the variables being entered in the following order: negative life events, social support, coping skills, life events × social support, life events × coping skills, social support × coping skills, and a conjunctive product score of life events × social support × coping skills. Both linear and quadratic analyses were conducted. These analyses revealed no significant moderator effects involving either the life events × moderator product terms (disjunctive moderator tests) or the triple product term (testing conjunctive moderation) when all of the cases were analyzed together.

## Discussion

The results provide strong evidence for a conjunctive relation between social support and coping skills in increasing injury vulnerability from the impact of major negative life events. Within the subgroup of athletes scoring low in both social support and psychological coping skills, negative life events accounted for nearly triple (22%) the sum of the injury variance accounted for in the low social support (2.3%) and low coping skills (5.8%) groups when these variables were considered as separate (disjunctive) moderators of the stress-injury relationship. In contrast, minor negative events, minor and major positive events, and total life events failed to predict subsequent injury, nor were their correlations with injury influenced by social support or coping skills.

Turning to the converse of vulnerability, if resiliency is defined in terms of a lack of relation between life stress and injuries, the data suggests a disjunctive rather than a conjunctive pattern of moderator influences for social support and coping skills because all groups having moderate to high levels of social support or coping skills exhibited nonsignificant relations between stress and injury. Thus, having either of these psychosocial assets reduces vulnerability to stress as it relates to injury risk, which suggests that, from an intervention perspective, injury risk could be lowered either by increasing athletes' psychological coping skills or their social support.

Interest in person-situation interactions within psychological research has stimulated attempts to identify moderator variables and study their influence. The results of this study suggest the importance of theory-driven hypotheses in the selection of conjunctive moderator possibilities, because very specific patterns involving restricted subsamples may be frequently encountered. The study of conjunctive moderators can also provide valuable information regarding the manner in which personality variables interact with one another to affect behavior.

More powerful statistical techniques are required for assessing moderator effects. In this study, the researchers were able to proceed with a relatively straightforward correlational approach in their assessment of conjunctive and disjunctive moderator influences. As Arnold (1982) has pointed out, however, this approach requires extremely large sample sizes if one is to isolate subgroups of sufficient size to demonstrate an effect. This is particularly the case if a researcher wishes to select extreme groups on the moderator variable of interest. Although the analyses in the present study began with 451 subjects, the subgroups averaged only 30–50 subjects when extreme groups were selected on the moderator variables. Thus, the researchers were unable to meaningfully explore the contribution of other potentially important variables that deserve empirical attention, such as gender and nature of the sport. The researchers were also fortunate in that social support and coping skills were minimally correlated, making it possible to select subgroups of similar size. With more highly correlated variables, it would have been difficult to isolate particular subgroups for study. Moderator variables that are correlated with one another or with the predictor variable also present statistical and interpretive problems regardless of whether a correlational or a regression approach is taken.

As noted earlier, moderated regression analysis is the most frequently advocated approach to assessing moderator effects. However, many writers have noted the lack of power this approach has for revealing moderator effects even in the simplest case involving a single moderator variable (e.g., Bobko, 1986; Cronbach, 1987; Hedges, 1987). In this study, the data illustrate an instance in which moderated regression analysis resulted in a failure to identify moderator effects that were in fact present. The regression analyses based on the entire sample led to the conclusion that social support and coping skills, singly or in combination, did not affect the form of the life stress-injury relation. This kind of result may be especially likely to occur in instances in which a significant predictor-criterion relation occurs only within a small subsample, as in the case of the low-low subgroups in this study. Yet, this is precisely the type of circumstance that may occur with some frequency in vulnerability or resiliency research.

## Subsequent research and application

At least 40 studies have examined the relationship of life events to athletic injury risk since the original Holmes (1970) research. A recent review of these studies by Williams and Andersen (2007) reported that approximately 85% found some type of correlation between life event stress and injury. Athletes with high life event stress were two to five times more likely to be injured than athletes with low life event stress. They further reported that for researchers who distinguished between negative and positive life events, the majority found that only the negatively appraised life events put athletes at risk of injury but there also was some evidence for positive events and total events increasing risk of injury. The almost universal finding of a life event-sport injury relationship is even more compelling considering it occurred across sports (e.g., football, baseball, field hockey, soccer, gymnastics, wrestling, Alpine skiing, race walking, track, and field) and competitive levels (youth to elite level) and with diverse measures of life events (eight questionnaires) and definitions of injury (from requiring treatment from an athletic trainer with no loss or modification of practice to time loss of missing more than a week of practice) (Williams & Andersen, 2007).

Smith et al.'s failure to find that minor life events contributed to injury risk has been supported by almost all concurrent and subsequent research (Blackwell & McCullagh, 1990; Hanson, McCullagh, & Tonymon, 1992; Meyer, 1995; Van Mechelen et al., 1996), however, the results of all these studies, including Smith et al., are suspect because of a serious design flaw. They measured minor life events (also called daily hassles) at only one time. Instead they need frequent assessment throughout the athletic season because of their ever-changing nature, thus enabling researchers to then compare subsequent injuries to the immediately preceding score (Williams & Andersen, 1998). In the one study that employed such a design and statistical analysis (Fawkner, McMurray, & Summers, 1999), the injured athletes had a significant increase in minor life events for the week prior to injury whereas no significant changes occurred for the non-injured athletes.

Although Smith *et al.*'s key study provides an excellent prototype for studying multiple moderators and whether they act singly or in combination in moderating the major and minor life stress-injury relationship, no subsequent researchers have employed a similar design and statistics. The failure to do so may have resulted from the requirement to have a large number of participants.

For researchers who examined psychological coping skills using the same tool as Smith *et al.* (Byrd, 1993; Lavallee & Flint, 1996; Noh, Morris, & Andersen, 2005; Petrie, 1993; Rider & Hicks, 1995), only Noh *et al.* found a relationship to injury outcome. Their professional, university, and dance institute Korean ballet dancers who had more worries and lower confidence incurred more injuries. Most of the preceding studies were hampered either by a small number of participants or statistical issues. Although Petrie is to be commended for testing for both direct and interaction effects, he used the regression analyses that Smith *et al.* challenged because they might mask significant results when differences are expected primarily from individuals scoring on the extreme ends rather than across the entire continuum. More research is needed to determine the relationship of psychological coping skills to injury.

In terms of social support, research tends to support the stress-injury model's hypothesis that social support either directly affects injury outcome or it moderates the influence life stress has on injury vulnerability. For example, Byrd (1993), Hardy, O'Connor, & Geisler (1990), and Hardy *et al.* (1987) found athletes with high levels of social support had fewer injuries and those with low levels had more injuries regardless of life event stress. The preponderance of evidence, however, is that social support has a moderating influence on the life stress-injury relationship. For the most part, high levels of support lessened the harmful effects of high life stress on injury whereas low levels of support increased the harmful injury effects. For example, Petrie (1992) found that negative life stress accounted for 14 to 24% of the variance in minor, severe, and total injuries in gymnasts with low social support in contrast to no significant relationship for gymnasts with high social support. Patterson, Smith, and Everett (1998) obtained similar results, but in this case negative life events accounted for nearly 50% of the injury variance in ballet dancers who reported low levels of social support. Although researchers usually found social support moderated the life stress-injury relationship in the direction hypothesized by the stress-injury model, this was not always the case. See Williams and Andersen (1998, 2007) and Petrie and Perna (2004) for a more thorough review of the coping resources research as well as the personality component of the model.

Smith *et al.*'s disjunctive moderation findings led them to propose that injury risk for athletes with high life stress might be decreased by either increasing their social support or by teaching them psychological coping skills. To date, no researchers have tried to decrease injuries by improving social support, but there is considerable support for a reduction in injuries from psychological coping skills interventions (e.g., Davis, 1991; Kerr & Goss, 1996; May & Brown, 1989; Perna, Antoni, Baum, Gordon, & Schneiderman, 2003). The injury reductions found through enhancing psychological coping skills are particularly impressive considering none of the studies targeted athletes at risk of injury. Even stronger findings might occur with at-risk athletes.

In one such study, Johnson, Ekengren, and Andersen (2005) provided interventions (e.g., stress management, relaxation, self-confidence training) for high-risk soccer players (many life events, low coping, high sport anxiety). The control group ($n = 13$) received 21 injuries spread across 10 of the 13 participants whereas only three injuries (one each for three of the 16 athletes) occurred in the intervention group. In a similar study, Maddison and Prapavessis (2005) found less time loss due to injury, decreases in worrying, and increases in coping for high-risk athletes (low in social support or high in avoidance coping or both) who received a stress management intervention compared to those assigned to the control condition.

In summary, the Smith *et al.* key study advanced understanding regarding the relationship of life events to sport injuries and how multiple coping resources moderate that influence. In the process they identified populations of athletes most in need of interventions to reduce injury risk and what those interventions should include. Their contribution regarding design and statistical prototype for studying the effects of multiple moderator variables, however, has unfortunately not influenced subsequent research in the sport injury area.

## Additional readings

Fawkner, H. J., McMurray, N. E., & Summers, J. J. (1999). Athletic injury and minor life events: A prospective study. *Journal of Science and Medicine in Sport*, 2, 117–24.

Johnson, U., Ekengren, J., & Andersen, M. B. (2005). Injury prevention in Sweden: Helping soccer players at risk. *Journal of Sport & Exercise Psychology*, 27, 32–8.

Passer, M. W., & Seese, M. D. (1983). Life stress and athletic injury: Examination of positive versus negative events and three moderator variables. *Journal of Human Stress*, 9, 11–16.

Petrie, T. A., & Perna, F. (2004). Psychology of injury: Theory, research and practice. In T. Morris & J. Summers (eds.), *Sport psychology: Theory, application and issues* (2nd ed., pp. 547–71). Milton, Australia: Wiley.

Williams, J. M., & Andersen, M. B. (1998). Psychosocial antecedents of sport injury: Review and critique of the stress and injury model. *Journal of Applied Sport Psychology*, 10, 5–25.

## Study questions

1   What are moderator variables and, when it comes to multiple moderator variables, can you distinguish between possible conjunctive and disjunctive effects?

2   According to Andersen and Williams' (1988) stress and injury model, (a) how do most psychological variables influence sport injuries, (b) how might stressful events, personality variables, and coping resources influence injury risk, and (c) what implications are there for interventions to reduce sport injuries?

3   What did Smith *et al.* find regarding the relationship of social support and psychological coping skills to injury vulnerability and resiliency (discuss in terms of conjunctive and disjunctive effects)?

4   When is it appropriate to use Smith *et al.*'s correlational statistical analysis for assessing moderator influences and when is the more commonly used moderated regression analysis particularly likely to fail to identify moderator effects that in fact are present?

5   What do research findings indicate regarding (a) the relationship of life events to sport injuries, (b) how coping resources might moderate that relationship or directly influence injury risk, and (c) interventions that might decrease injuries due to psychosocial factors?

## References

Andersen, M. B., & Williams, J. M. (1988). A model of stress and athletic injury: Prediction and prevention. *Journal of Sport & Exercise Psychology*, 10, 294–306.

Arnold, H. J. (1982). Moderator variables: A clarification of conceptual, analytic, and psychometric issues. *Organizational Behavior and Human Performance*, 29, 143–74.

Baron, R. M., & Kenny, D. A. (1986). The moderator-mediator variable distinction in social psychological research: Conceptual, strategic, and statistical considerations. *Journal of Personality and Social Psychology*, 51, 1173–82.

Bergandi, T. A. (1985). Psychological variables relating to the incidence of athletic injury: A review of the literature. *International Journal of Sport Psychology*, 16, 141–9.

Blackwell, B., & McCullagh, P. (1990). The relationship of athletic injury to life stress, competitive anxiety, and coping resources. *Athletic Training*, 25, 23–7.

Bobko, P. (1986). A solution to some dilemmas when testing hypotheses about ordinal interactions. *Journal of Applied Psychology*, 71, 323–6.

Booth, W. (1987). Arthritis Institute tackles sports. *Science*, 237, 846–7.

Bramwell, S. T., Masuda, M., Wagner, N. H., & Holmes, T. H. (1975). Psychological factors in athletic injuries: Development and application of the *Social and Athletic Readjustment Rating Scale* (SARRS). *Journal of Human Stress*, 1, 6–20.

Byrd, B. J. (1993). *The relationship of history of stressors, personality, and coping resources, with the incidence of athletic injuries*. Unpublished masters thesis. University of Colorado, Boulder.

Cauce, A. M., Felner, R. D., & Primavera, J. (1982). Social support in high-risk adolescents: Structural components and adaptive impact. *American Journal of Community Psychology*, 10, 417–28.

Coddington, R., & Troxell, J. (1980). The effect of emotional factors on football injury rates – a pilot study. *Journal of Human Stress*, 6, 3–5.

Cohen, J., & Cohen, P. (1983). *Applied multiple regression/correlation analysis for the behavioral sciences* (2nd ed.). Hillsdale, NJ: Erlbaum.

Cohen, L. H. (ed.) (1988). *Life events and psychological functioning: Theoretical and methodological issues*. Newbury Park, CA: Sage.

Cohen, S., & Edwards, J. R. (1989). Personality characteristics as moderators of the relationship between stress and disorder. In R. W. J. Neufeld (ed.), *Advances in the investigation of psychological stress* (pp. 235–83). New York: Wiley.

Compas, B. E., Davis, G. E., Forsythe, C. J., & Wagner, B. (1987). Assessment of major and daily stressful events during adolescence: The *Adolescent Perceived Events Scale*. *Journal of Consulting and Clinical Psychology*, 55, 534–41.

Cronbach, L. J. (1987). Statistical tests for moderator variables: Flaws in analyses recently proposed. *Psychological Bulletin*, 102, 114–17.

Crossman, J. (1985). Psychosocial factors and athletic injury. *Journal of Sports Medicine and Physical Fitness*, 25, 151–4.

Cryan, P. O., & Alles, E. F. (1983). The relationship between stress and football injuries. *Journal of Sports Medicine and Physical Fitness*, 23, 52–8.

Davis, J. O. (1991). Sports injuries and stress management: An opportunity for research. *The Sport Psychologist*, 5, 175–82.

Edwards, A. L. (1984). *An introduction to linear regression and correlation* (2nd ed.). New York: Freeman.

Fawkner, H. J., McMurray, N. E., & Summers, J. J. (1999). Athletic injury and minor life events: A prospective study. *Journal of Science and Medicine in Sport*, 2, 117–24.

Garrick, J. G., & Requa, R. K. (1978). Injuries in high school sports. *Pediatrics*, 61, 465–73.

Hanson, S. J., McCullagh, P., & Tonymon, P. (1992). The relationship of personality characteristics, life stress, and coping resources to athletic injury. *Journal of Sport & Exercise Psychology*, 14, 262–72.

Hardy, C. J., & Crace, R. K. (1990, May–June). Dealing with injury. *Sport Psychology Training Bulletin*, 1, 1–8.

Hardy, C. J., O'Connor, K. A., & Geisler, P. R. (1990). The role of gender and social support in the life stress injury relationship. *Proceedings of the Association for the Advancement of Applied Sport Psychology, Fifth Annual Conference (Abstract)*, 51.

Hardy, C. J., Prentice, W. E., Kirsanoff, M. T., Richman, J. M., & Rosenfeld, L. B. (1987, June). Life stress, social support, and athletic injury: In search of relationships. In J. M. Williams (Chair), *Psychological factors in injury occurrence*. Symposium conducted at the annual meeting of the North American Society for the Psychology of Sport and Physical Activity, Vancouver, BC.

Hedges, L. (1987). The meta-analysis of test validity studies: Some new approaches. In H. Braun & H. Wainer (eds.), *Test validity for the 1990s and beyond* (pp. 191–212). Hillsdale, NJ: Erlbaum.

Holmes, T. H. (1970). Psychological screening. In *Football injuries: Papers presented at a workshop* (pp. 211–14). Sponsored by Sub-committee on Athletic Injuries, Committee on the Skeletal System, Division of Medical Sciences, National Research Council, February 1969. Washington, DC: National Academy of Sciences.

Holmes, T. H., & Rahe, R. J. (1967). The *Social Readjustment Scale. Journal of Psychosomatic Research*, 11, 213–18.

Irvin, R. F. (1975). Relationship between personality and the incidence of injuries to high school football participants. *Dissertation Abstracts International*, 36, 4328-A.

Jackson, D. W., Jarrett, H., Bailey, D., Kausek, J., Swanson, M. J., & Powell, J. W. (1978). Injury prediction in the young athlete: A preliminary report. *The American Journal of Sports Medicine*, 6, 6–12.

Johnson, U., Ekengren, J., & Andersen, M. B. (2005). Injury prevention in Sweden: Helping soccer players at risk. *Journal of Sport & Exercise Psychology*, 27, 32–8.

Kerr, G., & Goss, J. (1996). The effects of a stress management program on injuries and stress levels. *Journal of Applied Sport Psychology*, 8, 109–17.

Lavallee, L., & Flint, F. (1996). The relationship of stress, competitive anxiety, mood state, and social support to athletic injury. *Journal of Athletic Training*, 31, 296–99.

Lazarus, R. S., & Folkman, S. (1984). *Stress, appraisal, and coping*. New York: Springer.

Lysens, R., van den Auweele, Y., & Ostyn, M. (1986). The relationship between psychosocial factors and sports injuries. *Journal of Sports Medicine and Physical Fitness*, 26, 77–84.

Maddison, R., & Prapavessis, H. (2005). A psychological approach to the prediction and prevention of athletic injury. *Journal of Sport & Exercise Psychology*, 27, 289–310.

May, J. R., & Brown, L. (1989). Delivery of psychological services to the U.S. alpine ski team prior to and during the Olympics in Calgary. *The Sport Psychologist*, 3, 320–29.

Meeuwisse, W. H., & Fowler, P. J. (1988). Frequency and predictability of sports injuries in inter-collegiate athletes. *Canadian Journal of Sport Sciences*, 13, 35–42.

Meyer, K. N. (1995). *The influence of personality factors, life stress, and coping strategies on the incidence of injury in long-distance runners*. Unpublished masters thesis, University of Colorado, Boulder.

National Collegiate Athletic Association (1992). *1991–1992 Women's volleyball injury surveillance system*. Overland Park, KS: NCAA.

Noh, Y. E., Morris, T., & Andersen, M. B. (2005). Psychosocial factors and ballet injuries. *International Journal of Sport & Exercise Psychology*, 3, 79–90.

Passer, M. W., & Seese, M. D. (1983). Life stress and athletic injury: Examination of positive versus negative events and three moderator variables. *Journal of Human Stress*, 9, 11–16.

Patterson, E. L., Smith, R. E., & Everett, J. J. (1998). Psychosocial factors as predictors of ballet injuries: Interactive effects of life stress and social support. *Journal of Sport Behavior*, 21, 101–12.

Perna, F. M., Antoni, M. H., Baum, A., Gordon, P., & Schneiderman, N. (2003). Cognitive behavioral stress management effects on injury and illness among competitive athletes: A randomized clinical trial. *Annals of Behavioral Medicine*, 25, 66–73.

Petrie, T. A. (1992). Psychosocial antecedents of athletic injury: The effects of life stress and social support on female collegiate gymnasts. *Behavioral Medicine*, 18, 127–38.

Petrie, T. A. (1993). Coping skills, competitive trait anxiety, and playing status: Moderating effects of the life stress-injury relationship. *Journal of Sport & Exercise Psychology*, 15, 261–74.

Petrie, T. A., & Perna, F. (2004). Psychology of injury: Theory, research and practice. In T. Morris & J. Summers (eds.), *Sport psychology: Theory, application and issues* (2nd ed., pp. 547–71). Milton, Australia: Wiley.

Requa, R. (1991, April). The scope of the problem: The impact of sports-related injuries. *Proceedings from the Conference on Sport Injuries in Youth: Surveillance Strategies*. Bethesda, MD: National Advisory Board for Arthritis and Musculoskeletal and Skin Diseases, National Institute of Arthritis and Musculoskeletal and Skin Diseases, and Centers for Disease Control.

Rider, S. P., & Hicks, R. A. (1995). Stress, coping, and injuries in male and female high school basketball players. *Perceptual and Motor Skills*, 81, 499–503.

Sarason, I. G., Levine, H. M., Basham, R. B., & Sarason, B. R. (1983). Assessing social support: The *Social Support Questionnaire*. *Journal of Personality and Social Psychology*, 44, 127–39.

Sarason, I. G., Sarason, B. R., & Johnson, J. H. (1985). Stressful life events: Measurement, moderators, and adaptation. In S. R. Burchfield (ed.), *Stress: Psychological and physiological interactions* (pp. 241–61). Washington, DC: Hemisphere.

Schroeder, D. H., & Costa, P. H. (1984). Influence of life event stress on physical illness: Substantive effects or methodological flaws? *Journal of Personality and Social Psychology*, 46, 853–63.

Smith, R. E., Smoll, F. L., & Schutz. R. (1988). *The Athletic Coping Skills Inventory: Psychometric properties, correlates, and confirmatory factor analysis*. Unpublished manuscript, University of Washington.

Thoits, P. (1983). Dimensions of life events that influence psychological distress: An evaluation and synthesis of the literature. In H. B. Kaplan (ed.), *Psychosocial stress: Trends in theory and research* (pp. 33–103). New York: Academic Press.

Valliant, P. M. (1981). Personality and injury in competitive runners. *Perceptual and Motor Skills*, 53, 251–3.

Van Mechelen, W., Twisk, J., Molendijk, A., Blom, B., Snel, J., & Kemper, H. C. G. (1996). Subject-related risk factors for sports injuries: A 1-yr prospective study in young adults. *Medicine and Science in Sports and Exercise*, 28, 1171–9.

Vinokur, A., & Selzer, M. L. (1975). Desirable versus undesirable life events: Their relationship to stress and mental distress. *Journal of Personality and Social Psychology*, 32, 329–37.

Williams, J. M., & Andersen, M. B. (1998). Psychosocial antecedents of sport injury: Review and critique of the stress and injury model. *Journal of Applied Sport Psychology*, 10, 5–25.

Williams, J. M., & Andersen, M. B. (2007). Psychosocial antecedents of sport injury and interventions for risk reduction. In G. Tenenbaum & R. Eklund (eds.), *Handbook of research in sport psychology* (3rd ed., pp. 379–403). Hoboken, NJ: John Wiley & Sons.

Williams, J. M., Haggert, J., Tonymon, P., & Wadsworth, W. A. (1986). Life stress and prediction of athletic injuries in volleyball, basketball, and cross-country running. In L. E. Unestahl (ed.), *Sport psychology in theory and practice*. Orebro, Sweden: Veje.

Williams, J. M., Tonymon, P., & Wadsworth, W. A. (1986). Relation of stress to injury in inter-collegiate volleyball. *Journal of Human Stress*, 12, 38–43.

# 21

## Burnout

Gould, D., Udry, E., Tuffey, S., & Loehr, J. (1996b). Burnout in competitive junior tennis players: II. Qualitative analysis. *The Sport Psychologist*, 10, 341–66.

**Written in collaboration with Kate Goodger**

### Background and context

Although originally identified in the work setting as *staff burnout* (Freudenberger, 1974) this metaphor has found significant resonance within the sport community where it is now considered a colloquialism. Anecdotal accounts, together with significant media attention, have created a recognizable image of the burned out athlete as young protégé, or former sporting legend, who has fallen from greatness as a result of this process of exhaustion.

The academic exploration of burnout in sport by researchers in the field of sport psychology first began with an examination of burnout in coaches by Caccese and Mayerberg (1984). Studies since have extended the target group to include athletic directors (e.g., Martin, Kelley, & Dias, 1999), officials (e.g., Taylor, Daniel, Leith, & Burke, 1990), and athletes (e.g., Raedeke, 1997). Cohn (1990) and Silva (1990) published the first investigations of burnout in athletes. Cohn conducted a qualitative study that explored the sources of stress and athlete burnout in high school golfers, whereas Silva examined burnout in relation to physical training. Resultant findings from Silva's study led to the advancement of the *Negative Training Stress Response Model* which proposes that physical training generates both physical and psychological stresses that may have a positive or negative impact upon an athlete. Positive adaptations to training result in positive training effects such as improved strength or speed, but negative adaptations lead progressively to staleness, overtraining, and finally, burnout.

Silva's model was not the first theoretical explanation of athlete burnout. Smith (1986) originally extended the notion of burnout to athlete populations through his *Cognitive-Affective Stress Model*. The model explains burnout through a four-stage stress process. In the first stage demands are placed on the athlete such as a grueling competition schedule. At the second stage the athlete appraises these demands and their ability to cope with them. Appraisal of the demands as threatening results in a physiological response at the third stage (e.g., fatigue) which in turn leads to a coping and task behavior such as reduced performance or withdrawal from the activity, in the final stage. The relationship between the stages is described as reciprocal and overall cyclical, with the coping and task behavior feeding back into the demands at Stage 1, and personality and motivational factors (e.g., self esteem) are proposed to have an overriding influence on the burnout (stress) process. In addition to his model, Smith – in the same article – is also heralded as offering a definition of burnout that historically has become one of the most frequently cited. He describes burnout as "a psychological, emotional and at times physical withdrawal from a formerly pursued and enjoyable activity in response to excessive stress or dissatisfaction" (Smith, 1986: 39).

Shortly after the work of Silva (1990), two other theoretical explanations were published which, alongside Smith (1986) and Silva, comprise *traditional* theories of athlete burnout. In 1991, Schmidt and Stein proposed a commitment perspective through which the burnout athlete was identifiable by an entrapment-based profile. A year later, Coakley (1992) offered a sociological explanation for athlete burnout through the *Unidimensional Identity Development and External Control Model.* Coakley proposes that the athletic experiences of young athletes result in identity "foreclosure" where the development of their identity is limited to the athletic sphere of their life. In addition, they experience a loss of autonomy over their life and decisions they make. These latter perspectives of athlete burnout are considered to be non-stress-induced burnout perspectives, as stress is not the principal cause but rather may be a symptom. Until the advent of such work, the literature had been dominated by a stress-induced perspective of burnout. It was this previous research that set the stage for the key study in this chapter.

## Key study

The key study by Gould, Udry, Tuffey, and Loehr was the second in a series of three published articles from the original research program commissioned by the Sport Science Division of the United States Tennis Association. The study represented one of the first empirical investigations of athlete burnout, and remains one of the most in-depth explorations within the existent literature. Arising from considerable debate at the time concerning the competitive pressures being placed upon junior tennis players, and the consequences of such pressure, the purpose of the study was to identify and describe in psychological terms junior players who had experienced burnout, in contrast to equivalent players who had not experienced burnout. In so doing, the authors intended to learn more about the burnout experience from those who had actually lived with it. The intent was also to gather information to inform future preventative and management strategies.

The study was divided into two phases of investigation. Phase one consisted of the completion of a battery of psychological and social psychological inventories, the results of which were contrasted across the comparative samples in the first article (Gould, Udry, Tuffey, & Loehr, 1996a). In addition, a sub-sample ($n = 10$) of burned-out players were selected from the findings of phase one to participate in in-depth interviews during the second phase of the study. This part of the research comprised the key study presented in this chapter. It reports physical and mental characteristics of burnout, recommendations for preventing burnout and an examination of three existing models of athlete burnout. The key study also promoted the novel suggestion of the existence of different types or strains of burnout. The final article in the series (Gould, Tuffey, Udry, & Loehr, 1997) presented three case studies of the experiences of individual burnout players.

## Method

### Participants

The participants were 10 junior elite tennis players who reported the highest levels of burnout and perfectionism in the initial, larger study (Gould et al., 1996a) and who agreed to participate in this part of the study. The sample consisted of six females and four males who ranged in age from 12 to 23 at the time of the interview. Of these 10 participants, seven had burned out of tennis and were no longer playing while three had burned out, but were again playing.

## Interview Guide

Based on an integrated working model of burnout derived by the authors of the scientific and practical sport psychology literature, an interview guide was developed with questions related to: situational demands and resources; signs and symptoms or characteristics of withdrawal; response/behavior to burnout symptoms; cognitive appraisal; training loads; involvement of significant others; social relationships; and advice for others. The interview guide was pilot-tested on several individuals and minor changes were made before it was used in the present investigation.

## Procedures

Participants were contacted by phone, informed of the nature of the investigation, and asked to participate. The investigator emphasized at this time that all information would be kept confidential. All interviews were conducted by phone (50–90 minutes long) and with the same investigator who was trained extensively in qualitative research methodology as outlined by Patton (1990) and Lincoln and Guba (1985). Special emphasis was placed on qualitative interviewing techniques – types of questions to ask, the wording of questions, rapport, and neutrality (Patton, 1990: 277–368) and Lincoln and Guba's work on implementing naturalistic inquiry and establishing trustworthiness. A pilot interview was conducted, tape recorded, and analyzed by three of the members of the investigative team with the interviewer given feedback and constructive criticism. The interviewer was a 26-year-old female with an extensive athletic background including time spent playing competitive junior tennis.

Because of its negative connotation in the tennis community, a concerted effort was made to use terms such as "withdrawal," "motivation problems," and "tennis difficulties," instead of the term "burnout." Each participant responded to an identical sequence of questions from the interview guide, with probing questions asked as needed. The probes were determined a priori in an attempt to minimize interviewer bias by ensuring that all follow-up questions were similar, thus facilitating comparison across participants while still allowing for flexibility in individual responses. All interviews were tape recorded and later transcribed verbatim.

## Data Analysis Procedures

Hierarchical content analysis, as recommended by Patton (1990), was used in this investigation. Specifically, the following six-step data analysis procedure was used:

1   All 10 tape-recorded interviews were transcribed verbatim resulting in 214 pages of single-spaced text.
2   Three of the four members of the investigative team, each of whom had a background in qualitative research methodology, read and reread all 10 transcripts to become very familiar with each participant. The investigators also listened to each taped interview to gain additional insight that the printed word cannot provide, such as tone of voice, pauses, and the use of sarcasm.
3   Idiographic profiles of two- to three-page written summaries of each participant's interview were independently developed by the three investigators. Each profile was then discussed

extensively by the three investigators until consensus was reached and a single profile developed.

4   In addition to the idiographic profiles, each investigator independently identified raw-data themes that characterized each participant's responses within each section of the interview. Raw-data themes are described as quotes or paraphrased quotes that capture a distinct idea or concept provided by the athlete. After each investigator had independently identified raw-data themes for a given participant, they met to discuss the identified themes and came to triangular consensus. Triangular consensus had to be reached for each raw-data theme to be used in analysis. This validation process resulted in a list of agreed upon data themes from all 10 participants for each section of the interview. To facilitate further analysis of these themes, each raw-data theme was written on a separate $3 \times 5$ notecard.

5   Using the raw-data themes developed in Step 4, an inductive analysis was conducted to identify common themes or patterns of greater generality. Higher level themes were labeled "First-Order Themes," "Second-Order Themes," and "Third-Order Themes," in order of increasing generality. The highest level, therefore, represents common themes of the greatest generality, meaning that no links emerged between these themes. As with the idiographic profiles and raw-data theme generation, triangular consensus had to be reached on all identified higher order themes.

6   Lastly, after all higher order themes had been identified, the investigators reviewed the emergent patterns to ensure the descriptors made intuitive sense and could be easily understood. Again, consensus had to be reached.

## Results

The interviews were analyzed using idiographic profile and hierarchical content analysis methods. Based on the preplanned structure of the interview and a review of information provided by the participants, distinct categories of responses emerged that were used to organize and analyze the data. These categories were labeled: Signs and symptoms (characteristics) of tennis burnout; How burnout feelings were dealt with; Factors leading to burnout; Preventing tennis burnout; Involvement of significant others; Advice to others; and Other findings.

Because of space limitations, only results pertaining to signs and symptoms or characteristics of burnout, factors leading to burnout, and advice for preventing burnout, and selected other findings were discussed in the article. Results of inductive-data analysis procedures summed over all 10 participants are described and explained separately for reach of these categories. These findings are presented first. Quotes from participants are weaved throughout the results in order to highlight particular themes. Next, results are presented from an analysis that involved examining the idiographic profiles of the 10 participants relative to the major tenants of existing burnout models. Based on this analysis, the degree of support for the varying theoretical models will be shown.

### Content Analysis

*Characteristics of Tennis Burnout.* During the interview, it was explained to the participants that each athlete who withdraws from tennis experiences unique feelings leading up to his or her withdrawal. The focus of this category of questions, therefore, was on identifying and understanding the specific signs and symptoms (characteristics) experienced by each of the athletes. Each participant was asked to describe the feelings he or she experienced in the six months prior to leaving tennis. Specifically, participants were asked to recall the physical and mental signs and symptoms they manifested. Elaboration probes involved the investigator identifying some common characteristics, such as fatigue and lack of motivation, to stimulate the athlete's memory. In the content analysis of this data, raw-data themes addressing burnout symptoms emerged into two separate areas – "mental" and "physical" characteristics.

*Mental Characteristics.* Thirty-six raw-data themes were identified by 10 participants. The raw-data themes emerged into nine first-order themes and six general dimensions (see Figure 21.1). These six dimensions represented mental symptoms or characteristics related to staying motivated, low motivation-energy, negative feelings and affect, feelings of isolation, concentration problems, and experiencing highs and lows.

A general "lack of motivation" was a powerful theme mentioned by six of the 10 participants within the motivation dimension. The following quote captures this theme:

> "I think I was pretty burned out. I just never wanted to practice anymore and, I don't know, it just wasn't there for me. So, I think I was just burned out. I think I felt like I don't want to do this anymore and it is just wasting my life. I didn't want to be there so I didn't feel like trying."

| Raw-data theme | 1st Order | General dimension |
|---|---|---|
| No loss of desire to play/compete<br>Still motivated to play | Stayed motivated | STAYED MOTIVATED |
| Lack of motivation ($N = 6$) | Lack of motivation | LOW MOTIVATION/ENERGY |
| Mentally & emotionally drained<br>No mental energy | Low emotional energy | |
| Aggressiveness<br>Frustrated ($N = 5$)<br>Moody/irritable ($N = 5$)<br>Bad attitude toward tennis<br>Depressed<br>Started getting nervous<br>No confidence | Negative feelings/affect | NEGATIVE FEELINGS/AFFECT |
| Felt alone on court<br>Embarrassed & ashamed<br>Kept things inside<br>Not as outgoing | Feelings of isolation | FEELINGS OF ISOLATION |
| Inability to concentrate out of tennis | Inability to concentrate out of tennis | CONCENTRATION PROBLEMS |
| Wasn't there<br>Dropped gradually out of game mentally | Poor tennis concentration | |
| Inappropriate ranking locus ($N = 2$) | Inappropriate ranking focus | |
| Highs and lows | Highs and lows | HIGHS AND LOWS |

**Figure 21.1** Mental symptoms of burnout hierarchical analysis results

Conversely, it is interesting to note that two of the athletes mentioned still being motivated to compete, but not necessarily to practice; the opposite of what is generally assumed to be true regarding burnout. This seems to confirm the notion that burnout is experienced differently by different individuals.

Within the negative feelings and affect dimension, a number of participants indicated they felt frustrated ($n = 5$) and moody/irritable ($n = 5$) during this time. Others discussed nervousness and no confidence as negative feelings they believed to be symptomatic of burnout. One participant noted depression as a salient symptom:

> "I went through depression. I mean, I started, um, as far as being depressed . . . that was all I started thinking about. It was taking away from my school work. I mean I was kind of falling apart in a way."

Another recurring theme was labeled "concentration problems" and was reflected in such statements as "I felt zoney" and "I wasn't there mentally." The participants often had a difficult time expressing how they felt in this regard: it seemed that they intuitively knew something was wrong, yet it was evident from listening to the interviews that words often could not capture their experiences:

> "I had no mental game. Like, you know, you are supposed to go out on the tennis court and supposed to be confident and you're supposed to think that you are going to win, but I was just mentally gone, like I had no energy, I had nothing to give it seemed like."

The "feelings of isolation" general dimension emerged from four raw-data themes, such as feeling alone on court and keeping things inside. Lastly, the "highs and lows" general dimension was a unique theme dealing with an athlete's feeling of experiencing sporadic days with tennis.

*Physical Symptoms.* Twenty-three raw-data themes related to the physical symptoms or characteristic category of questions were identified by all 10 participants (See Figure 21.2).

| Raw-data theme | 1st Order | General dimension |
|---|---|---|
| Knees and ankles hurt<br>Minor injuries<br>Weird Injuries | Injuries | PHYSICALLY SYMPTOMATIC |
| Illness from pressure ($N = 2$) | Illness | |
| Low energy ($N = 2$)<br>Fatigue<br>Tired all the time | Lack of energy<br>Negative feelings/affect | |
| No physical symptoms | No physical symptoms | PHYSICALLY ASYMPTOMATIC |
| Not fatigued<br>No low energy | No lack of energy | |
| Not sick ($N=4$)<br>No injuries ($N = 6$) | Not sick | |

**Figure 21.2** Physical symptoms or burnout hierarchical analysis results

Because one of the probes asked participants if they experienced physical symptoms, such as injury or illness, 14 of these themes related to the athletes reporting not experiencing a particular symptom.

These themes, therefore, emerged into two dimensions – physical symptoms or characteristics and lack of physical symptoms or characteristics. The most often mentioned physical symptom ($n = 4$) related to a lack of energy:

> "Looking back now, I felt that it was just overtraining and wanting to do too much all the time, you know, just sort of sapped all my energy and there was, you know, nothing left . . . I was overtraining, I know that for a fact, and I was just not getting enough sleep and trying to do too much – I had to be #1 in my section."

A salient physical symptom experienced by one participant was getting physically ill before matches. In fact, this characteristic was noted by the athlete to have greatly influenced her decision to quit tennis:

> "Like, you know, I used to get sick a lot. I think a lot of it had to do with the pressure because I couldn't handle stress very well and that is when I would get sick."

In comparison to the mental characteristics, physical characteristics did not appear to be prominent characteristics of burnout in these junior tennis players. Only nine raw-data themes were identified that related to being injured, ill, or lacking energy, whereas 18 raw-data themes made up the physically asymptotic category. Three athletes noted being injured prior to withdrawing from tennis, but these were reported as relatively minor. However, for some of the athletes who noted physical symptoms, these negative symptoms had a profound effect on their tennis experience.

*Factors Leading to Burnout*. The process of burnout is thought to occur as a result of a plethora of individual characteristics and situational factors. In interviewing these 10 participants, the aim was first to understand the manifestation of burnout in each individual, then to analyze across individuals for consistencies and commonalties. Specifically, athletes were asked to identify and discuss factors or incidents they felt influenced their decision to withdraw from tennis. As this was a primary focus of the investigation, participants were urged to identify *all* factors, with predetermined probes asked to stimulate their thinking.

A total of 83 raw-data themes were identified by all 10 participants as factors affecting withdrawal from tennis. Inductive data analysis revealed four fourth-order themes or general dimensions: five athletes identified 10 raw-data themes that resulted in a "physical concerns" dimension; eight participants identified 11 raw-data themes related to "logistical concerns"; nine athletes identified 20 raw-data themes that comprised a "social/interpersonal concerns" dimension; and 10 participants identified 42 raw-data themes that represented a "psychological factors" dimension (see Figure 21.3).

*Physical Concerns Dimension*. The physical concerns dimension encompassed the higher order themes of physical problems and poor play. The physical problems higher order dimension included data themes such as injury, illness, and physical fatigue. A lack of physical energy as a contributor to burnout is exemplified in the following quote:

> "You know, looking back, I feel now that is was just overtraining and wanting to do too much all the time, you know, just sort of sapped all my energy and there was, you know, nothing left."

| Raw-data theme | 1st Order | 2nd Order | 3rd Order | General dimension |
|---|---|---|---|---|
| Problem with eating<br>Being sick wasn't fun<br>Lack of physical development<br>Injury<br>Overtrained<br>Way too tired all the time | Physical problems | Physical problems | Physical problems | PHYSICAL CONCERNS |
| Getting beat by people I used to beat<br>Wasn't winning<br>Not satisfied with play<br>Erratic nature of play | Poor play | Poor play | Poor play | |
| Tennis plus academics took too much time<br>Gave up all time for tennis | Time demands of tennis | Time demands of tennis | Time demands of tennis | LOGISTICAL CONCERNS |
| Tennis overwhelmed life (N = 2) | | | | |
| Sole tennis focus<br>Conflicting interests | | | | |
| Didn't like travel | Travel concerns | Travel concerns | Travel concerns | |
| Never home because of travel | | | | |
| Travel<br>Travel grind | | | | |
| Adjusting to school | Adjusting to school | Adjusting to school | Adjusting to school | |
| No social life (N = 2)<br>Wanted to be with friends (N = 3)<br>No one to relate to | Dissatisfaction with social life | Dissatisfaction with social life | Dissatisfaction with social life | SOCIAL/ INTERPERSONAL CONCERNS |
| Parents down on me | Negative parental influence | Negative parental influence | Negative parental influence | |
| Father gave me negative personal evaluation | | | | |
| Never got a chance to breathe – suffocated by dad<br>Compete for parent attention with brother | | | | |
| Tennis people really mean<br>Sick of people involved (N = 2)<br>Monotony of playing same people (N = 2) | Dissatisfaction with those involved | Dissatisfaction with those involved | Dissatisfaction with those involved | |

**Figure 21.3** Factors loading to burnout hierarchical analysis results

| Raw-data theme | 1st Order | 2nd Order | 3rd Order | General dimension |
|---|---|---|---|---|
| Cheating by competitors<br>No friends<br>Negative team atmosphere<br>Coach not helpful<br>Family problems | | | | |
| Emphasis on ranking | Outcome goals | Unfulfilled/ inappropriate expectations | Unfulfilled/ inappropriate expectations | PSYCHOLOGICAL CONCERNS |
| Going pro emphasis | | | | |
| Goals screwed up | Expectations too high | | | |
| Talent expectations | | | | |
| Realized not going to be pro (N = 2) | Realized going pro unlikely | | | |
| Limited long-term opportunities | | | | |
| Did not get better | Lack of improvement/ talent | | | |
| Not talented enough | | | | |
| Scholarship pressure<br>Pressure to satisfy others<br>Grade pressure | Other pressure sources | Pressure | Lack of enjoyment | |
| Coach pressure to practice & win<br>Pressure from coach to have a winning attitude | Coach pressure | | | |
| Self-pressure to win (N = 3)<br>Self-pressure to play well (N = 2)<br>Self pressure | Self-pressure | | | |
| Parental pressure to practice | Parental pressure | | | |
| Parental pressure from critiques<br>Uncertainty of parental support<br>Pressure from parents' expectations | | | | |
| Too competitive (N = 3) | Too competitive | | | |
| No fun (N = 4)<br>Boring drills/got repetitive | No fun | No fun | | |

**Figure 21.3**—*continued*

| Raw-data theme | 1st Order | 2nd Order | 3rd Order | General dimension |
|---|---|---|---|---|
| Sick of tennis | Lack of motivation | Lack of motivation | Motivational concerns | |
| Interest in basketball<br>Having golf to fall back on | Other competitive interests | Wanted to pursue other Interests | | |
| Wanted to try other activities (*N* = 3)<br>Interested in trying to find something else<br>Had other options | Interest in developing other nonsport activities | | | |
| My character really wasn't competitive<br>Didn't like the way I acted on court<br>Self-esteem tied too much to tennis<br>Kept everything inside | Personality not conducive to competitive tennis | Personality not conducive to competitive tennis | Personality not conducive to competitive tennis | |

**Figure 21.3**—*continued*

The other higher order theme, comprising the physical concerns dimension, was poor play. Athletes identified items, such as not winning and erratic play, as factors influencing their burnout of tennis. One athlete discussed the frustration of getting beat as affecting his decision to withdraw:

"I think if I had been winning constantly – you know when I was 15 I was beating everybody – I would have stuck with it. I think winning was a part of it [reason for quitting]. And I was getting beat by people that I just used to have no problem with . . . they were beating me, you know, and I think that got to me a lot."

*Logistical Concerns Dimension.* Eight athletes identified factors related to "logistical concerns" as affecting the process of burnout. This general dimension consisted of three lower order dimensions: time demands of tennis, travel concerns, and adjusting to school.

The time demands of tennis, which often infringed on participation in other activities, was a powerful factor influencing burnout in five of the athletes. The following quote reflects this dimension:

"It's not the fact that you have to go somewhere, it is the fact of how often you have to do it, and sometimes like the timing is very bad and you have to make decisions about if you want to stay in town and do something, you know, that would be fun as opposed to going to a tournament and playing tennis . . . There is so much else going on that it almost seems like a waste of time to be playing tennis when there is so much else to do.

Traveling concerns were noted by four athletes that included raw-data themes related to not liking the "grind" of traveling as well as dissatisfaction with being away from home all the time. Lastly, one participant mentioned adjusting to school as a logistical concern affecting the process of burnout.

*Social/Interpersonal Concerns Dimension.* The social/interpersonal concerns dimension was comprised of 20 raw-data themes from nine participants. Three second-order themes emerged from the data: dissatisfaction with social life, negative parental influence, and dissatisfaction with those involved.

Six athletes mentioned dissatisfaction with their social life as a salient factor affecting burnout and influencing their decision to withdraw from tennis. Several individuals identified not having a social life and wanting to be with friends as salient factors:

"I think I wanted more of a social life, you know, getting to do stuff with some of my friends . . . Well, it [social life] kind of lacked the whole time I played tennis."

The perception of negative parental influence, such as over control, negative evaluation, and expectations regarding performance, also played a role in tennis burnout. One such theme is reflected in the following quote:

"He [my father] always kind of considered me kind of a weakling . . . I think he always considered me a failure. I had a father who was, you know, a typical tennis parent. I didn't even know if I liked tennis, um, but my dad really pressured me a lot, you know, to keep on training and I didn't know what for. I was just kind of suffocating."

Ten raw-data themes were identified that related to dissatisfaction with others involved in the tennis environment. These "others" included an array of tennis people, mean or cheating competitors, and other opponents often played against in tournaments. One participant talked in detail about this dissatisfaction:

"I think it's really hard to be a tennis player because it's such an individual sport and people can be really mean, especially in my age group and when I played up, there's some really mean, mean people. I think I was just sick of dealing with it, I mean it wasn't fun for me anymore . . . Like on the line calls and they were just known for accusing you of cheating and just stupid things like that, and like parents would get so involved in it, like they would be yelling at their kids and doing all these things, and it was just like I just got sick of it.

*Psychological Factors Dimension.* By far, the largest dimension comprising factors affecting tennis burnout in these participants were raw-data themes related to psychological factors. These 42 raw-data themes mentioned by all 10 participants coalesced into four third-order higher order themes: unfilled/inappropriate expectations, lack of enjoyment, motivation concerns, and personality characteristics not conducive to tennis. Each is discussed in detail below.

*Unfilled/Inappropriate Expectations.* This higher order theme contained data themes related to a focus on outcome goals, high expectations, the realization a professional career was unlikely, and perceptions of a lack of improvement or talent. Three participants mentioned the realization that a tennis career was improbable as influencing their burnout; one stated the following:

"But as far as what I was going through, struggling to make it on the pro tour and doing whatever, and I was definitely giving it my all . . . I mean I have friends that aren't even in the top 2000 in the world and they're trying to make it into the pro tour. I mean, it just seems like almost a waste for me to struggle like that and for me to spend so much money, so thank God for golf."

Relatedly, an emphasis on tennis ranking and high expectations were bothersome to one individual:

"My goals got out of focus and it got to where I . . . when you get to where you can't attain a goal, it's like you just feel like quitting. Sometimes your goals get out of whack. I didn't have a good goal structure. I had like a long-term goal and nothing else. I had a long-term goal. Everything was long-term, I didn't have enough immediate things . . . My biggest goal was to play professional tennis at a high level and I just realized that just wasn't going to happen."

*Lack of Enjoyment.* A theme salient to all 10 participants related to the perception of pressure and lack of fun. The following quote capture the pressure participants felt from themselves and others:

"It was the pressure that I was putting on myself. It was the pressure that my coach was putting on me to, I mean not a lot, but she was pressuring me a little bit. Um, the pressure from my parents that came not as much as it had in the past but it was still there. It wasn't fun anymore, it was more like a job and tennis was, I guess, my means of evaluating myself sort of. My self-esteem completely depended on how I did in tennis."

In addition to pressure, the lack of enjoyment dimension also encompassed themes related to the participant's perception that tennis just wasn't fun anymore:

"I stopped having fun with it and I don't really know the reason why, but I just did, and for me like once I stopped being completely committed to it, it was really hard for me to just go back and play for fun . . . Like I wish I wouldn't have made such a big deal out of it, 'cause I mean it's just a sport and it should be for fun. If you're not having fun with it, I would just say don't do it because, I mean, the reason I wanted to play a sport is to make friends and have a good time and be competitive and stuff."

Conversely, it should be noted that a lack of fun was not experienced by all the athletes, although that is often assumed to be a primary characteristic of burnout. One individual who quit tennis and took up competitive golf noted:

"Even at the end, I really enjoyed the competition. Even when I'd lose and I would be really angry, later on I'd look at it and know that I enjoyed it. I would have rather been there than any place else, I think."

*Motivation Concerns.* A lack of motivation and wanting to pursue other activities were factors affecting burnout in several participants. For some of these athletes, other competitive sports were attractive – primarily because they were more talented in these other sports or felt less pressure and had more fun in a team as opposed to individual sport. Additionally, some individuals were interested in just trying other activities:

"I had kind of an interest in trying to find something else. Maybe there is something else to do besides be on the tennis court all day. You know, try to get a little interested in something else for a change. That was a big part of it. A desire to get away from it and try to see what is on the other side of what it's like to be a person that just goes to school."

*Personality Characteristics.* Three participants identified personality characteristics that were not conducive to tennis as impacting their burnout. This dimension included data themes of having a noncompetitive character, acting out on court, perception of self tied to tennis, and a tendency to keep feelings to self.

## Advice for Others

One of the major purposes of this study was to develop a better understanding of burnout in an effort to help prevent other tennis players from experiencing similar problems. To aid in accomplishing this objective, participants were asked if they had any advice to give to other athletes to help them deal with some of the stresses of competitive tennis. Additionally, they were asked if they had any advice or suggestions to give to coaches and parents of elite junior tennis players. Data obtained from this line of question was rich in information and extremely helpful. The athletes were able to assess their experiences and identify how athletes, coaches, and parents can change or modify their behavior to prevent similar burnout experiences.

*Advice for Other Players.* Nine athletes cited at least one of the 24 raw-data themes regarding advice for competitive tennis players dealing with similar stresses. The raw-data themes emerged into seven general dimensions that focused on "playing for own reasons," "balancing tennis with other things," "if not fun, don't play," "making it fun," "relaxing," "taking time off," and an "other" dimension (see Figure 21.4).

*Advice for Parents.* Seven participants offered advice to parents on how to better interact with their tennis-playing children in an effort to prevent burnout. Twenty raw-data themes were identified that emerged into six higher order themes, plus a category containing three unique raw-data themes labeled other (see Figure 21.5). The six themes were labeled: "recognize optimal push," "lessen involvement," "reduce importance," "provide support and empathy," "separate parent-coach roles," and "solicit player input."

One higher order theme discussed by four of the participants was a suggestion to "recognize and provide an optimal amount of pushing." This theme also was mentioned in data related to positive parental influence. The following quote reflects this notion of a positive push:

"I think that there is a real fine line that parents have between pushing for what is best for the kid and pushing more for themselves. Or not even so much that, but pushing for performance or the overall mental health or growth of their child or whatever."

The suggestion for parents to "lessen involvement" also was mentioned by four participants. These athletes suggested that parents "back off" and "mellow out" in terms of the involvement in their child's tennis. One athlete nicely summarized this suggestion:

"They might want to stay out of . . . from my point of view . . . kind of stay out of the competition a little bit more. You know, like staying on the sidelines and watching every tennis match and every point and everything. You know when you are playing and your parents are sitting right there, it is like you want to do good and everything."

| Raw-data theme | General dimension |
|---|---|
| Play for yourself<br>Do what you want to do<br>Remember why playing | PLAY FOR YOUR OWN REASONS |
| Concentrate on things other than tennis<br>Be flexible if tennis doesn't work out<br>Balance – learn to do other things<br>Don't specialize unless you have to | BALANCE TENNIS WITH OTHER THINGS |
| If it is not fun, don't do it (should be happy with what you are doing)<br>If not fun, don't play | NO FUN – NO PLAY |
| Keep tennis more recreational<br>Find a way to start enjoying game<br>Realize tennis is just a game – have fun<br>Don't make such a big deal out of it | TRY TO MAKE IT FUN |
| Relax and try to enjoy tennis<br>Learn to relax | RELAX |
| Take time off ($N = 3$)<br>Take a break | TAKE TIME OFF |
| Have a goal structure<br>Be as patient as you can<br>Leave things on court<br>Let people know how you feel<br>Make as many friends as you can<br>None | OTHER |

**Figure 21.4** Advice for other players hierarchical analysis results

Other higher order themes mentioned by two or more participants included "reducing the importance on outcome," "providing support and empathy," and "soliciting player input."

Worthy of mention is the suggestion by one athlete for parents to try to avoid being the coach. This athlete suggested if the parent must be the coach, then an effort should be made to separate the roles of coach and parent in interaction with the child. This particular athlete experienced many relationship difficulties with her father who also was her coach. There was no role clarification, so she felt as if she was always an athlete in her father's eyes and never a daughter.

*Advice for Coaches.* Seventeen raw-data themes were identified by nine participants regarding advice to coaches of junior elite tennis players. These themes coalesced into four general dimensions, plus an "others" category comprising four unique raw-data themes. As can be seen in Figure 21.6, the five general dimensions included: "personal involvement with player," "two-way communication with player," "utilize player input," "understand player feelings," and other.

Four athletes suggested that coaches have more "personal involvement with players." This theme is reflected in the following quote:

"Maybe to be more involved, with their players, I mean, to maybe know their players more better on and off the court. Like you really have to know your player's personality to know what their problems are or to help them."

| Raw-data theme | General dimension |
| --- | --- |
| Don't push too much<br>Fine line between pushing for performance and overall growth and mental development<br>Push positively but at appropriate time<br>Give limited push | RECOGNIZE OPTIMAL AMOUNT OF "PUSHING" NEEDED |
| Mellow out<br>Back off<br>Stay out of player competition more<br>Observe, be quiet | LESSEN INVOLVEMENT |
| Reduce importance<br>Don't place emphasis on win/loss | REDUCE IMPORTANCE OF OUTCOME |
| Be supportive ($N = 2$)<br>Relate to how kid feels | SHOW SUPPORT/EMPATHY |
| Avoid being coach<br>Separate roles of coach and parent | PARENT-COACH ROLE SEPARATION/CLARIFICATION |
| Ask and involve kids – don't just tell them<br>Talk to children | SOLICIT PLAYER INPUT |
| Do nontennis activities with kids<br>Think more about kid – not money and time<br>Allow kids to be kids<br>None | OTHER |

**Figure 21.5** Advice for parents hierarchical analysis results

| Raw-data theme | General dimension |
| --- | --- |
| Be there for things in and out of tennis<br>Have personal relationship with player<br>Go through it together<br>Be more involved | CULTIVATE PERSONAL INVOLVEMENT WITH PLAYER |
| Communicate better with players ($N = 3$)<br>Try to understand player's decision | HAVE TWO-WAY COMMUNICATION WITH PLAYER |
| Compromise<br>Let players decide more | UTILIZE PLAYER INPUT |
| Know players more<br>Find out how player feels<br>Help player understand feelings | UNDERSTAND PLAYER FEELINGS |
| Good personality and knowledge of motivation needed in coach<br>Coach at level right for you<br>Foster right atmosphere<br>Talk to parents if they're pressuring player<br>None | OTHER |

**Figure 21.6** Advice for coaches hierarchical analysis results

The need for better coach-athlete communication also was a powerful theme mentioned by four participants. One athlete stated this piece of advice as follows:

"I would say just communication and talk about it 'cause the more you talk about it the more, 'cause like, I didn't even understand the feelings I had, I still don't understand them, you know, and it really helps to just talk about it and maybe you can like reach an understanding, and then I think the player would feel better if they know their coach understood."

Other higher order themes included "utilizing player input" and trying to "understand player feelings."

Although the higher order themes are distinct dimensions, it is probably the case that implementation of one suggestion would cross over into other dimensions as well. For instance, if coach-athlete communication is enhanced, the coach will undoubtedly come to better understand the athlete's feelings and have more personal involvement with the individual.

## Other Findings

*Training Loads.* Burnout is often assumed to be caused by excessive training and competitive loads leading to overtraining and feelings of physical exhaustion. To address this assumption, the participants were asked to identify their training and competition schedule prior to burning out of tennis. An analysis of the data indicated few commonalties across athletes indicating burnout is not necessarily due to overtraining. For example, related to typical training loads, a range of six to 42 hours a week in training was evidenced by these athletes. Oddly enough, the athletes who spent six hours a week practicing indicated this amount of training was adequate while an athlete who put in 35 hours of practice felt it was not enough. Thus, training and overtraining should be evaluated relative to the individual.

The competitive schedule of these athletes varied as much as their training schedule. The athletes reported participating in as few as six to as many as 24 tournaments per year. Additionally, half of the athletes indicated they felt they participated in too many tournaments.

*Performance Effects.* The participants were asked if and how the burnout process affected their performance on court. Most participants experienced a decrease in performance or were dissatisfied with how they were playing. However, this was not always the case as one athlete continued to play well.

*Singles Versus Doubles.* Although not a direct suggestion by the athletes, a review of the information provided by the athletes regarding preference for doubles versus singles indicates this is an area where coaches can have an influence by altering competitive schedules. The majority of athletes indicated a preference for doubles because it is "funner," "less pressure," and "not as competitive."

*Idiographic Profiles.* In an effort to determine the utility of the three existing models (Coakley, 1992; Silva, 1990; Smith, 1986) used to explain burnout, after all other analyses were completed, the researchers examined each individual case or profile relative to each burnout model. For example, each case (idiographic profile) was discussed and examined in light of basic premises of Smith's cognitive-affective stress model of burnout (e.g., tennis formerly enjoyable, chronic stress evident, alternative activities involved), Silva's negative training adaptation view (e.g., overtrained physically, exhausted), and Coakley's unidimensional identity development and external control model (unidimensional identity, high-tennis identity, little control over decisions). Through discussion of each case, the researchers reached consensus relative to whether each model appeared to best reflect the opinions expressed in the individual case. This procedure did not allow for an adequate and detailed test of each model, but it allowed the researchers to determine how useful each model may be in explaining actual cases of burnout. This was deemed a very important step in light of the fact these models were developed in the absence of almost any athlete burnout data.

Table 21.1 contains a summary of this analysis. An inspection of the table reveals that some support was garnered for all three models of burnout. Smith's (1986) and Coakley's models, however, were found to explain the most cases, with Smith's model being slightly more powerful. It was also somewhat surprising that Silva's (1990) negative-training stress model did not explain more cases (only 30% were fully or partially explained and 70% not explained), given the notions of physical overtraining causing burnout in the popular tennis literature.

**Table 21.1** Burnout model idiographic profile explanatory analysis

| Model** | Fully explained | Partially explained | Not explained | Unclear |
|---|---|---|---|---|
| Smith (1986) | Loren* Tara Lee Kathy | Joan Katie Jan Tommy Drew Brian | — | — |
| (frequency, %) | (4, 40%) | (6, 60%) | (0, 0%) | (0, 0%) |
| Coakley (1992) | Jan Drew Brian | Loren Tara Katie Lee Kathy Tommy | — | Joan |
| (frequency, %) | (3, 30%) | (6, 60%) | (0, 0%) | (1, 10%) |
| Silva (1992) | Jan Tommy | Joan | Loren Tara Katie Lee Kathy Drew Brian | — |
| (frequency, %) | (2, 20%) | (1, 10%) | (7, 70%) | (0, 0%) |

* Names of the participants have been changed in these idiographic profiles for the purpose of protecting the identity of the participants

** Because the three models are not mutually exclusive, a participant can be classified as providing support for more than one model

## Discussion

An important finding gleaned from the content analysis portion of this phase of the investigation focused on the identification of characteristics or symptoms of burnout in junior tennis players. A number of varied symptoms were identified ranging from increased aggressiveness on and off the court to feelings of embarrassment and shame. The most frequently cited characteristics included: a lack of motivation; frustration; being moody and irritable; and physically lacking energy.

Unfortunately, the design of this investigation did not allow the researchers to reach any final conclusions relative to the causes of burnout in junior tennis. However, strong suggestive evidence was solicited. For these players, burnout seemed to result from an interaction of personal and situational factors, and not solely from some sort of personality weakness (e.g., not being mentally tough) or aversive environment (e.g., overzealous parents; excessive tournament schedule). In both studying and designing programs to prevent burnout in junior tennis players and other athletes, then, the complex interaction of personal and situational factors must be considered.

Although it is important to recognize that burnout is caused by the interaction of personal and situational factors, a surprising finding resulting from this investigation was how salient social psychological factors were in the burnout process. Table 21.2, for example, shows that all 10 participants cited psychological factors as leading to burnout and 52% of all raw-data themes emitted were classified as psychological in origin. This was surprising because, based on the review of the burnout literature, it was expected that physical overtraining, injury, and physical exhaustion would characterize almost all cases of athlete burnout. Some participants' burnout was certainly characterized by high physical demands, but the Phase 1 results revealed that, as a group, the burnouts did not engage in excessive training, practicing on average only 2.3 hours a day for 5.3 days a week (Gould et al., 1996a).

The importance of the social environment surrounding the young athlete must not be denied when studying burnout. The results of this study emphasized the importance of having friends and being with friends for maintaining motivation in junior tennis. Yet, unfortunately as tennis became more competitive, opportunities for friendship and affiliation seemed to diminish. This had a three-pronged negative effect: lessening a player's ability to combat stress by reducing social support; reducing the fun of tennis; and making competing alternative activities where a player could spend time with friends more attractive. As a result of these

**Table 21.2** Factors lending to burnout general dimensions raw-data theme frequency and citation occurrence

*General dimension (% of all raw-data themes)*

Physical concerns (12%)
  • 10 raw-data themes
  • Cited by 5 (50%) of the players
Logistical concerns (13%)
  • 11 raw-data themes
  • Cited by 8 (50%) of the players
Social/interpersonal concerns (24%)
  • 20 raw-data themes
  • Cited by 9 (90%) of the players
Psychological concerns (51%)
  • 42 raw-data themes
  • Cited by 10 (100%) of the players
Total = 83 raw-data themes

findings, the researchers concluded that most all the cases of burnout examined in this study could be fairly well explained by using Smith's (1986) cognitive-affective stress model of burnout. This most likely results from the fact that Smith's model is the most comprehensive of the three examined. In addition, it emphasizes both personal and situational factors as determinants of burnout, and places a premium on the athlete's interpretation of the events causing chronic stress. This is not to say the Coakley (1992) and Silva (1990) models are not appropriate explanations of athlete burnout. The Coakley model explained almost as many cases as the Smith model, and the Silva explained several of the cases.

Given all of these findings, the researchers developed a conceptualization of burnout as a general process best thought of in terms of Smith's general stages. However, the results of this investigation also suggest different "strains" of burnout may exist within this process. In particular, a "social psychologically driven" form of burnout existed, and was actually the dominant form in this investigation, as the vast majority of athletes had very low on and off the court physical training loads. The social psychologically driven burnout further divided into athlete perfectionism and situational pressure substrains. This resulted from the fact that perfectionism was found to be such a strong factor of influence in the first phase of study (Gould et al., 1996a).

In contrast to the athlete perfectionism substrain of burnout, several athletes in this study did not seem to be highly perfectionistic or have unusual trouble dealing with perfectionistic tendencies. Rather, they were placed in situations where tremendous psychological stress was generated from others, particularly parents. In most cases, this stress resulted from expectations to win in an effort to please others and feel worthy. It also should be noted that at times this parental pressure was very subtle, so it might not always be obvious to the casual observer.

Finally, while less frequently identified in this study, a "physically driven" strain of burnout appears to exist as well. That is, as Silva (1990) has suggested, players get placed in a training environment where they cannot meet the physical training demands placed on them, experience considerable physical and psychological stress, and burnout.

## Subsequent research and application

The publication of Gould et al.'s study of burnout among elite junior tennis players represented a landmark piece of research within the field. The research questions posed, as well as the design of the study, has had a significant impact to the advancement of knowledge and understanding in this area of sport psychology. One of the recognized pitfalls of burnout research is locating individuals who have actually experienced the syndrome. By its very nature, burnout dictates that these individuals reach a point where they no longer wish to be part of the activity associated with their feelings of being burned out, and as a consequence, choose to withdraw from the activity. Gould and colleagues actively sought out these individuals, and contrasted them with others who had not experienced burnout.

The qualitative component of the key study enabled the researchers to probe in greater detail the experiences and burnout study of these athletes. In addition to the results that emerged relating to causes and characteristics of burnout, two further significant outcomes of the qualitative inquiry was the identification of different strains of burnout (i.e., physically-driven and socially-driven), and support for both Smith's (1986) and Coakley's (1992) models of athlete burnout. Although the notion of different strains of burnout had not previously been considered, it is an intuitively appealing proposition due to its implications for treatment and intervention.

Gould and colleagues also argued that not all individuals who experienced burnout withdrew from the activity as previously thought. Growth in professionalism and sport as a source of livelihood, coupled with the emergence of younger sports stars with life experiences that revolve predominantly around sport participation, has set the scene for potentially greater entrapment amongst athletes and involvement on a "have to" rather than "wanting to" basis (Raedeke, 1997).

Burnout research that explored models of athlete burnout has been limited to date, and Gould *et al.*'s interview study is one of the few published attempts. With the results supporting both Smith's (1986) and Coakley's (1992) models, an important conclusion was made that burnout is a product of the interplay between personality and situational factors. The qualitative accounts of athletes within the key study made the case clear that sport organizations and significant others including administrators, coaches, and parents have a role to play in reducing both stress and potential burnout in young athletes. This has implications for applied practice in preventing and treating burnout.

A number of other important advancements in the burnout field have more recently occurred. One of the principle advancements has been the introduction of a multi-dimensional definition of burnout, which is based on the most popular conceptualization in the professional domain by Maslach and Jackson (1984). Maslach and Jackson proposed that burnout comprises three dimensions, namely emotional exhaustion (EE), depersonalization (DP), and reduced performance accomplishment (RPA). Developed within the context of helping professions, Maslach (1993) warns of the contextual differences that may affect the appropriateness of applying this definition to other spheres of life. Acknowledging these concerns Raedeke, Lunney, and Venables (2002) sought to develop an athlete specific version. Through a study conducted with swimming coaches, Raedeke *et al.* offered the following definition of burnout among athletes: "A withdrawal from sport noted by a reduced sense of accomplishment, devaluation/resentment of sport, and physical/psychological exhaustion" (2002: 181). The authors also modified the burnout dimensions to reflect characteristics of the sport context. Physical/emotional exhaustion is associated with intense training and competition. Reduced athletic accomplishment relates to skills and abilities when athletes are unable to achieve personal goals or perform below expectation. Sport devaluation reflects one of the major contextual differences in that it replaces depersonalization as this was not identified as a salient dimension in athlete burnout (Raedeke & Smith, 2001). Instead, sport devaluation refers to a loss of interest, "don't care" attitude, or resentment towards performance and the sport.

A universally agreed definition and valid measurement tool of burnout for use among athlete populations have historically been two of the major challenges for burnout researchers (Dale & Weinberg, 1990; Raedeke & Smith, 2001). At the time of the key study, Smith's (1986) definition was the most well recognized but no measurement tool for use with athlete populations had been published. Gould *et al.* employed one of the few self-report instruments that have been developed – the *EADES* measure (Eades, 1991). This measure remains unpublished to date, however. Raedeke *et al.*'s (2002) definition has made a significant contribution to the field not only through the possibility for gaining conceptual agreement, but also the operationalization of the definition through the development of the *Athlete Burnout Questionnaire* (ABQ) (Raedeke & Smith, 2001). Although used in limited studies to date (e.g., Cresswell & Eklund, 2004, 2005a, 2005b; Raedeke, 1997), the ABQ has received positive reviews by researchers. Cresswell and Eklund (2006) recently examined the convergent validity of the ABQ with the *Maslach Burnout Inventory General* (MBI-GS; Maslach & Jackson, 1986). The MBI-GS is a modified version of the original

*Maslach Burnout Inventory* (MBI: Maslach & Jackson, 1986), which was developed for the assessment of burnout in human care settings. The MBI is the most widely used measure of burnout, appearing in over 90% of professional burnout studies (Schaufeli & Buunk, 2003) and the development of the MBI-GS has enabled burnout to be assessed in other contexts including sport. Essentially, the authors examined the degree to which the three dimensions of burnout outlined in the ABQ are similar to (or converge on) those in the MBI-GS (i.e., was emotional exhaustion in the ABQ really measuring emotional exhaustion as identified in the MBI-GS?). Cresswell and Eklund (2006) found the ABQ to be valid and supported the use of it in assessing burnout among athlete populations.

The key study remains one of the few attempts to explicitly examine different theoretical explanations of burnout. Newer, theoretical alternatives have been proposed for both athlete (Kallus & Kellmann, 2000; Kentta & Hassmen, 1998) and coach (Kelley & Gill, 1993; Kelley, 1994; Kelley, Eklund, & Ritter-Taylor, 1999) burnout. A major theme that has emerged in the athlete-based literature is the relationship between burnout, stress, and recovery. Proponents of this perspective (Kallus & Kellmann, 2000; Kentta & Hassmen, 1998) suggest that burnout is the product of accumulating stress (both training and non training based) without appropriate and/or sufficient (quality) recovery. Although reminiscent of some of the tenants of Silva's (1990) model (i.e., burnout through overload training), the stress and recovery approach adopts a "psychosociophysiological" frame-work. Rather than simply being the result of an athlete's failure to adapt to physical training, the stress and recovery approach considers that sources of stress may be psychological, sociological, and/or physiological in nature. The combination of these factors, together with an individual's ability to cope with stress and the provision of quality recovery predisposes athletes to burnout. Consistent with the key study findings, the stress and recovery approach provides the opportunity to consider burnout that is derived from social psychological factors, as well as burnout that is physically driven. The emphasis placed upon effective mental and physical recovery has high practical relevance to coaches and other practitioners working with athletes, and could be instrumental in preventing and managing burnout.

The work of Gould and colleagues has paved the way for the modern face of burnout research in sport in that it put the agenda of athlete burnout firmly on the research table. Although the empirical base remains small, it is growing, and with the advances that have taken place in terms of the definition and measurement of burnout, the future for burnout research looks optimistic. The value of Gould *et al.*'s work in interviewing athletes who actually lived with burnout has offered much to the literature in terms of insight. Research following a similar path is beginning to emerge (Cresswell & Eklund, 2004), but more work of this nature is needed if burnout in sport is to be better understood and effective interventions developed.

## Additional readings

Cresswell, S. L., & Eklund. R. C. (2006). The nature of player burnout in rugby: Key characteristics and attribution. *Journal of Applied Sport Psychology*, 18, 219–39.

Goodger, K., Lavallee, D., Gorely, P. J., & Harwood, C. H. (2006). Burnout in sport. In J. M. Williams (ed.), *Applied sport psychology: Personal growth to peak performance* (5th ed., pp. 541–64). New York: McGraw-Hill.

Gould, D., & Dieffenbach, K. (2002). Overtaining, underrecovery, and burnout in sport. In M. Kellman (ed.), *Enhancing recovery: Preventing underperformance in athletes* (pp. 25–35). Champaign, IL: Human Kinetics.

Raedeke, T. D. (1997). Is athlete burnout more than just stress? A sport commitment perspective. *Journal of Sport & Exercise Psychology*, 19, 396–417.

Smith, R. E. (1986). Toward a cognitive-affective model of athlete burnout. *Journal of Sport Psychology*, 8, 36–50.

## Study questions

1 Describe the models of burnout in sport proposed by Smith (1986), Silva (1990), and Coakley (1992).

2 List the data analysis procedures employed in the key study, as recommend by Patton (1990).

3 Outline the factors leading to burnout identified in the key study.

4 Explain the three dimensions of burnout as outlined by Maslach and Jackson (1984) and describe how Raedeke and colleagues have applied this within sport.

5 Describe some of the measures used in sport burnout research.

## References

Caccese, T. M., & Mayerberg, C. K. (1984). Gender differences in perceived burnout of college coaches. *Journal of Sport & Exercise Psychology*, 6, 279–88.

Coakley, J. A. (1992). Burnout among adolescent athletes: A personal failure or social problem. *Sociology of Sport Journal*, 9, 271–85.

Cohn, P. (1990). An exploratory study on sources of stress and athlete burnout in youth golf. *The Sport Psychologist*, 4, 95–106.

Cresswell, S. L., & Eklund, R. C. (2004). The athlete burnout syndrome: possible early warning signs. *Journal of Science and Medicine in Sport*, 7, 481–7.

Cresswell, S. L., & Eklund, R. C. (2005a). Motivation and burnout among top amateur rugby players. *Medicine and Science in Sports and Exercise* 37, 469–77.

Cresswell, S. L., & Eklund, R. C. (2005b). Changes in athlete burnout and motivation over a 12-week league tournament. *Medicine and Science in Sports and Exercise*, 37, 1957–66.

Cresswell, S. L., & Eklund, R. C. (2006). The convergent and discriminant validity of burnout measures in sport: A multi-method multi-trait analysis. *Journal of Sports Sciences*, 24, 209–12.

Dale, J., & Weinberg, R. S. (1990). Burnout in sport: A review and critique. *Journal of Applied Sport Psychology*, 2, 67–83.

Eades, A. (1991). *An investigation of burnout in intercollegiate athletes: The development of Eades Athletic Burnout Inventory*. Paper presented at the North American Society for the Psychology of Sport and Physical Activity National Conference, Asilomar, CA.

Freudenberger, H. J. (1974). Staff burnout. *Journal of Social Issues*, 30, 159–65.

Gould, D., Udry, E., Tuffey, S., & Loehr, J. (1996a). Burnout in competitive junior tennis players: I. Quantitative psychological assessment. *The Sport Psychologist*, 10, 322–40.

Gould, D., Tuffey, S., Udry, E., & Loehr, J. (1997). Burnout in competitive junior tennis players: III. Individual differences in the burnout experience. *The Sport Psychologist*, 11(3), 257–76.

Kallus, K. W., & Kellmann, M. (2000). Burnout in athletes and coaches. In Y. L. Hanin (ed.), *Emotions in sport* (pp. 209–30). Champaign, IL: Human Kinetics.

Kelley, B. C. (1994). A model of stress and burnout in collegiate coaches: Effects of gender and time of season. *Research Quarterly for Exercise and Sport*, 65, 48–58.

Kelley, B. C., Eklund, R. C., & Ritter-Taylor, M. (1999). Stress and burnout among collegiate tennis coaches. *Journal of Sport & Exercise Psychology*, 21, 113–30.

Kelley, B. C., & Gill, D. L. (1993). An examination of personal and situational variables, stress appraisal, and burnout in collegiate tennis coaches. *Research Quarterly for Exercise and Sport*, 64, 94–102.

Kentta, G., & Hassmen, P. (1998). Overtraining and recovery: A conceptual model. *Sports Medicine*, 26, 1–16.

Lincoln, Y. S., & Guba, E. G. (1985). *Naturalistic inquiry*. Newbury Park, CA: Sage Publications.

Martin, J. J., Kelley, B. C., & Dias, C. (1999). Stress and burnout among female high school athletic directors. *Women in Sport and Physical Activity Journal*, 8, 101–16.

Maslach, C. (1993). Burnout: A multidimensional perspective. In W. B. Schaufeli, C. Maslach, & T. Marek (eds) *Professional burnout: Recent developments in theory and research* (pp. 19–32). Washington, DC: Taylor & Francis.

Maslach, C., & Jackson, S.E. (1984). Burnout in organizational settings. In S. Oskamp (ed.), *Applied social psychology annual: Applications in organizational settings* (vol. 5, 133–53). Beverly Hills, CA: Sage.

Maslach, C., & Jackson, S. E. (1986) *Maslach Burnout Inventory Manual* (2nd ed.). Palo Alto, CA: Consulting Psychologists Press.

Patton, M. Q. (1990). *Qualitative evaluation and research methods*. Newbury Park, CA: Sage Publications.

Raedeke, T. D. (1997). Is athlete burnout more than just stress? A sport commitment perspective. *Journal of Sport & Exercise Psychology*, 19, 396–417.

Raedeke, T. D., Lunney, K., & Venables, K. (2002). Understanding athlete burnout: Coach perspectives. *Journal of Sport Behavior*, 25, 181–206.

Raedeke, T. D., & Smith, A. L. (2001). Development and preliminary validation of an athlete burnout measure. *Journal of Sport & Exercise Psychology*, 23, 281–306.

Schaufeli, W. B., & Buunk, B. P. (2003). Burnout: An overview of 25 years of research and theorizing. In M. J. Schabracq & C. L. Cooper (eds), *The Handbook of Work and Health Psychology* (pp. 383–425). London: John Wiley & Sons.

Silva, J. M. (1990). An analysis of the training stress syndrome in competitive athletics. *Journal of Applied Sport Psychology*, 2, 5–20.

Smith, R. E. (1986). Toward a cognitive-affective model of athlete burnout. *Journal of Sport Psychology*, 8, 36–50.

Taylor, A. H., Daniel, J. V., Leith, L., & Burke, R. J. (1990). Perceived stress, psychological burnout and paths to turnover intentions among sport officials, *Journal of Applied Sport Psychology*, 2, 84–97.

# PART 5

## Professional practice and ethics

# 22

# Professional practice of applied sport psychology

Gould, D., Murphy, S., Tammen, V., & May, J. (1991). An evaluation of U.S. Olympic sport psychology consultant effectiveness. *The Sport Psychologist*, 5, 111–27.

## Background and context

Ever since Norman Triplett's (1898) ground-breaking publication on social facilitation (as outlined in Chapter 7) psychologists from all sub-disciplines of the profession have taken an interest in sport. For example, Patrick (1903) and Howard (1912) were social psychologists who used sports as one of many contexts in their publications on the psychology of spectators. Coleman Griffith was an educational psychologist who worked as a consultant for university and professional sports teams in the USA in the 1930s, and published two groundbreaking textbooks (*The psychology of coaching* in 1926 and *Psychology and athletics* in 1928). Numerous other prominent psychologists around the world also began to apply their theories and research in sport settings during this early period, but this work was conducted sporadically and did not begin to have a noteworthy impact – from an applied perspective – until the 1960s.

At this time, several important developments occurred that provided the platform for applied sport psychology to develop. Psychologists began to accompany several eastern European teams to the Olympics as early as 1960 in Melbourne (Roberts & Kimiecik, 1989). Two psychologists, Bruce Ogilvie and Thomas Tutko, also published their ground-breaking book in 1966 entitled *Problem athletes and how to handle them*. Despite some criticism of this book, as well as their *Athletic Motivation Inventory* which became established as the most commonly-used inventory for measuring the personality of athletes, their work quickly gained popularity within the world of sport. The academic subject of sport psychology subsequently began to grow rapidly during the 1960s and 1970s within physical education departments in the USA. It was during this time of growth that many broad themes were defined that underlie the practice of sport psychology and that still concern many sport psychologists today, including motivation, competitive anxiety, psychological characteristics of successful athletes, psychological skills training, cognition and imagery, team dynamics, and leadership behaviors (Lavallee, Kremer, Moran, & Williams, 2004; Williams & Straub, 2006). Several professional organizations were established during this period specifically for sport psychology. These included the International Society of Sport Psychology (ISSP) in 1965, the North American Society for the Psychology of Sport and Physical Activity (NASPSPA), and the European Federation of Sport Psychology (FEPSAC) in 1968. Following the development of these professional organizations several sport psychology journals were launched during the 1970s, including the *International*

*Journal of Sport Psychology* in 1970, the *Journal of Sport Behavior* in 1978, and the *Journal of Sport Psychology* in 1979 (renamed the *Journal of Sport & Exercise Psychology* in 1987).

In the 1970s the primary goal of sport psychologists in North America was to advance sport psychology's knowledge base through experimental research (Williams & Straub, 2006). In 1979, however, Martens published an influential article entitled "About smocks and jocks" that called on sport psychology researchers to not limit their studies to within laboratories (smocks) but to also conduct research in the field where people play sports (jocks). This provided the impetus for an increase in research into performance enhancement via psychological interventions, and thus a documentation of the effectiveness of psychological interventions at enhancing performance (Greenspan & Feltz, 1989).

Professional practice began to move toward the forefront of sport psychology during the 1980s and 1990s (Gill, 1997). This was accomplished with the start of specialized training programmes in applied sport psychology (Andersen, Van Raalte, & Brewer, 2001), as well as the establishment of professional organizations devoted more to applied issues, including the Association for the Advancement of Applied Sport Psychology (AAASP) in 1985. The United States Olympic Committee established a registry of qualified sport psychologists in 1983, with sport psychology playing an increasingly prominent and visible role in the 1984 and 1988 Olympics (Williams & Straub, 2006). It was also during this time that publications were launched that focused predominantly on applied work, including *The Sport Psychologist* journal in 1987, the *Journal of Applied Sport Psychology* in 1989, and the textbook *Applied sport psychology: personal growth to peak performance* (Williams, 1986). In addition, in 1991, 48 psychological skills training books were identified in a review (Sachs, 1991).

It was during this time that researchers also started to evaluate the effectiveness of sport psychology consultants and practices. In the first article published in the first issue of *The Sport Psychologist*, Orlick and Partington (1987) presented the results of a study in which Canadian Olympic athletes identified the attributes and activities of effective sport psychologists. In this study, effective consultants were identified as those who worked individually with athletes, had good listening skills, and were interested and caring, whereas less effective consultants lacked interpersonal skills, had poor sport psychology application skills, and did not establish ongoing programs by providing follow-up meetings. These researchers also published a related article in the same year that focused on coaches' views of what qualities make an effective sport psychologist (Partington & Orlick, 1987a). In this study, effective sport psychologists were characterized as being good listeners, flexible, and hard working.

The key study by Gould, Murphy, Tammen, and May was designed to extend these findings by evaluating sport psychologists who worked with Olympic athletes in the USA. In order to examine effective consultant characteristics, these researchers obtained data from not only Olympic athletes and national team coaches, but also sport science and medicine administrators and the sport psychologists themselves.

## Key study

Applied sport psychology has experienced tremendous growth over the last 15 years. Today sport psychology specialists work with countless athletes and coaches at all levels of competition. There has been a dramatic increase in the number of applied sport psychology self-help texts (Vealey, 1988). *The Sport Psychologist* journal was developed to facilitate both research and professional practice in applied sport psychology. These indicators not only reflect the growth of the field but also demonstrate the great need for applied sport psychology services.

Accompanying the increased interest in applied sport psychology have been calls for greater accountability. Dishman (1983) argues that the professional model of sport psychology "assumes that there is something to deliver which produces clearly defined and reliable results." He goes on to state, "Under close scrutiny the validity of this assumption is presently unclear" (1983: 126). Similarly, Smith (1989) has recently argued that the future development and ultimate credibility of the field "will be influenced by its degree of success in responding to standards of scientific and public accountability" (1989: 166). While recent reviews (e.g., Greenspan & Feltz, 1989) have shown that applied sport psychology interventions can be effective, it seems clear that if applied sport psychology is to develop further, greater attention must be given to program evaluation and professional accountability.

Given these accountability concerns, it is surprising that so little sport psychology evaluation research has been conducted. There is a special need to examine the effectiveness of those consultants who provide psychological services to athletes and coaches; only scant attention has been paid to the topic (Orlick & Partington, 1987; Partington & Orlick, 1987a), despite increasing concern over the qualifications of those providing such services (Silva, 1989; Weinberg, 1989). Hence this study was designed to evaluate the effectiveness of a highly visible group of sport psychology consultants, those working for U.S. Olympic teams.

Some attention has been given to the description of services provided by U.S. Olympic sport psychology consultants. Suinn (1985), and more recently Gould, Tammen, Murphy, and May (1989) have examined these individuals and the types of services they provide. While these studies have furnished valuable information on techniques used and problems encountered, they are limited in that they only assessed the self-perceptions of sport psychology consultants relative to these issues. We need to examine consultant effectiveness as viewed by all those involved in these programs – the coaches, athletes, administrators, and consultants themselves.

Fortunately, two recent studies (Orlick & Partington, 1987; Partington & Orlick, 1987a) have begun to advance knowledge in this area by identifying the characteristics of effective consultants versus those of less effective ones. These studies have also led to the development of a sport psychology *Consultant Evaluation Form* (CEF; Partington & Orlick, 1987b). However, these findings must be replicated and extended further. This study, therefore, was designed to evaluate the service provided and effectiveness of a highly visible group of sport psychology consultants, those working for U.S. Olympic teams. Also examined were effective consultant characteristics and future sport psychology program and consultant needs.

## Method

### Sport Psychology Consultant Survey

The sample used in this portion of the investigation consisted of 44 sport psychology specialists who had consulted with coaches and athletes in over 25 U.S. Olympic sports. The sport psychology consultants ranged in age from 29 to 67 years, with a mean of 42.6 (*SD* = 7.7). There were 36 males (81.8%) and 8 females (18.2%). These consultants were identified by sports administrators from each Olympic National Governing Body (NGB) that reported having a sport medicine/science program.

The U.S. Olympic Committee (USOC) survey for sport psychology consultants comprised a series of objective and open-ended questions and was divided into three sections: a Demographic and Background Information section (e.g., age, education, professional membership/associations, and how the consultant became associated with the NGB); a Sport Psychology Services section which assessed types of psychological services offered, hours of service provided per year, and to which groups inside the NGB the consultant provided services; and an Evaluation and Future Directions of Sport Psychology Services section which assessed the perceived effectiveness of the psychological services, problems encountered in providing services, how the USOC could better aid the NGB sport psychology program, and future research directions. Each sport psychology consultant was also asked to include a list of four typical coaches and athletes he or she had consulted with while working with the sport.

## Sport Science/Medicine Administrator Survey

The sample used in this section of the investigation consisted of 26 sport administrators from 25 NGBs. The sports and/or organizations represented in the survey included archery, athletics, biathlon, bobsled, canoe/kayak, equestrian, fencing, women's field hockey, men's gymnastics, ice hockey, judo, luge, shooting, soccer, speed skating, swimming, table tennis, tennis, women's volleyball, weight-lifting, yachting, U.S. disabled skiing, Special Olympics, and the Cerebral Palsy Athletic Association. The administrators ranged in age from 29 to 56, with a mean age of 39.7 ($SD = 7.4$) years. There were 22 males (84.6%) and 4 females (15.4%). Of the 32 administrators who were identified and agreed to participate, and who were then mailed an appropriate survey, 26 (81%) returned completed questionnaires.

The sport science/medicine administrators' questionnaire comprised a series of objective and open-ended questions, and like the consultants' survey was divided into three sections: a Demographic and Background Information section, a Sport Psychology Services section, and an Evaluation and Future Directions of Sport Psychology Services section. While the administrators' survey was not as lengthy as the consultants' instrument, all items used for comparison purposes in this investigation were identical to the consultant survey. Each NGB administrator was also asked to provide a list of four typical NGB coaches and four athletes who had received psychological services.

## Coaches Survey

The sample used in this section of the investigation consisted of 45 coaches representing 20 U.S. Olympic sports: archery (3), athletics or track and field (3), bobsled (2), cycling (3), diving (1), equestrian (1), fencing (1), men's gymnastics (2), women's gymnastics (1), ice hockey (4), luge (1), shooting (1), tennis (3), women's volleyball (2), weight-lifting (4), wrestling (7), yachting (1), U.S. disabled skiing (2), Alpine skiing (1), and Nordic skiing (2). Of the 45 NGB coaches who responded, the ages ranged from 24 to 52 and the mean age was 38.2 years ($SD = 7.6$). There were 41 males and 4 females. The coaches were also well educated, as 21 had a bachelor's degree, 14 had a master's, and 3 had a doctorate. Two others had a junior college degree and four had completed high school. Fifteen of the coaches (33.7%) had coached during the previous Pan American or Olympic Games and 19 (42%) had coached a U.S. Olympic Festival (multi-sport national competition) team. On average the coaches had coached their respective sports for 14 years ($SD = 6.9$).

The 45 coaches were among those identified through lists supplied by NGB sport administrators and sport psychology consultants who had stated that these coaches had participated in the psychological services offered to coaches and athletes. Of the 54 coaches who agreed to participate and were mailed questionnaires, 45 (83%) returned completed questionnaires. The survey for coaches comprised a series of objective and open-ended questions and was divided into the same sections as the two previous instruments.

## Athlete Survey

The sample used in this section of the investigation consisted of 47 athletes representing 19 U.S. Olympic sports: archery (8), athletics or track and field (1), bobsled (2), cycling (1), diving (3), fencing (2), figure skating (3), ice hockey (1), judo (1), luge (3), shooting (3), swimming (1), table tennis (6), tennis (1), women's volleyball (2), weight-lifting (2), wrestling (2), yachting (1), and Nordic skiing (4). The athletes surveyed ranged in age from 13 to 42, with a mean age of 25.1 (SD = 6.1) years. There were 30 males (63.8%) and 17 females (36.2%). On average, the athletes had competed in their respective sport for 10.9 years (SD = 5.0) and began competing at the age of 13.6 (SD = 5.4). Eleven athletes had competed in the Olympics, with two of the 47 respondents placing in the top three positions. Only 29 athletes responded to the question on educational attainment. Responses revealed that educational attainment varied: 1 had finished junior high, 18 had finished high school, 1 had a junior college degree, 4 had a bachelor's degree, 2 had a doctorate, and 3 had no degree as of yet.

The 47 athletes were among those identified through lists supplied by NGB administrators and sport psychology consultants who had indicated that these athletes had received psychological services. Of the 64 athletes who agreed to participate and were mailed questionnaires, 47 (74%) returned completed questionnaires. The athletes' questionnaire was divided into the same three sections as for the previous instruments. It took approximately 30 minutes to complete.

## Variables Assessed

Comparisons among selected variables were made across all or various combinations of the subsamples. In all cases each variable was assessed in an identical way in all surveys in which it was contained. Variables that will be the particular focus of this investigation are explained below.

Partington and Orlick's (1987b) CEF was included in all four surveys. The CEF was developed for use with Canadian Olympic athletes and requires that the respondent rate perceived consultant effectiveness relative to the "effect on you" (rephrased "effect on athletes" for consultant, administrator, and coach surveys) and "effect on team" using an 11-point numerical scale with +5 representing "helped a lot," −5 representing "hindered/ interfered," and 0 representing "no effect." In this study, for data analytic purposes, a response of −5 was coded as 1 ("hindered/interfered") while +5 was transformed to 11 ("helped a lot"). This instrument also included 10 consultant characteristics (e.g., had a positive, constructive attitude) which were rated on 11-point numerical scales ranging from 0 ("not at all effective") to 10 ("yes, definitely effective"). Partington and Orlick's findings revealed that the scale was internally consistent and reliable.

Finally, several additional consultant effectiveness ratings were utilized. All respondents were asked to rate the overall effectiveness of the sport psychology consultant on a 10-point Likert scale with 1 signifying "not at all effective" and 10 "very effective." The coaches and athletes were also asked to rate the effectiveness of the consultant on the coach, using an 11-point scale paralleling those contained in the CEF. The final rating asked the coaches and athletes whether they would recommend retaining the consultant for work with them or their athletes/coaches.

All four subsamples completed a series of open-ended questions. In particular, they were asked how the consultant could satisfy the needs of athletes more fully and to identify the three most important research questions needing attention for coaches and athletes in their sport.

In an effort to better understand the types of sport psychology information desired, the coach and athlete subsamples rated 22 topics (e.g., goal setting) in importance. All ratings were made on a 10-point scale with 1 signifying "not important" and 10 "very important."

The administrators, coaches, and athletes were asked to respond to a series of questions focusing on desired roles that sport psychology consultants could play on teams in their sport. Respondents simply indicated "yes" if they desired or "no" if they did not desire each of the following roles: work with national teams, travel with teams to international events, travel with teams to Pan American and Olympic Games, be involved in research, work with junior development program, and be involved in coaching education.

## Results

### Evaluation of Consultant Effectiveness

The responses of the consultant, administrator, coach, and athlete subsamples were compared to determine whether they differed in their evaluation of the sport psychology services being delivered to NGBs. In particular, comparisons were made between subsample responses to the consultant effectiveness and consultant characteristic ratings.

Table 22.1 contains the mean ratings of the consultants, administrators, coaches, and athletes on Partington and Orlick's (1987b) 11-point effectiveness scales. Overall, the consultants were rated favorably. To determine whether there were differences between the subsamples, a one-way multivariate analysis of variance (MANOVA) was conducted using the four subsamples as levels of the independent variable and the overall effectiveness, effect on individual athlete, and effect on team ratings as dependent variables. A MANOVA was necessary because of the correlations between the various effectiveness ratings. Results revealed that no significant differences were evident between the groups, $F(5,120) = 1.95$, $p < .09$. Hence the consultants were evaluated as being of considerable help regardless of the source of the rating. In addition, no significant differences were found between the coaches' and athletes' evaluation of the consultant's effect on the coach, $t(1,76) = 1.26$, $p < .47$.

The consultants', administrators', coaches', and athletes' 11-point ratings of consultant characteristics were also compared and are listed in Table 22.2. A MANOVA comparing the

**Table 22.1** A comparison of four subgroups' ratings of psychological services

|  | Consultant | | Administrator | | Coach | | Athlete | |
|---|---|---|---|---|---|---|---|---|
|  | M | SD | M | SD | M | SD | M | SD |
| Overall effectiveness | 7.18 | 1.65 | 6.95 | 1.43 | 7.15 | 2.05 | 7.35 | 2.71 |
| Effect on individual athlete | 9.40 | 1.04 | 9.2 | 1.15 | 9.58 | 1.81 | 9.69 | 1.40 |
| Effect on team | 8.71 | 1.60 | 8.6 | 1.54 | 9.13 | 1.85 | 8.46 | 2.07 |
| Effect on coach | – | – | – | – | 9.42 | 1.70 | 7.79 | 2.00 |

**Table 22.2** A comparison of consultant characteristic ratings between four subgroups

| Consultant characteristics | Consultants | | Administrators | | Coaches | | Athletes | |
|---|---|---|---|---|---|---|---|---|
| | M | SD | M | SD | M | SD | M | SD |
| Useful knowledge | 8.97 | 1.50 | 8.57 | 1.33 | 8.36 | 2.02 | 8.78 | 2.01 |
| Individualized mental training based on athlete needs | 9.19 | 1.05 | 8.15 | 1.63 | 8.26 | 2.07 | 8.68 | 2.25 |
| Flexible – ready to collaborate/ cooperate | 9.16 | 0.99 | 9.24 | 1.33 | 9.17 | 1.49 | 8.98 | 1.97 |
| Positive-constructive | 9.19 | 0.97 | 9.33 | 0.97 | 9.44 | 1.41 | 9.37 | 1.12 |
| Trustworthy | 9.49 | 0.73 | 9.33 | 0.91 | 9.54 | 1.05 | 9.24 | 1.38 |
| Easy for athletes to relate to | 8.78 | 1.21 | 8.24 | 1.51 | 9.09 | 1.81 | 7.91 | 2.65 |
| Fitting in with team | 8.43 | 1.52 | 8.15 | 1.27 | 8.58 | 1.72 | 8.72 | 2.03 |
| Help draw on strengths | 8.92 | 1.21 | 8.32 | 1.37 | 8.32 | 1.80 | 8.83 | 2.18 |
| Help athletes overcome problems | 9.01 | 0.96 | 8.47 | 1.17 | 8.66 | 1.72 | 8.89 | 1.98 |
| Provided clear, practical, concrete strategies | 8.92 | 1.01 | 8.24 | 1.26 | 8.36 | 1.99 | 8.67 | 1.81 |

four group centroids across the 10 variables approached but failed to reach significance, $F(20,170) = 1.56$, $p > .07$. Hence the four subsamples were consistent in their favorable evaluations of the consultants' characteristics. Moreover, they rated the consultants favorably on all characteristics.

When asked if they would retain their consultant to work with the athletes, 33 (79%) coaches and 42 (91%) athletes indicated that they would. In addition, 36 (80%) coaches expressed a desire to retain the consultant for work with other coaches, while 38 (84%) athletes indicated a desire to retain the consultant for that purpose.

## Effective Consultant Characteristic Analysis

Coaches and athletes are the ones most often in the best position to observe and evaluate sport psychology consultants. Hence the relationship between each group's consultant characteristic and effectiveness rating was examined. Unfortunately, because of a great deal of multi-colinearity in the data, it was not possible to use multiple regression analyses to determine which consultant characteristics were most strongly related to perceptions of consultant effectiveness. Only simple correlations between variables are reported.

*Coaches' Perceptions.* Table 22.3 depicts the correlations between the coaches' Partington and Orlick CEF ratings on consultant characteristics and their ratings of consultants' effectiveness on individual athletes and the team. This table reveals that all the correlations were significantly different from zero. Hence all the characteristics are related to effectiveness perceptions by the coaches.

The consultant characteristics of fitting in with an athlete's team, the ability to draw on an athlete's strengths, and trustworthiness were the ones most strongly related to effect on individual athletes ($r = .79$, $r = .78$, $r = .67$, respectively). The best predictors of effect on the team included the ability to draw on strengths $r = .78$) and fitting in ($r = .75$).

*Athletes' Perceptions.* The correlations between the athletes' ratings of consultant characteristics and effectiveness are contained in Table 22.4. Highest correlations between

**Table 22.3** Relationship between consultant characteristics and consultant effectiveness ratings as perceived by NGB coaches

|  | Effect on athlete | Effect on team |
|---|---|---|
| Useful knowledge | .56 | .63 |
| Individualized mental training and needs | .32 | .41 |
| Flexible – ready to collaborate/cooperate | .56 | .54 |
| Positive – constructive attitude | .62 | .58 |
| Trustworthy | .67 | .65 |
| Easy to relate to | .55 | .54 |
| Fitted in | .79 | .75 |
| Draw on strengths | .78 | .78 |
| Help overcome problems | .59 | .64 |
| Provided clear, practical, concrete strategies | .51 | .61 |

Note: all correlations were found to be significantly different from zero, $p < .01$

**Table 22.4** Relationship between consultant characteristics and consultant effectiveness ratings as perceived by NGB athletes

|  | Effect on athlete | Effect on team |
|---|---|---|
| Useful knowledge | .61 | .29 |
| Individualized mental training and needs | .58 | .12 |
| Flexible – ready to collaborate/cooperate | .68 | .34 |
| Positive – constructive | .76 | .47 |
| Trustworthy | .61 | .46 |
| Easy to relate to | .65 | .43 |
| Fitted in | .43 | .58 |
| Draw on strengths | .74 | .34 |
| Help overcome problems | .67 | .23 |
| Provided clear, practical, concrete strategies | .74 | .28 |

Note: all correlations were found to be significantly different from zero, p < .01

consultant characteristic and effect on athlete ratings were found for positive-constructive ($r = .76$), draws on athlete strengths ($r = .74$), and provides clear strategies ($r = .74$). The best predictors of effect on team ratings were found for the characteristics of fitting in with athlete's team ($r = .58$), positive-constructive ($r = .47$), and trustworthiness ($r = .46$).

## Future Consultant and Program Needs

A series of comparisons were made between the various subsamples regarding the roles that sport psychology consultants should play, sport psychology topic importance ratings, ways of satisfying athletes more fully, and research topics needing further study.

The sport science/medicine administrators, coaches, and athletes indicated what roles they would like sport psychology consultants to have. Table 22.5 compares the results across the subsamples and reveals a great deal of consistency in the responses "to work with national team" and "be involved in research" between the three subsamples. Some inconsistency between sample responses was found on the other role items, however. Most

**Table 22.5** Roles that administrators, coaches, and athletes would like sport psychology consultants to play

| | Frequency of response | | | | | |
|---|---|---|---|---|---|---|
| | Administrators (N = 26) | | Coaches (N = 45) | | Athletes (N = 47) | |
| Role | Yes | No | Yes | No | Yes | No |
| Work with national team | 23 (88.5%) | 3 (11.5%) | 39 (86.7%) | 6 (13.3%) | 42 (89.4%) | 5 (10.6%) |
| Travel with teams to international events | 16 (61.5%) | 10 (38.5%) | 24 (53.3%) | 21 (41.7%) | 29 (61.7%) | 18 (38.3%) |
| Travel with teams to Pan American and Olympic Games | 13 (50.0%) | 13 (50.0%) | 22 (48.9%) | 23 (51.1%) | 31 (66%) | 16 (34%) |
| Be involved in research | 19 (73.1%) | 7 (26.9%) | 34 (76.6%) | 11 (24.4%) | 35 (74.5%) | 12 (25.5%) |
| Work with junior development program | 22 (84.6%) | 4 (15.4%) | 39 (86.7%) | 6 (13.3%) | 36 (76.6%) | 11 (23.4%) |
| Be involved in coaching education | 25 (96.2%) | 1 (3.8%) | 40 (88.9%) | 5 (11.1%) | 35 (74.5%) | 12 (25.5%) |

notable was that 66% of the athletes – compared to only 49% of the coaches and 50% of the administrators – favored having sport psychology consultants travel with teams to Pan American and Olympic Games. Additionally, 96% of the administrators, as compared to 89% of the coaches and 75% of the athletes, felt that the consultants should be involved in coaching education.

Importance ratings of a number of sport psychology topics were compared between the coach and athlete subsamples, as they are the primary targets of sport psychology consulting. Table 22.6 summarizes the coaches' and athletes' ratings of these topics. A MANOVA revealed no significant differences between the groups, $F(22,69) = 1.46$, $p < .12$. Hence, topics rated most important across the subsamples included imagery/visualization techniques, concentration/attention training, relaxation training, stress management, and arousal regulation.

Results for the four subsamples' responses to the open-ended item asking them to indicate how the sport psychology program could satisfy them more fully revealed a powerful and clear pattern for a perceived need to individualize, to spend more time with athletes; this item was identified by 60 respondents across the groups. The need to use sport-specific psychological skills and to have consultants increase their knowledge of the sport was recognized as an important concern by 3 administrators and 6 coaches. However, the consultants and athletes did not perceive this as a problem.

In the subsample responses to the open-ended item concerning the identification of future

**Table 22.6** A comparison of coaches' and athletes' ratings of the importance of sport psychology topics

| Topic | Coaches' ratings | | Athletes' ratings | |
|---|---|---|---|---|
| | M | SD | M | SD |
| Facilitate team cohesion morale | 7.61 | 2.13 | 6.63 | 2.86 |
| Improve interpersonal athlete/coach communication | 8.40 | 2.24 | 7.19 | 2.17 |
| Arousal regulation | 8.36 | 2.15 | 8.27 | 1.91 |
| Imagery/visualization techniques | 8.72 | 1.72 | 9.13 | 1.64 |
| Relaxation training | 8.41 | 2.11 | 8.55 | 2.05 |
| Stress management | 8.45 | 1.81 | 8.25 | 2.08 |
| Biofeedback | 6.73 | 2.70 | 6.13 | 2.26 |
| Concentration/attention training | 8.68 | 1.71 | 8.96 | 1.37 |
| Self-talk strategies | 7.41 | 2.48 | 8.51 | 1.71 |
| Thought management training | 7.46 | 2.15 | 7.73 | 2.07 |
| Motivation training | 7.34 | 2.48 | 7.29 | 2.64 |
| Behavior modification | 7.05 | 2.12 | 5.89 | 2.47 |
| Cope with foreign travel | 5.58 | 2.33 | 5.59 | 2.60 |
| Depression | 5.92 | 2.36 | 6.30 | 2.36 |
| Career termination/planning | 5.69 | 2.69 | 5.69 | 2.61 |
| Psychological recovery from injury | 6.66 | 2.89 | 6.07 | 2.77 |
| Eating disorders | 5.17 | 3.05 | 5.16 | 2.52 |
| Crisis management | 6.35 | 2.42 | 5.84 | 2.69 |
| Substance abuse | 5.85 | 2.79 | 5.29 | 2.99 |
| Personal self-esteem improvement | 7.46 | 2.36 | 5.84 | 2.69 |
| Family and marital concerns | 5.83 | 2.51 | 7.38 | 2.44 |
| Interpersonal conflicts | 6.54 | 2.16 | 6.90 | 2.82 |

research questions needing study, little consensus was seen across the groups. However, 6 consultants and 5 coaches identified methods of building self-confidence/esteem as an important research issue while 11 coaches and 10 athletes identified questions focusing on stress, anxiety, and fear reduction.

## Discussion

The evaluation of results were encouraging, as the coach, athlete, and administrator sub-samples as well as the consultants themselves all viewed the psychological services and personnel providing those services very favorably, whether rating the effect on the individual athlete, the team, or the coach. Most noteworthy were the findings that 73% of the coaches and 91% of the athletes indicated that they would retain their consultant(s) for further work. In addition, consultants received high evaluations on the Partington and Orlick (1987b) CEF across the subsamples. This is important since these characteristics were found by Canadian Olympic athletes to be critical considerations in the positive and negative evaluations of sport psychology consultants.

Roles most desired by NGB athletes, coaches, and administrators included work with national teams, involvement in coaching education, and work with junior national teams (cited by over 80% of respondents across the three subsamples). It was also encouraging to find that over 70% of the administrators, coaches, and athletes wanted sport psychology consultants to be involved in research. Travel with teams to international events and Pan American/Olympic Games was supported by over 50% of the respondents.

A strength of this study was the use of a previously developed instrument, the *Sport Psychology Consultant Evaluation Form*, to rate the consultants. Across 117 respondents from the three subsamples who use consultants' services (NGB administrators, coaches, and athletes), the sport psychology consultants were rated very positively on a diverse set of skills such as "has useful knowledge," "has a positive attitude," "helps athletes overcome problems," and "provides clear, practical, concrete strategies." A strong conclusion from this study was that, as a group, the sport psychology consultants being employed by NGBs at that time were perceived in a very positive light by some of the people they work with.

While the consultants were viewed favorably, it is important to recognize that all groups gave the consultants slightly higher ratings in working with individual athletes as opposed to when working with teams. For their part, the consultants themselves reported that team consultation situations are more difficult and that more variables need to be considered. Also, this survey found that the lowest rated characteristic of all consultants was "fitted in with the team." This suggests that in the American amateur sport setting, where team coaches have traditionally also been the team motivators and amateur psychologists, there may be a less clearly defined role for a sport psychologist. This would certainly explain some of the difficulties in being effective in a team situation. Current applied research in sport psychology focuses largely on individual interventions, and more research and theory development concerning team interventions is urgently needed.

When the correlations were examined between the 10 CEF consultant characteristics and the athletes' and coaches' ratings of individual athlete and overall team effectiveness, all 10 characteristics were found to be related to consultant effectiveness. This provides further validity for including these items in Partington and Orlick's (1987b) CEF. However, the present findings also suggest that additional psychometric data should be collected on the CEF because of the high levels of multi-colinearity between the 10 consultant characteristics. If this finding is replicated, it suggests that many of the consultant characteristics are tapping highly similar constructs. Hence, it would be important to reduce the current number of characteristics or include new variables that are found to be largely independent. Multiple regression analyses examining the relationships between consultant characteristics and effectiveness ratings would then be possible.

Simple correlations between the coach and athlete CEF consultant characteristics ratings and the "effect on athlete" and "effect on team" ratings suggested that fitting in with the team and drawing on the athletes' strengths were especially important characteristics of effective consultants. Being perceived as trustworthy, as having a positive-constructive attitude, and as providing clear strategies were also found to be most highly correlated to effectiveness. These findings validate professional practice or experiential knowledge of many contemporary applied sport psychology consultants (May & Brown, 1989; Ravizza, 1988; Salmela, 1989) who have emphasized and outlined strategies for fitting into the athletic environment and creating trust with athletic personnel. The importance of drawing upon athletes' strengths further supports the recommendations of Orlick (1989) and Halliwell (1989), who emphasized the need to respond to individual athlete needs and strengths as opposed to forcing a predetermined program on them, and offering clear and concrete psychological skill training strategies.

When asked which sport psychology topics they would like more information about, the coaches and athletes listed imagery and visualization techniques, concentration and attention training, stress management, relaxation training, self-talk strategies, and arousal regulation as most important. Least important topics, although all were still rated moderately important in an absolute sense, were substance abuse, family/marital concerns, career termination and planning, crisis management, personal self-esteem development, coping with foreign travel, and eating disorders.

These findings are important in that they inform sport psychology consultants about the types of information that coaches and athletes most desire at this stage of their career. Thus, consultants can better meet the needs of coaches and athletes, especially since substantial sport psychology research has been conducted in many of these areas (e.g., stress management). However, other topics such as concentration and attention training and self-talk interventions, which have not been extensively studied, should be given greater research attention.

It is also interesting to note that coaches and athletes focus on performance related concerns as being of primary importance, with nonperformance personal issues being judged less important. While this is not surprising, given their commitment and dedication to excellence, it suggests that consultants may need to emphasize nonperformance personal development concerns to a greater degree since these will not be the primary focus of athletes and coaches at this point in their lives.

When asked to respond to the open-ended question of "In what ways can the consultant satisfy you more fully?" 60 respondents across the subsamples cited the need to individualize sport psychology strategies and spend more time with athletes. This clearly indicates that while the respondents were generally satisfied with the consultants' effectiveness, further improvements could be made by individualizing techniques and programs for specific athletes. Therefore it is highly recommended that efforts be made toward this in the future. Consultants who are just beginning to work with sports groups should consider from the outset how best to provide individualized services to their clients.

Nine consultants also felt that they could better satisfy the needs of athletes and coaches by traveling with teams to competitions. Research and experiential knowledge is needed on the role of sport psychology consultants at competition sites and on the effectiveness of such on-site consultations. Athletes and coaches may be in a better position to determine this need than the consultants themselves. Three administrators and 6 coaches also indicated that consultants should increase their knowledge of the sport and/or focus on sport-specific psychological skills and strategies. The problems that arise when consultants do not possess adequate sport-specific knowledge have been well documented (Partington & Orlick, 1987a, b).

Finally, sport psychology researchers should use the findings of studies like this and the Partington and Orlick (1987a, b) investigation as a source of information when selecting future research questions. The individuals surveyed in this investigation, who were all involved in elite levels of athletic competition and training, suggested that we need to learn more about stress/anxiety/fear reduction and ways of facilitating self-confidence/esteem. Providing answers to these questions could greatly facilitate applied sport psychology service efforts for elite athletes and coaches.

## Methodological Considerations

The results of this study must be interpreted in the light of several methodological considerations, some of which are strengths and others of which are limitations. Among the strengths of the investigation was that it examined 4 diverse groups of individuals who were involved with sport psychology training for elite athletes and that an exceptionally high (overall 80%) return rate was achieved on each of the 4 subsamples. The high return rates are especially surprising, given the extensive nature of the questionnaires the subjects completed. Hence, the extensiveness of the survey itself was a major strength of the investigation.

The quality of athletes and coaches who completed the survey was also a strength of the study. For example, one third of the coaches had been or were currently a Pan American or Olympic Games coach, and 42% had coached a national sports festival team. Similarly, 23% of the athletes had competed in the Olympic Games, 55% in the World Championships, and 68% were national champions in their own sport. These coaches and athletes represented top level U.S. amateur sport participants. Finally, the administrator and consultant samples were selected using every name identifiable through USOC records. Thus these subsamples were drawn from the entire population of NGB personnel in these positions.

The investigation was not without limitations, however, two of which focus on the athlete and coach sample sizes and the selection procedure employed to identify these samples. At the outset, we had hoped to obtain, by requesting this information from the administrators and the consultants themselves, the names and addresses of all coaches and athletes who had participated in NGB sport psychology programs. Unfortunately, many NGB administrators did not have this information or did not have the time or staff available to locate it. Hence they were asked to submit the names of 4 coaches and athletes who had participated in the program. This, then, was not a random sample.

Similarly, when the sport psychology consultants were asked to provide names and addresses of participants in the program, some were hesitant to do so because of concerns of violating consultant/client confidentiality. Even though this investigation was conducted in a completely confidential manner and the strictest procedures were followed to ensure subject confidentiality, we honored those consultant requests not to give names and did not further pursue the issue with them. Thus this investigation is limited in that not all sports that had programs were represented, or were represented equally, in the investigation. It is possible that a bias toward favorable ratings was caused by consultants knowingly or unknowingly referring the researchers to athletes who had a positive experience with the consultants.

Future research should try to sample all participants in a sport psychology consultation program, as was done in the Orlick and Partington (1987) study. That is, they sent a survey (the CEF) to all 1988 Olympic athletes in Canada and requested that all those who had contact with a sport psychology consultant respond to the CEF.

## Subsequent research and application

Since the publication of the key study, applied sport psychology has grown tremendously and become incredibly diverse in its practice and knowledge base. This is reflected in many ways, including the increase in the publication of journals and books in applied sport psychology. For example, in 1997 *The Sport Psychologist* journal started a subsection on professional practice. The *International Journal of Sport and Exercise Psychology* (launched in 2003 as the new official publication of the ISSP) and the *Psychology of Sport and Exercise* journal (initiated in 2000 by FEPSAC) also promote the publication of articles on professional practice. Books such as *Sport psychology interventions* (Murphy, 1995), *Applying sport psychology: Four perspectives* (Taylor & Wilson, 2005), the *Handbook of research in applied sport and exercise psychology* (Hackfort, Duda, & Lidor, 2005), and new editions (1993, 1998, 2001, 2006) of *Applied sport psychology: Personal growth to peak performance* have helped pull together accumulating evidence in the field. The books *Doing sport psychology* (Andersen, 2000) and *Sport psychology in practice* (Andersen, 2005) examine the process of professional practice service delivery in sport psychology through dialogues from actual interactions between sport psychologists and clients. In terms of sheer numbers of sport psychological skills training books, Burke, Sachs, and Smisson (2004) indicated a growth to 187 books by 1998 and 282 by 2004.

Across the globe, it is unlikely that the demand for sport psychology has ever been higher. As teams and individuals constantly strive to find the winning edge it becomes increasingly likely that a sport psychologist will be involved to help find that edge (Lavallee *et al.*, 2004). Despite this growth, however, some athletes and teams remain reluctant to use sport psychology because of previous negative experiences or stereotypical images (Brewer, Van Raalte, Petitpas, Bachman, & Weinhold, 1998; Leffingwell, Rider, & Williams, 2001). Consequently, research has been conducted with the aim of understanding athletes' attitudes towards sport psychology so that services can be tailored to best meet the needs of athletes and increase overall usage (e.g., Martin, Lavallee, Kellman, & Page, 2004). These studies have explored how athlete characteristics such as nationality, gender, age, competitive level, and previous experience with sport psychology can influence attitudes towards sport psychology services.

The evaluation of the professional practice of applied sport psychology has continued to grow in importance since this key study was published. Two areas of focus have been to assess the effectiveness of interventions that enhance athletes' performance or that increase the physical activity levels of all types of individuals. For example, see Meyers, Whelan, and Murphy (1996) and Dishman and Buckworth (1996) for a meta-analysis of these intervention studies. A third focus has been the same as this key study, that is, assessing the effectiveness of sport psychology consultants and the factors that influence their effectiveness. Some sport psychologists have employed the CEF in research and applied practice (Gentner, Fisher, & Wrisberg, 2004; Hardy & Parfitt, 1994; Poczwardowski, Sherman, & Henschen, 1998). Weigand, Richardson, and Weinberg (1999) examined the effectiveness of an intern consulting with a university women's basketball team in the USA. Through quantitative (open-ended questions) and qualitative (interviews) methods, they were able to identify several attributes and activities related to consultancy effectiveness, including being knowledgeable about the sport, helpful, understanding and trustworthy, and aware of boundaries of expertise.

In an interesting case study, Lloyd and Trudel (1999) identify the content of the verbal interactions between an eminent applied sport psychologist and five elite-level athletes during ten sessions, and then compare the analyzed sessions with the consultant's approach to sport psychology as outlined in two published journal articles. Results revealed the consultant's verbal behaviors during the sessions accounted for 39% of the total coded behaviors leaving 60% for the athletes and 1% for silence. The content analysis revealed that up to 24 topics were addressed in each session, with certain issues having a more frequent word count. The analysis of the content and process revealed that the consultant followed an athlete-centered approach, which corresponded to the consultant's published perspective.

In another study, Anderson, Miles, Robinson, and Mahoney (2004) interviewed 30 athletes in the UK in order to identify factors pertinent to the effective practice of applied sport psychologists. They found themes related to characteristics (personable, good communicator, knowledgeable about sport, honest and trustworthy, exhibits professional skills) and activities (provides feedback, uses appropriate formats) of effective practitioners. Evaluating the sport psychologist is useful because the knowledge, delivery style, and characteristics of the individual practitioner can have a central influence on the overall effectiveness of the service provided. Evaluation of the consultant by athletes and coaches is just one component of a thorough evaluation of professional practice in sport psychology (Anderson *et al.*, 2004). Public reflection upon practice is growing in its importance, as reflecting enables sport psychologists to be accountable not only to others but also to themselves. Several journal articles (e.g., Anderson & Cecil, 2006; Holt & Strean, 2001) and book chapters (Clarke, 2004; McCann, 2000) have been written in which sport psychologists demonstrate the importance of reflection in their practice.

Although the development of psychological skills to enhance performance has historically served as the foundation for professional practice in sport psychology (Andersen *et al.*, 2001), applied sport psychologists today also work in the broad areas of psychological testing and counseling interventions (Danish, Petitpas, & Hale, 1995). Psychological testing is an area in which there has historically been a considerable amount of attention given by sport psychologists. Psychologists in many sub-disciplines are trained as both practitioners and researchers, with psychological assessment providing the bridge between the research and professional practice (Lavallee *et al.*, 2004). As researchers they are sensitive to applied issues, while as practitioners they are sensitive to research findings. As suggested in Nideffer and Sagal (2001), however, training in sport psychology has historically tended to be either research-focused or applied-focused. While this may have contributed somewhat to a decline in the actual use of psychological tests over the years, there has been a renewal in interest in this area among practicing sport psychologists recently. This is reflected in the publication of the books *Advances in sport and exercise psychology measurement* (Duda, 1998) and *Assessment in sport psychology* (Nideffer & Sagal, 2001), as well the *Directory of psychological tests in the sport and exercise sciences* (Ostrow, 1996), which summarizes information on 314 psychological questionnaires that have been reported in the literature since 1965.

For some applied sport psychologists, the delivery of psychological care and development of athletes above and beyond performance enhancement has become the focus of their work. In this model, the development of life skills, coping resources, and attention to counseling issues often seen in the sporting domain (e.g., retirement, injury, burnout) are important. Indeed, the launch of the *Journal of Clinical Sport Psychology* in 2006 suggests that counseling approaches are becoming more prevalent than ever before. This journal seeks to promote an understanding of theory, technique, and empirical findings specifically related to the integrated practice of clinical, counseling, and sport psychology, and includes topics relating to psychological health and well-being of athletes and coaches, psychological aspects of athletic performance, as well as issues and concerns that connect physical and psychological functioning.

There has been a dramatic increase in the number of sport psychologists in professional practice worldwide in recent years (Lidor, Morris, Bardaxoglou, & Becker, 2001), as well as the establishment of more than 100 postgraduate degree programs in applied sport psychology around the world (Sachs, Burke, & Loughren, 2007). Practicing sport psychologists are also beginning to recognize the needs of others outside of sport and exercise, particularly groups that can benefit from different kinds of psychological support to help them excel at the highest levels, including business professionals, military and emergency personnel (Asken, 1993), performing artists (Hanrahan), medical service providers (Brown, 2001), and astronauts (Orlick, 2000).

## Additional readings

Andersen, M. B. (ed.) (2000). *Doing sport psychology*. Champaign, IL: Human Kinetics.

Anderson, A. G., Knowles, Z., and Gilbourne, D. (2004). Reflective practice: A review of concepts, models, and practical implications for enhancing the practice of applied sport psychologists. *The Sport Psychologist*, 18, 188–203.

Green, C. D. (2003). Psychology strikes out: Coleman R. Griffith and the Chicago Cubs. *History of Psychology*, 6, 267–83.

Martens, R. (1979). About smocks and jocks. *Journal of Sport Psychology*, 1, 94–9.

Williams, J. M. (ed.) (2005). *Applied sport psychology: Personal growth to peak performance* (5th ed.). Columbus, OH: McGraw-Hill.

## Study questions

1 What is the *Consultant Evaluation Form* (CEF) and how was it used in the key study by Gould and colleagues?

2 What differences were found in the ratings of the consultants, administrators, coaches, and athletes in the key study?

3 What did the athletes and coaches identify as effective consultant characteristics in the key study?

4 What are the three broad areas that sport psychologists work in?

5 Following the publication of the key study, what are some other ways in which applied sport psychologists have been evaluated?

## References

Andersen, M. B. (ed.) (2000). *Doing sport psychology*. Champaign, IL: Human Kinetics.

Andersen, M. B. (ed.) (2005). *Sport psychology in practice*. Champaign, IL: Human Kinetics.

Andersen, M. B., Van Raalte, J. L., & Brewer, B. W. (2001). Sport psychology service delivery: Staying ethical while keeping loose. *Professional Psychology: Research and Practice*, 32, 12–18.

Anderson, A. G., & Cecil, S. (eds) (2006). Reflections on practicing sport psychology at the 2004 Athens Olympic and Paralympic Games (special issue). *Sport & Exercise Psychology Review*, 4.

Anderson, A. G., Miles, A., Robinson, P., & Mahoney, C. (2004). Evaluating the sport psychologist's effectiveness: What should we be assessing? *Psychology of Sport and Exercise*, 5, 255–77.

Asken, M. J. (1993). *PsycheResponse: Psychological skills for emergency responders*. London: Prentice Hall.

Brewer, B. W., Van Raalte, J. L., Petitpas, A. J., Bachman, A. D., & Weinhold, R. A. (1998). Newspaper portrayals of sport psychology in the United States, 1985–1993. *The Sport Psychologist*, 12, 89–94.

Brown, C. (2001, August). *The cutting edge: Performance psychology with surgeons*. Paper presented at the Annual Convention of the American Psychological Association, San Francisco, CA.

Burke, K. L., Sachs, M. L., & Smisson, C. P. (eds) (2004). *Directory of graduate programs in applied sport psychology* (7th ed.). Morgantown, WV: Fitness Information Technology.

Clarke, P. T. (2004). Coping with the emotions of Olympic performance: A case study of winning the Olympic gold. In D. Lavallee, J. Thatcher, & M. V. Jones (eds), *Coping and emotion in sport* (pp. 239–54). New York: Nova Science.

Danish, S. J., Petitpas, A. J., & Hale, B. D. (1995). Psychological interventions: A life developmental model. In S. Murphy (ed.), *Sport psychology interventions* (pp. 19–38). Champaign, IL: Human Kinetics.

Dishman, R. K. (1983). Identity crisis in North American sport psychology: Academics in professional issues. *Journal of Sport Psychology*, 5, 123–34.

Dishman, R. K., & Buckworth, J. (1996). Increasing physical activity: A quantitative synthesis. *Medicine and Science in Sports and Exercise*, 28, 706–19.

Duda, J. L. (ed.) (1998). *Advances in sport and exercise psychology measurement*. Morgantown, WV: Fitness Information Technology.

Gentner, N., Fisher, L., & Wrisberg, C. (2004). Athletes' and coaches' perceptions of sport psychology services offered by graduate students at one NCAA Division I university. *Psychological Reports*, 94, 213–16.

Gill, D. L. (1997). Sport and exercise psychology. In J. Massengale and R. Swanson (eds), *History of exercise and sport science* (pp. 293–320). Champaign, IL: Human Kinetics.

Gould, D., Tammen, V., Murphy, S., & May, J. (1989). An examination of U.S. Olympic sport psychology consultants and the services they provide. *The Sport Psychologist*, 3, 300–12.

Greenspan, M. J., & Feltz, D. L. (1989). Psychological interventions with athletes in competitive situations: A review. *The Sport Psychologist*, 3, 219–36.

Griffith, C. R. (1926). *The psychology of coaching*. New York: Charles Scribners.

Griffith, C. R. (1928). *Psychology and athletics*. New York: Charles Scribners.

Hackfort, D., Duda, J. L., & Lidor, R. (eds) (2005). *Handbook of research in applied sport and exercise psychology*. Morgantown, WV: Fitness Information Technology.

Halliwell, W. (1989). Delivery of psychological services to the Canadian sailing team at the 1988 summer games. *The Sport Psychologist*, 3, 313–19.

Hardy, L., & Parfitt, G. (1994). The development of a model for the provision of psychological support to a national squad. *The Sport Psychologist*, 8, 126–42.

Holt, N. L., & Strean, W. B. (2001). Reflecting on the initial intake meeting in sport psychology: A self-narrative of neophyte practice. *The Sport Psychologist*, 15, 188–204.

Howard, G. E. (1912). Social psychology of the spectator. *American Journal of Sociology*, 8, 33–50.

Lavallee, D., Kremer, J., Moran, A., & Williams, M. (2004). *Sport psychology: Contemporary themes*. London: Palgrave.

Leffingwell, T. R., Rider, S. P., & Williams, J. M. (2001). Application of the transtheoretical model to psychological skills training. *The Sport Psychologist*, 15, 168–87.

Lidor, R., Morris, T., Bardaxoglou, N., & Becker, B. (eds) (2001). *The world sport psychology sourcebook*. Morgantown, WV: Fitness Information Technology.

Lloyd, R., & Trudel, P. (1999). Verbal interactions between an eminent mental training consultant and elite level athletes: A case study. *The Sport Psychologist*, 13, 413–33.

Martens, R. (1979). About smocks and jocks. *Journal of Sport Psychology*, 1, 94–9.

Martin, S. B., Lavallee, D., Kellmann, M., & Page, S. J. (2004). Attitudes toward sport psychology consulting of adult athletes from the United States, United Kingdom, and Germany. *International Journal of Sport and Exercise Psychology*, 2, 146–60.

May, J. R., & Brown, L. (1989). Delivery of psychological services to the U.S. Alpine Ski Team prior to and during the Olympics in Calgary. *The Sport Psychologist*, 3, 320–9.

McCann, S. C. (2000). Doing sport psychology at the really big show. In M. Andersen (ed.), *Doing sport psychology* (pp. 209–22). Champaign, IL: Human Kinetics.

Meyers, A. W., Whelan, J. P., & Murphy, S. M. (1996). Cognitive, behavioural strategies in athletic performance enhancement. In M. Hersen, R. M. Eisler, & P. M. Miller (eds) *Progress in behaviour modification* (pp. 137–64). Pacific Grove, CA: Brooks/Cole.

Murphy, S. M. (ed.) (1995). *Sport psychology interventions*. Champaign, IL: Human Kinetics.

Nideffer, R. M., & Sagal, M. (2001). *Assessment in sport psychology*. Morgantown, WV: Fitness Information Technology.

Ogilvie, B. C., & Tutko, T. A. (1966). *Problem athletes and how to handle them*. London: Pelham Books.

Orlick, T. (1989). Reflections on sport psych consulting with individual and team sport athletes at the summer and winter Olympic Games. *The Sport Psychologist*, 3, 358–65.

Orlick, T. (2000). *In pursuit of excellence*. Champaign, IL: Human Kinetics.

Orlick, T., & Partington, J. (1987). The sport psychology consultant: Analysis of critical components as viewed by Canadian Olympic athletes. *The Sport Psychologist*, 1, 4–17.

Ostrow, A. C. (1996). *Directory of psychological tests in the sport and exercise sciences* (2nd ed). Morgantown, WV: Fitness Information Technology.

Partington, J., & Orlick, T. (1987a). The sport psychology consultant: Olympic coaches' views. *The Sport Psychologist*, 1, 95–102.

Partington, J., & Orlick, T. (1987b). *The sport psychology consultant evaluation form. The Sport Psychologist*, 1, 309–317.

Patrick, G. T. W. (1903). The psychology of football. *American Journal of Psychology*, 14, 104–17.

Poczwardowski, A., Sherman, C. P., & Henschen, K. P. (1998). A sport psychology service delivery heuristic: Building on theory and practice. *The Sport Psychologist*, 12, 192–208.

Ravizza, K. (1988). Gaining entry with athletic personnel for season-long consulting. *The Sport Psychologist*, 2, 243–54.

Roberts, G. C., & Kimiecik, J. C. (1989). Sport psychology in the German Democratic Republic: An interview with Dr. Gerd Konzag. *The Sport Psychologist*, 3, 72–7.

Sachs, M. L. (1991). Reading list in applied sport psychology: Psychological skills training. *The Sport Psychologist*, 5, 88–91.

Sachs, M. L., Burke, K. L., & Loughren, E. A. (2007). *Directory of graduate programs in applied sport psychology* (8th ed.). Morgantown, WV: Fitness Information Technology.

Salmela, J. H. (1989). Long-term intervention with the Canadian men's Olympic gymnastic team. *The Sport Psychologist*, 3, 340–9.

Silva, J. M. (1989). Establishing professional standards in applied sport psychology research. *Journal of Applied Sport Psychology*, 1, 160–5.

Smith, R. E. (1989). Applied sport psychology in an age of accountability. *Journal of Applied Sport Psychology*, 1, 166–80.

Suinn, R. (1985). The 1984 Olympics and sport psychology. *Journal of Sport Psychology*, 7, 321–9.

Taylor, J., & Wilson, G. (ed.) (2005). *Applying sport psychology: Four perspectives*. Champaign, IL: Human Kinetics.

Triplett, N. (1898). The dynamogenic factors in pacemaking and competition. *American Journal of Psychology*, 9, 507–33.

Vealey, R. (1988). Future directions in psychological skills training. *The Sport Psychologist*, 2, 319–36.

Weigand, D. A., Richardson, P. A., & Weinberg, R. S. (1999). A two-stage evaluation of a sport psychology internship. *Journal of Sport Behavior*, 22, 83–104.

Weinberg, R. S. (1989). Applied sport psychology: Issues and challenges. *Journal of Applied Sport Psychology*, 1, 181–95.

Williams, J. M. (ed.) (1986). *Applied sport psychology: Personal growth to peak performance* (3rd ed.). Mountain View, CA: Mayfield.

Williams, J. M., & Straub, W. F. (2006). Sport psychology: past, present, future. In J. M. Williams (ed.), *Applied sport psychology: Personal growth to peak performance* (5th ed., pp. 1–16). Columbus, OH: McGraw-Hill.

# 23

# Ethics

Petitpas, A., Brewer, B., Rivera, P., and Van Raalte, J. (1994). Ethical beliefs and behaviors in applied sport psychology: The AAASP ethics survey. *Journal of Applied Sport Psychology*, 6, 135–51.

**Written in collaboration with Martin I. Jones**

## Background and context

The field of applied sport psychology is in a constant state of evolution, learning from and integrating practices from psychology, philosophy, physical education, and sport and exercise science. Sport psychologists participate in similar activities and services as professionals in other areas of psychology (e.g., education, counseling, enhancement, etc.), however, subtle nuances and distinctions between sport psychology and other disciplines of psychology have resulted in the field of sport psychology striving for professional autonomy away from the other disciplines (Whelan, Meyers, & Elkin, 2002). This is evident in the initiation of the International Society of Sport Psychology (ISSP) in 1965, the foundation of the North American Society for the Psychology of Sport and Physical Activity (NASPSPA) in 1967, and the formation of the Association for the Advancement of Applied Sport Psychology (AAASP; renamed AASP for the Association for Applied Sport Psychology since the key study was conducted) in 1985. Similarly, this is apparent in the development of profession-specific ethical codes targeting the needs of the emerging field of applied sport and exercise psychology.

Ethics are defined as knowing and doing what is good and right as opposed to what is bad and wrong. Albert Schweitzer, the 1952 Nobel Peace Prize recipient, said: "Let me give you a definition of ethics: It is good to maintain and further life. It is bad to damage and destroy life." In the context of sport psychology, ethics are about helping people and doing no harm.

The essence of an ethics code in any profession or organization is to guide practitioners in deciding between right and wrong. When developing an organization or field-wide ethics code the fundamental nature of the code is a shared sense of values and responsibilities (i.e., what is right and wrong for most people). Moreover, an ethics code demonstrates to the public that an organization regulates itself, professionals associated with the organization can be trusted to act responsibly, and the dignity of the client is respected and guaranteed (Whelan, Meyers, & Elkin, 2002). Previous to the publication of the key study in this chapter there had been an ongoing discussion regarding the need for a professionalization of sport psychology (e.g., Gould, 1990; Silva, 1989; Weinberg, 1989) and a related development of a specific code of ethics. The existence of the *Ethical Principles of Psychologists and Code of Conduct* published by the American Psychological Association (APA) (1992) initiated the debate that sport psychology organizations should adopt the ethical standards to which all other disciplines of psychology adhere. The APA code was first developed in 1953 as a result of a polling of APA members for dilemmas they had faced that related to ethical conduct. The result was a document more than 170 pages long. Since 1953 the code has been revised several times to meet the ever changing needs of the profession to the current 16-page document (APA, 2002). At the time of the Petitpas *et al.* study the APA (1977) ethics code had been adopted by AAASP. However, with the publication of the 1992 code and increasing calls for professionalization of sport psychology, it was questioned whether AAASP should adopt the newly revised APA (1992) code. The 1992 code consisted of six general principles: competence; integrity; professional and scientific responsibility; respect for people's rights and dignity; concern for others' welfare; and social responsibility. In addition to the general principles the code included specific standards which were practical applications of the general principles or the rules of ethical behavior (Whelan *et al.*, 2002). Although seen as an improvement over previous publications of the code (Bersoff, 1994), the 1992 publication had its critics. Specifically, in sport and exercise psychology the guidelines lack the specificity to be practical and interpretable to service providers in applied sport psychology. For instance, the 1992 code did not address the needs of non-psychology professionals from physical education and sport science backgrounds, did not account for the multiple relationships existent in sports contexts and the associated boundaries (e.g., working as and with coaches), and did not address the use of the term "sport" psychologist. As a result the members of an ethics committee created by AAASP believed that it would be imprudent to recommend adoption of the 1992 code or to develop a new sport psychology code of ethics without first gathering data specific to the practice of sport and exercise psychology and the ethical beliefs and behaviors of those practicing it. As such, Petitpas *et al.* carried out an assessment of the ethical beliefs and behaviors of the AAASP membership specific to the practice of applied sport psychology in order to provide members of AAASP and the AAASP ethics committee with the resources to make an informed decision regarding the ethics code issue.

## Key study

Members of the AAASP ethics committee initially reviewed the literature associated with ethical beliefs and behaviors in applied sport psychology. This led to the identification of seven general questions that eventually provided a framework for the study. Whereas the first four questions concerned the appropriateness of the APA (1992) ethical standards for the membership of AAASP, the last three questions focused on issues related to the development of applied sport psychology as a profession and the role of an ethics committee.

1   Are there differences in beliefs and behaviors of AAASP members related to the ethical practice of applied sport psychology as a function of the academic discipline from which the individual received his or her degree?
2   Are there specific sport psychology related behaviors that are difficult to judge or highly controversial in terms of ethical practice?
3   Do members of AAASP observe sport psychologists engaging in behaviors that would be considered ethically questionable?
4   If ethically questionable behaviors are observed, what actions do the observers take?
5   What is the extent of supervision received by student and professional members of AAASP for their applied work in sport psychology?

6    What percentage of the professional membership of AAASP "makes a living" exclusively through the practice of applied sport psychology?

7    What does the membership of AAASP believe the role of the Ethics Committee should be?

To obtain preliminary data addressing these seven general questions, the AAASP Ethics Committee surveyed the membership.

## Method

The AAASP Ethics Survey, a cover letter, and a return envelope were mailed to 508 professional and student members of AAASP in April of 1992. These individuals constituted the entire paid membership of AAASP at that time.

Items on the survey were adapted from previous surveys of ethical issues in a variety of subfields within psychology (Pope, Tabachnick, & Keith-Spiegel, 1987; Pope & Vetter, 1992; Tabachnick, Keith-Spiegel, & Pope, 1991). Original items pertaining to ethically challenging sport situations were also developed. Items were designed to identify common ethical dilemmas in applied sport psychology and difficulties in applying the APA Ethical Standards to the practice of sport psychology. Both quantitative and qualitative approaches were used in the questionnaire.

In the structured response portion of the questionnaire respondents were asked to rate each of 47 behaviors in terms of: (a) the extent to which they had engaged in the behavior in their work as a sport psychologist; and (b) the extent to which they considered the behavior ethical. Interpretation of the term "sport psychologist" was left up to the individual respondents. Response options for the first category of ratings were *never* (1), *rarely* (2), *sometimes* (3), *fairly often* (4), and *very often* (5). Response options for the second category of ratings were *unquestionably not* (1), *under rare circumstances* (2), *don't know/not sure* (3), *under many circumstances* (4), and *unquestionably yes* (5).

In the open-ended response section of the questionnaire, respondents were asked to: (a) ". . . describe, in a few words or more detail, an incident that you or a colleague have faced in the past year or two that was ethically challenging or troubling to you." (b) ". . . list questionable ethical practices in applied sport psychology that you have observed" and ". . . mention any actions that you may have taken in response to these questionable practices." (c) describe their beliefs about the role and function of the AAASP Ethics Committee (i.e., education, enforcement) and provide recommendations on how to implement these beliefs.

Participants were asked to respond to items requesting demographic information (e.g., gender, age, degree, AAASP membership status, AAASP certification status, discipline, specialization, primary work setting, hours per week in applied sport psychology work, average monthly income derived from *non-teaching* applied sport psychology activities, membership in professional organizations). Additional items addressed respondents' exposure to ethical standards and supervision in applied sport psychology. Copies of the questionnaire are available from the first author.

## Results

### Demographic Characteristics

A 28% response rate was obtained, as 165 (113 professional members, 52 student members) questionnaires were returned. Demographic characteristics of the respondents (and of AAASP members in March 1994) are presented in Table 23.1. This data shows that the respondents

**Table 23.1** Demographic characteristics of respondents to the AAASP Ethics Survey

| Characteristic | N | %[a] | AAASP %[b] |
|---|---|---|---|
| Sex | | | |
|   Female | 64 | 38.8 | 40.7 |
|   Male | 101 | 61.2 | 59.3 |
| Age group | | | |
|   35 and under | 75 | 45.5 | – |
|   36 to 50 | 71 | 43.0 | – |
|   Over 50 | 12 | 7.3 | – |
| AAASP membership status | | | |
|   Professional | 113 | 68.5 | 52.2 |
|   Student | 52 | 31.5 | 47.8 |
| AAASP certification status | | | |
|   Certified | 18 | 10.9 | 9.8 |
|   Not certified | 147 | 89.1 | 90.2 |
| Discipline | | | |
|   Physical education/exercise science | 70 | 42.4 | 44.5 |
|   Psychology | 54 | 32.7 | 49.2 |
|   Other | 41 | 24.9 | 6.5 |

[a] May not sum to 100% due to missing data
[b] Percentages refer to AAASP membership figures in March 1994. AAASP does not record the age of its members

are largely representative of those who belong to AAASP at the time of the study. Professional members and members in disciplines other than physical education/exercise science and psychology appear to be slightly overrepresented and student members and members in psychology appear to be slightly underrepresented in the current sample.

Respondents reported engaging in an average of 6.04 ($SD = 8.62$, median = 2) hours per week of direct applied sport psychology service. This distribution was positively skewed, as over 70% ($N = 116$) of respondents reported five or fewer hours per week and over 90% ($N = 149$) of respondents reported 17 or fewer hours per week. In terms of average monthly income derived from *non-teaching* applied sport psychology activities, the modal response ($N = 101$, 61%) was $0. Eighteen respondents (11%) reported monthly incomes of greater than $1,000.

## Exposure to Ethical Standards

Nearly a third of the sample (30%, $N = 49$) indicated that they had taken a specific course in ethics (e.g., ethics course in psychology or counseling). Seventy respondents (42%) reported that they had taken one or more courses in which ethics were covered. A small portion of the sample (22%, $N = 36$) indicated that they had gained information on ethical standards in a workshop context (e.g., at professional conferences). Approximately half of the respondents (46%, $N = 76$) reported that they had been exposed to ethical standards through independent study (e.g., reading journal articles, textbooks, ethical guidelines).

## Supervision

Overall, 50 respondents (30%) indicated that they were being supervised in their applied sport psychology work. Most of the students (62%, $N = 32$) and only a small portion of the professionals (16%, $N = 18$) reported that their work was being supervised. Of the respondents who indicated that they were receiving supervision, students tended to report being supervised by faculty members (88%, $N = 28$) and professionals tended to report being supervised by peers (100%, $N = 18$). Patterns of supervision were similar for both students and professionals, as approximately half of the respondents who reported receiving supervision (47% [$N = 15$] of students and 56% [$N = 10$] of professionals) indicated that they obtained supervision on a regular basis. Reports of "as needed" supervision were common for both students (63%, $N = 20$) and professionals (83%, $N = 15$). Of the 49 respondents who stated that they were supervising the applied work of others, 28 (57%) reported that they had received training in supervision. The most commonly cited source ($N = 21$) of supervision training was a specific course in supervision ($N = 10$ in counseling/psychology, $N = 3$ in physical education, $N = 1$ in teacher supervision, $N = 7$ in an unspecified area).

## Ethical Beliefs and Behaviors

The percentage of respondents' ratings for each of the 47 behaviors in terms of occurrence in their own work as a sport psychologist and the degree to which they consider the behavior to be ethical is presented in Table 23.2.

Chi-square analyses were performed on responses to the 47 items to examine differences in ethical beliefs and behaviors as a function of gender, AAASP membership status (professional vs. student), and discipline (physical education/exercise science vs. psychology). Because of the large number of comparisons in these analyses, $p < .001$ was used as the criterion for statistical significance. No significant gender differences in ethical beliefs and behaviors were found. No differences in ethical beliefs between AAASP professional members and student members were obtained, but professional members were significantly more likely than student members to acknowledge "Publicly claiming to be a sport psychologist," "Practicing without supervision or peer consultation," and "Omitting significant information when writing a letter of recommendation for a student." Respondents in physical education/exercise science differed from respondents in psychology in only one belief and one behavior. Respondents in physical education/exercise science were more likely than those in psychology to report believing it ethical to accept "goods/services in exchange for sport psychology consultation" and to report "serving concurrently as college instructor and psychologist for a student-athlete."

Procedures developed by Pope et al. (1987) and Tabachnick et al. (1991) were used to examine the relationship between beliefs and behaviors and to identify rare behaviors, nearly universal behaviors, difficult judgments, and controversial behaviors.

*Relationship between Beliefs and Behaviors.* Because "the frequency with which the respondents reported engaging in a behavior was less than the frequency of instances in which the behavior was ethical in their judgment" (Pope et al., 1987) for all 47 items, the data suggest that the AAASP members in this sample are practicing largely in accordance with their beliefs.

*Rare Behaviors.* A rare behavior was defined as one acknowledged by less than 5% of the respondents. Only four behaviors met this criterion: "Including unverified claims in promotional materials," "Claiming affiliation with organizations that falsely implies sponsorship or

**Table 23.2** Percentage of AAASP members responding in each category

| Item | Rating[a] Your work | | | | | Ethical? | | | | |
|---|---|---|---|---|---|---|---|---|---|---|
| | 1 | 2 | 3 | 4 | 5 | 1 | 2 | 3 | 4 | 5 |
| 1. Publicly claiming to be a sport psychologist. | 46.1 | 18.8 | 10.3 | 9.7 | 9.1 | 18.8 | 15.8 | 10.9 | 25.5 | 22.4 |
| 2. Advertising sport psychology services. | 57.0 | 12.1 | 10.9 | 5.5 | 9.1 | 13.9 | 12.1 | 8.5 | 33.9 | 26.7 |
| 3. Including athlete testimonials in advertising. | 86.1 | 3.0 | 4.2 | 0.6 | 1.2 | 38.8 | 24.2 | 13.3 | 14.5 | 4.8 |
| 4. Promoting unjustified expectations through advertising. | 93.9 | 0.6 | 0.0 | 0.0 | 0.6 | 89.1 | 3.6 | 0.0 | 0.0 | 3.6 |
| 5. Including unverified claims in promotional materials. | 93.3 | 1.8 | 0.0 | 0.0 | 0.6 | 88.5 | 4.2 | 0.6 | 0.0 | 3.6 |
| 6. Practicing without continuing education to upgrade applied skills and knowledge. | 73.3 | 13.9 | 4.8 | 1.2 | 1.8 | 51.5 | 29.7 | 7.9 | 5.5 | 1.2 |
| 7. Practicing without supervision or peer consultation. | 37.0 | 15.2 | 20.0 | 13.9 | 9.1 | 21.8 | 21.8 | 21.2 | 23.0 | 7.9 |
| 8. Practicing without clearly defined financial arrangements. | 69.7 | 14.5 | 5.5 | 3.6 | 1.8 | 49.1 | 24.2 | 11.5 | 7.3 | 4.2 |
| 9. Accepting goods/services in exchange for sport psychology consultation. | 60.6 | 20.0 | 12.1 | 2.4 | 0.6 | 23.0 | 28.5 | 20.0 | 15.8 | 9.1 |
| 10. Providing inadequate supervision to trainees. | 84.8 | 6.1 | 1.2 | 0.0 | 0.6 | 86.1 | 4.2 | 1.8 | 0.6 | 2.5 |
| 11. Practicing without clarifying who is and who is not the client (e.g., coach, athlete, management). | 77.6 | 12.1 | 4.8 | 0.0 | 0.0 | 72.7 | 10.9 | 9.1 | 0.6 | 3.0 |
| 12. Consulting with an athlete who is concurrently receiving sport psychology services from another professional. | 78.8 | 10.3 | 4.2 | 0.6 | 0.0 | 37.0 | 29.1 | 15.8 | 9.7 | 3.6 |
| 13. Sharing athlete data with coaches without the athlete's written consent. | 82.4 | 7.9 | 3.6 | 0.6 | 0.0 | 76.4 | 14.5 | 1.8 | 1.8 | 1.8 |
| 14. Reporting recruiting violations to appropriate officials. | 83.6 | 3.6 | 1.8 | 0.0 | 0.6 | 20.6 | 13.3 | 24.8 | 12.7 | 17.0 |
| 15. Reporting an athlete who uses cocaine. | 84.2 | 0.6 | 2.4 | 1.8 | 2.4 | 20.0 | 15.8 | 21.8 | 17.0 | 17.6 |
| 16. Reporting an athlete who uses steroids. | 84.2 | 0.6 | 2.4 | 1.8 | 2.4 | 20.6 | 15.8 | 19.4 | 18.2 | 18.8 |
| 17. Reporting abusive coaching practices. | 72.7 | 8.5 | 4.5 | 3.6 | 2.4 | 10.9 | 12.1 | 17.0 | 26.7 | 26.1 |
| 18. Reporting an athlete's gambling activity. | 84.8 | 0.0 | 2.4 | 1.2 | 2.4 | 23.6 | 15.8 | 26.7 | 16.4 | 10.3 |
| 19. Reporting an athlete who committed burglary. | 83.0 | 0.0 | 2.4 | 0.6 | 3.6 | 21.2 | 12.1 | 20.0 | 14.5 | 23.6 |
| 20. Reporting an athlete who acknowledged committing rape in the past. | 83.6 | 0.0 | 3.0 | 0.6 | 1.8 | 22.4 | 13.3 | 23.6 | 14.5 | 17.0 |

**Table 23.2**—continued

| Item | Rating[a] Your work | | | | | Ethical? | | | | |
|------|---|---|---|---|---|---|---|---|---|---|
| | 1 | 2 | 3 | 4 | 5 | 1 | 2 | 3 | 4 | 5 |
| 21. Working with an athlete whose sexual or religious practices you oppose. | 47.9 | 7.9 | 18.8 | 9.7 | 7.9 | 15.2 | 5.5 | 12.7 | 20.6 | 40.0 |
| 22. Working with client problems for which you have had no formal training. | 69.7 | 18.2 | 4.8 | 1.2 | 0.0 | 58.8 | 28.5 | 3.0 | 2.4 | 3.0 |
| 23. Using psychological tests without attaining appropriate user qualifications. | 89.1 | 2.4 | 1.8 | 0.0 | 0.6 | 78.2 | 8.5 | 4.2 | 0.6 | 3.6 |
| 24. Consulting with athletes in a sport that you find morally objectionable (e.g., boxing). | 73.3 | 7.3 | 6.7 | 3.6 | 1.2 | 15.2 | 18.8 | 27.9 | 18.2 | 15.2 |
| 25. Consulting with individual athletes without training in counseling/clinical skills. | 73.3 | 7.9 | 4.8 | 3.6 | 2.4 | 53.3 | 20.0 | 10.3 | 6.1 | 4.8 |
| 26. Practicing while obviously affected by personal concerns. | 54.5 | 24.8 | 10.3 | 1.8 | 0.6 | 26.1 | 35.8 | 20.6 | 10.3 | 1.2 |
| 27. Using illegal substances in your personal life. | 78.2 | 10.3 | 3.0 | 0.0 | 0.6 | 50.3 | 14.5 | 18.2 | 7.3 | 3.6 |
| 28. Insulting or ridiculing a client in his or her absence. | 83.6 | 7.3 | 1.8 | 0.0 | 0.0 | 83.6 | 4.2 | 3.6 | 0.0 | 3.0 |
| 29. Using profanity in your professional work. | 39.4 | 32.1 | 16.4 | 4.2 | 2.4 | 31.5 | 29.1 | 13.9 | 12.7 | 7.3 |
| 30. Omitting significant information when writing a letter of recommendation for a student. | 66.1 | 15.8: | 7.9 | 0.6 | 0.0 | 40.0 | 30.3 | 18.2 | 3.0 | 1.2 |
| 31. Criticizing all theoretical orientations except for those that you personally prefer. | 63.6 | 21.8 | 6.1 | 1.2 | 0.6 | 52.1 | 23.0 | 10.3 | 6.7 | 3.0 |
| 32. Continuing to use intervention techniques for which empirical evidence is lacking. | 38.2 | 27.9 | 19.4 | 6.7 | 3.0 | 23.6 | 29.1 | 19.4 | 19.4 | 5.5 |
| 33. Practicing without evaluating the effectiveness of your work. | 44.2 | 33.3 | 12.1 | 4.8 | 0.0 | 39.4 | 38.2 | 9.1 | 9.1 | 0.6 |
| 34. Ignoring unethical behavior by colleagues. | 53.9 | 23.0 | 13.3 | 2.4 | 0.6 | 48.5 | 24.8 | 15.8 | 3.6 | 2.4 |
| 35. Claiming affiliation with organizations that falsely implies sponsorship or certification. | 91.5 | 0.6 | 0.0 | 0.0 | 0.0 | 83.6 | 4.8 | 3.6 | 0.0 | 2.4 |
| 36. Serving concurrently as coach and sport psychologist for a team. | 76.4 | 2.4 | 7.3 | 3.0 | 4.2 | 21.8 | 24.8 | 18.8 | 19.4 | 11.5 |
| 37. Socializing with clients (e.g., partying with the team). | 46.7 | 21.2 | 20.6 | 4.8 | 1.2 | 15.2 | 26.7 | 24.2 | 21.2 | 9.1 |

| | 1 | 2 | 3 | 4 | 5 | 1 | 2 | 3 | 4 | 5 |
|---|---|---|---|---|---|---|---|---|---|---|
| 38. Serving concurrently as college instructor and psychologist for a student-athlete. | 55.8 | 12.7 | 15.8 | 5.5 | 3.6 | 16.4 | 24.2 | 16.4 | 23.6 | 15.2 |
| 39. Traveling with a team. | 44.2 | 15.8 | 14.5 | 9.1 | 9.1 | 5.5 | 4.2 | 7.3 | 30.3 | 46.7 |
| 40. Being sexually attracted to a client. | 46.7 | 28.5 | 12.1 | 2.4 | 0.0 | 30.9 | 13.3 | 19.4 | 10.9 | 15.2 |
| 41. Becoming sexually involved with a client *after* discontinuing a professional relationship. | 92.7 | 0.6 | 0.6 | 0.6 | 0.0 | 34.5 | 15.8 | 21.8 | 12.1 | 10.9 |
| 42. Allowing out-of-town clients to reside in your home while services are being provided. | 83.6 | 6.7 | 1.2 | 2.4 | 0.6 | 81.2 | 3.6 | 5.5 | 1.8 | 4.8 |
| 43. Betting on a team or individual with which or whom you are working. | 92.1 | 1.8 | 0.6 | 0.6 | 0.0 | 81.2 | 3.6 | 5.5 | 1.8 | 4.8 |
| 44. Using institutional affiliation to recruit private clients. | 70.3 | 10.9 | 9.1 | 0.0 | 1.2 | 35.2 | 18.2 | 18.2 | 16.4 | 6.1 |
| 45. Entering into a business relationship with a client. | 84.2 | 5.5 | 1.8 | 0.6 | 1.8 | 41.2 | 18.2 | 20.6 | 8.5 | 7.9 |
| 46. Working with an athlete who uses steroids. | 64.8 | 17.0 | 9.7 | 0.6 | 1.2 | 16.4 | 15.2 | 24.8 | 17.0 | 22.4 |
| 47. Refusing to continue consulting with a client after you discover that he or she is involved in illegal activity. | 83.0 | 4.8 | 2.4 | 0.6 | 1.2 | 12.7 | 13.9 | 25.5 | 20.0 | 23.6 |

[a] Responses 1–5 sum to less than 100% because of missing data

certification," "Becoming sexually involved with a client *after* discontinuing a professional relationship," and "Betting on a team or individual with which or whom you are working."

*Nearly Universal Behaviors.* In accord with Pope *et al.* (1987) and Tabachnick *et al.* (1991), the criterion for a nearly universal behavior was to be acknowledged by at least 90% of the respondents. None of the 47 behaviors met this criterion.

*Difficult Judgments.* Tabachnick *et al.* (1991) defined a difficult judgment as "one in which 25% of the respondents indicated 'don't know/not sure' in terms of whether the behavior was ethical" (pp. 512–13). Applying this definition to the current study, eight behaviors were identified as difficult judgments. These items are shown in Table 23.3.

*Controversial Behaviors.* Tabachnick *et al.* (1991) defined a controversial item as "one in which the ethical judgments were so diverse that the *SD* > 1.25" (p. 513). Using this criterion, over half of the 47 items were identified as controversial. These 24 controversial behaviors are displayed in Table 23.4.

**Table 23.3** Items identified as difficult judgments

| Item |
| --- |
| 14. Reporting recruiting violations to appropriate officials. |
| 18. Reporting an athlete's gambling activity. |
| 20. Reporting an athlete who acknowledged committing rape in the past. |
| 24. Consulting with athletes in a sport that you find morally objectionable (e.g., boxing). |
| 37. Socializing with clients (e.g., partying with the team). |
| 42. Allowing out-of-town clients to reside in your home while services are being provided. |
| 46. Working with an athlete who uses steroids. |
| 47. Refusing to continue consulting with a client after you discover that he or she is involved in illegal activity. |

**Table 23.4** Items identified as controversial behaviors

| Item |
| --- |
| 1. Publicly claiming to be a sport psychologist. |
| 2. Advertising sport psychology services. |
| 3. Including athlete testimonials in advertising. |
| 7. Practicing without supervision or peer consultation. |
| 9. Accepting goods/services in exchange for sport psychology consultation. |
| 14. Reporting recruiting violations to appropriate officials. |
| 15. Reporting an athlete who uses cocaine. |
| 16. Reporting an athlete who uses steroids. |
| 17. Reporting abusive coaching practices. |
| 18. Reporting an athlete's gambling activity. |
| 19. Reporting an athlete who committed burglary. |
| 20. Reporting an athlete who acknowledged committing rape in the past. |
| 21. Working with an athlete whose sexual or religious practices you oppose. |
| 24. Consulting with athletes in a sport that you find morally objectionable (e.g., boxing). |
| 29. Using profanity in your professional work. |
| 36. Serving concurrently as coach and sport psychologist for a team. |
| 38. Serving concurrently as college instructor and psychologist for a student-athlete. |
| 40. Being sexually attracted to a client. |

| Item |
| --- |
| 41. Becoming sexually involved with a client *after* discontinuing a professional relationship. |
| 42. Allowing out-of-town clients to reside in your home while services are being provided. |
| 44. Using institutional affiliation to recruit private clients. |
| 45. Entering into a business relationship with a client. |
| 46. Working with an athlete who uses steroids. |
| 47. Refusing to continue consulting with a client after you discover that he or she is involved in illegal activity. |

## Ethical Dilemmas

Eighty-four respondents identified 89 ethically challenging or troubling incidents that they or a colleague had faced in the past year or two. In accord with procedures outlined by Strauss and Corbin (1990), responses were categorized by three independent raters using the APA Ethical Standards (1992) as categories. Frequencies of incidents corresponding to the eight ethical standards are displayed in Table 23.5. Most of the incidents pertained to general Standards and Confidentiality. Frequently cited issues in the general standards category included providing services without proper training, having students working with athletes without supervision, engaging in dual role relationships, and failing to make appropriate referrals. Frequently cited issues in the confidentiality category included dealing with coaches who want information about their athletes and responding to coaches who verbally and/or physically abuse their athletes.

Seventy-five respondents identified 136 questionable ethical practices. As shown in Table 23.6, the majority of these responses pertained to General Standards and Advertising and Other Public Statements. Frequently cited issues in the General Standards category included practicing outside of areas of competence, serving as both course instructor and sport psychology consultant to the same person, and failing to refer appropriately. Frequently cited issues in the Advertising and Public Statements category included claiming responsibility for client success and identifying clients during professional presentations.

The leading action reported in response to the questionable ethical practices was to do nothing ($N = 57$, 35%), followed by talking with or confronting the person involved ($N = 39$, 24%). Other actions listed were talking with colleague or supervisor ($N = 10$, 6%), reporting the

**Table 23.5** Frequencies of ethically challenging or troubling incidents identified by respondents

| Ethical standard | N |
| --- | --- |
| General standards | 40 |
| Evaluation, assessment, or intervention | 1 |
| Advertising and other public statements | 5 |
| Therapy | 3 |
| Confidentiality | 38 |
| Teaching, training, supervision, research, and publishing | 1 |
| Forensic issues | 0 |
| Resolving ethical issues | 1 |

**Table 23.6** Frequencies of questionable ethical practices identified by respondents

| Ethical standard | N |
|---|---|
| General standards | 56 |
| Evaluation, assessment, or intervention | 2 |
| Advertising and other public statements | 52 |
| Therapy | 4 |
| Confidentiality | 14 |
| Teaching, training, supervision, research, and publishing | 8 |
| Forensic issues | 0 |
| Resolving ethical issues | 0 |

questionable ethical practice ($N = 9$, 5%), educating prospective consumers about ethical practices ($N = 8$, 5%), and referring to a qualified professional ($N = 2$, 1%).

Respondents were split regarding their beliefs about the role and function of the AAASP Ethics Committee. Fifty-eight respondents (35%) advocated that the committee perform both education and enforcement functions, while 46 respondents (28%) suggested that the committee provide only education. Recommendations for education focused primarily on promoting awareness of APA standards (tailored specifically to sport psychology) through such avenues as workshops/group supervision at professional meetings, continuing education, increased coverage of ethical issues in sport psychology courses, and a workbook/casebook highlighting ethical dilemmas in applied sport psychology. Respondents advocated that educational efforts present formalized ethical standards, define competencies in sport psychology (i.e., *who* can practice *what*?), and address client-practitioner boundary issues. The need for consumer education (of athletes, coaches, parents, etc.) on ethical issues was also noted.

Regarding the role of AAASP in the enforcement of ethical standards in sport psychology, responses ranged considerably. Some respondents strongly opposed AAASP's involvement in enforcing ethical standards, while others argued fervently for AAASP to adopt an active role in monitoring the professional conduct of its members. Several respondents noted that avenues for enforcing ethical standards already exist for APA members and for unlicensed or uncertified practitioners violating title restrictions. AAASP-specific options suggested for enforcement of ethical standards included installation of a peer review board that could recommend disciplinary action for ethical violations, arbitration of alleged ethical violations by unbiased parties, and creation of a reporting system for victims of ethical violations (e.g., athletes, coaches). Some respondents, citing the financial and logistical difficulties in establishing enforcement mechanisms, argued instead for such options as peer enforcement, ethics hotlines, and educational programs providing proactive recommendations for change in identified problem areas.

## Discussion

The results of this survey indicate that the ethical beliefs and behaviors of AAASP members are consistent with the APA Ethical Standards. The overall lack of differences by gender, professional/student status, and academic discipline offers initial support for the adoption of the APA Ethical Standards. However, the relatively large number of "controversial behaviors"

($N = 24$) and "difficult judgments" ($N = 8$) indicates a need for continuing education in identifying and discussing appropriate conduct related to these so-called "gray areas."

All of the 89 ethically challenging or troubling incidents and the 136 questionable ethical practices that were identified by respondents fell within the general categories outlined in the APA (1992) ethical principles. In particular, the respondents identified many incidents related to dual role relationships, limits of competence, confidentiality, and public statements that are sport specific and beg further clarification. This lack of clarity may also have accounted for some members (35%, $N = 57$) taking no action in response to questionable ethical practices that they observed.

In examining the Ethics Committee's second general question related to aspects of the "professionalization" of applied sport psychology, the survey data are alarming. Over 70% of the respondents reported five or fewer hours of direct applied sport psychology services offered per week and 61% reported a monthly income of $0 derived from *non-teaching* applied sport psychology activities. Only 18 respondents (11%) reported monthly incomes of greater than $ 1,000. These data call into question the ethics of continuing to accept large numbers of students into a field that may not have an adequate number of non-teaching employment possibilities (Teetor Waite & Pettit, 1993).

Equally troubling is the finding that only 30% of the respondents reported that they were receiving supervision for their applied sport psychology work. Regular supervision is an important element of the learning process in the overall preparation of applied sport psychologists (Sachs, 1993). It is during supervision that individuals often learn the specifics of "how" to consult with athletes, exercisers, and coaches that are necessary supplements to the theories and techniques taught in the classroom. Supervision is not just for students. It should be an important element in the continuing education of all sport psychologists. Yet only 16% of the professionals reported that they received any type of supervision. This apparent lack of "quality control" can create a negative image for an evolving field like sport psychology. In addition, failure to adequately protect the consumer by neglecting to provide supervision can have both legal and ethical ramifications for students' advisors and affiliated institutions.

Another concern regarding supervision is the lack of training reported by those individuals who are supervising the applied work of others. AAASP now requires a supervised experience with a "qualified person" as one of the criteria to become a Certified Consultant. It would seem imperative for AAASP to provide continuing education to insure that these "qualified persons" gain training in providing *sport psychology* supervision.

Respondents were split regarding their beliefs about the functions of the Ethics Committee, with slightly more respondents ($N = 58$, 35%) advocating both education and enforcement functions than education only ($N = 46$, 28%), but both groups clearly advocating the provision of sport psychology specific information. AAASP appears to be committed to fulfilling this need, as evidenced by the three invited "Ethics" presentations at the 1993 AAASP Conference and the inclusion of a specific ethics continuing education requirement for renewal of Certified Consultant status within AAASP.

## Validity and Interpretation Issues

First, it should be noted that a 28% response rate is relatively low for a within organization survey on an important topic, but it is consistent with the return rates of ethics surveys of other professional groups (e.g., Percival & Striefel, 1994). It is possible that the survey length may have discouraged participation in the study. Second, it is impossible to determine if the 6.04 hours per week of direct applied sport psychology consultation reported by respondents is typical of most professionals in the field. The sample in this study appears to have been made up largely of faculty members and private practice clinicians who do applied sport psychology work "on the side." Third, the same individuals rated both the frequency of their own behaviors and their judgments about the ethicality of those behaviors. There is some evidence that this procedure does not bias results (Borys & Pope, 1989), but caution in interpreting these findings needs to be exercised. Fourth, many of the 47 items represent complex issues that may not be best represented by the brief descriptions provided. Finally, this survey contained items pertaining to ethically challenging sport situations that were generated by the authors to gather initial data about the ethical beliefs and behaviors of AAASP members. This survey should be replicated and expanded to include other examples of ethically challenging and questionable behaviors, such as those identified by respondents in the open-ended response section of the survey.

## Conclusion

It is understandable that members of AAASP not affiliated with APA might be skeptical about having their sport psychology practices regulated by a code of ethics that was developed for psychologists, who typically work in traditional clinical settings. Unfortunately, this skepticism may lead some AAASP members to reject the APA Ethical Guidelines before they have thoroughly examined the document. As pointed out by Tabachnick et al. (1991), "A crucial aspect of the maturation and moral development of any profession is the collective openness and dedication of its membership to study and critically examine itself" (1991: 515). Based on the results of this survey, the APA Ethical Guidelines appear to provide an excellent framework for AAASP's self-evaluation process.

The APA Guidelines can provide a vehicle to more closely examine the similarities and differences between sport psychology practices and psychological interventions in more traditional settings. For example, many sport psychology consultants work in settings with high public visibility and environmental expectations that are much different than those typically associated with seeing a client in a private professional office (Danish, Petitpas, & Hale, 1993). Just as the nature of a student-professor relationship may violate traditional "clinical boundaries" (Tabachnick et al., 1991), so too might the sport psychologist-athlete relationship, which frequently requires more time spent interacting with athletes and coaches in a variety of settings.

The APA Ethical Guidelines provide a framework for self-evaluation that is generally comprehensive but open to interpretation. The Ethical Guidelines are subject to both external influence, as evidenced by the recent Federal Trade Commission rulings on the legality of APA's standards for public statements, and internal modification, as witnessed by the adoption of "Specialty Guidelines for the Delivery of Services" for Clinical, Counseling, Industrial/ Organizational, and School Psychologist subgroups (APA, 1981). AAASP may best be served by adopting and using the current APA Ethical Standards while discussing the "gray areas" specific to the practice of applied sport psychology through a process of critical self-examination.

## Subsequent research and application

Since the Petitpas et al. key study the issue of ethics, and more specifically adoption of ethical guidelines, have remained popular topics in the field of sport psychology. For example, Kremer (2002) stated: "Sport psychologists should not forget that ethical considerations are just as important in this branch of applied psychology as in any other. Hence codes of conduct which govern the work of all applied or practising psychologists must operate with equal force in this domain" (2002: 18).

A major finding of the key study was that most of the ethical practices reported by members of AAASP violated the APA guidelines for ethical practice. One potential explanation for this finding is that many sport psychologists regards themselves as psychologists with an interest in sport, whereas an equal number regard themselves as sport scientists with a specialization in psychology. As such, there is confusion as to which professional standards (psychology vs. sports science/kinesiology) should guide practice (Kremer, 2002). To add to this uncertainty Kremer notes there are different ethical guidelines for psychology and sport science organizations depending on the practitioner's nation of residence. To help reduce the confusion, AAASP developed a code of ethics for sport and exercise psychology that all members of AAASP, regardless of their training in psychology or sports science, must adhere to. The AAASP ethics code is largely based on the APA's (1992) code of conduct. However, it was not only limited to the APA code. Over 50 other organizational ethics codes including sport science, sport medicine, and international psychology organizations, were also examined and many influenced the new document (Whelan, 2006). The AAASP ethics code is made up of the same six general principles in the APA (1992) code of ethics (competence, integrity, professional and scientific responsibility, respect for people's rights and dignity, concern for others' welfare, and social responsibility), but it also included 25 general standards. (A full copy of the AAASP code of ethics is available from www.aaasponline.org/governance/committees/ethics/standards.php.)

Numerous book chapters (e.g., Andersen, 2005b; Heyman & Andersen, 1998; Kremer, 2002; Whelan *et al.*, 2002) and professional practice journal articles (e.g., Andersen, 1994; Andersen, Van Raalte, & Brewer, 2001; Taylor, 1994) have been written since the Petitpas *et al.* study, however there are very few examples of applied articles that actually investigate and assess the ethical beliefs and behaviors of practicing sport psychologists to gain an understanding of what is actually happening in the field.

Following the establishment and implementation of the AAASP ethics code, Etzel, Watson, and Zizzi (2004) set out to replicate the work of Petitpas *et al.* with the AAASP membership of Autumn 2001. Etzel *et al.* stated that the key study by Petitpas *et al.* was limited in relation to its contemporary application. Specifically, the ethical dilemmas were particularly relevant to the 1980s and early 1990s (e.g., the over-examination of the use of recreational and performance enhancing drugs) and may not be as relevant to practice in the early 2000s. Furthermore, issues that may not have been applicable or relevant in the early 1990s may be extremely relevant due to advances in technology and changes in society.

A total of 322 AAASP members (29% of AAASP membership compared with 28% in the Petitpas *et al.* study) completed the web-based survey which asked about questionable ethical practices participants had observed, what actions participants had taken in response to those ethical practices, what participants believed the role of the AAASP ethics committee should be, what suggestions participants had for making the AAASP membership more aware of ethical principles and behaviors, and what suggestions did participants give for any potential revisions to the current ethics code? Etzel *et al.* (2004) concluded that there appeared to be less controversy in 2001 than during the early 1990s perhaps as a result of the adoption of the AAASP ethics code, the ease of access to the code on the internet, increased exposure to ethical issues in the AAASP newsletter, regular ethics workshops at the annual AAASP conference, and the more frequent inclusion of ethics into education and training.

Furthermore, when studying the characteristics of the current sample Etzel *et al.* found several differences in the ethical beliefs and behaviors between men and women, professionals and students, AAASP Certified Consultants and non-Certified Consultants, and individuals from physical education and psychology backgrounds. Interestingly, it was found that Certified Consultants were more likely than non-Certified Consultants to have practiced without supervision or peer consultation, to have been sexually attracted to clients, and to have allowed clients to reside in their home during service provision. Etzel *et al.* suggested that these results revealed that AAASP's ethical principles are not always followed consistently by the membership. Thus, it appears that the rule that membership in the AAASP commits members to adhere to the AAASP ethics code may not be effective in maintaining the ethical standards of its members.

Hays (2006) reviewed the primary ethical issues involved in the broader field of performance psychology. Performance psychology typically refers to the psychology of any performance in which excellence is sought and performers are required to meet certain performance standards (e.g., sport, business, performing arts). Hays described preparation for practice, competence, interpersonal and relations issues, and presentation to the public as primary issues in performance psychology. Preparation for practice and competence refer to accruing relevant qualifications, experiences and training to practice psychology in the performance realm and the ability to practice these skills and/or acknowledging boundaries of competence based on training, experience, and qualifications. Interpersonal and relational issues included gaining informed consent, ensuring confidentially, managing multiple role relationships, and maintaining appropriate boundaries. Moore (2003) stated that practitioners are required to give all the information necessary for a client to make an informed decision about the benefits and deficits of specific intervention strategies and the development of a working relationship with a sport psychologist. This includes obtaining written informed consent and explaining the aforementioned interpersonal and relational issues. Failure to fully elucidate these issues can potentially lead to both ethical and legal problems (Moore, 2003). Finally, Hays noted presentation to the public with reference to advertising, marketing and the use of the title "psychologist." For instance, performance psychologists should avoid deceptive or false statements regarding their training, experience, credentials, services, associations, and competence. Furthermore, the term "psychologist" is often protected by specific state, provincial, or national laws. Moreover, the term may conjure up the typical "shrink" image and may serve as a barrier to practice (Gould & Damarjian, 1998). Consequently, practitioners may choose the title coach or consultant with an associated prefix (e.g., sports performance consultant or mental coach).

Moore (2003) suggested that the APA Code of Ethics be incorporated into applied sport psychology thinking, assessment, and intervention in order to serve athletes both holistically and ethically. Practitioners can stay informed of ethical issues and how they pertain to their practice by becoming ethically self-aware. This can be achieved by reflective practice (cf. Anderson, Knowles, & Gilbourne, 2004) or by using the *Ethical Self Awareness Checklist for Sport Psychologists* (Moore, 2003: 608–10). This checklist is comprised of a series of questions that can be answered by yes, no, or N/A. For example, "Am I thoroughly aware of APA's Code of Ethics and how it pertains to my work?"; "Have I consulted with a colleague or another professional in the field"; and "If applicable have I contacted a lawyer regarding this issue?" Similarly, reflective practice can be employed to increase self-awareness and highlight ethical issues. Practitioners require sufficient time and space to retrospectively examine previous experiences and to critically examine determinants and consequences of action. This is known as retrospective reflection on action (Schön, 1987). By reflecting on action practitioners develop a repertoire of experiences that allow them to "think on their feet" and therefore allow them to foresee ethical dilemmas and take appropriate action. Reflection on action can be augmented by keeping a reflective journal, through supervision, and through structured questioning, and by doing so can increase a practitioner's ethical self-awareness.

In conclusion, ethics are a key issue in applied sport psychology as the ethical beliefs and behaviors of a practitioner form the backbone of his or her practice and are the foundation upon which everything else is built. To ensure the people sport psychologists serve, the practitioners themselves, and the field of sport psychology are protected, it must be ensured that practitioners adhere to a strict code of ethics with the overall aim of doing no harm (Andersen, 2005a). Although research has shown that to date that this is not always the case, to guarantee the progression of applied sport psychology and the safety of clients the field should incorporate ethical awareness and ethics training into the earliest stages of education in sport psychology.

## Additional readings

Andersen, M. B. (2005a). "Yeah I work with Beckham": Issues of confidentiality, privacy and privilege in sport psychology service delivery. *Sport & Exercise Psychology Review*, 1, 5–13.

Andersen, M. B, Van Raalte, J. L., & Brewer, B. W. (2001). Sport psychology service delivery: Staying ethical while keeping loose. *Professional psychology: Research and practice*, 32, 12–18.

Hayes, K. F. (2006). Being fit: The ethics of practice diversification in performance psychology. *Professional psychology: Research and practice*, 37, 223–32.

Sachs, M. L. (1993). Professional ethics in sport psychology. In R. N. Singer, M. Murphey, & L. K. Tennant (eds), *Handbook of research in sport psychology* (pp. 921–32). New York: Macmillan.

Whelan, J. P., Meyers, A. W., & Elkin, T. D. (2002). Ethics in sport and exercise psychology. In J. L. Van Raalte & B. W. Brewer (eds), *Exploring sport and exercise psychology* (2nd ed., pp 503–23). Washington, DC: American Psychological Association.

## Study questions

1   What is an ethical code and what were the six general principles put forward in the 1992 APA ethical code?

2   Why did the AAASP look to develop a specific ethical code?

3   How was a difficult ethical judgment defined for the purposes of the key study? Describe some of the items identified as difficult judgments by the researchers.

4   Thirty percent of participants in the key study reported that they were receiving supervision for their applied sport psychology work. Do you consider this percentage to be high or low? Please explain the reason for your answer.

5   What did Etzel *et al.* (2004) find in their replication of the key study by Petitpas *et al.*?

## References

American Psychological Association (1977). *Standards for providers of psychological services.* Washington, DC: APA.

American Psychological Association (1981). Specialty guidelines for the delivery of services. *American Psychologist*, 36, 640–81.

American Psychological Association (1992). Ethical principles of psychologists and code of conduct. *American Psychologist*, 47, 1597–611.

American Psychological Association (2002). *Ethical principles of psychologists and code of conduct.* Washington, DC: APA (available from www.apa.org/ethics/).

Anderson, A. G., Knowles, Z., & Gilbourne, D. (2004). Reflective practice: A review of concepts, models, and practical implications for enhancing the practice of applied sport psychologists. *The Sport Psychologist*, 18, 188–203.

Andersen, M. B. (1994). Ethical considerations in the supervision of applied sport psychology graduate students. *Journal of Applied Sport Psychology*, 6, 152–67.

Andersen, M. B. (2005a). "Yeah I work with Beckham": Issues of confidentiality, privacy and privilege in sport psychology service delivery. *Sport & Exercise Psychology Review*, 1, 5–13.

Andersen, M. B. (2005b). Touching taboos: Sex and the sport psychologist. In M.B. Andersen (ed.), *Sport psychology in practice* (pp. 171–91). Champaign, IL: Human Kinetics.

Andersen, M. B, Van Raalte, J. L., & Brewer, B. W. (2001). Sport psychology service delivery: Staying ethical while keeping loose. *Professional psychology: Research and Practice*, 32, 12–18.

Bersoff, D. N. (1994). Explicit ambiguity: The 1992 ethics code as oxymoron. *Professional Psychology: Research and Practice*, 25, 382–7.

Borys, D. S., & Pope, K. S. (1989). Dual relationships between therapist and client: A national study of psychologists, psychiatrists, and social workers. *Professional Psychology: Research and Practice*, 20, 283–93.

Danish, S. J., Petitpas, A. J., & Hale, B. D. (1993). Life development interventions for athletes: Life skills through sports. *The Counseling Psychologist*, 21, 352–85.

Etzel, E. F., Watson, J. C., and Zizzi, S. (2004). A web-based survey of AAASP members' ethical beliefs and behaviors in the new millennium. *Journal of Applied Sport Psychology*, 16, 236–50.

Gould, D. (1990). AAASP a vision for the 1990s. *Journal of Applied Sport Psychology*, 2, 99–116.

Gould, D., & Damarjian, N. (1998). Insights into effective sport psychology consulting. In K. F. Hays (ed.), *Integrating exercise, sports, movement, and mind: Therapeutic unity* (pp. 111–30). Binghamton, NY: Haworth.

Hays, K. F. (2006). Being fit: The ethics of practice diversification in performance psychology. *Professional Psychology: Research and Practice*, 37, 223–32.

Heyman, S. R., & Andersen, M. B. (1998). When to refer athletes for counseling or psychotherapy. In J. M. Williams (ed.), *Applied sport psychology: Personal growth to peak performance* (3rd ed., pp. 359–71). Mountain View, CA: Mayfield.

Kremer, J. (2002). Ethical considerations. In D. Lavallee & I. M. Cockerill (eds), *Counselling in sport and exercise contexts* (pp. 18–26). Leicester: British Psychological Society.

Moore, Z. E. (2003). Ethical dilemmas in sport psychology: Discussion and recommendations for practice. *Professional Psychology: Research and Practice*, 34, 601–10.

Percival, G., & Striefel, S. (1994). Ethical beliefs and practices of AAPB. *Biofeedback and Self-Regulation*, 19. 67–93.

Pope, K. S., Tabachnick, B. G., & Keith-Spiegel, P. (1987). Ethics of practice: The beliefs and behaviors of psychologists as therapists. *American Psychologist*, 42, 993–1006.

Pope, K. S., & Vetter, V. A. (1992). Ethical dilemmas encountered by members of the American Psychological Association. *American Psychologist*, 47, 397–411.

Sachs, M. L. (1993). Professional ethics in sport psychology. In R. N. Singer, M. Murphey, & L. K. Tennant (eds), *Handbook of research on sport psychology* (pp. 921–32). New York: Macmillan.

Schön, D. (1987). *Educating the reflective practitioner.* San Francisco: Jossey-Bass.

Silva, J. (1989). Toward the professionalism of sport psychology. *The Sport Psychologist*, 3, 265–73.

Strauss, A., & Corbin, J. (1990). *Basics of qualitative research: Grounded theory procedures and techniques.* Newbury Park, CA: Sage.

Tabachnick, B. G., Keith-Spiegel, P., & Pope, K. S. (1991). Ethics of teaching: Beliefs and behaviors of psychologists as educators. *American Psychologist*, 46, 506–15.

Taylor, J. (1994). Examining the boundaries of sport science and psychology trained practitioners in applied sport psychology: Title usage and area of competence. *Journal of Applied Sport Psychology*, 6, 185–95.

Teetor Waite, B., & Pettit, M. E. (1993). Work experiences of graduates from doctoral programs in sport psychology. *Journal of Applied Sport Psychology*, 5, 234–50.

Weinberg, R. S. (1989). Applied sport psychology: Issues and challenges. *Journal of Applied Sport Psychology*, 1, 181–95.

Whelan, J. (2006). *AAASP ethics code*. Available from www.aaasponline.org/governance/committees/ethics/standards.php.

Whelan, J. P., Meyers, A. W., & Elkin, T. D. (2002). Ethics in sport and exercise psychology. In J. L. Van Raalte & B. W. Brewer (eds), *Exploring sport and exercise psychology* (2nd ed., pp. 503–23). Washington, DC: APA.

# Index